D1259217

Laurence K. Shook

ETIENNE GILSON

This biography is the story of the distinguished Christian philosopher Etienne Gilson, based on a large collection of privileged correspondence, documents and personal recollections. It presents not only his immensely productive life as a writer, teacher and lecturer in France and North America but also something of the substance, nature and originality of his thought. It acknowledges one man's contribution to the welfare of mankind.

Son of a Parisian shopkeeper and his Burgundian wife, Gilson received a gentleman's education in private Paris schools, in the Lycée Henri IV, and in the Sorbonne during the second period when Emile Durckheim was inventing a new sociology, and Henri Bergson's lectures on creative evolution were attracting large crowds to the Collège de France.

Having studied successfully the revolutionary writings of René Descartes and modern French philosophy, Gilson became through private study a leading if eccentric authority on Christian medieval thought.

Gilson held university posts successively in Lille, Strasbourg and Paris, becoming the Sorbonne's inimitable historian of the philosophies of the middle ages. Named a delegate to international meetings in London, Naples and Cambridge (Massachusetts), and achieving thereby world-wide recognition, he refused invitations to move from Paris to another university. Encouraged, however, by French External Affairs he accepted special cultural missions in the Americas at Harvard, Toronto and Rio de Janeiro. In 1929 he founded in Toronto a research institute which later became the Pontifical Institute of Mediaeval Studies.

Gilson's life had other facets. When World War I broke out he at first served his country as a sergeant drilling recruits. Despatched to Verdun as a machine-gunner, he was promoted to lieutenant. In 1916 he fell prisoner, working out his frustrations by learning new languages (including Russian) and reading Bonaventure. In World War II he gave courses in the Collège de France through-out the occupation, refused to collaborate, and earned an honorary membership in the *résistance*. He subsequently represented France at post-war conferences at San Francisco (the United Nations), London (UNESCO) and The Hague. For two years he was a *conseiller* or senator in the French government.

A second lifetime facet was to accept special lecture series when they offered a challenge. Thus he delivered the Gifford Lectures in Aberdeen, the Henry James Lectures at Harvard, the Powell Lectures at Indiana, the inaugural series of ten lectures in the Mercier chair at Louvain and the Mellon Lectures at the National Gallery, Washington.

Gilson's most cherished of many awards was his election in 1946 into the Académie Française.

ACKNOWLEDGMENT

This book has been published with the help of a grant
from the Canadian Federation for the Humanities,
using funds provided by the Social Sciences
and Humanities Research Council of Canada.

CANADIAN CATALOGUING IN PUBLICATION DATA

Shook, Laurence K. (Laurence Kennedy), 1909-
   Etienne Gilson

(The Etienne Gilson series, ISSN 0708-319X ; 6)
Includes index.
ISBN 0-88844-706-X

1. Gilson, Etienne, 1884-1978.   2. Philosophers - France - Biography.
I. Pontifical Institute of Mediaeval Studies.   II. Title.   III. Series.

B2430.G474S56 1984   194′.0924   C84-098152-X

PRINTED BY UNIVERSA, WETTEREN, BELGIUM

Contents

Preface

During the last but one of Etienne Gilson's some forty visits to Canada, I asked him whether he would approve of my undertaking to write his biography. His first reply was negative. Biography, he said, is not a suitable preoccupation for a scholar. On reflection, he hedged a little. "If my life story has to be written," he said, "I should prefer that it be done in North America where I have established viable institutions for the advancement of medieval studies. I am afraid that a European biographer might overlook significant aspects of this side of my activity. There is also something to be said in my case for a biographer who is neither a professional philosopher nor a theologian. He can more easily deal objectively with the controversies which have so often beset me." Gilson-like, he then recalled that Bernard Shaw had once said there is no better reason for undertaking a project than wanting to do so. With this he gave his approval to my project and said he would help me. This was in 1971.

When my term as president of the Pontifical Institute of Mediaeval Studies came to an end in 1973 and my retirement from teaching in the University of Toronto was imminent, I began to do research on Gilson's life. His own extra-ordinary contribution to my undertaking came in 1974 when I visited him in Cravant, his place of retirement in Burgundy, where he was living with his elder daughter Jacqueline. Accompanying me on this first of two visits was Mary Diane Shook, who took over the task of taping my interviews with Gilson; Mary Diane broke down the tired old man's natural reserve by exploiting that incredible love of domestic animals which the two of them shared. When we left Cravant in May 1974 we brought with us the gift of hundreds of letters and documents. The letters were those of Gilson himself written to his mother and wife during his absence from Paris. Other collections of letters already existed in Toronto in the files of St Michael's College and in the Gilson Archives at the Pontifical Institute of Mediaeval Studies. Two other private collections of letters have been loaned to me: those belonging to the Pegis family in Toronto and the Thibaudeau family in Montréal.

Also important for the present biography are the interviews I was privileged to hold with many of Gilson's relatives, friends and scholarly acquaintances : with Jacqueline, Cécile, Bernard and Lucie Gilson; with Thérèse d'Alverny and Henri Gouhier; with M.-D. Chenu and Yves Congar of the Dominican convent on rue des Tanneries, Paris; with Fernand Van Steenberghen and Gérard Verbeke of Louvain; and with other scholars across Europe and North America.

Two economies affect the structure and content of this book. The first of these incorporates into it (where feasible and Gilson-oriented) information which will one day serve the making of a history of Gilson's Toronto Institute. The second incorporates bibliographical references into the main text of the book in an attempt to keep its cost within the reach of at least the moderately rich. Since most references are to letters and are easily coded, and since relatively few secondary sources are called upon, the reader will not suffer much inconvenience from the incorporations. The use of the abbreviation "tr." after some references indicates that the preceding citation has been translated into English by the author; the abbreviation "McG" plus number refers the reader to the appropriate listing in Margaret McGrath's *Etienne Gilson: A Bibliography* (Toronto, 1982).

A third device has been employed, unobtrusively I hope, which introduces into some chapter-headings the terms used by St Thomas and others to designate the successive ages of man. Since Gilson often used these terms himself to mark his passing years, they seem somehow to belong in his biography.

I should like to acknowledge the valuable assistance provided by librarians in Toronto, Paris, and Cambridge, Massachusetts; by the many persons in North America and Europe who have generously sent me information and anecdotes to illustrate some aspect of Gilson's life and work; also by those who have read and corrected my original manuscript, especially Armand A. Maurer and Janet MacLean, both of Toronto.

Financial assistance to enable me to gather data and to meet the costs of typing and publishing my long manuscript has been provided by St Michael's College and the Pontifical Institute of Mediaeval Studies, Toronto, by the University of St Michael's College Alumni Fund, by the Michaelmas Conference and by the Canada Council and the Canadian Federation for the Humanities, Ottawa.

1

Infantia, Pueritia, Adolescentia, 1884-1904

1 BIRTH AND BAPTISM

Etienne Henry Gilson was born at noon on Friday 13 June 1884. The birth took place in his parents' apartment over the draper's shop they owned at 25, avenue Lamotte-Picquet, Paris vii^e. Etienne was the third child of Paul Anthelme Gilson and Caroline Juliette Rainaud. His birth was registered in the *mairie* of the *arrondissement* on the following day, 14 June. As was common enough, this was undertaken by the midwife Sophie Girard, a widow who lived nearby on avenue Duquesne, and by two other neighbours, Adèle Diquerre, a wine merchant, and Auguste Roussin, a barman. Indeed, as the infant's mother was the daughter of a successful innkeeper, it is hardly surprising that, among his later accomplishments, Etienne should become a supreme connoisseur of wines.

The baptism took place in two stages. In a private ceremony in the Gilson home on 7 July 1884, water was poured by Abbé Escaré. The public ceremonies were supplied on 17 August in the lovely Church of Saint-Pierre du Gros Caillou on rue St-Dominique; the church had been rebuilt by Godde in 1826, and had not yet been enlarged or modernized. *Ondoiement*, the practice of baptizing children at home soon after birth and postponing the ceremonies until later, was largely a matter of convenience for sponsors, especially when they had to come from a distance. Although it was very common, it was sometimes regarded as an abuse of the sacrament; in 1914, when Etienne was twenty-nine, the practice was formally forbidden by the Holy See except in cases of danger of death.

The formal ceremony conferred upon the infant his all-important Christian names. As a Rainaud and a Burgundian, the child could fittingly carry the name of Etienne, once Burgundy's most popular saint until supplanted by the Blessed Virgin; the spelling of the second name, Henry, with a *y* was a distinguishing mark of the Gilson family. The baptism also appointed Etienne's communal Christian parentage. His *marraine*, or godmother, was Marie Octave Leroy; his *parrain* or godfather, Henry Charles Gilson, was a young family hopeful who had recently graduated in medicine and would later become head of medicine in the hospital of Angoulême. The official signature of H. Eguerre, *vicaire*, acknowledged the baptism on behalf of the local parish. One unusual detail attaches to the simple conferring of the sacrament; the infant passed water on Abbé Escaré's shoes, an episode the family never allowed Etienne to forget.

In the truest sense of the word, the baptism "took." As long as they lived, Etienne's *marraine* and *parrain* remained as close to him as his immediate family did. Moreover, although the promises made by them in his name during this sacramental initiation would occasion Etienne some soul-searching over the years, they became for him increasingly vivid and conscious commitments. Indeed, he would later write:

> A day comes when [the philosopher] has only two choices: either to make in his own name the promises once made for him by another, or formally to refuse to subscribe to them. Had I decided on the latter course, I do not know what I would think today; but I do know that in the full awareness of what I am doing and with the inner certainty of making a free choice, I still formally renew today the vows made in my name, a few days after my birth. (*The Philosopher and Theology* [New York, 1962], p. 9; McG 105).

Ultimately, however, as Etienne would say more than once, baptism is not a "philosophical situation" but a family occasion. In a Christian family "one becomes a Christian without being consulted."

2 THE GILSONS AND THE RAINAUDS

Etienne's father was only the fourth traceable generation of Parisian Gilsons. His father's family was one of those many, described as *fixée à Paris depuis la révolution*, whose distant family records had been lost through unprecedented displacement and excessive fear of self-exposure. Etienne's direct traceable Gilson ancestors, then, are limited to his great-grandfather, "Grandpère Charrette" Gilson; his grandfather, Jacques Michel; and his father, Paul Anthelme.

"Grandpère Charrette" may or may not have been the first Gilson to come to Paris. He acquired the sobriquet "scaffold" from the family legend attaching to him. As a young man in 1789 he reputedly stood at the head of a cue of dispensable persons awaiting his turn at the guillotine; by sheer good fortune, the machine broke down and the cue never re-formed. Whatever the truth, Grandpère Charrette certainly survived the revolution. He became a shopkeeper in Melun, made enough money to live on, and married Marie Pimard. He also became the father of five children: Jean Jacques died a bachelor; Félastine became Mme Anthelme Gay; Emilie remained a spinster; Jacques Michel married and carried on the Gilson name; and Charles entered the seminary of the diocese of Meaux.

Like Grandpère Charrette, Etienne's grandfather also became a shopkeeper in Melun. Jacques Michel Gilson married Adèle Desmares, also of Melun. Their six children constituted the older Gilson family as Etienne knew it. Léon, the eldest, became an architect and, as Etienne would later do, married a Ravisé. Emile also became an architect, and designed Melun's City Hall; he married Louise Lamotte and officiated at the civil ceremony by which Emile's parents were married. Emilie-Lucille married Louis Henry Ravisé, and thus became the grandmother of the girl Etienne was to marry. Paul Anthelme, born in 1838, married Caroline Rainaud of Cravant and became the father of five sons, including Etienne. Adèle remained a spinster. Charles, the youngest, married Céline Quillard; his son Henry was Etienne's first cousin and, as we have seen, godfather.

Whether or not Grandpère Charrette was the first Gilson to come to Paris, the family name seems not to have been Parisian. Indeed, the name has a Viking ring to it; as a personal name, it turns up in more than one Scandinavian saga. As a family name, Gilson is not uncommon along the border between France and Belgium, appearing frequently in cities like Lille and Liège. In 1926 Etienne reported to his wife that a "postcard forwarded to Cambridge, Massachusetts, which enquires whether I am from Sedan, comes from an educated and delightful Protestant gentleman. I have always told you that our name was from the Belgian Ardenne; Sedan is not far from there." (EG to Thérèse, 26.11.6; tr.)

Etienne did not like to think of himself as a northerner; he preferred Parisian speech to Belgian. Nor did he admit much in common with southerners, whom he thought too unscholarly. Etienne chose to regard himself as a Parisian with roots in Burgundy, which was true enough through his maternal ancestors. He was thoroughly embarrassed when, on arrival in Lille in 1913 to take up his first university appointment, he was welcomed as a native son. Although the Gilson family may indeed have come originally from Lille, it more likely came from Liège. Even Etienne would grudgingly admit this when pressed; in 1967, while attending a celebration there, he could not forbear noting that "sixty-two Gilsons are listed in the Liège telephone book" (EG to Shook, 67.10.14).

Etienne's mother, Caroline Juliette Rainaud, was a Burgundian. She was born 17 April 1851 in Cravant, a small medieval village in the department of l'Yonne about halfway between Auxerre and Avallon. Her parents, Narcisse Rainaud and Joséphine Morizot, were innkeepers. Their inn could be found in the row of low buildings on the south side of the Route de Paris between the bridge over the Yonne and the eighteenth-century gate through the village's medieval fortification. Narcisse was from Cravant, Joséphine from Avallon.

Etienne's maternal grandmother was the key to his extraordinary and romantic attachment to the people, the language, and the soil of Burgundy. In a delightful, unpublished paper entitled "La Bourgogne," written after his retirement to Cravant, he describes Joséphine as "descended from a line of bakers and millers of Avallon whose beginnings are lost in the night of time" (p. 1; tr.). Her more immediate descent is not lost however; her father, François Morizot, was a baker; her paternal grandfather, a miller from Cousin le Pont; and her mother, Marie Lottin, was *bonne* rather than *petite bourgeoise*, the sister of a distinguished notary. Etienne was especially proud of this grandmother because she placed both his mother and himself, geographically and emotionally, clearly within the vaguely defined enclaves of that Burgundy which "one enters somewhere on the far side of Auxerre and leaves somewhere beyond Dijon" (ibid.). She was indisputably a Bourgignonne in speech – her *armagnac* was *armagnà*.

Narcisse and Joséphine had only two children: Caroline, Etienne's mother; and Céline, *femme* Leroy of Vermenton, whose daughter was the godmother of both Etienne and Maurice. How Caroline Rainaud came to move to Melun and Paris is unknown. Once in Paris, she married Paul Anthelme Gilson. In all, she bore seven children, though two of them, twins, died in childbirth. Emile was the oldest, followed by Paul, Etienne, André and Maurice. In addition to raising her five sons, Caroline helped her husband run his draper's shop; this was located first on rue du Temple and then at 25, avenue Lamotte-Picquet where Etienne was born.

Caroline was a lovable, cultured, completely capable, and deeply religious woman. In the hundred or so extant letters that Etienne wrote to her over some forty years, he unfailingly addressed her as "ma chère petite Maman." In her early married life Caroline was the backbone of the small respectable *mercerie* that she helped her husband operate. Neighbours and customers were drawn to her as they were not to the less sympathetic Paul Anthelme. People sauntering along Lamotte-Picquet would peer through the shop windows to see if Caroline was on duty. If they saw her, they would enter to chat and perhaps to buy; if they only saw Paul Anthelme, they would quicken their steps and pass by. Caroline possessed another attribute that was useful in the dry goods business: with deft twists of her hands and fingers she could transform remnants of fabric into hats, kerchiefs and other pleasing and useful objects.

Paul Anthelme seems to have owned his business at the time of his marriage; no doubt he was set up in it by his father, Jacques Michel. When Caroline married Paul Anthelme, she was thirteen years his junior. She brought to the business a fine education, endless energy and ingenuity, and some property of her own. As time went on, Paul Anthelme became increasingly dependent upon his wife. He may have been congenitally lazy – Gilson children who showed lack of industry were chided for acting "just like their father." Whatever the case, he certainly experienced poor health. When his three youngest sons were still in school, Paul Anthelme suffered a severe stroke. He remained an invalid until his death some twenty years later, by which time he was also blind. The three young boys really only knew their father as a dependent. Their mother was the provider and the real head of the family.

When Paul Anthelme became incapacitated, his business was turned over to his second son, Paul. Caroline then moved with her husband and three young children into a small house at 9, avenue Lamotte-Picquet. Not long after, she acquired a larger home on boulevard Port-Royal; over the next forty-five years, this served as the family seat. With her remaining funds, Caroline bought PLM and government bonds and a small house or two which she rented out for income. In this manner Caroline provided adequately, though in dignified poverty, for her family. She managed to see each of her three younger boys through university.

3 Primary Education: Ste-Clotilde's, 1890-1895

Etienne's religious education began in his parents' home. It was apparently supervised from a distance by an Ursuline nun, Mother Saint-Dieudonné, who had taught Caroline in the primary school in Cravant. Caroline was clearly a favourite student: "You are," she once wrote to Caroline, "one of my first daughters and one of the most faithful" (08.1.3; tr.).

Mother Saint-Dieudonné exerted a strong influence over the entire family; that all five Gilson boys went to Catholic schools is largely attributable to her. Her letters to Caroline are full of spiritual direction and wise counsel. Etienne always spoke warmly and gratefully of this nun. He attached to the tiny bundle of her surviving letters to Caroline this note: "All the sons of my mother are indebted to Mother Saint-Dieudonné for being Christians and (of course) Catholics."

The Gilson family was also close to the Abbé Escaré who had baptized Etienne. Gilson often stated that Escaré was the first of the many priests to play a role in his life. It was Escaré who suggested that Etienne attend the Christian Brothers' school in the lively, prosperous, bourgeois parish of Ste-Clotilde. In all these early educational decisions, Etienne's father played a passive role. Although Paul Gilson never objected to his children receiving a Catholic education, he himself had attended only national schools and would likely have sent his children to them as well.

Etienne was six years old when he was enrolled in the Christian Brothers' school. The experience made a deep impression on him, and he later often spoke gratefully of his good fortune in his early schooling. He was particularly pleased with the grounding the Brothers gave him in Latin, and with the love of that language which they helped him to acquire. He often expressed amusement that the Brothers, who were forbidden by their rule to teach Latin because they were not priests, should have been such extraordinarily good instructors in the language and should have introduced children to it at so young an age.

The Brothers' school exerted an influence on Gilson far beyond the teaching of Latin. There he was taught, and taught well, the catechism which became the food and sustenance not only of his faith but of his entire concept of education and even of his metaphysics. Although the main concern of these teachers was to explain to the children the meaning of their creed, they supplied the future philosopher with the "true answers" to most of the questions raised by his subsequent interest in metaphysics.

Well on in his life, when Etienne was a Conseiller de la République and found reason to probe the matter of primary schooling to its depths, he characterized independent schools such as Ste-Clotilde's as "free" schools in the true sense of the word. Indeed, Etienne maintained that only their existence allowed state schools to operate as "free schools" as well. In a paper entitled "Une véritable liberté de l'enseignement" (*Ecclesia*, 126 [Sept. 1959]: 15-16; McG 823), he argued that whenever independent schools were closed and choice in primary education was replaced by monopoly, freedom in education could no longer exist. Furthermore he claimed that *inventio*, or the discovery of new ideas and educational structures, had historically taken place independently of state control. The state might adapt successful innovations, but could not invent them: "It was not the state that invented the primary school: it was the Blessed Jean-Baptiste de la Salle" (ibid., p. 16; tr.).

Etienne's five years at Ste-Clotilde's culminated in two important religious acts: his first communion was taken 16 May 1895 and his confirmation was received a few days later, 21 May 1895. These events are recorded on a large steel engraving of a first-communion scene attended by a large fashionable crowd in the ornate Gothic church of Ste-Clotilde. The diploma was signed by O. Garday, curé of the parish and vicar-general of the archdiocese.

When Etienne left Ste-Clotilde's in July 1895, he also sat the state examinations for his certificate of studies. According to a humorous remark by Pasteur Vallery-Radot at Etienne's reception into the Académie Française, he was unsuccessful: "Your primary studies were crowned with a resounding check at the certificate of studies.... You failed, and to this day you possess no certificate of studies" (*Discours de réception*, 39; tr.). That Gilson should have tried for the civil as well as the private diploma is in accord with his later practice: Etienne was always first a Catholic, then with equal fervour of a different order, a Frenchman of the Third Republic.*

4 Notre-Dame-des-Champs, 1895-1902

In 1895 Etienne was admitted to the "Petit Séminaire de Notre-Dame-des-Champs" (NDC), probably the best Catholic secondary school in Paris. NDC, canonically a little seminary, was a progressive and "mixed" school; its programme was geared to the needs of boys proceeding to all professions, not just the priesthood. When the school was founded in 1810 it was staffed by diocesan clergy and located in Saint-Nicolas. In 1848, when tension between church and state had sufficiently relaxed, the school was moved to rue Notre-Dame-des-Champs. Etienne attended NDC from 1895 to 1902. Four years after his leaving, local laws again curtailed the operation of religious schools and NDC was once more forced out of Paris; it operated for one year in the former Collège Sainte-Barbe at Fontenay-les-Roses and for a further year at 14, rue de Madrid before closing forever in 1908.

During Etienne's enrolment as a "Champist," the school was enjoying its finest years, those of the long headmastership (1871 to 1908) of Abbé Piot. NDC's programme was extensive. It covered the entire gamut of pre-university education from *neuvième* down through rhetoric and *belles-lettres*, concluding with the customary two years of introductory philosophy. The special objective of the

---

* See also "The Eminence of Teaching," *Disputed Questions in Education* (New York, 1954), pp. 17-30; McG 270.

school was to apply the educational ideals set forth in Bishop Dupanloup's *De l'éducation*. Its programme was humanistic in its attempt to transmit Greek and Roman culture, and *libre* or "free" in that it opened the minds of its students to the Christian and the transcendent.

The best impressions of life in NDC can be found in the series of *Annuaires* published by its old boys. The Association Fraternelle des Anciens Élèves de NDC was established in 1875, and its meetings and published *Annuaires* continued for thirty-five or forty years after the closing of the school. The talks given at these meetings by former teachers and students, though often overly sentimental, clearly illustrate the nature of the school itself and the achievement of its graduates in various professions. Etienne was the Association's honoured member in 1934; his talk on that occasion focused on the school's dedication to the educational programme of Dupanloup.

Etienne was first taken by his mother to NDC as a boy of eleven in 1895. Under the normal procedure, he was entrusted to the matron of the school and assigned to a priest for spiritual and academic direction. From this point Etienne's life became a succession of classes, meals, study-hall sessions, assemblies and religious exercises. On his semi-weekly walkdays, he could visit his family and friends or go, often alone, to visit the Louvre and other cultural centres.

The academic programme at NDC embraced the languages, the histories and the letters of Greece, Rome and France; these were supplemented with some mathematics and science, and with considerable religion, liturgy and music. In general, teaching methods were textual and rhetorical; they relied heavily on *explication de textes* and *memoria*. Although today we are experiencing a revival of interest in rhetoric as a healthy pedagogical instrument, the trend has not yet effectively included *memoria*, which of all the major divisions of rhetoric is the most practical and useful. At ninety years of age Etienne was still able to recite extensively from Greek, Latin and French works read as a Champist. There were few significant passages in the great masterpieces of French literature that he could not call upon for an apt quotation. He often rolled these quotations off his tongue in their entirety, clearly, accurately, and with undisguised pride and relish.

Etienne's dominant memories of NDC focused on one teacher in particular, Abbé Victor Thorelle. Thorelle first imparted to Etienne a strong sense of the range and breadth of Christian and French culture. Thorelle came from Bourgogne, with which Etienne also identified. He had a cultivated taste for the finest music, a taste which Etienne first absorbed and then shared. Thorelle was in charge of Etienne's class for four years, in *septième, sixième, quatrième* and *troisième*. In a sense then the priest and his students passed through the school together.

Thorelle was born in Pont-sur-Yonne, not far from the Gilson's beloved Cravant, but closer to Auxerre. His parents were at one time the *concierges* of the Little Seminary of Joigny. When Thorelle was ordained, he said his first mass in the chapel of the Blessed Virgin behind the high altar of the Cathedral of Auxerre. These places became shrines to Etienne as he grew older, and he loved to tell his friends how and why to visit them, even as he sent them to Vézelay and La Cordelle and to simple, beautiful, medieval Noyers.

Thorelle's taste for music was, by modern standards, classical, controlled and refined. When he went to teach at NDC, he had a huge harmonium placed in his room; there he spent his leisure time playing the music he loved best. There also the students prepared their motets on the vigils before great feasts or came to hear the abbé play and talk to them about music. Thorelle frequently sharply criticized the musical tastes of Abbé Ganuza, the school organist, and of Abbé Rouffe, the teacher of plain chant. Thorelle had his own views on the singing of a mass, views that his student came to share. "Music for me," Etienne would say later, "that is, good music, was Thorelle; bad music was Abbé Ganuza."

Thorelle was almost totally responsible for Etienne's early and lifelong love of music and of the fine arts generally. It was Thorelle for example who insisted that Etienne, an alto, join the school choir. Ever afterwards, Etienne gladly sang in his own family circle; among his children's finest memories was their father's rendering of often-difficult arias to their mother's piano accompaniment. Thorelle also taught Etienne about his own favourite composers, particularly Richard Wagner and that "innovator," Claude Debussy. Possibly the supreme musical experience of Etienne's life took place during these Champist years when Thorelle sent him off to hear *Tristan et Yseult* conducted by the philosophizing composer, Gustav Mahler. Etienne was transported by the music, particularly by the inimitable "Prelude," and often referred to the experience afterwards.

At NDC Etienne formed the longstanding habit of going off alone one afternoon a week to study the treasures of the Louvre. Maman was pleased with this sign of her son's artistic development. On one occasion she asked him if he would like to learn to play some instrument. "Yes," he quickly responded, "I would like to learn to play the flute." However, although Maman offered to arrange lessons, Etienne backed down: "I realized," he said later, that practising the flute might leave me too little time for Latin." Etienne never lost his interest in the fine arts. One of his earliest articles, written in a prison camp in 1917, was on the foundations of aesthetic judgment. The idea for the paper arose out of discussions with Abbé Thorelle at NDC (interview, 1975).

Still another important influence of Thorelle on Etienne concerned the cultivation of a conscious literary style. During his four years as Etienne's classroom master, Thorelle worked to develop his student's writing abilities. According to Etienne:

> Thorelle was a crank about composition and style; he read everything I wrote and pointed out, not without acerbity, what was wrong and what right about it. He told me that for effective writing certain tricks were to be learned and used. The first trick is to set down everything you want to say in brief, unrelated sentences; this is an easy trick because it is nothing else than writing like a boy. Next you must learn to mull over the correct and exact meaning of the key words you intend to use. Next you must save your important matter for the later part of the piece and subtly prepare the reader for it in the earlier part. Finally you must carefully check all

> places that call for connectives: sentences and paragraphs must be properly linked if
> the piece is to become a single unit. (interview, 1975.)

Gilson was always to observe Thorelle's precepts of style, but he was also to enrich them with his own awareness that style is an act of making, a *poiesis*, which proceeds by way of skills and precepts. Ultimately he believed that the origins of style are contained in the author's act of being. (See below, pp. 326-327.)

Etienne's results at the end of his rhetoric year, his last at NDC, attest to his success. At the final *distribution des prix*, 21 July 1902, he received first prize for French oration; second prize for Latin sight translation; second prize for Latin oration; first *accessit* (honourable mention) for Latin poetry; third *accessit* for Greek sight translation; seventh *accessit* for history of science; second *accessit* for the final examination; and fourth *accessit* for general excellence (Gilson Archives, 02.7.21).

The documents recording these results at NDC were carefully guarded by Etienne throughout his life. Also surviving from his Champist days is the *diplôme d'académicien*, granted him by the Académie du Petit Séminaire; this bears the signatures of E. Nicolas, student secretary, and Anatole Béry, student director, as well as that of Père A. Piot, president of the academy and superior of the NDC. Etienne's admission to this academy on 16 December 1901 anticipated that into the great Académie Française by over forty years. Other documents carefully saved from his Champist days are his undated *diplôme d'admission* into the Congregation of the Blessed Virgin and his *lettre d'admission* to the Congregation of the Holy Angels dated 6 February 1898, Feast of the Purification, with the Congregation's fitting and applicable motto, *piété, docilité, travail*. These last two documents bear Etienne's signatures, *Et. Gilson* and *E. Gilson*; these are the earliest specimens of his hand.

5 Lycée Henri IV, 1902-1903

In 1902 Etienne transferred from Notre-Dame-des-Champs to the celebrated Lycée Henri IV. In *The Philosopher and Theology* (p. 16), he explained that, having decided to teach in the lycées, he saw it as only fitting that he first study in one. He also later admitted privately that he had grown weary of NDC's rigid discipline. There was probably a third reason for the change: with his father's stroke and subsequent paralysis, and the absence of his older brothers, Etienne felt that he ought to share Maman's responsibilities in the large house at 91, boulevard Port-Royal.

Etienne's departure from NDC apparently had nothing to do with the kind of philosophy he would have learned there; he did not even know exactly what he would have studied under Abbé Ehlinger. Nonetheless he later stated his belief that it would have been bad philosophy, little different from the deliberately secularized, systematized, impersonal philosophy of the lycées. After all, the year was still only 1902. Not he nor the Ministry of Fine Arts and Letters nor the directorates of seminaries yet had "the foggiest notion" that a philosophy exists in a philosopher. No philosophy can be purged of errors arising from its principles without being purged of its principles as well; the Suarezian programme of the Jesuits had failed to purge the philosophy of St Thomas, as had the Faculties of the Empire and Restoration failed to purge that of Locke ("Compagnons de route," in *Etienne Gilson: philosophe de la chrétienté* [Paris, 1949], pp. 288-289; McG 234).

Although Etienne did not go to Lycée Henry ɪᴠ to avoid studying "scholastic" philosophy, he was later pleased that he had never been taught from scholastic textbooks. "Had I been exposed in my youth to the kind of scholastic philosophy represented by the textbooks then in use in the schools, such teaching would have been for me a genuine catastrophe" (*The Philosopher and Theology*, p. 46). Etienne's antischolastic attitude developed later, after he had left Lycée Henry ɪᴠ and before the outbreak of World War ɪ (below, pp. 20-21).

At Lycée Henri ɪᴠ, Etienne's professor of philosophy was Henri Dereux. Although he was an acceptable teacher, Dereux's thinking tended to be colourless. Gilson later described him as propounding "a mild form of spiritualism that Victor Cousin himself would not have disowned" (*The Philosopher and Theology*, p. 17). A continual theme of Dereux' was apparently "the unifying functions of reason." Dereux prepared Etienne for his baccalaureate examination and encouraged his desire to become a philosopher by awarding him the lycée's prize in philosophy.

After retiring from Lycée Henri ɪᴠ, Dereux was to become a not undistinguished painter. Gilson's liveliest memory of his teacher was recorded years later, 7 March 1972, on acceptance in Paris of the Gulbenkian prize for philosophy from the Brazilian Academy of the Latin World:

> It was impossible for us to imagine that he had ever been young. So far as I remember he never came to class without his formal high hat and frock coat. He used to speak slowly and deliberately, seriously and thoughtfully, teaching us that the essential thing in philosophy was to demonstrate the unifying function of the mind. He was a solemn impressive man who knew how to keep perfect order in his classes. The idea never seemed to occur to him that a philosopher could take time off from thinking, nor did it occur to us to disturb in any way the progress of a university activity bordering on the religious.
>
> On one occasion one of the boys forgot himself and made a smart joke. M. Dereux had decided to avail himself of a privilege the Ministry of Education left open to him: he had announced that his next class would be extracurricular and devoted to the vice of alcoholism. When the day came, he solemnly entered the classroom, crossed in front of the blackboard to get to his rostrum, and hesitated like one befuddled. Drawn on the board with coloured chalk and with a nimble and steady hand, the hand of one already a master, was a huge glass and on it the lump of sugar melting drop by drop into the wretched brew. Hat in hand, standing before the masterpiece, M. Dereux murmured in a creamy voice, "only a Dunoyer de Segonzac could get away with a joke like that." How true! Up there before us, taking in his hand a moist sponge, completely unaware that he was destroying the first masterpiece displayed by a celebrated painter of the days ahead, M. Dereux

quietly erased a picture which today would have held art historians entranced. ("On receiving the Gulbenkian Prize," Gilson Archives, 72.3.7; tr.)

A further comment on M. Dereux was made by Jacques Maritain in a short letter to Gilson on receipt of a complimentary copy of *Le philosophe et la théologie*:

> I am deeply moved to learn that we studied philosophy at Lycée Henri IV with the same M. Dereux who was both so good and so inclusive. Do you remember his funny way of pronouncing certain words, adding an *f* to their final syllable? It is curious to learn so long afterwards that we may even have sat on the same benches, and were to meet one day after many an experience. (60.6.22; tr.)

The Lycée Henri IV brought Etienne geographically and intellectually to the mountain of Ste-Geneviève and the threshold of the University of Paris. While there he made his first contact with Professor Lucien Lévy-Bruhl at the very time that the already-famous philosopher and historian of philosophy (*L'idée de responsabilité* [1885]; *La philosophie de Jacobi* [1894]; *La philosophie d'Auguste Comte* [1900]) was in the process of becoming something new, a sociologist. In 1903 M. Dereux arranged Etienne's timetable so that he and other young philosophers could attend Lévy-Bruhl's public course on David Hume. In that year Lévy-Bruhl published what Gilson called his "almost incredible book," *La morale et la science des mœurs*. At the end of the academic year, Lévy-Bruhl examined Dereux' students for the baccalaureate. Etienne records one anecdote concerning this examination:

> [Lévy-Bruhl] asked me if I was especially interested in any particular philosopher. Naturally enough I replied, "Yes, Hume." My grade was *une juste moyenne*. Much later I related this episode to him. He replied with a laugh: "You were lucky I didn't flunk you." ("Le Descartes de Lévy-Bruhl," *Revue philosophique de la France et de l'étranger*, 147 [1957]: 432-451; McG 244; tr.)

Etienne's brief career at Henri IV ended with his receipt of two essential documents. A certification from the Faculty of Letters, University of Paris, dated 13 July 1903, judged him "worthy of the bachelor's degree in the classical secondary programme, Lettres-Philosophie, with *mention passable*." In addition he received a bachelor's diploma along with all the rights and prerogatives it conferred.

Shortly afterward Etienne left to complete his military requirement. Already he had long been resolved to continue in philosophy at the Sorbonne as soon as he was able.

6 MILITARY SERVICE, 1903-1904

In July 1903, fresh from his baccalaureate and his nineteenth birthday, Etienne began his full year of military service. In a sense this experience completed his pre-university education as it became the occasion for many new experiences and for a growing self-awareness. Although Etienne found his new world unfamiliar and often not to his liking, he quickly learned to observe it objectively with high good humour. During this year, he began his *lettres à Maman*, that broken series of letters written during frequent absences between 1903 and 1937, the year of Maman's death. Because Maman saved many of these letters, they now constitute an important entry into Etienne's private and domestic life. The first letters from Eu are especially revealing in their unabashed confidences and in the tone of responsibility that Etienne adopts as senior male in the household.

The first month or so of service was spent in Paris while the class awaited the opening of a new camp at Eu (Seine Maritime) in Normandy. Etienne arrived at Eu in the autumn of 1903. He was assigned to a *peloton des dispensées*, a detachment of non-combat troops in which he would remain until the end of the service year. In his first letter to Maman, Etienne described the barracks as "new and pleasant" and "located out in fields and bordered by lovely hedges and a river [the Bresle] rather than by camp walls" (03.12.13; tr.).

Indeed, more than once during the year, Etienne was deeply moved by the sheer beauty of the area. In April 1904 he described a delightful Sunday walk in the company of his friends Joye, Toulouse and Lejeune. Toulouse, an especially close friend whom Etienne had known in Paris, had been confined to barracks "for I know not what reason." As a result he could only join them as far as the church of Eu, where they attended the nine o'clock mass. After mass, in order to prolong Toulouse's permission a little, the boys visited the tombs of the counts of Eu in the crypt of the church. The remaining three then set off for le Tréport where they dined at the hotel and "were served, among other things, surmullets which were very good." Afterward they walked in the little wood beside the sea where the temperature was delightful and where the ground was covered with jonquils, violets and primroses: "We also ran into two snakes, but Joye and Lejeune, who were walking ahead, broke their back with sticks; we did not bring them home to claim the bounty." Returning to Eu by the Bois de Cisé, Joye put back on his way an abbé who was travelling by quadricycle and who had been delayed for a quarter of an hour by a breakdown. "I think this is one of Joye's rare actions likely to stand him in good stead on Judgment Day; helping out an abbé in this way will surely count for something" (EG to Maman, 04.4.nd; tr.).

Another description of a view from Berneval during practice manœuvres provides a fine example of Etienne's consciously artful early prose:

> Berneval ... is really delightful, and from the top of the cliffs along the shore there is a marvellous view over the approach to Dieppe eight kilometres away; when the setting sun shone on these approaches in the evening and seemed to wrap itself around them, I was able to detach myself from the spectacle, spending perhaps an hour and a half or two hours contemplating it, watching the fishing boats enter the harbour under full sail, or some steamer piercing the horizon with its tuft of smoke. When the time came to return and sleep, how difficult it was to go! (EG to Maman, 04.7.nd; tr.)

Military service cut into Etienne's intellectual and cultural development but by no means brought it to a halt. He later recorded in *The Philosopher and Theology* (pp. 17-18) that while in service he first read Descartes' *Les méditations méta-physiques* and Léon Brunschvicg's *Introduction à la vie de l'esprit*. He also wrote from Eu, in the letter recording his Sunday walk, of returning to barracks about six o'clock to read two books he had taken out of the municipal library and had not looked at during the week. One was a life of Marie-Antoinette, and the other a history of the Netherlands during the sixteenth century. "It took the librarian a long time to find this last volume because it had never before been asked for. Its pages had not even been cut – a service I rendered the municipality."

Etienne's general concern for languages remained highly practical in emphasis. Earlier, he had begun a correspondence with an Italian girl from Bergamo. Now, as he told Maman, he found he had two Italian pen-pals:

> I am buried in correspondence. My little Italian girl has written me that she can only write once a month because a boy with whom she used to correspond, and whom she thought must be dead, sent her another letter which arrived only the day after she invited me to be her correspondent. She now offers me one of her girlfriends as a substitute. I am writing back telling her that I accept in good part her auctioning me off this way but also that I am reminded of a line in Offenbach: "C'est un fichu cadeau que vous allez lui faire." [It's a rag of a gift you are to make.] I have to believe that I am not being quoted very high on the Italian exchange. However, I gallantly assured my young Bergamotte that in addition to reading her girlfriend's prose, assuming, that is, that she lets me, I will gladly continue to read hers too, be it only once a year. *Diable!* But my Italian correspondence is becoming complicated! (04.6.nd; tr.)

Etienne's interest in music was not altogether neglected during this period. The occasional leaves he spent in Paris usually included a concert. Closer to the barracks he attended a local production of *Carmen* in Eu. In addition, like a true disciple of Abbé Thorelle, Etienne directed an orchestra, apparently made up of men from the camp, for a local festival:

> I directed my orchestra, playing before a very elegant audience composed of the very chic of the town, and I came away with my little success. I am enclosing an article from the local press on this artistic occasion, also a programme which I ask you please to keep as a souvenir, for I will enjoy perusing it later on. (EG to Maman, 04.7.nd; tr.)

Etienne's military training went very well and he became a good soldier, as he would subsequently demonstrate. Like most army personnel he was, or pretended to be, irritated over policy on permissions and leaves. He characterized his lieutenant-colonel as "stingy" in the granting of leaves. On one occasion Etienne was told that special leave to attend a baptism in Paris would be deducted from his forthcoming regular eight-day vacation; no doubt the lieutenant-colonel was less impressed than Etienne by the significance of the occasion. Etienne also complained that, although military service kept him constantly occupied, the whole military programme was an *école de fainéantise*, a school of laziness. He deeply resented being so tied down and wrote with querulous envy of his younger brothers' mobility that summer: "It doesn't appear to me that André and Maurice

are of a mind to let moss grow on their shoes; they seem to want to become
vagabonds; Paris-Melun, Melun-Paris, Paris-le Tréport, le Tréport-Paris, Paris-
Cravant. Hell! They clearly don't intend to take root!" (EG to Maman, 04.7.nd; tr.).
He began to view the end of his year's service as his "liberation." He knew that on
the day of his release he would rush madly for Cravant: "I simply cannot go two
years without seeing again that mosquito villa of ours" (ibid.; tr.).

For all his discontent, Etienne's period of military service was a success. He
became excellent with the rifle and was placed in charge of a section of twenty-
eight riflemen. In one match he ranked eighth in the regiment, winning an
ashtray: "I will keep this ashtray. ... Without it as evidence, I don't think I could
ever believe I won it. Imagine! Eighth in the regiment! No small beer this!" (ibid.;
tr.). And just after the major manœuvres, he sent his mother his official
assessment by his superiors, not, as he hastened to add, out of self-esteem but
"because it will probably give you pleasure ... and be some part of your re-
compense in this life." The report contained the following remarks, approved by
both the officer-in-command and by the colonel himself:

> Exercise grade – *très bien*; conduct grade – *très bien*; aptitude for command –
> *grande*; comment of captain in charge – lively intelligence, open character, cheer-
> ful, full of high spirits, has had a most happy influence on his comrades, has shown
> much energy during the forced marches which fatigued him, will make an excellent
> reserve officer. (ibid.; tr.)

The year's training culminated early in the summer with war manœuvres
between the camp at Eu and the Normandy coast near Berneval. These war
games simulated actual war conditions and called for co-ordinated battle charges.
All the troops had to live in the open for three days and nights. In "Dans un
grenier qu'on est...," the poet Béranger had celebrated the sheer joy of sleeping in
a hayloft. Now, having experienced this at firsthand, Etienne cheerfully
denounced the poet as a fraud: "Even when you sleep well in straw, you hardly
get a rest. Shame on Béranger!" (ibid.; tr.)

After ten months in the *peloton des dispensées*, with tests and war games
behind them, the recruits were graduated. Etienne ranked tenth out of eighty-two
recruits, which pleased him. In a July letter, he told Maman that the first thirty in
the course were personally congratulated by the colonel, though not granted any
special leave. The young men received the new status of soldier, and were
assigned to new barracks. Etienne was moved from Caserne Morris to Caserne
Drouet and enrolled in a detachment of the Fifth Company of the Eighty-Ninth
Regiment of Infantry. As was the case at Lycée Henri IV, he emerged with two
documents. He received a certificate of aptitude for the rank of *sous-officier* in the
reserve on the basis of marks averaging 17.34. He also received a certificate of
good conduct which reports that on 21 September 1904, Etienne was 1 metre 710
millimetres tall with chestnut hair and eyebrows, grey eyes, a round forehead,
medium nose, medium mouth, round chin, oval face and no distinguishing birth-
marks.

Shortly after graduating, Etienne was moved from Eu to Rouen where, in succeeding summers, he was to qualify as a *chef de section*. It was from Rouen that he was finally "liberated."

During his year of service Etienne grew closer to Maurice and for the first time followed his brother's programme of studies with close attention. He urged Maman to "tell Maurice to read all the time he has nothing to do; he should read Lamartine, Musset, Merimée; he should not abandon the great classics; it is the only way for him to become an architect rather than a house-builder" (04.7.nd; tr.). Later, Etienne was thrilled to hear that Maurice had completed his best academic year to date and had obtained his baccalaureate. Etienne asked his brother to visit le Tréport to discuss plans for the future. He urged Maurice to do another baccalaureate, this time in philosophy, taking his written examinations in philosophy and mathematics, and his orals in science, philosophy and history. According to Etienne, such a programme would keep Maurice in touch with rhetoric, so basic in the mastery of the *beaux arts*. At this stage Maurice had not yet decided to enter medicine.

Etienne also had his own course of studies to consider, though he firmly intended to enrol at the Sorbonne next year. First he would study for his *licence*, or university diploma, then for his *agrégation*, or competitive state diploma, a sine qua non for teaching in lycées and universities. Etienne hoped to take these two diplomas in the absolute minimum time of three years – a rare though possible achievement in philosophy. He had two reasons for haste: the first was shortage of money in the Gilson household; the second was his desire to marry as soon as possible.

Etienne's need for additional funds led him to apply from camp for a bursary. Along with the required forms and documents from Lycée Henri iv, he attached a succinct informative statement about his family's situation. He explained that his father, at age sixty-six and with three of five children still to be educated, was no longer able to work because of age and paralysis of the right side. Etienne was generally sensitive and reticent concerning his father's stroke; he nowhere referred to it as directly as in this application. Even this statement was sent home to be read by both parents, and Etienne assured them that he would not submit it without their full approval.

At this time Etienne was also reticent on the subject of his cousin, Thérèse Ravisé, whom he would soon marry. In the letters to Maman from Eu he mentions her only once, briefly and as an afterthought; when writing to explain his absence from a recent family gathering, he cursorily adds that "I hope all went well and that for once Thérèse was not ill." Even at this stage, however, Etienne knew that he was going to marry this cousin; no doubt his reticence was partly due to some embarrassment about their consanguinity.

In an interview in 1975, Etienne revealed that before attending the Sorbonne he had already fallen in love with Thérèse. As a boy he had not known any girls at all; then he had met Thérèse. "I had never imagined," he confided, "that anything like that existed. My desire for her was so great that it drove me furiously through the Sorbonne in the shortest possible time. I could not marry her without a job." Perhaps this passion lay behind the anxieties that he recounted to Maman shortly before completing his military service:

I am passing through, in this final period of my military service, a kind of involuntary introversion, withdrawing somewhat into myself. There are even moments when I hardly recognize myself: no longer going out at all, speaking less, joking rarely, and turning more often than ever toward a future which frightens me and seems full of works beyond my strength. You cannot guess how hard it sometimes is to doubt oneself in this way, especially when one is moving with all one's soul toward a life that ought to render beautiful a perpetual effort toward truth. Don't worry, however; I won't let these passing doubts break me. I rather think they are the necessary condition for new and more vigorous efforts than before. God willing, and by His path, I shall reach my goal. (04.7.nd; tr.)

2

Student in the Sorbonne, 1904-1907

In the fall of 1904 Etienne enrolled as full-time student in the Sorbonne. Not once had he seriously considered pursuing higher learning anywhere else. Etienne loved the Sorbonne – for him it was a sacred place. Within its walls, scholars had long studied and taught "philosophy and theology in the continuing atmosphere of philosophy and theology themselves" (interview, 1975). No individual could undermine the sanctity of the Sorbonne chairs; as a *Sorbonnard*, Etienne felt himself swept into the mainstream of man's continuing intellectuality. Yet, though he ardently defended the university whenever occasion arose, he could also, like all Frenchmen, roundly criticize it.

When Etienne left the military camp for the Sorbonne, he committed his strength, health and intelligence to the quick and thorough completion of his formal education. During 1904 to 1905 he took all courses and examinations required for the *licence*, and in July 1905 he earned the Sorbonne's *diplôme de licencié ès lettres avec la mention philosophie*. From 1905 to 1907 he took two years of further study with a view to his *agrégation* and to the subsequent writing of his two doctoral theses. In 1906 he obtained his *diplôme d'études supérieures* from the Faculty of Letters, and in 1907 the coveted *agrégé des lycées et universités dans l'ordre de philosophie* from the Ministry of Public Instruction.

Etienne's achievement in these three years was remarkable. Although he attributed his haste to his impatience to marry Thérèse, a gnawing desire to rid himself of prerequisites was a characteristic he would never shed. Committed, for example, to give a course or a public lecture, he would almost invariably prepare a text immediately. Although he often revised the material, he rarely appeared for any commitment without a manuscript that had been ready for some time.

At the Sorbonne, Etienne took far more courses than he had to. Writing later from Bourg-en-Bresse to his brother Maurice, he remarked: "You are right to be taking courses; I think that excellent. Courses were my recreation. I am lost here in Bourg without them" (08.1.18; tr.). Two courses during his licentiate year were particularly memorable: a course on Descartes given by Lucien Lévy-Bruhl, and a series of lectures given in the Collège de France by Henri Bergson.

While still at Henry ɪᴠ, Etienne had attended Lévy-Bruhl's course on Hume. Now at the Sorbonne he attended the course on Descartes, and after only three lectures he made up his mind to write his doctoral thesis on Descartes and under Lévy-Bruhl. Like Durkheim, Lévy-Bruhl was a philosopher-turned-sociologist.

Although better known for his sociological publications, he was highly regarded as an historian of philosophy; the course on Descartes was given within a historical context. According to Gilson, philosophy and sociology met naturally in Lévy-Bruhl: philosophically, he distinguished between logical thought like Aristotle's and thought by participation like Plato's; sociologically, he dealt with primitive peoples as prelogical and ruled by the law of participation.

As a student of Lévy-Bruhl's, Gilson first committed himself to the history of philosophy rather than to philosophy strictly so called. A story he often told his classes records the decision:

> I asked Lévy-Bruhl to direct me in philosophy. He told me that I must under-take something positive, that speculative philosophy just wouldn't do. "All right," I replied, "I will do history of philosophy. That's positive enough, isn't it?" (memorandum, Joseph Owens.)

Apparently it was.

Gilson later wrote glowingly of Lévy-Bruhl's presentation of the Descartes course:

> The lectures took place, not unfittingly, in the Amphithéâtre Descartes on Thursday 4:45 to 5:45. The professor came in fortified with notes which, it appeared to us, contained, in addition to the lecture itself, the texts of Descartes on which it was based. He spoke in a voice measured and clear, moderately animated, in exactly the tone he kept in conversation. His lectures were masterpieces of order, lucidity, clarity. I was only a beginner then, but had no trouble following and noting down the essential points in his ideas. ("Le Descartes de Lévy-Bruhl," *Revue philosophique de la France et de l'étranger*, 147 [1957]: 433; McG 244; tr.)

Certainly the master's lecturing style set a pattern for his student's.

Etienne made complete notes on the Lévy-Bruhl courses during 1902 and 1904. His notes on the Descartes course, as revised in 1905 under Lévy-Bruhl's direction for a course paper on "Descartes and Scholasticism," constitute the most complete piece of work by Lévy-Bruhl on Descartes. When Lévy-Bruhl suggested that Etienne publish these notes, he demurred; it seemed inappropriate that the student publish the master's thoughts. Years later Etienne's conscience bothered him, and he realized that publishing the notes might have offered some slight return to his *maître* for many favours. He decided to compromise, and summarized the first three lectures of the course in his "Le Descartes de Lévy-Bruhl."

Although Etienne's early contacts with Bergson were not so personal or warm, they were intellectually all-important; Etienne later called Bergson's course "the highlight of my life." In Bergson he met for the first time an authentic philosopher in the very act of philosophizing.

Etienne made complete notes of the two fifteen-lecture courses given by Bergson in the Collège de France in 1904. The major course was entitled "The Intellectual Effort," and the *petit cours* was "Herbert Spencer's Theory of the Unknowable." Much later, Gilson recalled the major course:

Each lecture was one piece of doctrine on the intellectual effort; one lecture on intellectual effort in Henry James, one in ... Wundt, and so on – one system a day to the very end. The fifteenth effort was his own. He would come to the platform from below, and he had no papers with him, no notes. He spoke slowly, consideredly, sometimes prodigiously amused, as he so often was by certain philosophical positions. I think I had the best copy of those lectures made by anyone. It was stolen; at least, it disappeared from my library during the first German occupation of France. The notes had been written with great care and were well underlined. I have always felt badly about losing those notes. (interview, 1975.)

Some of the lost materials survive in the manuscript of a series of lectures on Bergson given first in a German prison camp and later in South America. In this form, however, Gilson did not consider them adequate replacements for the lost notes.

Etienne had many other professors during these Sorbonne years. He names most of them in *The Philosopher and Theology*. In each of his three years, he studied under Emile Durkheim. His other professors included Frederic Rauh, Victor Delbos, Brochard, Seailles, Egger and Lalande, as well as semi-retired men like Mauss, Lachelier and Boutroux.

Though he was not as greatly influenced by Durkheim as by Bergson or Lévy-Bruhl, Etienne still never failed to take any course Durkheim offered. In 1904, before he could enrol in the first of these, Gilson found to his surprise that he had to submit to an "orthodoxy test" to demonstrate his scientific objectivity. According to Gilson, Durkheim was a knowledgeable philosopher in the "regular French tradition," but as a positivist he was hostile to philosophy itself. Although Durkheim had begun with Comte, he had moved on in a very different direction; instead of concerning himself with religion, he had become involved with delineating those "social facts" which place restraint on men. Etienne later came to view Durkheimian sociology as essentially Judaic, "inspired by the Book of Leviticus and by the constraining character of the law" (*The Philosopher and Theology*, p. 26).

From one of Delbos' courses, a class paper of Gilson survives on "Malebranche's Polemic against Aristotle and Scholastic Philosophy." In his professorial comments, Delbos found the essay "done with intelligence and exactitude," though it occasionally failed to develop some of the points it introduced and offered no explanation of the intensity of Malebranche's polemic against the scholastics. This sort of penetrating criticism from his professors helped turn Gilson into a sensitive scholar. Delbos seems also to have sympathetically introduced Etienne to the work of Maine de Biran (below, pp. 124-126). Besides being a specialist on Maine de Biran, Delbos shared Maine's constant habit of searching everywhere for answers to personal questions of a religious nature. As a student Gilson did not know whether Delbos was Christian or Catholic; it surprised him to discover that Delbos was both, and took religion very seriously indeed. In later years Gilson was deeply moved by Delbos' deathbed regret that he had spent so much of his lifetime looking for answers that he already knew by faith.

During Etienne's student days at the Sorbonne, an unfavourable criticism charged that its sociologists, particularly its Jewish sociologists, wielded undue influence in appointments to chairs and other posts in the universities and lycées of France. Charles Péguy made this charge frequently, and the criticism bothered Gilson more as he grew older. Twice it brought him to the Sorbonne's defence: once in *The Philosopher and Theology* in 1962, and again in a letter to the director of L'Amitié Charles Péguy, 9 August 1970.

Péguy's criticism was directed against the use of Bergson's philosophy and Durkheim's sociology to support the French government's hard line against religious schools. As Daniel-Rops put it much later, the French government was generally quick to encourage the tendency of positivist rationalists to appeal to the secular arm. As we have seen, Etienne felt deeply indebted to Bergson's ideas. And, although he rejected Durkheim's hostility to philosophy, Etienne respected him as a scholar, as a social scientist and as a dedicated professor of the Sorbonne. He did not share Péguy's view that Durkheim represented a practical Jewish monopoly over chairs and teaching posts; nor did he believe all Bergsonians were as one in seeking to unify France ideologically by destroying religion and "liberating" philosophy.

Etienne was aware that the *sociologues* wielded a good deal of power in making university appointments; he was even apprehensive about his own prospects in the educational bureaucracy. Yet to him Péguy's villains were invariably both kind and just. They left him free to disagree with them in class, in his earliest articles and in his essential theses. Indeed, Etienne came to feel that public university education may well have been more genuinely free than could be politically demonstrated.

If the Sorbonne *sociologues* did not threaten Etienne's career, they nevertheless threatened his philosophical and methodological development in ways he only partly recognized at the time. The *sociologues* had two limitations: they rejected metaphysics as an avenue to truth; and they bestowed an authority on the rational interpretation of data so total as to negate the significance of research techniques. As a Sorbonne student, Etienne was aware of the first of his masters' limitations, but did not discover the second until he met Marc Bloch in Strasbourg in 1919 (below, pp. 93-95). For example, rather than become involved firsthand in field-work, Durkheim was content to accept data gathered by missionaries within various, sometimes unprofessional, contexts. In this respect he and the other Sorbonne *sociologues* were far behind their colleagues in such disciplines as egyptology, historical linguistics and textual criticism.

Despite their limitations the Sorbonne *sociologues* taught Gilson how to integrate classical learning and rational judgment in order to enlarge his perspective and enhance the beauty of whatever truth fell under his scrutiny. Just as Gilson's faith permitted his ideas to transcend the narrow materialism of his masters, so the open humanism that they generously shared with him elevated his work beyond that of many who shared his faith.

Gilson has told us more about his professors at the Sorbonne than about the fellow students and other influential persons who helped form his intellectual attitudes. One great exception was his priest-friend of these years, the Abbé Lucien Paulet, eight years his senior and already teaching philosophy in the Grand Seminary of Issy. The two often attended the Bergson lectures together, and held long conversations about Bergson and about philosophy generally.

Lucien Paulet was completely overwhelmed by Bergson; in his seminary teaching, he tried to present a Bergsonian scholasticism which, he felt, was true philosophy. Paulet was apparently the first to impart to Etienne that strong bias against manuals of philosophy that would remain with him all his life. On one occasion their conversation turned to the most recent manual, Sébastien Reinstadler's *Elementa philosophiae scholasticae* (Freiburg im Breisgau, 1904); neither Etienne nor Lucien could find any resemblance between the contents of this textbook and the nature of philosophy.

Paulet was already beginning to modify his own textbook presentation in the light of his newly-acquired Bergsonianism. Surprisingly, he eventually had to resign his post in the Sulpician seminary because some of his colleagues found him hostile to religion. Etienne later reflected in *The Philosopher and Theology* on the lack of metaphysical awareness that he and his friend suffered during their time together at the Sorbonne:

> I have often wondered about what would have happened if Lucien Paulet had been enlightened on the true meaning of thomism; that is to say, if he had known the metaphysics of being, as taught by Thomas Aquinas himself, which so often differs from what his disciples attribute to him. I have no doubt that today my friend would be an ardent thomist offering his students much more than Bergson was ever able to offer us. But my friend died without ever suspecting what metaphysics really is. I myself had no idea of it, and even now I search my memory in vain to find, among the philosophers I then knew, the name of someone who could have told me what it was. (p. 52.)

When Etienne passed his *agrégation*, Paulet was one of the friends whose assistance he formally recognized in a note of gratitude. Similarly, when Etienne published his two theses in 1912, Paulet received complimentary copies. The two men remained close up to the outbreak of war in 1914; Paulet joined the shock troops and was killed in action in 1915. Etienne regarded the abbé's death, like the war-deaths of Péguy and Pierre Rousselot, a tragic loss for himself personally and for philosophy. Among the few formal photographs that he carefully preserved among his papers is one of Lucien Paulet.

Little information about Etienne's cultural activities survives from these Sorbonne years. However, his interest in the fine arts was no doubt as intense as ever, and he was probably aware of whatever significant cultural events took place. We do know that he kept in touch with Abbé Thorelle, and that this resulted in at least one memorable musical experience.

While at the Sorbonne, Etienne used to attend the high mass in Ste-Clotilde's on most Sundays. He enjoyed this mass immensely because of the extraordinary improvisations of the organist, Charles Tournemire. Thorelle urged Etienne to become acquainted with Tournemire, who had been César Franck's chosen successor at Ste-Clotilde's. "He is," said Thorelle, "a lonely man and will appreciate your disturbing him." One day Etienne took up Thorelle's suggestion and visited Tournemire in his loft high above the nave of Ste-Clotilde's. To his surprise and joy, the great organist received him warmly. Before dismissing him, Tournemire again delighted his young admirer by announcing a special musical treat.

> "I am going to play César Franck's *Prélude, chorale et étude.* Listen carefully, because this is the only place in the world where this composition can be heard as Franck wished it to be, and from the organ for which he composed it. Franck wrote this composition for this organ because of its unique register, *la voix humaine,* a register for which he was personally responsible." So, [recounted Gilson] I heard Tournemire play César Franck's composition, and have never forgotten the experience. This may count for little in the long history of music, but it was certainly something special for me. Again my old Champist friend, Abbé Thorelle, had taken over my cultural life. (interview, 1974.)

Some time later, Etienne noticed an account in the Paris papers of a current musical competition sponsored by the city; the two leading contenders were Charles Tournemire and Gabriel Pirnet, frequently spoken of as the most outstanding musician in Paris. Tournemire won first prize for a three-part (symphonic-chorale-symphonic) composition, and Gilson was delighted beyond expression.

Among the papers that have survived from this period of Gilson's life is the programme for a public concert given in the Grande Salle, rue du Conservatoire, 20 November 1904. The piece presented was *Le sang de la sirène,* "a musical legend in four parts" by Marcel Brennure after the style of A. Le Braz; its music was composed by Charles Tournemire. Etienne must certainly have attended.

Although Etienne had learned his music from Thorelle, he was also able to enjoy it with his Sorbonne *maître,* Lucien Lévy-Bruhl. Like Thorelle, Lévy-Bruhl was particularly knowledgeable in orchestral music. Jean Cazeneuve, Lévy-Bruhl's biographer, records that when the professor was a student in Lycée Charlemagne, he "hesitated between two careers; that of philosopher and that of orchestra director" ([Paris, 1963], p. 1; tr.). Certainly Etienne and Lévy-Bruhl often discussed music and musicians.

A second organist and composer whom Etienne first came to know while a student in the Sorbonne was Alexandre Guilmant. Etienne was introduced to Guilmant primarily through Abbé Thorelle but also through Lévy-Bruhl. He occasionally attended Guilmant's private recitals, including one long historical series on organ music, "Les Grandes Orgues de Trocadéro." Etienne felt indebted to Guilmant for his knowledge of the history of music. During his first visit to Harvard in 1926, he was pleasantly surprised to hear on the Faculty Club's organ a full register he thought was Guilmant's. It turned out to belong to one of Guilmant's pupils, of whom he learned there were several around Cambridge. Unknown to Gilson, Guilmant had preceded him to Harvard, and for several years had been organist in the Memorial Chapel.

At the Sorbonne Etienne's love of Wagner reached fever pitch. His first Wagner experience had taken place in 1900 when he was a mere Champist: at the General Exhibition he had heard Wagner's *Prelude to Tristan* as conducted by Gustav Mahler. Etienne never forgot the experience and at the Sorbonne first made the claim, often repeated throughout his life, that "if the works of all composers but one had to be lost, I personally would save those of Wagner." Later, when he wrote the article "Art et métaphysique" at the Verdun front, he capped the piece with a Wagnerian motto borrowed from Gabrielle d'Annunzio: "Ah, Stelio, t'aspettavo! Riccardo Wagner è morte. Il mondo parve diminito di valore." ("Ah, Stelio, I was waiting for you! Richard Wagner is dead. The world seems to have lost some of its value.")

At the Sorbonne Etienne's appreciation of Claude Debussy, another of Thorelle's legacies, involved him in a public disturbance. After the opening performance of *La mer*, about 15 October 1905, Etienne and other Debussysts clashed violently with campus traditionalists over the composer's right to ignore the demands of accepted scales and chords. Etienne on this occasion was party, *mutatis mutandis*, to a cause which opened the way for the acceptance of jazz and then rock; he might well have been shocked had he realized what new uses of dissonance were to follow.

Besides meeting his academic requirements in three short years, Etienne also spent the intervening summers of 1905 and 1906 trying to qualify as an officer in the military camp at Rouen. During the second summer he fell into a depression; rather than taking the officers' qualifying examination, he decided to content himself with becoming a *chef de section*, or noncommissioned officer. For Etienne 1905 to 1906 had been especially difficult. Because André and Maurice were both doing their military service, he had been left alone with his parents to shoulder many family responsibilities. As Etienne became increasingly depressed, his brothers and Maman grew concerned about him. Maurice, now in medicine, diagnosed Etienne's condition as a case of *la fièvre sorbonnesque*. He prescribed a visit to Cravant and an additional simple remedy:

> Ample harvesting of butterfly species and composites. All that is required is a forty-centimetre box. If one of you will undertake to buy it, I will gladly furnish the braided strap from Etienne's table drawer to bind it. (Maurice to Papa, 07.6.27; tr.)

Two letters written by Etienne to Maman from the military camp offer us glimpses into his inner life during the Sorbonne years. In these letters, both written in July 1906, he referred briefly to his depression: "I am feeling absolutely down and out [*abruti*]." Although he had intended to visit Dieppe and Paris on two Sundays of his four weeks in camp, he was too unwell to make either trip. Instead he spent those Sundays visiting Rouen's antiquities, which he found surprisingly rich and extensive. Of the other men in camp, Etienne wrote that there was "too much conviviality, too little solid morality"; Maman's training and Thérèse's patient goodness had spoiled him for camp life. He reported his decision to take only the qualifying tests for *chef de section*. Four weeks was too short a time in which to qualify also as an officer; "Besides, in time of war it is probable I shall get that rank in any case as the army is short 18,000 reserve officers." (06.7.10 and 16; tr.)

These letters also mentioned Etienne's upcoming final year of study at the Sorbonne. In the first he wrote: "I have received the descriptive booklet for the *agrégation* in philosophy next year. The programme strikes me as being a little heavy but it is most interesting." In the second he commented on the previous year's candidates for the *agrégation*: "Five students from the Sorbonne, four from the École Normale have qualified. It is our triumph! I hope in my turn to help keep up this tradition."

In these letters Etienne revealed a preoccupation with his role as acting head of his family. He had a paternal comment for each of the three Gilsons who were summering in Cravant. He told Maman not to be scandalized by the novel she was reading: "It is not as evil as you think; indeed the book doesn't utter a tenth part of the truth ... of what is going on in our time." To Paul, who had decided to plant some fir trees to battle the mosquitoes around *la fausse rivière*, he addressed one of his typically informed quips: "I have the impression that now that Paul has thrown himself into tree-culture, he hopes to surpass even Chautedrinne in cultivation of firs. I wish him luck!" Etienne also suggested that André, with time on his hands, busy himself with his water colours, "letting the angel in the garden serve as a bowl."

By the summer of 1907 Etienne's three rugged qualifying years at the Sorbonne were over: his *licence* had been obtained in 1905, his diploma of higher studies in 1906, and his preparations were now complete for the written and oral examinations that preceded his *agrégé*. The family knew that Etienne's efforts had been Herculean. They awaited results with trepidation: although they hoped that Etienne could avoid the delay of an additional year, they knew such delays were the usual results of the Sorbonne's rigorous testing procedures.

In a postscript to a fine letter to Papa from Vermenton in June 1907, Maurice wrote: "Auntie and I are constantly thinking about Etienne. Success will surely crown his work, and what a success it will be!" (07.6.27; tr.) At the end of July, Etienne sent a cryptic telegram from Paris to Maman in Cravant: "We are *admissibles* the 16 August." His writtens over, he was eligible on that date to take the final oral for the *agrégation*. On the night of 16 August he wrote to Maman, who was still in Cravant, a stirring, half-wild *bonheur* letter:

> Chère petite Maman. It is one-thirty in the morning, but I have gotten back out of bed to write you.... I am irresistibly compelled to tell you about my happiness.... It is hard even to think about it; it must be affecting my brain a little because I have been talking to myself explaining all the happiness that has come to me in one swoop. First, and greatest, is knowing how happy you will be to see another of the tasks you have taken on accomplished. ... My second happiness, need I say it, is that Thérèse and her parents will be so happy. For two years I have been dreaming desperately of the day I would send her a one-word telegram: *agrégé*. Right now, as I write this letter, she is sleeping with that blissful telegram under her pillow, that is,

if she is sleeping at all. ... My third happiness is my own. I don't yet quite grasp all its significance: it is the peace of existing; it is the path ahead; it is the realizing of a five or six-year dream; it is the end of the yearly nightmare of examinations. What more can I say? ... Within the space of three years, [God] has given me the two greatest temporal joys left for Him to give me: the love of Thérèse and the *agrégation*. (07.8.16; tr.)

The Sorbonne years closed fittingly with a vacation at Maman's family home. The little village of Cravant lies halfway between Auxerre and Avallon in the Burgundy countryside, and preserves many lovely medieval and renaissance remains. It lies on the east bank of the Yonne, just below the point at which La Cure, having wound its way from Vézelay through Lucy-sur-Cure, Arcy-sur-Cure and Vermenton, empties its waters. Route Nationale 6, Gilson's "cette meurtrière nationale 6," enters Cravant from the northwest, passes the Hôtel des Deux Ponts, then crosses the Yonne and an old canal ("la fausse rivière" of the letters). The road then passes between Maman's house and garden on the right and the village post office on the left. Cravant and Vermenton, both dear to the Gilsons, are separated by only eight kilometres. Their setting is rural, restful and timeless. In the villages and the surrounding countryside are preserved the life, the language, the beauty and the culture that in all the world Etienne held most dear.

The Gilsons began vacationing in Cravant and Vermenton in 1895 or 1896, when Etienne was twelve or thirteen years old. By the time of his *agrégation*, Etienne had grown to love these villages deeply, and the entire Burgundian countryside with them. Cravant, Vermenton, Accolay, Arcy, Noyers (pronounced *Noyèrs*, as he invariably warned), and many others became his own villages. The abbeys also became his own: at Pontigny, "the second of the daughters of Cîteaux"; at Fontenay, "the second daughter of Clairvaux"; at Reigny, "on the dark-watered Cure, founded by hermits but gathered into the Cistercian fold by Etienne of Toucy"; and at Vézelay, "which we owe along with other masterpieces to the monks of Cluny." Etienne particularly loved the local speech, "so delightful on one's tongue and which I used to speak ... when I played *e gobelles* [marbles] with little boys of my own age." ("Les abbayes de Pontigny, de Fontenay et de Reigny," *Jardin des Arts*, 102 (March 1963): 32-61; McG 192.)

The three formal Sorbonne years came to a symbolic close with Maman's reception of a sad letter from Abbé Piot, still superior of Notre-Dame-des-Champs in its last years. Maman had written Father Piot to announce Etienne's *agrégé*. Piot replied: "As for Etienne, he has shown himself a man of character at a time when there are so few of them. He will certainly bring honour to his family and to those who have helped prepare him." He then turned to Abbé Thorelle who had taught Etienne the meaning of style, of study and of the arts, especially music:

I regret having to tell you that three days ago [August 26] I made a sorrowful trip into Bourgogne. I had to go to Pont-sur-Yonne to give the last rites to M. Thorelle who died there in his mother's arms. I recommend him to your prayers. (07.8.22; tr.)

3

Quarta Est Juventus

1 LYCÉE LALANDE, BOURG-EN-BRESSE, 1907-1908

On 24 August 1907 Gilson was issued his official decree from the Minister of Public Instruction naming him *agrégé des lycées dans l'ordre de la philosophie*. Two long months followed of apprehensive waiting during which he took a vacation, made remote preparations to get married, and worked a little on his thesis. Finally, a second official decree from the same minister named him, 10 October 1907, "provisional professor of philosophy (sixth class) in the Lycée of Bourg to replace M. Aymard, deceased." Gilson's salary was to be 3,700 francs. He probably knew about this appointment unofficially some days before the date of issue; by 12 October he was already installed in a rooming house at 29, rue Voltaire and teaching in Lycée Lalande.

Bourg, or more correctly Bourg-en-Bresse, lies in the foothills of the Jura mountains about fifty miles northeast of Lyon near the Swiss border. Gilson's first letter to Maman is informative, and amusing too in much of its detail, especially concerning the family's efforts to find him clothes befitting his new dignity:

> I got Uncle Alphonse's trousers, and they fit me well. I also took his lined jacket, and just as well, as it appears that when the wind blows from Jura during the winter, the temperature drops to twenty degrees below zero. (07.10.12; tr.)

In this letter Gilson also mentions "the little chickens of Bresse." In his next, of 18 October, he admits to eating them twice a day; he also tells Maman that he is sending a package of these *délicieuses volailles* for Papa, now facing, along with his other ailments, an operation for cataracts. "Don't," he warns her, "save the chickens until the whole family is around. They are very small and won't provide a biteful for everyone." In Cravant in 1974 Gilson was still crediting Bourg with teaching him "just how good *real* chicken can be."

In his early letters from Bourg, Gilson wrote with enthusiasm about his classes, about his colleagues and about Lycée Lalande. He was happy about everything pertaining to teaching: "They were actually paying me," he later reminisced, "to teach what I was so deeply interested in." He also enjoyed the camaraderie he found in the lycée among the staff and between staff and students.

Gilson's post in Bourg was hardly rated a "plum" by prospective candidates: the town was remote, its opportunities few. Yet Gilson loved Lalande. He said nostalgically in 1974: "I should never have left Bourg. I could have worked there creatively, been happy, and been understood." The teaching staff at Lalande was relatively large: it included M. Gros the *proviseur*; M. Martinand the *censeur* or vice-principal (*le bison* to students); M. l'abbé Reverdy the chaplain; a treasurer and his assistant; and forty-three teachers. Lalande's extensive programme included all levels from *classe enfantine* to baccalaureate; it chiefly concentrated on the usual eight elementary grades from *huitième* (for beginners) to *première* (for seniors), and on the four collège (secondary) years: rhetoric, belles-lettres, and first and second philosophy. Students could take entrance examinations for the Ecole Normale after *première*, and for the baccalaureate after the completion of philosophy. As the only professor of philosophy, Gilson was placed in charge of the twelve candidates for the baccalaureate.

Of all Gilson's courses, he found teaching *la morale* to students in *quatrième* and *troisième* most pleasant. He wrote Maman:

> I like the course because it is practical; it covers matters important for living: the lie, for example, and charity. In this course I give neither lectures nor homework, but tell stories with the objective of doing the students some good. The little rascals find it *très chic*. I put my heart into it and am rewarded because they listen and are interested. (07.10.18; tr.)

In December he wrote to Maman during his class in *la morale*; his students meanwhile wrote a composition on an assigned topic:

> "Jacques has passed into the lycée; his character is already hypocritical. How does he act? What does he say? What will be the consequences of his conduct for himself and others?" They are going to tell me how hypocrites belittle others before the professors. I shall find it all rather entertaining. (07.12.4; tr.)

Besides teaching, Gilson's predecessor had also advised the students in politics and in personal conduct. The first he had achieved through a *bulletin politique* in one of the town's newspapers, the second by counselling students and their parents. Gilson turned down the newspaper column when it was offered to him. As teacher of *la morale*, however, he reluctantly accepted responsibility for counselling. He found this responsibility worrisome, and spoke of his scruples to the *proviseur*. He was referred to the trouble-shooting *censeur*, Martinand, a man of good sense who kept himself at arm's length from parents; according to his colleagues, the *censeur* had made the only mistake of his life when he had catalogued a library book, *Architecture du sol de la France*, under fine art. "So," wrote Gilson, "I asked the *censeur* about my duties. He warned me to avoid subversive ideas, especially 'liberty of conscience', an idea my predecessor had worked to death thus rendering discipline impossible in the entire institution. Preach good conduct, he told me simply. So that's what I preached." (ibid.; tr.)

Gilson recalled one particular problem that arose in his counselling. One day he asked the *censeur* what to do about a certain baccalaureate student enrolled in his class in *la morale*. Each day when the boy came to school he was accompanied right up to the door of the lycée by a young woman of reputedly easy morals. The *censeur* replied that Gilson should only become involved if the girl actually entered the lycée. Gilson then naïvely asked: "Ought not his parents be told?" The *censeur* replied with his customary guarded good sense: "Here's what the parents would reply: 'What the boy is doing is not against nature, is it?' So, then, it's natural." Gilson had just discovered the foundation of practical morality. (*Sept*, 34.4.7; tr.)

When Gilson was later asked whether he had taught St Thomas in the lycées, he replied:

> No, I was not supposed to. I was hired to get the boys through their baccalaureate examinations. No examiner was ever going to ask them anything about St Thomas. I taught a vague philosophy: psychology, ethics, logic and so on, but all as quite general. The psychology I taught was the association of ideas, contiguity. I taught the boys what reasoning is, what a demonstration is, the logical sciences. I did not teach philosophy as a science. Science is too noble a word to describe what I was doing: I taught it much as Victor Cousin had; that is, as conversation. St Thomas was not taught in the lycées then, or now; the lycées never came to St Thomas. (interview, 1974.)

Gilson's praticality extended beyond his morality classes. He made a special trip to Lyon to let the rector of the university know that he was available as an examiner, a task that could net him an extra 100 or 150 francs. All he elicited from the rector was the wry comment that examiners were picked up as needed, usually at the last minute. The reply left him somewhat irked.

Once Gilson settled down in Bourg, he began to give all the time he could spare to the writing of his thesis. Having begun the research in Paris with Lévy-Bruhl, he was now ready to begin the writing in earnest: "My work goes rather well; about forty pages are already written. I will have only to tidy up my style. From my point of view, all goes well, and I am quite satisfied." (EG to Maman, 08.6.25; tr.) Each time he went to Paris, Gilson took his work, his doubts and his queries to Lévy-Bruhl. This procedure continued after he left Bourg, and throughout his years at the lycées of Rochefort-sur-Mer, Tours, St-Quentin and Angers.

During the fall of 1907, Gilson's life in Bourg-en-Bresse was strenuous and lonely. In addition to his teaching and his thesis work, important domestic arrangements had to be made in view of his approaching marriage. Moreover, he keenly missed boulevard Port-Royal and ached for the coming of Thérèse; in one early letter he confessed that he cried often.

A few anecdotes survive from these months and offer humorous glimpses into the pathos of Gilson's bachelor plight. One of these is the episode of the Besson stove. After he had chosen his apartment at 12, rue Bernard, and it had been duly visited and approved by Thérèse over the All-Saints holiday, Gilson set out to furnish it. Furnishings had to meet two standards: they had to carry a quality mark, and they had to be cheap. Because Bourg's climate was cold, his first need was for a stove, a Besson of course. He found a secondhand one in the shop of the friendly M. Deschet, 9, rue Centrale. Letters from November to January record a succession of new annoyances: first he couldn't keep the stove alight; then he couldn't get heat from it, and had to wear an overcoat to bed; then he poked a hole through the ashpan; and finally, no doubt in a burst of impatience, he dropped the entire grate and broke it. He took he whole mess back to M. Deschet who promptly shipped it off to the factory in Paris for repairs; among the Gilson papers survives a bill from the Société du Poêle Besson for fifteen francs, forty centimes. When the stove was returned to Gilson, however, it still refused to heat. He wrote dolefully to Maurice: "I have no fire. I am going to the marble-mason's to look for some sand to bank the Besson's belly." (08.1.13; tr.) Then suddenly, toward the end of the letter, a triumphant note was sounded: "Flash bulletin! The Besson is throwing off heat like the sun itself. All is well."

Then there was the pants episode, "la mémorable ruine de mon pantalon." Gilson went to Paris at Christmas to visit his family and see Lévy-Bruhl about his thesis. He ruined his good pants, the pair he wore with Uncle Alphonse's jacket for his classroom appearances. His younger brother André – referred to as l'abbé since deciding to enter the seminary – loaned his own best trousers to Gilson until Maman could pick up a new pair at the Bon Marché. Gilson wanted the store to send them directly to him as "the cost of sending them will be less that way, and it is easier to put in a claim in case the parcel gets lost in transit."

On the trip back to Bourg, a fellow traveller in the compartment, an Alsatian, kept everyone awake with "histoires assommantes" of his incessant adventures in the big city. The train was an hour and forty minutes late reaching Macon, and Gilson missed his connection for Bourg. When he finally got back to his apartment, he immediately mailed Maman his measurements. He asked her to hurry, for he was "standing at attention grimly waiting." Why grimly? He had left André's pants behind in Paris:

> I must have forgotten to bring the pair from André's suit, because I can't find them. How predictable! The weather is fairly mild, and I can wear my summer pants. I hesitate to dress up like a butterfly, to hoist my reseda, because the gaudy colours will serve notice of my penury to the whole world. I am happy all the same, dreaming of my dear Thérèse who will be beside me in another month. (08.1.10; tr.)

Typical of Gilson's wry humour during this period was the note he attached to a little New Year's gift for Maurice – le petit docteur, now that he was entering medicine. The gift was a heligravure, reproducing a work by the English painter, John Hoppner. Gilson quoted Faust's echo of Horace's Ars Poetica, 70: "Er ist tod und begraben und niedermals wird wiedergehen." "If you like it, hang on to it; give it a proper spot on your shelf. If you don't, shove it into a corner, or give it to an enemy." (08.1.13; tr.)

For Gilson the major event of this period was his impending marriage to Thérèse Ravisé, his second cousin:

> We were cousins issus de germains: her grandmother and my grandfather were brother and sister. She was probably the first woman I saw as a woman. ... I first

met Thérèse at Cravant when I was about eighteen. ... I decided on the spot I would marry her, but still had to pass the *licence*, the diploma of higher studies, the *agrégation*, and then get an appointment. (interview, 1974.)

Although by October 1907 he had obtained the necessary teaching appointment, his attempts to persuade the Ravisés to set an early date for the wedding were unsuccessful. February 10 and 11 was the earliest they would agree to.

On 10 February 1908 the marriage contract was drawn up before the Ravisé family notary, M. Auberge of Melun. The civil ceremony took place the same day. The financial arrangements were of the kind usual among *la petite bourgeoisie*; the Gilsons, after all, were shopkeepers, and the Ravisés were successful chocolatiers. Etienne and Thérèse elected for marriage under the joint-property system; this also allowed for the making of individual property deals with the other party's authorization. Thérèse's dowry was valued at 44,356.25 francs: this included the cost of her trousseau, 4,350 francs; a house at 6, rue de Ponthierry, Melun, 25,000 francs; and thirty-five registered three-percent PLM railway bonds, 15,006.25 francs. The trousseau came from the joint property of M. and Mme Ravisé, the house and bonds from M. Ravisé's own holdings. Ravisé reserved the right to live in the house as long as he lived, paying rental of 250 francs every three months.

For his part Gilson assembled money to rent and furnish their apartment. For this he had his salary; his 100-franc *indemnité d'agrégation*; some shares which Maman sold as his part of her dowry; and a further sum from rentals on Maman's few properties. Among these properties was the house on rue de Jura, Paris, whose chimneys were this year in worrying disrepair; this provoked Gilson to quip that the Jura had pursued him even to Bourg, which lay in the foothills of the Jura mountains (EG to Maman, 07.10.12).

Gilson's personal gifts to Thérèse were a Lachemal tea-service, a tablecloth, and a timbale (an earthenware cooking pot) that had come to him from his grandmother. For the apartment he bought a Louis XV bedroom and dining-room set (copies by Mercier and Krieger), a carpet, a stove and so on. He was very happy about the ring he had picked out:

> Don't tell Thérèse, and especially don't tell Marthe or Louise [the wives of his elder brothers]. Thérèse only knows that her ring is *en moderne, style modéré*. What she does not know is that the setting represents a chased-gold leaf, and on the edge of this leaf a diamond of the loveliest water symbolizes a dewdrop. I have been looking for a long time for a setting that represents something and I have certainly found one. (EG to Maman, 07.11.10; tr.)

The sacramental marriage and nuptial blessing took place at eleven-thirty *très précise* on Tuesday 11 February 1908 in the Church of Saint-Aspais at Melun. There was a dispensation from two banns in Bourg, obtained from the bishop of Belley. In Melun and Paris, however, all the banns were duly published on 19 and 25 January and on 2 February. The wedding took place as planned; a menu of the dinner that followed remains among the Gilson papers.

Gilson and Thérèse were very happy in Bourg but their letters to Maman from February to June for the most part have not been saved; this was probably owing to the upset caused by Papa's new illness, cataracts. A few details survive, however. We know for instance that the lycée gave Gilson leave for the wedding for the week of 9 February. We also know that the young couple came directly back to Bourg; by Saturday 15 February, when Gilson wrote to Maman, they had not so much as stepped outside their apartment. According to this letter they planned to go to the hotel for dinner on Sunday, no doubt after mass; we can guess that they ordered the *petits poulets de Bresse*. From a letter of Thérèse to Maman on 20 February we learn that Thérèse was overwhelmed by the luxury of the apartment, and that Gilson was ill with the grippe.

By June, vignettes of the couple's domestic life begin to appear. Gilson writes to Maman that he is watching Thérèse make jam. This experiment seems not to have succeeded for in July he writes again:

> Your advice on the subject of cherries for jam arrived just as we were enjoying a new ovenful of five or six pots. This time they were absolutely delicious. My little *cordon bleu* is becoming tops in preserving. Our cuisine here is invariably excellent, although right now we are eating as little meat as possible; the heat spell has put us on a Friday-abstinence diet because we discovered a number of spoiled spots in otherwise fresh pieces of meat and this has somewhat turned us off butchers. Right now eggs have top priority, particularly in the form of potato omelettes. (08.7.6; tr.)

The same letter provides two other glimpses into newlywed life. As Thérèse cuts out for herself "a blouse of white cloth," Gilson comments that the disarray of their living room "reminds me of the dining room at 91, boulevard Port-Royal during one of Maman's dressmaking bees." The other item is less pleasant:

> I have the satisfaction of informing you that the bedbug which has been devouring us was caught last Monday. It was enormous. Two others have since met the same fate, and I fear they may not be the last. On top of all this, we have found a moth in a hatbox. Our apartment is fast becoming a kind of zoo.

Much later in his life, Gilson recalled the newlyweds' difficulty in surviving on his meagre salary:

> One day when I brought home my pay, I found that I had been passed a bronze coin in place of a silver one. Thérèse said to me that I would simply have to pass the coin off on someone else or we could not make ends meet. Another month, when our cash had dropped to ten francs, she sent me off to a casino to see if I could build it up a little. I knew nothing of casinos, but she did: that side of her education surpassed mine. She explained to me how to gamble, so I went off to try. I lost much of our ten francs on the first play. I slowly built up what was left to eight francs but in the end went home broke. Fortunately I had a train ticket. (interview, 1974.)

In a letter dated 6 July 1908, Gilson told Maman that he had sent off an article to a learned journal: "I am sending seven large pages of copy to the *Annales de philosophie chrétienne*. It has been a lot of work, but it is also distracting, and reading for it helps to keep me *au courant.*" He did not describe the nature or content of the article and it seems to have been rejected by the editor: at any rate it was not printed in the *Annales.* It is tempting to speculate on the topic of this paper, particularly as the editor of the *Annales,* Lucien Laberthonnière, was soon to be in trouble with Rome over the political and religious positions taken by Action Française and *Le sillon.** Could Gilson have been arguing for or against some Laberthonnière position: for instance that the church ought not to have an official theologian or philosopher; that St Thomas' philosophy was essentially that of Aristotle; or that philosophers such as Edouard Le Roy and Maurice Blondel exaggerated philosophy's contributions to faith? Or was his theme more political, dealing with issues raised by Action Française and *Le sillon*? Gilson was already on the side of French democracy and would later become involved in social reform; he always believed in the right of scholars to probe social issues. He was ultimately to become critical of Pius x (below, pp. 66-67), to feel sympathy for Loisy (below, pp. 115, 206-207), and to join the Mouvement Républicain Populaire (MRP), that nonconfessional, left-of-centre political party of which Marc Sanglier, champion of *Le sillon,* was the first president.

June and July in the lycées were usually months of anxiety. If the students did not do well in the competitive examinations, their teachers would lose face with the ministry. Rumours of forthcoming changes abounded, heralding good news or ill. On 6 July Gilson told Maman that his baccalaureate students would take their written examinations the next day. Except for three classes a week to younger students, his teaching for the year was over. Although he noted that prize day was set for 30 July, he did not seem to know yet that he would be delivering the formal address. He wrote that he hoped to be left in Bourg for a second year: however he would "leave worrying about such things to God."

Gilson was called upon, as were many teachers in the lycée at the end of the year, to mark papers in French composition without compensation for supplementary service. The same had been the case earlier in the year when the town of Bourg had organized an extra-mural competition among the better students of the district: for his part in this project Gilson had received, as he put it, "zero francs, zero centimes." On yet another occasion, when invited to examine a group of students in psychology, *la morale* and pedagogy, he was paid only one franc per hour, a payment he called "derisory and a bad joke." Gilson thought

---

* Action Française, first a committee and then a league, was founded in 1898 during the Dreyfus affair to re-establish the monarchy in France. Action Française advocated integral nationalism as opposed to the kind of national centralization exemplified by the Third Republic. Dominated by such free-thinkers as Charles Maurras and Léon Daudet, it also attracted anticlericals. Action Française published a biweekly periodial and a daily newspaper, both called *L'action française.* Gilson, a republican, was never sympathetic to the organization. The Holy Office objected to Action Française almost from the beginning but issued no formal condemnation until 29 December 1926.

Le sillon was a political review founded in Paris in 1894. It was first edited by Paul Renaudin and then, in 1902, by Marc Sanglier. Like Action Française, *Le sillon* also espoused radical policies that Gilson found objectionable.

that a protest should be launched by the Bourg teachers union, l'Amicale de Bourg. Teachers should insist on payment for supplementary work, particularly when their sacrifice only served to make the books of Treasury and Accounts look good. He complained to Maman that, "Only baccalaureate exams are paid for, and for these no vacancies have turned up this year."

The prognostication proved overly pessimistic. Early in July Gilson was assigned to examine a class of thirty-two girls seeking the *brevet supérieur* (higher-school certificate). His description of these examinations will not surprise many who knew him as an examiner:

> I spent the entire day testing thirty-two girls for their certificate. It was a real experience for me. I had three of them burst into tears, and a fourth fainted. They were terrified, both at being tested by me and because psychology is reputed to be a difficult exam. Perhaps I should add that their tears were really caused by their fatigue and nerves, not by me. The principal of one school told me afterward that I had an excellent press among the girls, that I was even popular because, so he said, of my kindness. The kindness of little Etié is enough to make one die of laughter! I gave, the principal went on to say, every chance to those who were going under. I encouraged everyone, etc. Next day I was completely worn out, downright tired. Thus far the chronicle of my examining. (EG to Maman, 08.8.11; tr.)

All Gilson's students were highly successful. His record with baccalaureate candidates was almost perfect: of the twelve he prepared, eleven were declared *admissibles*. "The only failure," he wrote, "is by far the best student of my class. Such things happen. He hoped to become a teacher but must not be cut out for one, which may be a useful lesson to him." (08.8.8; tr.) Possibly even this boy's results were reconsidered: Gilson later recalled that all his 1908 baccalaureate candidates in philosophy had passed, including "even the local prefect's son who was a dunce" (interview, 1974).

As his last official duty as a professor in Lycée Lalande, Gilson delivered the *discours d'ouverture* at the Solemn Distribution of Prizes, 30 July 1908. This was a considerable honour, and indicates the respect in which *proviseur* Gros must have held him. Gilson's address, printed in the annals of the lycée, may well have been his first published article. His subject, "Hunting La Vouivre: A Remedy for Ennui and a Way to Rescue Local Traditions from Oblivion" (Gilson Archives), is a spirited defence of local folklore and Sorbonne sociology. Gilson presents two Bressan versions of how to hunt *la vouivre*. These he has adapted from two local authors, Gabriel Vicaire and Denis Bressan (alias de Berthillier). Etymologically *vouivre* is a puzzling word: it may well be a derivative of Bressan *voui*, cognate of French *oui* (see Robert, *Dictionnaire de la langue française*). In folklore however *la vouivre* is either a flying serpent or a mythical bird. On its forehead, like an eye, it carries a wondrous diamond.

With high humour and delicate sympathy, Gilson retells his stories, relating them to local language and customs and urging their importance for the young graduands seated in front of him. Though as students they have learned the wonderful language and customs of Paris, he tells them, there is no call for them to lose their own. In a variation on a Goethean theme, he explains that, although the present normally moves into the past, there is a sense – as on prize day – in which the past also moves into the present; and theirs is a Bressan past well worth saving, "un passé ... qui ressuscite." Gilson even lays claim to a bit of original research, naming the unknown farmboy who once stole a vouivre's diamond; who else could this clever fellow have been than "lou grand volé de Chai," the valet of Saix, the hero of quite another old Bresse song. All this folklore, embellished with a touch of scholarship, and embroidered with fine descriptions of Bresse farms, of the village of Domes, and of the mountain and valleys of Ain, made Gilson's *discours d'ouverture* one of the most unusual prize-day orations in any school's history.

2 ROCHEFORT-SUR-MER, 1908-1910

The first year of teaching in the lycées ended quietly in August 1908. Gilson and Thérèse took a trip north into the Vosges and the Swiss border, stopping briefly in Belfort and Mulhouse; they then returned to spend the rest of the month with their families in Melun, Paris and Cravant. So far as they knew, they would return to Bourg for 1908 to 1909. Their expectations were abruptly changed however when the Minister of Public Instruction informed Gilson, on the very late date of 30 September, that he had been provisionally appointed as professor of philosophy at the lycée in Rochefort-sur-Mer. Gilson was replacing a M. Robert, whose appointment had also been changed at the last moment.

In Bourg there was a scurry as Gilson and Thérèse prepared to move right across France. The Ravisés rushed from Melun to help with the moving of the foodstuffs. M. Deschet, who had sold Etienne the stove and other furnishings, honoured an earlier promise to pack and ship the couple's furniture. Gilson set off alone for Rochefort, taking residence in the Grand Hôtel de France while he arranged his classes and searched for a place to live. Thérèse joined him there a few days later. Before long they rented the apartment on rue Thiers in which they would live for the next two years. Rochefort was the only lycée, of the seven Gilson taught in, in which he remained for over a year.

At first Gilson liked Rochfort-sur-Mer. Located at the mouth of the Charente and on the Atlantic shore, it was close to the St-Cyr Military School for Infantry and Cavalry and to the Naval College; both were national institutions which attracted many substantial visitors to the area. Rochefort's lycée also gained prominence because it provided unique academic services, including the teaching of Naval's two-year preparatory programme. Gilson was immediately assigned both philosophy and mathematics at St-Cyr and Naval; as a new teacher, his assignment to three hours a week at Naval showed that the lycée's administration already had considerable confidence in him. Indeed, this very confidence meant that he was given too much to teach: seventeen classroom hours during the first semester, eighteen during the second. However his salary rose by 550 francs, which was "not to be sniffed at," and the post was rather a pretty one "for a toad of twenty-four years" (EG to Maman, 08.10.nd; tr.).

Gilson found the town of Rochefort "*gaie, ravissante et animée*, not stodgy like Bourg, and people there throng the streets at all hours." He enjoyed life by the sea, and had no regrets about exchanging the hills of Jura and the *volailles* of Bourg for Rochefort's tides and salt-water fish. Moreover Rochefort had splendid public gardens, especially le Jardin de la Préfecture Maritime, which reminded him and Thérèse of Versailles and the Luxembourg. They walked there constantly, mingling with the families of Rochefort's naval officers and *fonctionnaires*. Indeed, walking soon played a major and idyllic role in their daily routine. During the afternoon, Thérèse would take her needlework to the public gardens; Gilson would meet her on his way home from the lycée, and the young lovers would stroll homeward, arm linked in arm. (EG to Maman, 09.4.18; tr.)

Rochefort was fairly close to Angoulème where Gilson's first cousin and closest friend, Docteur Henry Gilson, was chief of medicine in the large hospital. Etienne was not in Rochefort ten days before he visited his cousin; Henry immediately treated him to a tour of Angoulème and gave him a rare volume by Descartes that he would cherish all his life. Subsequent visits to Angoulème were many and gladly taken. On one of these, Gilson and Thérèse were invited to join Henry, his wife and son for Mardi Gras 1909: "We had as usual *crèpiots et pets-de-nonne*, and we cut the pat of butter from both ends against the holy season of Lent when the reign of the bean begins" (EG to Maman, 09.2.25; tr.).

Unfortunately, Gilson soon learned that conditions at the lycée were not as healthy as they had first seemed, nor were the students so bright. The first sign of trouble arrived when Gilson lost his supplementary hours along with the subsidy that accompanied them: "Whatever happens, my supplementary hours will be and are cancelled." The young teacher voiced his objections strongly. Although he feared his angry protests might damage his career, he decided to stake his future on the excellence of his thesis rather than on the sweetness of his disposition:

> It is the necessary consequence of the "soup," the *purée noire*, in which the lycée finds itself, and the administration is cutting its expenses so as to remain afloat. It is throwing ballast overboard, and my trifling concerns are part of this ballast. There is nothing to be done about it. I simply wrote to Darlu telling him that the uniting of these two classes during the course of the year – they were not at the same point – was creating for me as a professor an inextricable situation; also I believe they intend later this year to divide the classes again and take something else away from me, possibly my Greek classes. My one student will be sacrified, and as he wishes to enter Normal School, he will have to shift for himself. I don't dare hope that they will release me from Naval, yet this would be the only solution that would do anything for me. (EG to Maman, 09.1.28; tr.)

The next day Gilson wrote in frustration that "If I am offered a good post anywhere, I will clear out, but I think I am screwed down here for at least three years" (EG to Maman, 09.2.25; tr.). The Inspector Darlu sent a noncommittal, though kindly, reply to Gilson's letter, urging him to be understanding. Gilson wrote Maman:

> I believe there is some truth in his remarks, and they will do me good. I had seized the opportunity when writing him to tell him that Rochefort was not as important a lycée as Bourg. "Since the matter has come up," I wrote, "the enrolment in the lycée here has dropped by 150 students and this had turned it into a minor lycée." To all this Darlu made no rejoinder. The future will tell what will come of all this, but I feel that I no longer belong here. The ministry remains silent. Not a word. I am going to write to the head of the bureau telling him that far from having received financial compensation here [to meet his last-minute moving expenses] I have just lost the supplementary hours which were the only advantage of Rochefort over Bourg. They will make fun of me, I believe, if I make no request or express no opinion. (09.4.4; tr.)

The inspector came and inspected, looking serious, but Gilson did not retrieve his hours. Notwithstanding their differences however, no personal animosity developed between Gilson and the principal. When the rumour spread that the principal would resign at the end of the year, Gilson could only respond: "It is a pity! I fear I shall never meet another man so friendly and accommodating." (4.18.09; tr.)

Despite his problems with the school's administration, Gilson soon proved himself an excellent teacher. One day in May the principal visited his class and was astonished at the ease with which his students expressed their ideas. Gilson urged him to return when one of the students would be conducting the class: "Some of them speak like little lawyers" (EG to Maman, 09.5.2; tr.).

At Rochefort, Gilson was no longer so preoccupied with his new marriage. He now assumed many responsibilities as real head of the Gilson and Ravisé families, and his affections deepened noticeably for both of them. He was especially concerned about Maman, who was becoming a prisoner to Papa's need for a fulltime nurse. Now that Papa was nearly blind, she had to read to him constantly. As a result Gilson's letters to his mother during this period contain much discussion of various novels. On one occasion, for example, Maman sent Gilson a romance by Martini for his opinion; although he found it naïvely simple and inferior to the same author's *Plaisir d'amour*, he confessed to enjoying it. Another time he announced that he had found just the kind of book Papa would enjoy, *Nouvelles génevoises* by Toepffer; although the first story was long and might tire his father, the second, "L'héritage," would certainly entertain him. Son and mother both became enthusiastic about Romain Rolland's Jean-Christophe series. Gilson promised to bring her *Dans la maison* the next time he visited: "I am glad you like Jean-Christophe. There are bits in his books, I should myself like to have written." He also praised a woman novelist, M. Ignayie, who "may not be a genius but is certainly talented" (10.12.1; tr.).

On another occasion Gilson wrote that he was sorry Maman had to take her walks on boulevard Arrago; if she only lived nearer the Luxembourg, she could take the kind of walks that he and Thérèse were enjoying in Rochefort. He promised to slip up to Paris, taking French leave – "je filerai à l'Anglaise" – between exams and prize day, to provide her with a little relief and to visit the Bibliothèque Nationale himself from time to time.

Gilson also worried about the domestic life of Marthe and Emile, his second-eldest brother. Marthe, he wrote, was too set on living in the fine house at 1, rue de Regrattier. The Monceau district was above their means, and something along Gros-Caillou, Duquesne or Bosquet would have been more suitable. "It is a general truth," he philosophized, "that the more one spends the less one gets." Marthe's real problem turned out to be a difficult pregnancy; she was forced to take to a wheelchair and to live under medical care in Autun to avoid a miscarriage. Thus the burden of Gilson's concern switched to poor lonely Emile:

> He will, from the time the child is three months old, be busy trying to make a man of him, because it will be a boy, never fear. If by some miracle it turns out to be a girl, it will still have to be a man, and at three years of age will go to Père Sertillanges [the young Dominican, much admired by all the Gilsons, who used to preach to full crowds in Lent in the parish church of Saint-Pierre du Gros Caillou]. Tell Emile not to torment himself. He will be the best of fathers with but one fault – worrying himself into a grouch. If only he could avoid being a Gilson to the end, and temper the hot blood of the Melunaises with the sangfroid of great-grandma Raynaud! (EG to Maman, 09.4.4; tr.)

Gilson could easily have been analyzing himself.

Etienne's two younger brothers, Maurice and André, hitherto his special wards, were now launching their own careers. In 1909 Maurice, *le petit docteur*, had at last met all the challenges of competition and had become a resident intern in a Paris hospital. He was seeing Jeanne Morel, whose father, Dr Morel, had recently been killed in a mountain accident; her mother had died some years earlier. Gilson was fond of Jeanne, and wrote for her his only surviving poem. In its last stanza, the fine poem anticipates his later presentation of the medieval romance of Héloïse and Abélard:

Souvenirs

L'Alpe rude et le roc mauvais; l'âpre chemin
Et des pas chancelants qui se perdent dans l'ombre.
Un cri désespéré déchire le val sombre;
De la mort dans la nuit; un regard qui s'éteint.

Voiles de deuil; les robes noires, et les larmes,
Et le gîte mauvais chez le mauvais berger,
Les yeux tristes levés vers l'azur mensonger
Et la prière vaine au milieu des alarmes.

Les jours passent; du sort que l'on ne peut fléchir
Les deux portes d'airain pèsent sur la captive
Et c'est la fuite enfin sur l'océan sans rive
Où la voix des perdus s'explose et vient mourir

Mais un soleil couchant ruisselle sur la plaine
Et du grand fleuve d'or qui s'embrase à ses pieds
Jusqu'au balcon de bois des aîtres familiers
Vers Elle un parfum monte en une chaude haleine.

Des cœurs battent près d'elle et jusqu'à défaillir
Des cœurs battent dans l'ombre ou la rose s'effeuille
Et dans le grand jardin dont l'âme se recueille
S'élève un rythme doux qui ne vient plus mourir.

L'or croule dans le ciel; voici la nuit divine.
Mais elle a vu surgir le vainqueur du destin
Il approche; Elle tremble, et le bras qui l'étreint
L'entraîne au beau chemin que l'amour illumine.

Souvenirs

The rugged Alpine plain, the vicious rock, the rough road
And hesitant steps stumbling into the shadows.
A despairing cry pierces the darkening vale;
Death in the night; a look that sees no more.

Veils of mourning; dark clothes, tears,
And the wretched slab in a wretched shepherd cot;
Sorrowing eyes raised to the deceiving blue;
The hollow prayer amid the terrors.

Days pass, from the judgment which no man escapes,
Two bronze doors stand heavy before the captive
In that final flight o'er the shoreless sea
Where the voice of the lost explodes and is heard no more.

But a setting sun streams down on the plain
And from the great river of gold blazing at its feet
A perfume ascends like a warm breath
Right up to the gallery rail of familiar faces – to Her.

Near her, hearts are beating, almost to the breaking point,
Hearts are beating in the shade where the rose is shedding its petals.
And in the great garden where the soul is one with God
A sweet rhythm revives and will die no more.

The gold in the sky dissolves, and now it is night divine.
She has seen ascending the conqueror of destiny.
He is approaching; She trembles; and her arm, embracing him,
Draws him along the lovely way which love illumines.

When Maurice and Jeanne were married, on 20 January 1910, Jeanne had to issue her own invitations to the guests. Unfortunately the wedding took place on the day between the death and the funeral of Madame Ravisé, Gilson's mother-in-law. Despite this unhappy coincidence, Gilson was happy about the marriage, particularly for André's sake. The young *abbé* had recently been ordained. Now, said Gilson, André would have two fraternal homes; these would allow him some measure of the family life that he would otherwise have to forego:

> L'abbé should enjoy going from time to time to Maurice's. Both Jeanne and Maurice are very fond of him. In their home he will be able to experience a touch of family life, so sweet in itself, so indispensable to life's happiness, but which priests like him have to give up. I will make sure when circumstances permit that André, whom I love a great deal, will have a place in our home too. (EG to Maman, 10.3.9; tr.)

In September 1909 Gilson and Thérèse had accompanied Eugène Ravisé and his second wife Marie-Gabrielle Boudinot on a trip into the mountains. In a letter to Maman, 3 September 1909, Gilson provided "le bilan de nos promenades"; in his liveliest narrative style he described a variety of experiences, including their journey over the glacier "de Trelatête, one of the finest in the Alps ... with its fleece of ice and its desolate solitude" (09.3.9; tr.). This trip had brought Gilson very close to Thérèse's parents. When Mme Ravisé died in Melun, 19 January 1910, at the age of sixty-five, he was deeply upset; no doubt he was little inclined to celebrate his brother's wedding on the following day.

If Gilson was upset by Marie-Gabrielle's death, his father-in-law Eugène was prostrated with grief. A few days after his wife's funeral, Eugène left Melun for a protracted visit to the Rochefort home of Thérèse and Etienne. Henceforth the nickname Papère – to distinguish him from Papa – appears constantly in Gilson's letters to Maman. Eugène quickly fell into the routine of the Gilson household. In June he returned briefly to his house and garden in Melun to attend to the processing of his wife's estate. He then returned to Rochefort and moved to Tours when Gilson received his appointment there.

Eugène remained with his daughter almost continuously until his death during the war years. According to Gilson he was a restless man: he loved to go walking and bicycling, and frequently spent his days alone in nearby towns. He often proved himself indispensable to Thérèse, as on the wretched day when the maid Lia spilt boiling water over herself, or during the harrowing flight to Vermenton with Thérèse, Jeanne, and their babies (below, p. 68).

The deepening love between Gilson and Thérèse eased greatly the burden of increasing family responsibilities. Both longed for a child and were beginning to worry that after two years of marriage there was still no sign; as Gilson somewhat enigmatically wrote, "I would like to commence soon, with my little Thé's help, a new work which would bring a new happiness." Meanwhile they passed their days in mutual consideration and respect. Both realized that to finish his theses Gilson needed a lot of time to himself:

> The finest part of it is as sweet as can be; my poor little wife sits beside me, working away thoughfully; so as not to disturb me she keeps her voice soft and gentle. ... She is well enough but she has a slight cough. We joke about this weakness with an expression of Papa's: "Even the most beautiful feline is still a cat." (EG to Maman, 09.2.25; tr.)

Gilson often remarked that there was a good deal of Sylvestre Bonnard in him; certainly, there was nothing pejorative in the word *cat*. Although his usual pet name for Thérèse was "Chouchette," in moments of endearment she also became "la plus belles des chattes" and "la chatte qui ne mange pas les oiseaux":

> Our little Rochefort birds are getting very much like those of Port-Royal in both number and effrontery. "The most lovely of cats," "the cat who does not eat little birds" puts out bread and seeds for them on the balcony of our bedroom. We sleep now with the shutters closed and windows open. The other morning the sparrows awakened us at four o'clock with unusual racket and commotion – chirping and the flutter of wings out on our balcony. We listened for a while to this charming little aubade, then carefully fell asleep again. (09.3.10; tr.)

During the two years at Rochefort, Gilson's thesis was of course the *pons asinorum*. Nonetheless he made great progress with it. The massive effort required is clearly revealed in a letter written in January 1909, after a Christmas break spent in Paris:

> I have [since returning] added seventy pages to my thesis. I have been writing like a madman – on coming home from class, before going to class; before, after and, I swear, even during my meals. ... As I am always starting some section over and over again, my right hand is limp from writing. I hope to finish the great part of my work by the long vacation, apart, that is, from correcting and revising. Then I will move on to the second or complementary thesis and, God willing, get my doctorate during 1911. (EG to Maman, 09.1.28; tr.)

The theses were not all chore, however. Gilson was clearly absorbed in and challenged by his work:

> It seems to me that my work will contain new and curious insights into Descartes, though I am not the one to be the judge of this. I only hope that those who look at the thesis will find reading it as interesting as I find writing it. (EG to Maman, 09.2.25; tr.)

Nearly three months later, he was beginning to sense how his whole life would be spent:

> I have plans for the second, minor thesis; and I see books and books after that. I will only have to make a selection. I dream especially of a defence of religious thought against philosophical and scientific objections. I don't know what I will decide upon, but first I have to finish my two theses. (EG to Maman, 09.5.2; tr.)

The desire to defend religious thought took concrete form during 1909 when Gilson published his first article in a learned journal. In a rejoinder to an article by Abel Rey, Gilson rejected the position of many scholars, including Lévy-Bruhl, who saw no scholarly role for philosophy apart from absolute positivism. The article, "Sur le positivisme absolu," was published in *Revue philosophique de la France et de l'étranger* (68 [1909]: 63-65; McG 463). It was primarily a defence of philosophical thought as such, though in its treatment of human and divine liberty it also extended this defence to religious thought. Gilson later claimed that this article effectively covered all he had to say on the subject (interview, 1974). He felt grateful that Lévy-Bruhl, then second editor of *Revue philosophique*, allowed the article to appear without objection even though it ran counter to all he stood for: "He was the most generous and objective of men." That Gilson dared to write the article almost on the eve of submitting his thesis to Lévy-Bruhl was indicative of his own selfless and objective scholarship.

From January to June 1910, Gilson laboured on his complementary thesis:

> I have begun to recopy scholastic texts for my dictionary. I have never seen such overwhelmingly boring labour. I take but one pleasure in it, that of discovering interesting texts. But copying them out after they have been found has no attractions. (EG to Maman, 10.3.9; tr.)

Later he added that: "this complementary thesis could turn out to be larger than the principal one. There is nothing wrong about this, quite the contrary." (EG to Maman, 10.5.2; tr.) At this stage he expected to complete his minor thesis by January 1911. He then planned to spend several months revising his major work on liberty in Descartes.

In the second of Gilson's two years at Rochefort, the lycée's administration functioned more smoothly. In May 1910 he heard indirectly that Inspector-General Compayre planned to assign him a better post at another school. In June and July therefore he was especially anxious that his students perform well in their baccalaureate exams. He found his students "with one exception, stupid as geese," and complained that "no one in the lycée is concerned about making students work." Nonetheless his students were successful.

Just before he left Rochefort, Gilson found himself in a better frame of mind:

> On 30 June I was visited by a baron who asked me to give his son private tuition twice a week during July. I told him I wouldn't be here during the entire month. "No matter," he said, "begin in any case." I made a commitment. I have now given the boy three tutorials and will give him three more before July 14. That is sixty francs of found money. Private teaching is not pleasant, but pocketing money is. (EG to Maman, 10.7.7; tr.)

The demand for Gilson's services was by no means confined to the baron. Boys and parents alike realized that, in the young M. Gilson, they had a matchless teacher. After leaving Rochefort, Gilson heard from Mme Larson, whose husband had replaced him, that the lycée was again a "dirty box" and that the staff were once more dissatisfied.

From the middle of August to late September of 1910, Gilson spent his time between Paris and Cravant. This summer there was no uncertainty to cope with. On 19 July 1910 he received his new appointment. For one year he would replace Maurice Halbwachs as professor of philosophy in Lycée Descartes, Tours.

4

From Lycées to University, 1910-1913

1 Lycée Descartes, Tours, 1910-1911

On 19 July 1910 Gilson was appointed to teach philosophy at Lycée Descartes, Tours, "for the duration of the leave of absence granted to M. Halbwachs." Halbwachs was six or seven years older than Gilson was senior in service. Both men were *agrégés* in philosophy; both were writing their doctoral theses; both would later defend their theses at the same time; and both were in competition for the same university post. Both men were also students of Lévy-Bruhl in philosophy; however, Gilson's interests were philosophical, while Halbwachs', like his master's, were sociological.

Thérèse's health had been precarious of late, and she was in need of rest. Therefore she, Gilson and M. Ravisé spent August and early September in "the little house" of Cravant, living in the two lovely back rooms that looked south over the garden. The three moved to Tours, 131, boulevard Heurteloup, in late September and, as usual, Gilson went on ahead and prepared the way. This was a particularly unpleasant chore on this occasion. He was forced to wrangle long and bitterly with his unco-operative and largely inactive Rochefort mover, and he found his new landlord in Tours very "distant," though not actively hostile (EG to Thérèse, 10.9.17). Moreover he couldn't seem to find the things he thought he had packed: Does Chouchette remember where the rings for the cretonne curtains are? Does she know where the window curtains are? Would she bring his notes from the Bibliothèque Nationale, now wrapped and possibly tied with a string in the more modest library on boulevard Port-Royal? And would she please not forget!

If moving was troublesome, so was establishing the smooth operation of the household. The Loire and the Cher had flooded, and mud had entered the kitchen and cellar. However, as Gilson wrote Maman,

> We ... will be perfectly happy when the house gets polished up, and when we get gas, and when we have bought a slave. Right now we are considering a sixteen-year-old girl-slave, called to my attention by a colleague. She is without an owner at the moment because a slight accident befell her mistress: someone strangled her. (10.10.5; tr.)

Whether this was the maid at whose "reception" Gilson and Chouchette "assisted" three days later is not clear. We do know however that the maid was sorely needed and had a much nicer room than Maman's alcove on boulevard Port-Royal (EG to Maman, 10.10.8; tr.).

The lycée in Tours was clearly a good one and had originally been founded in 1830 as a *collège royal*. Now it offered the regular baccalaureate programme and also special preparatory programmes for students who wished to enter either government service or the Military Academy of Saint-Cyr. Gilson was delighted to find that his courses during 1910 to 1911 included, besides *la morale* and philosophy, special mathematics and polytechnic for these special programmes; as he was never particularly good in math, he enjoyed boasting later that he had taught it.

Gilson's first impressions of his new position were happy ones:

> I have now sixteen students in philosophy and seventeen in mathematics. The latter, along with the Saint-Cyrians, make a class of twenty-five, a good number. This time I find myself in a truly important post. (EG to Maman, 10.10.8; tr.)

He took particular pleasure in the physical details of the room he would be working in:

> I saw my classroom. It is large, airy and – painted mauve! I writhed at seeing the colour, and will wear mauve ribbons on my pants. The professional chair is too tight and I won't be able to stretch my legs out as far as I would like. But there are positive advantages: central heating, so that I won't freeze as I did last year, and I won't have to tip the boy who brings the coal, as at Bourg. (EG to Maman, 10.9.17; tr.)

Although the school, with its sophisticated student-body, had discipline problems, these didn't seem to bother Gilson:

> The principal asked me if I wanted to split these classes, as such a number of trouble-making boys might frighten me. In effect, he was offering me supplementary hours. I thought I ought to refuse them partly to be smart, partly to see how I would make out. There were isolated attempts at independence for about fifteen minutes, but when it became clear that this wouldn't work, the trouble-makers gave up. You can't leave boys like this out of your sight for a moment nor can you turn your back on them; you have to be a kind of lion-tamer. But it's all rather funny. Since you can't punish them you have to use tact and guile, and this is fun. As for teaching them philosophy, I feel that I shall get somewhere with them. (EG to Maman, 10.10.13, tr.)

Gilson and Thérèse immediately warmed to Tours, with its lively cosmopolitan flavour. They found the surrounding countryside and the Loire incomparably beautiful and "so delightfully French." The region had a number of local food specialities, like *paté jambonneau de Tours*, and stuffed prunes that Gilson could not resist sending to Maman and Jeanne. Tours also had a thriving colony of English people who chattered away in their own language, to Gilson's delight.

Most important, Tours had a rich musical life. By November Gilson and Thérèse had attended three concerts, two of them featuring pianists, the third a violinist. "If ever music comes searching us out in Tours, all our possible and humanly realizable wishes will have come true" (EG to Maman, 10.11.17; tr.). In December Gilson actually found someone to teach him harmony:

> I am about to realize, for my personal distraction, a dream I have had for a long time; I am going to learn harmony so that, in the future, I will not merely love music but understand it. The professor of music here in the lycée, M. Arbelet, is going to give me lessons: he is also professor of harmony in the Tours National School of Music. He questioned me hard in his home on the solfeggio to find out whether I knew enough to begin harmony. My replies were good enough to convince him to give me lessons. Along with the many remarkable concerts we have here, these lessons will help remove the clinkers from my brain. My thesis, certainly a venerable work, is not one likely to develop my intelligence. (EG to Maman, 10.12.1; tr.)

Gilson's favorite colleague at the lycée was M. Guyot, professor of history. Guyot was a sociable young man of thirty-two, knowledgeable in the gossipy affairs of the Parisian *beau-monde* and well-connected both socially and academically. He too was busy finishing his thesis; now at the printing stage, it would have to be defended this very year. Guyot was a good friend to have. He helped Gilson find good domestic help and reliable tradesmen, and encouraged him to speed up the pace on his thesis. Guyot also taught his young friend to manœuvre effectively among administrators at various levels. Gilson's account of dinner conversation at the Guyots' home is gossipy for him:

> We dined at the Guyots' with M. Arbelet. Guyot is a cousin of the Baschets of the Annales family and of the *Illustration*. He knows the Brissons [a theatre family] well, and speaks of the famous cousin, Yvonne, as "not much good." He says she is not a very good mother, and that life in the Brisson family can only be described as Bohemian. Yvonne herself has had her "affairs"; her eldest daughter is going to marry a son of Paul Gimsby, former director of the Odéon; the young man is already divorced, and there is something shameful about this marriage. Guyot, who knows them well, speaks of their much paraded morality as a façade and a blind. The same goes for the Annales whose famous hotel actually belongs to the *Illustration*: the Annales only rent it. The social aura of all these illustrious collaborators is, apparently, disgusting. I don't *know* this, but have in my bones felt it to be so for a long time. (EG to Maman, 10.11.24; tr.)

Four months later, rumours about year-end changes in the lycée were just beginning to fly. Guyot, his doctorate complete, was transferred in mid-term to Henri IV in Paris. "Pretty nice!" commented Gilson. The movement of Guyot from Tours toward Paris was encouraging. Gilson recalled that Belot, the well-known philosopher at Lycée Louis-le-Grand, had moved directly from Tours to Paris. "If this establishes a long tradition, I only ask that it be continued" (EG to Maman, 11.3.12; tr.). Guyot's rapid advancement did not stop with Henry IV. At the end of 1912, when Gilson was teaching in Angers, Guyot was named head assistant in the cabinet of the Ministry of Public Instruction. "The appointment," wrote Gilson, "is a plum. He will do well in every sense of the word. His appointment cannot hurt me, but it won't help me either, because we Gilsons are not the kind of people who ask for things." (EG to Maman, 12.11.27; tr.)

In late June 1911 the principal of Tours, M. G. François, decided to hold a school reception at the Château de Langeais on the Loire. François asked Gilson to address the gathering. Thérèse was thrilled by the glamorous event and was thoroughly satisfied with the way everything went. Gilson's remarks, written a few days afterward, were more reserved:

> I delivered my talk and the principal said he was pleased with it. I am pleased too – at no longer having it over my head. The talk itself came off very well; afterward we had tea, champagne and cakes. The little festival was ever so proper: I was honoured (?) by being presented to Madame Siegfried, the owner of the Château de Langeais. She is closely associated with Père Laberthonnière, and trapped me into accepting a number of invitations from which I must try to disentangle myself. (EG to Maman, 11.6.26; tr.)

At this early date in her long career as mistress of Langeais, Mme Siegfried was sponsoring religio-political movements; she later settled for a more social role as hostess for the theatre crowd and a well-known personality. At the time of meeting Gilson, Mme Siegfried supported Lucien Laberthonnière's journal *Annales de philosophie chrétienne* and Marc Sanglier's *Le sillon*. Like other disciples of Lacordaire and Ozanam, she was a supporter of Ralliement.* After meeting Gilson she tried to attract him to the cause. Although Gilson's position was similar to Mme Siegfried's, he was keenly aware that his involvement with the Sorbonne and with public education in general already had cast suspicion upon his commitment to Catholicism. Madame Siegfried's invitations could easily have led to philosophical, political and religious entanglements which Gilson, on the brink of his career, did well to forgo.

Another, very different social event at this time provoked Gilson exceedingly for its political folly and its social gracelessness. When Gilson had first arrived in Tours, the new lycée had been nearly finished and the main building was expected to be ready for use the next month. Meanwhile the principal and vice-principal were living in town, awaiting completion of their splendid on-campus apartments. The formal dedication of the building and the inaugural festivities had been postponed until the following July, the end of the academic year. The top ministry officials travelled from Paris, and a full complement of local administrators and politicians were on hand. This time Gilson was clearly not invited to speak:

---

* Le Ralliement à la République was a movement among leftwing French Catholics who sought appeasement between the French church and the Third Republic in response to instructions issued by Pope Leo XIII in 1884. After the Dreyfus affair of 1898, the government expelled religious congregations from France and broke off diplomatic relations with the Holy See. Accordingly, in 1909, Pope Pius X countermanded his predecessor's instructions to seek appeasement, leaving Ralliement in confusion and disarray. Mme Siegfried was one of those who hoped to re-establish it.

> I went to the democratic banquet, and I venture to say I will never go to another. My democracy is a hot-house plant and will wilt if I carry it too often into the open air. The foolish noise of the talks and the manifest stupidity of conscious citizens truly stunned me.... It is the kind of thing one has to see once, but once is enough. The principal was counting on receiving the red ribbon [of the Legion of Honour], but apparently there was no ribbon left on the roll. The little blue flower did service all the day long and half a dozen of them were required: one for the prefect's wife, another for the principal's, another for his daughter, and another for his niece, and so on. The whole thing became dull. When I noticed at the end of the dinner people were beginning to quarrel and to abuse one another, I picked up my hat at the checkroom and returned to Heurteloup. There Chouchette's blue eyes drove away at once the plethora of ugly images. (EG to Maman, 11.7.nd; tr.)

Gilson gave two other talks that we know of during the year 1910-1911. The first was addressed to the Education League in Angoulême, by his cousin Henry's invitation, on the subject of "Pierre Loti's View of Life." No doubt Loti had come to Gilson's attention during his stay in Rochefort; the town now preserves Loti's house as a national monument. Maman had sent Gilson the article that had set him thinking about the nature of Loti's sadness:

> I have been tapped to give a lecture for the Education League, and I have it already in my head. I will speak on Pierre Loti's conception of life. That is to say, dear Maman, that your issue of the *Annales* has got among my papers, and at just the right moment. I will use particularly the little extract from Anatole France on Loti's sadness, and I will endeavour to show that France was mistaken about the fundamental character of this sadness. So, you have a share in the preparation of this lecture which it will be a pleasure for me to recall as I deliver it. (EG to Maman, 10.10.17; tr.)

The lecture was given on Annunciation Day in March 1911. When the time came to go to Angoulême, Gilson found that his cousin had arranged for him to travel at the league's expense, "first-class, of course." He travelled second-class and covered most of Chouchette's fare as well.

Before the lecture Gilson sent Maman a clipping of its announcement in the local newspaper. The article, he explained, had been drafted and submitted by her illustrious nephew himself:

> We are happy to announce for Saturday next, 25 March, an interesting lecture which will have for its subject the captivating work of Pierre Loti. The lecture will be given by M. Etienne Gilson, professor of philosophy in the lycée of Tours. We understand that this young teacher is closely related to the likable doctor-in-chief in the hospital of Angoulême. (undated clipping.)

Certainly, Gilson added, the "young teacher" and the "likable doctor" planned to go out on the town together after the lecture (11.3.20).

The following October Gilson returned to Tours from Saint-Quentin to give another talk, this time at the Solemn Distribution of Prizes. This *discours*, keyed for the occasion, was somewhat formal, even platitudinous; amid some flamboyant moralizing, it stressed that the lycée was not designed to turn out doctors, civil servants and businessmen in machine-fashion but to transmit genuine culture with its combined hellenic and native riches. If this lecture seems somewhat flat and uninspired, it may have suffered from Gilson's disappointment at his recent transfer to a less prestigious and pleasant post.

The year in Tours allowed Gilson to make important headway with his two theses. By early summer of 1911 he had become thoroughly sick of the task: "I gladly promise myself never to stick my nose back into this work again. It will be, when it is over, a good riddance." (EG to Maman, 11.6.26; tr.) However, trying as he found the thesis writing, he was beginning to see the end. His estimated date for finishing was now January 1912; he held so grimly to his task, and he was so anxious to move on to a university career, that he eventually beat this target by three months.

Already by June 1911 Gilson had reached the revision stage, which he found particularly taxing. He especially disliked the fussy work of ensuring that the texts he had gathered for the complementary thesis or dictionary were as accurate and complete as possible. One day Gilson found that Père A. J. Sertillanges had referred to a text unknown to him. He confided his problem to Maman, then wrote to Sertillanges whom Gilson had known as a peacher in St-Pierre-du-Gros-Caillou. Sertillanges wrote the following reply:

> Monsieur. Your letter is the occasion of my correcting an error. One ought never to rely on one's memory in making a reference. I could have sworn that the text I printed was from the *De concordantiis*. It was not. It was from the *De aeternitate mundi contra murmurantes*, opusc. 23 or 27, according to the editors. (Sertillanges to EG, 11.3.18; tr.)

The letter included a transcription of the text, in case Gilson had not the edition in hand. Unfortunately, however, the correspondence proved not to be helpful.

Gilson must have been involved in many exchanges of letters with scholars working on medieval texts. He was, of course, still approaching these texts as clarifications of Descartes' thought. Nonetheless his work and the direction of his theses were apparently becoming quite widely known. During this year Victor Delbos asked him to prepare some material for the *Bibliographie philosophique*. Gilson was thrilled to be asked, and thanked Delbos warmly for thinking of him (EG to Maman, 11.6.26).

During this summer Gilson discovered, much to his disappointment, that he would be leaving Tours for the lycée at Saint-Quentin. He had been given reason to think that Halbwachs, whom he had been replacing, would not return; this proved not to be the case. Gilson did not welcome the transfer. Saint-Quentin was located in the Picard area, which Gilson spurned. Moreover, the lycée was much less prestigious than that at Tours, and was ranked alongside that at Bourg.

A second piece of annoying news that arrived for Gilson this summer was a summons to report in September for twenty-three days of additional military training to be taken, ironically, in the camp at Tours. Gilson was to return to his unfinished officer's training programme. The summons was a nuisance, but at least the armies of the Republic had not washed their hands of him:

At any rate they haven't flunked me out, the rats! I am to report 31 August before 8:00 AM. This means calling off our plans for a tour across Europe. I hope we are not in for manœuvres during September, but I fear being disappointed. (EG to Maman, 11.6.26; tr.)

Before reporting for military service, Gilson managed to take Thérèse for a trip to Luxeuil-les-Bains to see if the waters might offer her relief from the digestive problems that were plaguing her. Gilson's own health had always been good, save for occasional grippe, an abscessed tooth, and of course his case of *fièvre sorbonnesque*. At Luxeuil however, probably because Thérèse's doctor mentioned it, he realized for the first time that he was getting too heavy. He wrote Maman: "As for me, I am on a diet, and I am eating less bread in order to reduce, for I am truly too fat. I hope to take off a few kilos, and the scales will tell me the results." (11.8.22; tr.) Although Gilson liked Luxeuil, his "thesis-obsession" interfered with complete relaxation: "There are moments when writing is becoming a kind of horror. I believe I have written 3,000 pages over four years. Fortunately, this disease is curable, but it is not to cure it that we are here in Luxeuil." (EG to Maman, 11.8.22; tr.)

The couple had planned to spend nine days at the resort, from about August 20 until Gilson's departure for the camp in Tours. However, Thérèse showed so much improvement that she prolonged her visit for another eight days after Etienne's departure. Gilson departed alone from the baths at the end of August "to take up once more, on Thursday morning at 8:00, *l'uniforme et le fusil*" (11.8.28; tr.).

2 The Lycées of Saint-Quentin and Angers, 1911-1913

By a decree of 18 July 1911 the Minister of Public Instruction named a disappointed Gilson to the lycée of Saint-Quentin to supply once more for a teacher on leave of absence. Although Gilson was unhappy with the move, he did not raise any formal objection. Lévy-Bruhl was also displeased and described the transfer as "extremely annoying." However there seems to have been an understanding that before long Gilson would be definitively appointed to Tours; in view of this, he kept his house on boulevard Heurteloup, no doubt subletting it for 1911 to 1912.

At the end of September Gilson wrote that he would be travelling to Saint-Quentin in a few days. During a brief stopover in Paris he planned to dine with Maman and to deposit his principal thesis with the dean of philosophy. The dean would then pass it on to Lévy-Bruhl, Picavet, Rébelliau and others for their judgments. All that remained for Gilson was to complete and revise his complementary thesis while at Saint-Quentin.

As *modus vivendi* for this year of waiting, the Gilsons decided to temporarily disband their household. M. Ravisé would return to Melun and Thérèse would divide her time between Melun and boulevard Port-Royal in Paris. Gilson would live *en garçon* in Saint-Quentin and spend Thursday to Sunday of each week in Paris or Melun. Thérèse of course could visit Saint-Quentin from time to time as she wished. According to Gilson, the arrangement was "less costly and less fatiguing" than any other, though costly enough for a makeshift (EG to Maman, 11.9.26; tr.). As it turned out, the makeshift was good for the thesis; having secured the co-operation of his principal, Gilson was able to be near the Bibliothèque Nationale for up to four days a week. Thérèse also benefitted: because she became pregnant about the time of leaving Tours, she found the Paris-Melun arrangement, with Gilson home four days a week, particularly congenial.

Gilson disliked the north because of his memories of Eu and Abbéville; moreover Saint-Quentin was an ugly town, even in the minds of its own citizens. Nonetheless his post there was an easy one and his teaching assignment, as he put it, "was a breeze." He had only four students in philosophy, as compared to twenty the year before, and only four in mathematics, as against seventeen, plus polytechnic and St-Cyr students, at Tours. He also had some twenty youngsters at the level of *les bambins de Bourg* in *la morale*.

Since Gilson was home so much, he wrote no letters to Maman between November 1911 and the following June. In June he wrote her three times, probably because she was at Cravant. In one of these, 6 June 1912, he told her he had received Picavet's written report or visa on his thesis. The comments were much as he had expected. Picavet's criticisms were few: he considered the thesis too long, the expression *scolastico-cartésien* too vague for a title, and some of Gilson's objections (such as to Chauvin's definitions) so petty as to be humourous. In all, Gilson found Picavet's criticisms rather trifling and easily coped with during the defence. When he passed these criticism on to Lévy-Bruhl, he was advised as follows:

> Follow his recommendations when they seem to you to be good. Otherwise, forget them. The essential thing is that he gave you the visa. He must be in bad humour, and it is my fault. I told him flatly that your thesis was now complete and that there could be no question of your adopting another plan or of proceeding in some other direction, etc. I deprived him of the pleasure of dictating to you. I hope my action does not embarrass you. If, however, he makes you angry, don't show it, and scrupulously observe all formalities. (Lévy-Bruhl to EG, 12.6.3; tr.)

In this same letter Lévy-Bruhl accepted the dedication of the thesis. Although he questioned a dedication of a thesis to its director in principle, he recognized that the practice was a Sorbonne tradition of long standing and did not feel it restricted his own liberty to criticize Gilson's work. Moreover, he considered the thesis particularly successful:

> It is a thesis with something to say, one which in methods and findings brings something quite new to bear on problems to which the old methods can no longer contribute anything. This is rare enough these days. Should you be confronted with harsh criticism (and you well may be), I will gladly stand behind you.

Some days later Gilson received a second letter from Lévy-Bruhl (see EG to Maman, 12.6.17). Now that he had carefully read both theses, Lévy-Bruhl's opinion of them remained high; indeed, at his suggestion, Alcan was prepared to publish them. Moreover Lévy-Bruhl considered it quite possible that Gilson would be awarded the *mention très honorable* at the defence, and might reach Paris by some other route than through the lycées. Despite such assurances, however, Gilson became uneasy at the lack of definite news from Tours concerning the coming year. By June he had heard nothing except the rumour that Halbwachs was contemplating leaving Tours for a post at Toulouse (EG to Maman, 12.6.24).

June, then, was a month full of expectation and promise, not least because the Gilsons were preparing eagerly for their firstborn child. Chouchette remained in Melun, and Dr Masbremer agreed not to leave town for a moment without looking in first. A midwife, *une sage-femme*, was engaged and a nurse, Sister Séraphim, agreed to live in over the period. That the birth ended four long years of childlessness made everyone doubly anxious: as Gilson laconically remarked, "Arrangements have been made as though for a battle" (EG to Maman, 12.6.17; tr.). The midwife predicted 25 June for the birth, warning that the first child might be delayed. Finally, on 27 June 1912, Jacqueline Marie Charlotte, "belle, grosse et brune," was born, to the joyful relief of her father.

The birth of Jacqueline was quickly followed by a dizzying series of events. On 8 July Gilson signed with Félix Alcan and R. Lisbonne to publish his principal thesis. The manuscript was to be in by 15 July and the book published by 15 October. On 9 July Gilson was appointed to the lycée at Orléans, which must have seemed a considerable disappointment. However on 18 July his appointment was changed to Angers, close to Tours, where he was to replace M. Reynier.

Early in August Gilson departed for a month of military service at a special officers' training camp in Sedan. The month was not a difficult one:

> I never had a period of military service under better conditions. I take the drilling exercises each morning and am free to make or not to make the two tiring marches. Between yes and no, I naturally choose no. If my stay in barracks cannot be called pleasant, neither can it be called painful. (EG to Maman, 12.8.30; tr.)

Sometimes, however, Gilson did march:

> This morning the regiment paid a visit to the battlefield of Sedan with explanations. It was interesting and not too tiring – about twenty kilometres in all. This is probably my last march. (EG to Maman, 12.8.31; tr.)

In September Gilson took a room in Angers and Thérèse and the baby moved to the house on boulevard Heurteloup in nearby Tours. All in all it was a hectic and a happy year. Some fifty-six years later Gilson wrote:

> I was for one year a professor of philosophy at the lycée of Angers. That was many years ago. I still remember it as a charming interlude. For the life of me I cannot remember where I rented a room. I do remember that the janitor used to sell cherry

turnovers (hot!) at the ten o'clock intermission and I always bought two of them. They were worthy of Mahomet's paradise. (EG to Maurer, 68.7.26.)

Following the birth of Jacqueline, Gilson entered into a long period of reflection on domestic life, child care, child psychology, family life and related subjects. This lasted beyond the birth of Cécile and well into the war years when he was deprived of his wife and children for long periods of time. The first little essay of this sort focuses appropriately on Maman:

> I very often think of you, chère petite Maman, and of the long days you pass with our poor Papa. How hard our life really is! It does not let us live near the people we love. The only consolation is knowing and understanding surely the hearts that love you. You know, dear mother, what you mean to me. I bless you every day from the bottom of my heart for having made me as I am – a little like yourself. I shall never imagine a lovelier moral ideal: to be as Maman wanted me to be.... I know now that we shall live always, as grandma lives in you, and as you live in me, and as we shall all live in our little Jacqueline. (12.8.30; tr.)

In a later piece, the subject is children, parents and love:

> They say that children can never return to their parents what they have received from them and this is true. But the reverse is true too. Parents can never love their children enough to give them back the happiness they have received from them. A month of parental care is not to be equated with even one of their smiles. (EG to Maman, 12.11.13; tr.)

In another letter Gilson recounted his first walk with Thérèse and the baby, their "première grande promenade." On Friday afternoon, 25 November 1912, Gilson and Thérèse proudly wheeled Jacqueline's carriage the four miles from Tours to Avertun. Jacqueline was a *biberon*, a bottle-fed baby, because Thérèse had not the milk to nourish her. Gilson describes with fine precision the sudden transformation of the angry, hungry *bébé* upon receiving its *biberon*:

> In very few seconds, the face becomes the colour of well-cooked brick; the forehead wrinkles into a vertical flange, the body curves into an arc, the navel reaching for the heavens is the centre of that arc. There is fearsome howling which drives you back panic-stricken, but which pursues you, fills your ears, removes the very haste which the circumstances seem to call for. As soon as the nipple of the bottle is in place, a beautiful smile breaks through the tears like a rainbow at the end of a storm. Chouchette has once more found "the little angel." (EG to Maman, 12.11.27; tr.)

The jury and complimentary copies of Gilson's thesis, 200 in all, were finally published as pre-edition, followed by a trade edition of 825 copies for 3,000 francs; he was then to be paid royalties of ten percent on the trade copies which carried a slightly modified title. The original thesis was entitled *La doctrine cartésienne de la liberté et la théologie*; the trade book was called *La liberté chez Descartes et la théologie*. Both were dated Paris, Félix Alcan, 1913 (McG 83).

Gilson quickly developed mixed feelings about Alcan. He wrote 25 November:

> I have received my bill from Alcan publishers. It was not slow in coming. I have the bill before the books, for up to now I have received one lonely copy of this thesis. That is all I have yet for 3,191 francs. It gives me a mad desire to begin all over again. How tempting the prospect of working for five years in order to have the right to pay 3,000 francs. (EG to Maman, 12.11.25; tr.)

Despite Gilson's irritation, however, the appearance of his one thesis copy pleased him:

> When stitched it will surely move the reader. Even I find it convincing now. Everything has now been deposited in the Sorbonne and I have only to wait. I told you, I believe, that the defence will take place at either the middle or end of January. (EG to Maman, 12.11.13; tr.)

An interesting copy of the major thesis can be found in the Gilson Archives at the Pontifical Institute in Toronto. It is the copy he gave his wife and is inscribed as follows: "A ma chère petite Thérèse en souvenir des longues et douces heures silencieuses passées l'un près de l'autre."

3 THESES AND THEIR DEFENCE, 1913

When Gilson went to teach in the lycée of Angers, he became almost totally absorbed in the printing of his two theses and in his forthcoming defence of them in January 1913. Two candidates for the doctorate of letters were scheduled for this year: Halbwachs' defence came in early January, Gilson's on 29 January.

Although Halbwachs' thesis was in philosophy, it was primarily sociological: "The Working Class and Standards of Living: Research into the Hierarchy of Needs in Contemporary Industrial Societies." Halbwachs was questioned harshly by two of his jury, Bouglé and Seignobos, who felt his conclusions were too general and hasty, lacking an analysis of other social groups, especially farmers. Nonetheless Halbwachs, though manifestly annoyed, made a good defence and received his *mention très honorable*. He then visited Durkheim, who belonged to the Committee of Higher Education; Halbwachs was always politically alert. Afterward he reported to Gilson that Durkheim had praised both their theses and had suggested that both graduates would probably find places in the universities during 1913. The rumour overwhelmed both Gilson and Thérèse, and keyed Gilson up to an even greater pitch of excitement during the ten days that remained before his defence.

Gilson was quite satisfied with the men on his jury when their names were known: Lévy-Bruhl, of course, director of the theses; Lalande and Delbos for philosophy; Picavet, *chargé de cours* for medieval thought in the University of Paris; Lalande for methodology and lexicography; Delacroix for theology; and Rebelliau, in Lévy-Bruhl's opinion the best all-round authority on Cartesian criticism. The task of sending out complimentary copies of his theses Gilson entrusted to Maman, his "sovereign dispensatrix" (EG to Maman, 13.1.16).

La liberté chez Descartes et la théologie was the first major work of Etienne Gilson, philosopher and historian of philosophy. It deals in a rigidly controlled fashion with Descartes' doctrine of liberty first in God, second in man. The work takes issue with other studies of Descartes, especially those by Espinas. According to Espinas, Descartes was highly influenced by the theology of his Jesuit teachers at the college of La Flèche and by theological controversies of the time. The Descartes of Espinas was benign, receptive and positive where theology was concerned, a metaphysician of the La Flèche kind, whose thought was essentially theological and whose focus was neither metaphysics nor physics, but religion.

Using the historical methods of Lévy-Bruhl, Gilson did not concur with this assessment of Descartes' philosophy. He closely examined such evidence as the courses and text-books used by Descartes at La Flèche; he also examined as best he could the new mathematics and physics in which Descartes was interested. He agreed that Descartes knew something about the theology of the controversialists as well as of earlier theologians. However, Descartes' metaphysical position was, unlike theirs, neither apologetic nor oriented to the defence of God's existence, creation, liberty and so on. Descartes' concern was to allow the older metaphysics and theology to shed what light it could on the new physics. He was not concerned about whether, in creating the world, God was necessitated in any way: indeed, Descartes agreed that He was not. He did not even care whether God could make a triangle whose three angles did not add up to two right angles, or whether twice four had to equal eight, or whether a mountain demanded a complementary valley. The "eternal truths" which concerned Descartes were the principles of physics and mathematics; these he was content to accept as laws in their physical and mathematical reality, independent of any metaphysics of creation and liberty.

Descartes left his metaphysics somewhat vague, partly because he hoped to avoid the doctrinal difficulties of a Galileo, partly because he wanted to focus his thinking on physics and mathematics independently of theological truth. As a true revolutionary, he espoused some of the metaphysical positions frowned on in the schools: for example, that God created the "eternal truths" as a king establishes laws in his kingdom, or that there is a radical distinction between soul and body. In adopting these, he was not profoundly new: he was just taking over the more neoplatonic of two currents of thought predating St Thomas. However, his physics was new. By trying to make his metaphysics acceptable, he sought to render his physics palatable: "recevoir la métaphysique, c'était faire recevoir sa physique" (p. 437).

Gilson's thesis is particularly notable for the clarity and impeccability of its scholarship, the precision and beauty of its language, and its effective use of the historical method. Brilliant, for example, in the early pages, is his concise, exact sketch of the subjects taught at La Flèche and of the schedule followed there; in the later pages the aristotelianism, thomism and suarezian molinism taught in those courses is presented with crystalline clarity.

For the most part, Gilson's treatment of texts in his thesis is objective and impartial. However, during the defence, Lévy-Bruhl did catch him out on one breach and asked:

> Don't you sometimes go beyond your text? Speaking of final causes, you say [p. 93] that for Descartes, the idea of the ends which God would propose for Himself is an idea impossible to sustain, absurd in its base: that is, *according to you*. When Descartes rejected the search for final causes, he was advising against searching for what does not exist. The Latin text says nothing to the effect that such an idea is absurd. (*Revue de métaphysique et de morale*, 21 [May supplement, 1913]: 19-32; tr.)

After some discussion of whether or not anthropomorphism was an absurdity, Gilson came round: "I admit that here I have gone beyond the text of Descartes." The admission did him no harm. Like Halbwachs, Gilson was awarded his doctorate with *mention très honorable*.

At the opening of the same defence, Gilson read the abstract of his minor or complementary thesis, his *Index scolastico-cartésien* (Paris, 1913; McG 71).* The *Index* was essentially a dictionary of scholastic terminology to be found in Descartes. In the abstract Gilson argued that Descartes drew heavily on scholastic terms, sometimes using them as the scholastics had done, sometimes adjusting their definition. This process of redefinition occurred not only within philosophy but in physics and the other sciences as well. Gilson drew no conclusions in the *Index*, and was content simply to "prepare the way for a complete study of the subject." He never regarded his minor thesis as a completed work of scholarship and years later, in 1964, was dismayed to learn that he was powerless to block an unauthorized reprint of it by Burt Franklin in New York (below, p. 366).

Although in 1913 Gilson was pleased with his theses and relieved to see them published, his chief pleasure lay in his little "Jacqueline-Poulet." In mock-thesis jargon, he wrote to Maman to express his delight in the real triumph of the hour: "As of 16 January 1913, Jacqueline weighs 6 kilos, 585 g, and her language à la mode is *Ia, ia, ia, ma, m-mma, ga. Quelle langue admirable que ce Turc!*" As John Wain wrote of a tiny addition to Johnson's *Dictionary*: "A little flower beside the dusty highway of lexicography!" (*Samuel Johnson* [1974], p. 274).

4 RECOGNITION AND WAITING

With the printing and defence of his theses Gilson became an established scholar. Although he had often referred cautiously to his career as that of "professor of philosophy in the stream of public instruction," there is no doubt he perceived himself as scholar first, teacher second. With Bergson as his first model, Gilson wanted to be a practising philosopher; nonetheless his theses under Lévy-Bruhl had been in the history of philosophy, and Gilson was always to insist that professionally he was an historian of thought. His primary interest in the medieval period was in the history of its ideas; he did not believe medieval philo-

---

* The text of the abstract of the *Index* can be found with a transcript of Gilson's defence in the *Revue de métaphysique et de morale*, 21 (May supplement, 1913): 19-32.

sophy could be isolated from the other intellectual disciplines of the period, particularly theology.

Some time before completing his theses, Gilson had become aware of his shortcomings as a medievalist. Two months before his defence he decided to learn how to read medieval manuscripts properly; without this skill he could neither call himself a true medievalist nor an authentic historian of the Middle Ages. To complete his education, Gilson began to back up systematically into the medieval world. Like Anatole France's celebrated character "he already liked cats, now he was taking to the reading of manuscripts." In November 1911 he wrote Maman from Tours:

> I am becoming more and more a Sylvestre Bonnard, but it is very difficult and I have only yet read a page and a half of manuscript. Fortunately, I have found a kindly professor, M. [Loiseau] de Grandmaison, well-known archivist paleographer, who is I believe delighted to have a pupil. He is instructing me in essentials, but I am always inclined to divine [the meaning of a text] before having read it, and I make mistakes as large as my thighs, which is saying a lot. (12.11.25; tr.)

Although Gilson would never become an outstanding paleographer (editor of texts), by the time of his defence he was well on his way to becoming a medievalist. Not only was he learning to read manuscripts, but while working on Descartes, he had made two important personal discoveries. First, he had realized that medieval thought, to maintain integrity, must not be isolated from theology. Second, he had learned that a knowledge of the neglected Middle Ages requires of the investigator a broad range of intertwining disciplines.

Following the defence of his theses, recognition of Gilson's scholarship greeted him from all sides. The first plaudits of course were received from those who had attended his lively examination. Lévy-Bruhl already knew his student's abilities and Delbos and Lalande had already written Gilson excitedly about his discoveries the moment they had finished reading the theses. Picavet, who despite his modest abilities was the Sorbonne's first professor of medieval thought, prepared a generous if somewhat guarded *visa*. And Léon Brunschwicg, professor of general philosophy in the Sorbonne, wrote a review of *La doctrine de la liberté chez Descartes et la théologie* which appeared in the May supplement of the *Revue de métaphysique et de morale* (pp. 7-8). Brunschwicg's review went into considerable detail, and welcomed the work as offering "notable progress in the study of Descartes' metaphysics"; he praised the thesis as "a detailed inquiry in which Gilson has proven himself to be a patient, honest and original historian."

Xavier Léon, editor of the *Revue de métaphysique et de morale*, invited Gilson to prepare at once an article for his journal. This was completed by early June and appeared in the *Revue* (22 [1914]: 456-499; McG 311) under the title "L'innéisme cartésien et la théologie." The article was highly significant in Gilson's scholarly development. Its subject, innate ideas in Descartes, had for two centuries puzzled and even embarrassed Cartesians. Although the paper's theme resembles that of his thesis, its perspective is different: it examines Descartes from the point of view of St Thomas, Descartes' "adversary."

In the first section Gilson offers an account of St Thomas' theory of knowledge using texts from the *Summa theologiae*, the *De veritate* and the *Summa contra gentiles*. He unfolds the doctrine to that point where he believes St Thomas begins to run into difficulties; he maintains that Thomas is hindered by the lack of any medieval physical evidence to support the role of the senses or to demonstrate those bothersome intermediaries, the intentional species. In the second section Gilson proceeds to show how certain sixteenth-century theologians and apologists associated with Descartes – Cardinal de Bérulle, Père Gibieuf of the Oratory, Silhon, Mersenne – returned to the old Platonist use of innate ideas to demonstrate, as Suarez had done against St Thomas, that the idea of God was innate in man. This position was doubly useful to Descartes. First, he found much protection in having established theologians on his side. More important however he found a metaphysics helpful to his physics; the concept of innate ideas meant "independence, aseity, sufficiency," not so much to his thought, but to the mechanistic physics of extension and movement. (See Octave Hamelin, *Le système de Descartes* [1921].)

Although Gilson's article was a logical extension of his doctoral thesis, it reflected a shift toward the study of St Thomas and away from Descartes. Around this time, no doubt as a result of writing the article, Gilson decided that, should he obtain a university post, one of his first courses would be on St Thomas. He wrote to Maman in April:

> While waiting [for news of university appointments] I am preparing a course on the philosophy of St Thomas Aquinas. This will cause a stir in the university, and it is by no means certain that the dean of the place will not ask for an explanation, though he can have no valid objection to confront me with. It seems not to have crossed anyone's mind that a university man might offer a course on St Thomas. I will have some funny stories to tell you. (13.4.26; tr.)

He would indeed offer such a course during his first year of university teaching.

On 24 May 1913 Victor Delbos formally presented copies of Gilson's two books to the Institut de France. At the time Delbos was permanent secretary of the Academy of Moral and Political Sciences in the institute, and the presentation marked an important recognition of Gilson's work. In a note to inform Gilson of the event, Delbos added that he had heard from Boutroux that Gilson had been officially inscribed among the professors destined to enter the universities (13.6.nd).

Other forms of recognition began to reach Gilson. F. A. Blanchet of Paris, a thomist and a professor of the history of modern philosophy at the Institut Catholique, wrote Gilson immediately on reading the book:

> I turned first to your conclusion, and I was happy to find there confirmation of what seemed to me, when studying Descartes, the close relation between his system and theology on a number of points. This but redoubled the interest which the very

title of the work aroused in me. The further my reading takes me into your work, the more I admire the awareness you have brought to the study of theological doctrines and the remarkable manner in which you present them. (Blanchet to EG, 13.1.25; tr.)

Around this time l'abbé Lucien Laberthonnière published Gilson's "Notes sur Campanella" in the *Annales de philosophie chrétienne* (165 [1913]: 491-513; McG 365). Just when this article was submitted and accepted is not clear, but is was published in the *Annales* shortly after the defence. The article describes Campanella's theory of knowledge clearly and objectively. Gilson found this theory particularly relevant to Descartes' interest in physics and to Bacon's in the observation of natural phenomena. Because he believed that Campanella's reputation had suffered because of prejudice against renaissance philosophers, he tried to soften this prejudice by simply working through Campanella's major ideas. In particular he presented Campanella's distinction between spirit (the corporeal) and soul (the immaterial), Campanella's analysis of sensation, and his conclusion that not only is knowledge of particulars superior to knowledge of universals but that philosophy must be founded on observation and experience. As Gilson argued, this approach, adapted from Telesio and Cosenza, remained pertinent to any study of the new science.

When Laberthonnière published the article, both he and the *Annales* were on the brink of ecclesiastical condemnation. On 5 May 1913 a decree placed on the Index all issues of the *Annales de philosophie chrétienne* which had appeared under Laberthonnière's editorship, between 1905 and 1913. Gilson's article made the *Annales* just in time to fall under the decree of condemnation. As is well known, Laberthonnière, desiring orthodoxy, dutifully submitted to the curial decision by giving up writing entirely.

Between his defence in January and the opening of the next academic year, Gilson was also busy with a number of domestic distractions. Early in the year Thérèse became pregnant for the second time. Though unwell, she was in better health than during her first pregnancy, and she remained for a time with Gilson at Maison Heurteloup in Tours. During June she moved with her father and Jacqueline to Melun, partly to prepare for the birth and partly to finalize a housing purchase. Gilson and Thérèse had both wanted a home near Paris against the day when Gilson would have a post there. Because Ravisé's health was failing, they had decided to acquire a house (8, rue de Ponthierry) and the bare land under it on Ravisé's larger property at 6, rue de Ponthierry. The purchase was connected somehow with Thérèse's dowry as she was to inherit the house eventually. At any rate, little money exchanged hands. Gilson and Thérèse gave Ravisé a mortgage for 12,000 francs, interest on it payable from three months after his death; on 8 April Gilson also paid costs of the transaction, 1,000 francs.

The Gilsons found the new house well suited to their needs. It was quite large, with a cellar, a main floor, a first floor, an attic and a high storeroom. The house faced a courtyard on which were found a stable, a coach-house, a storehouse, conveniences, rabbit hutches and a common well. Notary Auberge's document described the property as "standing from front and east along rue Ponthierry." It was about three minutes walk from the railway station and ideal for commuting. The Gilsons purchased the home at the end of April, and in June Thérèse, Jacqueline and Ravisé took possession.

By all accounts the move was a hectic one. A few days before it was to take place, the Gilsons entertained Professor du Roure, who would later arrange many lectures for Etienne at McGill University in Canada:

> We have had here [in Tours] my friend, du Roure, just back from Canada. ... He came to the house to dine, sleep and breakfast before going to Paris. He is a good friend, always likable, and makes charming company. (EG to Maman, 13.6.nd; tr.)

Preparations for the move were apparently extensive, and involved seeing to the needs of three separate generations:

> We are surrounded by packages and baggage. Ours is a veritable exodus, one in which we are carrying along things for parents and for children, present and future. Chouchette wishes to advise you through me that Jacqueline will be in the Gare de Lyon about twenty minutes to six. (EG to Maman, 13.6.26; tr.)

Throughout the spring and early summer of 1913 tantalizing rumours flew constantly concerning university openings and faculty changes. As of 1 April it was whispered that Radier of Montpellier might resign; other appointments were also possible in Caën and Poitiers to the posts held by Robin and Rivaud. As of 26 April a new opening was rumoured in Aix, Maurice Blondel's post: "Damn!" wrote Gilson, "Pardon the expression, but you know I can't stand southerners." As of 22 May openings were likely at Lille, Rennes and Aix: "I will take anything offered me." By early June, two veteran academics expressed opinions. Delbos, quoting Boutroux, claimed that Gilson was officially listed among "those destined to go to universities." Meanwhile Durkheim told Halbwachs that, although appointments had been held up until July, he and Gilson were the two candidates under serious consideration (13.6.nd.).

Around 19 June Blondel announced that he would not retire. As a result Lille become the only new post available; it was generally acknowledged that either Halbwachs or Gilson would get it. Gilson wrote from Tours:

> I am likely to come after Halbwachs, who is older, so I shall probably have to remain in the lycées until Blondel retires which, according to Lévy-Bruhl's letters, must be before long. I have, however, a request in to the ministry lest they get the impression I am abandoning the chase. (EG to Maman, 13.6.nd.; tr.)

To further his cause, Gilson sent a copy of his major thesis to the dean of the Faculty of Letters at Lille, and had Maman send the dean a copy of his *Index scolastico-cartésien*. On 26 June Gilson wrote Maman that he was very much annoyed. He had been asked by his chief competitor, Halbwachs, for help in obtaining the one vacant post:

> I have now sent a letter to Lévy-Bruhl saying that although I have not asked him to intervene for me, neither am I constrained to intervene for anyone else. We have,

each of us, our dossiers; let the authorities judge between us. I don't look for any protection but I do not intend to remove myself from the running for anyone – the consequences for the future are too great. On the ground that he is six or seven years older than I, some would appoint him *maître de conférences* at Lille and me deputy professor at Aix while Maurice Blondel is ill! If that is what happens, too bad! But I have no obligation to withdraw in deference to my rival whose doctoral defence all know was inferior to mine. It was because of him that I was planted at Saint-Quentin and at Angers, and I keep reminding myself of this. Moreover, I was angry that he should have written Lévy-Bruhl while I could not bring myself to do so. Now, however, I have good reason. I do not, I told Lévy-Bruhl, ask anything for myself, but I don't ask anything for Halbwachs either. Well! Let him make of it what he will; I am not going to worry about it; I will sit back and wait. (EG to Maman, 13.6.26; tr.)

The wait proved less than three weeks. Gilson left for Rennes on July 15 to serve for a few days as a member of the baccalaureate jury in the academy there. The next day he received word from his mother that he had been appointed *maître de conférences* (assistant professor) in philosophy and in science of education in the Faculty of Letters, Lille. She had heard that the appointments were out and had gone over to the ministry to pick up her son's. The official document, dated 11 July 1913 and signed by the minister, Louis Barthou, appointed Gilson to Lille from 1 October 1913 to 31 October 1914 at an annual salary of 4,500 francs. "I am as happy," Gilson wrote Maman, "as I was that time at the *petit séminaire* when I was able to tell you that I had stood first in my class" (13.7.16; tr.). The victim in the proceedings was Halbwachs, who stayed on for another year in the lycée at Tours.

Gilson left Angers and Tours as soon as his year's work was wound up. His last note from Tours, undated but certainly near the end of July, refers to his separated family: "We will be taking up our normal life again in about ten days." On 11 September 1913 his second daughter, Cécile, was born in Melun.

5 UNIVERSITÉ DE LILLE, 1913-1914

The summer of 1913 was particularly busy. After the move from Tours to Melun there was business to take care of in Paris and Lille and a visit to Maman at Cravant. The doctor's instructions to Thérèse created the usual flurry, and the household swelled with midwife, nurse and helping friends. Despite this bustle Cécile was born in relative peace and calm. Immediately afterward, however, Gilson had to find a home in Lille and move the furniture yet another time. The move was very expensive: as Gilson tersely commented from Lille, "We were bled" (EG to Maman, 13.10.nd.; tr.).

The house in Lille was at 44, rue Louis Faure, a short distance west of the old university. After the war Gilson remarked that it has been spared by German shells because it was "a bourgeois house in a poor district," not inviting destruction. The old faculty of letters and its library were then located at rue Jean Bart and rue Angelier near the historic Porte de Paris. Although perhaps not as grand as the buildings that later replaced them, for Gilson they were warm and friendly places in which to teach and study. He found friends there very quickly. In his first days at Lille, to "organize things" before the arrival of Chouchette and the babies, he received a warm and friendly reception. He wrote Maman that "everyone thinks I am a native of Lille because of my name which is decidedly Belgian" (13.10.nd.); no doubt he enjoyed the welcome more than the aspersions it cast upon his ancestry.

Gilson's letter of 1 November offers an amusing glimpse of the young philosopher struggling with child psychology. Gilson was clearly fascinated by the antics of his two babies, one only a year and four months, the other less than two months old:

> Jacqueline was a little devil in the train from Paris to Lille. Cécile slept, making her presence felt only when the train made its three stops. She let the Compagnie du Nord know that a *rapide* ought never to stop: she kept saying so in no uncertain terms and the whole car had to listen to her. We came to the house by carriage and put the babies to bed. They didn't so much as notice that they had changed homes. ... Cécile is a winning child ... as warm as a little quail, and a joy to hold. Jacqueline is now "our pretty Jacqueline"; she's lots of fun on our walks, although she is tricky to a fault. She tells us, with an angelic air, that she wants pipi or caca so as to get put down on the ground. When we don't pay any attention she lifts her clothes to join the action to the word. Since she so often does want to go we hardly know what to do. She is conscientious enough about it all, and usually produces a dropping about the size of a tiny half-pea, to console us. (EG to Maman, 13.11.1; tr.)

Gilson loved his babies immeasureably. During this year, almost as much as during the war years when he missed them constantly, his letters were those of a doting father:

> The two little sisters are the best of friends and thus far understand each other perfectly. Jacqueline keeps us informed about what is going on: *peu Céci* (Cécile is crying), *dodo Céci*, etc. We have tried to teach Jacqueline to give the bottle to her sister, but the job quickly bores her; when she thinks Cécile has had enough, she finishes off the rest herself. She's still not much of a nurse. Meanwhile Cécile gazes at her with admiration, thinking that whatever so important a person does simply had to be just, equitable and salutary. (EG to Maman, 14.3.6; tr.)

During 1913 to 1914, Gilson's programme of courses pleased him. Each week he delivered four hours of instruction to in-course philosophy students preparing for their licence; because one of these was supplementary, it earned him an additional thirty francs a lecture. On Fridays at three o'clock he offered a public course entitled "The System of Thomas Aquinas." During the second semester he gave a special public course of twelve lectures in the history of secondary education; this was authorized separately by the minister of Public Instruction and earned him a supplement of three hundred francs. Finally he also delivered one lecture in a *les-samedis* series in which professors from the arts faculty provided public lectures for the people of Lille in the university's Salle des Fêtes on rue Auguste Angelier.

Gilson found university teaching a pleasure after the purgatory of the lycées: "I have literally the kind of life I have always wanted – a life passed in free work" (EG to Maman, 14.1.26; tr.). However he was not particularly happy with his seven licentiate students whom he examined early in November. These candidates had all been prepared by his predecessor, Père Perijou, with possibly some supplementary tutoring by himself. Gilson told them flatly he would have "plucked" them in the lycée before their baccalaureates. Of the seven "dunces" whom he examined, he failed six, he found the seventh "not much better than the others." Not surprisingly, he quickly earned the reputation of being a "ferocious" examiner (EG to Maman, 13.11.9; tr.).

Gilson found his course in education a trial; he worked from scratch and spouted "undigested books" he would have preferred not to be reading (EG to Maman, 14.1.26). He probably spent a good deal of the course on the programme which Descartes had taken at La Flèche, and which he had already built into his doctoral thesis.

If his education course was a trial, his special public course on St Thomas' "system of philosophy" was a source of great pleasure. At this stage Gilson approached the work of St Thomas as a formal and objective system, maintaining a sharp focus on philosophy as such. Clearly Gilson was still far from his later, more mature understanding of Thomas as a theologian drawing on a unique philosophical competence. Moreover, the methodologies of the Sorbonne still held Gilson firmly in their grip: a glance through his first three lectures reveals various references to the work of such thomist scholars as Sertillanges, Mandonnet, Grabmann, Grunwald, De Wulf, Heitz and Baeumker. Gilson's presentation, however, cannot be dismissed as derivative. Not only were the lectures analytical, critical and perceptive, they revealed broad erudition and superb rhetorical skills. The lectures also had their political aspect: they were intended to reintroduce St Thomas' works meaningfully into the French universities and to return them to that traditional and Catholic stream of learning they had largely created. At Lille, then, Gilson possessed something of the dedication and zeal of a missionary.

Gilson expected some opposition to his course on St Thomas from Professor Lyon, the faculty rector. Instead he received positive encouragement. No doubt the rector was only too aware of how unfavourably his faculty's treatment of thomism compared with Louvain's a few miles across the border. But there was another reason for this enthusiasm. As Gilson learned after his first lecture, the rector believed that a course on St Thomas would "purify an infected faculty":

> I have discovered the secret of my public course on St Thomas. The rector told me that he had, two years ago, rented out the faculty's amphitheatre for a congress of freemasons who turned out to be very heretical freemasons. The initial objection was mild but it quickly became a storm and the local newspapers were full of it. I am now supposed to be purifying the faculty, thus far without success. I had approximately thirty persons at my first lecture, but not one ecclesiastic. Perhaps this will change, but the ecclesiastical trend to date is one of abstention. (EG to Maman, 13.11.17; tr.)

There was indeed a change. As word spread of Gilson's rhetorical brilliance, there were countless requests for copies of the first lecture; the rector himself asked for a copy for publication in the university's *Revue bleue*. Moreover, Fernand Strowski, editor of the bimonthly *Revue des cours et conférences*, asked Gilson for the entire course at the rate of twenty-five francs a lecture. Because Strowski normally featured lectures by professors of the Institut de France and the Collège de France, as well as members of the Académie Française, both Gilson and the rector were highly pleased.

Among those who began attending the St Thomas lectures was Thérèse:

> Chouchette came yesterday to hear about St Thomas: she was much diverted. My entrance made her laugh; then I laughed too. Then she sucked some licorice pastilles to prevent coughing, which provoked a fit of coughing I thought would never end. Feeling warm, she took off her hat-veil, etc.; I pass over the fact that a large gentleman grew less and less interested in my lecture and more in my wife. (EG to Maman, 13.11.22; tr.)

By mid-December Thérèse was still attending the course, and questioning Gilson so much at home that he felt he was giving the course twice. But she was good for business!

> Last Friday the big gentleman again tried to get into conversation with her – a delicate problem for her in that she prefers to be left alone, but doesn't want to drive away my clients. I am like one of those café managers who tries to keep a pretty cashier. (EG to Maman, 13.12.14; tr.)

The full course must have covered about twenty-five lectures. No doubt due to publication troubles at the outbreak of World War I, the *Revue des cours et conférences* succeeded in publishing resumés of only nine: "From Plotinus to Thomas Aquinas," an introductory survey; "Faith and Reason: The Object of Philosophy"; "The So-called Evidence for the Existence of God"; "The First Proof for the Existence of God"; "The Four Last Proofs for the Existence of God"; "God's Knowledge by Way of Analogy"; "God's Knowledge of Universals and Singulars"; and "Creation: Nature and Creative Activity." A lecture on "Creation: Angels" was also given in mid-February (EG to Maman, 14.2.6; tr.).

At Lille Gilson for the first time had the freedom to research a subject of his own choice. For his first project he chose the mysticism of St Bonaventure. He first mentioned this research to his mother at the beginning of November; by 17 November he reported that he was "splashing about as he pleased in Bonaventure and that the exercise was both hard work and a fine existence." In mid-December he asked Maman to "tell l'abbé André that I am conversing softly with St Bonaventure, and that I have ordered from Diez, the second-hand book dealer in Rome, two black-letter volumes, one of which, dated 1501, he will be much in love with" (13.12.14; tr.).

The Bonaventure project brought Gilson close to the university librarian, M. Van Rycke. He learned a great deal about the operation of a good library, and would later use the knowledge in the design of his own medieval institute:

> The university library is beautifully set up: it has a reading room for professors with access to the shelves, an extremely precious service. I have never known this kind of convenience for my work, and I promise you I intend to use it well. (EG to Maman, 13.10.nd; tr.)

Gilson's friendship with Van Rycke meant that he got the books he needed quickly: at least three hundred francs were spent on his behalf during the first month alone, and the spending continued. Van Rycke also became his source of university gossip. On one occasion Gilson learned that a disappointed colleague had been spreading bits of misinformation about himself:

> Luquel, who was appointed to Montpellier and who wanted to be named to the Faculty of Lille, told the librarian here, (1) that it was he who had indicated to Lévy-Bruhl my thesis subject and that I had stolen it from him, (2) that I was surely a Jew because I had dedicated my thesis to Lévy-Bruhl; (3) that I was anti-religious since I had announced my course as on Thomas Aquinas rather than St Thomas Aquinas. ... By his standard, M. De Wulf and Père Mandonnet would be anti-religious. The librarian had only smiled at Luquel, commenting on how penetrating his judgment was, and sent him off to Montpellier consoled. May Augustine and Bonaventure help him! (EG to Maman, 13.11.9; tr.)

Gilson's lecture in the *les-samedis* series of the Department of Letters was delivered in what a reporter for *L'écho du Nord* called "la coquette Salle des Fêtes." Taking as its subject "Pierre Loti," the lecture was the first of the series on "Figures Contemporaines." Succeeding lectures by Gilson's colleagues were on Verhaeren, Meredith, Hauptmann, Anatole France, Maeterlinck, Tolstoi and Hervieu. The closing lecture, with music, was on César Franck, a favourite of Gilson's through Tournemire at Ste-Clotilde's.

Gilson's lecture had little in common with that given by him on Loti two years before in Tours. The earlier lecture had been a flamboyant rejoinder to Anatole France's disparagement of Loti. The Lille lecture was measured, philosophical, and read without flourish. It explained the philosophical nature of one who was not formally a philosopher, yet for whom life revealed something far more lovely than all man's works, namely his soul (*L'écho du Nord*, 13.1.19; tr.). In 1973, at eighty-nine, Gilson would return to Loti for a third and final time, in a speech for the Académie Française (EG to Maurer, 73.11.26).

Gilson took on one more major assignment during this year. Xavier Léon, secretary of the Société Française de Philosophie, invited him to defend before the society his thesis on Descartes' doctrine of liberty and theology. "Reopening the defence," he wrote Maman, "doesn't make me happy, though the honour is great. I shall write Lévy-Bruhl and ask him what to do." (13.11.17; tr.) Lévy-Bruhl advised him to accept, and Gilson prepared to address the society's meeting of March 1914.

As was the custom, Gilson prepared a précis of his thesis for distribution before the meeting. He submitted his theses in seven statements:

1. Descartes' doctrine of liberty is based philosophically on the absence of any distinction between God's understanding and God's will.
2. Descartes' physics, in which creative action is simple and does not invoke final causes, requires this absence of distinction. Man has access to the finite but not to the infinite aspect of eternal truths.
3. Descartes' thought was opposed to but sometimes conditioned by the structure of scholastic thought. Therefore Descartes occasionally, at the suggestion of Cardinal Bérulle and Père Gibieuf, employed "distinction of reason" but affirmed at the same time God's absolute simplicity.
4. In his *Fourth Meditation*, Descartes presented the liberty of man in terms of a critique of the "liberty of indifference" which he had borrowed from Gibieuf.
5. Descartes later dropped this critique as a result of his desire to avoid the jansenist quarrel.
6. In reaction to jansenism, Descartes moved toward molinism.
7. Nonetheless, "liberty of indifference" is accidental to cartesianism.

The regular members of the Société Française de Philosophie present for the discussion of Gilson's thesis were Belot, Berthelot, Bouglé, Brunschwicg, Chabrier, Dauriac, Delbos, Drouin, Dunan, Guy-Grand, E. Halévy, Laberthonnière, H. Lachelier, Lalande, Léon, Lévy-Bruhl, Meyerson, Parodi, Robin, Roussel, Roustan, Tisserand, Van Biêma and Winter. Maurice De Wulf was also present as a guest of the society. Gilson had visited De Wulf at Louvain shortly before the session and had enjoyed the trip a great deal;* he had asked Léon to invite De Wulf to the meeting in return.

As Gilson's guest De Wulf asked the first question. Although he agreed with Gilson's general thesis concerning the continuity between medieval and renaissance thought, De Wulf was unable to see why *theology* belonged in the title. According to De Wulf, true theology must be concerned with revelation, a topic not treated at all in the paper: "You tend," he objected, "to describe as theological anything that concerns God." A discussion followed, the outcome of which remained unresolved. De Wulf and Lévy-Bruhl insisted that there was no theology in Descartes, but that there was room for finality. An additional objection to the thesis was raised by Parodi, who found it structurally flawed: he felt that the two parts of the thesis, one devoted to God's liberty, the other to man's, were merely juxtaposed and lacked interior integration. All in all, the meeting was successful and stimulating. Gilson realized how right Lévy-Bruhl had been to insist that he accept.

Gilson looked forward to remaining in Lille for the next year, and perhaps for several more. In July 1914 he was promoted within the rank of *maître de conférences*, and his salary increased accordingly. He felt he was now firmly

---

* In anticipation of the visit Gilson had written Maman: "I hope to be able to visit with him the Catholic University – the loveliest and most celebrated of them all. I understand it has an incomparable library. What a wonderful day it will be for me." (14.3.6; tr.)

entrenched and could calmly await the day when a position might open for him in Paris. He planned a restful vacation during August at his beloved Cravant; indeed, the previous December he had already arranged for the use of Maman's house there:

> If you foresee no inconvenience, we will go to Cravant for three weeks during the month of August, or even for the entire month. ... Thérèse and I will be happy to bring our little ones to Cravant and to see again the house where we first got to know each other. When I think of the little boy I was when I used to go to Cravant, I experience a deep and happy emotion in realizing that I am now about to take my own children there. From now until summer we shall be looking forward to this holiday. (14.2.13; tr.)

The holiday was never to take place. In July 1914 the Gilsons left Lille for their house in Melun expecting to go on to Cravant in August. On 27 July they visited Maman at boulevard Port-Royal. Thérèse revealed a premonition that war would soon break out and that all their happiness would end. Gilson denied there would be a war: mobilization perhaps, but no war. Mobilization however came almost immediately, and on 2 August he left Melun to report in Lille. Sergeant Etienne Gilson signed up in the 43d Division (infantry), 28th Company (*dépôt*) of Lille Nord. He was assigned to the instruction of recruits rather than to a territorial army. This meant that although he was on active service, he was not likely to be sent to the front immediately.

5

The Great War, 1914-1918

1 MOBILIZATION, LILLE, 1914

Gilson was not entirely surprised to be assigned to the instruction of recruits. He had performed well in his 1904 service course and his additional military training had brought him almost to the level of officer. Moreover for seven years he had been a successful teacher in the lycées and university. He was surprised, however, on the morning he signed in, to find that the university porter had been made an officer, while he, a *maître de conférences*, was only a sergeant. He at once applied for officer's rank and expected to receive it in about a month.

Gilson's first few days in the army were less than gratifying. Like many of the men called up, he had no uniform. He slept at home on Louis Faure, took his meals in a hotel, and went daily to the barracks to drill large numbers of recruits. Normally a company numbered about 250 men, but those raised in Lille ran to between 700 and 800. Many of Gilson's recruits were naturalized Belgians, some of whom Gilson knew were far worse off than himself. One of these was forty-eight years old with ten children, another was forty-seven with eight children.

Gilson was deeply concerned at this time for the welfare of Thérèse and Maman. Thérèse, with two babies to care for, was absolutely terrified. She had become convinced that because she and Gilson had been far too happy together, they were now never to see one another again. Maman meanwhile was disturbed that Papa did not even know that war had broken out. She was also concerned that when her five sons were called up, they would stray from the faithful practice of their religion.

Gilson's first letters from Lille and from Croix de Villers attempted to console the worries of his wife and his mother. To Thérèse he made light of the war: it would not be a real one, and certainly his *dépôt* would never be sent to the front. He then advised Maman against trying to tell Papa of the war. He also firmly clarified his position with the church:

> First of all, I promise you to do from tomorrow all you ask me. It would be a lot
> easier had I never got mixed up with our holy mother the church, as you think it to
> be. I have never failed to observe my religious duties. What is true is that I have not,
> since the present pope [Pius x] came on the scene, considered myself to be very
> orthodox. But I am doing my best. I am giving all my good will, and I don't believe

I can do much more. There is no need for you to be upset on this point. (EG to Maman, 14.8.16; tr.)

According to Gilson, Pius x had failed to understand the extravagant enthusiasm of those republicans and scholars eager to adapt the presentation of doctrine to the discoveries of science. Gilson felt that his friend Abbé Laberthonnière, though in philosophical error, had deserved at most a sympathetic reprimand. Other issues had also driven Gilson further from orthodoxy. The very issue of *L'écho du Nord* that had reported his lecture on Pierre Loti had also announced the *suspensio a divinis* of Abbé Lemire, the inflammatory republican editor of *Cri de Flandres*; although Gilson did not particularly admire Lemire, he did not think the abbé should be suspended and threatened with excommunication for promoting his version of the social doctrines of Leo xiii. When Pius x died a few days later on 20 August, Gilson wrote Maman that "I assure you again that all you have asked me to do, I have done. Besides, the pope is dead! I may be more comfortable with his successor." (EG to Maman, 14.8.21; tr.)

Gilson's first real awareness of serving in an army at war seems to have arisen when the 43d Company was moved to the lovely camp at Croix-de-Villers, about ten kilometres outside Lille. He had only been there a very few days when he wrote almost pathetically to Maman of Thérèse's desire to visit him: "We will have to wait until the great Belgian battle is under control – and then, will I still be here?" By the time he wrote these words on 21 August, the first German army under General von Kluck had already won the battle of Tirlemont and entered Brussels. Gilson must have known that his military *dépôt* could not be left at the Belgian border; any attempt by Thérèse to join him would have been sheer madness.

From 26 August the *dépôt* of the 43d marched westward night after night. Gilson managed to mail a few cards with postmarks like Loos and Pas-de-Calais; one bore a picture of a church interior in Aucky-lez-La Bassée. Throughout the march Gilson did not know his destination, though he thought it might be Rouen. Finally, on 2 September, he sent a more informative letter-card to Thérèse:

> I am in good health and still with the *dépôt* of the 43d. We are at Caen and leaving this evening for Limoges. There are some very hard marches, and we eat little, but as I have lots of money, I can't complain. I am constantly thinking of you who are probably going to go through another siege. It is terrible. But I have unshakable confidence in the final success of the war. Since we left Lille, I have received no letters, but I carry with me my memory of you. I am not badly off, indeed quite privileged.... PS I have not been writing recently because there have been no postal facilities anywhere. Also we have been marching every night. I love you very much (14.9.2; tr.)

The reference to a past siege might have meant the first German airplane raid on Paris, 30 August 1914. Certainly, as the 43d made its long hard way south to Limoges, Paris was preparing for another attack. On 3 September the government moved to Bordeaux. And on 11 November Thérèse wrote a dramatic and detailed description of her flight from Melun to Vermenton with her own two babies, with Jeanne and her baby, and with Papa Ravisé. Gilson received this letter, and over the years wore it thin with constant rereading:

> *Mon cher aimé.* ... At half-past twelve, we left the house for the station, Cécile in my arms, Lucie in Jeanne's, Jacqueline holding my father's hand, and with horribly heavy bags. ... A first train arrived and left without picking us up. A second let us on, and we were twelve in the compartment. At Laroche we had, with bags and little girls, to climb into a cattle-car where we remained until we got to Cravant. ... The next night there was a new alarm. Jeanne, I, and the babies had moved into the upstairs apartment: Jacqueline fell out of her improvised bed onto the floor. I lifted her up and she was covered with blood. ... It was not very serious. ... Now, all that is past, and only the memories remain. Melun [was] unrecognizable, and unusual panic reigned. ... Marie [the maid] set off for Britanny the day we left. She wanted to take us with her, but it was not practical. ... We had to drown our beautiful Mélisande in a basket with all her kittens. It was her own sleeping place. Never again will we have animals: it's too painful. So that's where we are now, *mon cher petit*. ... Right now I am leading two lives: one active, material, but it hides another life full of intense thoughts, ardent and burning memories. In it, I think of our long and loving talks, our walks in Belgium, in Touraine, I think of sweet artistic communions, of music, of everything divine that life has given us. And it makes me happy again! ... Your Jacqueline often asks me for those photographs lent to me by my cousin and which are on the clock in my room: the little soldier with the deep, sad look, the first communicant. Jacqueline covers these photographs with kisses and caresses, and talks to them endlessly. Her memory is remarkably precise: *petit papa partit gare avec Maurice!* She often speaks of Maurice to Aunt Jeanne. He is in the east on the Epinal coast, Martha is at Autun, Emile too, but he can be mobilized any day now. ... Cécile is one year old today! She is sweet and lovable, a dear little love. Jacqueline is a little woman with acquired nerves, sensitivity, impassioned. *Femmette* is a little lover who hopes and adores: her whole life belongs to you. My father loves you dearly too. ... Here's hoping for news from you soon. ... I send a long passionate kiss on your dear lips. *Thé.* (14.9.11; tr.)

2 BEHIND THE LINES, SEPTEMBER 1914 TO JUNE 1915

When Gilson reached Limoges shortly before 18 September 1914, he wrote Maman immediately to report receipt of Thérèse's letter. He was so relieved to learn that his family was safe in Burgundy that he took their hectic exodus lightly: the journey, he said, was "nothing at all." At Limoges Gilson began a nine-month stay far behind allied lines; he moved back and forth between Limoges and Camp de La Courtine (near Ussel, Creuse), and between La Courtine and Confolens. Until the end of March 1915 he continued as an instructor of recruits; he was a sergeant-instructor until early December when he became an adjutant-instructor. On 31 March 1915 Gilson was transferred from the 43d Regiment to the 165th and made an apprentice-head of a section of machine-gunners. From 1 April to 15 June he trained for special action on the front line, probably for Verdun.

Gilson's letters over these nine months provide a clear record of his life in each of the three camps. They chronicle his work and reveal mixed feelings at being far from the front lines. They also document his close concern for his family, his growing affinity with colleagues and *bleus* from Lille, and his intellectual and spiritual activities.

At Limoges Gilson again drilled and trained recruits, though this time he trained them specifically to be sergeants. In early December he was promoted to adjutant, and his duties became more congenial: while sergeants attended to details in a single section of troops, adjutants oversaw four sections, giving orders and ensuring they were carried out (14.12.18; tr.). At the end of March 1915, Gilson wrote from Confolens to tell Maman of his new posting:

> This morning I learned that I am to depart on the thirty-first of this month for La Courtine [where he had been from October to January] where I am to serve my apprenticeship as head of a machine-gun section. I will stay there fifteen days. I am extremely happy about this posting because machine-gunning is really interesting and allows for more independence at the front. (15.3.26; tr.)

The new posting meant that Gilson could no longer be transferred by his immediate superior officers. This was not always an advantage, and more independence did not mean more flexibility. He quickly discovered that to head a machine-gunners' section was to be a kind of concierge; he handled all complaints and arguments, kept the names of those who were to march each day, and was pestered continually because "everyone wants to know whether his name is on today's list" (EG to Maman, 15.5.7; tr.).

During these months in central France, Gilson was about as comfortably situated as an active soldier could be. In Limoges he lived out of barracks in the home of a prosperous doctor where he had "a good bed, café-au-lait in the morning, excellent meals, and fulltime employment in very interesting work" (EG to Maman, 14.9.30; tr.). Camp de La Courtine was extensive and well-built high in the hills where the air was healthy and sharp. Gilson had his own room in the congenial sergeants' quarters where he could read and study. On free days he sometimes went on hikes with his friends and took along a picnic lunch: "We are outside most of the time. Since I am doing what I want to do, no complaint is in order" (EG to Maman, 14.10.13; tr.). In Confolens Gilson was billeted in various places: first in the Château de Villevert just outside the city; then, to his amusement, in the home of a midwife, *une sage-femme*.

Confolens was near enough to Angoulême for Gilson to visit his cousin Henry. Henry's practice was thriving, and he offered to help any of the Gilsons who were in financial difficulties. According to Henry, his increased income was due to the new shortage of civilian doctors, to his recent purchase of an automobile that let him visit more patients, and to everyone's sudden eagerness to pay bills promptly lest they be cut off from medical help. Gilson found his own comfort and his cousin's wealth embarrassing. Their privileged situations bothered him when he thought of the recruits he had trained for front-line action and of the countless young officers already killed or wounded. "The situation is scandalous!" (EG to Maman, 15.2.8; tr.)

On one occasion Gilson found himself half-hoping in a letter to Maman that he would not become an officer; without a commission he was less likely to be sent to the front. He quickly reconsidered in a remorseful postscript:

> It is good all the same to purge France as my comrades are doing; the sink-hole of 1870 is about to be cleaned out, and how good that will be! The destruction of Reims and Louvain pain me grievously: I will go to Louvain the moment I can. I do hope M. De Wulf was not there when it happened. (EG to Maman, 14.9.30; tr.)

A few days later he wrote, still in the same vein:

> All of us [Maman's five sons] will gladly give our lives that our country may be free, because it is the most beautiful country in the world; my daughters will be happy here, and their husbands and children too. It is worth a father's while to go into battle. Perhaps in the long run the battle will bring him more honour than pain. At any rate I hope so. (EG to Maman, 14.10.7; tr.)

Gradually Gilson's gnawing ambivalence was resolved. It was not enough to tell himself that he would go wherever he was sent – his obligations to France were broader than those to his family:

> The 165th on the line is near Verdun, so I may shortly go there. I may thus see the doctor [Maurice] if fortune smiles on me. I have never asked to go to the front; I have not felt I could ask in view of my obligations to Thérèse and the children. But my going seems to be taking on a certain importance in that I, for my country, represent a social value which it will be quite easy to see when this war is over. Many things have to be done now if we are to gain from the victory, which we shall surely have, all the happy consequences it can bring with it. (EG to Maman, 15.2.5; tr.)

When Gilson first went to Limoges in September 1914, Thérèse had just made the frenetic journey with Jeanne, M. Ravisé and the three children to her aunts' home in Vermenton. When the siege of Paris stalled along the Marne in October, both Jeanne and Thérèse wanted to return to Melun. Jeanne had simply become restless but Thérèse had a nervously ill child on her hands. Separation from her father was driving Jacqueline frantic; her tantrums and nightmares had become impossible to handle in Thérèse's aunts' home. On 22 October 1914 the little group returned quietly to Paris, and settled down again in Melun. When he received this news, Gilson cried and could not finish his letter to Maman. It was one of his lowest moments.

There were also bright moments during this nine months. Thérèse visited her husband at least three times, usually with the help of Emile whose military posting was with railway transportation. Gilson and Thérèse had a few days together in the Hôtel Terminus in Ussel some time before 22 November 1914. On 21 January 1915 they met again at Limoges for twenty-four hours, and on 26 March they met at Confolens. There may have been one or two other meetings as well.

Some insight into the bond between Gilson and Thérèse can be had from Thérèse's lovely fourteen-page letter to her husband at Christmas 1914. She opens the letter with a touching description of Christmas eve and Christmas day in the house on rue Ponthierry, with *bottines et chaussons* in the chimney place, a modest dinner on the table, and a visit from Jeanne. She next touches on some of the religious problems posed by this wartime Christmas season. Thérèse then moves into a deeply personal vein, thanking Gilson for the spiritual comfort in his last letter:

> I know that in all life's circumstances I can lean on you, and truly you are for me more than my heart's love, you are my "creator"! This is a wonderful thing which I never tire of rejoicing in. You have drawn aside for me the curtain of life. It is you who have shown me the splendour and beauty of living. In you I believe. In you I have faith. You have led me Godward, toward Him whom I now worship more than ever before, and in whom I always confide. You have helped me to understand. (14.12. *ce jour de Noël*; tr.)

The letter goes on to another spiritual topic, the sufferings of Christ and sufferings for Christ. Then, as a domestic letter will, it turns to a discussion of the household budget and of finances generally; as acknowledged business head of the family, Thérèse had made a number of small investments. Finally the letter closes with anticipation of the January visit.

Someone else continually in Gilson's thoughts during this time was André. The young priest had been sent to the front line and was rarely heard from. Although Gilson was sure that his brother was a runner in battle-communication, he was actually in foods and provisions. Often in danger, André was the most exposed of the Gilson boys (EG to Maman, 14.9.30). During part of this nine months André was in Le Chaudail; at another time he was in the Bois-de-Prêtre along the Marne. When Gilson finally heard from him after months of silence, he wrote Maman that he was "singing all day long" (14.11.28; tr.). Four months later he heard from André again. This time, wrote Gilson, his brother had a request: "What do you think it is? Not food. The man wants some German music. He kills them but he still wants their music. And he is right!" (15.4.20; tr.)

Apparently Gilson did not get down to anything academic until he reached La Courtine about the middle of October 1914. No doubt in Limoges he had been far too busy providing military instruction to give much time to study. At remote Camp de la Courtine, however, there were more instructors and life was more relaxed. There was also more privacy: adjutants had private rooms in a large sergeants' unit. Gilson had taken his volumes of St Bonaventure to La Courtine and he read them whenever he could, "making notes as though finishing up a book" (EG to Maman, 14.12.18; tr.). He had begun reading with a pencil when quite young and never gave up the habit; he used to tell his students he could no more read without a pencil than he could write without one.

Even at La Courtine, however, Gilson's reading time was limited. Like his contemporary humanists Paul Elmer More and Irving Babbitt, therefore, he developed the principle of reading only the best. In camp his preferred journal was *L'écho de Paris*: with articles by men like Barrès and Bourget, it was "the best-edited journal in Paris today" (EG to Maman, 14.12.22; tr.). Gilson's brother Emile sent this journal to him fairly regularly, and Maman often sent him articles she knew he would like to read. He particularly enjoyed two articles they sent him, and immediately passed on one of them, by Sertillanges, "to one of my colleagues on the Lille faculty on the Haute-de-Meuse front"; this was probably Lieutenant Pauphilot, the machine-gunner whose place Gilson had taken at La Courtine. The other article was a resumé of one of the lectures in Jacques Maritain's *Cours sur l'Allemagne* series, 1914 to 1915, for the Institut Catholique de Paris (see *Documentation catholique*, 10 [1923]: 643-659). Gilson asked Emile for more of the lectures in resumé, though he apparently knew Maritain at this time: "It is true than I can ask Maritain himself to send them to me" (EG to Maman, 14.12.29; tr.).

In April Gilson wrote Maman from the barracks of Confolens that he had been reading some spiritual conferences by Père Janvier that she had sent him. He admired the pieces very much, "partly for their fine spirituality, partly because they never mention the war," and intended to send them on to Thérèse (15.4.20; tr.). Like similar intellectual and spiritual asides in his letters from La Courtine and Confolens, Gilson's account of his reading reveals a profound desire to preserve under adverse conditions some contact with the world of letters from which he was temporarily exiled.

3 VERDUN, JUNE 1915 TO FEBRUARY 1916

Gilson spent Thursday 17 June 1915 with Thérèse on boulevard Port-Royal. That night he left Paris to conduct three hundred troops to the Verdun front; to his disappointment he was still an adjutant. Thérèse travelled with him as far as Melun.

Gilson's first day at the front was spent in Verdun itself. It is fully described in his Verdun log, the detailed diary that he now ambitiously began to keep. From time to time he sent log entries to Thérèse, who then made another copy for Maman. Understandably the diary could not be kept up and was eventually abandoned. However, those entries that survive provide graphic accounts of Gilson's life in Verdun and reveal a cryptic style very different from that of his letters. The diary also shows that he had acquired an expert knowledge of procedures during his past nine months as an instructor.

Verdun was not a particularly active front during the three months following Gilson's arrival. The nearest heavy fighting was in Champagne, especially at Argonne where André was stationed. At Verdun the French and the Germans had dug themselves in. Although there were skirmishes and ambushes to keep the troops occupied and alert, each side was waiting for a strategic moment to launch a major offensive.

Gilson's first day at the front was described in his log:

18 June, 0230 hours. The sergeant major, who knows the region, shakes me to wake me up. "Come on, we are arriving in Verdun!"... We pull into the station. Sure enough, it is Verdun! Not a trace of war, not even in this station which was shelled by 420s only a few days before. A sergeant conducts the detachment toward Mirabel barracks. During the march some distant cannon fire is heard and, in the morning twilight, the sound of six French biplanes leaving on reconnaissance. Until 10:00 AM this is all. I detrain the men and have food distributed; I buy bacon and onions for three hundred men; I look around for newspapers, etc., etc. Thus the hours pass in the calmest, most silent, the dullest little city in the world. They tell us that large shells have been falling here and there; and they tell me to have my men go into hiding if an airplane is seen. But is what they say believable? We are in a kind of Vermenton fallen asleep or drowsing in the noonday sun.

1600 hours. A calm day. Cannon fire spaced and distant. Many planes and much sun. Meet an infirmarian who notices that I am reading *Le temps* and asks if I am a teacher. He is professor of natural sciences at the lycée in Angers, and he gives me some news: no news about Cheirel; Dulac has retired; Dusumier, my predecessor in philosophy, has been killed; my successor in philosophy, Schlegel, has also been killed. Let's hope I don't turn out to be the hyphen between them. ...

1700 hours. Received the order to awaken the men at midnight and to leave for Cumières at 1:00 AM. A lieutenant will lead us; five sergeants will line up the men. This will be a night-walk so as not to arouse enemy artillery. Everyone is now quite happy to get out of Verdun where the citizens are virtually prisoners; where soldiers don't leave their barracks day or night, morning or evening; where women are strictly and, apparently, effectively excluded. Moreover, I have already run into a good number of people who say they are going mad. Everyone wants to get out of here.

I am thinking about you, my dear, and about my little ones, above all of you. I am thinking tenderly not sadly. I am living with all of you, but I am living with you alone, my dear wife. I passed the last three night before leaving for Verdun within the warmth of your body. I went to you a hundred times and you received me. I simply had to have you. And you see? Women guess everything! I change the subject now. I have to go and repack what I have hardly unpacked.

1900 hours. I summon together my three hundred men to congratulate them on their behaviour during the trip and to give them their orders for the night departure. My report to them is interrupted here by a French plane which is passing over us to pay its respects. We watch it until someone shouts: "Taubes!" I see on the horizon two magnificent birds and suddenly the anti-aircraft defences surround them with projectiles – our first war spectacle, but one far from terrifying! You might describe it as delicious fire: the birds poise, then lift themselves in the white flack that is so graciously encircling them. They turn around and move away. The party is over. I recall the men whom I had dispersed, and go on with my report. (EG to Thérèse, log entries, 15.6.23; tr.)

The first card-letter from Verdun to Maman, written 19 June, continue this narrative with the arrival of the troops at an unnamed village, possibly Cumières or Forges, on the second line of defence:

I arrived this morning on the firing line in a very tranquil and peaceful place. From their trenches, some two hundred meters apart, French and Germans exchange occasional rifle fire to keep themselves occupied. The artilleries exchange shells which swish high above us. The village is in ruins, but a charming stream runs through it and, miraculously, its church tower is standing. Our normal schedule here is four days in the trenches and four days rest, the one amounting to about the same thing as the other. (15.6.19; tr.)

Gilson later added to this account:

That first day I stood up to survey the landscape. I heard a shot or two but paid little attention. The captain shouted at me: "Are you trying to become a war hero? Don't you realize they are sniping at you?" Surprised and chastened I slid down into my trench. (interview, 1974.)

Although Gilson arrived at Verdun as an adjutant, his commission was on its way. He had been posted to Verdun as highly competent personnel; his replacement as adjutant had already been named and was to join the 165th that summer. Of the three battalions of the 165th, Gilson's was the best; his company, the 10th, was also crack. The officers treated Gilson as one of themselves. They walked and chatted with him, borrowed his copy of *Le temps*, and admitted him to their mess at officer's rates.

Something of Gilson's strategic competence emerges in his log-entry for Friday, 2 July 1915. Gilson's ambush patrol was carrying out one of its exercises:

Friday 2 July 1915. This evening I am going to our cottage post: we have twenty men in it, 200 meters from here, in open country. It is a railway gatehouse along the line from Verdun to Contenoise. The next level-crossing gatehouse, towards Contenoise, is occupied by Germans. Tonight a patrol will go along the railway line and try to dislodge the Germans there. This means travelling 750 meters twice, risking ambush and a sentinel's rifle. I am not conducting this patrol: I am accompanying it to a point marked on a map. We will all leave here together through our barbed-wire entanglements by paths we know. Then, ready for flight if need be, we will cross Forges Creek on a plank already in place. From there this is the pattern: rails to our left, creek to our right, our gatehouse behind us, the German gatehouse ahead, although we cannot see it. We can, however, see the tops of two poplars nearby in profile against the sky. Some men will detach themselves from the others here and move cautiously in the tall grass, gun loaded, eyes ahead, yet still keeping sight of his buddy who can suddenly be asked for help or whose place may have to be covered. For my part I have only 350 metres to move, in order to reach the place I have picked out – but how far it is! This France is a whole world!

First we cross grassy patches where tall stalks, now dried out, crackle and sound. Next comes a long muddy ditch unexpectedly blocking our way and necessitating a short detour to the right. How long the detour seems! We move in the direction of the railway bank where the bole [clay] is firmer but where there are tall thistles propped straight up like peas in a kitchen garden. The higher ground is firmer. Here is the ditch again. I think I am there. Here along the railway there is a level crossing; and beyond it there is a large bush which I must examine lest someone come and cut off the patrol route and forestall us. Just a minute! The Germans come there too. Right where we are to stop is a large trampled area indicating that one of their patrols has stopped there before us; each patrol, without either catching sight of the other, is now busy with its own task. Our three men and their corporal will move up as far as the barbed wire which protects the German cottage and, at the usual signal, "fire," will throw through the window of the house the grenade each is carrying. Then there will be a salvo of shots and our men will return at triple gallop. They are starting off now, but slowly; the moon is coming up and the countryside is wrapped in an opal haze. Everything is blending into the milky mist. When near the German house they creep along, anxious not to make any noise, and they remove with a shake of their leg any brittle grass clinging to their foot. I can scarcely make them out, but would estimate they are about 8 metres from me. I have lost sight of them now.

Just a minute! Attention! The grass is covering over with wet dew. It is slowly wetting my clothes and, to get out of the cold, I go under some bushes. I find tracks left by some German patrol. A strange noise brings me up short – snippers clipping barbed wire. But where? Are we making it, or are the Germans? A mystery! But I distinctly hear the snipping of barbed wire and it is some distance off where the Germans are. There is also the driving of stakes into the ground with regular metal blows. I return to my observation point. Twenty-five minutes roll by – thirty-five – still nothing. But the decisive moment is drawing near relentlessly. Suddenly there is a gunshot – with the round, large flashes of two detonations. So our men have reached the German cottage without being seen. ... Silence! Then seven or eight shots. ... Who is this unknown person or persons causing rifle flashes some 30 metres along the tracks in front of me? Can it be a German sentry about to shoot the French patrol from the rear? I leap in the direction of the firing. A large man, low near the ground, leaps up. I say: "Halt, Halt! Or I will shoot." "Don't shoot; it's me!" "Who are you?" "Dechef!"

Fine! The corporal has left his patrol on the way and taken a position 30 meters in front of me. I softly congratulate him on his way of leading a patrol – 300 metres behind the soldiers. He is sweating and puffing, and I wonder why. Now the other men return. No damage. All is well. We go down on one knee in a line and shoot away at the cottage. Then we all leave laughing and talking freely. Suddenly bullets are flying. We all fall flat on our bellies. This is the Germans' first reply: they have taken their time recovering their spirits. But their bullets are wasted! They are shooting blindly. Bullets patter away; all the German posts around join in the firing, even from across the Meuse. We return quietly without so much as hearing a bullet whistle by. Meanwhile the Germans go on firing without knowing what they are firing at.

Back at out cottage, I telephone the captain that all has gone well. I then shake hands with the members of the patrol and start to leave: "Goodbye, adjutant!" "Goodbye, my friends!" As I rise to leave, I hear Corporal Dechef giving his account of the raid: "We were creeping forward, close together, right up to the barbed wire; there was a sentry there. ..." I believe it. (EG to Thérèse, 15.7.2; tr.)

On this first night of ambush Gilson was an observer only, though a sharp one. The following night, Saturday 3 July, he was in charge. The captain ordered a second patrol in the hope of taking prisoners should the Germans try to regain their gatehouse. Again Gilson described the patrol in detail. The men approached the cottage from the other side of the tracks through a swamp where the water was sometimes waist-deep. However, because the enemy did not attempt a return, no prisoners were taken.

Most of Gilson's assignments between June and October were those befitting an adjutant. He laid barbed wire and supervised digging operations and the excavation of rocks; he now understood why day-labourers worked slowly for "in their *métier*, it is a case of choosing between going fast or going on for a long time." He also attended to the exercising of men and animals. His work with the animals he found a bit tricky: with four horses and four mules to look after, he had first to learn to distinguish mules from horses. He also had to cope with one pretty mule that was especially difficult, at one moment capricious and stubborn, at the next sniffing Gilson's pockets for bits of food. One day he derived great satisfaction from his preparation of "a salve of lard and tincture of iodine ... excellent for treating cuts and scratches on horses" (EG to Maman, 15.9.30; tr.). The incongruity of such priorities for a philosopher amused him: "When cooking pots arrive, it is better to have one's mind on a double row of oak logs than on a system of metaphysics" (EG to Maman, 15.9.11; tr.).

Shortly after reaching the front Gilson was called to assist a man who had been mortally wounded. The dying man clung to him and called out for his mother and a priest: "I could not give him either, but I think from my memory of his eyes looking at me that I gave him some tenderness and sweetness at the moment of his death" (EG to Maman, 15.7.1; tr.). Gilson later told how, as he attended the man, he remembered an opinion of Albert the Great on confession in time of emergency:

> At such a moment there is no obligation to confess providing there is no contempt of religion and reception of the sacrament is impossible. Nor does then one have to confess to a person not empowered to absolve. Yet, if one does confess to such, the humility and embarrassment involved take away most of the guilt. (*In IV Sent.*, d. 17, a. 39)

Gilson told the dying man this and heard his confession. "The action," he added, "was a source of tremendous consolation to both of us."

From early September to early November 1915, the German and Allied armies at Verdun both waited uneasily for the enemy to open an offensive. Little news of the war penetrated through to individual soldiers. Gilson, who was expecting a promotion, was mystified in late September when he was transferred from the 165th Regiment to the 164th. He remained an adjutant and was placed in charge of a new machine-gunners unit. During September and October Gilson had little opportunity to prove himself as a soldier. He contented himself with a change of image: "I have cut off my beard and am smoking a pipe. I find the pipe smelly and dirty, but realize that becoming a genuine *poilu* is not easy" (EG to Maman, 15.0.30; tr.).

In September Gilson heard that Thérèse was unwell and intended to take the children to Luxeuil and try the waters again. Mail was slow and Gilson could not keep abreast of her recovery. His heart told him that Thérèse really needed her husband rather than a doctor. He was surprised to later learn that Thérèse returned from Luxeuil much improved; he was probably right, however, as she was ill again by December.

A few excerpts from a letter written to Thérèse on 26 September survive in an October letter of Thérèse to Maman. One of these reveals Gilson's boredom, his essential ignorance of the facts of the war, and his impatience to get it over with:

> Today is a Sunday, calm and very tranquil. Cannons are still. However ... we suspect in a confused sort of way something of what is going on at the moment. We are not without confidence as we wait for whatever they want to do with us, but we are awfully impatient about the precise time of the offensive. We would love to cleanse French soil before winter. (Thérèse to Maman, 15.10.2; tr.)

Clearly Gilson was largely unaware of the seriousness of events along the Verdun front and of the various strategies of the British generals and General Joffre.

In November Gilson was finally promoted to second lieutenant in the 1st Company of the Machine-Gunners of the 164th Regiment. During November he apparently moved back and forth between the front and a training camp, probably at Beaumark, where he instructed trainees in machine-gunning. On 29 November 1915 he wrote Maman from the cozy barracks of this mountain camp:

> Here we live in snow. The barracks are located much as though they were a sanatorium. It is a dream-place for one seeking a cure by fresh air. Since it is quiet here, I give myself to the joys of reading. I read at my table as long as I have coal or wood; and when out of fuel, I read in my warm little bed. I am reading everything, French, Italian, Spanish, and the days seem short. It is just a little scandalous to be leading this kind of existence at the front. As my men say, who are also sleeping in good beds in barracks, somebody has to be well accommodated (15.11.29; tr.)

Not only was Gilson well accommodated at Beaumark, but he returned to writing in a serious and productive vein. The important essay, "Art et métaphysique," was written "at Beaumark, near Verdun, between two shifts in the trenches"; an offprint preserved in the Gilson archives in Toronto is signed "on campaign, November-December 1915." The twenty-four page article appeared in the *Revue de métaphysique et de morale* (23 [1916]: 243-267; McG 200). It was first discussed in a front-page review-article, "Dans la tranchée," published in *Le temps* (16.5.8).

"Art et métaphysique" provides a common focus for many of the aesthetic concerns that had engaged Gilson up to this time. Bergson appears as the philosopher of creative intuition and human effort; Anatole France, the accusing artist, holds up a mirror in which Gilson finds many of his own idiosyncrasies; and Pierre Loti is present, a man whom Gilson loved for possessing tastes so close to his own. "Art et métaphysique" was the first of Gilson's articles and books on the fine arts; these were later to occupy a place of considerable importance in the non-professorial side of his long career.

The article is a profound one, utterly personal and contemporary, and excellent early Gilson. Of necessity it was assembled without scholarly footnotes, though Gilson did attach one note; this warned his readers not to interpret certain comments as arguments for or against either expressionism or formalism (p. 254). The most amazing aspect of the piece is that Gilson was able to write at all while on active service at the front. Although the reviewer for *Le temps* questioned some of the conclusions, he called the performance a "moral polyphony" reminiscent of Marcus Aurelius composing his *Thoughts* while on expedition against the Quales or Marcomans.

According to "Art et métaphysique," artistic creation is not comparable with any scientific undertaking, including metaphysics. Because some philosophers, most notably Plato, have produced works that are both philosophy and art, it is tempting to compare the two kinds of work. Nonetheless, philosophy is a trap for the artist, and can easily prevent him from producing anything at all; Anatole France recognized this with his character, Jacobus Dubroquens, who was always about to give birth to a world but who died before starting his first canvas. All science, including metaphysics, proceeds by making concepts, while art, which is not a science, proceeds by immediate intuition. Although the metaphysician is sometimes intuitive, his point of departure from the real is a scientific concept rather than an instinct.

A work of art can only be conceived and appreciated through a series of psychic experiences which are not identical in aesthetics and in creative art. Aesthetics arrives at a recognition of beauty; art creates an object that is beautiful. The art critic succeeds when he discovers beauty; the artist succeeds when he creates it. Aristotle then was correct. Art is not a theoretical or contemplative discipline, as pure science or metaphysics can be. Nor is it a practical discipline that regulates action upon physical, moral or social reality. Art is a "poiesis" an "activity which produces new realities."

Gilson further argues that any analysis of artistic activity must take into account the psychic consequences for the spectator. There are many such consequenes. First, the enjoyment of art requires the effort of cultural preparation; such preparation is interior and voluntary, even though it involves submission to the work of art. Second, the relation between the spectator and the artist's work is not unilateral, but is a dialogue. The spectator's "I" at first rejects the new creation, then only slowly and with effort proceeds to accept it. Gilson describes this movement toward acceptance as growth of, or nutrition for, the spectator's psychic existence. Third, the psychological change created by the enjoyment of a work of art is profound; although stimulated from outside, it takes place in the spectator's "existence" or "act-of-being," and affects all facets of his life. Moreover "the proper character of aesthetic intuition is an experience in one's own interior life of the enrichment that comes from the artist's 'I' through the intermediary of his work of art." Fourth, a work of art stirs up emotions, which the spectator supplies; each completes the other. Finally, the understanding of a work of art comes when the spectator allows it to render all the *sens et signification*, the meaning and import, with which the artist's vision has endowed it.

In his final comments Gilson urges all to aspire to the limitless enrichment offered through art. True art transforms the order and procedure of life in a manner totally unlike metaphysics. Pascal, adds Gilson, praised this special kind of transformation as separate from and superior to any that occurs in metaphysics.

Despite intermittent shifts in the trenches, the last months of 1915 were quiet, reflective and productive. Pascal was apparently much in Gilson's thoughts, which may account for his article's concluding reference. In thanking Maman for a handsomely bound copy of the La Mennais *Imitatio Christi*, he commented that, like Pascal's *Pensées*, it was just right for the long nights when it was difficult to sleep; one could read a page or two of either book, then reflect on the passage for some time afterward (15.12.11).

The quiet and inactivity that had engulfed Verdun since Gilson's arrival were rudely interrupted on Christmas Eve 1915. First there was a small incident that would nag at Gilson's conscience for many years. Walking through the camp in early evening, he came to a post with no sentry on duty. "Someone has gone for a Christmas beer," he mused, as he set this observation down in his report. A senior officer asked him if he really wanted to report the sentry, and Gilson replied that the man should be disciplined even if it were Christmas Eve. "He won't just be disciplined," said the officer. "He will be shot!" Gilson left the item out of his report. (Joseph Owens, *viva voce*.)

The missing sentry soon gave way in Gilson's thoughts to more momentous events, as the evening's peace was shattered:

> At 11:35 the Christ Child brought us out toys! Some thirty-five or forty shells fell round about us. The first fell through the roof into a barn right across from my house on the other side of the street. Most of the men were in bed at the time. Some had just left for midnight mass. This saved their life. Of all the rest there in the barn only three were uninjured. The one shell killed eight men and gravely wounded six others. It created a hellish scene: the wounded had to be searched out with the bombardment continuing all around. We lowered the wounded as best we could into a shelter full of mud and crowded with soldiers, and we stretched them out along the ground wherever there was room. I don't want to describe this scene for you but is was a real hell and worthy of Dante: a horrible butchery, ignoble and disgusting; and the scene included some old women who had remained in the district and some little children who watched our wounded men die. The medical officer who had come to us could only see the victims one at a time, while all around him groans, death rattles, plaintive appeals could be heard, and all could feel the presence above them in the loft of the four who had been instantly killed and whose bodies lay up there battered, gaping, torn. What a frightful horror! The 1st Company of the Machine-gunners of the 144th Brigade will never forget Christmas Eve 1915. Toward 9:00 Christmas morning I returned to my room and threw

myself on the bed. There were no window panes left, naturally enough, but it was not this that kept me from sleeping, it was the nightmares that came every fifteen minutes. The captain and Lieutenant Chauchoy were in the same state as I was. I tell you all this because I think you courageous enough to have the right to know whatever happens to me exactly as it happens. As for me, I have not been wounded. I haven't a scratch. The only soldier with rank who was wounded was a corporal. The shell which did all this fell in front of my house; the rest fell nearby or passed overhead. If I can survive a situation like this, I may very well survive to the end. (EG to Thérèse, 15.12.30; tr.)

For the first six weeks of 1916, life at the Verdun front returned to the pattern of the previous autumn. Despite continued anticipation of a major offensive, there was considerable time for reading and study along with occasional leaves of absence. Gilson still visited Beaumark from time to time to lecture trainees and he continued to read prodigiously. As late as 5 February he wrote Maman that he had received a book from Delbos: "I will read it at once because I am devouring the printed word more voraciously than ever" (16.2.5; tr.).

After 13 February the commanding officer, Captain de Sambœuf, kept his two lieutenants, Gilson and Chauchoy, constantly on call. Their battalion was defending a line at Bois de Ville-devant-Chaumont from the enemy troops at Herbebois. The German offensive at Verdun began on Monday 21 February. On Wednesday 23 February, Gilson, Chauchoy, and three noncommissioned orderlies were taken prisoner. Although Captain de Sambœuf was wounded, he was quickly pulled back among his own men. De Sambœuf sent a succinct statement of the circumstances to Thérèse on 3 March 1916:

Since 13 February, we [de Sambœuf, Gilson, Chauchoy] had been quartered together in a dugout waiting for the offensive which we knew to be imminent. From 21 to 23 February we were subjected to a bombardement more violent than can ever be described. Our company had already suffered some cruel losses but we three had by good fortune not received a scratch even though the wooden uprights of our dugout had literally been turned upside down. Toward 11:00 AM, 23 February, Gilson and Chauchoy were sitting in the dugout on the edge of a camp bed. I sensed an infantry attack and had just raisen to my feet to pick up my equipment. We were only a few steps from one another.

The bombardment had gone on for fifty-two hours (and was about to let up, as things turned out) when, by an unheard of piece of bad luck, a shell hit the base of our dugout from the outside and severed one of its corner posts, and the dugout fell in on us. I was cut off by earth and rubble from my two officers: I could hear them calling for help, and I too, helpless and half-crushed, was under the debris, but I called out to them. As I was nearer the exit from the dugout, I was the first to be released by the devoted attention of one of my noncommissioned officers, the same brave young man who then went to work with his pick and dug from the outside into the corner of the shelter where my two good friends were buried. (de Sambœuf to Thérèse, 16.3.19; tr.)

De Sambœuf went on to describe how, in his stunned condition, he only vaguely remembered some German footsoldiers stepping out from the bush.

Apparently the Germans had reached the dugout just as the two lieutenants, who were stunned but not wounded, were being extricated from the rubble. De Sambœuf had the impression that some shots had been exchanged to prevent his comrades' capture, but he was not sure. At any rate, he had himself been dragged back among his men. His two lieutenants and their rescuer had not.

4 Prisoner of War, February 1916 to November 1918

Much later, in 1974, Gilson offered a more dramatic version of his capture. First he described the opening of the offensive by the Germans, claiming that he could not improve on Jules Romain's description in *Verdun*:

> Boom! came the sound of a gun from the east. All three stopped as at a word of command. The sound had been deep and full-throated. It must have come from a gun of medium calibre, probably a 150. It broke with a more than usual solemnity on their ears by reason of the bright February stillness which it so markedly disturbed. How long the three men stood there it would have been difficult to say. They said nothing.
>
> Suddenly, *Boom, ban ban, ran, ran, ranranran* ... followed by an enormous sequence of explosions, as though thousands of mines had suddenly gone up, strung out along a half circle of the horizon stretching from north to northeast. Almost immediately came the crash of shells near at hand, in the air, in the branches, in the ground. Fragments of steel and wood, lumps of soil, stones of every description flew over their heads. Great columns of smoke jetted upwards from twenty different spots all round. The whole earth seemed to tremble. The air was filled with the smell of hot gun-breeches suddenly thrown open. (*Verdun*, tr. Gerard Hopkins [1940], p. 251.)

Gilson then began his own account:

> On the second day of the offensive I went with my sector and our two machine-guns down into a dugout. As I entered the shelter with my adjutant – who was my elder – I signalled him to come below with me. "Lieutenant," he said, "you should not do that. Stay with me near the entrance with the least possible space above us; if anything happens, perhaps we can get out." Sometime during the day we heard this one particular shell – our shell. It killed everyone in the dugout, except the adjutant and myself. The two of us returned to the captain, each carrying a machine-gun. He asked us what was going on. We are, we said, bringing back to you all that is left of the company.
>
> The next day, stupidly perhaps, I went all the way down into our own dugout quarters, and there a shell found us again. I was wearing my helmet at the time. How I would like to have brought that helmet back! I was hit by something, shrapnel perhaps, which made a hole in my helmet the size of my fist. I was unhurt, but completely buried.
>
> My orderly, who was my very close and dear friend, came over to where I was and began digging me out. He said to me as he was digging, "Take it easy, and above all don't shoot because some Germans are standing over us with flamethrowers poised." When I was sufficiently uncovered to get on my feet, a

German soldier, realizing how frightened I was, said to me, "Morgen, wir sind keine barbaren." I did not resist. I had no gun and couldn't shoot. They let my own orderly lead me away. The German soldiers were undoubtedly under orders to avoid brutality, no doubt because the Paris papers had been describing them as barbarians. At any rate, my captors were typically German: not only were they not barbarians, they made it clear they were not.

The next stage was terrible. We were taken through the French villages – our way of the cross – and, although I have no way of knowing how many thought the same way, one Frenchwoman jeered from her doorstep: "So you let them take you prisoners!" The most charitable word I heard was from a German soldier, an older man, who was guarding us on the train. He said: "You look sad." I said: "I *am* sad; I am a prisoner." "Being a prisoner," he replied, "doesn't much matter, what matters is being an officer. If you were a simple soldier, French or German, everything would be bad; but you are an officer, and for an officer, whether French or German, everything is good." (interview, 1974.)

Gilson was taken first to the prisoner-of-war camp at Mainz, where he remained until 3 March. He found the camp "not disagreeable," and immediately wrote brief cards to Thérèse and Maman. His first full-length letter was written to Thérèse from Mainz on 2 March, but was sent from Vöhrenbach, 30 March, nearly a month later; no doubt the delay was for vetting by the censors. Writing in pencil – ink was forbidden – Gilson assured Thérèse that he was well, if somewhat stiff and exhausted; the partial deafness that had followed the battle had passed. He asked her to buy him shoes and clothes and to have his uniform chest sent on if it still existed; he had no cap, and his battle-dress was worn and damaged. All he'd had with him when taken prisoner was the little pocketbook containing her photograph.

Because he was drawing half his army pay, Gilson did not need money; he was more concerned that Thérèse make sure she received the other half. However, he was unable to buy extra food and he asked Thérèse to send him a weekly parcel with one supplementary item, such as sardines, tunafish, corned beef or chocolate, for each day of the week. He also suggested that rather than sending bread she subscribe to the bread-delivery service for prisoners of war; for five francs monthly, payable in Paris, bread would be delivered to him three times a week by Pain du Prisonnier de Guerre of Switzerland.

In the letter, life at the Mainz camp was succinctly described:

> My knowledge of German has already served both me and my comrades well. Life is very quiet here. We are well lodged, sleep in beds, dine in large refectories. We are all of us officers from various nations: England, Russia, France, Belgium and so on, which imparts to the camp a picturesque character. From the terrace where we walk, we have a view of the monuments of the city, and of the Rhine and its banks. Walks are arranged on the basis of one a week for each officer. (EG to Thérèse, 16.3.2; tr.)

The stay at Mainz was short. In a card written a day later on 3 March, Gilson informed Thérèse that the prisoners were to be moved that night to an unknown destination. He was taken to Vöhrenbach in the Schwarzwald where he remained for the next four or five months. Virtually no letters survive from this period; most likely they were never delivered. Apparently these were trying months for Gilson psychologically. It was probably at Vöhrenbach where, in an effort to escape the wearisome companionship of his fellow prisoners, he contrived to be put into solitary confinement. In his quest for solitude, Gilson for the first time understood how a man could become a Carthusian:

> Being alone is not the worst situation a man can be in. Never to be alone is far worse. I found this out as a prisoner. I got so that I could not stand being with people all the time with never a minute to myself and I decided to get myself put into solitary. When I presented myself to the big German doctor, he said "You don't need medical help, do you?" "No sir," I said. "Then why are you here?" "Because I want to go to jail, I want to be put in a cell; I want to be alone for eight days." "That can be arranged," he said. And so it was! I was sent to a solitary cell for eight days. ...
>
> My predecessors in the cell had written reflections on the wall: a German thought, an English thought, a Russian thought. All were quite typical and I was much taken by them. I then asked the guard for a book to read. "No," he said, "reading is forbidden." "But," said I, "the walls of this cell are covered with newspapers; I am going to read those pages from beginning to end." "Just go ahead," the guard said, and went away. He returned shortly with two other men who removed every scrap of paper from the walls, with the result that I nearly perished from the draughts coming in through the cracks. My two little jokes turned out to be grim ones. This craving to be alone, however, stayed with me a long time. Even after the war, when I was back home in Melun, it sometimes returned to me, and Thérèse used to say that perhaps my experience had made me a little mad. (interview, 1974.)

Sometime during August 1916, Gilson was moved from Vöhrenbach to the officers' prison camp in Burg-bei-Magdeburg, where he remained until February 1918. He seems to have become more settled in mind at Burg, and acquired additional accomplishments which would enrich his subsequent career. Three brief letters to Maman in August and September 1916, along with three cards written in January 1917, are all the communications extant from Burg; there were certainly others, whether lost or undelivered. In general the Burg letters emphasized his excellent health and morale, and his persistent study of living languages, especially Russian. He apparently undertook to read aloud to his fellow prisoners his ex tempore translations of all journals and papers reaching the camp; a pact seems to have formed among the men to waste as little time as possible (16.8.14). The Burg letters also mentioned Gilson's busy schedule of study in philosophy, though he was "not in a place especially organized with such an end in view." Study, he wrote, was "the only thing I can now do for my country. Tell Émile and André that they can have no idea of how beautiful their situation looks from here." (16.9.15; tr.)

When later asked how he acquired his books, Gilson explained how simple it was. He was never without money, and local booksellers carried on a considerable business with prisoners of war. Some of the books acquired from these vendors have made their way into the library of the Toronto Institute; most notable is *De humanae cognitionis ratione*, a collection of short pieces by St Bonaventure and his disciples published at Quaracchi in 1883, which bears the stamp "Officier-Gefangenlager, Vöhrenbach. Geprüft."

Gilson wrote Maman that he was working as diligently in prison "as though her eyes were fixed on him." Evidence of concentrated work survives in the article "Du fondement des jugements esthétiques" which he was allowed to send to Paris for publication. The article appeared in *Revue philosophique de la France et de l'étranger* (83 [1917]: 524-546; McG 261) and was signed from the "Camp d'officiers prisonniers Burg-bei-Magdeburg, Allemagne." It constitutes a kind of campanion article to his "Art et métaphysique," written a year earlier while "on campaign."

"Du fondement" applies the themes of "Art et métaphysique" to art criticism. Not only can aesthetic experience profoundly alter a man's being, but it also bestows on him a duty to express this changed consciousness through the exercise of criticism. Indeed, in the truly great, a failure to exercise critical awareness is tantamount "to an unbearable mutilation of mind." Gilson supports his position with statements from Victor Hugo, Robert Schuman, Franz Liszt, Anatole France and George Bernard Shaw. Gilson found Shaw's statement particularly appealing, and quoted it more than once:

> I have sometimes been asked why anyone should read a philosophic treatise to find out the story of the Ring. I take this opportunity to reply publicly that there is, as far as we know, no reason why anyone should take any trouble in the matter at all unless they want to, and that the degree of trouble must be the wanter's capacity. (Shaw, *The Perfect Wagnerite*, ed. Tauchnitz, p. 7.)

Gilson referred again to Shaw's retort when asked to authorize the writing of this biography: "I don't think the task worth taking on," he replied, "unless, of course, someone wants to badly enough, and has a wanter's capacity."

At Burg-bei-Magdeburg Gilson also became involved in sports and dramatics. His souvenirs of Burg include a postcard photograph of the camp's two tennis courts; he became a better than average tennis player, and later surprised several younger men at Harvard by roundly beating them. Photographs of an actors' group also survive. On 31 December 1916 the group staged the puppet play "Guignol lyonnais: les cloches de Cornerville." On 5 January 1917 it followed with two of T. Bernard's short plays, "Une aimable lingerie" and "L'anglais tel qu'on le parle." Apparently, after these debuts, Gilson's acting skills were never tested again.

For all these diversions, family anxieties weighed heavily on Gilson during his imprisonment. His separation from his wife and daughters was torture to him. Thérèse was not well and her responsibilities were heavy. On 22 April 1916 she lost her father Eugène Ravisé; the old man had been in decline ever since returning to Melun from Vermenton. Although Jacqueline had recovered from her attack of nerves, she continued to fret for her papa. Cécile meanwhile was growing up without knowing her father at all; she later recalled her first impression of papa after the war as that of a strange and terrifying giant hovering menacingly over her.

One piece of news from Thérèse lightened Gilson's worries somewhat. After Eugène's death, she and the notary M. G. Auberge had straightened out the family's financial affairs. Thérèse had kept the Melun property, but had sold off as much unneccessary furniture as possible; this had increased her cash holdings by the comfortable sum of 4,000 francs. At least for the time being she had no financial worries.

While in the prison camp, Gilson was also keenly aware of Maman's concern for her husband and sons; indeed, many of her worries were his own. Although Maman could be proud of her sons' contributions to their country, she was often lonely and worried. Émile and André were still in dangerous posts, and André in particular was continually on the front lines of battle. Gilson's heart bled for his mother: "The news of my brothers, little and big, is always welcome because I am always thinking of them. Never have I sensed how completely we have been one. ... I still hope that the *grande table* on Port-Royal will once again be fully set when we all return." (16.9.15; tr.)

Paul Anthelme Gilson died on 25 May 1917. Although the *grande table* would be set again, Papa would no more preside at its head. The death notice sent out by Maman gives some idea of her isolation now in the absence of her sons:

> Paul Anthelme Gilson, mourned by his widow and her five sons: Émile, sergeant in the 223d Territorial Regiment, on active service; Paul, sergeant in the 20th Transport Squadron, on active service; Étienne, second lieutenant, 164th Infantry Regiment, prisoner of war; André, sergeant-major, 168th Infantry Regiment, croix de guerre, on active service; and Maurice, assistant medical officer, radiology laboratory, Val de Grâce.

In February 1918 Gilson wrote to Thérèse that he had just been moved from Burg-bei-Magdeburg to Strölen-Moohr, Kreis Sulingen, in lower Saxony (18.2.3). The circumstances surrounding this transfer are not clear. Judging from a rough diagram Gilson sketched for an illustrated causerie the next year in Paris, the prison was a rough one; Gilson was housed in what he called "a square hut." His move there was probably related to German reprisals for the mistreatment of German prisoners in Russia and elsewhere.

According to Gilson, Ströhlen-Moohr was a hurriedly constructed camp intended for reprisals against Ukrainian prisoners; of the four camps where he was imprisoned, Ströhlen was the only one in which he encountered reprisals himself at first hand. When Gilson arrived on 2 February 1918, all his books not bearing an official stamp were impounded. Nonetheless, at first the prisoners were assured the camp was not in reprisals. The poor conditions were convincingly attributed to winter weather and poor camp equipment; there was, for example, only one pump to serve the needs of everyone. And at first the food seemed normal enough. In the morning there was ersatz coffee, and in the evening, barley broth alternated with flour soup. For dinner at noon there was stew "said to be of meat" twice a week and potatoes mixed with turnips twice a week; on the other three days there were potatoes, occasionally served with horse-radish, cucumber and questionable fish. These dishes were supplemented by bread, jam, biscuits and so on where called for.

On 1 March 1918 the prisoners were told that reprisals were officially to begin. Prisoners were henceforth to have fewer orderlies, a smaller courtyard, less light, and delayed mail – when this last was announced a guffaw rose through the camp. Ten men rather than seven were assigned to each room, and the beds moved closer together. Prisoners were also forbidden to remain in their rooms during the day.

Gilson did not find the reprisals overly severe at this stage. Unfortunately however, the prisoners were also ordered to write three letters or postcards of the kind that would pass the censors. The prisoners' commanding officer, Colonel Perlier, advised them not to write the unpatriotic letters, and most agreed. As a result, biscuits, sugar, and the ersatz coffee were cut off, the bread allotment was reduced, and the cost of room and board was increased from three to four marks a day. When the prisoners continued to refuse to write letters, jam was cut off and parcels from home witheld; the prisoners were confined to barracks day and night, except for two trips to the refectory for dinner and supper. From then until 20 April the prisoners were restricted to bread and water, forbidden to wear shoes, and constantly summoned by unrelenting bells. Despite bland assurances in censored letters to Thérèse and Maman, Gilson later condemned his treatment at Ströhlen as outrageous, unpardonable and personally humiliating, a form of "refined slavery." In an effort to use the prisoners as means to their own propagandistic ends, the German had abused them, lied to them constantly, and stolen their property. On 4 May the policy was changed. Annoyances were lifted in stages and the prisoners were "liberated" in line with the Berne Accord relating to prisoners of war.

Gilson seems to have moved back and forth between Ströhlen and Burg at least once, giving lectures on Bergson in each camp. His marginalia on the surviving manuscript of the lectures note that they were delivered at Ströhlen on an unspecified date and at Burg-bei-Magdeburg on 27 October 1918. Whether there were two or three lectures is unclear; however the series comprised three lectures when it was repeated in a somewhat expanded form at Rio de Janeiro in 1936.

Appropriately enough for a prison-camp setting, Gilson began his lectures with a discussion of Bergson on liberty. Also appropriate was his frequent recourse to military metaphors in such passages as this one: "Evolutionary movement would be a simple enough thing if life, like a bullet, described a single trajectory. But it is a shell that has burst into fragments which in their turn burst into further fragments." Well into the 1920s, Gilson lectures continued to reveal a preoccupation with the imagery of war.

The lectures on Bergson were a landmark in Gilson's development as a "Christian philosopher." According to Gilson, Bergson regarded man's primitive knowledge as basic to and more wonderful than his scientific and artistic knowledge, immured in the vital movement of the universe. This led Bergson to conclude that liberty, spirituality of the soul, and creative power in the world together comprise what religion calls God. Clearly then Bergson's was not the God of Catholicism; Gilson, as a later and Christian philosopher, saw that he must go further than Bergson could take him.

Gilson loved Bergson for his sense of how the universe unfolds before us. He warmed to Bergson's appreciation of human thought as a continuing effort to draw from the real all that is in it. But, as Bergson had seen, the history of human thought is dialectical. Effort is followed by discouragement, and then by renewed effort: Plotinus had succeeded Aristotle; Pascal had succeeded Descartes; Bergson had succeeded Comte; Aquinas and Bonaventura had perhaps proceeded together. Gilson saw that within this dialectic he had his own role to play and his own efforts to expend. Just as Bergson had surmounted Comte, he must surmount Bergsonianism. Moreover, Gilson's efforts could only be realized in the practice of philosophy and not by way of either surrender or apologetic.

The Bergson lectures at Burg took place only two weeks before the collapse of Germany and the end of the war. As the liberation got underway, Gilson was impressed by the prevailing good order among prisoners, guards and quietly watching townsfolk. He was placed in charge of a group of men from a regular camp and returned to France a little earlier than most, by boat through the North Sea. He was home in Melun in time for Christmas. A story is told of how the postman, bearing the telegram announcing Gilson's arrival, ran down the street waving it in the air and shouting. He wanted to make sure that all the neighbours saw him deliver the message and with all the ceremony due it.

6

From the Armistice to the Sorbonne, 1919-1921

1 LILLE AGAIN, 1918-1919

At some time during the winter of 1918 to 1919, following joyous reunions with his family in Melun and Paris, Gilson returned to Lille where the 158th Infantry was based. He, Thérèse and the girls moved into their former home at 44, rue Louis Faure, and he began to renew his ties with the university.

Gilson was entitled to some financial compensation for his time in the prisoner-of-war camps; this was taken care of immediately so as to precede demobilization. The treasury department at General Headquarters (Laval) awarded him the difference between his prisoner's allowance and the more generous terms of recently approved compensatory grants: he received an additional 4,320 francs for his services up to 1 January 1918, and 2,160 francs for services between then and 1 January 1919 (Bureau of Accounts to EG, 19.4.5, 19.8.18). A year later he was also awarded 1,625.60 francs for loss of family belongings and other damages, especially those to his house in Lille (Préfecture, Nord Lille, to EG, 19.12.18). Gilson was pleased to receive these monies even though they did not begin to cover his losses. Postwar inflation and the evaporation of his investments had wiped him out financially; his two properties were all that remained.

Gilson was also entitled to formal recognition of his military exploits prior to capture. On 6 February 1919 Captain de Sambœuf mentioned him for the croix de guerre to the head of command of the 164th Regiment of Infantry. On 12 June 1919 Gilson was decorated, with citation, by the commander-in-chief of the French armies, Maréchal Pétain (order no. 18798 D).

Following demobilization, Gilson accepted Colonel Randier's invitation to join the 158th Infantry as a second lieutenant in the reserve. Although he was subject to recall, this never actually took place. A few years later, on 20 February 1924, he was raised to the rank of full lieutenant.

Classes at the University of Lille began shortly after the war ended, and Gilson resumed his lectures. He also began to review books for the *Revue philosophique de France et de l'étranger* on pressure from his old professor, Lucien Lévy-Bruhl. The *Revue philosophique* had been founded by Charles Ribot back in 1876 and had remained under his personal direction for forty years. Lévy-Bruhl had been a member of Ribot's editorial board, and had succeeded Ribot as editor in February

1917. Gilson must have appreciated the significance of the appointment for his own career. He had quickly submitted "Du fondement des jugements esthétique" to Lévy-Bruhl from the prison camp at Burg-bei-Magdeburg in time to be published in the June 1917 issue. Now, with his return to France, he immediately became involved, not entirely against his will, in the strenuous and distracting para-academic work of reviewing books for the *Revue*. Lévy-Bruhl "sent me many books that he did not know what else to do with," Gilson said much later. "He knew that I would never turn him down." (interview, 1975.)

In 1919 these books included two on religion and society by the modernist Alfred Loisy; two on general philosophy by the neoscholastic scholars Gonzague Truc, a non-Catholic, and Père Lumbreras, a Dominican; a neoscholastic journal, Agostino Gemelli's *Rivista di filosofia neo-scolastica*; and a rather dubious first volume of a multi-volume study entitled *L'évolution intellectuelle de saint Augustin* by the acclaimed scientific historian, a former priest, Prosper Alfaric. Each of these offered a particular challenge to a Catholic philosopher.

Although Gilson was later feared for his sharp, witty and impatient criticism, his early reviews were restrained, moderate, even kind. In the 1919 reviews, he was sympathetic toward Loisy's weary attempts at scholarship in the face of the Imprimatur, the Index, and rampant authoritarianism; he was gentle when pointing out the sectarian limitations of Truc and Lumbreras; and he was almost obsequious in his impartiality toward Alfaric, who had contrived to make Augustine's story shed favourable light on his own. Gilson later confessed that Alfaric's recanting of heresy on his sickbed only to relapse upon recovery had rendered his scholarship suspect.

Gilson reviewed books for Lévy-Bruhl until 1926, when his visits to North America forced him to discontinue a number of activities. During this period he gradually came to dislike book-reviewing. In 1939 he warned the editors of the newly created Toronto journal, *Mediaeval Studies*, that "research scholars should be writing books, not reviewing them." Most reviewing, he added, was a waste of time; important is not what is said about an author, only that his name be spelt correctly. Gilson never allowed *Mediaeval Studies* to have a book-review section. Nonetheless, his own book reviews for Lévy-Bruhl allowed him the opportunity to settle his own mind on many of the disturbing dilemmas that were confront-ating Catholic scholars at the time.

On 3 February 1919 Gilson's academic rank at Lille was raised from *maître de conférence* to *professeur adjoint*, or from assistant to associate professor. The promotion was put into effect retroactively to August 1914 to redress in part the delaying effects of the war on Gilson's academic career and to improve his seniority and increase his retirement pension. This promotion had little bearing on Gilson's already high status at Lille, but it strengthened his candidature for another appointment, to the "Strasbourg mission." Gilson received word that he was to take up residence in Strasbourg by 1 May to begin work in his new post. His expenses and salary were to be charged to the special budget providing for the extension of the French Republic into the new provinces; for further details he was to report to the inspector-general in charge of teaching in Alsace and Lorraine. (Ministry of Public Instruction to EG, 19.4.12, 19.4.18.)

Before moving to Strasbourg, Gilson prepared an address for 27 April to the Association pour le Rapprochement Universitaire in Paris. This association had been formed to promote a healthy esprit de corps among the university teachers of France. This particular meeting had been called to honour professors in the provincial universities, and Gilson was the selected speaker. His address detailed his experience of reprisals in the prison camp at Ströhlen-Moohr, and also dispensed some practical political philosophy. He discounted reports that Germany had been, since the Kaiser's abdication six months earlier, in the process of a genuine revolution. Although violent incidents had taken place, they had been sparked by the Germans' understandable desire to protect the poor by restricting the privileges normally usurped by the bourgeoisie in difficult times:

> Popular mentality, which is both cause and effect where governement is concerned, has not changed; there has been no movement of ideas. There has appeared in Germany, with the exception of Wolf and a few Frankfurt intellectuals, no genuine republicanism. Nor are the disorders we see, in themselves evidence of bolshevism. No new idea is in the air. ... So the mental attitudes making for war are going to subsist, and these are the tougher stuff. This does not mean that another war is inevitable, but it means that hope for lasting peace based on the notion that some kind of conversion has taken place is a mistaken one. (EG's lecture notes, 27.4.19; tr.)

This talk for Rapprochement Universitaire was Gilson's last function as a Lille professor; three days later he arrived at Strasbourg. The day he left Lille, the Council of the Faculty of Letters passed a special resolution congratulating him warmly on his new appointment.

2 STRASBOURG, 1919-1921

Gilson reported to the University of Strasbourg at the beginning of May 1919. He and Thérèse sold their house in Lille, just repaired after the ravages of neglect during the war years, and acquired another near the place de l'Université, at 3, allée de la Robertsau. This was undoubtedly the best-located of all Gilson's homes in its proximity to teaching and library facilities. It was paid for with capital from the sale of the Lille house along with the reparations money recently received for war damages.

Now that Alsace and Lorraine had been returned to France from Germany by the Treaty of Versailles, the French government was making a serious attempt to integrate the provinces into the fabric of French life. The University of Strasbourg had been built by the German government in 1882. In 1919 the French government began to restore the beautiful university buildings, to extend the university's facilities, and to purchase a wealth of books and equipment. In many ways Strasbourg was becoming the finest university in France.

In all probability Gilson began lecturing immediately upon his arrival at Strasbourg. Lectures had resumed on 15 January 1919, a mere two months after the armistice; on 20 January 1919 Christian Pfister, soon to be appointed faculty dean, had opened his course on "Alsace since 1648" (*Annuaire*, Faculté des Lettres, 1922).

Whether or not Gilson lectured, he was certainly kept busy for the six months preceding the university's grand reopening in November. As professor responsible for philosophy, he was in charge of removing introductory philosophy from the university's curriculum and restoring it to the lycées where in France it properly belonged. He also had to help find new senior professors to teach the advanced courses that were about to be introduced. A few of Gilson's own preferences are evident in the university's appointments. One appointment went to Maurice Halbwachs, whose seniority had once stood in Gilson's way. Another went to Charles Blondel, philosopher, psychiatrist, doctor of medicine, and Gilson's friend and fellow Bergson-addict. A third appointment, as senior consulant, went to Sylvain Levi, dear to Gilson from his university days.

Not surprisingly the Ministry of Public Instruction honoured Gilson during this period by appointing him an Academy officer and by naming him professor in the history of philosophy as of 1 October 1919. He also joined the board of examiners for students taking their *agrégation*. Lucien Febre leaves us a vivid account of one more of Gilson's functions, his chairing of the Committee to Elect the New Dean. This meeting was purely a formality, as everyone knew that Christian Pfister, *Alsacien de toujours*, who had been holding the university together since January, would certainly be chosen:

> There were forty of us there, most having only arrived the day before, barely out of our uniforms, already displaying that bashfulness – so very French – about our croix de guerre and our citations. Passionately French certainly, as we had been proving ourselves to be, guns in our hands during four years, but trying nevertheless to be the faithful servants of that lacerated Alsace whose moral health we well knew was going to be very dependent upon us and our efforts. Under the scintillating chairmanship of a still young Étienne Gilson, we were gathered together to agree on who was to be our dean. As a matter of fact we had already chosen him in our hearts, and he was, moreover, the choice of the entire University of France. (*Combats pour l'histoire* [Paris, 1953], p. 391; tr.)

On 22 November 1919 the French University of Strasbourg was officially inaugurated by the Republic. The date was chosen as the anniversary of "that vibrant and spontaneous plebiscite which welcomed French troops into the capital of Alsace" (*Fêtes d'inauguration*, 21, 22, 23 November 1919 [Strasbourg, 1920], p. 1; tr.). The inauguration was a gala affair with a civic parade and a public festival. During a large convocation honorary professorships and doctorates were given to outstanding scholars and university administrators from many countries: to Cardinal Mercier of Louvain and Malines; to Henri Pirenne of Ghent; to Lord Reay of St Andrew's and the British Academy; to Harvard's Laurence Lowell and Charles Haskins; to Nicholas Murray Butler of Columbia;

and to many others. Raymond Poincaré, president of the Republic, presided at the inauguration and, surrounded by the 180 professors of the university's seven faculties, gave the principal address. Gilson sat with the 38 professors of the Faculty of Letters referred to by the president, his eyes twinkling, as the "quarante professeurs d'élite." The entire affair introduced Gilson to a whole new world of scholarly celebrity.

After the inaugural festivities finished, the hard work of reconstruction and reorientation began. According to Dean Pfister, the first chore of the Faculty of Letters was "the wiping out of its German past" (Annuaire, 1922, 6). This would entail a new examination system for new students, more instruction in French, moderation of academic structures in line with those of the Republic, and the extending of university education to a larger portion of the local population. Gilson liked this sort of challenge, and set to work at once to effect the necessary changes.

The addition of first-class professors from the provincial universities of France guaranteed more instruction in French, and the removal of tuition fees as in other French universities offered greater accessibility for the local population. Not all German practices were eliminated however. Some aspects of the German seminar were adapted: the Faculty of Letters continued to be organized around "institutes" rather than disciplines; the autonomy of programmes was maintained; and professors were encouraged to participate in one another's courses.

Gilson was particularly affected by the decision to move introductory philosophy back into the lycées. This called for some temporary duplication, as introductory philosophy had to be continued for students recently admitted to he university. Louis Lavelle, professor of philosophy in the Lycée Fustel de Coulanges, was appointed to teach introductory philosophy during this period of transition; Gilson and others taught advanced philosophy and the history of philosophy. Mlle Marie-Thérèse d'Alverny (below, esp. pp. 139, 311, 382) entered the Univesity of Strasbourg in 1920 and took both programmes, preparing her BA-equivalent thesis under Lavelle and studying Greek and medieval philosophy with Gilson. She was very much devoted to both men, though they had very little in common:

> I liked Lavelle, but Gilson did not. ... Gilson esteemed him as a man, but not as a great mind. Lavelle was, philosophically, an idealist working in the tradition of Berkeley and Kant – terrain of minimal interest to Gilson. Lavelle has always been a kind of bone of contention between Gilson and me, not that I cared all that much for idealism, but I liked Lavelle. For me, both men had great gifts of intellect, and both men could express themselves with utmost clarity. (interview, 75.5.3.)

Whatever their differences, Lavelle and Gilson structured a creditable "institute," or department, of philosophy. As both men had hoped, it attracted many students from different faculties and programmes. By 1922, shortly after Gilson left Strasbourg, enrolment in philosophy courses reached its highest figure in the history of the university.

Gilson gave two full courses and part of a third during each of his two years at Strasbourg: "The History of Greek Philosophy since Socrates" (Tuesdays at four-thirty); "Descartes' *Discours de la méthode*" (Mondays at three-fifteen); and part of a public course offered with several colleagues in "The Major Directions of Contemporary French Philosophy" (Thursdays at three-fifteen). Gilson's course in Greek philosophy survives in a bookful of notes in the Gilson archives, Toronto. The course on Descartes can be found in large part in the commentary to his edition of Descartes' *Discours de la méthode* (1925). The public lectures seem not to have survived.

Two letters to Gilson from Maxime Alexandre, one of his Strasbourg students, written more than forty years later, reveal something of Gilson's impact as a teacher. The first letter invited Gilson to the ceremony in which Alexandre's daughter was to receive the Dominican habit; Gilson was invited "because your courses on St Thomas at the University of Strasbourg were an important step in my journey towards Catholicism, which, I believe, justifies this somewhat formal invitation" (64.3.16; tr.). The second attempted to account for Gilson's profound impact on his life:

> I should like to tell you – which I think I have never done – why I have retained so deep and lasting a memory of you. I was not very good in philosophy when I was your student in Strasbourg – the German school after all, which I left at fifteen, had scarcely prepared me for it at all. What moved me, what attracted me – and you will understand why I have waited so long to confess it – was to see Madame Gilson attending almost all the courses you gave us. In my eyes, the two of you made a model couple. I heard also, from my friend Léon Marchal, that you used to go to mass every morning in the cathedral. You can see what an impression such things made on me. (66.1.22; tr.)

This is one of the few references to Thérèse extant from this period. Not until Gilson's trip to America in 1926 does a clear portrait of her re-emerge through her husband's letters home.

Gilson also impressed his colleagues at Strasbourg, most notably two economic historians, Lucien Febvre and Marc Bloch. The careers of Febvre and Bloch had so far been not unlike his own. Febvre was six years older than Gilson, he had studied in the École Normal Supérieure of Nancy, had taken his doctorate from the Sorbonne in 1911, and had taught in the Faculty of Letters at Dijon. After mobilization on 3 August 1914, he had served in the war as sergeant, second-lieutenant, lieutenant, and finally as captain in a company of machine-gunners. He had been decorated with the croix de guerre by both France and Belgium, had received citations, had been wounded in 1916 but had returned to action, and had been admitted to the Legion of Honour. Bloch was two years younger than Gilson. A native of Alsace, he had taught in the lycée in Amiens, had been working on his thesis – "Rois et serfs" – when the war broke out, had been mobilized as a sergeant, and had emerged as a captain with four citations and the Legion of Honour.

Both Febvre and Bloch had experienced one advantage over Gilson: three-year scholarships from the Thiers Foundation had enabled each of them to train for their careers as free and uncommitted students. Thus Bloch had spent the years 1909 to 1912 acquiring informally the methodologies pertinent to his concept of medieval history as they evolved from those of Camille Jullian, Henri Pirenne and others. Gilson had received no comparable formal training. Although he had hoped after the war "to have the benefit of coming into close contact with the history of medieval philosophies and theologies under Klemens Baeumker and, perhaps, Count von Hertling," he was turned down for the bursary that would have made this possible (interview, 1974). His two years at Strasbourg with Bloch, therefore, provided him with valuable vicarious training as a medievalist. According to Febvre, Bloch was always eager to exchange knowledge with his colleagues:

> At the university, our seminar rooms [Bloch's and Febvre's] were close. Our doors faced each other. And they were open. There was no question of medievalists feeling in conscience bound to ignore modern times; nor, inversely, of moderns to deal at arms length with the Middle Ages. In fact, our students moved from one room to the other – and their teachers with them. We often went back to our lodgings together; and the walk down the center of allée de la Robertsau was the scene of many goings and comings, prolonged escortings and escortings back, in spite of the weight of bags bulging with books. (*Combats pour l'histoire* [Paris, 1953], p. 393; tr.)

And according to Gilson, Bloch made a point of attending his philosophy seminars and questioning him, both in front of his students and privately, on his evidence for many of his interpretative statements. Through these exchanges Bloch passed on to Gilson the benefits of his own training and selfdiscipline.

At Strasbourg both Bloch and Febvre began to move beyond traditional concepts of history. Although the French universities of the time recognized them only as historians in the old broad sense of the word, they viewed themselves as economic and social historians. The two men became almost obsessed with this matter of their identity within their formal discipline, an obsession that would later culminate in their efforts to gain the recognition of the Collège de France. Bloch was already describing himself as a "comparative historian of civilizations." He was focusing his interest less on origins and more on humanity's technological development, as Febvre also was doing. Bloch searched the past for keys to man in his present situation. As Pirenne had probed the wine-trade, textiles and cities, so Bloch was preparing to probe water-mills, harnesses, stirrups, coins, farming and the use of money, always with the eyes on modern man. Febvre later described Bloch's method as a blending of two approaches: the horizontal (international) and the vertical (then-to-now).*

---

* See Lucien Febvre, "Marc Bloch" in *Architecture and Craftsmen: Festschrift für Abbot Payan Usher* (Tübingen, 1956), pp. 78-84; see also J. A. Raftis, "Marc Bloch's Comparative Method," *Mediaeval Studies*, 24 (1962): 366-368.

Around this time Gilson was also beginning to see himself as a specialized historian, namely an historian of medieval philosophy. After his contacts with Bloch and Febvre at Strasbourg, he began to view medieval studies more broadly than he had learned to do through the doctrinaire methodologies of Durkheim and Lévy-Bruhl or through his own readings of St Thomas and others. He began to see medieval studies in a much wider context, free of the limitations imposed by disciplinary, methodological or intellectual isolation. He began, in short, to dream of his own institute where all medieval studies might be taught and researched in an integrated fashion, where philosophy and theology, history, literature, and so on could be pursued as related disciplines. Here the various branches of study could share their methodologies, both traditional and new. Why could not Aquinas, or Abélard, or Augustine, read with the precision of Bloch's scrutiny of the works of man, provide insights into humanity and civilization beyond anything yet achieved?

After Gilson left Strasbourg, direct contact with Bloch was limited to his vain effort to obtain for Bloch a chair in the Collège de France (see below, pp. 208-209). Gilson did, however, follow Bloch's last years fairly closely through their mutual friend, Thérèse d'Alverny. Common knowledge, of course, was Bloch's founding in 1929, along with Lucien Febvre, of the *Annales d'histoire économique et sociale*. Equally well-known were the many successes in the Oslo congresses and in lecture halls throughout Europe; these brought him in 1936 to Henry Hauser's chair in the Sorbonne. Bloch's brilliant progress ended tragically with the war years: his bold Jewish activism and his able role in the Resistance led to his arrest, torture and execution in 1944. Mlle d'Alverny corresponded with Bloch during these last years, and never failed to brief Gilson on the content of Bloch's letters.

Although Febvre and Bloch had the strongest impact on Gilson, other Strasbourg colleagues also influenced him. In particular the lively and imaginative scholarship of Gustave Cohen both challenged and puzzled him. In 1920 Cohen published his *Écrivains français en Hollande dans la première moitié du xviie siècle*. The book dealt with the activities of the many young Frenchmen who visited Holland in the early seventeenth century, some as voluntary mercenaries, some as university students, others as refugees from the intellectual controversies raging at the time in Paris. Cohen dealt at some length with René Descartes in a fashion that Gilson considered extravagant. Gilson reviewed the book in a critical article entitled "Descartes en Hollande" (*Revue de métaphysique et de morale*, 28 [1921]: 545-556; McG 245).

Cohen saw Descartes as the victim of persecution by arrogant Aristotelians; Gilson saw him as a man who simply wanted to be alone. Basing his conclusions on a diary entry by a young Hollander named Beeckmann, Cohen claimed that Descartes' persecution indirectly produced the "method" elaborated by him during the 1620s. Although Gilson warmed to Cohen's imaginative approach, he preferred to believe Descartes' own statements on the background of the "méthode": in the sixth chapter of his *Discours*, Descartes does not present himself as a persecuted man but as one who has found Parisian polemic hostile to personal repose. "Moreover," wrote Gilson, "Descartes has specifically warned his readers 'never to believe the things which some may claim to have from me unless I myself have divulged them' " (p. 548; tr.).

Cohen then passed from this to a discussion of Descartes' suspected and still undemonstrated association with the Rosicrucians. According to Cohen, the RC on Descartes' seal referred to Rose-Croix rather than to René des Cartes. Moreover, claimed Cohen, Descartes was also one of Fludd's Longlivers: instead of dying at fifty-four he had somehow changed his residence and disappeared. Although Gilson found Cohen's accumulation of data impressive, he did not accept it. According to Gilson, no single piece of Cohen's evidence was irrefutable, and Descartes himself had contributed none of it.

Despite his reservations concerning Cohen's theories, Gilson praised Cohen's "remarkable book" for its reluctance to furnish a synthetic portrait of Descartes and for its attempt to let the man's actions speak for themselves in a strictly biographical presentation: "Fact by fact, detail by detail, step by step, Cohen has set before the reader the fascinating features of a man who was frank to the point of brusqueness yet shy to the point of secrecy, a Frenchman nonetheless, towering and lonely" (p. 556; tr.). Gilson liked Cohen and continued to do so throughout his life, particularly when Cohen became deeply immersed in the theory and production of medieval drama. Much later, during celebrations at Cluny in 1949 to mark the thousandth and nine hundredth anniversaries of Saints Odo and Odilo, Gilson gave the keynote address in the town hall and Cohen directed, from his wheelchair, a memorable production of the *Jeu d'Adam* in the open-air Roman amphitheatre (below, p. 245 n.).

Once settled in Strasbourg and with his lectures underway; Gilson was at last able to make real progress with his long-projected programme of publication. First he turned his attention to the lectures on the philosophy of Thomas Aquinas given five years before in the University of Lille. Some of these lectures, about half of them, had been published from 1913 to 1914 by Strowski. Now they appeared independently in a work of thirteen chapters entitled *Le thomisme: introduction au système de S. Thomas d'Aquin* (Strasbourg, 1919; McG 155). This first edition of *Le thomisme* was important for Gilson, although it was not a very good book; as Gilson himself later wrote, "The book deserves to survive in this first edition as a monument to the ignorance of its author" (*The Philosopher and Theology*, 1960, p. 91). The volume was, however, the first of the six editions of *Le thomism* that would eventually record the evolution of Gilson's understanding of St Thomas.

The first edition of *Le thomisme* was cheap and unattractive. It was a rush job meant to come out late in 1919, though its preface bears the date January 1920. The publisher was not completely to blame, as postwar conditions were difficult. Moreover, Gilson was always a particularly awkward author. His early manuscripts were all handwritten, and he was constantly making alterations. After 1922 his usual publisher became Joseph Vrin, a bookseller on Place de la

Sorbonne; although the two men became close, lifelong friends, it was not without considerable forbearance on Vrin's part.

Apparently Gilson did little revision of the Lille lectures for the Strasbourg volume. Because the last six chapters appeared here for the first time, it is impossible to check their relationship to the original lectures. However the first seven chapters were printed almost verbatim from the text of Strowski's *Revue*, and only the first two show any alteration at all. In chapter 1, the title "From Plotinus to Thomas Aquinas" became the more modest "Le problème thomiste"; Thomas was frequently (*pace* Luquel) identified as a saint; and one belaboured rhetorical passage contrasting the methods of Sertillanges and Mandonnet, probably inaccurately, was deleted.

In Chapter 2, thirteen new paragraphs were added, four after the first paragraph, eleven just before the last. Both additions deal with the distinction between theology and philosophy and show that Gilson was disturbed to find both university rationalists and neoscholastic rationalists arguing from the same principle. The former ignored medieval thinkers because they allowed theology to contaminate philosophy, and the latter found in Thomas a genuine philosophy independent of his theology. Gilson suggested that "one might, at least provisionally, try a third procedure: set aside value judgments and work out the relation between philosophy and theology within St Thomas' system" (p. 16). This suggestion was to preoccupy him for years to come, even after he gave up the use of the word *system*, bowing to Mandonnet's objection that it designated method rather than doctrine.*

Maurice De Wulf had favourable things to say about this book. It seemed to support some of his own positions: that theology is distinct from philosophy; that there would still remain philosophy in thomism if all theology were taken out of it; and that St Thomas' system was an ensemble of philosophical demonstrations planned with a view to theological ends. However, in relating the volume to his own work, and to that of Grabmann, Sertillanges, Mercier and Mandonnet, De Wulf described it, rather inadequately, as an "introduction and initiation into the philosophy of St Thomas." He failed to point out that it was an introduction intended less for the students at Catholic universities than for Gilson's own colleagues and their students in the national lycées and universities. Gilson wanted *Le thomisme* "to put at their ease those with no idea of Saint Thomas' world" (p. 16). He wanted to show them that Thomas had not pursued

---

* Gilson later came also to feel that *system* placed the focus on philosophy rather than on the philosopher, who became increasingly important to him. This does not mean that he did not sometimes find so positivistic a word useful to describe the simplification of concepts to the fewest possible principles. However, as he came to espouse "Christian philosophy," he decided that "system" tended to over-denote the simplifying role of faith:

> Choosing man in relation to God as his central theme, the Christian philosopher acquires a fixed centre of reference which helps him to bring order and unity into his thought. That is why the tendency to simplification is always so strong in Christian philosophy: it has less to systematize than any other and it has the necessary centre for the system as well. (*The Spirit of Medieval Philosophy* [New York, 1936], p. 39; McG 33.)

philosophy as they would have done, highlighting such matters as monism, pantheism, ethical obligaton and moral conscience, metaphysical reflections on averroistic pluralism, the act of potency. Rather, Thomas had followed, in the *Summa theologiae*, a strictly theological order dealing successively with God, the angels and man. Gilson himself, strangely enough, had been conditioned into doing things this way: his wartime situation had forced him to proceed from author to author by way of *opera omnia* rather than by topic. Perhaps it was this special awareness that so deeply embedded in him an appreciation of St Thomas' own theological order.

From Strasbourg Gilson also published a second and more important volume. The *Études de philosophie médiévale* (McG 46) were published in a series established by the university's Faculté des Lettres as part of the general programme to strengthen the postwar institution. Gilson's *Études* appeared early in the series, 30 September 1921; they were preceded by two volumes on medieval music and art by Théodore Gérold of the Protestant Faculté de Théologie, and were quickly followed with volumes or facsimiles by Cohen, Lavelle, Prosper Alfaric, Bloch and others.

The *Études* is precisely the kind of book one might expect from the relatively young incumbent of an important chair in the history of philosophy. Of its eight explorations of philosophical problems in their historical contexts, four focus on St Thomas' medieval predecessors and four on his renaissance successors. This rationale works extremely well to organize the volume, although there is little attempt to integrate one *étude* with another. The first four *études* were newly written for this volume; the last four were reprints of articles written between 1913 and 1920 for *Annales de philosophie chrétienne*, for *Revue de métaphysique et de morale*, and for *Revue philosophique de la France et de l'étranger*.

The first four *études* established Gilson's reputation as an historian of medieval thought and are among the most beautiful pieces he ever wrote. The first, "The Meaning of Christian Rationalism," is a penetrating and cogent analysis of the so-called rationalism of John Scotus Eriugena, St Anselm and Peter Abélard. Gilson's procedure in this chapter would remain characteristic of him throughout his life. Before he began he first put aside much of what he had learned about faith and reason from his modern masters so that he would not obscure or falsify the medieval texts. He then tried to determine whether terms like "rationalism" and "pantheism" were even applicable to a John Scotus Eriugena and, if they were, in exactly what sense; to speak of Eriugena as pantheist without such precautions would, he judged, have been meaningless. Gilson conducted a thorough reading in good printed editions of the *opera omnia* of the authors concerned. He then extracted those passages pertinent to and illustrating Christian rationalism, and expounded his own understanding of what their authors meant by them, supplying the *ipsissima verba* in the footnotes. This whole procedure involved long hours of hard intensive work. Finally his tentative findings were dressed up in a literary composition that had, in the best rhetorical sense, a beginning, a middle and an end.

Gilson took similar care with the other three seminal studies: "Theology's Servant," "Double Truth," and "Thomism's Historical Significance." The latter *étude* is particularly noteworthy in that its opening section is devoted to St Bonaventure's illuminative way. De Wulf, in reviewing the *Études*, found this passage "ambivalent" and questioned whether St Bonaventure's illuminative way truly illustrated Christian rationalism; this issue was later developed in Gilson's first truly great book, on the philosophy of St Bonaventure. De Wulf also commented on the sheer beauty of certain passages dealing with the relation of soul and body (*Études*, pp. 106, 107). There were more of these than he could conveniently quote, and the following, overlooked by De Wulf, is perhaps the finest of all:

> The highest unity of the composite called man has assuredly to be maintained, but without forgetting that this composite will one day dissolve into two elements of very unequal value, each with a very different destiny. The soul is destined for immortality and happiness, and this, its end, explains all its properties. It is because the soul is destined for happiness that it is immortal; it is because it is immortal that it can be separated from the body; it is because it can be separated from the body that it is not just a form but a true substance. ... If the soul is by itself a substance, the body is too, and this is what keeps St Bonaventure from speaking of form in man the composite even at the very moment he is speaking most strongly of the oneness of that composite. (*Études*, 108; tr.)

The real issue raised in this passage – the nature of the impact of aristotelian philosophy on traditional augustinian thought – would arise again in Gilson's career. For Gilson, Bonaventure was creating his own scholastic system, his own unique way of coping with aristotelianism; he was not some kind of pre-thomist, nor did he care very much for the pagan Aristotle. The seeds of the later controversy with De Wulf and Mandonnet, then, were already being sown. (See below, pp. 127-128.)

It is not surprising that the *Études* sold well: it was simply a good book. When in 1930 Gilson wished to use once more some of the materials contained in it, he wrote apologetically to the Publications Committee of Strasbourg to ask for permission. The reply came from Albert Grenier, an old friend with whom Gilson had worked on the same committee some nine years earlier:

> Your volume has been our best seller. We have recovered all expenses. You owe us nothing. Your *Études* are entirely your own. I thoroughly understand your wishing to select from among them in republishing. This note provides me with an opportunity to renew an old friendship not only for myself but for our mutual colleagues, for you were a very active member of this committee when it was formed. We still have difficulties, new ones of course, and we find it increasingly difficult to get help. But the faculty remains a watchful parliament and our manuscripts are still unpretentious. (Grenier to EG, 30.2.20; tr.)

Gilson wrote one other book in Strasbourg, though it did not actually appear until he had moved to Paris. The first edition of the *La philosophie au moyen âge* (Paris, 1922; McG 109) perhaps reflected Gilson's Strasbourg lectures more accurately than did the *Études*. *La philosophie* was published by Librairie Payot et Cie in two small sextodecimo volumes and was part of Collection Payot under the direction of M. Batault. It was written under contract, and Gilson's royalties were set at ten percent of the selling price, three francs per volume. *La philosophie* was a financial success. It was reprinted in 1925 and 1930, and revised, enlarged and issued in one volume in the Bibliothèque Historique series in 1944.*

La Philosophie was Gilson's attempt to offer an overall view of medieval philosophy. It is not a learned guide like Ueberweg's, nor a systematic guide like De Wulf's, nor an analysis of the relation between medieval and Greek thought like Bréhier's. Rather it is an historian's day-to-day unfolding of the development of medieval thought between its first contact with Greek philosophy and culture and the end of the fourteenth century. *La philosophie* is marked by coherence of thought, sureness of experience and scrupulous attention to texts. Above all, as Lucien Febvre observed in his review of the 1942 edition, the work reveals "the kind of clarity which comes not from arbitrary simplifying of details but from mastery of the subject as a whole" (see *Combats pour l'histoire*, pp. 284-288).

At Strasbourg Gilson continued his involvement in music, and assisted with the production of symphony concerts in the Municipal Theatre of nearby Mulhouse. Gilson already knew Mulhouse from of old; in August 1908 he and Thérèse had stopped there briefly after their year in Bourg-en-Bresse. Now the two of them became involved in launching a series of symphony concerts to be given by Felix Delgrange, director of the Conservatoire Rameau and head of the Parisian orchestra "Pour la Musique." Delgrange was to be accompanied by some fifty-eight visiting musicians. Although Gilson's exact role is uncertain, he at least edited the printed programme for the second of these concerts, held Sunday 24 April 1921. He probably also had a hand in choosing the music: the selections included the "Prelude" and the "Death of Yseult" from Wagner's *Tristan* which had so impressed him as a Champist, and Debussy's *La mer* which he had once defended in a student riot at the Sorbonne.

Gilson's notes for the programme, five little prose gems, are interesting in themselves. Pedagogically they are pure Gilson, rich with arguments *ex convenientia*:

> The celebrated "Prelude" develops first the inseparable themes of Obligation and Desire, and then the impassioned ones of Glance and Potion. ... Near the end of the "Prelude" comes a new theme, Deliverance by Death. The end of the work is anticipated in its beginning. Thus can the last scene of *Tristan* be legitimately joined to its prelude.

La mer is the occasion for a little lecture defending the legitimacy of the great French innovator:

> 1. Melody has become completely liberated from scale. ... Melody is always correct if it expresses something.

---

* Two sets of these little volumes are in the library of Toronto's Pontifical Institute, one inscribed "À ma chère Thérèse en tendre hommage," the other "À M. Bréhier en hommage cordial."

2. All chords and tones are legitimate if they are employed in such a way as to satisfy the ear and stir the imagination.
3. Musical composition from such chords and melodies is not predetermined by a pre-existing frame, but is subject to the impression it will awaken in the soul of the listener.

Observations like these may well have been born in conversations with the musicians that Gilson and Thérèse gathered around them near concert time. For the first time since Tours, regular cultural sessions became possible for the Gilsons; the birth of the children, two changes of residence, and the Great War had previously interfered with this side of their lives. On allée de la Robertsau the Gilsons entertained a great many musicians, both local and visiting. Thérèse's role in these gatherings was a prominent one. Attractive, gifted and intelligent, she was invariably the darling of the evening.

During the summer of 1921 life for Gilson was beginning to fall into the pattern he liked: preparing and giving courses in philosophy; serving on academic juries; becoming involved with Strasbourg's two faculties of theology;* and, above all, writing and publishing books. He could easily and contentedly have settled in Strasbourg for the rest of his life. In late October, however, he had a major decision to make. He was invited to replace François-Joseph Picavet, *chargé de cours* for medieval philosophies in the University of Paris, who had died suddenly that April.

Gilson must have known that he was under consideration as Picavet's replacement. In May he had received some extraordinary confidences from Louis Rougier, a professor five years younger than himself. Rougier had been professor in the Lycée Français de Rome and was at the time living in Lyon; he had originally approached Gilson for ideas on the role of the University of Paris in the Middle Ages. In May he had written Gilson:

> Back in Lyon I read in yesterday's *Le temps* the announcement of Picavet's death. The fact that his chair in the Collège de France is now open immediately raises the question of his successor.
>
> I don't think it indiscreet to ask you whether you will be a candidate, because if you are you have every chance of getting it. If you do, and your chair in Strasbourg becomes vacant, I would be minded to canvas for it. ... Indeed, right now, my only opportunity is Besançon. ... Please do let me have the details about your chair, whether you would be able to designate me as your successor, and especially who has the right to nominate. I am led to understand that at Strasbourg it is *le fait du prince*, that is, is up to M. Charlety or M. Alapetit. I should also like to know the salary: I believe it is special, not the same as in other provincial faculties.
>
> Excuse, dear sir and colleague, the eagerness and urgency of my questions, but I have learned to my cost that relying on one's own rights is not enough to get you

---

* Gilson's friends in the Protestant Faculty of Theology asked him to clarify the medieval meaning of *abêtir* as used by Pascal; they placed his clarification in the first volume of their *Revue d'histoire de philosophie religieuse* (1 [1921], pp. 338-344; McG 446).

there, and that no opportunity to try one's luck should be overlooked. (Rougier to EG, 21.5.22; tr.)

It is tempting to speculate on the meaning of Rougier's mistaken reference to the Collège de France. Was it a Freudian slip? Or was it consciously planted as bait to whet Gilson's appetite for Paris? Rougier was a man of great ambition and incredible devices; this letter was but a harbinger of troubled waters ahead (below, p. 348).

Many of Gilson's friends, most notably Bergson, emphatically advised him to stay at Strasbourg: why should a professor consent to become a mere *chargé de cours*? But Gilson wanted to be in Paris. He wanted to be near his mother once more, and to live with Thérèse and the girls in the old Ravisé home in Melun. Although he would lose status, he would not lose any salary: in Strasbourg he earned sixteen thousand francs a year, while at the Sorbonne he would earn fourteen thousand for his regular courses plus two thousand for teaching in the École des Hautes Études. His decision made, he moved to Paris in November 1921 for the opening of the new term.

7

The University of Paris, 1921-1925

1 TEACHING IN THE SORBONNE

There is a certain irony in the circumstances that Picavet's death made possible
Gilson's appointement to the Sorbonne. François-Joseph Picavet (1851 to 1921)
had come to the Sorbonne in 1906 after serving for two years as secretary of the
Collège de France. Gilson had just begun his third year as a student; under
happier conditions he might have welcomed the appointment of a *maître de cours*
in the history of medieval philosophies, a field into which his studies were already
taking him. Unfortunately, however, Gilson soon found that Picavet's courses on
St Augustine revealed little understanding of their subject. This lack of understanding also extended into other courses, because Picavet used the then-popular
comparative method of instruction, employing Augustine as the basis of his
comparisons. Picavet, Gilson said later, should have been persona grata at the
Sorbonne: he was not a Catholic and, more importantly, he was filling a key
position in a previously neglected field. Despite these advantages, however,
Picavet's service to the university amounted to little more than pointing out that
medieval thought existed: he was quite unable to shed light on that thought or to
demonstrate its role in bridging ancient and modern philosophies.

If Picavet's limitations frustrated Gilson, they did help him to define what his
own role in the University of Paris should be. He saw this role as an authoritative
one calling for a thorough knowledge of Augustine and Aristotle, as well as of
modern philosophy. His approach to each writer should be exhaustive: the *opera
omnia* of each one was to be read on its own terms and with the fullest possible
knowledge of its historical context.

The ministry's official appointment of Gilson to the Faculty of Letters,
University of Paris, was dated 16 November 1921. A month later the further
appointment followed to the École Pratique des Hautes Études; lectures at the
École, discontinued since the war years, were scheduled to resume in April 1922.
The distinction between the two roughly resembles that between undergraduate
and graduate departments in North America and Britain. Gilson viewed the
distinction as largely one of instructional method. In the Sorbonne he taught more
or less ex cathedra, presenting his discipline definitively and authoritatively. In the
École, however, he taught from a single or very limited number of texts and, as

far he was temperamentally able, dealt with his students as peers. For him the École existed for the advancement of his discipline and, indeed, of knowledge itself. He later explained the distinction:

> In the Sorbonne, I lectured on the philosophers of antiquity, the Middle Ages, and modern times in the continuing atmosphere of philosophy and theology itself. In the École, I studied texts by means of new technologies and methodologies. In both I was interested in doctrine rather than in the making of critical texts. The method of the École des Chartes was not interested in doctrine as such. (interview, 1975.)

At the Sorbonne Gilson was forced to adopt Picavet's official rank of *chargé de cours*. It clearly smarted to surrender the status of professor, despite a later disclaimer that "distinction of rank in a university is a device to get people to teach without paying them for it" (interview, 1974). Gilson rather expected promotion before long, and became increasingly annoyed as it was postponed. After two years he was finally raised to *maître de conférence*, or assistant professor; and on 1 November 1926 – the year he went to Harvard as visiting professor – he became *professeur sans chaire*.

Gilson's craving for recognition in the Sorbonne was embedded in a practical idealism that Cardinal Newman would have understood, one that can be found in volume 1 of Gilson's own *La philosophie du moyen âge* (2 vols. [Paris, 1922]; McG 109). There he wrote that the University of Paris was, in some mysterious way, a kind of miracle. Founded by popes for the health of religion, and by crowned heads for the health of the nation, it had always been a thorn in the side of popes and governments alike. Yet in the thirteenth century it had been the home of St Thomas, and in the twentieth had become the home of Henri Bergson. Gilson had always wanted to be part of the Sorbonne mystique. But, although he was gratified to be teaching there, he was disappointed that the Sorbonne adamantly refused to establish a chair in the history of medieval philosophies.

The École was quicker to recognize Gilson's worth than was the Sorbonne. Gilson joined the Section of Religious Sciences of the History of Doctrines and Dogmas as one of two course directors in medieval theologies and philosophies. Gilson was a director of the second class, while Paul Alphandéry was a director of the first class. The distinction was based on past service and was financial only. Gilson received a salary increment each year; by 1924 he became a director of the first class with a stipend of nine thousand francs.

Since its establishment in 1886, the Section of Religious Sciences had been mistrusted by religious persons. From the start it had been widely viewed as a liberal attempt to undermine the older, conservative faculties of theology. Suspicions were reinforced by two notorious cases: Maurice Verne had been forced out of the Protestant faculty of theology in 1882 and four years later had found a place in the newly-created section; and Bishop L. Lacroix of Moutier-en-Tarantaise had been appointed to the section after being forced to resign his see for supporting the 1904 law separating church and state. Tensions had subsequently eased, especially after Verne became the section's president in 1913 and ably shepherded it through the wartime suspension of seminars and through the difficult period of reopening. Nonetheless, when Gilson was appointed to the École's Section of Religious Sciences, many wondered whether he too might be a liberal. Fortunately Gilson's appointment turned out to be an embarrassment to noone.

In April 1922 the École reopened for the first time since the war. The programme included two sets of courses in the religious thought of the Middle Ages: Alphandéry's on "Greco-Latin Mythology" and "Cathar Mysticism"; and Gilson's on "Divine Illumination in Augustine" and on "The Franciscan Spirit in Medieval Theology." The two directors were in no sense rivals and maintained cordial though not close relations; Gilson once noncommittally described his older colleague as "a good man, a liberal Jew who lectured in the Sorbonne on the crusades and gave seminars on historico-doctrinal subjects in the École." Meanwhile, for close friendship among his colleagues at the École, Gilson turned not to Alphandéry, but to the Indianist, Sylvain Lévi, who became president of the Section of Religious Sciences in 1923.

Some years later, in his remarks during the obsequies of Paul Alphandéry (1875 to 1932), Sylvain Lévi traced the section's struggle for academic respectability:

> Today one can hardly imagine the explosion of rancour, hatred and fury which greeted the appearance in the École des Hautes-Études of a section devoted to religious sciences. The Faculty of Catholic Theology, which the Sorbonne had sheltered up until that time within the traditional structure of the university, had just disappeared. Frustrated persons, and, even more, ignorant persons, thought they could see in this newly created section a diabolical device that would war on all kinds of belief and propagate every form of official atheism. More than one scholar, invited to occupy a chair, felt compelled to turn it down; others only accepted after a period of anguish. Years have passed since then, and generations of masters. Four presidents before me have carried out the functions which now devolve on me. Our École now approaches its fiftieth year and its time of probation has passed. Never in its course of forty-six years has any incident disturbed our peaceful research; never has the most suspicious adversary been able to scowl at a discourse held in our lecture halls. Priests, Protestant pastors, rabbis teach side by side with laymen, some of them no doubt sceptics and nonbelievers, because we are under no obligation to probe the intimate beliefs of anyone. It is everywhere understood that outside the domain of faith itself which commands respect, the study of religions, of facts and doctrines can and must be treated with the same liberty, with the same independence of spirit as the history, archaeology and sociology with which religion is so intimately joined. (*Annuaire* [1922-923], pp. 30-31; tr.)

Gilson's first two years at the University of Paris, 1921 to 1923 were intellectually aggressive ones. During this period he sorted out his philosophical positions and became the Sorbonne's informal historian of medieval Christian philosophy. He acquired some disciples, most notably Henri Gouhier, and began to reach out to the international community of scholars through his publications and congress papers.

Although Gilson felt that his faith offered him some sympathetic advantages in his field, he was aware that these carried their own dangers. He continually worried that his will might warp his intellect by encouraging him to see only what he wanted to see. This concern frequently cropped up in his writings during these years.* It is for this reason that theologians have on occasion found him rigid in dealing with the *revelabile*; he sometimes leaned backward to ensure that his faith did not control his reason. At this time Gilson was also deeply involved in his research on St Bonaventure and was struggling with those confusing primacies, the love of God and the intellect of man. Bonaventure taught him many things, not least "how man moves toward God through other things" ("quo modo homo per alias res tendat in Deum") and how the scholar's task "is not to stand in the way of the new but to reaffirm things commonly and rightly held" ("non ... novas opiniones adversare, sed communes et approbates retexare"); these texts were both cited in the first volume of Gilson's *La philosophie au moyen âge* (pp. 145, 143).

The four seminars Gilson offered in the École des Hautes Études between 1921 and 1923 not only expressed his ideals concerning the role of research in the university but also foreshadowed the direction of his future work as an historian of philosophy and as a philosopher. The seminars dealt with four quite separate topics: philosophical problems arising in the study of man's knowledge in the work of St Augustine; the influence of Franciscan spirituality on the history of thought during the Middle Ages; Augustine's thought as presented in the work of St Thomas; and Descartes and the religious thought of the sixteenth century. Yet despite the apparently disparate topics, the seminars had much in common. Gilson dealt with each subject through primary texts and in each case emphasized what the author meant by them. And running throughout all the seminars was the issue of Augustine's significance for Christian thought during the Middle Ages. Gilson's seminars examined what Augustine had meant in a number of his texts, what the role of faith had been in the thought of medieval Christians, and whether more than one manner of Christian thinking could be described as philosophical. These issues established the pattern of Gilson's philosophical (and theological) thinking during the next half-century.**

Gilson's courses at the University of Paris from 1921 to 1923 bore a significant relationship to the books on which he was already working, his *Saint Bonaventure*, his *Saint Augustine*, and his edition-with-commentary of Descartes' *Discours de la méthode*. Throughout this important formative decade, Gilson was also to give courses on such diverse topics as Albert the Great, Duns Scotus, Avicenna, Scotus Eriugena, twelfth-century platonism, St Anselm, mysticism from St

---

* See for example his first chapter of *Le thomisme*; his "Essai sur la vie intérieure" (*Revue philosophique*, 89 [1920]: 23-78; McG 274); "La religion et la foi" (*Revue de métaphysique et de morale*, 29 [1922]: 359-371; McG 428); and "Le bilan religieux du xixe siècle français" (*Foi et vie*, 26 [1923]: 1179-1202; McG 568).

** For an English rendering of Gilson's anticipatory summaries of these four seminars, see the appendix, pp. 395-397.

Bernard to Dante, mathematical sciences and optics, and Luther. The growing popularity of Gilson's courses, the publications they led to, and his international congresses established Gilson as a scholar of international reputation.

The sharp increase in the number of Gilson's students at the École tells its own story. In 1922, the École's first postwar year, Gilson had only eight students and Alphandéry nine; this was average for the Section of Religious Sciences, which generally attracted four to twenty students altogether. In Gilson's second year at the École, attendance of his courses rose to thirty-one students, twice Alphandéry's enrolment and the highest in the section. By 1924[*] enrolment was up to fifty-one, and the following year it reached sixty-four; in 1929 it was still a high fifty-nine, much to the delight of Sylvain Lévi, who had become president of the section in 1923.

Gilson and Sylvain Lévi were the closest of friends. Sylvain's family came originally from Auxerre; so far as Gilson was concerned, this by itself was enough to recommend him. The Lévis had been tailors in Auxerre and the town's only Jewish family; like Gilson, however, Sylvain had been born in Paris. The two men had been thrown together a great deal at the University of Strasbourg. It had been the older Lévi who had deepened Gilson's understanding of eastern spirituality:

> I remember a passing visit of Tagore to the University of Strasbourg. In the *aula magna* of the university, before an incredibly packed house, the Indian Magus had just delivered a lecture on the "Message of the Forest." With wonderful poetic grandeur, and not without some disdain for us pale Westerners, he had shown how India was indebted to its religion for a feeling for nature and universal brotherhood that Christianity had been unable to instil into any Western poet, not even Shakespeare. After the lecture, the professors crowded about to meet him and passed one by one under his somewhat inattentive stare. Sylvain Lévi presented one little man to him simply as Paul Sabatier. Tagore was unmoved. Gently insistent, Lévi repeated: "Sabatier, the author of the life of St Francis!" Suddenly Tagore's face lit up. "Ah! St Francis, I know him well. And how I love him! He is really one of ours." I don't think, indeed, that Tagore's "message of the forest" had anything to all to teach St Francis! It is a lesson of great value. The first contact between the Hindu poet and one of the most perfect incarnations of the Catholic spirit had the effect of making us aware of our own spiritual riches by showing us incarnate in the person of St Francis a feeling for the brotherhood of beings in God which even India knows it has not surpassed. ("Une heure avec Étienne Gilson," *Les nouvelles littéraires*, 25.1.3; tr.)

Lévi was Indianist in the Collège de France and in the École des Hautes Études, and professor of Sanskrit in the Sorbonne. He knew many ancient and modern languages. He pioneered with Antoine Meillet the study of the Tocharian of Chinese Turkestan, and later published a number of West Tocharian fragments of texts from the region of Kucha. Gilson later recalled:

---

[*] During this year Richard McKeon of Chicago, later dean of Gilson's North American students, was enrolled in Gilson's course.

> What a linguist he was! I remember him telling me once that it is only the first ten languages that require effort. On one of the many occasions I visited him he put a box in my hand. "You are now holding," he said, "three fragments, all that remains of a great civilization, that of the oasis of Kucha in India. I found one of these fragments myself, the Japanese government sent me another, and the Indian government the third." Sylvain Lévi once even thought he might have discovered the birthplace of Buddha. If so, his discovery was achieved by sheer erudition. Certainly, he came to love this birthplace of Buddha which was, since the discovery, become a place of pilgrimage. Though Lévi did not believe in Buddhism, still the birthplace of Buddha was as dear to him as Jerusalem itself. (interview, 1975.)

Not surprisingly, it was Lévi who, a few year later, recommended Gilson for the Collège the France. All his life Gilson remembered his friend with the warmest respect and affection: "Sylvain Lévi meant everything to me. If I had a chance to come back as someone else, I would want to come back as Sylvain Lévi. " (interview, 1975.)

Another friendship that endured to the end of Gilson's life developed during this period with Henri Gouhier, who first attended Gilson's Sorbonne classes in 1921. Gouhier became a regular auditor and soon a regular assistant. "He was," said Gilson later,

> less like my student and rather more like my son, like one of my own family. He came from Auxerre where he had made a brilliant course in the lycée. He attended my courses in the École shortly after leaving the army and was still wearing his uniform. He studied with me, then began teaching under me. (interview, 1975.)

Gouhier's thesis in the University of Paris was, like Gilson's, on Descartes. It was published under the title *La pensée religieuse de Descartes* in 1924 in Gilson's series Études de philosophie médiévale (Paris; McG 182). Gouhier's subsequent career, like Gilson's, was in the history of modern and medieval philosophy, with forays into the fine arts and theology. However, his focus was more obviously modern than Gilson's and he produced many monographs on Descartes, Malebranche, Comte, Saint-Simon and others. Like Gilson he was intrigued by Maine de Biran, some of whose works he edited. And like Gilson he was curious about the relationship between philosophy and history. Two of his books in this area are vital to an understanding of Gilson: *La philosophie et son histoire* (Paris, 1944) and *L'histoire et sa philosophie* (Paris, 1952). Indeed, when, in 1949, Gouhier contributed to *Étienne Gilson, philosophe de la chrétienté* (Paris, 1949; McG 943), he entitled his piece "De l'histoire de la philosophie à la philosophie" (McG 1002), in deference to the major point of intellectual contact between him and his master. Gouhier's personal orientation was less international than Gilson's, and was confined more or less to the Sorbonne where he taught, his reviews in *Les nouvelles littéraires*, and his appointment to the Institut de France. Nevertheless he remained all his life a superb historian of philosophy.

Another of Gilson's distinguished students at the University of Paris was Alexandre Koyré. Koyré attended Gilson's first seminars in the École and went on to a noteworthy career as a publishing professor. Although Koyrés thesis, "Essai sur l'idée de Dieu et les épreuves de son existence chez Descartes," was almost completed when Gilson came to Paris, Gilson apparently influenced its fourteen-page appendix on Cartesian inneism and illumination as related to St Augustine, St Thomas and St Bonaventure. At the École, Gilson and Koyré developed a friendship that, although not particularly close, lasted throughout Gilson's lifetime.

2 Russian Relief and the Nansen Committee

During the summer of 1922, at the end of his first year in the Sorbonne, Gilson became involved in a private programme of Russian relief with a non-affiliated group known as the Association for Aid to Russian Children. The association was formed by professional people in Paris and worked in co-operation with the Nansen Committee of the League of Nations.

Severe famine had struck Russia and the Ukraine during the winter of 1921. Aid had been despatched from most countries, but not from France where people were disposed to distrust stories about Russian famine. The French were of two minds about revolutionary Russia. In principle, most French republicans were sympathetic to the revolution which had much in common with their own of 1789. More practically, however, Russian nationalization had meant repudiation of Czarist debts, and the assets of many French investors, including Gilson and the Ravisés, had been frozen in Russian banks. Crop failure and hunger might require relief, but the Soviet's desire for credit in the capitals of Europe placed them beyond consideration. As the winter of 1921 came and went, no French aid reached Russia from either the state or the church. The French believed the Russians had betrayed them, and steadfastly refused to send money.

In the summer of 1922, the League of Nations reported that still another crop failure was expected in the Ukraine and that the coming winter could be as bad as the last. The Nansen Committee was reactivated. In addition the Hygiene Committee of the League of Nations reported that plague had struck the Black Sea area and was spreading into Europe with each departing refugee ship; the plague took the form of cholera and typhus, and was especially rampant among children.

An important letter appeared on the front page of *Le Figaro*, 21 July 1922, from Dr Maurice de Fleury of the Academy of Medicine, Paris. It referred to the epidemiological report recently issued by the League:

> An epidemic situation of disastrous proportions is raging in Rostov [today Rostov-on-the-Don] and in Novorossiisk where thousands of refugees have gathered. There are 3,000 cases of cholera in Odessa and the hospitals there are overcrowded; 40 cases a day are being reported in Rostov; and the situation is worsening throughout all districts of the Ukraine.

Dr de Fleury appealed not only to medical corporations but to professional and academic bodies to take up the challenge of relief. The Academy of Medicine followed up de Fleury's appeal with additional facts and figures. According to the academy, cholera had broken out in Russia on 3 May 1922, and at Odessa and Novorossiisk on 25 May 1922; all Europe was now threatened as refugees fled these centres (*Le Figaro*, 22.7.16). Once again, missions for the relief of children in Russia and the Ukraine were formed in several countries; in July, for example, the Holy See sent a mission from Bari to Moscow, Rostov and Ekaterinoslav (today Dniepropetrovsk). A French mission was now organized by a number of professional groups while the government continued its inactivity. These groups established headquarters at 10, rue d'Élysée under the presidency of Mme René Dubost. Funds were collected privately and a mission was dispatched to Russia and the Ukraine in August 1922. In charge of this mission was Étienne Gilson of the Sorbonne.

Gilson later explained why he was chosen for this work:

> One thing I did in the language line [in the German prison camps] was to learn Russian fairly well by working at it with some thirteen Russian prisoners. This, of course, proved useful when I went to Russia to work among the famished children. In fact I was selected for this work because I could speak Russian. Then too I wanted to see Russia about which I had come to know a good deal from fellow prisoners of war. (interview, 1974.)

Although Thérèse did not accompany her husband to Russia, she was a friend of Mme Dubost and was almost certainly involved in the work of the local relief committee.

There is no complete record of Gilson's itinerary and work during the mission of 1922, only two telegrams published in *Le Figaro*:

> *Odessa, 1 September.* Between Odessa and Kherson [along the Dnieper], for some 150 kilometers inland, the famine promises to be more terrible than last winter. There is no harvest. The situation of children is particularly tragic. A redoubled effort is needed. The French cantines between Odessa and Kherson are functioning excellently. Each cantine badly needs showers and overnight shelter if the children saved from hunger are not to die from cold and epidemics. I will send a table giving the exact situation. (22.9.13; tr.)

> The general situation has improved, thanks to the season and to aid provided since last winter. Predictions for next winter remain quite pessimistic. Districts served by French kitchens have enough grain for two or three months. Famine will strike there during January. I have personally taken part in a distribution of food and clothes sent here from Saint Étienne and Villeurbain. Villagers are begging for continued aid without which they would have died last year and will die next. Within the governorship of Samara the situation is worse yet; in the district of Pugachev famine has already begun again. Autumn seeding moves slowly because there are not enough horses; the situation will go on deteriorating from January to next June. (22.9.22; tr.)

Gilson's work on the mission took him into the Ukraine and into Russia proper. He visited already-established cantines at Viasovsk, Elshensk, Kluchersk,

Marinsk, Pristan, Radishchovsk, Sokvorsk and Shchirikinsk, and opened new ones in the Ukraine at Marioupol (today Zhdanov), Karkow, Ekaterinoslav, Kherson, Berdiansk, and in one unspecified industrial centre, Odessa or Saratov (associaition memo, 22.8.4). During the 1930s Gilson was accused of showing an uninformed bourgeois prejudice against Russian communism. He immediately retorted that he had personally witnessed conditions that warranted this aversion:

> It was not in the Ukraine that a Russian scholar, when I asked if there was anything I could do for him, said to me: Yes, two things. Give me a shirt, and get me out of this country for half an hour, so that I may recall what human life is. Then I will gladly die. ("Intermède soviétique," *Sept*, 34.5.19; McG 687; tr.)

Not all of Gilson's observations of Russia were negative ones, however. "One day when in an industrial centre," he recalled, "I noticed that the factories were all closed. I asked a passerby what was the matter. 'Don't you know,' he replied, 'that today is Sunday? We don't work on Sunday here.' " Gilson also found that his education in the Russian language had been limited in an unexpected way:

> There was a decided male quality to the vocabulary and sound of the Russian I had learned in prison camps. I learned the language without ever having spoken to a Russian woman or even hearing a Russian woman's voice. When I got to Russia and met Russian women for the first time, I not only found them fascinating, as men do women, but I was amazed at the rich, warm, new and unsuspected music which their voices brought to the language. I came to experience in Russian something of that aesthetic quality which women impart to intelligible sound and to know why men can listen long and quietly to a woman's chattering without so much as intervening with a single sound. (interview, 1974.)

In July 1926, when Gilson was sailing for America aboard the *Le Havre*, he encountered a sharp reminder of the Russian episode. He wrote about the coincidence to Thérèse:

> The ship's officer asked if there was aboard anyone who knew Russian. Five passengers required help with their customs declaration. Since no one else spoke up, I offered my services. The first passenger to present himself was a Ukrainian from Karkow; I looked at him. He was the Bolshevik government representative with whom I had journeyed in 1922 from Warsaw to Karkow. He did not appear to be pleased by the meeting. There he was, a Bolshevist diplomat who knew not a word of English, could not even transliterate his name into Latin characters. What a tiny place this world is! This man's name was Priernougfor, that is, ancient sailor. He had anchors tatooed on one arm. (26.7.20; tr.)

3 JOSEPH VRIN AND THE SECOND EDITION OF *LE THOMISME*

Shortly after the Russian journey the second edition of *Le thomisme* (Paris, 1922; McG 156) was issued through the bookseller Joseph Vrin. The experience convinced Gilson that he could best present his steadily unfolding ideas through continual revision and re-editing of his Lille-Strasbourg work on St Thomas. This was also Gilson's first professional dealing with the philosophical bookseller and publisher who would later become perhaps his closest friend.

Gilson had not been happy about the 1920 Vix edition of *Le thomisme*. It had been prepared in haste for lectures in Lille, then published in Strasbourg without further reflection. His brief "Preface to the Second Edition" sums up many of his misgivings:

> I have tried, in re-editing this work, to retain that introductory and initiatory character which I tried in the first edition to give it. However, I have also tried seriously to take into full account the observations, sometimes so absolutely right, which people have made to me about it. Wherever my language was inexact, whether by excess or defect, I have corrected it. Where comments seemed, in my opinion, themselves to deserve criticism, I have quietly introduced into my text references or explanations which seem to me to justify my view. I have also added to my original treatment of thomism some data on the life and works of St Thomas [chapter 1, section a]. I have added also the beginnings of a bibliography of thomism and a fundamental treatment of habits and virtues [chapter 13]. I still welcome further suggestions and corrections. Nothing is healthier than good criticism: *removere malum alicujus, ejusdem rationis est sicut bonum ejus procurare.* I am indebted to my readers for many favours, and I look forward to receiving more. (p. 6; tr.)

The second edition of *Le thomisme* improved considerably on the first, and fairly reflects Gilson's understanding of St Thomas as of 1921. In the additions found in chapter 13, it also reveals a refinement of technique. Except for a general reference to de la Barre and Sertillanges, these additions almost totally disregard secondary sources and depend much more heavily on the bare text of the *Summa theologiae*.

Gilson's friendship with Joseph Vrin apparently began soon after his return to the Sorbonne. At any rate, by the time the two men drew up the contract for *Le thomisme*, they seem to have become firm friends. Typically, this contract was signed well after the release of the book; although the preface to the second edition was signed April 1922 at Melun, and the book itself bears the date 1922, the contract was not signed until 1 February 1923. The contract simply stated that the manuscript was already in the publisher's hands, that the royalties were to be two francs for each volume sold, that 2,000 copies would be for sale, and that the author's corrections would be at the expense of M. Vrin.

Temperamentally, Étienne Gilson and Joseph Vrin were most unlike. Although Gilson was self-sufficient as a scholar, he was hardly so in domestic or business affairs. For the former he relied on Thérèse, and for the latter he needed Vrin almost as much as he had needed Maman when he had first become a scholar. Vrin was at first reluctant to answer that need. He was a bookseller, who preferred selling books across the counter to people he knew than across oceans to clients he had never met. No one was more surprised than Vrin to find himself becoming an international publisher, a role for which he had neither training nor taste. When orders began to come in to 6, place de la Sorbonne from around the world, he would shove them to one side of his desk until Gilson or some other friend called in and helped him with his replies. Yet with all their differences – Vrin used to refer to Gilson as *mon calvaire* – the two men became fast friends. They had one overpowering bond, a total dedication to the Catholic faith against which other issues appeared minor.

4 RELATIONS WITH CATHOLIC SCHOLARS

During the early years of the 1920s Gilson communicated very little with the Catholic scholars of Louvain and the Institut Catholique. No doubt his station within the secular fortress of the Sorbonne generated some suspicion on their part, some apprehension on his.

At Louvain scholastic philosophy had long been taught. As early as 1893, Louvain had set up its successful Institut Supérieur de Philosophie (École Saint Thomas d'Aquin) to pursue scholastic thought in the context of scientific research. The goal of this institute was to probe the philosophy of the Middle Ages in order to orient its principles to contemporary needs, to vigorously pursue the directives set forth by Leo XIII in *Aeterni patris* (1878), and to discover and teach scholastic methods. It also paid considerable attention to new methodologies, particularly to experimental psychology and sociology. Thus the Institut Supérieur was fashioning a new scholasticism on the valid principles enshrined in the old.

An excellent policy of publication supported the institute's work. At its founding the institute already had access to the *Revue néo-scholastique* for its shorter studies. In 1912 it set up the *Annales de l'institut supérieur de philosophie* for items of intermediate length; it immediately initiated its series on the philosophy of Aristotle under the general title Aristote: œuvres philosophiques: traductions et études. The founder and first president of the institute was Cardinal Mercier, and the list of its distinguished scholars included Mansion, Noël, Michotte, Lottin, Colle, Lemaire, Jacquart and Deploige. Louvain also had Maurice De Wulf, premier historian of philosophy, who had received Gilson so graciously in 1913 and had attended the presentation of Gilson's thesis to the Société Française de la Philosophie.

The Institut Catholique de Paris had been created in 1876 as a protest against the French government's overhaul of traditional education. It was founded to restore a home for Catholic philosophers and theologians, and to supply integral courses in Christian thought beyond the lycée level. Although the Catholic Institute sometimes described itself as the "free University of Paris," it existed outside the national educational structures and depended upon practising Catholics for inspiration and suppport. From its beginning the Catholic Institute taught psychology, ethics and logic. It attracted scholars who, like Jacques Maritain, wanted to work as Catholics within aristotelian and scholastic traditions. Institute professors taught "the existence of God, creator and providence; the spirituality and immortality of the soul; the objective values of reason, free will, and moral obligations as the bases of belief rather than, as was the case in the French universities when these things were taught at all, in order to demolish them" (*Revue thomiste*, 21 [1913]: 579-587; tr.).

Gilson was close to some of the professors of the Institut Catholique, especially to Sertillanges and Rousselot. He shared their concern for the true bases of faith, appreciated their support of the church, and shared their respect of the *Aeterni patris*. He was not however part of their circle, and developed no close relationships like those he shared with Sylvain Lévi, Henri Gouhier and Lucien Lévy-Bruhl. Moreover, Gilson had never studied philosophy with the object of bolstering or promoting his faith. He read philosophers in order to know what they taught and in order to expand his knowledge of the history of philosophy. And just as his faith had not come to him through philosophy, philosophy was not going to deprive him of it.

Gilson was not altogether sure that his Sorbonne colleagues were incorrect when they spoke of Thomas as a medieval theologian rather than a philosopher. Possibly the professors of Louvain and the Catholic Institute, in their attempt to use thomist or scholastic philosophy to solve the problems of modern philosophy, were victims of a passing euphoria. At any rate Gilson was clear on one point: there appeared to be several medieval philosophies and, as the Sorbonne's course director in "medieval philosophies and theologies," he was contracted to teach them all.

One embarrassment for Gilson was the tone of an earlier assault by Father Simon Deploige on the sociological positions of Lévy-Bruhl and Émile Durkheim. In 1911 Simon Deploige, president of Louvain's Institut Supérieur de Philosophie, had published his successful *Le conflit de la morale et la sociologie*. Deploige's book had been directed against Lévy-Bruhl's widely published *La morale et la science des mœurs* (1903). Lévy-Bruhl had challenged moralists to choose between moral philosophy and its defective methodology; according to Lévy-Bruhl, moral philosophy was merely a projection of the practice of a given society at a given time, whereas the sociology of Durkheim was a much-needed and still developing science of morality which would one day allow man to control his social environment. Deploige's work had defended the validity of moral philosophy and of natural law. He had focused his attack on the inconsistencies of Durkheim who, sometimes as a sociologist, sometimes as a moralist, sometimes as a metaphysician, proposed an amoral approach to morals. Deploige had also accused Durkheim of dishonestly laying claim to ideas which had first come out of Germany. This slur on Durkheim's scholarly integrity had introduced a vein of bitterness into an otherwise legitimate confrontation; it was this that offended Gilson.

Deploige's book had been an instant success in Catholic circles and was reprinted the following year, 1912. The issue, perforce, was neglected during the war. In 1923, however, the work was published for the third time in Jacques Maritain's Bibliothèque française de philosophie, with a new preface by Maritain himself. Maritain praised Deploige's volume and upheld Deploige's criticism of Durkheim's sociology as valid, though no longer needed. He was reprinting the book because he valued highly its outline of St Thomas' "method in moral and social philosophy" as provided in chapters 7 and 8. In these chapters "M. Deploige has succeeded in disengaging the leading ideas in St Thomas' method."

Deploige had mined St Thomas for ideas that he felt could be put to work again. Gilson was sceptical of this claim, and wondered whether Deploige had found in Thomas what Thomas had put there. Gilson was beginning to believe that the best scholars were misreading St Thomas, and misreading him precisely because their focus was on contemporary situations. Moreover, they were making too much of systems in their preference for philosophies rather than philosophers. For Gilson, the assumptions and prejudices of systems always tended to obscure the reality of God; whittling St Thomas down to a permanent philosophical system did little but obscure Thomas' theology.

In general, Gilson held aloof from controversy with the neoscholastics, whether philosophers or theologians. Like von Döllinger, Möhler, Loisy, Tyrrell and others, he was disposed to think that theology should be permeated with scientific history and philosophical speculation. Indeed, like St Thomas himself, Gilson believed theology to be a science and felt that the force and impulse of scientific thinking ought in some sense to purify faith. Gilson knew however that this kind of integrism had for many scholars meant severance from Rome. Principles of historical research had not protected Loisy from sanction when he had written as a "free exegete" that the only one of the twelve articles of faith acceptable on historical principles was that Jesus was crucified under Pontius Pilate. Loisy's case had touched Gilson deeply.

If Loisy was a dissident Catholic, another of Gilson's colleagues, Maurice Blondel, was an overzealous and prejudging one. Blondel had taken his doctoral degree at the Sorbonne in 1893, and had written his thesis on human "action," not in concept but *in se*. He wanted to use philosophy to serve apologetics, to "do better than our modern students in the light of the gospel." Blondel's apologistic stance got him into trouble with Sorbonne professors and with the Ministry of Public Education, which suspended him briefly from lycée teaching. He eventually modified his apologetic line and, after many years of struggle with his professors, had his thesis accepted. Gilson always had serious doubts about the philosophical integrity of Blondel's procedure. Relations between the two remained amicable, however, until 1931 when Blondel's *Lettre* roundly criticized Gilson's stance on Christian philosophy (below, pp. 199-201).

In Europe after World War I, a revival was taking place in thomist and neoscholastic research. In the early 1920s Gilson played only a small part in this revival, which occurred largely within Catholic institutions. Louvain's Institut Supérieur, of course, continued its important advanced work. At the Institut Catholique, the dean of philosophy, Abbé E. Peillaude, revived the old nineteenth-century Société Philosophique, originally founded by Mgr Maurice d'Hulst; the Société offered many series of excellent discussions, such as Maritain's critical analysis of Maurice Blondel's position on intelligence (23.4.32). In 1921 the Dominicans of the French province opened in Belgium their high-powered Institut Historique d'Études Thomistes where they offered courses by such competent thomists as Mandonnet, Roland-Gosselin, Margueritte, Synave, Schoff, Chenu and Théry. In Germany, Munich's long-established programme of textual and doctrinal criticism by Klemens Baeumker and Georg Friederick, and then by Martin Grabmann, was augmented by the 1921 establishment by Professor Switalski of a new research centre, the Albertus Magnus Akademie, at Cologne. Such disciplinal foundations as these, as well as the research activities of centres, institutes and private individuals in Italy and Spain, created a thomist renaissance.

Although the resurgence of thomism exercised an immense influence over Gilson, he was not really party to its development. During his first three years at the Sorbonne he contributed only a few items to Louvain's *Revue néo-scholastique*,* nothing at all to the Catholic Institute's *Revue de philosophie*, and little or nothing at all to other Catholic journals. Nor did Gilson offer lectures or courses in the programmes of Catholic centres, and no close contacts were established. Gilson's contribution to the thomist renaissance lay in the momentum provided by his books and by his presence as a defender of St Thomas within the national universities. Significantly, when the *Bulletin thomiste* reviewed his work along with that of his students Gouhier and Koyré, it entitled the review "Le thomisme et les non-scolastiques" (2 [1925]: 317). Gilson was probably pleased by the distinction.

If Gilson had few close friends among Catholic scholars at this time, he also had few enemies; the few opponents he did have were largely only sceptical critics. One such critic, Abbé J. Bricout, after briefly reviewing Gilson's *La philosophie au moyen âge*, added apprehensively:

> I wonder whether many readers won't conclude that modern thought is the legitimate daughter, the normal development, from Christian thought. [Gilson] actually writes that "modern thought has been suckled on the ideal of a society of minds as universal as reason itself. Just as theology's heir is Reason, so is Christianity's heir Humanity." This is a false conclusion. Our Catholic philosophers have to correct it for the good of rasher spirits among them. Our philosophers will also have to give serious consideration to those details on which Gilson establishes the general theme running through his volumes. ("Les sciences religieuses à la Sorbonne," *Documentation catholique*, 8 [1922]: 563.)

5 EARLY INTERNATIONAL MEETINGS, 1921-1924

Gilson's stature as an international scholar started to grow as he began to attend postwar congresses and to accept invitations as a visiting lecturer. Between September 1921 and May 1924 he attended three international congresses and delivered six visiting lectures. More specifically, he attended a congress in Oxford

---

* These were a divided article in 1920 and 1921 entitled "Météores cartésiens et météores scolastiques" (McG 348), and two articles in 1923, "Le platonisme de Bernard de Chartres" (McG 398) and "Saint Bonaventure et l'évidence de l'existence de Dieu" (McG 436).

from 24 to 27 September 1921; participated in the international session of the Société Française de Philosophie in Paris from 27 to 31 December 1921; delivered six lectures in Brussels during December 1923, later repeating them in London; and visited Naples for the Fifth International Congress of Philosophy from 5 to 9 May 1924.

The 1921 Oxford congress gathered a limited number of English, French and American philosophers in an attempt to reinstitute international meetings after the war. The congress was built around a substantial core of philosophers – Henri Bergson, Sir James Eddington, Alfred North Whitehead, Bertrand Russell, Baron von Hügel. It attracted many scholars and was highly successful. Gilson attended as a member of the French delegation from Strasbourg, just before taking up his appointment in the Sorbonne.

Bergson gave the inaugural paper and spoke again at the closing dinner. His paper, "Expectation and Change," dealt with distinctions between the possible and the real. Gilson later recalled with enthusiasm Bergson's contributions to the congress:

> At the Congress of Oxford, 1921, I felt most vividly that [Bergson] was the prince of the mind. Some hundred philosophers from all over the world were there. Bergson had already delivered his dazzling inaugural on "Prévision et Nouveauté" when, at the parting banquet, he set forth what he thought was the present task of philosophy. To make his point he sketched a striking picture of the story of the soul as related to what he called "the body of humanity." He developed the theme that men have unconsciously been partial to exaggerated forms of the mechanical and industrial and have allowed their "body of humanity" to overdevelop. Now we have to wonder whether the soul has strength enough to keep this monster of a body under control. (Frédéric Lefèvre, "Une heure avec Étienne Gilson," *Les nouvelles littéraires*, 25.1.3; tr.)

Thérèse was able to accompany her husband to Oxford, and they stretched the visit into ten memorable days. Gilson had a glorious chance to polish up the English he had learned from books and from fellow prisoners in Germany. His acquisition of fluid English became a private joke between Thérèse and himself. He later wrote to her from Harvard:

> When I was congratulated on my English [by an entomologist at the home of Professor Ralph Barton Perry], I did what I always do now: I admitted that I had lived a long time in England. There was a time when I was inclined to tell the whole truth, namely, that I had spent some ten days there – you remember them – and people were incredulous and visibly convinced that I was either posing as a man who had been born into the world knowing English, or who had a genius for languages. With this new system, a single answer suffices and discussion becomes unnecessary: "Oh, yes! A very long time." People are satisfied and that's that. How simple! It is curious to be reduced to telling a lie in order to seem to be telling the truth! (EG to Thérèse, 26.10.19; tr.)

During the Oxford congress Gilson became especially friendly with Edward Bullough and with Professor and Mrs Whitehead. When Bullough, of Caius

College, Cambridge, subsequently produced in 1924 an English translation of *Le thomisme*, Gilson permitted him to use the third French edition even before it appeared in Paris. The friendship with Alfred North Whitehead and Mrs Whitehead was renewed in 1926 at Harvard when Whitehead and Gilson found themselves colleagues in the same philosophy department.

Two months after the Oxford congress, from 27 to 31 December 1921, the Paris-centered Société Française de Philosophie invited representatives from American, English, Belgian and Italian societies to attend a special session. On the closing day Gilson, now teaching at the Sorbonne, delivered a paper entitled "La spécificité de la philosophie d'après Auguste Comte" (*Congrès des sociétés américaine, anglaise, belge, italienne et de la Société Française de Philosophie* [Paris, 1921], pp. 382-386; McG 453). This controversial paper clearly demonstrated that he was ready to come to grips with French university philosophy as a scholar arguing among his peers. It reconstructs Comte's system logically and chronologically, concluding that positivism, which must perforce deny the possibility of metaphysical knowledge, adds to the "ordre intellectuel" and "ordre sentimental" which enable a positivist to specify philosophy in relation to science: "If my interpretation is correct," Gilson wrote, "then it is the intrusion of a subjective and human principle into the domain of the sciences which specifies positive philosophy as such." The paper was successful and provoked much discussion among such audience members as Pécaut, Lord Ashbourne, Lenoir, Lévi-Bruhl and Charles Blondel. (See below, p. 217.)

Gilson's success with his paper ensured him more such invitations. It also developed in him a special affection for Comte. Strangely enough, Comte, the darling of French systematic philosophers, was sympathetically received even by Catholic thinkers in France. Léonce de Grandmaison, for example, wrote at about the time Gilson was giving his paper:

> Apart from a few isolated thinkers (Maine de Biran is an illustrious example), French philosophy – ought I not say European philosophy! – has accomplished very little. Only the positivism of Auguste Comte strikes me as a system put together by the hand of a skilful artist, with coherence and incontestable vigour. ... Apart from two or three Catholic philosophers, Gratry, Olle-Laprune, Maurice Blondel, whom do we have? (*Documentation catholique*, 8 [1922]: 431.)

Although Gilson might not have approved of all three examples, he did agree with de Grandmaison that Comte's system was worthy of respect. Gilson felt this system was as far as philosophy could go toward fashioning its own religion. Nonetheless, as Gilson was to maintain repeatedly, true religion can only come to man as a gift from God. Over thirty years later, on the centenary of Comte's death, Gilson wrote:

> Those of us who are furthest from [Comte's] doctrine but who still believe in the value of philosophical speculation have a fraternal feeling toward this man for whom the requirements of theory are imposed as the condition of everything else. Comte has no objection to using medieval theology to tie society together. His difficulty is that it does not in fact do so, that it no longer has social efficacy. And his

criticism of socialism and communism is on the same ground. ("Le centenaire d'Auguste Comte," *Le monde*, 57.9.4; McG 581.)

Philosophically then, Gilson maintained his Sorbonne-inspired interest in Comte and Descartes even as he began to probe more deeply into medieval thought. For Gilson, the study of medieval philosophy cast essential light on the origins of modern philosophy. He developed this theme in a series of six lectures on "Descartes and Scholastic Metaphysics" at the Free University of Brussels in December 1923.* This was probably the first course he gave at an outside university, and he repeated it in London. The lectures clearly reveal Gilson's wide-ranging familiarity with modern philosophy. They also demonstrate how, within Gilson's orthodoxy, the study of medieval thought constituted an authentic revolution in philosophy. The brief introduction to the lectures is illuminating:

> The complete break which for too long a time has separated the history of modern from medieval philosophy is nowadays disappearing. Any opposition to rejoining the two domains would no doubt cease if a certain prejudice could be removed; that is, that studying modern philosophy in relation to medieval philosophy means studying what modern philosophy had borrowed from medieval philosophy. This is not necessarily what is meant. The relation between the two calls for some far more general statement: that it is impossible to grasp the meaning even of what is original in a philosophy without knowing the doctrines the author of this philosophy had constantly before him while elaborating his own original doctrine. These lectures aim at demonstrating the truth of this statement. Also, in order not to dissipate your attention, I propose simply to reflect upon a few essential points in Descartes' metaphysics and then to examine whether anything more can be learned about them by putting them into the context of scholastic-metaphysics. (*Revue de l'Université de Bruxelles*, 29 [1923-1924]: 105-106; tr.)

Gilson's first lecture in this series was entitled "Methodical Doubt and the Critique of Substantial Forms." He elaborated this topic under six headings: methodical doubt; the experience of Descartes; the biological character of aristotelianism; the purgative function of doubt; historical counterproof; and a conclusion. The remaining five lectures were as meticulously organized and as succinctly set out as the first, and were entitled: "Descartes' Critique of St Thomas"; "Descartes and St Anselm"; "Descartes and the Scholastic Principle of Causality"; "God as Guarantor of Certitude"; and "Scholastic and Cartesian Man." Throughout these lectures members of the audience were nowhere invited to become either a cartesian or a thomist; they were simply asked to consider historically certain events and processes. In this the lectures were decidedly different from the one Gilson delivered in Naples a few months later.

---

* This course was twice printed by the university, first in its own *Revue*, and then in a separate pamphlet. It was subsequently incorporated into *Études sur le rôle de la pensée médiévale dans la formation du système cartésien*, Études de philosophie médiévale, 13 (Paris, 1930), volume 2, chapters 2-7; McG 47.

The congress in Naples was called for a threefold purpose: to celebrate the seventh centennial of the founding of the university; to conclude the past year's celebration of the six-hundredth anniversary of the canonization of St Thomas; and to host the Fifth International Congress of Philosophy. The fourth congress had been held in Bologna in 1911 and the fifth had been scheduled for London in 1915 but had been postponed because of the war. When the Congress Committee asked Naples to expand their celebrations into the long-delayed Fifth International, the university gladly agreed. For Gilson, the Naples congress offered the most representative and international gathering in his experience to date.

Gilson was among those officially nominated by the French Ministry of Public Instruction to represent France at the celebration; this meant that he could bring Thérèse, expenses paid, and could stay at the Institut Français of Naples. Other philosophers attending from France were Léon Brunschvicg and Victor Delbos from Paris, and Maurice Blondel from Aix en Provence. Besides the distinguished Benedetto Croce, the Italians present included Agostino Gemelli, university rector and well-known editor of Milan's *Rivista di filosofie neo-scolastica*, which Gilson had been reviewing for *Revue philosophique*. Other delegates came from North and South America and from every country of Europe. Gilson had never before functioned at the heart of so a large group of international scholars.

Gilson's paper for this congress was on "The Humanism of Thomas Aquinas." The paper demonstrates most of the traits that characterized Gilson's writing in the 1920s. A eulogy of Gemelli and a laudatory exordium on Romanesque architecture reveal his masterful use of opening rhetoric. His precision and clarity of style are apparent throughout, particularly in a contrast of the meanings of sovereign good in Aristotle and St Thomas. Gilson's wide learning, especially in the area of philosophical humanism, informs his presentation of an all-embracing religion as the fundamental reality, served and presented by philosophy within the context of Western civilization and culture. Finally, Gilson's "sustained awareness that he is professionally an historian of thought" leads him to a consideration of modern philosophies and to Auguste Comte:

> Philosophies of illumination, of the science of nature, of sociology, predicted the disappearance of religion, appealing to principles. This went on right down to the time of Auguste Comte, whose error was to reverse the procedure. He thought he could pick up all the pieces of that edifice which eighteenth-century critiques had demolished, and that he could produce a religion out of positive philosophy. But such a religion refused obstinately to be born from such philosophy. No philosophy has ever given birth to even the tiniest bit of religion. What religious living seeks of philosophical speculation is a set of formulas which will tell it just a little about itself, and which will above all provide a clearer and purer awareness of what religious living both is and does. (*Atti del V congresso internazionale di filosofia*, [1925], p. 987; McG 303; tr.)

In this lecture, early in 1924, a more human and warmer tone prevails than in the highly organized business-like Brussels lectures. In part the change can be attributed to the presence in the audience of many neoscholastic and thomist philosophers. But the new tone also indicates that Gilson had become more deeply involved in thomism than formerly. Like Catholics everywhere, Gilson had clearly been deeply moved by Pope Pius xi's recent promulgation of the anniversary of Thomas' canonization.

6 Saint Thomas

On 7 March 1923, the feast of St Thomas Aquinas, the master-general of the Dominicans, Louis Thessling, had circulated throughout his order a letter calling on all Dominicans to honour the "stability," "clarity" and "utility" of the teachings of the Angelic Doctor during this sixth-hundredth anniversary of his canonization at Avignon by Pope John xxii. The General's letter was followed, on 29 June 1923, by Pius xi's encyclical *Studiorum ducem*. This document invited Christians to that "pondering of truth" which produces "more perfect and embellished virtues." He warned that to desert the metaphysics of Thomas was "to risk disaster," and he urged respect for philosophy, that "most noble of human studies" so near to that higher sphere, theology. Pius also bestowed on Thomas a new title: the "Common and Universal Doctor of the Church." The celebration of Thomas' canonization must have seemed particularly timely to Gilson as a corrective to other celebrations marking the anniversaries of Ernest Renan (b. 1823), Voltaire (b. 1723), and even Blaise Pascal (b. 1623).

The actual celebrations marking the canonization consisted for the most part of testimonial meetings. One of these, a gala event, took place 19 July 1923 at Le Saulchoir, the Dominican theologate of the Paris province in Belgium. Cardinal Mercier attended this session, as did Mgr Lesne of Lille, and Père Gardeil delivered the address. As a result of this gala, the great French Dominican labours on behalf of thomism got their second wind. A "Thomist Week" was held in Rome by the Academy of St Thomas Aquinas with papers by Cardinal Billot, Jacques Maritain, Simon Deploige, Martin Grabmann and others. Some time later Maritain spoke on "St Thomas the Apostle of Modern Times" at a triduum in Avignon. Most important perhaps for subsequent scholarship was the founding of the Société Thomiste de Saint Thomas d'Aquin with Mandonnet, Maritain, Roland-Gosselin and Destrez among its founding councillors; in 1924, under Mandonnet and Théry, the society created the *Bulletin thomiste* as its official organ.

Gilson gave no papers at these early gatherings and was not among the founding members of the Société Thomiste. Nonetheless, in his Naples paper he spoke like a member of the thomist constituency. Certainly he was coming to be regarded as a thomist, though not as a scholastic. Nor was he a neoscholastic: he considered himself simply an historian of thought and of thinkers. Although at the time of the congress in Naples Gilson was as concerned with university philosophy as with the thomist renaissance; no thinker, not even Bergson, touched him as deeply as did Thomas. His explorations of thomist thought would soon attain a passionate intensity.

In response to Pius xı's relating in *Studiorum ducem* of truth to virtue in philosophy, Gilson hastened the following year, 1924 to 1925, to offer at the Sorbonne
a course in "The Moral Teaching of St Thomas Aquinas." He also accepted a
request to place a volume on Thomas' moral teachings in the series *Les moralistes
chrétiens*, edited by Gabalda. Gilson's *Saint Thomas d'Aquin* (Paris, 1925; McG
142) nicely complements the metaphysical emphasis of the second edition of his
Le thomisme. As his first major excursion into "moral philosophy," it assumes an
atypical format: within a kind of Menippean satire, Gilson's translations of
various excerpts from Thomas alternated with his own prose commentary.

Gabalda insisted that Gilson provide a translated text with neither the Latin
original nor scholarly footnotes. Gilson finally agreed but only reluctantly.
Certainly he agreed with Gabalda concerning the importance of first-hand
translation. In his own seminars he refused to accept any quotations until the
student had first presented them in his own words; "if you cannot put a text into
your own words," he would caution, "you don't know what it means."
Nonetheless Gilson did not want to dispense altogether with the original text.
Moreover he felt he might mislead the reader by presenting Thomas' moral
doctrine as separable from his metaphysics. Thus he wrote, somewhat
apologetically:

> The doctrine of the Sovereign Good, which comes first in my presentation, is the
> keystone of the entire moral arch. It shows how moral philosophy blends with
> metaphysics. What this metaphysics is I have tried to demonstrate elsewhere [*Le
> thomisme*, 2nd ed., Paris, 1924]. There I found it quite impossible to include the
> infinite practical detail of the system's moral implications. As St Thomas himself
> says, moral doctrine does not take on its full meaning until it has advanced to a
> stage where it can control its detail. Thus I readily agreed to present St Thomas'
> moral teachings in this collection, *Les moralistes chrétiens*, when my friend and
> colleague, M. l'Abbé Baudin, professor at the University of Strasbourg, asked me to
> do so. (*Saint Thomas d'Aquin*, pp. 12-13.)

Vrin meanwhile was apparently quite content to serve for once as Gilson's agent
for another publisher. Gabalda wrote Gilson:

> We agree to print your manuscript of Saint Thomas as it stands, with the addition of
> the short introduction you mention. We shall increase the numbers of the first
> printing. Because there are so many additional pages, we shall have to increase the
> list price in order to cover the difference in manufacturing costs. However, your
> royalties will increase accordingly. We hope to give you entire satisfaction and not
> to burden you with the work of revision. We have today sent your manuscript over
> to Librairie Vrin as you request. (Gabalda to EG, 24.7.7; tr.)

Saint Thomas d'Aquin appeared in late summer, and had to be reprinted twice
before the end of the year. Subsequent editions appeared in 1930 and 1941. Like
Le thomisme, it was among the early Gilson items to be translated into English.
The translation was made by Leo Richard Ward, csc, of the University of Notre
Dame, and was published in 1931. Gilson objected strongly to the English title,

Moral Values and the Moral Life (McG 143). In his opinion, the word "values" was out of place in a philosophy of being in which good was transcendental. To speak of good as a value, he felt, was to uproot it from its ontological origins and to assign to it subjective connotations unfaithful to St Thomas' meaning. When the English version was reprinted in 1961, Ward maintained the word "values" but added the subtitle "The Ethical Theory of St Thomas Aquinas."

In spirit, Gilson's introduction to *Saint Thomas d'Aquin* is very close to his Naples lecture. After briefly surveying Thomas' life, and insisting that his moral teaching is inseparable from his metaphysics, Gilson moves into an analysis of Thomas' humanism: he points out that Thomas had proclaimed the whole of Hellenism, including Aristotle, perfectly fulfilled and satisfied in Christianity fully three centuries before the position was argued in what has become its *locus classicus*, William Bude's *De transitu Hellenismi ad Christianismum*. Gilson next suggests that moral philosophy offers a working solution to the difficulty of most scholars in reconciling augustinism and thomism. According to Gilson, this problem arises from an initial focus on man as substantially soul in Augustine and as soul and body in Thomas; once however the initial focus is directed, as in the moral teachings of Thomas, to the beatific vision, all conflict tends to disappear. Therefore, moral philosophy in *Saint Thomas d'Aquin* opens with reflection upon the sovereign good and then proceeds through human acts, good and evil, the passons, virtues and vices, law, charity, the cardinal virtues, and political societies or states.

In the "notes bibliographiques" of the book, Gilson provides an illuminatiing series of directions for the convenience of the uninitiated reader. These notes were intended to compensate for the absence of scholarly notes insisted on by Gabalda. They display Gilson's pedagogical method at its clearest and best, and stress the five methodical steps that he urged throughout his career.

1. Read, reread, reflect on the text of St Thomas. He is one of those true philosophers whose writings at first reading seem to be obscure but with more reading and reflection become increasingly clear. He is not one of those who seem clear at first, but obscure on reflection.
2. Remove the initial obscurity by resorting to *explication de texte*, taking care to learn the author's technical terminology and his characteristic style and vocabulary.
3. Observe particularly how Thomas uses the analytic order: he poses a thesis, presumes that it has already been demonstrated, then works back to the principle which supports it.
4. No text is understood nor explained until one (a) has established the meaning of the technical terms to which the reason has appealed, (b) has established the reasoning in the synthetic order from principle to consequences, (c) has separated from the reasoning process the example which, after all, is only there as an illustration.
5. Nothing keeps faith with a philosopher's thought, no historian's treatise, no translation however carefully made, nothing except the philosopher's own text in the very languages in which he wrote it. (p. 16; tr.)

Although thomism was looming larger in Gilson's intellectual and moral world in this period, it would be a mistake to suggest he was now becoming a thomist. Gilson was never to commit himself to the philosophical school called thomism. His commitment would never be to anything other than the text that Thomas left behind, and his objective would simply be to understand the meaning of that text.

7 MAINE DE BIRAN

Gilson was by nature an independent thinker, always chary of philosophical schools. While at the Sorbonne, both as student and professor, he never adapted the sociology of his professors of philosophy. He respected Durkheim's methodology, but not his rejection of philosophy and religion. He felt the same toward Lévy-Bruhl, despite his warm affection for the man. Personal gratitude never entailed intellectual discipleship. As for the neoscholastics, while he gladly shared their faith and their love of Thomas, he read his texts for himself.

Not surprisingly then, Gilson began in the 1920s to experience sympathy for another private and independent philosopher, François-Pierre Gonthier, Maine de Biran (1766 to 1824). Maine, so named for a property he owned, had in civil life been a bodyguard for King Louis xvi; then, during the Revolution, an underprefect in seclusion on his Domaine de Grateloup near Bergerac; finally during the two Restorations he had become a senior civil servant. Privately however Maine was his own philosopher. He submitted papers to European academies, kept an intimate journal, and gathered with other idealists at the Maison d'Auteuil, the continuation of the salon of Mme Helvetius. He also wrote a number of treatises for his own satisfaction, and stored them away for later generations.

Maine de Biran began philosophizing as a cartesian, then as an idealist in the manner of de Condillac and Locke, although he was never the disciple of any school. His constant struggle was to set forth a unique philosophy of man's interior life. To establish that man's knowledge was fully immaterial, he maintained that man's sensations – the origin of his ideas – were also immaterial. Nor was man's active moral life material: for Maine, the happiness of man derived from moral philosophy and from interior virtue. Maine hoped one day to be able to discover within himself a faculty of believing, where faith and philosophy might meet. Late in life he concluded that no bridge could exist between faith and philosophy, and he turned seriously to Catholicism. Gilson could not help approving of a man like this, but was far from accepting Maine's philosophy.

Gilson had encountered Maine's unusual manner of philosophizing several times during his career. He had met it in Bergson who admitted to having been influenced by him: Maine's analysis of spiritualism, which held that the life of the spirit originates elsewhere and has to be sought and lived, resembled Bergson's own concern with active, motive and voluntary efforts in thinking, his "élan vital." In addition, Durkheim and Lévy-Bruhl had been very taken by Maine's "Mémoire sur l'habitude"; this prizewinning submission to the Institute of France, written in 1799 and revised in 1802, had become very important to certain sociologists, as had Maine's unfinished "Essais d'anthropologie." And in 1910 to 1911, Victor Delbos had delivered a course of lectures on Maine at the Sorbonne. As permanent secretary of the Institute of France, Delbos was in effect custodian of Maine's papers. Beginning in 1910, he published a number of articles on Maine in *L'année philologique* and elsewhere. Interest in Maine de Biran reached its peak in 1924 with the centenary of his death: Pierre Tisserand was already publishing the *Opera omnia*, and Maurice Blondel was preparing his text of Delbos' Sorbonne lectures.

At around this time Gilson, searching among Vrin's second-hands books, discovered Coventry Patmore's personal copy of Ernest Naville's study of Maine de Biran. This copy, copiously annotated in the English poet's hand, became the basis of Gilson's first draught of "Une philosophie de la vie intérieure: Maine de Biran." He delivered this paper in 1925 in the municipal building of the Sixteenth Arrondissment at the request of the mayor; it was subsequently reworked and updated with texts from Henry Gouhier's three-volume edition of Maine's *Journal intime* (Neuchatel, 1955-1957) for a lecture to the Alliance Française de Toronto. Patmore's annotated Naville volume, along with the two draughts of Gilson's paper, are in the Gilson Archives, Toronto.

Gilson's paper on Maine de Biran falls into four parts. The first, "La réinvention du moi," presents Maine as a sensitive and independent philosopher, irritated by his contemporaries' focus upon society and on external nature. Concerned that society and nature were moulding him into a reflection of themselves, he felt driven to ask questions about himself, his interior sensations, his "moi." The second section, "L'effort volontaire," deals with Maine's attempts to show that through the force of his effort his faculties in some way caused his sensations, memories, concepts and so on. It is by effort, said Maine, that one lifts a finger, or makes the best of external nature. This "voluntary motive effort" seems to be the one basic irresolvable faculty of the "moi" by which man assumes power over his life. If effort is a faculty, it is one by which man takes possession of himself. The third part of Gilson's lecture, "De la volonté à la grâce," maintains that, from the stoics to Pascal, man's experience is most often miserable because no succession of efforts yields permanent reward or enduring satisfaction. Man needs something that transcends his will. Must this something also transcend nature itself and philosophy too?

In his fourth section, "La grâce," Gilson explores the nature of the transcendence that Maine enigmatically embraced late in his life. Although Gilson fully accepted the credibility of Maine's conversion, he hesitated somewhat concerning his ultimate conclusions. Gilson's summary however is sympathetic, if a little deflating:

> On 17 February 1822, just over two years before his death, [Maine de Biran] wrote what will remain the best-balanced statement of his final convictions .... "How is one to penetrate an idea like God, duty, immortality? The stoic will say that the will can always reproduce these ideas and keep them alive; the Christian will attribute

everything to grace. The observant philosopher will not dismiss the influence of supernatural grace; he will attribute to his unknown cause anything grand, beautiful, lofty etc. which he notices suddenly producted *within him* but *without him* ...; but doing so he will recognize how much the spontaneity of organizing his experience, of the principle of life arousing and calming him, may contribute to his pure and elevated state of soul." Certainly, this is grace. However, the fluctuations in the spiritual level are not attributable to the presence or absence of grace, because these are part of our natural condition, in large part even of our body. (pp. 12-13; tr.)

According to Gilson, Maine de Biran's goals were beyond the power of man to achieve. Nonetheless, in his struggle, Maine advanced the cause of philosophy in France:

> In the history of French philosophy, his work opens the way for the teachings of Ravaisson, of Lachelier, and more particularly, perhaps, of Bergson who seeks to grasp the "moi" under the even more stringent conditions in which the sense of effort is also an experience of liberty. It is the trial of philosophers of this kind to be working on a rich, inexhaustible and endless subject. The grandeur of their struggle is in exploring a mystery not by dreaming about it like poets, but like scholars and sages, by thinking it out. (ibid.)

8 THE TWO GREAT BOOKS OF 1925

In the year 1924 to 1925 Gilson published two other books, probably his greatest achievements of the decade. The first was his magistral study of St Bonaventure, and the second was his edition, with notes and commentary, of Descartes *Discours de la méthode*. Both were the culmination of long years of intensive study.

La philosophie de saint Bonaventure (Paris, 1924; McG 118) had been gestating since 1913 when Gilson had first approached the topic as a private research project in Lille. He had continued the project during the war years behind the lines, in the trenches, and as a prisoner. Some of his work on St Bonaventure had appeared incidentally in his Strasbourg *Études* and in the *La philosophie au moyen âge*; he had also published one short article on the existence of God according to St Bonaventure in Louvain's *Revue néo-scolastique de philosophie* (25 [1923]; 237-262; McG 436); this article was incorporated into chapter 5 of the book.

Gilson's St Bonaventure was a Christian philosopher whose philosophy was expounded from within the theological order. He was not an aristotelian, but an authentic augustinian. Aristotle sought the sufficient reason of the universe in natural things, and placed great confidence in humanistic science and culture. Bonaventure, on the other hand, like Augustine, accepted the self-consciousness of the soul; his thought was God-centred and mystically oriented, and his doctrine essentially religious. Although Bonaventure employed some aristotelian doctrines, especially those concerned with the modes and processes of human knowledge and with the theory of abstraction, he employed them only as useful adjuncts to his own positions, and notably to illumination. Gilson's Bonaventure respected Aristotle but held him accountable for the humanistic error that later corrupted the medieval aristotelianism of the Dominicans and others. In his concluding chapter, Gilson brilliantly denounces the portrait proffered by De Wulf and the neoscholastics of the Middle Ages as intellectually aligned:

> St Bonaventure's doctrine marks, in my eyes, the peak of Christian mysticism, and forms its most complete synthesis. Hence will be seen without any difficulty that it is not in any rigorous sense comparable on any point to St Thomas' doctrine. Certainly to deny the two any fundamental agreement would be absurd: both are Christian philosophies, and any assault on faith finds them one in resisting it. Let pantheism rear its ugly head, and both are there teaching *creatio ex nihilo* and insisting that there is an infinite distance between being *per se* and participated being. Confronted by ontologism, both deny *formaliter* that God can be reached by human thought from this life. ... They are in profound indestructible agreement where they are supported by long tradition and the test of time, and in matters not contested in even the bitterest doctrinal disputes. If their two philosophies are equally Christian and satisfy the conditions of revelation, they remain notwithstanding two distinct philosophies. This is, no doubt, why Sixtus v in 1588 and Leo xiii after him in 1879 ... spoke of them as two sources of nourishment and light: *duae olivae et duo candelabra in domo Dei lucentia.* (pp. 472-473; tr.)

Non-Catholic and university philosophers were generally puzzled by *Saint Bonaventure* when it appeared. Among Catholics it had a mixed reception. A number of thomists were largely in agreement with the book.* One of these, Gabriel Théry, drew very close to Gilson, and in 1926 became his associate in launching the *Archives d'histoire doctrinale et littéraire du moyen âge*.

In its presentation of Bonaventure as an anti-thomist Christian philosopher, Gilson's book was unacceptable to his friends De Wulf and Mandonnet. Both men had a considerable stake in the development of Bonaventurean scholarship. De Wulf had consistently maintained that the thirteenth century was marked by a scholastic synthesis that reached its peak in Thomas. He considered St Bonaventure a pre- or incipient thomist, an imperfect representative of the high scholasticism of the late augustinian or early thomist stream. He was certainly not prepared to accept an augustinian Bonaventure who was unreceptive, even hostile, to Aristotle. Mandonnet meanwhile had long taken Bonaventure to be a neoplatonic augustinian who, in his failure to distinguish the object of theology from the object of philosophy, was not a philosopher at all. De Wulf eventually made a concession to Gilson in the fourth edition of his *Histoire de la philosophie médiévale* (1926): he ceased to speak of a "scholastic synthesis," modifying his terminology in line with Baeumker's *Gemeingut* to "common patrimony." Mandonnet, however, remained adamant: because philosophy was not to be confused

---

* See John F. Quinn, *The Historical Constitution of St Bonaventure's Philosophy* (Toronto, 1973), p. 27, n. 26.

with religion, no disciple of St Augustine could be called a philosopher (*Bulletin thomiste* 3, 2 [March 1926]).

The controversy surrounding Gilson's interpretation of St Bonaventure was later renewed in the 1930s and 1940s over the application of St Augustine's "Christian philosophy." Eminent scholars, such as Fernand Van Steenberghen of Louvain and the Franciscan Père Robert, used further research into Bonaventure's writings and into the methods and quarrels of the schools of Paris to range themselves against Gilson and to disagree with one another.*

Gilson's second important book in the mid-1920s was his *René Descartes: Discours de la méthode: texte et commentaire* (Paris, 1925; McG 177). Again, Gilson had been working on this book for a long time; its ideas can be traced through the courses on Descartes he gave at Lille, Strasbourg and Paris, all the way back to his doctoral theses. The work reflects Gilson's intense and continuing interest in French university philosophy.

Léon Brunschvicg had first suggested to Gilson that he prepare this volume. After Gilson took it on, he decided the chore could better be performed collectively by the members of the Société Française de Philosophie. In 1924 he proposed that the Société take over the project, and pointed out that they had collaborated on this kind of work before. In 1902 they had collectively undertaken to produce the now-published *Vocabulaire de la philosophie* under the general editorship of André Lalande; the work had increased its authority with such official authors as Conturat, Delbos, Belot, Egger, Halévy, and Lachelier, and with names such as Maurice Blondel, Laberthonnière and Bethelot in its supplementary *rez-de-chausée* footnotes. However, the Société as a group disagreed with Gilson. Even Lalande opposed the idea, maintaining that collaboration made for conflicting interpretations, unclear submissions and a slower schedule. In the course of his argument Gilson quoted Descartes from part 1 of the *Discours*: "Good sense is the most widely shared thing in the world because everyone thinks himself to be so well provided with it" (p. 1, l. 18). When Gilson added, innocently perhaps, that the statement was "certainly ironical," some members disagreed. The subsequent dispute made collaboration a dead issue. And indeed, when Gilson's own commentary on the line appeared, his long and erudite explication did not include a word about irony.

Gilson described his commentary as "personal reflection" and anything but definitive. In the first edition he acknowledged indebtedness to Lucien Lévy-Bruhl, Léon Brunschvicg, André Lalande and Henri Gouhier. In the second edition he added the names of Ch. Adam, M. le Dr Lecène, Charles Blondel, Abbé Émile Bautin, P. Villey, Gustave Cohen and Cornelis de Waard, all of whom had submitted corrections. The change in Gilson's note to p. 11, l. 11 offers an example of this delayed collaboration. Descartes describes himself here as "en-

---

* For the history of these controversies, along with a detailed and extensive analysis of the pertinent doctrinal issues in the writings of St Bonaventure, see once again John F. Quinn's *The Historical Constitution of St Bonaventure's Philosophy* (Toronto, 1973).

fermé seul dans un poêle" all the day long. In the first edition Gilson, perhaps re-
calling his own days in Bourg-en-Bresse, interpreted this, German manner, as "in
a stuffy room heated by a cook stove." The second edition however incorporated
Bautin's suggestion that the expression "dans un poêle" refers to more than
warmth and designates an actual room:

> However large a house was, it never contained more than one *poêle* – the room
> behind the kitchen. This room is warmed by the kitchen stove which is built right
> into the intervening wall. This is why the room is called the *poêle*. It is the best
> room in the house. Such rooms are still found in Lorraine and are kept for
> distinguished visitors. I prefer to think of Descartes as being put up in such a
> guestroom all the day long, his hosts never intruding, not even to rebuild the fire.

Gilson's commentary in the *Discours: texte et commentaire* is encyclopedic in
breadth – four hundred pages against less than one hundred of text. His
explication is highly personal and illustrates that simply to read the *Discours* is by
no means to understand it. Countless scholars around the world regard Gilson's
commentary as among the most enjoyable and rewarding reading of their lives.

Shortly after the publication of *Saint Bonaventure*, Gilson had been offered his
first honorary degree. It was awarded to him by the University of St Andrew's,
Scotland, for his considerable contribution to medieval studies. Two amusing
incidents attended the convocation. At the dinner in Gilson's honour, the
chancellor, with soccer in mind, proclaimed, "We are delighted to welcome to
Scotland a scholar from that country which, like ours, sometimes administers real
lickings to the English." And at the convocation, after a dignified and flattering
citation had been read over Gilson by a dour dean, a student, conscious of St
Andrew's golfing prestige, cried out: "What's his score?"*

Gilson was clearly moved by the honour tendered him in Scotland. *Discours:
texte et commentaire* carried the dedication: "To the University of St Andrew's: in
grateful homage. Étienne Gilson, LL.D." He was so pleased with the international
recognition that for once in his life he even identified himself as an LL.D rather
than his usual "Professor Gilson."

9 OTHER EARLY CONTROVERSIES

As has been seen, the appearance of *La philosophie de saint Bonaventure*
involved Gilson in a scholarly difference of opinion with De Wulf and Mandonnet, and later forced him to enter a debate concerning the nature of Christian
philosophy. Scholarly progress depends on healthy debates such as these, and
Gilson entered them with relish. However, *Saint Bonaventure* also gave rise to
another, less-healthy controversy.

---

* When Gilson recalled the anecdote in 1975, he insisted that "I had not then, nor have I ever
since, even so much as held a golf club in my hand;" no doubt he had forgotten his try at golf in the
summer of 1926 at Charlottesville.

Abbé O. Habert strongly resented the dabbling of a wicked Sorbonne professor in the delicacies of Christian mysticism and Catholic thought. On 24 October 1924 he placed a virulent anti-Gilson article entitled "Notes à propos d'études médié-vales" in *La vie catholique*. The attack opened with an ironic expression of satisfaction that the Sorbonne was finally beginning to examine medieval texts in depth. But, wrote Habert,

> Let us not be dupes. The professor admires the architecture of the temple, he lets himself be stirred by its sacred chants and moved by its thought as caught and shaped by modern philosophy. But he is himself still a stranger in that temple. ... I will never accept his distorted thomism. (pp. 9-10; tr.)

Habert then pretended to be shocked that Gilson, in a book review for the *Revue de métaphysique et de morale* (September 1922), had shown only praise for Delacroix' *La raison et la foi*:

> It I can be permitted to read between the lines, M. Gilson's real sympathies for a thomist aristotelianism and for a bonaventurian augustinianism might, to put it bluntly, boil down to only this: the one appears to bear the precious seeds of a rationalism to come ... the other to be a forerunner of Pascal and contemporary pragmatism. ... Generous and kindly as we should be to our fellow travellers, we still have to keep our wits about us. (ibid.)

Gilson was quick to respond. In perhaps his sharpest piece of writing to date, he showed how his words had been twisted and falsified into "a collection of theses which I don't recognize as my own." As for the review of Delacroix, Gilson admits to having employed the reviewer's technique of simply restating an author's arguments:

> Indeed, Habert's methods and mine are different: I wrote an analysis or review of Delacroix's book, presenting his ideas without criticizing them, a procedure unacceptable to the abbé whose method is, rather, to criticize my ideas without presenting them. ("Pour travailler tranquille," *La vie catholique*, 24.11.1; McG 759; tr.)

Gilson was equally incisive in his replies to the charges that he was "a stranger in the temple" and that he read the early Franciscans and Dominicans in a modern context.

At about this time another controversial situation arose in which Gilson was the agressor. Gilson published two critical articles, one dealing with François Villon and the other with Rabelais, in order to demonstrate "the interest which the history of religious ideas has for the study of French literature" ("Rabelais franciscain," *Revue d'histoire franciscaine*, 1 [1924]: 257; McG 415; tr.). Gilson wrote both articles partly with a view to criticizing his colleagues and partly to state a scholarly need for the strengthening of an interdisciplinary approach to medieval studies. Gilson eventually supplied this need himself with the founding of the *Archives d'histoire doctrinale et littéraire du moyen âge* and of the Toronto Institute of Mediaeval Studies.

The first of these controversial articles was "De la Bible à François Villon" (*Annuaire de l'École Pratique des Hautes Études* [1923-1924], pp. 3-24; McG 241). The article demonstrated Villon's copious use of sacred scripture and the strictly medieval character of his usage. It was not really offensive, but merely suggested that Gilson's literary colleagues were not so well informed in matters literary as they should be. The second article was less innocent. Entitled "Rabelais franciscain," it was patently critical of Abel Lefranc of the Collège de France, an authority on Rabelais.

Gilson and his good friend Henri Lemaître had planned together how best to illustrate through Rabelais the indebtedness of Renaissance and modern French literature to the scholastic thought of the Middle Ages; the article would be included in the first number of Lemaître's *Revue d'histoire franciscaine*. In November 1923, Lemaître wrote twice to Gilson on the subject outlining the kind of article called for:

> The first point to be dealt with is to show that Rabelais was a Franciscan, that he received a Franciscan education, that he lived a good part of his life among the Franciscans, and that this part of his life has not been given any importance by M. Abel Lefranc and his school. It has, however, been noted and commented upon by the Franciscan chronicler Lucas Wadding.
>
> Next, I think it will be easy for you to call to the reader's attention passages which can be clarified from an understanding of the Franciscan Doctors. Such passages are certainly numerous. Without citing all of them I am sure that a rapid inspection will produce enough of them to be convincing. This is important. If you prove that Rabelais' basic thought is medieval thought, that his position is not inconsistent with that of his predecessors, and that he was only critical of their methods with a view to ameliorating and improving them, Lefranc's theory which places Rabelais in modern times will collapse as worthless.
>
> Moreover, it would perhaps be better to postpone until a second article the question of Rabelais' style and presentation of thought. The public should not be left bewildered by the titillations of this subject. I am sure that your literary study on the Rabelaisian manner will be a lively success, but I do believe it will be even better if properly timed. It should be your trump card. It will finish off the Society for Rabelaisian Studies. It will dissipate in a fit of laughter all those *pissintunicos* who have no idea what Franciscan joviality is like. (23.11.6; tr.)

As a reading of "Rabelais franciscain" quickly shows, the entire plan of Gilson's article is covered here. The article proceeds in four stages. First, Rabelais is shown to have been a Franciscan. Next, "scholastic notes" are supplied for fifteen terms found in *Gargantua* and *Pantagruel*, all of them echoing medieval terms of technology and philosophy. Third, examples of Franciscan "salt" are taken from Salembene and others, not as evidence that Rabelais had ceased to be a Christian and was a rationalist in the modern sense, but only to demonstrate that Rabelaisian "salt" was typically Franciscan. Finally, Rabelais is shown to have been known among chroniclers of the order as one of its writers. In general, Gilson focussed less on franciscan and more on scholasticism than Lemaître suggests, and he includes the salty section which Lemaître would have saved for a later article. Otherwise, he follows Lemaître's suggestions to the letter.

Has Gilson *proved* that Rabelais was not an atheist? His own answer is clear:

> Not at all. I have, I think, simply shown that the norm of what was in those days acceptable, what excessive, in the matter of jokes, even religious jokes, escapes us. Moreover, it is not going to be settled by the impressions of some professor of the Sorbonne [Gilson himself] or of the Collège de France [Abel Lefranc] in this year of grace 1924 merely by reading the text of Rabelais. In truth scholars are a very long way at present from being in a position even to ask such questions. Rather, the Middle Ages must be studied first as one of the principal data conditioning any solution. ("Rabelais franciscain," p. 289; tr.)

Gilson was afraid that his bluntness in "Rabelais franciscain" might have hurt Lefranc's feelings, and with misgivings he sent him an offprint with an explanatory letter. Lefranc's reply, from his summer home in Bellevue, was quick and courteous:

> Need I tell you that your article in the *Revue d'histoire franciscaine* was of great interest to me? I believe that your explanations and interpretations must be kept and made use of. Thanks to your deep knowledge of the scholastic vocabulary, you have recovered the exact and special meaning of a whole series of expressions which successive editions of the Master, up to and including my own, have not made clear with all the justice one might desire. I have not yet taken these up with the particular collaborator whose task it was to explain these various expressions. You have managed to present your results with great courtesy, as I am fully aware. For my part, reading you, I had somewhere back in my mind that kind of satisfaction which a new and convincing solution creates. As for what touches on the question of the rationalism of Rabelais (I employ the word because it is the most useful) I have still a number of things to say. I stick with my conclusions and can support them with new arguments. Besides, you have not thought it necessary to take sides. (Lefranc to EG, 24.7.26; tr.)

Although Lefranc and Rabelais the Franciscan were dropped for the time being, the issue later provided Gilson with at least one impromptu lecture, before the Alliance Française in Boston, January 1927. The Franciscans also played an instrumental role in Gilson's first visit to Canada in the spring of 1926.

8

Annus Mirabilis, 1926

In many ways 1926 was Gilson's *annus mirabilis*, his year of crowning achievement. During this year his reputation in France became assured, and even the sceptical among the Catholics softened toward him. He also at this time established his *Archives d'histoire doctrinale et littéraire du moyen âge*, a learned journal totally dedicated to medieval thought and its history. Finally, Gilson dominated two important 1926 congresses, a national one held in Canada and an international one in the United States. These initiated his life-long activities to promote the study of medieval thought and to organize medieval studies.

Gilson's year got underway with an exciting meeting of the Société Française de Philosophie, 13 February 1926. At this meeting Léon Brunschvicg presented a somewhat alarmist paper on "Conditions for the Existence of Graduate Instruction in Philosophy" (*Bulletin de la Société Française de Philosophie*, 26 [1926]: 1-27). In 1926 French universities were feeling the effects of a new apathy in philosophical studies. Brunschvicg argued that too many universities were teaching philosophy and that good professors were too thinly spread throughout the many provincial universities. He maintained that a concentration of teaching strength in a very limited number of centres was required. Gilson and others disagreed. Brunschvicg, observed Gilson, wants to provide students with good professors. Surely the problem is the reverse: there are not enough properly-prepared students for existing professors to teach. Gilson could not put this problem out of his mind, and took it to North America with him. Speaking in April before the French Benevolent Society, he invited Premier Taschereau, who was present with Colonel Georges Vanier, to encourage more French-Canadian students to study philosophy in Paris. And at Harvard the next fall he began to seriously consider emigrating to the United States which seemed to possess so many more appreciative students.

Gilson's first voyage to North America apparently came about when Rector Gabriel Lapie was unable to attend a congress in Montréal. On 25 March 1926 Dean Ferdinand Brunot wrote Gilson:

> The rector has informed me that, in conformity with your expressed desire, he is granting you the necessary leave of absence to attend the Congress on Moral Education in Montréal, Canada. (26.3.25; tr.)

In a letter written 7 April 1926, when Gilson was already in Montréal, Brunot added that the Minister of Public Instruction had no objection to his attending "the meeting of the National Council to be held in Montréal (Canada)." Gilson had only one week, then, in which to prepare for his trip and write his address.

If Brunot's two letters revealed some uncertainty about the name of the congress, there was good reason. The Canadian National Educational Council, which sponsored the conference, had no formal connection with the universities of Canada. The council was the creation of the Canadian Industrial Reconstruction Association which had been formed after World War I to encourage domestic industry, imperial ties, and resistance to postwar socialism. The leading personalities in the Canadian National Educational Council were neither university administrators nor professional scholars; rather they were industrialists like W. J. Bulman of Winnipeg, Vincent Massey of Toronto and Henry Cockshutt of Brantford, and financiers like James Richardson of Winnipeg and Sir Edward Beatty of Montréal, president of the Canadian Pacific Railway. The council wanted to produce better Canadian citizens by means of education; it was particularly influenced by John Dewey, whose recent writings were very popular in Western Canada, the home of many of the council's founders.

The National Council had decided that, in order to improve education in Canada, an educational lobby should be established in Ottawa, the national capital. Because education in Canada was a provincial rather than federal matter, this decision had created considerable controversy, particularly in Québec. The council's first two eductional conventions, in Winnipeg and Toronto, had taken the theme "Education and Citizenship." However, because the third convention was to be held in Montréal, the theme had been modified to "Education and Co-operation" in deference to the French Canadians.

The third convention took place 5 to 10 April 1926. Speakers included foreign delegations from the United States, Britain and France. The French delegation consisted of three speakers, each representing some new development in education. First was Senator André Honnorat, former Minister of Public Instruction and now the official protagonist for the Cité Universitaire; he was to speak about La Maison Canadienne, currently under construction in the Cité. Second was Professor Jean Brunhes of the Collège de France, whose chair was in the newly recognized discipline of human geography; his presence was particularly appropriate as the University of Montréal, former succursal of Laval University, had just appointed Canada's first professor of geography. Third was Étienne Gilson, with his ground-breaking approach to the history of medieval philosophy. Equally avant-garde in academic circles were the speakers from Britain and the United States.

Gilson sailed to Canada on the CPR steamship *Montcalm*. He disembarked at the winter port of St John, New Brunswick, on 2 April 1926. He then travelled by boat-train to Montréal, and stayed at the Mount Royal Hotel where sessions of the conference were held.

On 5 April Vincent Massey delivered the opening presidential address and announced that the council had abandoned its plans for an Ottawa lobby; Massey was shortly to leave the council's executive to become Canada's new minister to Washington. The next morning, Tuesday 6 April, the two first papers were given. Sir John Adams, professor of education at University of London, gave the first on "The Importance of Language in Education," a subject combining the theme of the congress with his own emerging speciality.

By the time Gilson rose to give his paper, two sour notes already had been struck. Just before the opening of the congress, representatives from the Association Catholique de la Jeunesse Canadienne-Française and from Laval's campus newspaper had raised strong objections on constitutional grounds to the very notion of a national education conference. Then, while reading his paper, Sir John Adams quite unconsciously offended many Québecois by emphasizing the superiority of a pure language, like Parisian French, over local dialects; apart from its dubious linguistic validity, this theory was politically simplistic and highly provocative. Thus, although Gilson's paper was successful, it could not compensate for Adams' gaffe any more than could subsequent statements by Vincent Massey, the Duchess of Athol, Thomas Hunt Morgan and by Gilson himself.

Despite these awkward circumstances, Gilson's paper on thomism was warmly received at the congress. Both Laval and Montréal had long since embraced St Thomas; indeed, Laval's interest in the philosopher dated back to 1884, the year of Gilson's birth. Nowhere in North America, and in few places in the world, could an audience have been found more capable of understanding Gilson's approach to thomism. Gilson's insistence upon essential thomism, shorn of modern applications and Catholic bias, was warmly appreciated for the breakthrough it was (*Le devoir*, Montréal, 26.4.7). Many present must also have found a paper on essential thomism an ironic choice for an assembly inspired philosophically by John Dewey.

On Wednesday 7 April a special convocation was called by the University of Montréal in honour of Brunhes and Gilson. Present at the affair were the university's rector, Mgr Piette, his administrative officers, some fifty members of his teaching staff, and a number of guests including Colonel Bovey (representing McGill), Baron de Vitrolles (consul-general of France), and C. F. Delage (Québec's superintendant of education). Gilson valued the honorary degree and carefully preserved the diploma, the second of the score or more he would receive in his lifetime.

On Thursday 8 April, Le Cercle Universitaire tendered a luncheon to Gilson and Brunhes. Gilson took the opportunity to redress Adams' blunder. He described his friendship in a German camp with a fellow prisoner who was originally French-Canadian; together they had taught French to their non-French fellows. This man had inspired in Gilson a longing to visit Québec. And now that he was here at last, he realized that French-Canadians were "plus nous-même que nous-même" – more ourselves than ourselves (*Le devoir*, 26.4.9). From this luncheon, and from visits to a few Montréal homes, came Gilson's earliest Montréal friendships, with the Thibaudeaus, the Beaulieus and Édouard Montpetit. Indeed, the seventy-eight guests named in the newspaper account encompassed much of the elite of French-speaking Montréal society.

On Saturday 10 April, the day after the congress closed, Gilson gave a public lecture in the auditorium of the Grand Seminary of Saint-Sulpice. The lecture was at the invitation of the University of Montréal philosophy faculty as well as of the Canadian province of the Franciscans; the Franciscans were initiating a cycle of celebrations marking the seven-hundredth anniversary of the death of St Francis of Assisi. Gilson's address remains a highlight in his North America career. Its topic was "Saint Thomas et la pensée franciscaine" (*Orient*, 10 [1926]: 247-253, 268-291, 329-335; McG 442). In his introduction to a published version of the lecture, the editor of *La revue franciscaine* wrote:

> This lecture actually created Gilson's reputation in Canada, even as it filled all who heard it with admiration for those masters of Franciscan thought who drew their authentic inspiration from St Francis himself (*Le VIIe centenaire de la mort de saint François* ... [Montréal, 1928], p. 45; McG 205).

The lecture also provided Gilson with an opportunity to call attention to the major thesis of his recent *La philosophie de saint Bonaventure*, by arguing that the Seraphic Doctor was not a thomist but a valid Christian philosopher in his own right.

The lecture reads today as a brilliant if extravagant rhetorical discourse. It opens quietly enough, referring to St Thomas whom "the University of Montréal has chosen as its guide and master." It then contrasts the movement of St Thomas' thought with that of the Franciscan masters: "St Thomas sets out from man's actions and moves on to the perfection of his contemplative life in humility; the Franciscans, however, moved from an "apotheosis of humility to the existence of a Franciscan philosophy – *a fide inchoans ad speciem tendans*." Gilson finally maintains that the scholar cannot possibly analyze St Francis as he does St Thomas, and appeals to the wise counsel of Bergson:

> Look how all developments return to certain principal theses, and how these theses return to one alone, and how this one thesis can be reduced to a kind of first image born from the unique and ineffable intuition from which the whole system flows. (*Orient*, p. 253; tr.)

Gilson strains in search of this "first image," invoking a metaphor familiar to the Québecois, who have just emerged from maple-syrup season:

> There can be seen ... under the bark of dialectic, without which there can be no philosophy at all, a plentiful sap which circulates, the source of which I am trying to point out to you in the spiritual life of St Francis (p. 247; tr.)

Frédéric Lefèvre later recorded an incident that took place on this same platform of Saint-Sulpice:

> Jean Brunhes told me about the success of his friend and companion Étienne Gilson, their fraternal co-operation, Gilson's lecture on St Francis of Assisi, and the episode when the rector of the University of Montréal unexpectedly called upon

Brunhes to talk about human geography in the thirteenth century. Gilson, upset by the distress of Jean Brunhes, prompted him in a hoarse whisper: "The routes of the Middle Ages!" Brunhes, taking off from there, spoke for three quarters of an hour on the routes, the methods of transport, the pilgrimages, peaking with the creation of the University of Oxford "which had only been created because the war had closed the route across the English Channel." ("Une heure avec Jean Brunhes," *Les nouvelles littéraires*, 26.10.30; tr.)

When Gilson read Lefèvre's account in the copy of *Les nouvelles littéraires* that Thérèse sent him at Harvard, he wrote back as follows:

I even supplied him with the story about the founding of Oxford, which he had not known. I drew up the outline of his talk in the minute during which the rector was finishing his remarks; may I add that Brunhes did not follow my outline very closely. (26.11.18; tr.)

Both Brunhes and the editor of *La revue franciscaine* specifically referred to Gilson's "success" in Montréal. Certainly he emerged from the National Congress with a considerably widened public reputation. He did not exactly "save" the National Council: it only survived one more congress, in Victoria and Vancouver in 1929. He did, however, prove himself an able emissary for two barely compatible causes: *Le thomisme* and *La république*.

After a state dinner held in Montréal's Ritz Carlton, the three members of the French delegation travelled to Québec City. There they attended the fiftieth-anniversary meeting of the French Benevolent Society and a regular meeting of the Institut Canadien at Université Laval. In the world of international scholarship, Gilson's career as an informal ambassador-at-large for France was underway.

2 Spring and Early Summer, 1926

In mid-April Gilson returned to Europe aboard the CPR liner *Melita*. He at once resumed his struggle with the Ministry of Public Instruction for a university chair. This time he won a partial victory: the ministry compromised by naming him *professeur sans chaire* effective November 1926. This concession was probably influenced less by Gilson's success in Montréal than by a request from Harvard that he be named its next exchange professor from the Sorbonne. It would hardly have been appropriate for the Sorbonne to send a mere *maître de conférence*; since 1911 the university had sent to Harvard such esteemed scholars as Legouis, Lévy-Bruhl, Feuillerat and Jeanroy. The official decree naming Gilson *professeur sans chaire* is dated 6 May 1926, and the official appointment from the president and fellows of Harvard is dated 12 May 1926. On 25 June 1926, Gilson's salary category was also raised, from third class to second.

Between his first visit to Canada in April 1926 and his first to the United States at the end of July, Gilson devoted much of his time and energy to launching his *Archives d'histoire doctrinale et littéraire du moyen âge*. The journal was originally the brainchild of Père Gabriel Théry OP of the Saulchoir. According to Gilson, Théry was gifted with a "mind overflowing [*regorgeant*] with projects which he was always ready to take on, gifted as he was with a rare facility for work and for expressing himself with the uninhibited freedom of a man unable to remain silent about anything striking him as right" ("In memoriam," *Archives*, 26 [1959]: 7; tr.).

Théry suggested the magazine and its title in a brief chat with Gilson outside the door of the Salle des Manuscrits of the Bibliothèque Nationale. Within ten minutes, the two very different men agreed to establish a publication dedicated to healing the rift between the history of medieval thought and the history of medieval letters. Over the next few weeks, they talked the project over with Joseph Vrin. They then announced the *Archives* in a short brochure which, strangely enough, they printed and circulated without title, author or date.

Vrin was to be the "editor" of the *Archives*, totally responsible for its publication, management and financing. The two founding-directors assumed joint responsibility for policy decisions and for reading submitted manuscripts. The *Archives* was to provide medieval philosophy and letters with their own periodical, a back-burner on which the discoveries of researchers could simmer until historians and other scholars were ready to deal with them. The list of caveats was typical of Gilson's dislikes: no book reviews, no abstract doctrinal discussion, no polemics. The periodical was to be a researcher's tool, and was to offer historical and scientific detachment; espousing no causes, it was simply to render scholarly achievement visible.

Each of the two directors placed an article in the first number. Gilson's lead-article was entitled "Why St Thomas Criticized St Augustine" (*Archives*, 1 [1926]: 5-127; McG 405). It summarized his daily classroom work on Thomas-Augustine relations and foreshadowed both his monograph on Augustine in 1929 and his flurry of articles and papers in 1930. Théry's contribution was the critical re-edition of a text from a Soest manuscript recording the famous trial of Eckhart, an important text in the history of medieval thought. The first issue also included the text of a group of works by Franciscan masters prepared by Ephrem Longpré, a Canadian scholar much commended by Gilson during his April visit to Canada. Indeed, the content of the *Archives* throughout Gilson's lifetime frequently reflected episodes from his life.

The Gilson-Théry collaboration lasted until Théry's detainment in Africa at the outbreak of World War II. It was a profitable relationship, though not an easy one. Each man was critical of the other. Théry felt that Gilson was intellectually rash in using scholarly methodology to probe the interior life and mystical experience of St Bonaventure (*Revue des sciences philosophiques et théologiques*, 13 [1924]: 252). And Gilson considered Théry too offhand in practical matters; on his frequent nonacademic missions to the East and to Africa, Théry often left no address where he could be reached, even by his own master-general. Even in Gilson's warm "In Memoriam" he could not refrain from mentioning Théry's absences:

I have sometimes a kind of feeling that Père Théry has just gone off on one more absence, as he used at times to do for a year or two, and that he will be returning with the same simplicity that marked all his returns: first, a warm and friendly word that went straight to your heart; then, suddenly, some great new project which he could hardly wait to tell you about. ("In Memoriam R. P. Gabriel Théry OP [1890-1959]," *Archives*, 26 [1959]: 7; McG 306.)

The long-suffering victim of both Gilson and Théry was Joseph Vrin. According to his grandson, Gérard de Paulhac, Vrin often spoke of Gilson as "mon purgatoire."

Théry was one of those rare intellectuals who never failed to charm. He brought *Archives*, with its circulation of less than nine hundred, a considerable percentage of its subscribers. He even cajoled the master-general of the Dominicans into soliciting subscriptions from all the order's houses. Gilson often remarked with amusement how a full run of *Archives* could be located: "There was always," he said, "somewhere a small Dominican house in possession of a complete run of the journal, neither constantly in use nor indispensable."

Despite their differences the two directors and the editor founded a first-class journal of interdisciplinary medieval research. During the years following World War II, Thérèse d'Alverny became associated with it, kept it healthy and gradually took over, with the result that it survived the death of all three founders.

3 The University of Virginia, Summer 1926

Two separate incidents turned Gilson's thoughts to teaching in America. The first was the meeting of the Société Française de Philosophie, 13 February 1926, in which Léon Brunschvicg had called attention to the lack of teachers and students of philosophy (above, p. 133). The second was a conversation with Albert G. A. Balz, Corcoran Professor of Philosophy in the University of Virginia. When Balz asked Gilson why he didn't visit the United States, Gilson replied that his English was poor. "That makes no difference," Balz assured him. "We all speak bad English; in America you simply go ahead and speak it in your own way." (Interview, 1974.) Thus, when Gilson agreed to attend the Sixth International Congress of Philosophy at Harvard in September 1926, he arranged with Balz to go to Charlottesville first and give a summer course in French philosophy at the University of Virginia. He also arranged to stay on at Harvard for the semester after the congress as visiting professor from the Sorbonne.

Shortly after the close of the school year in July, the four Gilsons went from Melun to Maman's house in Paris for a short visit. On 20 July Gilson and Thérèse said their tearful goodbyes; because Thérèse was too upset to risk a separation in public, only Maman and the girls accompanied him to the station. Gilson took the train to Le Havre and sailed first class on the *Savoie*, "expenses paid," for New York. Thérèse, Jacqueline and Cécile set off in the opposite direction for two months holiday at Clos des Hirondelles, Golfe-Juan in Alpes-Maritime. This separation was the first of many to interfere with Gilson's family life in the next years.

Gilson was travelling on a diplomatic visa as a member of France's official delegation to the congress. Just after he boarded the *Savoie* at Le Havre, he wrote to Thérèse and reflected upon the changing horizons of his life. Twenty years earlier, in 1904, he had visited this seaport during his military service:

> I remember at that time hearing people whose way of life was different from mine talking about their crossings. The limits of my world then were three: Le Havre in the west, Avallon to the east, Angoulême to the south. (26.7.20; tr.)

Even the ship's newspapers seemed like omens, and he cut two clippings for Thérèse and Maman. One was a photograph of last year's Harvard exchange professor to the Sorbonne, J. D. M. Ford, surrounded by a group of fifteen Sorbonne professors. The other was a photograph of Mme Léon Brunschvicg, the suffragette wife of Gilson's Sorbonne master and colleague, who was now campaigning for the right of Frenchwomen to vote. Both Gilson and his world were changing!

When Gilson arrived in New York for the first time, he knew no one. He spent his day visiting Columbia University and the University Club, and touring the city by bus. Gilson carried a letter of introduction to Columbia from Richard McKeon, an American student at the École. But although he had no trouble at the club or the university, the visit was not memorable. By evening he was tired, and dined alone in a restaurant. He caught the night train for Charlottesville and retired early to the sleeper. The next morning Professor Balz met him at the station, took him home for breakfast, and escorted him to the Colonnade Club where he was to live for the next month.

Gilson's first impressions of life in Charlottesville and in Thomas Jefferson's University of Virginia were not especially favourable. Shortly after reaching his room in the Colonnade, he wrote a number of rather ill-humoured observations for Thérèse. The weather produced "the impression of living in a steambath." The students, whom he had only seen walking across the campus, "all drive cars and carry no books; they appear to regard the university as an occasion for meeting one another in a country setting, courses being an afterthought." As for Prohibition, "people here drink grape juice, coca-cola and water. ... A colleague kindly invited me to taste a drink that was as alcoholic as it was prohibited. I declined. I am afraid of alcohols I don't know." All this, of course, was to change. Gilson quickly grew to love Virginia's climate and mountains, and he came, as always, to respect his students. Nor did he fatigue himself greatly declining either food or drink.

Charlottesville introduced Gilson to a different and less sophisticated academic climate. The relaxed summer tempo and Charlottesville's graceful southern civility soon won him over. At first he lectured for the entire hour, concentrating on his English delivery: "My delivery," he wrote, "is both bad and good, perhaps bad rather than good. No matter! No deaths have been reported yet." After about four lectures, he began using the last ten minutes of each period for a summary of the lecture in French; this device attracted a few new students who wanted to keep up their French. Gilson's students were a varied lot, mostly eager young men, two "girls philosophiques," three professors, and a number of married women, such as Mrs Blake, Mrs Randolph, Mrs Godwin, Mrs Neff, Mrs Balz and Mrs Forsythe. These women soon began to invite Gilson to lunch and dine in their homes. They arranged for him to accompany their families on trips into the nearby countryside, and persuaded him to take the classic excursion to Monticello, the beautiful mountain home of Thomas Jefferson. All in all life became very satisfactory:

> My students are most gracious and seem to be interested in the course in spite of my atrocious English. Two of the girls, with infinite good will, are lost in these philosophical systems we are examining and which do seem to spin out one after the other with little stability. Apparently I have to set an examination. So goes my humble life – at one time putting questions to my own Jacqui and Céci, at another to American college girls. The philosophers lot! (EG to Thérèse, 26.8.17; tr.)

Occasionally at Charlottesville classes were held on the lawns under a tree, decidedly a new experience for Gilson. One day, he reported, a "colossal dog" joined an open-air class. Gilson introduced the lecture: "Today we are going to deal with the sceptics." Much to the delight of class, the dog howled. Gilson continued: "I observe that the philosophy I am to deal with today is offensive even to a dog."* Gilson found the laughter of his students gratifying. He wrote Thérèse that "I am now beginning to make people laugh, even speaking in English" (26.8.28).

Gilson gave two courses at Virginia, with thirty lectures each: "The Development of Thought from the Twelfth to the Sixteenth Centuries" and "The Evolution of French Thought Since the Sixteenth Century." In both he supplemented his formal lectures with tutorials in which students translated specified passages of French philosophy into English, and provided a succinct summary of the philosophical point raised in each. In the final examination for "The Evolution of French Thought" Gilson asked the students to write a general account of one the the systems. He was agreeably surprised when he read the answers, which repeated the points made in the lectures without distortion. Clearly the students had learned something about French philosophy and he was coming to know English.

Gilson much appreciated his students' help with the language. A decade later, when he returned to Virginia to give the Richards Lectures in 1937, he gratefully acknowledged in the foreward to his published lectures, his "students of the Summer School of 1926 who kindly helped me through a difficult task" (*Reason and Revelation* [1938]).

---

* A related dog story comes much later in Gilson's career. In the 1960s a dog regularly accompanied its owner to Gilson's course at Berkeley (below, pp. 380-381). Suddenly the dog no longer came. "Why not?" asked Gilson. "We had just reached the transcendentals!"

Gilson seems at first to have found life in Charlottesville too quiet and lonely: "I generally dine at 6:30 or 7:00, rather too close to lunch time. After dinner I don't know what to do other than play billiards and bridge. When I go to bed I fall asleep thinking about everything in the world, but particularly about my *femmette*." (EG to Thérèse, 26.8.22; tr.). He missed Thérèse a great deal: "How far away you are, my well-beloved! How empty our lives would be if we thought we were really alone, that we were one only without the other." (26.8.29; tr.) In the first weeks his activities, apart from teaching, were limited to reading the proofs of the third edition of *Le thomism*, sent to him by Vrin: "I am reminded of my normal occupation and everything somehow seems strange." He also read a new American novel, *Babbitt*, by Sinclair Lewis:

> It is the portrait of an American businessman; the caricature is very entertaining, and the intellectuals are enjoying it immensely. I think it will be untranslatable; a good deal of its humour is dependent upon language and details familiar to Americans. The humour smacks a little of the farmyard. (EG to Thérèse, 26.8.17; tr.)

After the middle of August, social events became more numerous. Gilson was thrilled by his glimpses into Charlottesville society. His letters to Thérèse describe many events in detail, and offer an interesting social portrait of the mid-1920s. The letters focused on Mrs Blake and her circle and on the family of Professor Balz, subjects likely to interest Thérèse.

The Blakes were influential businesspeople in Charlottesville. Both husband and wife were independently wealthy; Mrs Blake's father had made his fortune in Chicago as a designer and decorator for department stores. Mrs Blake spoke French fluently. Normally she spent about three months of the year in Charlottesville at her mother's home and spent the other nine months commuting between her villa at Cap Martin near Nice and her appartment on rue Montpensier near the Palais-Royal. This summer she attended all Gilson's lectures, and particularly enjoyed the French summaries. In late August she arranged a dinner for Gilson, through the mediation of Professor Balz.

When Gilson received his invitation to dinner, he asked Balz how he should dress. A day later, Mrs Blake stopped in at the Colonnade to tell him that dress was to be "tuxedo." Gilson was unfamiliar with this term; he was surprised to learn that the expression "un smoking" was unknown, and that one usually spoke simply of a "tux" or, more elegantly, of a "evening jacket." In any event, when Gilson learned that a "tuxedo" was de rigueur, he was delighted. "I will hoist my medal," he wrote "I haven't lost it yet." To embellish the medal, he asked Thérèse to "please send me in one of your letters a few centimeters of croix-de-guerre ribbon. Just a little, and put it in flat. I don't want the customs to open the letter suspecting there is lace in it. If they ever open the letter, my ribbon will be gone forever."

Gilson described the dinner to Thérèse in detail:

> Cocktails – *bien entendu*. A young woman, most pleasant, sips hers, finds it too strong, offers it to me. I say *merci non* politely. She insists. I simply have to take it.

Later I hide it in a corner. How bewildering! At table I am between Mrs Blake and her mother. No tablecloth. Netted mats under plates and glasses. *Potage* served in red lacquered bowls each with its own cover, brought from China by Mrs Blake herself. One roasted pigeon per person, served with sugared tomatoes, mashed potatoes, slices of fried eggplant. Lemon icecream. Coffee. Obligatory bridge, in English, from 8:30 to 11:00: four ladies, four gentlemen. Thanks to you, I was fairly well dressed. ... A charming little girl of eight years was introduced to me as Marie Laurentin, daughter of one of Mrs Blake's sisters. The little girl was wearing a long, silk, bright-blue dress. She asked me with a blush if I had a little girl. When I admitted to having two, she asked me, dropping her head, if I had brought them with me. I could only say "no." Then, after a brief pause, she begged me in a low voice to bring them next time. (EG to Thérèse, 26.8.24-26; tr.)

Gilson probably had an ulterior motive in passing along this moving little episode. Thérèse never came to like North America. Gilson did everything he could to attenuate that dislike, constantly writing to her about the pleasures of life as an American professor, about fine schools for little girls in the Boston area, and about the stream of French visitors that passed through the United States. "Existence here goes on in a tranquil routine which amazes me. Why wasn't I born in Virginia? And why haven't I been teaching philosophy to young Americans?" (EG to Thérèse, 26.8.20-22; tr.)

Although Gilson had many loftier reasons for accepting his posts in America, he was concerned that his separation from his family be financially worthwhile. Indeed, whenever he was separated from Thérèse in this and subsequent years, he was anxious to let her know whether the anguish of their loneliness was balanced by some improvement in their position. The first such accounting appeared when Gilson received his salary of $600 for the summer courses at Virginia:

During the afternoon of 3 September, I saw people standing around the cashier's office. I went in myself and timidly asked if there was a cheque for me. "It may be so" was the cashier's phlegmatic reply. After foraging through a packet of cheques, he tendered me one in the amount of $600. Now, my dear, listen closely: *I didn't steal it*. I am extremely proud of earning this money, not only by the sweat of my brow, but by the sweat of my entire body, and even, I dare say, of my mind. For once I award myself a high mark.

Gilson then produced an example of his unique book-keeping; this must have amused Thérèse, an expert in this department:

At present my finances are as follows:

Receipts:		
	Personal from royalties	920
	In the bank in Canada	200
	From Ministry Foreign Affairs	806
	From University Virginia	600
		2,026

Expenses:	Re preparation and crossing	186
	Travel and expenses, August	115
		301
Balance:		$2,225

My expenses before sailing were actually taken out of money brought back from Canada, which means that I have had more money on hand than is shown. The $186 shown has not actually been drawn from receipts shown. In fact, I have $1,600 in the bank, a cheque for $600, $200 in Canada, and $10 in my pocket: that is, $2,400 exclusive of pocket money. (EG to Thérèse, 26.9.3; tr.)

The living expenses to be deducted from this accounting were minimal: as an honorary member of the Colonial Club, his bill for room and board came to a total of $45 plus gratuities.

Gilson needed to find his trip profitable in order to justify his cruel separation from Thérèse. Shortly after he arrived in Cambridge, he wrote to her:

I see that our present separation is a bitter grief to you. You can be sure that I am not happy about it either. I have to go over and over again in my mind all the reasons I once had for our present situation just to explain to myself how I happen to be here at all. I believe I acted reasonably; I am not at all sure I acted well. What I feel confident about is that the way I have taken is the only escape open to us to a material future less wretched than our past life has been. Only time can tell how right or wrong our calculations were; and this in no way has any bearing on my present anguish in trying to live without you. I am lost, my dear, without your love and without our life together. (26.9.19; tr.)

A few days later he estimated that he would return to France with savings of 100,000 francs, "two little dowries for our young ladies" (26.9.24; tr.).

The last few days in Charlottesville, at "cette université au bois-dormant," were among the most delightful he had known. Professors Balz and Ecols entertained him and his summer students presented him with a new work by an American philosopher. He also received affectionate farewell notes from Mrs William Hall Goodwin and Mrs Wagenheim. During quiet and dreamy days in the deserted university, he completed his paper for the upcoming congress. He found the unfamiliar solitude a little daunting:

I spent my morning and afternoon, save for mass and breakfast, writing my communication for the Congress of Philosophy. I have just finished it and hope it will be tolerable, even though the subject I have been asked to write on is hardly an inspiring one. Besides I am so sluggish and lazy in this unfamiliar solitude that I cannot summon up courage to pass judgment on my work. (EG to Thérèse, 26.9.5; tr.)

On Thursday 9 September, Gilson travelled by train to Washington, where he stopped over for a day. On Saturday morning he arrived at South Station, Boston, where he was to board the rapid transit train for Harvard Square.

4 THE INTERNATIONAL CONGRESS OF PHILOSOPHY, 1926

When Gilson arrived at Boston, he found one of his students from Paris waiting for him. Gilson knew Zimmerman as a disturbed and sometimes bothersome young man. He was not altogether pleased to see him again, though he was grateful for company on the train to Harvard Square. Zimmerman proved himself a considerable nuisance over the next four weeks as he hovered possessively and made continual demands on Gilson's attention. Indeed, the young man's presence was perhaps the only sour note struck during this first period in Cambridge.

At Harvard Square, Professor Ralph Barton Perry met Gilson, delivered him from Zimmerman, and took him to his home at 133 Irving Street. Perry then turned Gilson over to his wife and rushed off on congress chores. For two days, Sunday and Monday, Mrs Perry introduced Gilson to the mysteries of Cambridge, including the skilful civic art of coping with prohibition. Gilson had met the Perrys before, at the Oxford Congress and at the French follow-up in 1921. They probably understood him, and his intense loneliness, better than anyone else in America.

The first scheduled event of the congress was an opening meeting and smoker at eight o'clock Monday evening. Gilson spent his Sunday and Monday afternoons familiarizing himself with his surroundings. Returning to the Perrys' from a leisurely walk on Monday afternoon, he found that he and Perry had been invited to an early dinner at the Harvard Club. Clearly Perry was opening doors for him. The other guests included President Lawrence Lowell of Harvard, President Nicholas Murray Butler of Columbia, and his own rector, Paul Lapie, who had just arrived in Cambridge with the French delegation. Gilson was flustered by this last-minute invitation to join so illustrious a group; "I reached for my black silk ultra-transparent socks and tried to pull one of them on, only to have it stick in my hand. Forget it!"

After a hasty but sumptuous dinner, Gilson found himself in Gore Hall awaiting the addresses of welcome. There were five of these: by Nicholas Murray Butler on behalf of the organizing committe; by A. Lawrence Lowell for Harvard; and by W. E. Hocking, R. C. Lodge and H. W. Stuart, on behalf of the respective Eastern, Western, and Pacific divisions of the American Philosophical Association. Irreverently Gilson complained to Thérèse: "*Discours... discours... discours.*" When these were over, and Lapie had replied at length, the reception began. "Thereupon, from some fifty strangers came: 'Oh yes, Professor Gilson. So glad to meet you!' etc. etc. At 11:30 one of these strangers wanted, or so it seemed to me, to march me right back to Toronto with him. The university there is set on getting me." This enthusiastic Toronto recruiter was probably Father Joseph T. Muckle, in Cambridge that September to work with E. K. Rand.

Gilson delivered his papers on Wednesday 15 September. He presented his major paper at a general session entitled "Le rôle de la philosophie dans l'histoire de la civilisation" (*Proceedings of the Sixth International Congress of Philosophy*

[New York and London, 1927], pp. 529-535; McG 433). Four other scholars also addressed this topic: Henry Osborne Taylor, John Dewey, Sarvepalli Radhakrishnan, and Benedetto Croce, whose paper was read by Raffaelo Piccoli. Gilson also read a shorter paper of twenty minutes at a sectional meeting of the historical group on a subject of his own choice, the role of Arab philosophers in the interpretation of scholasticism.

In its probing of the relations between philosophy and civilization, Gilson's major paper provided an interesting contrast with the views of the other four contributors to the session. In general terms Gilson was at odds with Croce, who rejected metaphysics, the transcendent, and all closed systems. He also disagreed with Dewey, who assigned philosophy no relation to any truth other than scientific statement and historical fact; Dewey preferred to consider thought in relation to meaning, a different and more transient concept than truth. Gilson was reasonably in accord with Radhakrishnan, a realist for whom religion was "not a life transforming but a life transcending" (p. 548). And he admired Taylor's astute presentation of a broad general thesis that defined the role of philosophy in the history of civilization as the application of reasons and definitions to the countless absorbing matters which have successively pressed upon the human mind.

Gilson presented his arguments strictly as a philosopher, refusing to take refuge behind the screen of his particular field of specialization. His arguments were threefold. First, he maintained that philosophy is shaped by, and has an external source in, history and society. Second, he insisted that philosophy, through the free effort of a few individuals – such as Plato, Aristotle, Thomas, Descartes, Bergson, or William James – has helped to actually create that history and society. Finally, he argued that philosophy, quite beyond its relation to history, penetrates through to those timeless truths and spiritual riches which are the accumulating treasures of humanity, and which at least describe if not define civilization. Whatever the objections of his opponents to this conclusion, especially to its openness to the possibility of a divine revelation consistent with the nature of man, none could accuse Gilson of begging the question or of flaunting his own lifelong convictions before the congress.

The second paper, "L'étude des philosophes arabes et son rôle dans l'interprétation de la scolastique" (Proceedings..., pp. 592-596; McG 277), was entirely different and concentrated on methods of pursuing medieval studies. Gilson argued that scholars were far too uncritical in their acceptance of current views on the influence of Arab thought in Europe. Even the best authorities, such as Klemens Baeumker, were guilty of a fundamental error. Historians of philosophy were consistently presenting Arab thought in a thomist perspective. Such distortion, warned Gilson, is only too common in scholarship. In Germany historians automatically dealt with all German thinkers as preparing for or continuing Kantian critiques. And in modern French philosophy, Malebranche, Leibniz and Spinoza were continually dealt with as Cartesians.

Gilson provided several examples of how a thomist perspective distorted scholarly views of the Arab influence. According to the thomist perspective,

Aristotle became known to the Latin world in the thirteenth century in "the contaminated and impure form" given his thought by various Arab philosophers, notably Avicenna and Averroes. The thomists maintained that St Thomas, after preparatory work carried out by Alexander of Hales and Albert the Great, succeeded in separating authentic aristotelianism from the foreign elements introduced by the Arabs. The thomists argued that Averroes, who came later than Avicenna, therefore replaced Avicenna. So they had to conclude that when Duns Scotus used Avicenna, he was following an older and less authentic tradition than was Thomas. Gilson found this very neat but wrong. Indeed he and his students had turned up evidence to the contrary in a recent seminar. But, stressed Gilson, no theories of Arab influence would be proved until scholars studied Arab thought in itself and not simply through the surviving works of European thomists. Essentially, Gilson's methodology, here as always, was to read a work first on its own terms.

Gilson ended his minor paper with a series of suggestions: that philosophers work on Arab philosophy on its own terms; that Arab writings be properly published, including the Latin translations in which they were known in the Latin Middle Ages; and that philosophers work collaboratively and internationally. Such counsel was timely and well-directed, especially as Gilson's audience included many local members of the recently-founded Mediaeval Academy of America.

Gilson was a great success at the congress, and emerged as its dominant personality. As always, he related this success to the work, concern and support of his students. The day after he gave his papers, he wrote to Thérèse:

> I am now quite at ease in English. The proof of this came yesterday when everyone began putting questions to me. I did not want to reply at all, pleading that there was no time. But I had to go on: repeating the questions, putting them in order, replying to them – all this in English and on the spur of the moment. Everything went well: McKeon stayed close to me, his eyes drinking me in. How like he is to our young friend Gouhier! The friendships of the young are so total, so spontaneous, that they do your heart good. (26.9.16; tr.)

The other four members of the French delegation to the congress were all Sorbonne colleagues and friends of Gilson, some quite close. Paul Lapie, Lucien Lévy-Bruhl, Léon Robin and C. Bouglé arrived at the congress together just before it opened, were housed with other delegates, and left together shortly after the congress closed. Gilson appreciated all their papers, with the exception of Bouglé's. His comments on his colleagues to Thérèse are informative, especially concerning his rector Lapie, whose health was rapidly failing:

> Lapie is visiting some schools in the company of M. Desclos, his interpreter, a former teacher of English at Rochefort. Robin is having a grand time with automatic equipment: his communications were, incidentally, remarkable; his ambition is to learn English by the Berlitz method, then to come back here on a visit in a year or so. Bouglé is telling jokes which don't always come off, any more than

did his papers; he is a charmer, however. Lévy-Bruhl is still repeating constantly: "My God! What English!"

Lapie is appreciated everywhere for his simplicity. His communication was interesting. During the discussion period which followed it, an American professor put a series of six or seven questions to him. Fortunately I was near him, wrote out the questions and passed them over. This enabled Lapie to reply as though he understood what was asked. He was most kind in his gratitude. (26.7.19; tr.)

Gilson had agreed to write up an account of the congress for the *Revue de métaphysique et de morale*. He took the commitment seriously, and each night before retiring dutifully wrote up the day's proceedings. The day after the congress closed, he mailed the packet to Paris, complete save for the papers of Léon Robin of Paris and Coriolano Alberini of Buenos Aires, which he had neither heard nor read. A short time later, Xavier Léon, editor of the *Revue*, wrote from Paris:

> I thank you for sending me some news of yourself and your fine review of the proceedings. I do reproach you for being too reticent about yourself. I have heard from elsewhere that you were the darling of the congress, which doesn't surprise me at all. I should like to hear more. ... Happily, our rector [Lapie], whom I met on his return, was overwhelmed by his journey, his stay in Cambridge, and his return.

Léon hereupon reverted to the ugly role of editor: "I shoud like to have your review ready for the next number, so do complete those two parts you left blank" (26.10.14; tr.).

5 Courses and Lectures at Harvard and Elsewhere

From late September through early January 1927, Gilson gave two regular courses at Harvard; the second course, on scholasticism, was repeated at Radcliffe College. Harvard men during the Lowell "modification," along with Radcliffe women during the "enlightenment" of the Comstock years, were for Gilson an entirely new educational experience.* Some aspects of this experience were wonderful, but others raised in him grave doubts about the quality of higher education in America.

From the first, Gilson found the students' degree of choice in their course of study disconcerting:

> Today I have been on duty all day long admitting students to my courses. It is an intriguing system. The students choose the courses in which they wish to enrol. Once enrolled they are obliged to attend. Thus, before enrolling, they have the right

---

* C. W. Eliot, president of Harvard from 1869 to 1909, invented and introduced the elective system by which Harvard students selected their own courses within subject groups. A. Lawrence Lowell, president from 1909 to 1933, modified the elective system by requiring certain basic courses judged necessary for a well-rounded education. The Harvard elective system revolutionzed American higher education. Dr Ada L. Comstock was president of Radcliffe College from 1923 to 1943, when the education of women was undergoing rapid reform.

to be informed. "Good day, sir! I am so-and-so, student of such-and-such year. I am looking for information about course 13a (the number of one of my courses). Will your course be difficult? Will you lecture in French or English? Must one know Latin?... – mm – Will you be dealing with St Augustine? For how many lectures?" And so on. (EG to Thérèse, 26.9.29; tr.)

And at least one of his female students found him as strange as he found them:

> This morning at nine I opened the second course, on scholasticism; about forty students attended. My best lecture yet in English. ... I repeated the lecture at noon at Radcliffe, where twelve students, serious, unsophisticated, attended. One of them was so upset when she heard the sound of my voice that she broke into a silent, silly laughing spell, which I quite understood: after all, she was the one who was paying for the course with her own money; and it was I who was going to collect the $500. (EG to Thérèse, 26.9.30; tr.)

Gilson's courses were on "Descartes and French Philosophy" and "Medieval Scholasticism." His regular schedule consisted of nine hours a week. He taught French philosophy at noon on Mondays, Wednesdays and Fridays, and taught scholasticism on Tuesdays, Thursdays and Saturdays at nine o'clock in Harvard and at noon in Radcliffe. His classes were highly successful, both as instruction and as entertainment – the students loved listening to Gilson and he loved talking to them. A number of professors also began attending, Whitehead among them. In October, as interest in the classes began to grow, Gilson found:

> Students seem to be more and more interested and remain after class to discuss things that have arisen. The professors present get into the fray, including Whitehead, who is to a large extent an English-speaking Brunschvicg. You can see how easy this makes things. (EG to Thérèse, 26.10.18; tr.)

Despite his popularity as a professor, Gilson was not satisfied that he was really involved in "higher education." He felt that he was merely opening up to innocent minds the existence of philosophy; his students were not yet ready to perform as scholars. Gilson suspected that he was wasting his time on American under-graduate education; perhaps he felt a keener responsibility to the advancement of philosophy than to the teaching of novices. In early January 1927, when Gilson was considering the offer of a permanent post at Harvard, he reflected at length upon this issue:

> People have been asking me frequently how to get results like mine into their lectures. I always reply that doing so would entail changing their teaching methods. They want me to launch a campaign in order to bring this about. I refuse absolutely to get involved in what is not my business. This very morning I was asked to explain my views to one of Harvard's five administrators, and I refused. It is not up to me to reform Harvard. I say what I think should be done, but it's up to them to do it! Thereupon, I am being asked if I will return to put my ideas into operation. But my stock answer, and I gave it once more this morning, is that the kind of teaching I am doing here is not higher education. What would you do, they say, if you were permitted to have your own way entirely? In that case, I reply, I would seriously

consider the material offers you are making me. This must be the tenth time they have brought up this challenge. This gives you an idea of the kind of preoccupation confronting me. I am trying to achieve something without awakening too much jealousy, without wounding tender susceptibilities, and this is not easy. (EG to Thérèse, 27.1.2; tr.)

The philosophy department at Harvard did not only want Gilson for his views on teaching. Gilson had convinced the department that it was neglecting the history of philosophy in its failure to read the philosophical texts of all periods and peoples on their own terms. Gilson did not consider a survey of a century or two in the context of some philosophical system to be history of philosophy at all. When he first arrived at Harvard, he was frustrated by the lack of appreciation for his discipline:

> As for the history of philosophy, they don't see any use for it. Perry is quite upset. He thinks that too much studying of the systems of others prevents young people from finding one of their own. It's like saying that visiting museums and studying the masters prevents one from becoming a painter. For those who have real genius, nothing gets in their way; and for those who don't have it, going to the masters is only to their profit. Such, you see, is the milieu I am working in: it is a desert waiting to be cultivated. (EG to Thérèse, 26.10.6; tr.)

And a few days later:

> I am frightened by the ignorance of professors. Perry has no notion of what it is to read a text. He wanted me to have my students read two hundred pages of St Augustine in one month. I can't read forty pages of Augustine myself in that time. *Que faire?* I say "yes," and let it go. Why struggle? I would be fighting in a void. (26.10.9; tr.)

By the end of the semester, however, understanding of the subject had grown. On 20 December Professor William E. Hocking, an empirical idealist in the manner of Josiah Royce, invited Gilson to speak on the neoscholastic movement and the study of scholasticism to a large gathering of philosophy students in his home. Two days later Gilson wrote:

> On another front I have won a complete victory. When I arrived I observed a decided hostility toward the history of philosophy. Several Harvard professors considered the subject mortally dangerous to philosophic originality. Some of them dropped in on my courses and continued coming. Yesterday, the most inveterate objector of them all [unnamed] invited me to give a lecture on the method of studying the history of philosophy, and he found an hour when he and his students could attend. So I have won my battle here for the history of philosophy. ... As [James H.] Woods put it – the wake of my passing will be visible here after my departure. (EG to Thérèse, 26.12.22; tr.)

A few days after this, the philosophy department proved beyond doubt that it recognized Gilson's contribution:

> An hour ago [on Wednesday 10 January 1927] Woods came to offer me, in the name of the department of philosophy, a full professorship for as many years as I

would like, with a salary beginning at $6,500 or 162,500 francs. There is no need to tell you that I did not accept it, but I am free to take up the offer whenever I wish. (EG to Thérèse, 27.1.10; tr.)

This offer eventually led to Gilson's compromise arrangement to teach at Harvard as visiting professor during the first terms of 1927-1928 and 1928-1929. The department of philosophy was not alone, however, in pressing for Gilson's return. American medievalists in general welcomed Gilson's presence, particularly Charles Homer Haskins, president of the newly formed Mediaeval Academy of America. And Lawrence Lowell, president of Harvard, also wanted Gilson at his university.

Gilson spoke frequently with Lowell while he was at Harvard. In early October he dined with the Lowells at their home. During the conversation he gained considerable sympathy for Mrs Lowell, a Puritan from Old England referred to affectionately throughout the Harvard yard as "Old Roast Beef." Gilson also confided to the Lowells his intense loneliness in the absence of Thérèse. Shortly afterward, Lowell sent him a memo:

> In accordance with your suggestion, the Corporation has voted to appropriate in future years, so long as the rate of exchange remains in its present condition, $1,200 a year to compensate the Exchange Professor from France for the loss that he would incur in coming to this country; an amount that would be raised to $1,500 if his wife comes with him. I shall write this to M. Petit-Dutallis and to the Recteur of the University of Paris without delay, hoping at the same time to send the name of the professor we propose to send to France. (26.12.15.)

With some amusement Gilson commented that "I so cried about the absence of my wife, that they are going to take pity on my successors."

On arrival at Cambridge, Gilson had found a number of invitations to lecture waiting for him at the Perrys'. By the end of the congress he had received requests from Québec, Montréal, Toronto, Ottawa, Chicago, Urbana, Bryn Mawr, Smith, Providence, Washington, Minnesota, New York and others. Gilson appreciated the honour paid him by these invitations, and anticipated the revenues from them as some justification for his prolonged separation from his family.

Commitments to lectures fell sharply into two categories. Some were scheduled during the semester in nearby locations. Others were postponed until the lecture tour that would take place between 15 January, the last day of term, and 5 February, when he would sail for France.

Gilson's first outside lecture was in French to the Salon Français de Boston, and was arranged by Professor Mercier of Harvard's French department. Mercier called one afternoon at Gilson's quarters in Gray's Hall, and the two talked for two hours on Claudel, Mauriac, Ramuz and Bernanos. Gilson promised Mercier a lecture he truly wanted to give, and chose the topic "Spiritual Movements in Contemporary French Literature." He was pleasantly surprised during his research to find Widener Library so well stocked with Claudel, Jammes, Valéry and Mauriac, though he was disappointed that he could find no Ramuz, Pourrat,

Bernanos or Sylvestre. As he prepared this lecture Gilson came to appreciate
Valéry more than ever, finally building the entire lecture around him. "I swear,"
he wrote Thérèse:

> I cannot understand Charles Blondel's attitude towards Paul Valéry. The beauty of
> Valéry's language is patent, and he is as "spiritual" as can be. He is full of original
> ideas and knows how to present them in an original way. Take, for example, what
> he says about love, how if it is to avoid being something ordinary, it requires
> troubles or ideas to sharpen it. ... You and I have been pretty smart organizing our
> own little troubles, but around February we may get some ideas. (EG to Thérèse,
> 26.10.30; tr.)

Gilson gave the lecture in a Boston hotel on October 30. Although he missed a
football game to do so, he received an honorarium of fifty dollars, "which put me
in good humour."

Soon after this first outside talk, Gilson attended a lecture to the Alliance
Française in Boston by a French compatriot, Jules Bois. The subject of this lecture
was "Le miracle moderne"; it was delivered with a musical accompaniment,
Méditation de Thaïs. Gilson was disgusted. He described Bois as a "little Tartarin
de Tarascon," with black goatee and a round little paunch, spluttering and
blundering from beginning to end:

> How I wished myself a hundred feet under the earth! The Americans were
> laughing at him and many walked out in disgust. I would like to have done the
> same but unfortunately I knew Bois and had already been at a meeting with him
> and some Protestant ministers (a friendly gathering). This Tartarin of a mystic is a
> frightful man. France must be stable to survive such ridiculous delegates. The one
> bright result is that the vice-president, a charming woman who speaks perfect
> French, asked me to give a lecture on 8 January. My subject will be "Le visage de la
> France dans l'œuvre de Jean Giraudoux." On this trip to Boston, I shall have no
> other objective than to regain the ground just lost. I can be as bad as Jean Bois, but
> not worse. (EG to Thérèse, 26.11.18; tr.)

Gilson planned his next special lecture for Cornell University on 22 November.
Although normally he would not have accepted an engagement so far from
Cambridge, he found that Harvard would be closed for a week; its football game
with Yale was scheduled for 20 November and Thanksgiving was to fall five days
later. Besides, what European could possibly leave North America without
visiting Niagara Falls, which was not far from Ithaca. Sunday 21 November
found Gilson stranded on the international bridge between New York State and
Canada. Eventually he got back into the United States, but only after suggesting
that the immigration officer telephone President Lowell and ask him if the stupid
professor out on the bridge belonged to him.

Gilson was determined to do especially well at Cornell. His lecture was to be in
French on Jean-Jacques Rousseau; referring to the Bois lecture, he joked to
Thérèse that his own musical background would be the ballet from *Sylvia*. On
Monday afternoon, safely arrived in Ithaca, he chatted informally in English to a

classroom full of students. He was pleased at his facility with English, and regarded the afternoon as a tour de force.

Gilson's lecture on Rousseau was a great success:

> The lecture at Ithaca seems to have pleased people. Guerlac, professor of French there, told me that as diction it was not even approached by the professors of diction sent out by France. (I discount that...!!) It is more pleasant to hear this kind of thing said than its contrary. I was taken for an automobile ride by a young professor whose wife had been a student of mine in Paris. ... She is a little philosopher busy with Auguste Comte as she awaits her children. I also met, after my lecture, a young Protestant minister who had driven seventy miles (one hundred km) to be present and was driving back that same night. You discover unexpectedly now and then the things people do and which you otherwise never know about. Another young Cornell professor was looking for my article on the medieval sermon. I tell you such things because I know they please you. Sometimes I am much amused by the very exaggeration of the things people say to me, and don't dare repeat them. They would too much resemble the boastings of a super-Tartarin de Tarascon. (EG to Thérèse, 26.11.25; tr.)

After the lecture Gilson returned from Ithaca by way of New York. He managed to spend a few happy hours in the Metropolitan Museum:

> I was most impressed by the Manets; they are prodigious; they carry the art of existing by themselves to a point rarely achieved in painting. There are good Goyas too, and two fine Rembrandts. There are splendid things in all departments. There is in the Egyptian section a necklace from 2000 BC that took my breath away: an enamelled plaque set in gold and suspended from a collar of gems – alternating blues, yellows and reds – incredibly lovely. The medieval section is less successful. The Roman section, my dear, you would like. It houses a huge, reconstructed, Pompeian atrium with its columns, its pond surrounded by little lawns, with marble tables placed here and there displaying precious objects. The whole thing is enclosed in glass with Naples and Vesuvius visible in the distance. When I saw all this, there you were again at my side! Do you remember that sparkling wine of Pompeii? (EG to Thérèse, 26.11.26; tr.)

Gilson then returned to Cambridge for Thanksgiving dinner with the Homer Haskins.

On 30 November 1926, eight days after the Cornell lecture, Gilson gave his first lecture in English to a group of students not his own. In a talk to the girls of Wellesley College, Gilson lectured on "The Evolution and Meaning of Medieval Philosophy." Again the lecture met with success. In his account of his drive back from Wellesley, Gilson revealed his empathy with ordinary struggling citizens, and particularly with female academics:

> I was taken back to Cambridge by a delightful little Frenchwoman, a teacher of French at Wellesley and the wife of an American student who was without means. She had by economizing managed to buy a small Ford car, and she was proud of it. "Deep down," she said, "I don't think much of it. But I had to have it in order to get to Wellesley for my classes. What I really want is a maid!" "Oh yes," I said, "I

understand – you don't like housework." "Housework be damned," she said, "we live in two rooms and a kitchenette. It's the dishes!" So this little Mrs Chamberlin spoke several times about her future maid. I assured her she will have one, and a Buick too, to replace her Ford. It is somewhat distressing to see a courageous little Frenchwoman trying to make herself over into an American. But what kind of life can she expect in France? If she's lucky she might find a secondary-school job in a place like Melun or Issoudun. ... "This Ford," she told me, "is the first auto in my family! Maman said to me: 'It looks like a sedan chair.' " (EG to Thérèse, 26.12.1; tr.)

Gilson enjoyed his trip to Wellesley, and made it a point to return whenever he could.*

On 1 December Gilson attended a tea offered by the university preacher. Among the fifty or so present were the Lowells and an "Admiral," no doubt Samuel Morison. Gilson gave a brief talk on an assigned subject, "Religious Sociology in France," though without much enthusiasm.

Next day, 2 December, Gilson repeated his Wellesley lecture before a large public audience at Brown University in Providence, Rhode Island. The invitation to lecture at Brown had come from Professor Everett early in October. Everett already knew Gilson indirectly; he had fallen ill when in Angoulême and Henry Gilson had treated him. Etienne's note to Thérèse was faintly sardonic:

> I owe this invitation to this professor's good impression of Henry. I shall write Henry and thank him. Neither philosophy nor the reputation of the professor accounts for it, but surgery! Henry's wife will be triumphant! She will no doubt in time come to believe that she even gave the lecture. (26.10.19; tr.)

When Gilson arrived in Providence, he was met by Everett and taken home to dine before the lecture. Everett introduced Gilson to the audience as the cousin of Henry, and drew a charming portrait of "le médecin humaniste." Gilson stayed overnight with the Everetts, and returned to Boston in time for his class at noon.

Gilson gave five more lectures while at Harvard. On 8 December he addressed a *cercle* of French-Canadian students in Boston. Although the lecture carried no stipend, it rewarded him with special insight into the French-Canadian will-to-survive: the boy who drove him back to Cambridge earned his living by selling in Boston the blueberries that children picked for him in the country. On 15 December Gilson addressed the Philosophical Club at Harvard. This was followed on 8 January by his "post-Bois" lecture for the Alliance Française de Boston on the playwright Jean Giraudoux.

On Sunday 9 January 1927, at Albertus Magnus College in New Haven, Gilson gave a philosophical talk on the doctrine of free will in the work of Albert the Great. The professor of philosophy of the college wrote the following day:

---

* On January 11, before leaving Cambridge for his Canadian tour, he gave a second lecture there. Later, in the fall of 1927, he lectured in French on St Bernard; when he received his stipend of fifty dollars, he remarked with amusement to Thérèse, "This combination of dollars and St Bernard lacks elegance, but St Bernard was not married and had no daughters" (27.10.27; tr.).

My students today were all most enthusiastic about your lecture; to arouse undergraduate enthusiasm is the greatest of tests. Also you inspired the rest of us to sit up
very late talking about free will! I hope that you will keep the notes [actually texts
from Albert's works] and that when you return to France you can find time to write
it out for us. (Nicholas Moseley to EG, 27.1.10.)

In New Haven Gilson met a group of Dominican nuns who had once been exiled
from St-Brieuc; they cried with joy that a compatriot was successfully lecturing in
English in America.

On 11 January Gilson kept his return engagement at Wellesley, lecturing on
contemporary French literature. He was almost stopped by a heavy snowstorm
from which he had to be rescued, as he claimed, like Charlie Chaplin in *The Gold
Rush*.

6 HARVARD FRIENDSHIPS

While Gilson stayed at the Perrys' home, he grew very close to them. As
realists, he and Perry held related philosophical positions: Gilson's was a thomist
realism, while Perry's was the presentative or new realism popular in America
after 1900. During the congress the two men constituted an informal subcomittee
on day-to-day arrangements, and Gilson was highly impressed by Perry's
competence in practical matters. He was also puzzled by Perry's forbearance and
was amazed when his host sequestered himself the day before the congress dinner
"to write the speeches that the politicians were supposed to deliver" (EG to
Thérèse, 26.9.16; tr.). Wellington Wells, president of the Massachusetts senate,
was chairing the dinner and had to introduce eight very disparate scholars; as
chairman of the local committee, Perry was probably the one man in Cambridge
capable of briefing the poor senator. Gilson, however, probably never in his life
sought assistance with a speech or a lecture, and would have found even a
briefing objectionable.

Like Father Carr in Toronto, Perry probably had designs on Gilson; at any rate,
he was behind President Lowell's generous offer later in the term. Mrs Perry also
got along famously with Gilson. The first day of his stay, she pretended to be at
her wit's end in search of some liquor for him. Would he please be so good as to
go out and find a bootlegger? Gilson immediately reached for his hat and started
out the door — much to her amusement, Mrs Perry had to run into the street to cut
him off.

Over the years Gilson was a frequent guest at the Perrys' table. Mrs Perry
inevitably placed him at her right, and to the left of some woman whose family
she wanted him to know. As a result, Gilson was never in Cambridge without at
least one dinner invitation in hand, a situation that he sometimes protested. Perry
teased him on the point, telling Gilson, in the jargon of the football they both
enjoyed, that his defence was not nearly so strong as his offence.

When Gilson first arrived in America, he found many customs distateful. He
cringed at the very thought of eating corn from the cob: "They butter it with a

knife, salt it, take in in their two hands and gnaw it as a dog gnaws a bone. It's disgusting. Gnawing corn disgusts me: it is ignoble." (EG to Thérèse, 26.8.3; tr.) Through the Perrys, however, Gilson grew to appreciate American politesse. He discovered that it was not undignified for university students to work as part-time domestics, nor was it a breach of decorum for guests to help out with the serving at dinner parties. He even found that buffet meals, in which guests sat helter-skelter all over the house, could be "sometimes both highly practical and deeply human." The Perrys gave a particularly unusual dinner party: thirty-two guests sat at four tables, four men and four women at each, and the men changed tables after each course, serving the next course while on their feet. Gilson enjoyed it thoroughly:

> All this took place most gracefully. I pass it on to you to give you an idea of how customs differ. These people have in reality a deep simplicity which sometimes gets expressed in a crude manner, but sometimes, as in this case, with pleasing inventiveness and lovable spontaneity. They have, of course, like us their ultra-refinements: nobody touches what is on his plate until everyone is served. Gracious enough, to be sure, but silly too, since all the while they wait, the cuisine is growing cold. (26.11.10; tr.)

Gilson's friendship with Harry Wolfson was of a very different order. Not only did the two men share what they felt to be an enlightened attitude toward Eastern philosophies, but they both like to end long philosophical discussions with a drink, a dinner and a play. On the day before Gilson's first lecture in Harvard College, he entertained Wolfson in his new apartment at 89 Gray's Hall. They debated philosophy strenuously, then adjourned to Wolfson's favorite Jewish restaurant, the Premier Cafeteria (the Prime) at Berkeley and Washington Streets in Boston: "c'était très bon, très différent comme cuisine, et très amusant comme têtes." At the restaurant the philosophers discussed how Jewish people were coping with the harsh immigration laws, "les anciens font les petits." They followed this with a stage show, *The Jazz Singer*, which later became the first talking picture starring Al Jolson. Gilson summarized the sentimental plot for Thérèse: the son of a cantor is a great success in the music halls but, when his old father is dying, is persuaded by his mother to return to a life in the synagogue. Gilson wittily closed the account, like a true Bergsonian, with the *élan vital*: "The drive of the race has broken the American *effort*" (26.9.29; tr.).

Another close friendship that was quickly renewed was with Alfred North Whitehead, a philosopher whom Gilson never ceased to admire. He was also very fond of Mrs Whitehead who, though raised in France, was nonetheless very English. On 13 September, the third day of the congress, Gilson wrote home to Thérèse:

> I have been invited to tea at the home of Professor Whitehead. ... His wife was raised in France up to the age of twenty-one. Whitehead himself is a delicious old gentleman. I have a standing invitation to call on him every Sunday, and at any other time I feel like doing so. (26.10.13; tr.)

Whitehead became one of the several professors who regularly attended Gilson's Harvard lectures. And after New Year's, when Gilson had just given the first of four well-attended special lectures, Whitehead said to him: "You have done more for France here than all your predecessors taken together." Gilson called this "a kindly exaggeration, but pleasant nevertheless!" (27.1.3; tr.)

One of Gilson's best Harvard anecdotes concerned Mrs Whitehead. It was told to him by James H. Woods, Harvard professor of philosophy:

> The other day, Woods asked Mrs Whitehead, who is English, this question: "What do you think of this statement of Erasmus: 'the English are charming – they always treat you as an equal, provided you acknowledge their superiority'?" (*Entre-nous, c'est bien joli!*) Mrs Whitehead reflected, then after a pause said: "No, I think not. We are not proud. We are not arrogant. Only, you see, it's that we have had in our affairs so often to deal with inferior races." *Incroyable, mais vrai!* (26.10.22; tr.)

Through his friendships at Cambridge Gilson became a sympathetic and puzzled observer of American life. This is especially true of his experiences with the Henry Copley Greenes, the Perrin T. Wilsons, the Jean-Jacques Haffners and the John L. Saltonstalls. These four families all became dear to Gilson, and each of them numbered at least one French-speaker among its members. Other families too, the Porters, the Merciers, the Borings and the Pickmans, welcomed him into their lives.

The Greenes were among the first families to be mentioned in Gilson's letters. Henry Copley Greene was unlike anyone Gilson had met: "I have taken pains to find out the profession of Mr Greene, my host of yesterday: he does nothing! Which hardly explains how he happens to own two homes and a van for transporting calves!" (EG to Thérèse, 26.10.26; tr.) Greene's full and varied life was of the kind only possible for the son of a wealthy father. *Who's Who in America* classified him simply as "author," and in his early days he had published translations from French and Latin, English versions of foreign plays, and many items bearing on children and childhood – the introduction to Greene's *Childhood of Christ* had been written by Alice Meynell. His career included posts with the Red Cross in Boston and in France during World War I, with the French War Emergency Fund in 1916 to 1917, and with French Reconnaissance in 1918. He had a croix de guerre with a silver medal, and knew a great deal about medicine, the blind and philosophy. From 1926 to 1928 Greene held some kind of instructorship in Harvard's department of philosophy; this explains how he first met Gilson and why his eldest daughter, Francesca, was enrolled in Gilson's first course at Radcliffe.

Gilson's friendship with the Greenes indirectly began with an interesting dinner at the Perrys:

> In all, eight persons were present, one of them Miss Comstock, president of Radcliffe. She is a lovely, simple person, without affectation, unabrasive. She was quite insistent that I stir up her students and be strict with them. No doubt I wore a sceptical smile because she broke into a laugh and said there would seem to be little

hope on that score. So I told her the following story, This morning I was at my barber's in Cambridge and was watching a young man who, like myself, was having his hair cut. I thought to myself, I know that young man, but where have I seen him ? Eventually the barber removed the cloth covering his customer and I recognized in this young man one of my Radcliffe students. The boy was a girl, but a girl who no longer had her flowing locks. Miss Comstock was anxious to get off the subject of this anecdote. (EG to Thérèse, 26.10.19; tr.)

On the following Sunday, Gilson and Whitehead were driven in a big car to the Greenes' farm in Ipswich. Their driver was a young man named Johnson, one of Gilson's Harvard students and Francesca Greene's current boyfriend. They were to dine at the Greenes' at two o'clock:

These Greenes live on an old farm. They had just returned from France. They brought out a box-lunch containing some ham, a pat of butter, some salad, a bottle of mayonnaise, some bread and bacon. They installed themselves in a rough and ready way at a rustic table. Three daughters were there, but the eldest was not; she was back in Boston as they told me, she was not feeling well. At 4:30 the entire family took off, carrying with them fallen apples they had gathered, in a Ford van fitted out for transporting calves and which they had just bought in France (!!!); they drove back very carefully. We had gone ahead in the big car and stopped for tea at their home – a fine one – in Cambridge [10 Longfellow Park]. The first person to greet me was Francesca, no more sick than you or I. She was in a red sheath dress trimmed with pearl grey cordova leather. I recognized her at once, not only as one of my Radcliffe students, but as the same young man who was getting his hair cut at my barber's. Cambridge is indeed small, because as Mrs Greene was taking her place in the big car for the trip back she said to me quietly: "This place does remind me of the countryside at Avallon!"* Is there any point at all in travelling? (EG to Thérèse, 26.10.22; tr.)

The Wilsons were another family that figured prominently in Gilson's life in Cambridge. Mrs Wilson first met Gilson at a dinner, probably at the Perrys':

I sat beside a pleasant woman dressed in white and began speaking to her in English, but she soon switched to perfect French. She is Mrs Wilson, wife of a Boston surgeon. I congratulated her on her impeccable French. "Oh," she replied, "I am the daughter of Réjane." (EG to Thérèse, 26.12.3; tr.)

Réjane, or Gabrielle-Charlotte Réju, had been a leading French actress at the turn of the century. She had played lead roles in many theatres including the Odéon, the Vaudeville and the Théâtre-Nouveau. She had been married to the comic actor and director, Jacques Porel, between 1893 and 1905; after her divorce she had bought the Théâtre-Nouveau and changed its name to Théâtre-Réjane. Gilson and Thérèse had met Réjane in Strasbourg at the home of Mme Dubost; in fact, when the University of Strasbourg had reopened in 1919, one of the dishes at the formal banquet had been called "cœur de filet de Charollais Réjane."

---

* Avallon was the home of Gilson's maternal grandmother Morizot.

When Gilson found that Mrs Wilson was the daughter of Réjane, he felt as though he were meeting a part of his past. He was soon invited to her home for dinner:

> I dined at Mrs Wilson's home, in a lovely Louis xv setting, a pastel of Réjane by Bernard on the wall. She spoke softly of her *maman* and was completely simple and refined. The other day I had told her how I ordered scallops in a restaurant thinking I was ordering *escalopes de veau*. I actually got shellfish or, more specifically, fried clams, which are popular here. To compensate for my past disappointment, Mrs Wilson now had served up some magnificent veal cutlets with mushrooms. A little American woman at my right, wearing red and very blonde, asked me: "What kind of meat is this?" Veal is almost unknown in the United States. So Mrs Wilson had a triumph: *pâté de foie gras, salade, crème fourchettée*, a male server, a woman cook. Thus did the daughter of Réjane see that I got my veal cutlets. To what will St Thomas bring me next?
>
> Then we left for the Pro Arte concert. ... I chatted with the Quartet, and they recognized me quite well and at once. They told me that Xavier de Grunne's father died two months ago. I learned from others that Motte-Lacroix had become professor of piano with the Boston Conservatory (naturally). Mrs Wilson told me too that Germaine Tailleferre was in New York, and had just married an American – she is his third wife. Mrs Wilson then invited me over to dinner again on Saturday to meet M. et Mme Darius Milhaud who are (naturally) in America. (EG to Thérèse, 26.12.7; tr.)

The *naturallys* reflect Gilson's wonderment at the almost excessive number of French celebrities daily turning up in America. Milhaud of course, composer extraordinaire, was by demand on an extended world tour.

Gilson's social life at around this time seems to have been assuming a byzantine complexity. The Saturday invitation was soon complicated by others:

> The dinner for M. and Mme Darius Milhaud which I shall be attending at Mrs Wilson's will be at 1:30 sharp. Then Saturday evening there will be a concert [by Cécile Sorel] to which I have been invited by one of my students [Johnson] who is very rich and has several subscriptions. He told me he would be bringing Francesca Greene too. That's the American way.* To complicate things, another woman is holding a reception right after the [Sorel] concert for Darius Milhaud and has invited me to attend it. So I must get Johnson invited too as I could hardly drop him. ... Everything is getting complicated like something out of Proust. (EG to Thérèse, 26.12.14; tr.)

Saturday was a full day, and very long:

> What a life! This morning my own two lectures, plus Perry's which I attended. My last lecture ended at one. At 1:30 I was at Wilson's and dined with the Milhauds who are simple and likable. We talked about the Xavier Léons, and then about Mme Dubost who amuses both Milhauds enormously. Darius described her as a "combination of a clever poodle and Marie Laurencin." Mrs Wilson couldn't place

---

* The comment refers to the practice of keeping company without any parental involvement.

her at first, then suddenly cried out: "Oh! That's the blond woman with the blue ribbons!" Right. Paul Boncœur did not get there at all, nor did that gentleman who lives in Mme Dubost's house, whom nobody knows, who eats a few sandwiches, looks disdainfully over the crowd invading the room and takes his leave – M. Dubost! Darius Milhaud played two of his own pieces for piano, not very well. If he is playing like that this evening he would do well to get a replacement. (EG to Thérèse, 26.12.19; tr.)

With the Wilsons, Gilson was plunged into the heart of *la vie mondaine*. He was not sure whether he really liked it, and he became quite uncomfortable as he slowly recollected stories about Mrs Wilson's *maman*, her brother Jacques, and her sister-in-law:

I remember now very well the beautiful Mme Jacques Porel. I wish I could forget her when I see Mrs Wilson. Mrs Wilson has spoken of her brother several times. When I complimented her on her magnificent table service (all the plates and other dishes were Sèvres porcelain with blue and gold lines), she told me that her mother had gradually put it together with the "goodies" given her by the presidents of the Republic. At her mother's death, she had kept all the dishes and left the unglazed Sèvres porcelain to her brother. Not exactly silly! But she never made the least allusion to her sister-in-law. Mrs Wilson is charming, completely unspoiled, very busy with her children, and with as little theatre as possible. Everyone regards her highly, and thinks well of her. Not a word, however, about her sister-in-law. (26.12.31; tr.)

Apparently Mrs Wilson did eventually let Gilson into her confidence. She told him at least one story about her infamous sister-in-law:

It is not always funny to be an elegant women. (I think you remember her, the daughter-in-law of Réjane whom we met at the home of Mme Dubost.) She is clothed by Jean Patou at extremely low prices, on condition that the papers tell about her clothes, and on the prior condition that she never let her weight pass determined limits, that her chest, hips, thighs conform to determined measurements: one centimetre more and the furnishing of her dresses and cloaks ceases automatically. The unfortunate woman must, it appears, spend her time weighing herself, measuring herself, reducing. Hers in sum is the plight of the fashion model. (EG to Thérèse, 27.11.1; tr.)

Another Cambridge family Gilson came to know well during this year was the Haffners. They too were international figures, French Huguenots who knew and loved the world of art, theatre and music. Haffner was something of a sculptor and designed for a firm of architects; in 1925 he had been named the Nelson Robinson Jr Professor of Architecture at Harvard. He was as at home in Paris as in Cambridge, though his wife, a de Quatrepage, was more completely French than he. Gilson enjoyed spending time with the Haffners. In their home he was sure to meet someone he had run into before in Europe. Once at tea there he met Mrs Haffner's father and was promptly asked if he was related to this gentleman's friend, Henry Gilson of Ste-Barbe; as Gilson remarked later, "le monde est minuscule!"

On Boxing Day 1926, Gilson was somewhat embarrassed to find himself accompanying Mrs Haffner to a Motte-Lacroix concert in Boston:

> Saturday afternoon I had tea with the Haffners. I was invited, somewhat awkwardly and deferentially, to stay for dinner. I wondered why, until they showed me "Une heure avec ..." sent by Mrs Haffner's parents, which explained everything. I stayed for dinner and accompanied Mrs Haffner to the concert. She suggested to her husband that she and I go by taxi. *He froze, and so did I.* I remained calm and took her off by tram and returned the same way. She was quite content but did not care to go to the lobby during the intermission. She was wearing overshoes, she said: "I don't like going to the lobby having to shuffle along clumsily." "Neither do I," I replied. So we didn't appear in the lobby. However, Motte-Lacroix came to us, so that – again as in Proust* – I was finally able to congratulate him in Boston for the concerts he had given us in Strasbourg. Mme Motte-Lacroix, a blond Swiss, will soon be as stout as Blanche Selva. (EG to Thérèse, 26.12.27; tr.)

A few days later, New Year's Eve, Gilson dined again with the Haffners. This time, sensitivities of a different nature appeared:

> We played bridge until midnight waiting for the New Year. At midnight all the sirens of the port of Boston, the ships, the churches and their bells, combined to create an infernal uproar to greet the arrival of the New Year. Then everyone went home. During the evening little Françoise Haffner said to her mother: "Maman, I hate to go shopping in the stores with you because you have such a funny accent." Frightening isn't it? As a matter of fact the accent of the two young Haffner girls is absolutely perfect. (EG to Thérèse, 27.1.2; tr.)

The "two young Haffner girls" were young twins, Françoise and Monique. Gilson watched them playing one day in the snow, fighting with some boys: "These girls speak half-French, half-English; they knew only *holly* for *houx* and *Christmas* for *Noël*" (EG to Thérèse, 26.12.12; tr.). Mrs Haffner worried about her daughters' French. She privately suggested to Gilson that if he were to teach at Harvard a semester each year, his wife might tutor the girls, and others as well, in spoken French. Gilson's friends at Cambridge increasingly spoke of Thérèse coming to America. But although Gilson dutifully relayed these conversations to her, they failed to evoke much response.

The next fall Gilson watched Haffner redecorate his new house in Cambridge; the Haffners had just moved that summer. Gilson found the finished house "lovely throughout," especially in its use of colours. An unfortunate exception, however, was the attic. Mrs Haffner had decided to let the two unused attic rooms to two Harvard students. The young men asked to be allowed to decorate their own rooms. One of them, a young Jewish boy with aesthetic ambitions, redecorated his room so extravagantly that Haffner was quite embarrassed; in fact, the room became a conversation piece around Cambridge.

---

* Gilson was continually citing Proust at this time, having recently heard Edouard Champion, the French publisher, give a lecture on him in Boston, and having consequently just read *Albertine disparue*.

Wherever it was located, the Haffners' home was a stopping place for visitors passing through New England. Gilson was frequently sent for to help entertain these guests. In the Haffner's newly decorated house, Gilson met a talented young woman who had quietly accompanied her two nephews to Cambridge. She was just about to set off on an extended European tour:

> It was Ruth Draper, the celebrated actress who plays, completely alone, little scenes in which several persons are involved, scenes which she composes with great powers of observation. She is leaving for London, Berlin and Rome. She has been offered the Théâtre de l'Œuvre in Paris but finds it unsatisfactory, too remote from everything. How completely unassuming a person she is! (EG to Thérèse, 27.10.13; tr.)

Haffner's work had brought him into touch with so many fields of art that he constantly surprised Gilson with his knowledge. An incidental remark about the marriage of Mariel, for example, caused Haffner to explain to Gilson that the seated nude outside Mariel's studio was a work by Delamarre, in the style of Clodin; Haffner knew this, because he had attended the Villa Medicis at the same time as Delamarre. Gilson, out of interest, closely followed one particular art exhibition that Haffner organized through a licensed art dealer in Boston. No doubt Haffner had bought the paintings in Europe during the summer and was now selling them to cover his expenses:

> Haffner is preparing his exhibition. Here one can sell only watercolours. Americans are not, it appears, fussy about French oils. The dealer in whose gallery the exhibition takes place makes an advance deduction of thirty percent of the sale price; This is the Paris tariff, and a jolly good deduction it is! (EG to Thérèse, 27.10.29; tr.)

Haffner may have been partly responsible for Gilson's ultimate decision to move from Melun to Paris. Haffner planned to acquire a property in central Paris and build on it a combination studio, gallery and home – a sort of private mansion. Gilson asked Thérèse whether they might also consider a move to Paris; they could let their house in Melun and rent a Parisian apartment (27.11.12). However, when Thérèse eventually agreed to move to Paris, she chose an apartment on rue Collet, a considerably more pretentious address than any Gilson had ever considered.

Haffner and Gilson eventually became close enough for Gilson to discuss his finances without embarrassment. One of these discussions led Gilson to offer Thérèse advice about her investment of their money, an area in which he had sworn never to interfere. The franc was quite low – twenty-five to the dollar – and Thérèse had placed money in certain equities she regarded as promising. Haffner was not impressed by her selection, and assured Gilson that the franc would strengthen, possibly reaching fifteen to the dollar: "We should sell the Quilmes," Gilson wroter her, "and put money into French income. ... If the franc strengthens, the value of some of our other things will tumble." On Haffner's advice, he also urged Thérèse to place half their two hundred thousand francs into French, half into foreign investments, replacing their Paris Lefrancs, Haut Congo, Quilmes and other stocks with Bank of France notes or French annuities. Ultimately of course, given the crash of 1929 and the outbreak of World War II, there was little to choose between the strategies. Thérèse however was not impressed with Haffner's advice and said so forthrightly. Gilson refrained from contradicting her, and tactfully abandoned the subject:

> Your scepticism about Haffner's theories is amusing. His wife telephoned me some good news that they have just received. He has been commissioned to design plans for a new skyscraper university in Pittsburgh. It is to be fifteen storeys high. He is very happy and it is a stroke of good fortune. (27.11.21; tr.)

On 18 December 1926, at the Wilsons' reception for Milhaud, Gilson met for the first time Mrs John L. Saltonstall, the former Gladys D. Rice. Gilson immediately warmed to her as a "petite" and gracious friend and an excellent teller of funny stories. She was also forthright. Seated on the floor at the Wilsons', her back to the fire, she complained to Gilson that the French had not the same deep affection for Americans that Americans had for them; "I tried to rid her of such a 'dangerous error' but with no success because, after all, she was only too right."

Mrs Saltonstall invited Gilson to attend her large New Year's Day dinner party at "Huntwicke" in Topsfield, Massachusetts, her country home. Her house was one of the few Gilson saw in America in which the furnishings were almost as interesting as the architecture. His description to Thérèse reveals his fascination with furniture:

> We came upon a large dwelling built on a hill and overlooking a beautiful valley. The house was surrounded by a park of lawns, trees, ponds, etc. The furniture in some rooms was antique, in some modern – by Dim. The finest room of all is modern; a vast, vaulted, lime-white hall furnished by Dim, some Marie Laurencin paintings, and one by Jacques Blanche entitled *L'héritage du capitaine* which depicts a collection of varied objects described by Jean Cocteau in *Potomac*. Mrs Saltonstall had a copy of this book but admitted she had never read it. I easily found the page which her painting so faithfully illustrated. She gathered everyone around her to point out the marvel. She was very happy. Mr Saltonstall is a likable fellow. An ardent hunter, he showed me through his library filled with guns and with books on hunting, mainly of wild fowl. Somewhat awkwardly he enquired about that "philology" dealt with recently by a congress at Harvard. He had no idea of what a "philologist" is.

That New Year's Day, the Saltonstalls' entire party of twenty-five people went on a hike in the snow with sleighs and unleashed dogs; "I was," wrote Gilson, "supplied with snow-packs and a leather jacket." On the hikers' return they enjoyed a huge meal of red kidney beans, sausages, bacon, rice cooked in water and apple fritters. The men served the meal without any protest from the ladies. "In France one would have to use domestics to serve twenty-five people."

During this meal Gilson witnessed an episode he would never forget:

> Betty Saltonstall, fifteen years old, said to her mother, in my presence, that [Mrs
> Saltonstall] would never acquire real Boston social grace. Her mother replied
> pleasantly: "I tried for five years to acquire it, but I got nowhere. I got bored and
> gave up." "My reason for saying this to you, Mother, is that I am now at the age
> when I must choose my way of life." "I believe, my dear," her mother said gently,
> "that you will succeed better than I with Boston manners: you have a presence full
> of dignity, and I wish you every happiness." I wouldn't have missed the scene for
> an empire. (27.1.2.)

Gladys had indeed given up on acquiring Bostonian respectability. For some
time, to Gilson's surprise, Saltonstall had been "freeing" his wife for two months a
year as she travelled unattended to Paris. When Gilson returned to America the
next September, he found the Haffners also aboard. They told him that this year
Gladys had decided to remain in Paris while she asked her husband for a divorce.
Gilson was dismayed, and could only wonder helplessly what would become of
her Dim furniture and her Laurencin paintings. He wrote Thérèse sadly that "I
suppose I won't be going to Topsfield any more" (27.10.13; tr.).

7 LA TOURNÉE CANADIENNE

Harvard's first semester ended at one o'clock on Saturday afternoon, 15
January 1927. On the same afternoon Gilson took the overnight train from
Boston to Chicago and continued on to Urbana and the University of Illinois. At
Urbana he was the guest of Dean and Mrs Daniels, who pampered him "like a
spoiled child."

Gilson had carefully prepared three lectures in English on medieval theories of
knowledge. He delivered these at the University of Illinois at four o'clock on
Monday, Tuesday and Wednesday. Gilson approached his topic through a close
examination of texts from St Bonaventure, St Thomas and Duns Scotus against
the more general background of Augustine's thought. In Gilson's view, theories
of knowledge offered the most practical illustration of the revolution that took
place in philosophical thought during the thirteenth century. He was particularly
close to the subject at the time, having just written his lengthy article for the first
number of his *Archives* on "Pourquoi saint Thomas a critiqué saint Augustin."
Early in the article he had underlined the significance of theories of knowledge to
that revolution:

> Before St Thomas Aquinas, there was almost unanimous agreement supporting St
> Augustine's doctrine of divine illumination; after St Thomas there was no longer
> any such agreement and even John Duns Scotus, the Franciscan doctor, on this
> essential point abandoned the Augustinian tradition which up until then his order
> had stoutly supported (p. 5; tr.).

Immediately after his third lecture, Gilson returned to Chicago. He left Urbana
with three hundred dollars; he was counting on his lecture tour to raise his

earnings in North America to a hundred thousand francs. This would render his family's style of living "very different from the decent poverty in which we have been living" (EG to Thérèse, 27.1.19; tr.).

At Chicago Gilson was met by Professor Moore and driven to the Quadrangle Club. The next day, Thursday 20 January, he made a quick tour of the city and delivered a single lecture on the same topic at three o'clock at the University of Chicago. At five-forty he caught the flier to Montréal. On Friday at around six in the afternoon he was met at the Montréal station by Madeleine Thibaudeau and driven to her parents' home at 62 Rosemount, Westmount.

Gilson had been introduced to the Thibaudeaus by Jean Brunhes on his trip to Montréal the previous April. When Mme Thibaudeau learned from the university registrar that Gilson was expected, she immediately wrote and invited him to be their houseguest. Gilson had already been invited by Secretary Montpetit to stay at the Club Manquille, but he preferred the family atmosphere in the Thibaudeaus' home. He also found it gratifyingly elegant to have a limousine at his disposal, as well as a chauffeur in the person of Madeleine, the daughter of the household. For her part Madeleine loved accompanying Gilson wherever he went in Montréal; it provided her with an entrée to the male-dominated university world, otherwise inaccessible to her.

The Thibaudeaus were originally Acadian, with European origins in Poitou. Some of the family had been deported to Louisiana during "le grand dérangement," and had given their name, with a slight change in spelling, to the town of Thibaudaux. Alfred A. Thibaudeau and his wife, Eva Rodier, both had fathers who had been Canadian senators; Alfred's father had been a Liberal, and Eva's a Conservative.

In addition to their home in Westmount, the Thibaudeaus had large holdings in Beauharnois on Lake St Francis. Over the years, Gilson came to know both places well. The Beauharnois property, La Pointe, was the scene of the great fishing triumph of Gilson's life. Out in a boat one day with Jacques, Madeleine's brother, he hauled in a fourteen-pound muskellunge. Jacques, who had himself caught only a few perch, tried to land the fish but it tore the net to shreds. Gilson stubbornly hung on and the two men eventually, tugging hand over hand, pulled the fish into the boat. The head of the fish, dried and varnished, for years adorned the wall of Gilson's home in Vermenton; a photograph of it still remains.

Three days after his arrival at the Thibaudeau home, Gilson wrote the following in their family guest-book:

> Having a clean heart is willing what God wills.
> Willing what God wills is willing God Himself.
> Willing God Himself is winning all things else,
>   never to lose them again if
>   never again separated from Him.
> It is apprenticeship to eternal joy.   (27.1.24; tr.)

Gilson's first Montréal engagement was both cultural and ambassadorial. On the morning of Saturday 22 January, in Salle Saint-Sulpice, he read the inaugural paper for the Institut Scientifique Franco-Canadien. The new institute was part of France's general effort to assist the spread of French culture wherever possible; there was already an Institut Franco-Américain in the United States with its own regular publication. Gilson had been chosen to inaugurate the institute's first formal session. He took for his topic "Saint Bernard, Founder of Medieval Mysticism."

The large and distinguished audience included Archbishop Gauthier; Monseigneur Piette, rector of the University of Montréal; Monseigneur Maurault, rector of Notre Dame; Senators Raoul Dandurand and F. Beique; Baron de Vitrolles, the consul-general; and a host of scholars from Montréal's two universities. M. J. L. Dalbis, the institute's first president, introduced Gilson and affirmed the reasons for choosing a philosopher to speak at the first meeting. It was, said Dalbis, fashionable in some circles to downgrade philosophy in favour of pure science. This was a mistake, especially for those seeking guidance in reconciling faith with new discoveries.

Gilson took his lead from Dalbis' remarks and opened his address on the theme of guidance in Dante's *Divine Comedy*. Dante's first guide, of course, was Virgil, the guide of poetry and science, the "symbol of guidance by reason alone." Virgil was followed by Beatrice, "symbol of reason illumined by faith," the guide for scholars, theologians, martyrs and contemplatives. But the guide who alone could lead Dante into final ecstasy was Bernard, the "symbol of burning charity" and the great authority on the philosophy of love.

Gilson went on to present Bernard as a theorist and analyst of divine love, notably in the *De diligendo deo* and the *De gradibus humilitatis*. He invited scientists and scholars generally to look steadily with Bernard at the ultimate end. This focus upon the ultimate end had characterized French culture, at certain times and at its best. When Abélard was France's supreme logician, Bernard the mystic was there as well. When Descartes was the thinking man par excellence, not far away was Blaise Pascal. And sometimes these poles had met, as they did in the thirteenth century in the minds of Bonaventure and Thomas Aquinas.

That night members and friends of the new institute dined together at Le Cercle Universitaire. As guest of honour, Gilson again addressed the group. This time he spoke on the French spirit of modern French literature. Entitled "Idealism in Contemporary Literature," this was essentially the same talk he had given to the Salon Français de Boston in October.

According to Gilson contemporary literature, as seen in the poetry and criticism of Paul Valéry and Paul Claudel, was returning to its traditional concerns after the digressions of such nineteenth-century *romanciers naturalistes* as Flaubert, de Maupassant and Zola. The naturalists had been stung by biting despair through their preoccupation with blind instinct and the dead weight of matter. The younger writers were rejecting this preoccupation with matter and returning to the "true French spirit" by focusing upon the ideas and the intelligence of man.

Gilson's Valéry was a symbolist, drawn into the *idea* of pure poetry, disengaged from the didactic, the descriptive and the rhetorical. Like Bergson before him, Valéry was intrigued by the laws of intellectual effort. Gilson's Claudel, meanwhile, took his cues from Mallarmé and Poe, along with his religious orientation. For Claudel the poetic act was analogous to God's creative act: while God speaks the Eternal Word and calls beings into existence, the poet uses words to bring thoughts into consciousness. The poet's art then, is a creative one, not essentially a recording one.

Gilson concluded his talk with a comparison of the aims of the new writers with the aims of the new institute. Both were attempting "a vigorous reconstruction of the French soul, a conscious return to its most profound traditions, a liberation from matter, and a will to serve spiritual forces." Gilson's optimism was contagious and won him long and enthusiastic applause (*Le devoir*, 27.1.24; tr.). On Thursday of the following week he gave an English version of the talk in the Salle Moyse of McGill University; he had received the McGill invitation from his friend Professor René du Roure before leaving Cambridge.

On 24, 25 and 28 January in Salle Saint-Sulpice, Gilson delivered a course of three evening lectures for the University of Montréal. Their general title, "The Theory of Knowledge According to St Thomas," allowed Gilson to delve more deeply into thomist philosophy than in the series recently given in Urbana. The first lecture examined the sources of human knowledge according to Aristotle, Augustine and Thomas. The second presented the thomist concept of man's knowledge of individuals as the product of his God-given reason exercised on the evidence of his senses. The third explored the problem of how man, whose knowledge is derived through his senses, can ascertain the existence of the soul or of God. These were rich lectures, well reported in Montréal's *Le devoir*. They probed aristotelian participation, augustinian illumination and thomistic abstraction and analogy.

On Wednesday 26 January Gilson made a hurried trip to Québec City to deliver an evening lecture for the Institut Canadien at Laval University; his subject was "Le thomisme." He then returned to Montréal to complete his commitments there. On Saturday he went to Ottawa to speak for the Dominicans and the Alliance Française; the request for this lecture had been supported by no less a dignitary than "M. King le Premier Ministre" (EG to Thérèse, 27.1.19).

Gilson arrived in Toronto on Sunday 30 January 1927. He was scheduled to speak at St Michael's, a small Catholic college located, anomalously from his perspective, in a state university. To his surprise, he found there a lively group of thomist scholars. For some ten years Father Henry Carr and his Basilian colleagues had been attracting to Toronto such distinguished Catholic educators as Sir Bertram Windle and Gerald B. Phelan.

Gilson spent three days at St Michael's living in community in a way that recalled his happy years at Notre-Dame-des-Champs. Each afternoon he repeated one of the three public lectures already given at Urbana. He also held a lively evening discussion with the University of Toronto Philosophical Society. Gilson enjoyed his time at St Michael's, and thought he recognized a favorable setting for the medieval institute he had dreamt of since his Strasbourg days. He promised to visit the college and university again in the fall.

Gilson left Toronto for New York in time to catch the *S.S. Paris*, which was to sail for France on 5 February. While in New York he gave two lectures: one at Columbia on French philosophy for his friend Professor Bush, and one at Barnard College on scholasticism. He left America a tired and happy man, hungry for the company of his wife and family.

9

A Year of Change, 1927

1 Late Winter and Spring in Paris

The next five months, February through June 1927, were very full. In Paris Gilson took on an increased teaching load while he developed a new approach to the works of St Augustine and Duns Scotus. Thérèse complained to her husband about his timetable even before he returned from North America. She believed that his teaching schedule in Paris would keep them apart almost as much as his absence had done. Gilson tried to make light of her complaint:

> It is ... not all that easy at this time [9 December 1926] to rearrange my lectures. They were fixed last July. ... The situation as it stands won't be too bad: we shall be together Monday afternoons, Tuesday and Wednesday evenings, all day Thursday, all day Friday. Saturday will be complicated right over into Sunday. Not ideal, to be sure, but not bad either in a working family! You can get your hooks on me as often as polite society permits. Note too that I only go back to teaching on 1 March (which, if I read aright your pretty little red calendar, is Mardigras) and so in fact I return to lectures on 2 March. Then there will be holidays from 9 to 28 April. The academic term will be short enough. Don't be upset! (26.12.9; tr.)

Gilson did not yet realize that he would have to assume extra teaching while his colleague Robin spent the term at the University of Pennsylvania; the letter appointing Gilson and Emile Bréhier to cover Robin's course on ancient philosophy was waiting when he arrived home.* Besides his heavier teaching load, he was also faced with a backlog of articles to read for the *Archives*.

Despite his crowded schedule, Gilson was determined to know more about St Augustine and Duns Scotus. In the Ecole he arranged his seminars in "The Philosophy of Duns Scotus" and "The Latin Avicenna and Duns Scotus." Ever since he had composed his article for the *Archives* on "Why St Thomas criticized St Augustine," Gilson had been furiously revising all his writings on Augustine. In future he planned to devote as many courses and lectures as possible to Augustine's ideas.

---

* In this letter the ministry for some reason described both Gilson and Bréhier as *maîtres de conférences*. Possibly the ministry had made a mistake and forgotten that Gilson was *professeur sans chaire*. Perhaps too the new title was euphemistic. Or the terminology may have been merely ad hoc, relating only to this special assignment and to the level of compensation (3,600 francs) attaching to it.

Gilson's new focus on Augustine concurred with a new confidence in his own authority as a scholar. Up until now he had tended to show considerable deference to the Sorbonne colleagues who had once taught him; he had also shown great care and patience in his dealings with the Catholic thomists. After his return to Paris in 1927, this deference became far less apparent. Perhaps his teaching success in America had given him a keener sense of his own abilities.

This new security is illustrated in an episode involving Gilson's formidable *maître et ami* Léon Brunschvicg. Apparently Gilson had an appointment with Brunschvicg in his home. He called at the proper time and was ushered un- announced into the library, where he found Frédéric Lefèvre in the midst of interviewing the philosopher for an upcoming "Une heure avec ...." In the final paragraphs of the interview, Gilson can be seen imperturbably usurping Lefèvre's control:

> At this moment a friend of the philosopher's was shown in. I recognized one of my former victims [25.1.5], M. Etienne Gilson. "Ah! Lefèvre." exclaimed the smiling Gilson, "since you have the ear of my master and friend, don't forget that you are dealing with more than a philosopher, but with a writer too. In my opinion his *Introduction à la vie de l'esprit*, and still more perhaps his *L'idéalisme contemporain*, are finely wrought examples of what the French mind can with genuine artistry bring to the presentation of philosophical ideas.
>
> "Besides, my *maître*'s inquisitive mind extends beyond the abstract problems of philosophy into matters of aesthetic production."
>
> And turning towards Brunschvicg, he asked: "Aren't you working on aesthetics in the Ecole Normale Supérieure?"
>
> "Yes, I have a lecture in the Ecole Normale..." and went on to explain what he and his students there had been doing and had now published. "Now that you have finished this work," Gilson asked, "what are you doing to do next?" "I think I'll turn to philosophy." (*Les nouvelles littéraires*, 27.5.14; tr.)

According to Henri Gouhier, Gilson's relations with Lefèvre were warm and generous. When Lefèvre wrote up his interview with Brunschvicg, he asked Gilson to check it over as he was not himself comfortable with philosophy.*

Although Gilson had not yet lost patience with neothomists, the beginnings of his quarrel with them are discernable in the third edition of *Le thomisme* (Paris, 1927; McG 157). Gilson had proofread the text in America and it appeared in book-form during February 1927. The moment Père M.-D. Roland-Gosselin read the new edition, he began writing Gilson frantically:

> I read the third edition of your *Thomisme* yesterday. Naturally I turned first to its new passages, and especially to chapter 13, "Connaissance et Vérité." ... It is neither what I expected nor wished it to be. ... You have allowed yourself to be misled by the two opuscula *De natura verbi* and *De intellectu et intelligibili*. ... I must say, in

---

* Professeur Henri Gouhier provided this information. He also said that Lefèvre had in 1925 submitted to Gilson beforehand a draft of his "Une heure avec Etienne Gilson." This indicates that the compliments paid Maritain by Gilson in this article were considered and deliberate.

spite of Grabmann and Peltzer, these opuscula ought not to be taken into consideration in an historical discussion of St Thomas' thought. ... Moreover, apart from the question of their authenticity, I don't recognize St Thomas ... in your way of explaining the relation between the thing known and the *species*. ... This has always seemed to me to be for St Thomas, not as you put it a kind of moving on or extension of the object, and not really distinct from it, but rather a distinct substitute for it just as the *verbum mentale* is. *Applicatio cogniti ad cognoscentem ... non est intelligenda per modum identitatis, sed per modum cujusdam repraesentationis.*

As to Maritain ... I don't think he will be any happier with your explanation than I am. ... I think you will be attacked by both of us. (27.3.5; tr.)

Although Roland-Gosselin's view on the authenticity of the two opuscula was well taken, his other point was not. His disagreement with Gilson hinged on whether Thomas believed that man knows things in themselves or in some similitude or representation of themselves. According to Roland-Gosselin, St Thomas held that man known only a similitude or representation of things; he believed that this position had direct bearing upon a problem of knowing later raised by Locke. For Gilson this position read far too much into Thomas' occasional use of the terms *similitudo* and *repraesentatio*; he believed that a careful reading of all the texts made this clear.

Gilson replied graciously to Roland-Gosselin, and received from him two more letters on the same point (27.3.9; 27.4.9). However the issue of the relation between the *res* and *species* was not resolved. When Roland-Gosselin later reviewed the third edition of *Le thomisme*, he did not modify his position (*Bulletin thomiste*, January 1929). Nor did Gilson substantially alter his treatment of the issue in the fourth, fifth or sixth editions of *Le thomisme*. Gilson believed that the use of Thomas' ideas to address modern questions that Thomas had never dreamed of asking would do nothing but hinder modern metaphysics. He never considered cartesian, kantian, lockeian or phenomenalist thomists to be authentic thomists. This quarrel with Roland-Gosselin contained, in embryonic form, the debate between methodological and critical realism that would preoccupy Gilson throughout the 1930s.

One of Gilson's strongest allies during this spring of 1927 was his old student Henri Gouhier. Gouhier was reviewing new books in philosophy this year for *Les nouvelles littéraires* and his attitudes both reflected and influenced Gilson's own. Gouhier's review of the first volume of Emile Bréhier's *Histoire de la philosophie* raised two objections that Gilson certainly shared: Gouhier criticized Bréhier's contention that the arrival of Christianity had not much affected philosophy, as well as his denial of the development of a "Christian philosophy." As well, Gouhier's review of Maritain's *Art et scholastique* agreed entirely with Gilson's position on Thomas. Gouhier challenged Maritain's reference to Thomas as "apôtre des temps modernes"; "for St Thomas," wrote Gouhier, "to be the apostle of modern times, he should be answering questions posed by them. And since times never cease to be modern [Thomas'] interpreters must in each generation show forth the youthfulness of his thought."

Although the ministry and the Sorbonne still refused to create a chair in medieval studies, they did begin to recognize, along with Gilson, the contributions of American culture. On 25 January 1927, shortly before Gilson's return, the chair of American Literature and Civilization was inaugurated with Professor Cestre as its first incumbent. In May, the Ministry of Public Instruction wrote:

> The development of intellectual relations between France and the United States has so expanded that further consultations in the matter of naming exchange professors had now become indispensible. (J. Cavalier, 27.5.3; tr.)

A committee was quickly formed to advise on the means for best expanding academic relations between the two countries.

Shortly after the first meeting of this committee, Gilson was authorized by the ministry to be absent from the Sorbonne during November and December 1927 "to teach the history of philosophy at Harvard University" (27.5.30). Gilson either knew about this authorization beforehand or immediately telegrammed Professor Woods at Harvard. At any rate Woods wrote two days later, 1 June, to say how pleased he was that Gilson could come. Woods thanked Gilson for permission to announce a seminary on Leibniz: "This will fill a great gap in our historical courses." He added that he would see Gilson in France in July.

2 SPECIAL HONOURS

During this period Gilson received two deeply appreciated honours. At its second annual meeting, 29 to 30 April 1927, the Mediaeval Academy of America elected him a corresponding fellow. At Harvard Gilson had become close to the academy's president, Charles Homer Haskins, and was in full sympathy with Haskins' desire to advance the academy's inquiries into "every phase of medieval civilization" (*Speculum*, 2 [1927]: 233). Other French scholars named corresponding fellows at this meeting were Joseph Bédier, Alfred Jeanroy, Charles Victor Langlois, Emile Mâle and Henri Pirenne; at the first annual meeting, those named had included Gilson's friend, Maurice De Wulf.

Gilson was also invited this spring to receive the degree of Doctor of Letters, *honoris causa*, from Oxford University. The convocation took place on June 30, and Gilson revelled in the elaborate and learned fun of the ceremony. He was also gratified to find himself honoured along with two great field marshals, and especially with Ferdinand Foch, his former commander-in-chief. Foch's brief interrogation of Gilson was perhaps a little anticlimactic however:

> "What do you do?" asked Foch.
> "I am a philosopher," said Gilson modestly.
> "How goes philosophy?"
> "Very well."
> "Have you ever been here before?"
> "Yes."
> "Bien," muttered the field marshal. "Où est le cabinet?"

3 HARVARD AGAIN: SAINT AUGUSTINE

In the summer of 1927 Gilson returned with his wife and children to the Alpes-Maritimes, staying at Villa Menie, Golfe-Juan, near Cannes. As he was not committed this year to giving a summer course in America, he was able to stay on with the family into the second week of September. When he left them, he went first to Cravant to visit Maman, *marraine*, his niece Lucie, and others. At Auxerre he saw Gouhier, and at Melun he picked up all the local gossip from the maid, Victorine, who was minding the house and the two Gilson cats. Still at heart a Sylvestre Bonnard, Gilson described his reception by Roussette and Poumoume:

> Roussette's kittens, the one we found a place for last year, and also this year's, are both dead. This did not stand in the way of her raising another, a black kitten, tinged with brown and with blue eyes, which is quite cute. Roussette paid no more attention to me than to a block of wood. She wanted to eat in the kitchen and had no time for me. Poumoume, aware of the presence of a stranger, sought refuge upstairs on the sewing machine. Victorine went after her, and Poumoume hissed when she came near. When she had been forcefully lifted down, she at last looked at me and apparently recognized me. She quickly stretched her head forward and from then on would not let me out of her sight. *Déjeuner* was for her a delicious pleasure; she went right to her place, curled up with her back against my left hand, and purred with all her might. When I was leaving, she sat on the staircase, mortally sad, still without taking her eyes off me for a moment. Roussette had gone back to her kitten. (27.9.14; tr.)

Gilson went from Melun to Paris and wrote Thérèse from Gare St-Lazare. He caught the boat-train for Le Havre where, on 15 September, he boarded the *S.S. Paris* for New York.

Gilson was firmly resolved to take things easier than last year; although he had brought back some $4,000 from North America, he had also returned utterly exhausted and dissatisfied with his scholarly achievements. This year he would remain in America for three months instead of seven; he would lecture seven hours a week at Harvard instead of eight; he would take on very few outside lectures; and he would work long hours in his study in Widener. Fortunately Harvard had substantially increased his salary; for three months lecturing he would receive a half year's payment:

> When I leave here in December, I will have cashed three salary cheques, that is $554 × 3 = $1,662. After I return to France, the same amount will be paid into my bank account in the Cambridge Trust Company. (EG to Thérèse, 27.10.19; tr.)

Gilson's arrangements at Harvard turned out to be more complicated than he had foreseen. In the first place, he had promised Woods that he would take a "seminary." He wasn't quite sure what a seminary was, except that it reduced his classroom load by an hour as it met for only two hours a week. He soon learned however that assigning topics to students allowed them to raise philosophical problems that concerned them, leaving him somewhat at their mercy. He found that a seminary required more preparation than a lecture and wrote Thérèse that "it is a kind of exercise in mental gymnastics and lasts for two hours. It is not nothing." (27.11.29; tr.)

Gilson was no longer a novice on staff, but a quasi-member. He found he had been selected this year by President Lowell to address the returning students, first at Radcliffe on 29 September, then at Harvard the next day. He spent his first few days in Cambridge preparing this assignment, then had Mrs Perry adjust his English prose. The Radcliffe session flustered him somewhat; he was more nervous than usual and was dissatisfied with his talk, though the audience was "kind and indulgent." He recovered his spirits during the more social events. He stood in the reception line with President Comstock, Dean Brown and the librarian, and attended a tea "of which I took none lest I lie awake all night"; during both these functions he immensely enjoyed the way the girls lionized him. (EG to Thérèse, 27.11.29) The talk at Harvard went better, and was subsequently printed as "The Ethics of Higher Studies" in the *Harvard Alumni Bulletin* (30 [1927]: 127-130; McG 656). On Saturday he attended the opening football game with Perry and was delighted when Harvard won.

During these first days at Harvard, Gilson was troubled by an inability to get down to work. He did not understand his problem, though he knew it was more than the loneliness he had suffered last year after leaving his family. After Saturday's football game, he walked over to his study in the Widener, but had a bad session. At nine o'clock he shoved his books aside in disgust and returned to his quarters in Gray's Hall. By Sunday morning Gilson was desperate. After mass he walked into Boston, dined alone in a cheap restaurant, dropped in to see a "wretched Raymond Novarro film," and walked back to Cambridge:

> I then worked in the university library but with no taste for it. I left at 5:00, discouraged, having got nowhere. This evening it seems to me I shall never again write a decent book, and so I am melancholy. (EG to Thérèse, 27.10.2; tr.)

Gilson called this short period of dejection his *journée de cafard*. In the Widener, he had been attempting to revise what he had written on Augustine in the first volume of his *La philosophie au moyen âge*. Gilson had been working on Augustine for some years; he had written two good articles on him for the *Archives* and planned to make him the subject of his next major book. Now he found himself suddenly unable to explain Augustine simply and clearly, whether in class or in his own work. The philosophy of Augustine, Gilson later wrote Thérèse, is "a dangerous thing to write about. No one has ever succeeded, and I know perfectly well I have not succeeded either. Nor did St Augustine himself succeed. There is something in this man which completely defies systematization." (27.10.27; tr.)

The melancholy of Sunday 2 October eased a little after Gilson wrote to Thérèse about it. On the next day it left him entirely:

> I have given my two hours of lectures and am free for the rest of the day. My spirits are much better today, and I shall return to work less discouraged. I hope my

bearcub will finally take shape. But, God, how I will have to lick it. It is frightening how much patience is required to bring forth these spiritual children. Even then they sometimes turn out to be ugly.

Later in the day he was himself again:

> Now this was a day that ended to my complete satisfaction. Almost complete, that is, because I have the impression I missed fire in my class on St Augustine. But I shall do better the day after tomorrow because I know now what went wrong. Otherwise, my work went smoothly. I was in the library from 2:30 to 5:00. Then I visited Mrs Hocking, the wife of the philosophy professor. I went back to work in the library from 6:00 to 8:00, and I finished the chapter which yesterday had made me despair about ever writing my book. I don't think what I have done is brilliant, but I will polish it when I have time. Certainly, this evening my courage is restored. (27.10.3; tr.)

For all that Augustine eluded him, Gilson continued to be fascinated by the man. The few outside lectures he agreed to give this fall were exclusively devoted to augustinian thought. Some of the depth of Gilson's involvement emerges in his letters to Thérèse: "St Augustine is a prodigious being for the very reason you say. He desired everything violently, had everything, and left everything. Pascal, who loved him, did the same." (27.11.7; tr.)

Not surprisingly Thérèse herself expressed a desire to read St Augustine. Gilson urged her to start with the *Confessions*, at least the first ten books, in Labriolle's translation: "You have it in the house, two volumes in red, Guillaume Budé" (27.10.27; tr.). He then advised her to proceed to the *Soliloquies* (27.10.22; 27.11.6). Clearly Gilson's book on Augustine was already struggling toward the light.

4 Visits to Toronto and Montréal

Gilson's fall visits to Toronto and Montréal were his most significant undertakings outside Harvard this term. Both universities had counted on at least a week with Gilson; they were disappointed when he told them he couldn't miss any of his scheduled Harvard lectures, and that he would not tour later as he had done last year. In late October, Gilson wrote St Michael's College at the University of Toronto with a proposal he was not sure they would accept. A Friday had unexpectedly become free because lectures were to make way for term tests. Gilson could be in Toronto for three days only – Thursday, Friday and Saturday, 3 to 5 November. St Michael's gladly accepted as long as Gilson was willing to give his four lectures on Thursday and Friday, leaving Saturday free for informal conversations about a proposed medieval institute; Saturday was the first day of the Canadian Thanksgiving holiday and could not be used for lectures. Gilson was quite agreeable, and gladly accepted the offer of three hundred dollars for the engagement. He was not anxious, however, to give four lectures in two days, especially as they were not yet written; as he told Thérèse, "if I don't produce something worthwhile, they are not the kind of people who won't notice it" (27.10.27; tr.).

Gilson left for Toronto on the afternoon of 3 November with three lectures prepared on the "Psychology of St Augustine." The lectures were entitled "The Nature of Sensations," "The Origin of Ideas," and "Memory and its Metaphysical Meaning." The fourth lecture, which was for the Philosophical Society, would deal extemporaneously with some matter arising out of these.

Gilson was met in Toronto at Union Station by Father William Murray, a professor of French who had known Gilson's priest-brother, André, in Paris. Murray took Gilson to the college for breakfast. Entering the priests' diningroom, Gilson cavalierly ordered two "dropped eggs." When the waitress stared at him blankly, he realized he had used American slang: "I had forgotten," he explained, "that I was in England."

The three lectures took place on Thursday afternoon at two o'clock and five o'clock, and on Friday morning at nine; the club discussion followed on Friday evening. On Saturday Gilson entered into his "conversations" with the college administration concerning their proposed Institute of Mediaeval Studies. The conversations concerned the nature of the proposed institute and how it could best be administered within the structure of the University of Toronto with which St Michael's was federated. Gilson became so involved in this discussion that he almost missed his six o'clock train for Boston.

Gilson wanted an up-to-date, professional, interdisciplinary institute, "a model laboratory of the history of medieval civilization" ("St Michael's Establishes Institute of Mediaeval Studies," *University of Toronto Monthly,* 28 [December 1927]: 119-121; McG 794). His institute would have a private specialized library with convenient access from offices and classrooms; a programme of mandatory introductory courses; research seminar courses in as many areas as feasible; and a collaborative methodology that would emphasize primary texts and documents. The institute would be neither a theologate nor a school of philosophy but a place for all medieval studies. Gilson had nurtured this ideal for many long years and kept it to himself "in more than one illustrious university of both the old world and the new."

When the conversations were over, Gilson was satisfied: of Toronto he declared, "the institute will be there or will be nowhere!" (p. 120.) When he left Toronto that evening, his mind was virtually made up, though he still wished to consult with his wife, with his Harvard friends, and with the Sorbonne.

Gilson's trip back to Cambridge was arduous; heavy rains had washed out the rail-line between Albany and Boston. He found a letter waiting for him from Thérèse – after some fourteen years, she was once more pregnant. Gilson was ecstatic. "We will spare nothing to assure its health," he wrote. "Jacqueline will be its *marraine*." Subsequent letters were so solicitous that Thérèse twitted him with being jealous of "la petite chose." Gilson opened his soul to her in a long warm letter which closed: "I hope the little boy or girl about to make us three will bring as much happiness to us as have our two beautiful bigger children" (27.11.17; tr.).

On Monday 7 November, the day after returning from Toronto, news arrived that the University of Montréal had also accepted Gilson's offer to spend three days there. Apparently he had initially suspected opposition:

> Montréal agrees to my lecturing on St Augustine. This is a real novelty, an interesting eventuality. Ideas do take their course, minds slowly expand, provided there is no show of force. With time and patience, anything can be accomplished.

Gilson was doubly pleased at the invitation, as it gave him a chance to meet with old friends:

> Madeleine Thibaudeau also informs me that my chauffeur, limousine and room are at my disposal. The poor girl adds that I will even be able to go out alone if I want to. ... Jean Brunhes must have been teasing her. I wouldn't put it past him. (27.11.7; tr.)

The visit to Montréal called for three lectures on St Augustine and ten public appearances in all; these were to be crammed into three days, Thursday to Saturday, 1 to 3 December. Ottawa also wanted Gilson for a talk, but Montréal decided it could not be squeezed into the schedule. In the midst of Gilson's hectic visit, an additional talk was sprung on him unannounced by René du Roure; Gilson found this "thoughtless [*abusif*] to say the least."

Gilson sent Thérèse a "brief recapitulation" of the last half of his hurried visit:

> How glad I was to have the automobile as everything was snow-covered. Dined at 1:00 with Mr Edouard Montpetit, and at 5:00 gave my lecture at McGill. After dinner, at 8:00, I lectured at the University of Montréal. The public was as loyal and attentive as ever – one of the most knowledgeable publics in medieval philosophy I could have. Friday dinner [abstinence] at the home of M. Matthys: we did penance with oysters – *bouchées à la reine* – two roasted wild ducks, Sauterne, St Emilion. In the evening I gave my second lecture, and Saturday morning at 10:00, the third. Dinner with the Dominicans. Evening meal at Le Cercle Universitaire, and afterward the talk on pure poetry. Following, there was a reception at the home of M. and Mme Doret, champagne etc. Returned to the Thibaudeaus at 1:00. Up Sunday morning at 7:00. Mass at 8:00. Train departure at 9:00. (27.12.5; tr.)

This three days marked Gilson's true entry into the intellectual and political life of Montréal, and indeed of all Québec. The visit was reported in "Etienne Gilson: historien de la philosophie" by Hermas Bastien, philosophy professor at the University of Montréal; this article appeared in the sensitive and nationalistic *L'action canadienne-française* (19, 1 [1928]: 37-44; McG 1091), the mouthpiece of the Ligue des Droits Français.* Bastien particularly noted Gilson's control of the fundamentals of the art of discourse, his intellectualism, his *luminosité* and his ability to examine the minds of others from their own point of view, all qualities pertinent to the ultimate objectives of the Ligue.

---

* The Ligue had been founded in 1913, and was still very active under the direction of Abbé Philippe Perrier, Abbé Lionel Groulx, Emile Bruchési and others.

5 Claudel, Gouhier

Immediately after his return from Montréal, Gilson went to Boston to hear
Paul Claudel lecture at the Alliance Française on "Le regard américain vers la
France." This was Claudel's first visit to Boston since his appointment as France's
ambassador to Washington the preceding April. Gilson was invited to attend the
lecture and a reception on 5 December, as well as another lecture at Wellesley
College and a dinner in Boston the next day. He was determined to attend all of
these; to avoid missing classes, he had already declined an October invitation to
join Claudel in New York in celebration of the centenary of French scientist and
author, Marcelin Berthelot.

Claudel and Gilson had much in common. They were both exemplary
Catholics who lived in the public eye, and both were active in the French cultural
mission. Despite different interests they were both involved with literature. And
in their respective modes of thought, both were realists. Some years ago Claudel
had declared his philosophical realist sympathies in a preface to Jacques Rivière's
A la trace de Dieu:

> God, and religious truth whose source God is, are neither of them constructions of
> our own mind. God is a fact, a person, a reality in some way exterior and concrete
> presenting himself to us. ... Whether it is a question of God or a tree, we can never
> get all of either of them into a definition. (tr.)

The subject of the lecture in Boston was an American's impressions of France;
Gilson had given a similar lecture in Québec City and elsewhere. Claudel's talk,
built around his own poems, struck a chord with Gilson's own family concerns:

> I am pleased that you attended Claudel's *L'annonce faite à Marie*. ... The play must
> have been very beautiful even though unactable. Violame defies interpretation – an
> impression of mine which some great young artist will come along one day and
> disprove. ... Claudel's lecture the other day in Boston was quite simple. ... I wish
> you could have heard him. His daughter, who is very dear to him, was there. After
> he read "L'enfant Jésus de Prague," he said with a touch of emotion in his voice: "I
> think I wrote that for the child who is here today!" And his daughter is indeed a
> lovely girl. What a life this man leads! He is away from his family: the education of
> his boys keeps them all in Paris. (EG to Thérèse, 27.12.9; tr.)

Both Claudel and Gilson found their long absences from home painful and
dehumanizing; Gilson referred to his exile as a *brutalité* (EG to Thérèse, 27.10.19).
In a later piece of writing Claudel declared that his life had made him

> a kind of perpetual amateur; ever a guest lingering at the threshold of precarious
> hospitality, one whose life is spent between one waiting-room and another, one
> who never has time to unpack his valise before a handshake cuts off his
> conversation with some fellow-traveller ("Non impedias musicam," *La vie intellec-
> tuelle*, 36.6.10; tr.).

Gilson always retained his empathy with Claudel. Much later, in retirement in
Cravant, Gilson often told visitors how Claudel had taught him to appreciate the

town's beauties. He would read aloud from Claudel's *Journal* an account of the poet's 1939 journey from Belgium to Brangues: "*Déjeuner* in Cravant, facing the tower of a Renaissance church of great beauty; the bells from its beautiful stone, the swallows in the blue sky" (p. 273; tr.). Do you know, Gilson would say, I had never noticed that quality of the bells before.

Between Gilson's visit to Boston and his departure for Europe on Christmas Eve, little time remained. On 10 December he visited Cornell for the second time. He liked Cornell and thought that Henri Gouhier might be happy there. Gilson was worried this year about his old student. Feeling unsettled, Gouhier was going to take a summer post in Middlebury, Vermont, to find himself:

> He sent me a rather sad letter. His being turned down by Poitiers is an injustice. He is disgusted, and rightly so. I think he plans marriage *pour sortir de ses bouquins*, a risky solution. He is also thinking about politics. ... And I know why. Universities have become more ossified. ... The registrar, A. Moritze, directed him to telegraph *negouhier* if he refused their offer, *acgouhier* if he accepted. Wouldn't you know? The wire came through *accoucher*! (EG to Thérèse, 27.11.17; tr.)

Gilson decided to return on the *S.S. Majestic* so that he would be with Thérèse and the girls by New Year's Day. The *Majestic* also offered the new cheap "tourist" accommodation, tailored to the pocketbook of the scholar. By travelling tourist class, Gilson could save enough money to bring Cécile out with him next fall. Pleased with his business acumen, he smugly reported his calculations to Thérèse; in reply, she teased him that he had chosen a ship not even mentioned on *Le Figaro*'s traveller's page which he had once advised her always to consult.

Gilson felt that at long last he ought to acquire a new trunk. His luggage was very battered; this, along with his disreputable hats, had become almost a trademark. And this year he had more presents to bring back than previously. Mme Thibaudeau was sending stockings for Thérèse as well as a bonnet and a knitted rose-coloured sweater for the baby: "Here I am before it is even born become the personal carrier for *numero trois*!" Gilson coveted a fashionable Hartmann trunk with built-in drawers and racks, but at forty-two dollars he was inclined to deny himself. He wrote to Thérèse, who apparently told him to do whatever he wanted: "You tell me to buy the trunk without holding a conference about it. What I wrote you was that I was going to hold a conference about it and not buy the trunk."

Gilson eventually resolved the issue in true thomist fashion. He developed three arguments in all, two from convenience and a third from divine intervention:

> I finally bought the trunk. I thought: first, that the old one was not up to the return trip and I would have to buy a new one in France when it was really an American trunk I wanted; second, I was afraid of being caught out by my wife (not easy-going when angered); third, a cheque for thirty-two dollars from a Radcliffe student who is auditing one of my courses just fell out of heaven into my hands. This turned the scale. I added ten dollars from my own pocket and bought the trunk. (EG to Thérèse, 27.10.9; tr.)

The wardrobe trunk turned out to possess its limitations. It was heavy to haul and not immune to the knocks and blows that beset all trunks. It also had a compartment for women's dresses, a sad reminder to Gilson that he was travelling alone.

6 Decision on the Institute

Before returning to Paris, Gilson felt he must decide what to do about the offer from Toronto to establish his institute:

> The superior of St Michael's [E. J. McCorkell] writes that he is coming to Boston to discuss the matter with me. I shall not avoid the discussion. Certainly the project interests me very much because it is the first time that my concept of the Middle Ages has taken form on a foundation that will make possible its surviving me. On the other hand, I fear the work involved. Nor do I want to desert Harvard where I have become so perfectly accepted; but the work in Toronto holds the greater interest. (EG to Thérèse, 27.12.16; tr.)

After the visit by Father McCorkell, Gilson met privately with President Lowell and told him that, although he would be at Harvard next year, he would not be there again on a regular basis. Lowell was disappointed but understood the decision. His comment lingered in Gilson's memory all his life: "After all, you are going back to your own." In part, Lowell was referring to Gilson's decision to work at St Michael's in a Catholic atmosphere. But Lowell also understood that by accepting St Michael's offer Gilson could remain in Paris and continue to explore medieval philosophy within the Sorbonne. Lowell wanted to make Gilson part of Harvard's world; St Michael's wanted Gilson to introduce it to his.

Gilson found his decision to discontinue teaching at Harvard emotionally difficult. During January and February he received warm letters from Woods, Perry, Miss Comstock and others urging him to reconsider. In January, however, both Father McCorkell, superior of St Michael's, and Sir Robert Falconer, president of the University of Toronto, wrote strong letters to M. Cavalier, Director of Public Instruction. They told Cavalier of their plan to make "the University of Toronto a centre in America for the study of the medieval period," and asked him to allow Gilson "to come to us for the fall term of each year until such time as in his judgment the work is sufficiently advanced to develop on its own" (McCorkell to Cavalier, 28.1.12). In the end Cavalier authorized Gilson to leave the Sorbonne and "to go to the United States and Canada for the purpose of giving instruction in Harvard University, in the University of Toronto, and in St Michael's College of that University" (Charety to EG, 28.7.4; tr.).

10

France and America, 1928-1930

1 THE QUARREL OVER ATHEISM

Back from North America in January 1928, Gilson embarked upon the rigorous three-year period that would cap his career in the Sorbonne and lead to his entry into the Collège de France. No sooner had he returned to Paris than Xavier Léon, secretary of the Société Française de Philosophie, asked him to serve as antagonist in a forthcoming meeting. Léon Brunschvicg was to make a presentation to the société entitled "La querelle de l'athéisme." Some time earlier Brunschvicg had argued in favour of atheism in a review of Gilson's edition-with-commentary of the *Discours de la méthode*; when Léon had asked Gilson to reply to the argument, Gilson had refused. In the intervening years, however, Gilson had come to feel a keener responsibility to his faith. He agreed to tangle with Brunschvicg when the société met 14 March 1928.

Brunschvicg's presentation of his thesis at the meeting was masterful. He set forth the claim of radical rationalists that in a non-a-priori scientific idealism, or "true spiritualism," knowledge of the real is to be identified with the activity of the human mind alone. There can be no problem of God within immanent reflection divorced from the transcendence of revelation. Philosophically therefore, there is no God.

Gilson handled his presentation competently, although the best historian of the event, Cornelio Fabro, gave him little credit for it.* Brunschvicg, said Gilson, has accepted at face value Pascal's assertion that the God of Abraham, Isaac and Jacob, the God of the imagination, is very different from the God of reason that has occupied recent philosophers. For Brunschvicg, as for Voltaire and others, the philosophers' God or reason is merely the clockmaker who constructed the world and set it into motion. Brunschvicg throws out this God because, in a valid philosophy, knowledge of the real can only be identified through the activity of the mind itself. Immanent reflection divorced from the transcendence of revelation

---

* For Fabro's account see his *God in Exile: Modern Atheism* (tr. Arthur Gibson [Glen Rock, N.J.], pp. 61-65). Rather than examining the actual transcription of the meeting, Fabro seems to have accepted the later account given by Brunschvicg himself in *De la vraie et de la fausse conversion* (Paris, 1950), pp. 214 ff.

presents neither any problem of God nor any God. This is a classic argument, and on its own terms unanswerable.

As antagonist, Gilson chides Brunschvicg for assuming that Pascal's God of Abraham was no more than the God of common sense. Pascal's God, argues Gilson, was a mystical one whom men both experienced and touched, not an intra-philosophical but a supra-philosophical God. Indeed, Pascal should not have been introduced into the quarrel at all. Moreover, Brunschvicg's clockmaker God is a double misconception. A clockmaker is not a creator. Nor is he a mystic's or a metaphysician's God. At most a clockmaker is a God of nature.

Gilson deals with his opponent's various statements as little more than postulates. He disputes Brunschvicg's contentions that there is only one kind of knowledge; that this world of becoming contains within itself the sufficient reason of its own being and operation; that only the rational in man, and not the irrational and sensible, calls for explanation; and that spiritualism and dogmatism are incompatible. Gilson's trump card, perhaps understated at this time, is his claim that if Brunschvicg could not philosophically speak of *God*, neither could he of *no God*. Atheism has no more place in his philosophy than has theism.

Once Gilson and Brunschvicg had presented their respective arguments, each began to inspect words, phrases and ideas used by the other. The two were left arguing at cross purposes. Gilson argued in the language of Aristotle, Augustine and Thomas, where analogy means something more than metaphor; Brunschvicg used the language of the more recent mathematical and physical philosophers, in which the appeal to analogy is utterly banal. Each described the language of the other as naïve. Certainly, the question at issue was not resolved.

If Gilson did not actually win the debate, he did succeed, unlike many philosophical opponents of contemporary atheism, in demonstrating that philosophers could not validly close the case for God before it was even opened. The need for opposition to growing atheism convinced Gilson that his presence in Paris was important. Throughout his career his involvement with the question of atheism never flagged and his skill in approaching it continued to grow; as late as 1968 he prepared papers on the topic (below, p. 378). Gilson's enduring support for his position remained Auguste Comte, as Henri Gouhier sensed in his response to one of Gilson's later papers:

> Your article on the difficulties of atheism brings to light an important and often forgotten problem. Comte was aware of it and did not want the word to be so much as mentioned. Positivism defines a state in which the problem of the existence of God has no more place than has the existence of Juno or Jupiter. This got him into a rather different difficulty, that of ill-founded prophecy. At least, however, he had the good sense to understand that atheism in no way shares the privilege of rationality. (Gouhier to EG, 70.9.5; tr.)

Gilson's debate with Brunschvicg was not a hostile one, and the two men remained good friends. For Gilson, the effort was reassuring; he now knew that he need never fear confrontation with brilliant intellectuals.

On the day after the debate, 15 March 1928, Gilson's third child, his first and only son, was born in Paris. Jacqueline was fifteen and Cécile fourteen when Bernard was born, and Thérèse and Gilson were forty-three and forty-four. The birth, to use a well-known Gilsonism, gave an "entirely different" dimension to the whole family by placing an infant boy at its centre. The effect on Gilson himself was dramatic, increasing his sense of the totality of human experience and considerably mellowing his confidence in the autonomy of the intellectual life.

2 European Invitations

During this period a flurry of European and particularly British requests came to Gilson for lectures and courses. Europe was conscious of the new approach toward medieval thought emerging from the Sorbonne and wanted to meet it at first hand. The first of these invitations came from the University of Aberdeen in Scotland, which asked Gilson to give the Gifford Lectures on natural theology. Between 1928 and 1931, Gilson was asked to lecture in the University of Cambridge on the "Middle Ages and the Renaissance"; in the University of London on "God in Descartes"; in the Universities of Leipzig and Marburg on "Cistercian Mysticism"; in the University College of Wales on "St Bernard and the Love of God"; and in Lady Margaret Hall at Oxford to inaugurate the P. M. Kinder Lectures. There were other invitations too, which he was unable to accept.

The invitation to become Aberdeen's fifteenth Gifford lecturer was particularly noteworthy in that it was a call to function directly as a philosopher. Moreover few philosophers outside Britain – only Josiah Royce in 1898 and Hans Driesch in 1907 – had received invitations from Aberdeen. The preliminary feeler came in early March 1928 from A. S. Ferguson, Aberdeen's professor of logic:

> As you will doubtless hear from official sources, the *senatus* of this university elected you this afternoon to the Gifford Lectureship, which is within its gift. It was the strong desire of my philosophical colleague, Professor John Laird, and of myself, that we should add your name to the list of distinguished men who have held this office, and we are delighted with the remarkable vote of the *senatus*, which showed (as I think) a wish to do honour to an eminent philosopher and to France. (Ferguson to EG, 28.2.28.)

Ferguson enclosed a list of the distinguished men who had previously given the lectures, the most recent being Dr E. M. Barnes, the brilliant and controversial bishop of Birmingham. Gilson would be the first Gifford lecturer to focus his attention on the thought of the Middle Ages.

The formal invitation to Aberdeen came from H. J. Butchart of Marischal College, the university registrar. Butchart outlined the nature and conditions of the lectures as set forth by the donor Lord Gifford: they were to deal in a general way with "natural philosophy"; to consist of twenty lectures extended over two successive years; to carry a stipend of £550 each year; and to be published in fifty copies of unbound sheets for the university. A postscript for Gilson's benefit added that they were to be delivered in English; as things turned out, the lectures were actually delivered in French.

Gilson replied immediately that although he was "disposed to accept," the early suggested date and his heavy fall commitments to Harvard and Toronto had caused him second thoughts. Laird and Ferguson immediately sent back two very different replies:

> [*Laird*:] We are profoundly sorry to hear that you may have some hesitation. ... We think very seriously that Scotland ought to know about medieval philosophy in this present time. ... We need this knowledge quite as much as Harvard or Toronto. ... Inform me whether I could see you somewhere in Paris (or Melun) ... on Friday 16 or Saturday 17. ... If the main difficulty is one of dates ... a certain delay would be no great matter. (Laird to EG, 28.3.9.)

> [*Ferguson*:] I am delighted that you are disposed to accept. ... Professor Laird (who originally suggested your name) tells me that he has written offering to meet you when he passes through Paris. (Ferguson to EG, 28.3.10.)

Two days before sending his acceptance to Butchart, Gilson wrote Perry at Harvard telling him about the invitation. Through Perry, Gilson's Aberdeen lectures were provisionally accepted by Charles Scribner's and Sons as early as 14 May 1928. The lectures were delivered in Aberdeen during 1931 and 1932. They were published in French by Vrin in two volumes in 1932, and were translated into English by A. H. C. Downs for joint publication by Scribner's of New York and Sheed and Ward of London. For a time Scribner's became Gilson's major American publisher.

Gilson's choice of subject for the lectures was "Medieval Philosophy and Its Present Value." This title stood until the lectures were given and was changed for publication to *The Spirit of Medieval Philosophy* (McG 32); as an historian, Gilson was never comfortable with the notion of value. Although the preparation of the twenty lectures placed a heavy burden on Gilson, it also provided him with the opportunity to sharpen and specify his own philosophical stance. Essentially he found himself forced to explain what he meant by medieval philosophy. As he slowly pulled the lectures together between 1928 and 1931, he clarified his own positions to himself and began to assert those positions through his regular university courses, his private discussions, and his incidental articles and lectures. The Gifford Lectures slowly brought to light, as no other experience had done, the metaphysician and the philosopher who lay behind the historian of thought.

The invitations to lecture in Germany in 1929 also had special significance for Gilson. Marburg, once a leading Kantian stronghold, had since 1924 been witnessing the attempt of Heinz Heimsröth to build a bridge between Kant and scholasticism. Peter Wust had reported Heimsröth's work in "Die Rückkehr des deutschen Katholicismus aus dem Exil" (*Kölnische Volkszeitung*, 24.5.21-22); this article had been picked up in France by *Documentation catholique* (12 [1924]: 101-118). According to Wust, Heimsröth had been following the pattern set by Gilson in proceding from Descartes back into the Middle Ages, and had been using both

Gilson's and Koyré's work. In the light of all this, Gilson's invitation to Marburg was not surprising.

As for Leipzig, a letter survives from Professor G. Friedmann requesting the necessary information to introduce Gilson and his topic, Cistercian mysticism, to his audience. Friedmann wrote that interest in the lecture was running high and that the university's largest amphitheatre had been engaged to cope with the expected crowd. After the lecture a small gathering of professors was planned, which would include Hans Driesch, Israel Freyer and others interested in philosophy; Gilson already knew Driesch from his work on the Permanent Committee of International Congresses in Philosophy.

Gilson lectured in Marburg on 12 May 1929 and in Leipzig two days later. However, although the lectures were important in themselves, Gilson's German visit was most notable for inspiring two articles for *L'européen*, a newly founded journal which was attempting to focus the attention of French intellectuals on European thought. Gilson's articles were the first of hundreds of serious popular writings he would eventually submit to daily, weekly and monthly papers; he soon came to regard this form of journalism as his duty, both as a republican and as a man who regarded himself as temperamentally close to the ordinary citizen.

The titles of these first two pieces were not terribly inviting: "Autour de Benda: la mare aux clercs" (29.5.29; McG 557), and "Vues prises de Marbourg" (29.6.19; McG 827). Gilson had been growing increasingly impatient with French intellectuals since 1926 at Harvard when he had read an article on Julien Benda by Henri Gouhier in *Les nouvelles littéraires*. Gouhier had taken issue with a thesis first proposed by Benda in 1910 and recently reprinted. Benda had argued that the general public adopts its morals more by emotion than by reason, picking up ideas proposed by philosophers, distorting them, then living by these distortions. He had maintained that historians of philosophy did less than their duty to their fellow men by failing to take into consideration how the great ideas have fared among *le vulgaire*. Gouhier's article had replied that historians, in dealing with the various philosophical schools, actually did show concern for what becomes of great ideas. Gilson had not considered Gouhier's an adequate response and had resolved to read for himself Benda's *Mon premier testament*, *La trahison des clercs* and *La fin de l'éternel*. Like many others in and outside France, he became very impressed with Benda and felt considerable sympathy for his ideas.*

"Autour de Benda: la mare aux clercs" deals with Benda's thesis in *La trahison des clercs*. According to Benda, scholars and intellectuals ought to be investigated, as they have somehow lost sight of the philosopher's vocation to seek and love

---

* One of those who read Benda in the 1930s, possibly at Gilson's suggestion, was Frank Pickersgill, a young graduate student at the University of Toronto who was executed as a spy in the war. In 1937 Pickersgill wrote to his friend Ford: "Oh say, if you have any spare time this winter, take Julien Benda's *Trahison des clercs* from the library; it is very good indeed, I consider, and the most interesting diagnosis of the trouble with modern intellectuals that I have ever seen" (George H. Ford, *The Making of a Secret Agent*, 2nd ed. [Toronto, 1978], p. 58).

truth. Benda, writes Gilson, is the first person since Malebranche to rise and defend the idea of truth; philosophers now refuse to discuss the issue, and are incensed with Benda for raising it. Benda labours on the level of pure truth only, asking "whether, yes or no, the word truth signifies all universal and necessary knowledge"; meanwhile modern intellectuals only consider how best to employ truth in some other cause. Gilson upholds Benda's "absolute value of the true" and equates it with that idea of wisdom which the dying Victor Delbos felt he had wasted his life rediscovering. Gilson also takes Benda's condemnation of intellectuals one step further and blames them for yielding to the temptation of original sin, defined by Augustine and Bonaventure as that desire within every man to lay his hand on a temporal good, to feel himself as somehow distinct, and to be ruled by self-interest and pride.

The second of the first two L'européen articles, "Vues prises de Marbourg," is a serious attack on French critical scholarship by an unnamed Marburg interlocutor. When the article was published, many felt that there was no such person and that Gilson was really speaking for himself; however, on his own copy of this number of L'européen, Gilson named the critic as the scholarly Leo Spitzer.

The interlocutor begins by expressing strong regrets that French scholars have so extravagantly adopted the "positivist method" of research through the systematic use of fiches or tabulating cards, and have almost entirely abandoned the older French system of "fearless construction and synthesis." In this positivist method, says the interlocutor, a positive fact becomes a "fetish before which one is expected to bow respectfully, even with superstitious fervour, as though there is to be found in facts something more than the mind is capable of putting there." Certainly scholars must gather facts and classify them, but this can only be a beginning. The constructive mind must then take over and must synthesize the facts, building bridges between them. Why, he asks, do you in France in your positivist rationalizing have to renounce synthesis?

The interlocutor goes on to accuse the French of confusing scientific positivism with inexorable rational logic. How France has been impoverished by a Littré! You think you are following Comte, but Comte never destroyed without compensating. Where now are your metaphysicians? Where your philosophers? When you make progress on one front, you feel you have to amputate on another. You call this "using your reason" and "simplifying," but it amounts to cutting yourself off from half the truth.

Gilson's article excited considerable response. Among the readers who wrote in to comment were Senator Léon Bérard, F. Baldensperger of the Sorbonne, Lacour-Goyet of the Institute of France, and Daniel-Rops of the Lycée d'Orléans. Gilson was encouraged by these reactions and wrote a number of subsequent articles for L'européen throughout its two-year career. In general these focused on the point at which philosophy and the fine arts meet.

During the late 1920s, then, Gilson was as involved in the scholarship of France and Europe as he had become with that of Harvard and Toronto. His strengthening thomism was not separating him from contemporary issues; in his own way, he was bringing it to bear on them. The challenges now faced by Gilson were as diverse as they were forthright. His involvement with *L 'européen* forced him to confront the sociological issues that arose in current trends in scholarship. His preparations for Scotland presented him with a doctrinal challenge, to define medieval philosophy. And in Canada he faced a pedagogical and structural challenge as he began to design his own programme for studying the Middle Ages.

3 TORONTO PLANS, AUTUMN 1928

The fall of 1928 found Gilson in Cambridge for the third successive year. His activities followed the pattern set during the two previous years: the teaching of two courses in philosophy at Harvard; active participation in campus events; special evenings with his Cambridge and Boston friends; and lively lecture visits to Wellesley, Cornell, Montréal, Ottawa and Toronto. There were however two important differences. Everyone at Harvard was aware that this was to be Gilson's last regular semester as visiting professor. And Gilson was not in Cambridge alone – his daugther Cécile was with him.

Cécile, now fifteen, studied English from Mondays to Fridays in Arlington Heights Academy, and on weekends joined her father and his friends. For her the experience was exhilarating; for Gilson life was less lonely. Cécile kept a record of the places she saw and the people she met, a record she later burned during the occupation of Paris. She also wrote most of the letters home for herself and her father, but these were not saved.

On 1 to 3 November Gilson visited Toronto for a third time. The primary purpose for the visit was to give further shape to the new Institute of Mediaeval Studies, which was to open in 1929. During these three days Gilson also delivered four lectures. Two were historically and textually based, probing the thought of Roger Bacon in a manner suitable for graduate students to emulate. The third was an evening session with the wider-based University of Toronto Philosophical Society on what was soon to become a highly controversial subject, medieval realism. The final lecture was more oriented toward public relations, and was delivered to Toronto clergy on "Early Christian Philosophers."

Whereas last year Gilson's conversations with Gerald Phelan had dealt mainly with the new Institute, this year the two discussed Louvain and neoscholasticism. Gilson found a lot of himself in Phelan: strong faith, keen intelligence, broad culture, training in languages and music. Both men were highly professional teachers, and both possessed enough vanity to bluff a little when bluff seemed called for. But Gilson also found in Phelan much that was new, particularly his Catholic academic background and his circle of neoscholastic friends; Gilson knew the world of neoschalisticism well enough from the outside but had never really penetrated it.

Gerald Bernard Phelan was a native of Halifax, Nova Scotia. He had been a brilliant student in St Mary's College, Halifax, during the experimental period,[*] and then in the bilingual Holy Heart Seminary conducted by the strongly France-oriented Eudist Fathers. Ordained in 1914, he had worked for a time in St Mary's Cathedral and its Bermuda mission. After the war he had gone first to the Catholic University of America for his MA, then to Louvain for his PhD and *agrégé*. At Louvain he had studied advanced philosophy with Maurice De Wulf, Léon Noël and Auguste Mansion, and had done his experimental psychology and dissertation with Albert E. Michotte; he had become close to these scholars and their neoscholastic circle, and remained so all his life. In 1925 Phelan became professor of psychology at St Michael's in Toronto. Henry Carr was already buiding his department of philosophy; indeed, both Phelan and Gilson came to Toronto because Carr was willing to give them their heads. Phelan was crucial to the development of the new Institute; if Carr and the Basilians were the Institute's soul, Phelan and Gilson were its experience and intellect.

From the start of their relationship Phelan encouraged Gilson to react flamboyantly to what both men regarded as a temporizing tendency toward idealism in current neoscholasticism. Phelan urged Gilson to respond strongly to Roland-Gosselin, Noël and others who were taking issue with his third edition of *Le thomisme*. Phelan also encouraged Gilson to select as his topic for the meeting of the Philosophical Society the pertinent subject, "The True Meaning of Medieval Realism." Although the text of Gilson's talk seems not to have survived, it was apparently close in substance to his article entitled "Le réalisme méthodique" (below, pp. 219-221). This was the first of many articles on realism that eventually culminated in *Le réalisme thomiste*.

Gilson referred obliquely to Phelan's role in the genesis of his own position in the postscript of a letter the following March: "PS – I have sent for the Joseph Geyser Mélange, an article on "le réalisme méthodique" which will please you. I discuss in it the position of Canon Noël." (EG to Phelan, 29.4.29.) Moreover, Gilson's dedication of a later volume of essays on realism "to my friend, the Rev. G. B. Phelan" represents not only friendship but indebtedness. The raising of the issue of medieval realism was the first fruit of collaborative work within the Institute circle.

In 1928 Gilson and Phelan also began to assemble the book collection that would later become one of the research glories of North America. The basic books were turned over to the Institute from the eclectic Priests' Library of the Basilian Fathers; this library's original holdings had been assembled over some seventy years and had been expanded considerably during the 1920s when Carr and others were making philosophy a specialty within St Michael's.

---

[*] During this period St Mary's faculty included a colourful group of laymen such as W. F. P. Stockley, Maxwell Drennan, Bernard Gavin and John Cobb. See L. K. Shook, *Catholic Post-Secondary Education in English-Speaking Canada* (Toronto, 1971), pp. 63-65.

In their pursuit of books for the Institute, Gilson and Phelan formed a kind of team. Phelan was the acting librarian and Gilson, in effect, was his European agent. Vernon Bourke was Phelan's assistant. A letter from Gilson to Phelan early in 1929 shows the two hard at work:

> Tomorrow I shall pass your request on to Vrin. Many books are out of print and cannot be found at the moment, but Vrin is keeping his eye open and trying to acquire them. He has been unable, though searching for a whole year, to put together a complete set of the *Revue thomiste*, for example. Monceaux is out of print, etc. Thus you will find among the books I am sending several not immediately needed. I bought them because I found them. You may not be able to find them later when you need them. I am going to try to get the three volumes of Monceaux through the ministry, if any remain. (29.4.29.)

In 1978 Vernon Bourke compared his experience working on the Institute's collection with his current complicated efforts to establish a new graduate programme of philosophy in Texas:

> When I think of how quickly and simply the Institute was started in 1928 at St Mike's, I find the elaborate organization details of the 1970s amusing. For instance, [in 1928] I checked over the Migne *Patrologia latina et graeca* for the new library (Father Phelan was librarian, I did the work), and I ordered the missing volumes directly from Paris for thirty-five cents a volume unbound. At that time there were still some of the original printing in stock. (Bourke to R. J. Scollard, 78.8.15.)

4 GILSON'S *SAINT AUGUSTINE*

Gilson was back in Paris for New Year's Day 1929. Shortly thereafter his formidable and somewhat controversial *Introduction à l'étude de saint Augustin* (Paris, 1929; McG 73) appeared. Gilson's preface to this book was dated Melun, 1 June 1928, and had been written shortly before his final trip to Harvard as regular visiting professor. The book's dedication suggests how difficult his wrench from Harvard must have been: "To the Teachers and Students of the Department of Philosophy of Harvard University: E.G., who remains one of theirs."

In his preface Gilson writes that he has approached the study of Augustinism through Augustine's own texts and has attempted to uncover the spirit of Augustinism from Augustine's own point of view; these are the same principles that earlier informed his work on St Thomas. In calling his book an *Introduction*, Gilson means that he is not yet through with the subject. Therefore he includes, beyond the usual table of proper names and themes treated, various useful tools for further study: an up-to-date bibliography that goes far beyond his own reading; personal assessments of many of the bibliographical entries; and a table of contents so controlled as to offer a tentative systematization of an author whose writings have defied systematic analysis. Gilson makes it clear that his work requires more refining; he does not feel that he had said the last word. Henri Gouhier acknowledged this in his sympathetic review of the book for *Les nouvelles littéraires* (29.11.30):

Six or seven years ago, M. Et. Gilson gave a first sketch of his triumphant synthesis in a public course in the Sorbonne. Between that synthesis of yesterday and this of today came the patient analysis carried out in the Ecole Pratique des Hautes Etudes, and between today's synthesis and that of his second edition still to come, other analyses will continue to be made.

As Gouhier observed, Gilson's *Saint Augustine* takes the form of an "itinerary of the soul to God." It sets forth for the first time themes essential to grasping Augustine's personal experience and philosophical principles. It also traces Augustine's quest for God through his intellect, his will and his contemplation of God's works. Although Gilson's *Saint Augustine* predates the surge of profound research on him in the 1940s, it rightly recognizes Augustine's eclecticism and his function as "an inhibitor rather than transmitter of neoplatonism."* Of most interest to Gilson, however, is the late medieval perspective on Augustine's contributions to the development of Christian thought, a perspective which interestingly contravened Gilson's own principles for the study of figures of the past.

Gilson's main conclusions are succinctly incorporated into the final chapter entitled "Augustinism." First he argues that Augustinism is not philosophy in the usual sense of a rational and theoretical effort to resolve general problems posed by man and the universe; nonetheless, it *is* philosophical, a Christian philosophy which transfers problems to a higher plain. Second, Augustinism is not susceptible to organization into a closed linear synthesis, but has its own order centred in grace and charity. Third, Augustine's presentation is characterized by control of digression through supreme rhetoric. Fourth, this presentation functions in two perspectives, the Platonic and Judeo-Christian cosmologies which it is always seeking to reconcile. Finally, although Augustinism has a true metaphysics, it is strongly psychological and best described as a "metaphysics of conversion" or of "interior experience."

Gilson's *Saint Augustine* drew a good deal of criticism both from secular and Catholic philosophers. As represented by Brunschvicg, university philosophers refused to accept Gilson's notion of a Christian philosophy in the context of St Augustine. The Louvain philosophers also found it impossible to accept Augustinism as a Christian philosophy.

Perhaps the most thorough piece of analytical criticism was written by Fernand Van Steenberghen in Louvain's *Revue néo-scolastique* (34 [1932]; 35 [1933]). Although Van Steenberghen considered Gilson's *Saint Augustine* the best and most authoritative work produced for Augustine's jubilee, he did not accept its thesis. He argued that Augustine's doctrine was not, either in fact or in Augustine's own opinion, a philosophy; when Augustine had called his work a pure philosophy to differentiate it from Aristotle's pagan philosophy, he had not used the word in a scientific sense. Augustine's work, in so far as it was scientific at all, was strictly theology. Van Steenberghen's judgment reflected a general

---

* This judgment was expressed by the authoritative Augustine scholar, John O'Meara, *viva voce*.

Louvain position which held that scientific philosophy and theology had been considered separately in the Middle Ages and that philosophical reflection on revealed truth had been adequately provided for within the discipline of theology. Although Van Steenberghen's criticism of Gilson's thesis was not actually in print until 1932 and 1933, it was widely known by late 1930. In part this criticism explains why Gilson now began to develop his thesis of Christian philosophy in earnest, and would spend most of the 1930s demonstrating it in a variety of ways.

In his *Introduction to the Study of Saint Augustine* Gilson consciously said little concerning the foray into manicheism that had given Augustine his sense of evil, or the involvement with neoplatonism that had given him his philosophical spiritualism, his respect for being, and his philosophical vision of the God whom he had already accepted by faith. Gilson felt that the tracing of these intellectual developments was unnecessary, as neither of them had produced the slightest philosophical change in any of Augustine's essential theses. He had however once called an article by Charles Boyer shallow for precisely the same omissions, and he now found it necessary "to retract expressly this reproach as ill-founded."

Gilson was indebted to Boyer's work on Augustine; in particular he considered Boyer's *Christianisme et néoplatonisme dans la formation de saint Augustin* (1920) a decisive demonstration of Augustine's direct conversion to Catholicism prior to his involvement with neoplatonism. Perhaps as penance for his unfair criticism, Gilson now accepted Boyer's invitation to participate in the Augustine-Thomist Week to be held in Rome from 23 to 30 April 1930; this celebration would mark the fifteen hundredth anniversary of Augustine's death. Gilson was not overly enthusiastic about the invitation. He was inclined to agree with the Dominican editors of the *Revue thomiste* that this linking of Thomas with Augustine was an artificial instance of *concordisme*, an "awkward way of serving a not-disinterested end, a double blemish in a scientific undertaking" (*Revue thomiste*, 7 [1930]: 126-127). Gilson's paper for Augustine-Thomist Week was entitled "L'idée de philosophie chez saint Augustin et chez saint Thomas d'Aquin" (*Vie intellectuelle*, 8 [1930], 46-62; McG 305). The paper was easy to prepare and safely noncommittal; it contrasts unfavourably, for example, with his "The Future of Augustinian Metaphysics" (McG 207) in Bullough's *A Monument to Saint Augustine* (1930), written for the Augustine celebrations in London later in the year.

As things turned out Gilson was unable to go to Rome in late April, and his paper was read in a shortened version by Père Théry, his co-director of the *Archives*; this permitted an unannounced paper by Josephus Ricciotti to be squeezed in at the last moment. Gilson's absence from Rome seems not to have been a form of protest but a genuine case of pressing family concerns. There had recently been a lot of illness in the house: Jacqueline had been operated on for appendicitis, Bernard had whooping cough, and he himself had undergone surgery for a cyst. Moreover, he and Thérèse had been house-hunting in Paris and were planning an April move to 11, avenue Constant-Coquelin. For reasons that are not clear, this move did not take place; however, later in the year the Gilsons did move to avenue Emile-Accolas in the Champs de Mars.

5 HISTORIEN MANQUÉ

One of the great historical projects in progress in 1929 in France was the *Histoire de l'Eglise* by Fliche and Martin. The celebrated authors, conscious of the conjunction of conventional history with the history of ideas, tried to involve Gilson in the volume on doctrinal movements in the Middle Ages. Gilson apparently hesitated, and Fliche wrote to him from Montpellier:

> Your letter disappoints me. Although I understand your reasons to the contrary, I still insist that you agree to undertake personally two or three chapters of the volume in question and to distribute the others between Théry and Chenu (29.6.14; tr.)

Gilson replied on June 16, apparently accepting on the condition that he assume responsibility for the entire volume. He wanted to invite some of his students to collaborate with him in preparing it. He received Fliche's reply upon his return from Canada early in 1930:

> Now the situation is that we have among our collaborators several Jesuits but no Dominican. Since we see no possibility of finding a friar-preacher for the properly historical section, Mgr Martin and I feel that we should ask you whether you could not as of now envisage one Dominican collaborator (you have mentioned Théry and Chenu) whom we might announce, so as to maintain the wide-open character of the collection. (30.2.7; tr.)

Ultimately Gilson did not take on the work for Fliche. The volume on doctrinal movements was produced by André Forest for the twelfth century, Fernand Van Steenberghen for the thirteenth, and M. de Gandillac of the Sorbonne for the fourteenth.

6 FOUNDING OF THE TORONTO INSTITUTE, AUTUMN 1929

In the late summer of 1929 Gilson left Paris for the official founding of the Institute of Mediaeval Studies in Toronto. His decision to base his North American activities in Toronto was regretted in two places. Perry and his colleagues would like to have held Gilson at Harvard, and Gilson's friends in Montréal, Ottawa and Québec would have liked to see him set up his institute in French Canada. Gilson picked Toronto partly because of its willingness to comply with his plans and partly because it did not desire him to sever his ties with Paris.

Gilson arrived in Toronto on Sunday morning, 29 September 1929. On 30 September he attended the academic mass to formally open the Institute of Mediaeval Studies, and he immediately assumed his new duties in the non-administrative post of the Institute's director, a title he would hold until his death. Gilson was to provide a lecture course and a seminar, lasting roughly three months. He was also to assume the personal direction of the Institute's students, to assemble research personnel, and to arrange if possible for the Institute to be formally approved by the Holy See. These duties set a general pattern for Gilson's Toronto activities for the next ten years.

During the fall of 1929 Gilson gave a lecture course on "The Thirteenth-Century Oxford School" and a seminar on "The Psychology of Thomas Aquinas." The lecture course was open to auditors from the graduate school, while the seminar was restricted to candidates proceeding to degrees. Both courses were intended to indicate suitable fields of research work; this concern was to characterize all of Gilson's Toronto offerings. When he wasn't teaching, Gilson worked with his colleagues to develop the Institute within the structural framework of the University of Toronto.

Gilson's activities this fall were not entirely confined to Toronto, as the following letter illustrates:

> I shall be giving two lectures for the Institut Pédagogique where I shall read Claudel's poems with commentary, and one talk to Le Cercle Universitaire, and perhaps a lecture at McGill. I shall be going to Québec where I shall speak on my Ottawa subject, "Le sentiment d'amour au moyen âge." In Ottawa I shall be giving three lectures, one each on St Bernard, St Francis and St Dominic. I shall finish off with lectures at Cornell and Illinois. (EG to Mme Thibaudeau, 29.8.22; tr.)

The fall semester in Toronto passed quietly and to the satisfaction of all. On the day Gilson left for France he wrote: "My work here is drawing to a close in a spirit of mutual affection which affords me deep pleasure. Never before in [North] America have I had such positive results, and I am encouraged. ... As for the Ottawa project; it is now ready and will definitely be realized." (EG to Mme Thibaudeau, 29.12.15; tr.)

The "Ottawa project" requires some explanation. In 1926, when the church was marking the fiftieth anniversary of Leo XIII's encyclical *Aeterni patris*, there was a strong feeling among a number of Catholic colleges and universities that they ought to be implementing the directives of the encyclical more vigorously. In Montréal, the Institut Scientifique Franco-Canadien marked the anniversary by sponsoring lectures, including Gilson's, on medieval philosophy; Montpetit, the university secretary, also hoped at that time to persuade Gilson to set up his institute in Montréal. The Dominicans of Ottawa also had hopes of sponsoring Gilson's institute when they first invited him to speak in 1927; Père E. A. Langlais, the order's Canadian provincial, later claimed that he had dreamed in 1927 of establishing courses that would make "the originality of St Thomas" better known in Canada, possibly leading to a Dominican institute in Ottawa or Toronto.* In Toronto, St Michael's tried to implement *Aeterni patris* by strengthening its department of philosophy in the 1920s with De Wulf, Noël, and Phelan; then, after 1926, by aggressively pursuing Gilson. Laval marked the anniversary with the founding of its Ecole Supérieure de Philosophie and with a

---

* See Benoît Lacroix, "Notes sur les premières origines de l'Institut," Dominican Provincial Archives, Notre-Dame de Grâce, Montréal.

series of five special lectures in thomist philosophy. Unlike the other institutions, Laval was not avidly pursuing Gilson; with excellent philosophers and theologians of its own, it was not disposed to turn to the Sorbonne for reinforcements.

When Toronto engaged Gilson, then, Laval did not much care, Montréal was disappointed, and Ottawa decided to modify its plans for an institute. Gilson suggested that Langlais enlist support for the "Ottawa project" from the Dominicans in France. Langlais received from France promises to lend him a medievalist and to help with the training of some of Ottawa's younger men. Langlais also received the detailed plans for an *institut* drawn up by Gilson's co-founder of the *Archives*, Père G. Théry. The French provincial even designated Roland-Gosselin to give courses the next year for Langlais in Ottawa and Montréal; illness prevented Roland-Gosselin from acting on his Canadian appointment, and no French Dominican was actually able to go to Ottawa in 1929. Père M.-D. Chenu agreed, however, to go to Ottawa in 1930, and assured his good friend Gilson that he would also provide a course for him at the Toronto Institute.

The Ottawa project became a reality in 1930 as the Institut Saint-Thomas d'Aquin. It was subsequently moved to the University of Montréal when the Dominicans became responsible for teaching philosophy there; in Montréal it became known as the Institut d'Etudes Médiévales. Gilson's role in bringing the formal study of medieval thought to Canada, then, was a major one.

By the time Gilson was preparing for his second autumn in Toronto, he had arranged to have some young Basilians – Vincent L. Kennedy, Alex J. Denomy, George B. Flahiff, Terence P. McLaughlin – designated for medieval studies. He had also begun to look about for established personnel. Among the names to come up were Ephrem Longpré and Jacques Maritain. Longpré would have been a fine acquisition but was not available. As for Maritain, Gilson was not sure he would welcome the invitation – when Phelan suggested Maritain's name, Gilson hesitated.

A few years earlier Gilson had been interviewed by Frédéric Lefèvre for "Une heure avec Etienne Gilson" (*Les nouvelles littéraires*, 25.1.3). Lefèvre had pointed out that Gilson's approach to philosophy was very different than Maritain's. Gilson had responded by characterizing Maritain's method as one that set bare ideas in juxtaposition, submerging the individuality of the philosophers who espoused them: "It is more important," said Gilson "to try to understand ideas through men ... in order to judge in a way that unites. ... Pure ideas, taken in their abstract rigour, are generally irreconcilable." Gilson feared that Maritain, who had little sympathy for Sorbonne philosophy, might have been offended. As it turned out, Maritain had actually liked this particular interview and had written Lefèvre immediately to tell him so, though defending his own method vigorously: "It is not the psychology but the critique of philosophers that brings truth to light" (25.1.3; tr.). However, Gilson did not find out about Maritain's friendly response until many years later, when Henri Massis gave him a copy of the letter at an Académie meeting.

Despite Gilson's trepidations, he dutifully, even timidly, passed Phelan's invitation on to Maritain when he arrived in Paris early in 1929. To his surprise Maritain was keenly interested. Although prior commitments ruled out work at the Institute in 1929 or 1930, Maritain promised Gilson that he would come in the early 1930s.

7 Activities in the University of Paris

The years 1925 to 1932 marked the peak of Gilson's career as a teacher of philosophy in the Sorbonne. During these years Gilson also won recognition as a noted thomist, not so much as a disciple but as a researcher into the nature of Thomas' doctrine. In 1928 Juan Carvalhos visited Gilson's classroom in order to see what lay behind the reputation for brilliance and flamboyance that had spread throughout Paris. "The enchanting world of ideas," wrote Carvalhos, "comes to life in the soft harmonics of his voice as one sequence of reasons blends into the next. Clear ideas, rich in form and new meaning, tumble and sparkle. ... 'I strive to understand my authors, not to be critical of them.' " (L'avenir, 28.6.18; tr.)

A much more precise insight into Gilson's courses at this time can be found in the two sets of lecture notes taken by André, Gilson's priest-brother. André attended Gilson's courses at the Sorbonne for two academic years, from 1929 to 1931. Although the courses were by no means identical, both carried the same title: "Grandes thèses de la philosophie médiévale." The first, given in 1929-to-1930, consisted of ten two-hour lectures:

1. What is meant by Christian philosophy? Augustine and revealed truth.
2. The coming of thomism; the averroist double-truth in which the philo-sophic was absolute.
3. Being and the transcendentals.
4. The structures of particular beings: matter and form, potency and act, essence and existence.
5. Substance and its properties.
6. Realities of the physical world: la causalité, species.
7. The problem of knowledge.
8. L'être et le connaître: epistemology and criteriology.
9. Theory of the concept: science, the theory of truth.
10. Knowledge of God.

The second series, given in 1930-to-1931, consisted of sixteen lectures. Although these bore heavily on psychology, they also proceeded logically from the earlier series:

1. Problems arising in thomist psychology on the nature of the soul and on the soul as substance.
2. The nature of the soul: the soul as form.
3. The nature of sensation.
4. The senses and sensation.

5. The *sensus communis*.
6. Imagination.
7. Intellect: distinct from soul or a faculty of the soul?
8. *Intellectus agens*. [André's references, to pp. 1-244 in Maritain's *Les degrés du savoir*, would seem to have been added later.]
9. Abstraction. The cognitive process: idealism and thomist realism.
10. Intellection and conception.
11. The nature of the *verbum* and of the intellect.
12. [Missing from André's notes.]
13. Relations between concept and judgment.
14. The object of knowledge.
15. Knowledge of incorporeals: God and the soul.
16. *Habitus* (*les habitudes*).

Whether Gilson was himself responsible for the textbook structure of the lecture series, or whether André superimposed it, is uncertain. Whatever the case, Gilson clearly exercised a masterly control over the content of his Sorbonne lectures, and the result is a design for the sort of comprehensive textbook that Gilson never wrote. André's notes also reveal Gilson's immediate intellectual concerns, namely the definition of Christian philosophy and the issue of medieval realism.

In its Sorbonne-classroom lecture stage, the question of medieval realism appears simply and without reference to contemporary neoscholasticism. According to André, Gilson presented the problem as follows:

> Briefly, the criteriological problem consists in asking how to escape from doubt, how to attain certitude. The epistemological problem, the conditions under which knowledge is possible, the conditions making possible the fusing of an object and a subject to the degree that they become one, is anterior to this criteriological problem. You won't discover these conditions by analyzing the act of knowing in which object and subject are united. You will find them rather in the metaphysics of being, that is, by searching out the constitutive elements of being. If you establish yourself within thought, you will never connect with things, because everything will show up as thought. Neither, if you install yourself in the thing, will you connect with thought, because everything will show up as thing. In either case you will only get a partial view of the real. However, you must make metaphysics the condition of the problem of knowledge.
>
> You must take your position from the ensemble of experience and nature. In such an ensemble there are not only things but knowledge of these things. Before you ask yourself how thought can be connected with things (the criteriological problem) you must ask how there can be a presentation of these things. You must stop asking how to come to a knowledge of things (an idealist point of view) but ask how the knowledge of things is given to you. The idealist point of view has to be turned right around. (André Gilson, lecture notes, 1929-1930; lecture 8, p. 8; tr.)

During the second series of lectures, in 1930-to-1931, the psychological aspects of medieval realism were introduced. André's notes for lecture 10, on intellection and conception, reveal Gilson as an incisive and lucid teacher, and show how close he had already come to the core of his *Le réalisme méthodique* and *Réalisme thomiste et critique de la connaissance* of the later 1930s. According to the idealists, "it is thought that makes the truth of things, hence one can never exit from the order of thought, nor ever enter the order of things." For Gilson's Thomas, the point of view is entirely different: "the given does not have to be proven, and the mind does not have to fashion a critique of its own knowledge in order to know whether, in the act-of-knowing, it reaches something other than self because the given is not thought but thing" (André Gilson, lecture notes, 1930-1931, lecture 10, pp. 5-6; tr.). Here Gilson is speaking as a philosopher rather than as a historian. Clearly Maritain was right when he wrote to Frédéric Lefèvre that he considered Gilson's "purely historical position" to be only a "provisional" one (25.1.3).

11

Philosophical Methodologies, 1930-1939

1 CHRISTIAN PHILOSOPHY AS METHOD

In the early 1930s Gilson made a strenuous attempt to convince philosophers that his use of the expression "Christian philosophy" was a valid one. Gilson used the term to specify that part of Christian medieval thought which was authentically philosophical, that is, was the work of human reason functioning autonomously within the context of divine revelation. The term itself was not new, and had sometimes been used theologically. Augustine had used it to distinguish Christian from pagan wisdom; Erasmus to accentuate the infinite possibilities for development which God's wisdom extended to men; Luther and Calvin to designate the full salvation in Jesus of man and his arts; and Pope Leo XIII had used it in the title of his encyclical *Aeterni patris*. Gilson felt the expression could be useful in designating the kinds of rationalization constantly present in medieval works. On two occasions he defended his usage with particular skill and vigour: in 1931 before the Société Française de Philosophie, and in his Gifford Lectures in Aberdeen during 1931 and 1932.

The meeting of the Société did not first introduce Christian philosophy as a controversial issue. Back in 1924 Mandonnet had taken strong exception to the term in his review of Gilson's *Saint Bonaventure*; Mandonnet had insisted that if there were a Christian philosophy, it could only be found in St Thomas who alone among medieval thinkers had provided a proper rational basis for thought. When Gilson had found still another Christian philosophy in St Augustine, he had come under further attack.

Emile Bréhier, Gilson's fellow historian of philosophy at the Sorbonne, had in 1928 argued strenuously in three lectures for the Institut des Hautes Etudes de Belgique that the Middle Ages contained no movement that could be called a Christian philosophy. Augustine had simply grafted what he could of Greek philosophy onto his Christianity, as had others after him. And Thomas had simply drawn on the principle of contradiction to affirm that philosophical truth could never contradict revealed truth and must therefore be seen as only the *ancilla theologiae* to Christian revelation. In Bréhier's view, thomism was not the product of an autonomous reason, but of committed clergy and monks during a period when they controlled intellectual development. When that control ended

Thérèse Ravisé   Etienne Gilson

Possibly their wedding portraits, 1908

"Au rapport" 1914
"I am at the extreme right,
marked with a black dot."

Portrait as Prisoner-of-War
(1916-1918)

One of the prisoner-of-war camps in which Gilson was interned

Prisoners-of-war: group portrait
Gilson is eighth from the left in the middle row

Thérèse

Cécile and Jacqueline
as young children

"En famille": Jacqueline, Etienne, Cécile
Probably about 1929

The Family at Melun, ca. 1930
Etienne, Thérèse, Maman with
Bernard, Jacqueline and Cécile

Maman :
Caroline Juliette
Rainaud Gilson

Maman just before her death, 1937

Jacqueline, Thérèse
and Cécile, ca. 1935

Gilson and Jacques Thibaudeau
Montreal, 1927

The author and Thérèse
at the *fêtes* at Cluny, 1949

The muskellunge caught at
La Point which, mounted, hung
in Gilson's study at Vermenton

The Academician
with his sword

Gilson, Rev. L. J. Bondy CSB,
Joseph Vrin, at Vrin's Farm, 1956

Dr. William Walton, Fr. Frank Lescoe and Etienne Gilson, 1953

Rev. Albert R. Jonsen sj (left) of the University of San Francisco
confers the honorary degree of Doctor of Humane Letters on Gilson,
6 February 1970. Looking on is Rev. Philip P. Callahan sj.

Gilson and three of his former pupils:
Vincent Moran, Desmond FitzGerald, and Rev. Edmond J. Smyth sj.

The Lecturer
(California, 1969)

in the sixteenth century, no philosopher continued to work within the framework of theology. No historian of philosophy, argued Bréhier, who asked himself the right questions could possibly conclude philosophically that there had ever been a Christian philosophy.*

Gilson disagreed with Bréhier, and believed in the existence of authentic medieval philosophies. He believed that Christian theologians had done more than simply append Greek philosophy to Christian beliefs; they had created a philosophy that was Christian both in its form and in its content.

The meeting of the Société took place on 21 March 1931. In a letter to Phelan a few days earlier, Gilson outlined the structure of the debate:

> I have a meeting of the Société de Philosophie coming up this Saturday dealing with "The Notion of Christian Philosophy." Bréhier will be there (contre), Maritain (pour), Brunschvicg (contre), et alii complures. Quelle salade! (31.3.18.)

The alii complures included Xavier Léon, Edouard Le Roy and Raymond Lenoir. Although Maurice Blondel and Jacques Chevalier submitted letters, they were not present.

At the Société debate Gilson employed three basic arguments to demonstrate Christian philosophy. First he maintained that in Christianity there is, over and above practical, speculative elements, a Christian exercise of reason which is not divorced from faith; much is to be gained by turning to "the Bible and the Gospel as sources of philosophic inspiration," especially for pure philosophy and metaphysics. Second, there is an early history of this exercise of reason, especially in Justin, Lactantius, Augustine and Anselm. And third, this Christian philosophy gives precise expression to a unique understanding of the Supreme Being, the *Ego sum qui sum* of Exodus, thus affirming a metaphysical primacy of being.

Unlike Bréhier, Gilson was finding that philosophical systems meant less and less to him. Philosophers on the other hand, such as Aristotle, Thomas and Bergson, were coming to mean more and more. It was the act of philosophizing, Gilson was beginning to feel, that constituted true philosophy. On the surface this conclusion seems somewhat similar to the position of Maurice Blondel, who approached philosophy as primarily action. There was, however, a basic difference: while Blondel's "philosophy of action" was apologetic, Gilson's was autonomous speculation on known truth.

Blondel did not attend the Société's historic meeting, but submitted his objections to Gilson's position in a letter. According to the rules of the Société, such letters had to be submitted in advance so the presenter of the thesis could incorporate his responses into his presentation. Blondel submitted his letter, then somehow persuaded Xavier Léon, the secretary, to let him read Gilson's responses beforehand. Blondel then substituted a second letter for his original one, thus depriving Gilson of any opportunity for rebuttal. Gilson found Blondel's

---

* See "Y a-t-il une philosophie chrétienne?" *Revue de métaphysique et de morale*, 38 (1931): 133-162.

actions irregular and surreptitious, and could never afterward regard him as an honest scholar. The text of Blondel's long original letter can be found in the Gilson Archives, Toronto; to his own copy, Gilson attached the note: "First version of [Blondel's] remarks; he substituted a second for it after reading my reply which my excellent and dear friend, X. Léon, imprudently communicated to him."

Blondel's second, substituted letter was sharper in tone and less considerate than his first. Blondel charged that Gilson was still trying to conceptualize everything within a closed system, and was therefore not truly a philosopher. Blondel called for an "open philosophy," one less historical and more philosophical in posture, and at the same time truer to Catholic doctrine which is definite and specific. Why not, he asked, speak of a "Catholic" rather than a Christian philosophy? Most damaging to Gilson, however, was the charge of historicism:

> In exegesis, in apologetic, even in theology, [Gilson] has signalled over and above his excellent intentions, the deviations of *historicism*. Let us avoid falling into philosophic historicism. History in the technical sense of the word is not itself qualified to discern that supreme reality carried along by those facts and ideas that have been grasped in time and space. (*Bulletin de la Société Française* [1932], p. 89.)

For the rest of his career Gilson would repeatedly face this charge of historicism. It is hardly surprising then that he became cool, and perhaps a little bitter, toward Blondel; some of Gilson's friends, however, including Père de Lubac, were not aware of the reasons for this coolness (interview, 1975).

Gilson had never, even in the early days, subscribed to Blondel's philosophy of action. Now in 1931 he felt more strongly than ever that Blondel was too much of an apologist to be a good philosopher. A letter to Phelan in early 1932 makes this clear:

> Maurice Blondel holds for a Catholic rather than for a Christian philosophy, meaning by Catholic, I believe, a non-Christian philosophy or one that is Christian only in so far as it is true. (EG to Phelan, 32.3.11.)

From this time one or other aspect of Christian philosophy was to set Gilson apart from various neoscholastics, thomists and other Catholic scholars. Certainly Christian philosophy is the touchstone that best facilitates comparisons and contrasts between him and them. Gilson and Jacques Maritain always remained reasonably close on the issue. Although Maritain felt that it was better to approach Christian philosophy doctrinally than historically, he admitted that Gilson had brought both "vigorous impulse" and "historical clarification" to the subject. Maritain also acknowledged "fundamental agreement" with Gilson. When he wrote formally on the subject in his "De la notion de philosophie chrétienne" (*Revue néo-scolastique*, 34 [1932]: 155-186), Maritain declared his support for Gilson's position. Unlike Gilson, however, he was "mustering the elements of a solution of a doctrinal kind" and distinguishing "between the *order of specification* and the *order of exercise*," that is, between nature and state: "I say that we have to distinguish between the nature of philosophy, what it is in itself, and its state within the human subject at the historical period of its making" (p. 160). Maritain did not agree with Blondel that philosophy's sphere is purely natural, and felt that Blondel frequently misunderstood Gilson's positions.

Following the Société meeting, while university philosophers continued to dismiss Christian philosophy, a good many Catholic philosophers decided they could live with both the term and the concept. Many, however, disagreed with Gilson as to the exact meaning of the expression and how it could be used most effectively.* Some, like Fernand Van Steenberghen and Gabriel Marcel, suggested that *Christian philosophy* was but another term for theology. Others, like Père M. D. Chenu, employed the expression much as Gilson did, as applicable to any system of philosophy or any authentic way of philosophizing which was de facto richer and more fertile because pursued in the context of religious doctrines. According to Chenu, Christian philosophy had an essential rational component not necessarily present in theology. On 11 September 1933 at Juvisy the entire issue of Christian philosophy was aired by neoscholastic, thomist and other scholars at their Journées d'Etudes de la Société Thomiste.

As Gilson grew older he sometimes wondered whether his struggle to explain Christian philosophy had been worth his effort. Yet had he yielded to weariness in the 1930s he would not have produced two masterpieces: the Gifford Lectures on "The Spirit of Medieval Philosophy" and the William James Lectures on the "Unity of Philosophical Experience."

2 Delivering the Gifford Lectures, 1931-1932

During 1930 Gilson was constantly in touch with John Laird of Aberdeen to ensure that the Gifford Lectures would be a success. Gilson now knew that he wanted to lecture on medieval philosophies as authentic and distinct from ancient Greek and modern Western philosophies. He did not know, however, how he was going to work a series of twenty lectures over two years into his Paris and Toronto commitments. Laird advised him to follow the "Bishop Barnes plan" and subdivide each year's series. Thus the Gifford Lectures were delivered in four five-lecture series on February 16 to 20 and May 29 to June 2 of 1931, and on February 8 to 12 and May 30 to June 3 of 1932.

Gilson was bothered by the general title he had given his lectures – "Medieval Philosophy and Its Present Value." He failed to solve the problem however and delivered his papers under the announced title. In 1932 he turned the manuscript over to Vrin for publication in two volumes as *L'esprit de la philosophie médiévale* (Paris, 1932; McG 32). Although the word *esprit* was somewhat noncommittal, it did leave a role for faith in medieval philosophy.

---

* See Van Steenberghen's reviews in *Revue néo-scolastique*, 34 (1932): 366 ff.; and 35 (1933): 106 ff., 230 ff. See Marcel's review in *Revue des jeunes*, 32.4.15, pp. 308 ff. For Chenu's comments, see "Note pour l'histoire de la notion de la philosophie chrétienne," *Revue des sciences philosophiques et théologiques*, 21 (1932): 231-235.

Gilson opened his First Gifford lecture with a brief discussion of "scholasticism," those bodies of doctrine created by Christian, Jewish and Mussulman scholars in order to reconcile the teachings of Aristotle, Plato and the Greeks with divine revelation. Although the scholastics were not hostile to Greek philosophy, they considered it lacking in the revealed notion of a personal God and of creation *ex nihilo*; the scholastics believed that revelation made good sense of most Greek philosophy once its errors were corrected. These scholastics regarded themselves as philosophers in that they stood for right reason as opposed to erroneous reason. Revelation could redeem Greek thought as it was redeeming world paganism.

Modern philosophers had begun to ask themselves whether these scholastics should be properly understood as philosophers or as theologians. Gilson was coming to think of them as theologians who philosophized as well. He argued for their authenticity as philosophers in order to justify the philosophical contribution of scholars like Thomas, Bonaventure and Augustine, and was quite confident that philosophical speculation could be the healther for beginning where faith left off.

Other questions had also arisen concerning the scholastics. Did medieval scholars really view themselves as philosophers? How much did modern scholars really know about medieval speculation? And were not many modern philosophers also guilty of buiding their philosophies on some degree of faith? As to this last question, Gilson already knew from his own early research that Descartes had been dependent upon faith for his philosophical stance. Malebranche and Leibniz, and even Kant, were dependent on faith; those who identified Kant only with his *Critique of Pure Reason* were forgetting that he had also written a *Critique of Practical Reason*. Even the ultra-modern contemporary, W. P. Montague, author of *Belief Unbound* (1930), who had rejected divine omnipotence and the "crude hypotheses of our ignorant ancestors," had ultimately settled for a new religion that "is a pretty example of biblical folklore complicated with Greek folklore. ... recollections of the Gospel absorbed in his childhood" (*The Spirit of Medieval Philosophy*, pp. 16-18).

Gilson's second lecture attempted "to interrogate the Christian philosophers themselves as to their own idea of Christian philosophy" (p. 19), and to place their answers into a historical setting. In Justin, Lactantius, Augustine and Anselm, Gilson found a true appreciation of what these early scholars had meant "when they spoke of the debt of reason to revelation" (p. 41). The next lectures offered a consideration of the great medieval theses: the third lecture dealt with the scholastic idea of God as being and its necessity, and succeeding lectures explored such matters as contingency, analogy, causality, finality, Christian personalism, love and free will.

Gilson summarized his lectures with the stirring statement that "the more one reads the medieval commentaries on Aristotle, the more one is convinced that their authors knew exactly what they were about" (p. 424). The scholastics were, at the very least, "commentator-philosophers"; for Gilson this meant that they were in fact philosophers. He concluded that if, as some have said, "St Thomas was a child and Descartes a man, we, for our part, must be very near decrepitude" (p. 426).

The first series of lectures was highly successful. The Scottish philosophers accepted Gilson's presentation of the philosophizing of medieval Christians, and Scottish Catholics were not disturbed by his collaboration with Aberdeen's militantly Protestant university. No doubt the general interest in his lectures contributed to Gilson's decision to continue the use of the term "Christian philosophy."* Gilson was happy about the first series, and said so excitedly in his letters to Mme Thibaudeau, Dr Phelan and Father McCorkell. The presence of Bishop George Bennett was particularly gratifying in the Protestant university: "For the first time since the Reformation the Catholic bishop entered the university. ... Protestant and Catholics are equally satisfied. ... I am teaching St Thomas as (I suppose) a philosophical justification of the Confession of Westminster. (EG to McCorkell, 31.3.18.)

Gilson's second series of Gifford Lectures coincided with a convocation to mark the quincentennial of the university's founding by another Catholic bishop, William Elphinstone; Gilson, Bishop Bennett and a large group of Protestant ecclesiastics received honorary degrees. These May celebrations were decidedly religious and Protestant, and reminded Gilson that his Christian philosophy also had implications for Protestant thought – just as it threatened the autonomy of neoscholastic philosophy, so it also threatened the autonomy of Protestant theology. Not surprisingly, then, Gilson began to turn his attention to Protestant ideas. Significantly he did not allow this to find its way into any of the later Gifford Lectures; his own historical principles did not allow him to introduce such a relatively modern phenomenon as Protestantism into any examination of medieval thought. Nevertheless, around the time of the Gifford Lectures, Gilson was seriously probing not only the philosophical and historical validity of neoscholasticism and neothomism, but of the neochristianity of the sixteenth century as well. And Christian philosophy had profound repercussions for them all.

Gilson's intensified interest in Protestant theology got underway with a course in the École Pratique des Hautes Études on Luther – not Luther as Gilson had lectured on him in the early 1920s, but Luther in the context of Christian philosophy. Shortly after completing the third series of Gifford Lectures, Gilson wrote Phelan that he had twenty Protestant theological students enrolled in his Luther course. He was also deeply into Karl Barth whom he found an excellent theologian:

> We are discussing Karl Barth, a true theologian, who knows his calvinism and lutheranism. Indeed, he has just published a book on St Anselm to which Scholz is preparing a reply. Peter Wust is carrying on a brisk controversy with the Protestants, and he too has just written an article on Christian philosophy in which

---

* Interestingly, however, when Gilson stopped over on his return to Paris to lecture at Oxford, he used the expression *philosophes de la grâce* to describe St Bernard, Pascal and Maine de Biran.

he makes the case (a good one, I think) that since Protestants no longer have a "nature" they have no right to a philosophy, not even to a moral philosophy. This goes far and deep! (32.3.11.)

The following year, 1933, Gilson extended his analysis of Protestant theology to include calvinism and gave a course of lectures in the Protestant Faculty of Theology, Paris, on "The Nature of Theology or *Fides quaerens intellectum.*" During 1934 Karl Barth gave a similar course in the same faculty, replying to Gilson's course lecture by lecture; Gilson gave his complimentary tickets to Father O'Donnell, who was working with him in Paris, and asked O'Donnell to report back.

By 1925 one Protestant apologist, Pierre Jaccard, had already seen that the direction of Gilson's teaching was a threat to Protestant theology. Speaking of Rome as intransigent and the various thomist movements as continuations of the counter-reformation, he had added that Gilson was beginning to change the battlefield by getting thomism into the French universities, by re-establishing it in the history of philosophy, and especially by recognizing that medieval philosophies were not unified but fundamentally different from one another. "He is getting along with the neothomists, but will this last? I doubt it." Jaccard had been very concerned about the implications of Gilson's probing, his thomist offensive, "and his brilliant strategy." Then, after the Gifford Lectures were over, Wilhelm Rotte described Gilson's Christian philosophy as a change of front from Greek rationalism to a metaphysics of Exodus, altering the Greek outlook and re-orienting the biblical.* Many Protestant theologians wrote careful and major reviews of *L'esprit de la philosophie médiévale*, up to and including Reinhold Niebuhr's important review of 1936.

During this period Gilson also pushed his investigation of Christian philosophy beyond history into theology. By analyzing nature, lutheranism, calvinism, Catholicism and theology itself in the context of philosophy, Gilson hoped to discover the theoretical roots of Christian philosophy within the very essence of the Catholic faith. He published the results of this analysis in *Christianisme et philosophie* (Paris, 1936; McG 7), and the note accompanying his complimentary copy to Phelan shows that he expected to stir up controversy with the Louvain philosophers: "I will send you a little book which I have just published, *Christianisme et philosophie*. It is pure theology, but I have an imprimatur. After this, as you will see, it will be impossible for me to set foot in Louvain." (36.7.10.)

Gilson apparently expected Louvain to react unfavourably to his questioning of some of Mercier's assertions. Most notably, Gilson had objected to Mercier's claim that "the existence of God cannot be made the object of an act of divine faith"; if this were true, then the Catholic faith would be reduced to "a pure and simple intellectual adhesion to the doctrine of the infallible church" as the

---

* For Jaccard's view see "La mêlée thomiste en France en 1925," in Lausanne's *Revue de théologie et de philosophie*, 14 (1926): 51-75. For Rotte's, see "Der Neuthomismus in Frankreich: Im Anschluss an Jacques Maritain und Etienne Gilson," *Theologische Literaturblatt*, 12 (1933): 78-90.

calvinists had charged. Gilson sent a copy of his book to Mgr Noël at Louvain and received the following information in reply:

> The texts you quote from Cardinal Mercier surprised me at first. I afterward found they were not in my edition of the *Manual*. They were added later when Mercier was archbishop, and this surprises me greatly because he was then no longer revising his philosophical books, so I am not sure that the phrases are his.
>
> I don't think I would myself have said quite that. However the fact that Mercier may have made such an addition – or have had such an addition made – to his text while he was a bishop and in the apostolic ministry, is quite interesting. One would have expected him to take objection to "modernist" ideas. But what he says is very much like the logic of theologians of the day on the act of faith and the motives of credibility. (Noël to EG, 36.8.18; tr.)

Ralph MacDonald's translation of *Christianity and Philosophy* (New York, London, 1939; McG 8) no longer attributed the texts in question to Mercier but to "one of Mercier's disciples" (p. 129). It is not known whether Gilson or Phelan authorized this change.

With the publication of *Christianisme et philosophie*, the full case for Christian philosophy had been put and the Gifford Lectures were rounded off. When Maurice Posul, the dean of the Faculté Libre de Théologie Protestante, received complimentary copies of the work from Gilson, he replied graciously:

> I am happy to think that the evening you were so good as to spend with us last spring occasioned the publication of this beautiful book. I have read it with lively interest and admired not only its vigour and clarity but above all its sincerity. ... I, who am not a dogmatist ... am always trying to confront Christian positions with primitive Christianity, and I don't find in the days of Christian origins anything justifying the idea of Christian philosophy. No doubt I am a heretic on this point as on a number of others, but it seems to me that Christianity and philosophy are located on two different planes, and I would revere a Christian philosophy which, without claiming any objective value, would serve for a given time and milieu as a symbol for Christianity. I remain a disciple of Sabatier, and I could even go a little further than he and say not that religious knowledge is symbolic but that there are only religious symbols. In going this far, I tell myself that I am remaining faithful to Pauline Christianity, at least to the "now in a glass darkly, then face to face" of 1 Cor. 13.12. (Posul to EG, 36.9.18; tr.)

3 ELECTION INTO THE COLLÈGE DE FRANCE, 1932

Most successful professors in the French universities have aspired to the Collège de France, and Gilson perhaps more than most. For Gilson the prestige of recognition and the increased opportunities for personal research were secondary. Primarily he desired the flexibility of the Collège, its ability to accommodate his regular absences in Canada. In addition he thought he would have a better chance for a full chair in medieval philosophy at the Collège than at the University of Paris.

There was also enough of the showman in Gilson to equip him for the role of a Petit de Julleville, though hardly to the same extravagant degree.* Like Petit de Julleville, Gilson revelled in certain formalities. He was acutely aware of the dignity which the role of *maître* brought with it from the Middle Ages, and of the courtesies it owed to its audience. He always came into the lecture hall as if pleased to be there, with his text prepared and in his hand. He regarded his lecture period as a contract to begin on time and to end on time; if he was diverted from his lecture for any reason, he would compensate by omitting certain passages leading to his conclusion that had been carefully marked beforehand for this purpose. He neither invited nor objected to questions if they were to the point, but if he suspected the intentions of the interrogator he could and would brush him off with chilly disdain.

Gilson later explained some of his reasons for seeking a chair at the Collège:

> Getting a chair in the Collège de France was my greatest honour. ... I wanted the chair: one only had to deliver thirty lectures a year at the rate of two a week, one general, one more technical and scientific. I have always liked the Collège, ever since following two of Bergson's courses there, one on "the intellectual effort," one on Spencer's "theory of the unknowable." To accept a chair one has to resign from the Sorbonne, but not from the École. I resigned from the École too because I could not continue to carry so much work. I am not referring to my work in America. I mean there was too much work involved by courses in the Collège and École at the same time: the same course could not be given in both places. Lévi was sad about my resigning from the École. (interview, 1975.)

Although Gilson was made-to-order for the Collège de France, he was not at first confident he would be admitted. During 1930, however, he started to think of himself as a prospective candidate and began canvassing the professors of the Collège for their vote. The reaction of those approached was so positive that he began to feel his election was a foregone conclusion. One of these preliminary visits was to Alfred Loisy. Old, sad and disappointed, Loisy had become a chronic hypochondriac and was just about to resign:

> Loisy reassured me: "You will be all right. You will get your appointment. Later you will become a member of the Institut de France and of the Académie Française. Now, you must be careful; don't go off on visits during bad weather. Look at Mgr [name unclear], he made all his visits during the winter, caught a very bad cold and died." Ironically, Loisy was *vitandus* ["to be avoided"]; perhaps I should not have visited him, but it is unlikely that he was *vitandus* in this particular context. This reminded me that Loisy told me that he once received a book from Abbé Brémond inscribed *a vitando ad vitandum*. (interview, 1975.)

---

* De Julleville was an extreme case of accentuated eccentricity and formality. According to legend, he always entered the lecture hall of the Collège wearing gloves, top-hat and a cane. He first set down his cane as a call to attention, carefully placed his top-hat near the podium where it could serve as the visible sign of his ominous presence, then slowly removed his gloves summarizing his previous lecture as he did so. He always synchronized his unvesting to the length of this summary so that the lecture began when the gloves were on the table.

By 1931 Gilson was speaking confidently of his candidature to his friends in North America. After the first short series of Gifford Lectures, he wrote to McCorkell: "Nothing will be done in the Collège de France before November, and I shall go to Toronto [in September] as usual" (31.3.18). He had by this time canvassed the professors and submitted his *Exposé de titres*, a descriptive statement of his entitlements for a Chair in the History of Medieval Philosophies in the Collège de France. The brochure outlined why such a chair should be established and why Gilson was the suitable candidate to fill it. First, he argued, it was high time that a chair be created with a view to methodic exploration, in the spirit and tradition of Emile Boutroux, Victor Brochard, Victor Delbos and Lucien Lévy-Bruhl, of French medieval philosophies during and before the twelfth century. Second, these philosophies possess a historical reality not covered by designations like "scholasticism," "thomism," "averroism," and "avicennism," a reality coming to light as more and more university teaching notes became available. Third, his own work to date, such as his *Bonaventure*, has called attention to the existence of original syntheses, none of them to be dismissed as a *thomisme manqué*. Fourth, Gilson hoped to present as a future project at least one more such synthesis by reconstituting cistercian mysticism as still another historical reality. Fifth and finally, he urged attention to three special relationships in researching the medieval philosophies: between the thought of the Christian world and of the Judaic and Mussulman worlds; between the history of philosophy and the history of the sciences; and between philosophy and the world of letters. Gilson's request for a chair in the Collège, then, was based on the interests and concerns that had already occupied much of his career.

Sylvain Lévi was probably responsible for Gilson's nomination. In the fall of 1931 the preliminary election took place in which the chair was discussed within the Collège. There was a short delay while the professors debated the name of the chair. Then, in November, Gilson wrote to Mme Thibaudeau from Toronto: "The election in the Collège de France was a success; all that remains is to designate its titular, and that will be me. So, all goes well and the only cloud on the horizon has dissolved." (31.11.16; tr.) Although there had apparently been another possible candidate, Rougier, his name did not stand (see EG to Bellisle, 32.1.1).

The final election took place 17 January 1932:

> I have been appointed today to the Collège de France as professor of medieval philosophy, thirty votes against seven. It was difficult to hope for a better result. There have been some reservations as to my going *regularly* to Toronto, but such clauses are more theoretical than practical and the net result will certainly be a greater freedom on my side. It is absolutely sure that I shall be back in Toronto around 29 September. (EG to Bellisle, 32.1.17.)

Writing to Phelan, Gilson was more jubilant: "My nomination to the C. de F. will be signed tomorrow 12 March by the Président de la République: *sonnez clairons, battez tambours*" (EG to Phelan, 32.3.11). On 5 April 1932 Gilson gave his inaugural lecture in the Collège on "Le moyen âge et le naturalisme antique"

(*Archives*, 7 [1932]: 5-37; McG 352). On 24 May 1932 he was officially named an honorary professor in the University of Paris. A new era in Gilson's life had begun.

From 1932 to 1951 Paris was Gilson's focus and the Collège de France the seat of his intellectual activity. His courses in the Collège from 1932 until the outbreak of the war were as follows: in 1932, "L'esprit de la morale médiévale"; in 1933, "L'école cistercienne et l'influence de saint Bernard" and "La doctrine de saint Anselme"; in 1934, "L'idéal social du moyen âge" and "La métaphysique de Duns Scot"; in 1935, "Etude sur la psychologie d'Albert le Grand" and "Les théories de la connaissance au moyen âge"; in 1936, "Les fondements du réalisme médiéval" and "Les origines médiévales de l'humanisme"; in 1937, "L'idée d'humanité: recherche sur l'histoire d'un idéal médiéval" and "Humanisme et philosophie de Jean de Salisbury à Pétrarque"; in 1938, "Saint Augustin et le néo-platonisme" and "Les grandes crises de la pensée médiévale." In 1939 courses were announced in "La culture libérale selon Cicéron et sa survivance au moyen âge" and "Logique et théologie chez saint Anselme"; these were suspended because of the war.

In 1933 Gilson attempted to sponsor the nomination of Marc Bloch to the Collège. Bloch had been close to Gilson at Strasbourg and the two men had considerably influenced each other's scholarship (above, pp. 93-95). Bloch badly wanted into the Collège so that he could devote himself more fully to his research and to the editing of the *Annales*. Lucien Febvre, Bloch's associate in the *Annales*, did not feel he should sponsor his friend; Febvre had himself been elected only recently, and was too closely associated with Bloch for the nomination to be credible. Bloch and Febvre first persuaded France's senior historian, Camille Jullian, to sponsor Bloch, but Jullian died during December 1933 before discussion of Bloch's candidature came up. They found a new sponsor in Alexandre Moret, professor of Egyptology in the Collège, but Moret suddenly realized that he would be out of the country for the coming election. Finally Bloch wrote to Gilson from Strasbourg at the end of December:

> I beg you, most earnestly, to replace [Moret]. A long explanation of why I wish with all my heart to have you accept this chore is unnecessary. Among your colleagues [in the Collège] no one appears to me, at this distance, capable of pleading my cause with such authority and hope of success; and how can I hide from you that if you find a favourable reply impossible, I shall be frightfully embarrassed. (33.12.28; tr.)

Gilson demonstrated his friendship and took on the sponsorship; Febvre provided him with the necessary information.

Bloch's nomination was plagued with difficulties. There were two other candidates for a chair at this time, both also from Strasbourg, and both also good friends of Gilson's: Albert Grenier had worked with Gilson on the Committee of Publications at Strasbourg and had been Jullian's *suppléant* at the time of his death; Charles Blondel, philosopher and psychiatrist, had been Gilson's friend for many years. Apparently Bloch, noted for his caustic remarks, indiscreetly referred to the Collège's "national antiquities." Although the phrase was harmless enough in itself, it echoed the title of Jullian's chair to which Grenier was now aspiring. Bloch was charged by some with campaigning against Grenier, a charge he strongly denied to Gilson (Bloch to EG, 34.2.15).

A further hurdle to Bloch's nomination could neither have been expected nor forestalled. In the *Annuaire* of the Collège for 1934 the following entry occurs: "The professors met on this day [34.3.18] to consider the assignment of funds made available following the death of M. Camille Jullian. Their deliberations were brusquely interrupted by the death of M. Camille Matignon which took place during the meeting." As a result of Matignon's death, the election was postponed until April 1934. At the April meeting no action was taken, and the nomination expired. Gilson was most upset at the Collège's inaction and was sure that his presentation of Bloch had been somehow inadequate. Bloch assured him that Febvre had described Gilson's presentation as superb. Indeed, Bloch asked for Gilson's sponsorship a second time, in the fall of 1934 for selection in 1935. Gilson declined because he had already committed himself to support his lifelong friend, Charles Blondel.

Gilson was so fond of Blondel that he was willing to forego his regular trip to Toronto in the fall of 1934 to help his friend get elected. He explained this to the head of St Michael's, Father Bellisle:

> My friend Dr Blondel of Strasbourg told me in January that he would be a candidate at the Collège de France in the fall of 1934, if he believed I would be there to help him. This is his only chance to get there, and I am his only chance of getting there. I could afford to go to Toronto [in the fall of 1932] while my own career was at stake because I was young enough to find other opportunities if I missed that one, but Dr Blondel would not have the friends I have in Paris if I was not there, for I am his only one reliable friend. For this reason, as he will then be fifty-eight, I would like to do for him what I have not done for myself and stay in Paris in the fall of 1934. (33.1.8.)

The fall election was never held because the Collège was forced to cut out four chairs for financial reasons. Gilson went to Toronto as usual. Neither Bloch nor Blondel were ever admitted to the Collège; in the next election, February 1935, Albert Grenier was appointed to Jullian's chair. In 1936 Bloch's disappointment was somewhat alleviated with an appointment to Henri Hauser's chair in the Sorbonne.

Gilson's next action on behalf of a candidate was more successful. In 1938 he, along with Paul Valéry, sponsored the election of the engraver-philosopher Henri Focillon. On this occasion all went perfectly, and at the end of the election-meeting Gilson and Valéry rushed hilariously up rue Saint-Jacques carrying the good news.

Gilson loved the Collège de France and loved his colleagues in it, even when he fought with them. Of all his colleagues, Valéry was perhaps his favourite. In his eulogy before the Académie Française at the time of the poet's death, he reminisced on Valéry's role at the Collège. When Valéry had first been elected, everyone had asked "But what will Valéry teach?" The entire Collège quickly came to the same conclusion: "A chair for Paul Valéry means Paul Valéry's chair, a Chair in Poetics." Valéry was no mere *faiseur* but a *maker* in the best Greek sense of the work. At meetings of the professors of the Collège, he would sit throughout sketching away on the blank sheet provided for notes by an *administration prévoyante*. For Valéry, "empty white held an irresistible attraction" because "art abhors a vacuum," because "designing is a manner of listening," because "the mind thinks with its hands too" (cf. below, p. 359). Gilson often longed to get hold of the sheet on which Valéry had been doodling, "but I was too far away from him, directly across the table to be exact, while his close neighbour was Paul Hazard, *esprit ailé et grand maître en notre langue*, who deftly lifted the page of designs as he left each meeting."

4 Director of Studies, Toronto

When Gilson opened the Institute of Mediaeval Studies, he realized he would have to train many of its original professors himself. He planned to offer in 1935 his first full medieval programme with, if possible, pontifical accreditation. Among his early wards were five young Basilian Fathers: George B. Flahiff, Terence P. McLaughlin, Vincent L. Kennedy, Alexander J. Denomy and J. Reginald O'Donnell. Between 1929 and 1935 Gilson supervised their studies in medieval history, law, liturgy, vernacular literature, and paleography, respectively.

Because of its dependence upon the availability and location of the various scholars he wanted his men to work with, Gilson's training procedure may have seemed somewhat capricious. Flahiff, McLaughlin and Kennedy he sent first to Strasbourg – where his own vision of the institute had been born – for initial orientation. He then moved them elsewhere to acquaint themselves with other institutions at first hand and to work with selected scholarly researchers. Thus Gilson moved Flahiff from Strasbourg and Professor Muench to the École des Chartes with its roster of specialized professors; he also provided for Flahiff to take trips to London to consult with Professor Powicke and to use the London Records Office. McLaughlin was moved from Strasbourg to the École Pratique des Hautes Études where he could be near Gabriel Le Bras of the Collège de France. Kennedy was transferred from Strasbourg, where he had worked with Michel Andrieu in liturgy, to Rome where he could continue in archeology with Mgr Kirsch and Leo Cunibert Mohlberg. Denomy was sent directly to Harvard to take his doctorate in Old French with J. D. M. Ford, then to Paris to work with Ford's Sorbonne friends. O'Donnell went first to Cracow to continue his paleographical studies with Alexandre Birkenmayer, then to Paris to be near the documents of the Bibliothèque Nationale and the libraries of western Europe generally.

Gilson enjoyed guiding the research and study of the young medievalists whose work would enrich his Institute. Typical of the correspondence from them is this letter from Denomy at Harvard, where he was just beginning his critical edition of the *Life of St Agnes*:

> The way [Ford] outlined the work was this: a critical edition based on our manuscript, together with a collation of the British Museum and the Carpentras manuscripts ... then a grammatical and philological study of the poem. The dialect seems to be that of Picard, and since *Aucassin et Nicolette* seems to be the only Old-French document wherein there is a study of the dialect as such, Professor Ford felt that this *Life* would afford an interesting survey of it. The second part of the thesis would be a study of the sources and analogues. (Denomy to EG, 32.10.26.)

For Gilson, Denomy's project represented the proper movement of authentic medieval thought outward into the area of literature, using the contemporary techniques both of linguistics and of philology.

Gilson's function as director of the Institute also included the selection of outside scholars. Jacques Maritain's first courses at the Institute were given from January to April 1933, two years before Gilson's formal programme was put into operation. They were eminently successful, and Gilson agreed with Phelan that Maritain should be invited to become a permanent member of the staff:

> As for Maritain, he is delighted, and wants nothing more than to return, but has not made a definite decision. I believe he is considering leaving the Institut Catholique for St Michael's but is still hesitating. In any case he is very grateful for all you have done for him. I believe his friendship for you equals my own, which is to say a good deal. Likely you will see him again at St Michael's, even annually. I am not pressing this, just letting the idea come to a head, so well disposed do I find him. (EG to Phelan, 33.5.18.)

Gilson soon had some complaints about Maritain that had little to do with philosophical differences. Maritain seemed unnecessarily difficult in his failure to decide the timing of his visits to Toronto. Gilson blamed Maritain's wife, Raïssa, for his dilatory manner. In May 1935, when Maritain still had not returned to Toronto for the second visit, Gilson wrote Phelan:

> As for the delicate point you touch on in your letter, I am embarrassed. ... I wrote you on this subject a letter which I threw in the waste-basket. ... I would not like to write it over again, but just let me tell you to be on your guard. I don't want to risk a psychological analysis, it would certainly be wrong, but I don't think I am exaggerating when I say that the Toronto Institute should take care not to let Maritain come simply when it suits him. Besides, there is behind this Mary (who has a bit of Martha in him) a Martha (who is also a Mary) and she seems to me to be endowed with a well enough sense of the concrete. When I telephoned her this year to tell her that, since Jacques' mother had recovered, perhaps Jacques might go to Toronto at least for April and May, she proposed May *only*, and "with a lecture tour in the United States!" (35.5.5.)

Phelan eventually simply arranged for Maritain to "maintain a permanent tie with the Institute and come there when he wished."

Gilson also tried to involve other European scholars in his Institute. Philotheus Böhner, André Combes and Ephrem Longpré were all editors of significant medieval texts. Böhner had published two translated adaptations of some of Gilson's work: *Der heilige Bonaventura* (Leipzig, 1929; McG 120); and *Die Mystik des heiligen Bernard von Clairvaux* (Wittlich, 1936; McG 153). Gilson liked Böhner's willingness to take on difficult projects. He wrote Phelan that Böhner was his "best German friend" and had "several times urged me to undertake at the Institute a critical edition of Ockham's *Sentences*" (38.7.9). Finally, in 1938, Böhner accepted Gilson's invitation. Gilson was elated: "If we procure an edition of at least the prologue of the first book the Institute will rank among the indisputable seats of medieval learning" (ibid.). Böhner did not stay at Toronto for more than one year. He no longer wanted to work on the *Sentences* but on Ockham's *Logic*; nor was he at ease politically in Toronto. After leaving the Institute, he joined his Franciscan confreres at St Bonaventure University in New York State. There he enjoyed a long and productive career, not just as a competent editor of Ockham but also as a distinguished professor of biology and botany.

In his preparations for the Institute's programme, Gilson tried to avoid creating simply another school of thomism. He also made a strong effort to incorporate the newer technologies of the best recent medieval scholars. These two objectives were evident in the courses and seminars he offered at the Institute during 1931 and 1932. The two lecture-courses reflected Gilson's own changing interests: "An Introduction to Christian Philosophy" (1931) and "Christian Moral Philosophy" (1932). Both revealed a deepening sense of the spiritual which did not pass unnoticed; Yves Congar, following Gilson's courses in Paris, wrote him:

> People now have a good deal to say about obedience to the magisterium. But who today is moved to say that the unity of the church consists first in faith, hope and charity. ... I am not the only one who is saying that your teaching has spiritual value and falls in the category of things which are only complete when imitated. (32.3.3; tr.)

The seminars of these years most clearly reflected Gilson's interest in the new technologies. "The Philosophy of Duns Scotus" (1931) and "St Bernard and Cistercian Mysticism" (1932) were both handled through the intensive analysis of pertinent texts. In these seminars, the seed-ground of the books ahead, Gilson was analyzing medieval man through his spirituality much as the better historical scholars, led by Marc Bloch, were analyzing him through his ploughing, his methods of irrigation, his harness-making. Gilson had only contempt for scholars who, like G. G. Coulton, examined the past only by exhuming the police-court news: "I am reading Coulton's *Saint Bernard* and feel glad I bought it while the pound was low. To do the work full justice, the pound should have been very low." (EG to Bellisle, 32.3.11.)

In 1933, following Maritain's first courses at the Institute, Gilson modified his seminars a little. This year he decided to augment *explication de texte* with a practical exercise in compiling a text. He wrote Phelan in January to announce that his fall seminar would not examine the *De substantiis separatis* of St Thomas as planned but would instead consist of a "practical introduction to an edition of a medieval text: ... the unprinted *Hexaemeron* of Robert Grosseteste. The seminar will ... cover the various phases of editing an unprinted text: collation of manuscripts, selections of readings, *apparatus criticus*, etc." (33.1.9.) This seminar, though unusual for Gilson, indicated one kind of work he wanted to see achieved in his programme.

In this year Gilson also collaborated on his lecture-course for the first time. He asked Phelan to take part of his course on "The Social Function of Christian Philosophy":

> I will speak exclusively of Christian wisdom as agent, *facteur*, of social unity without getting into any specific political theory. I will not touch relations between church and state: these will be your business. You will study the concrete modalities of this social unity in a Christian setting. (33.5.18.)

As Gilson's medieval programme began to acquire permanence, his family began to show more interest in Toronto. In 1932 Cécile accompanied him to Canada, met the Thibaudeaus, and lived during the fall with Lady Windle. The following year Thérèse decided at long last to accompany her husband to North America, bringing Bernard but leaving the girls in France. On 21 July 1933 Gilson wrote to ask Father Bellisle for the rear apartment of 5 Elmsley Place* to be set up as a housekeeping apartment for them as of 3 October. Gilson wrote to Mme Thibaudeau to express his emotional relief at this turn of events and to supply details of this year's crossing. To Mme Thibaudeau's generous offer to meet them in Québec, Gilson replied happily: "I don't think we have any objections to riding around in a Cadillac" (EG to Mme Thibaudeau, 33.7.21: tr.).

The three Gilsons disembarked at Québec City, 2 October. They were picked up by the Thibaudeaus and driven to Montréal. Thérèse and Bernard spent a week at the Thibaudeaus' summer home, La Pointe, near Beauharnois, while Gilson went directly to Toronto to deliver his first lecture, 4 October. He also wanted to check the accommodations at 5 Elmsley Place to ensure that nothing went wrong. Nothing did, neither when Thérèse arrived nor throughout the very happy fall. By 1933 Gilson had made many close friends in Toronto, and all were delighted to see Thérèse. Besides the faculty and students of the Institute, these friends included the Gordon Taylors, the Alex Sampsons, the Roeslers, the Larkins, the Arthur Kellys, Lady Windle and Marjorie Nazier, Mlle Marguerite McDonald and many others. Toward mid-December the three returned to Montréal for Gilson's regular lectures, this year a series of three in Salle Saint-Sulpice under the auspices of l'Institut Scientifique Franco-Canadien. Père Lamarche complimented Thérèse in thanking Gilson for these lectures, noting that it was fitting wisdom should travel in the company of "la grâce française" (*Le devoir*, 33.12.18; tr.).

---

* This was the residence on the campus of St Michael's College in which Gilson and other visitors usually stayed. During the 1920s it had been the home of Sir Bertram Windle.

These Montréal lectures on "La société chrétienne universelle" pulled together the essence of the course he and Phelan had just completed in Toronto. Gilson praised scholasticism's great dream,

> Christianity grateful to God, Father of all men, Author of all that is, turning all men into brothers and children of the same father, and into God's servants in a shared religion. And because this religion established, as the necessary condition for reaching a supernatural end, the practice of justice, of the moral law, of charity, it supplied the only rules which make possible man's obtaining happiness in this world.

According to Gilson this dream of a great Christian social order had been broken by an averroism which had decreed faith and reason to be irreconcilable, and which had established two empires, the one directed by the pope, the other dependent upon princes. Nostalgia for a universal society had been transmitted across the centuries, and Protestants, positivists and theologians − Leibniz, Comte and Campanella − had sought to restore it. Yet, although these efforts had failed, a universal Christian society might still be revived, *un ordre catholique*, in which faith is the light of reason. This theme had run through Gilson's course with Phelan in Toronto; in 1934 and 1935 it found further expression in his articles for *Sept*.

The fall of 1933 closed with the Gilson's lively visit to New York. The proud parents had to buy a new trunk just to find room for the fleet of ships, lighthouses, trains, Lindy-and-Ann airplanes, and other toys that Bernard had by now acquired:

> Today we visited Radio City. ... Bernard was almost kidnapped by a chorus girl. I tried to explain that he was not a girl but a boy, and that she had better be careful. ... Then the whole chorus wanted to have him. ... We watched the show from the stage and again from the audience. ... We spent six hours there. O *ubi* Thomas Aquinas! I attended midnight mass in St Patrick's sitting in a confessional, such was the crowd. I am writing foolish things (foolish but true) in order to avoid so many more serious subjects, particularly one; my wife thinks she may not come back next year. (EG to Bellisle, 33.12.29.)

Thérèse apparently reconsidered, and in 1934 she and Bernard returned with Gilson. However, because of the construction of new buildings on Queen's Park Circle, the Gilsons found everything in turmoil:

> The superior had asked that our apartment be made ready but nothing was done about it. Everything we left behind last year is broken or missing, anything we left clean is dirty. All has to be put in order again. I am spending my time supervising the painters. When they leave the rooms will have to be somewhat refurnished. When I go out I am not sure the beds will be made when I return. All things considered, it is best I stay right here supervising the job. (EG to Mme Thibaudeau, 34.10.3.)

Eventually the new buildings would house Gilson's Institute.

Other than the domestic chaos, the fall of 1934 went well. As last year, Gilson had introduced from Paris a last-minute change into his announced courses: instead of "The Notion of Nature in the Middle Ages" and "A Study of Documents and Texts Concerning the Place Ascribed to Theology in the Thirteenth Century," he substituted "Epistemological Doctrines in the Thirteenth Century" and a seminar on "The *Itinerarium mentis in Deum* of St Bonaventure." He had arranged with Vrin to send ten copies of the *Itinerarium* for the students, and had written to Phelan that he wanted "the seminar to be a small one so that it may be a real one" (34.6.8). Already Gilson was aware that he was establishing permanent patterns.

5 REQUEST FOR PONTIFICAL APPROBATION

Gilson's personal plan for the Institute was primarily directed toward research, not to the granting of higher degrees. Phelan and Carr thought otherwise however and wanted the Institute to seek a charter that would allow it to grant degrees suitable to its purpose and character. They proposed applying to the Holy See for a charter that would establish the Institute as a pontifical faculty of philosophy.* Phelan wrote Gilson in early 1934 asking if he would object to such a petition and Gilson replied:

> Needless to say, I have no objection to a faculty of philosophy, provided we can make a go of it. I know you well enough to be sure that since you are of the opinion that we should have one, nothing will stop you. Assuredly, if a faculty is possible, it is desirable. So I subscribe to the project. Father Carr [who was to take the project to Rome] will bring me up to date on the details of the project. (34.2.24.)

Although Gilson's support of the project was not at first enthusiastic, it was real enough. When Carr and others began to hold meetings in Rome with the administration of the Sacred Congregation of Seminaries and Universities, Gilson gladly joined them. He became genuinely enthusiastic after Mgr (later Cardinal) Ruffini expressed the opinion that what Toronto really wanted was not a faculty of philosophy but an institute of medieval studies. Even though there was no provision for such an institute in *Deus scientiarum Dominus*, it was better to ask for something they wanted rather than for something they did not want. After exploratory meetings late in March 1934, Gilson arranged for a private audience with Pope Pius XI and asked Jacques Maritain to accompany him. As a result of this frank discussion, their request for a charter for an institute of medieval studies was placed firmly on the Sacred Congregation's agenda. (EG to Bellisle, 34.4.3.)

Gilson was quick to realize that the charter would not come at once. In a letter to Phelan in August 1934, he described Rome's likely procedures accurately and in almost every detail:

---

* The original application was for a faculty of philosophy. *Deus scientiarum Dominus* (1929), the Holy See's latest Sacred Constitution governing such matters, recognized as eligible for such degree-conferring charters only Catholic universities, Catholic faculties of theology and Catholic faculties of philosophy.

This will be our last preparatory year. I am much less certain of our erection into a pontifical institute than Father Carr seems to be. ... They are going to wait to see how we are doing. ... My only hope to the contrary is that someone may just want truly and strongly to encourage and please us. Mgr Ruffini is capable of this, for he is a man of great intelligence with a big heart. If he does not succeed, we are in for a long wait. Our wisest procedure is to work on as though the whole question had never been raised. (EG to Phelan, 34.8.31.)

In June 1936 the Sacred Congregation issued a "provisionary refusal" to which was attached a *nota bene* which justified a course of hopeful waiting. When he learned of the refusal, Gilson wrote Phelan:

They want the Institute to actually function before giving it approval. ... You are right to conclude that the Institute is to be organized under the direction of the archbishop of Toronto. ... Rome's approbation of the idea is certainly something; it [remains] to authorize the archbishop to take the direction of the enterprise and ... to protect it. (EG to Phelan, 36.7.15.)

When the Institute finally received its charter, 21 November 1939, Gilson recalled to students and faculty "how vividly the workings of Divine Providence were evident at every stage of the progress over a number of years toward the happy event being celebrated today" (minutes, 39.11.21; below, p. 240).

6 CATHOLIC ACTION: *LA VIE INTELLECTUELLE* AND *SEPT*

The condemnation by Pius XI in 1926 of Action Française was followed in France by a sharp change in the quality and character of Catholic journals. The old *Nouvelles religieuses* had been a well-written journal of information, a cut above the clipping service offered by *Documentation catholique*. In October 1928 its editor, Père M.-V. Bernadot, transformed it suddenly into *La vie intellectuelle*, and a new era began in Catholic journalism. The Dominicans pushed the new journal hard, and an elite of Catholic contributors supported it: Brémond, Gillet, Chenu, Glorieux, Ghéon, Mandonnet, Massignon, Massis, Maritain, Roland-Gosselin, Théry and many others. But not at first Gilson who was still, in his own view and among aggressive Catholics, considered an outsider, a *professeur de la Sorbonne*.

In June 1929 Gilson's attitude began to change, and he began to place occasional articles in *La vie intellectuelle*. There were several reasons for this, including his strengthening friendships with the Saulchoir people and the church's promotion of "Action Catholique."* He also read an article on one of his papers by R. Dalbiez, "Souvenir d'un Congrès de Philosophie" (*La vie intel-*

---

* "Catholic action" is a generic term used to describe lay participation in the apostolate of the bishops of the church. Pius XI had made a special plea for Catholic action within the various national churches. Gilson's response, generous and enthusiastic, was to participate within his special competence, that is, as a French Catholic intellectual.

lectuelle, 9 [1929]). The article looked back eight years to the international meeting of philosophers convoked by the Société Française de hilosophie in December 1921. This *congrès* had never attracted much attention; its proceedings had been slow in coming out and, if Dalbiez caught its true spirit, it had been a pitiful demonstration of the breakdown of communication among philosophers.*
According to Dalbiez, Gilson's paper had been the one bright spot at an otherwise dispirited assembly. His "La spécificité de la philosophie d'après Auguste Comte" (above, p. 118) had been a knowledgeable analysis of Comte's three successive states of philosophy: the theological, the metaphysical and the positive. Gilson's main argument had been that Comte's "absolute positivism is the absolute negation of positivism."

When Gilson read Dalbiez' article, he began to think that, through *La vie intellectuelle*, he might like to reach a wider audience of Catholic intellectuals. At around this time Père Bernadot, a friend of Gilson's, invited him to republish or even prepublish a number of the articles he was already planning. This would allow Gilson to reach for the first time those Catholic readers who had no access to *acta*, learned journals and so forth, and to encourage those readers to look at his books. Gilson liked the idea and many of the seventeen items he ultimately contributed to *La vie intellectuelle* were of this category. His first two articles for the journal, for example, were "L'idée de philosophie chrétienne chez saint Augustin et chez saint Thomas d'Aquin" (8 [1930]: 46-62; McG 305), which had not yet been published in the *Acta hebdomadae augustinianae-thomisticae*; and "Le problème de la philosophie chrétienne" (12 [1931]: 214-232; McG 408), which was shortly to appear as chapter 1 of *L'esprit de la philosophie médiévale*.

A few years later Père Bernadot began to edit the more popular and much more circumscribed journal, *Sept*. Not surprisingly Gilson became a contributor to this as well. Indeed, it was Gilson who prepared Bernadot's policy-statement for *Sept*, delivering it as an address to Les Amis de *Sept*, and then publishing it in *La vie intellectuelle* (31 [1934]: 9-30). The objective of *Sept*, said Gilson, was to bring decision and unity into the ranks of French Catholics and to induce the French Republic to abandon its present educational policy of secularization. As a result of this address Gilson came to involve himself for two years in the political and social problems of French Catholics. The statement is also the background of his collected *Sept* articles on education, *Pour un ordre catholique* (Paris, 1934; McG 125).

---

* Few contributions to the conference appeared to hold much conviction. No one, complained Wildon Carr in his paper on "The Nature of Scientific Knowledge," knows whether the philosophy of Henri Bergson is a neo-realism or a neo-idealism. Bergson, who was presiding at the session, raised an arm, then dropped it wearily as though to say, "Do I even know the answer myself?" For many, the rug seemed to have been pulled out from under philosophy. Carr even raised the whimsical issue of reality's role in the astronomer's knowledge of extinct constellations whose light after millions of years has not yet reached earth. Ralph Barton Perry made lively ridicule of sociology. Only Gilson's paper, according to Dalbiez, offered any real contribution.

Gilson's first article for *Sept* was more formal than subsequent ones, perhaps because it was aimed at French intellectuals; it recalled the subject and style of his earlier sophisticated journalism in *L'européen*. Entitled "En marge de Chamfort" (34.3.3; McG 634), the article attacks the self-interested littérateur – the *clerc-laïc* – who viciously ridicules the nobility and defames the priesthood with witty remarks cribbed from Sébastien Chamfort's pre-revolutionary *Caractères et anecdotes*. Like Chamfort, the *clerc-laïc* longs to claim the power of the nobility and the clergy for himself. The intellectuals have formed their own "priesthood" for controlling government, one which assumes privileges and eschews self-denial.

Gilson's next article for *Sept* was a review of G. K. Chesterton's *St Thomas Aquinas*, "Chesterton, le moyen-âge et la Réforme" (34.3.17; McG 585). Gilson was shaken by Chesterton's grasp of his subject: "How can that man, who never really studied philosophy, say the right things about St Thomas and in just the right way?" He learned from Chesterton that paradox could become literature in the grand manner, and could teach lessons in history. He also learned that modern historians often write history backwards: just as Chesterton saw English Protestants writing history from the perspective of the Reformation, so Gilson now saw French historians writing it from the vantage point of seventeenth-century rationalism.

After reading Chesterton, Gilson's popular articles acquired a new optimism. The rest of the *Sept* articles of 1934 offered simple and credible views on practical Catholic social issues. These papers were quickly gathered into *Pour un ordre catholique*, a book that did much to strenghten Gilson's reputation in Rome:

> My book, *Pour un ordre catholique*, is well received in Rome, including the approval of Mgr Pizzardo [of the Congregation of Seminaries and Universities] and the Holy Father. So all is well. It is being translated into Spanish and English. (EG to Phelan, 35.3.8.)

Gilson's articles for *Sept* in 1935 reveal the onset of disillusion. Bernadot and Gilson had intended the journal to unite French Catholics, a prospect that began to seem less and less attainable. Malaise crept into Gilson's articles, most noticeably in "Par delà le Sillon et l'Action Française" (35.6.21; McG 729), "Action politique et action catholique" (35.6.28; McG 540) and "En marge de l'Action Française" (35.7.5; McG 635). As Gilson grew less hopeful of mending rifts among French Catholics, he became more convinced that the church could not be committed to any particular party. This point runs through his last *Sept* articles, "Les catholiques et l'action sociale" (35.8.2; McG 577), "Qui est mammon?" (35.8.9; McG 777) and "Action catholique et action politique" (35.8.16; McG 538).

In *Sept*, Gilson was attempting to serve the church in the area of popular Catholic action; he was not formulating theoretical social philosophy. Social philosophy was the emphasis of quite another Catholic periodical, Emmanuel Mounier's *Esprit*. Jacques Maritain, who was always inclined toward philosophical social doctrine, contributed a number of articles to *Esprit*; not so Gilson, who instinctively as a republican distrusted socialism in all its forms.

7 REALISM AS METHOD

During the 1930s Gilson entered his second strictly philosophical controversy, this time over the so-called critical realism of many neoscholastics.* He addressed this issue in two important books. *Le réalisme méthodique* (Paris, 1936; McG 131) collected a number of Gilson's papers written since 1930; it was published in Yves Simon's "Cours et documents de philosophie." *Réalisme thomiste et critique de la connaissance* (Paris, 1939; McG 134) was prepared by Gilson to make clear that any thomism that used the arguments of the critical realists was not the thomism of Thomas Aquinas. Interestingly Gilson produced these works, which contain some of his finest philosophical writing, at the same time he was writing his popular articles for *Sept*.

The clarion call to the realism controversy was Gilson's paper "Le réalisme méthodique" which he published in the Geyser Festschrift (*Philosophia perennis* [Regensburg, 1930], 1: 743-755; McG 417). The article was a criticism of the positions taken in Désiré Mercier's *Critériologie générale* and Léon Noël's *Notes d'épistémologie thomiste*. Although Gilson had misgivings about publishing so severe an analysis of these positions, he was apparently encouraged to do so by Gerald Phelan.

Gilson's article disposes of Mercier quickly. Like Descartes before him, Mercier has appealed in his *Critériologie* to the principle of causality in order to proceed from thought to things; that is, he has introduced an illation, or inference, between thought and the real. Mercier's realism is mediate and contrary to the realism both of medieval scholastics and of the Greeks. It is therefore nonthomist.

Noël is not so easily disposed of. His is an immediate realism, like the idealists, and especially like Kant, he has proceeded from the "I" through to things as perceived. This, argues Gilson, is not an authentic realism because it terminates with the *percipi* not with the thing. Noël has followed the method of Descartes, the source of idealism. He has also used the critique of Kant and can therefore never reach the real; a kantian critique is a philosophical method and never emerges into the real world.

According to Gilson, realists, like neoscholastics, deceive themselves when they make their epistemology a necessary preamble to philosophy. Realists have to use the method of realism and start from things rather than thoughts. Idealists may smile at such a method and call it naïve, but in its modern form scholastic realism

---

* "Critical realism" is a term that was brought into common use through the title of the book *Essays in Critical Realism* (New York, 1920). It was a co-operative reaction by Durant Drake and six American philosophers against the "new realism" of which Ralph Barton Perry was the leading protagonist. The characteristic tenet of critical realism is that knowledge of the real external world is upheld by critical study of the internal data immediately present to the mind.

is anything but naïve. Modern scholasticism is fully aware of the existence of idealism, and takes into account the nature of the problem of knowing:

> Scholasticism is a self-conscious, a considered, a willed realism. It is not based on a solution to a problem posed by idealism for the very reason that the givens in such a problem necessarily imply the solutions of that same idealism. In other terms, surprising as a thesis like this at first-hand appears, scholastic realism is not a function of the problem of knowledge – the contrary is rather the case – but the real is put there as something distinct from thought, the *esse* is put there as distinct from *percipi*, and this because of a definite idea of what philosophy is, and even as a condition of the very possibility of philosophy. It is a methodic realism. (*Le réalisme méthodique*, p. 11; tr.)

Scholastic realism is realism as method, wherein the real is given as distinct from thought, and *esse* is given as distinct from *percipi*. The realism of the Greeks and medievals may have been naïve, but scholastic realism is not.

Neoscholastics generally resented the methodic restrictions Gilson wanted to impose upon them. Some, particularly M. D. Roland-Gosselin, felt that modern scholastics should carry on their battle with idealism using methods approved by idealists. There was also a certain advantage in being able, like idealists, to proceed from epistemology into ontology. Roland-Gosselin wrote furiously:

> Will "the eminent historian of medieval philosophy" succeed in persuading modern disciples of St Thomas of the need to change their front in the struggle against idealism ? As an entry into the lists on the terrain of philosophical discussion properly so called, this can certainly be called a fine success! Mgr Noël is the scholar most quaified to be a judge of this. If I may express frankly my personal opinion, I think it will require something more than the hasty sketch boldly put out by M.G. (*Revue des sciences philosophiques et théologiques*, 20 [1931]: 137; tr.)

Roland-Gosselin bluntly put two questions in his paper. Does not the problem of knowledge create for philosophy some need for looking at "the point of view and the method of idealism"? And is it more in line with the realism of St Thomas simply to adopt the realist method, or is it not wise for the intelligence to reflect upon its own act? Gilson did not need to reply to these questions. His answer had already been given in his conclusion to "Le réalisme méthodique":

> The philosopher as such has only one duty – to put himself into agreement with himself and with things. He has no reason to suppose *a priori* that his thought is the condition of being; he has no obligation *a priori* to make what he is going to say about being, dependent upon what he knows by his own thought. (*Le réalisme méthodique*, p. 14; tr.)

And further:

> With a sure instinct for the right way, the Greeks took resolutely the road of realism, and the scholastics did so too because it led somewhere. Descartes tried a different road. Once walking it, he saw no obvious reason for not going on. We today, however, know this way leads nowhere, and so we have to leave it. (ibid.; tr.)

In the same Dominican *Revue* in which Roland-Gosselin had attacked him, Gilson published his longer and more devastating sequel, "Réalisme et méthode" (21 [1932]: 161-186; McG 416). This article became the second chapter in *Le réalisme méthodique*. It offers perhaps the best statement of Gilson's position and best exploits his profound familiarity with the entire range of French philosophy.

At the time of writing "Réalisme et méthode," Gilson became aware that Noël's position had been less a statement of his own thought than a defence of Mercier's:

> I have just received a moving letter from Mgr Noël which I will bring with me. This marvellous friend wanted to defend and cover Cardinal Mercier, his master, and at the same time present his authentic thought. Like everyone else, I fell into the trap, and accused him of a mistake which was really only, on his part, loyalty and friendship. (EG to Phelan, 32.6.29.)

Nonetheless, Gilson thought Noël may have read some of his own ideas into Mercier's. For the moment he assumed this was so and that Noël's was really an "immediate realism." Like so many of the neoscholastics, Noël was disposed to emulate the idealists in beginning the epistemological demonstration from the "I," speaking even of the *cogito*; these neoscholastics claimed they only did this to facilitate conversation with the idealists. Gilson found this tactic misleading and almost dishonest, and contrary to the method used by Thomas himself: "Why, I ask, as indeed Noël asks, does St Thomas always start from the real, and not from the apprehended? And why doesn't St Thomas start from God?" (*Le réalisme méthodique*, p. 44; tr.)

These questions led Gilson to frame one of his most cogent statements about *la méthode thomiste*. First, and *pace* Spinoza, scholastics don't start from God because a metaphysical gap between God and things separates God, the necessary, from the real, which is contingent: the real therefore cannot be deduced from God, nor can the human intellect have God as its proper object. Second, for St Thomas the essence of realism is "ab esse ad nosse valet consequentia" ("it is proper to move from being to knowing"); for Descartes it is the opposite, "a nosse ad esse valet consequentia." These methods are in opposition, as is clear from Thomas' claim that thought has the wherewithal for knowing, but not for knowledge of itself. Thought, in St Thomas, only extends to self when it knows things *in actu* (*Summa theologiae*, 1.87.1). Without things there is no knowledge. Indeed, the first step in knowledge is the thing as being, "ens est quod primum cadit in intellectu" (1.5.2); apprehension of the thing is only the second step. Thomist reason does not begin with the "I"; to pretend it does is a mistake. Toward the end of "Réalisme et méthode," Gilson writes:

> Scholastic realism is not based on metaphysical reasoning. If this reasoning starts from God, it has to fail because of the impossibility of deducing the contingent from the necessary. If it starts from thought in Descartes' sense, it also fails, but for a different reason. Between one contingent being and another there is always a metaphysical rupture because of the analogy of being: if the being from which one departs is heterogeneous to the other, one never reaches the other because the being of that other will never be anything more than that of a representation of itself.

Thus the only solution left is to admit, even as experience suggests, that the subject does not find its object in an analysis of knowledge of it, but it finds its knowledge, and itself too, in an analysis of its object. (*Le réalisme méthodique*, pp. 47-48; tr.)

A third article, "Autour de la philosophie chrétienne: la spécificité de l'ordre philosophique" (*La vie intellectuelle*, 21 [1933]: 404-424; McG 202) makes up chapter 3 of *Le réalisme méthodique*. This article is an analysis of the failure both of Greek and medieval thinkers to provide a science of the real for each order of the real, and of seventeenth-century thinkers to provide correct ones. The chapter is not however set squarely within the context of the controversy. Chapters 4 and 5 of *Le réalisme méthodique* are two short pieces: "La méthode réaliste" (*Revue de philosophie*, 5 [1935]: 97-108; McG 347) and "Vade-mecum du débutant réaliste" (*Revue de philosophie*, 5 [1935]: 289-301; McG 490). The five chapters together reveal why Gilson would shortly make a major appeal to contemporary philosophers to abandon idealism entirely.

Critics of *Le réalisme méthodique* complained that its discussion seemed arbitrarily confined to Mercier and Noël. They also maintained that Gilson's invalidation of the use of kantian critiques by realists effectively turned the existence of the exterior world into a postulate. Gilson deals with these criticisms in his fuller, better organized *Réalisme thomiste et critique de la connaissance*. Here Gilson works more like an historian reorganizing his own philosophical reflections. He skilfully presents the notions of "common sense," "I am," and "I think" within an historic context, and extends his criticisms past Noël and Mercier to M. D. Roland-Gosselin, J. Maréchal, Charles Boyer, B. Picard, Père Descoqs and a few others. In chapters 6, 7 and 8 he examines the kantian critique to show why he finds an internal contradiction in the use of it by thomists; thomists can make critiques, but not of realism itself. Finally he focuses sharply, from his own point of view, on both object and subject in relation to the apprehension of existence. He concludes wittily with his own version of the formula of his friend A. N. Whitehead: any philosophy which excludes the real from the object of the act of knowing commits "the sophism of the misplaced existence" (p. 229). Like Yves Simon, Gilson stands by an "ontology of knowing"; he accepts through epistemology the possibility of an act of knowing and leads it into metaphysics, its natural term.

In his *Distinguer pour unir, ou Les degrés du savoir* (Paris, 1932, pp. 137-138) Jacques Maritain had substantially agreed with Gilson on "critical realism," but had felt the term itself was not necessarily self-contradictory. Always open to the modern instance, Maritain did not favour abandoning the term to the exclusive use of the idealists, and thought it could be developed to describe some transition from the implicit to the explicit. According to Maritain, the term could be redefined to reduce Gilson's objections to it. In *Réalisme thomiste* (p. 37, n. 1), Gilson returned to the issue, claiming that if his objections were reduced, the term "critical realism" would designate no distinct philosophical position whatever. Maritain returned once more to the point in a letter written from Fontgombaud, Indre, after the appearance of *Réalisme thomiste* in early 1939:

Cher Ami. I have had to wait for the summer break to read your *Réalisme thomiste*. I have done so admiringly and with great pleasure. Not only because you are emitting a well-deserved volley at *cartesiano-thomisme* and *kantiano-thomisme*, but because you are on this occasion making us penetrate to the very substance of the realism of St Thomas. You have made me *vehementius et profundius intelligere* some essential points which I am putting all my heart into teaching. I thank you warmly.

I thank you further for the way you speak of my positions. I am more than ever convinced that we are in substantial agreement (although I still defend the expression critical realism, understanding it in my own way, which is just as paradoxical as your calling your realism dogmatic but not critical!) (Maritain to EG, 39.8.16; tr.)

8 SPECIAL LECTURES, 1935

In 1935 Gilson was called upon to deliver an unusually large number of special lectures over and above his courses in the Collège de France and the Toronto Institute. The trend started early. On 13 February he read a paper on "Saint Thomas Aquinas" to the British Academy for its annual lecture on a "master mind" (*Proceedings*, 21 [1935]: 29-45). Gilson was honoured by the invitation and took his son Bernard, now almost seven, with him to London for the event.

A few weeks later Gilson was named a Chevalier de la Légion d'Honneur. He responded dryly to Phelan's congratulatory note:

Thanks for your felicitation to the *chevalier*. I was named *chevalier* because a minister of the government wished to have me named *officier*.* It was discovered that I had never been named *chevalier*. For once I was in full agreement with my minister on the importance of the thing, and it does please the ladies! Moreover, Bédier was exquisite, even succeeding in giving meaning to something which in itself has none. (EG to Phelan, 35.3.8.)

A deluge of official lectures followed these events. By a decree of November last (34.11.3), Gilson had been designated Membre du Conseil Supérieur de la Recherche Scientifique (section eight: philosophical and social sciences). This meant that he was to stand ready to participate in the Service des Œuvres Françaises à l'Etranger at the nod of several ministries, including National Education, Public Instruction, and External Affairs. Thus in early 1935 Gilson found himself committed to three special series of lectures: to the Institut Français de Vienne, 13 to 17 May; to the Faculté Catholique de Salzbourg, 17 to 21 May; and, through the Brazilian embassy, to the planned Faculté des Lettres of the university in Rio de Janeiro, late July to 19 September. Although Gilson was not the only French scholar to get caught in this web, he apparently got more than his share of such assignments. The foreign services were looking for lecturers who could draw a crowd, a bill Gilson obviously filled: M. Réau, directeur de l'Institut

---

* Gilson did not become an *officier* until 1949.

de Vienne, had to move the lectures from the Salle de Conférence de l'Institut to the large Amphithéâtre de l'Université (Réau to EG, 35.2.22).

Gilson's first briefing on what was expected of him in Rio came from the undersecretary at External Affairs in March:

> For Rio, you must realize that up to now the Faculty of Letters only exists on paper: I mean by this that it is difficult to consult it. What the public and university will expect from you is above all a history of French philosophy. This will not prevent your giving some lectures in medieval philosophy. (35.3.11; tr.)

At first Gilson was at a loss to understand why External Affairs was so determined to send him to Rio. The answer was not particularly flattering: "I had until yesterday no idea why they were so insistent that I go. As it turns out, it is to prevent someone else who has been moving heaven and earth to go there." (EG to Phelan, 35.5.5; tr.)

Gilson travelled to Rio in the summer of 1935 with Thérèse, Jacqueline, Cécile and Bernard. The trip began with a farewell visit to Maman at Cravant to console her for the family's absence over the next five months. Before even leaving Paris for Le Havre, Gilson wrote Maman a short letter describing "la bousculade de départ" as the Gilsons scurried to meet the sailing hour, eleven o'clock Friday morning, 5 July.

The ship moved southerly from Le Havre, calling at La Coroque and Vigo in Spain and passing along the coast of Portugal. A great many Russian, Lithuanian, Czech and Spanish emigrants were on board, packed together in dormitories of fifty. On 10 July the ladies took advantage of a full day's stopover at Casablanca to do some shopping; Gilson found these buying sprees at all the ship's ports of call incomprehensible, especially considering the four trunks and six valises already aboard. He also found his family's supply of medicines mystifying: "We are a kind of mobile hospital unit: their love of médicaments is unbelievable!" (EG to Maman, 35.7.8-9; tr.)

On July the ship's stokers went on strike to celebrate "the national feastday," ostensibly to win "the right to make up their own menus." And as the Gilsons crossed the equator for the first time, they found they had to be baptized by Old Father Neptune:

> Since the Gilson family had no desire to be dipped into a tub, they elected for the more dignified sprinkling with eau de Cologne. We nevertheless received our five baptismal certificates assuring us of dispensation from the ceremony on crossing the equator again on some other ship. (EG to Maman, 35.7.31; tr.)

In Rio de Janeiro the Gilsons were met by Mme Escare and her daughter Josiane, and taken to their rooms in Pensão Castelo da Glória (Ladeira da Glória 108). On account of the excessive heat, the Brazilians slept on hard pallet beds under only a sheet; Gilson found this "chilly enough" during the night if the breeze blew in through the shutters of their unglazed windows.

In accordance with the ministry directive, Gilson gave a survey course of fourteen lectures on the history of French philosophy; no doubt he also touched effectively on medieval philosophy. There survives from Rio, carefully saved by Gilson, a series of six pencil sketches on small slips of cheap paper. Each sketch bears a caption, no doubt taken from the talk, and one of them places the lecture at Petroplis, 4 August 1935. In the first sketch Gilson's arms are straight and stiff as his hands press down on the podium; it bears the caption "quidditas des choses." The second reveals Gilson glowering into his notes, its caption "logicus considerat omnia." In the third, Gilson's shoulders are hunched, his elbows are pressed into his ribs, and his hands are extended questioningly; the caption reads "seulement: Duns Scot." The fourth, with Gilson's right hand pointing at the audience, reads "une prise directe." The fifth outlines the head of a bewildered auditor with the inscription "intelligentia separata." And the last, of another puzzled auditor, asks "non est probari Deum esse vivum?"

Besides this course, Gilson also gave two special talks on "L'action catholique" and "L'ordre catholique." He found that he was easily understood by his audiences, but he did not find the people he met representative of Brazilian society:

> French is marvellously understood in *haute société*. It is my opinion that there are Brazilians and Brazilians, but I am not certain because apart from the rector of the university (M. Peixoto), whom I went to see as soon as I got here, I have not yet visited a single Brazilian in Rio de Janeiro. We have been guests of our ambassador [M. Hermite], and of old friends of these friends, but neither my wife nor I has yet, in fifteen days, had any conversation whatever with a native of the country. Hence my conclusion that Brazilians are much like Frenchmen. (EG to Mme Thibaudeau, 35.8.8; tr.)

On 19 September the Gilsons set sail from Rio de Janeiro for New York aboard the *Northern Prince*. From New York they flew to Montréal where Thérèse and the children remained for a holiday with the Thibaudeaus at La Pointe. Gilson returned alone to Toronto to open his autumn lectures and to launch at last the Institute's expanded programme.

The syllabus for this year, more elaborate and elegant than previously, listed six executive officers and eleven professors (later to be called fellows). The expanded programme covered theological and philosophical thought, history, law, liturgy, archeology, medieval Latin, paleography, and the vernacular languages and literatures. The Institute hoped to include some reference to pontifical degrees, but this could not be done; the rubric stated simply that the lecture-courses were "prescribed for all students of the Institute" and that the work of the Institute was still, "for the most part, of a private and personal character carried on under the direction of the staff." The students were all registered in the University of Toronto and eligible for the university's degrees of MA and PhD when they satisfied the requirements of its graduate departments.

The first meeting of the new council was held on 15 October:

> Dr Gilson welcomed the new members of the staff and expressed his pleasure in the fact that the Institute could now begin to function according to the *statuta* which

had been submitted for approval to the Sacred Congregation of Seminaries and Universities (council minutes, 35.10.15).

Apparently Gilson had privately hoped for more fanfare to mark the programme's implementation. In a letter to Mme Thibaudeau he promised there would be some kind of solemnity the next year:

> There will be a solemn inauguration, 29 September 1936. As I will then have just been at Harvard for its tercentenary festivities, and as my courses will commence about the 29th, I shall just have time to return from Toronto to begin [the William James Lectures] at Harvard. ... Let us hope no European war interferes with these projects. The year then will begin with two university festivals. How many discourses and how much bad cooking to look forward to! But Harvard's festival will be a very beautiful one, and Toronto's a dream come true. (EG to Mme Thibaudeau, 35.10.18; tr.)

In late September Gilson began his regular Toronto courses. In both his seminar and his lecture-course he emphasized Duns Scotus, convinced he had finally broken through to an authentic understanding of the *doctor subtilis*. Earlier he had written Phelan:

> My Toronto course, which will begin with Duns Scotus, will probably not get much beyond him because I am in the process of discovering him – at long last! I have such unexpected and, I think, important results that they ought to be presented at the Institute in Toronto while they are new. I am sorry Dan Walsh won't be there. (35.3.8; tr.)

Gilson had discovered, largely through internal evidence, that Scotus' *Theoremata* were authentic. He first presented his findings in his Toronto lectures of 1935, and repeated them a few weeks later in two Ottawa lectures, largely for the benefit of Chenu, who was there this year. In Montréal he gave the same two lectures for the Capuchins. He also prepared an article on the subject and sent it to France and Germany.*

This year Gilson had also committed himself to deliver, in collaboration with Dean George Brett of the University of Toronto's School of Graduate Studies, several lectures on cartesian thought; he had promised Phelan that these would also include some treatment of the thirteenth century (35.3.29). Yet, despite all his Toronto commitments, Gilson was constantly on the road this fall. In addition to the Scotus lectures in Ottawa and Montréal, he gave many others in Canada and the United States. In October he lectured at Assumption College in Windsor. In November he went to Notre Dame University for several days, and delivered talks to chapters of the Alliance Française in Washington and New York on the way home. In response to long and continuous pressure from Mlle Sturm, he also spoke at Smith College in Northampton, Massachusetts.

---

* See Gilson's "Les seize premiers *theoremata* et la pensée de Duns Scot," *Archives*, 11 (1938): 5-86; McG 445; also "Metaphysik und Theologie nach Duns Scotus," *Franziskanische Studien*, 22 (1935): 209-231; McG 346.

Gilson's annual Montréal lectures for the Institut Scientifique posed a problem for him in 1935. Would the two Scotus lectures for the Capuchins satisfy the institute? Indeed, had they even invited him this year? Gilson could not remember. Not wishing to offend his Montréal friends, he despatched a cautious letter to Mme Thibaudeau and offered to deliver a series of five new lectures:

> Pardon me for calling on you, but you know better than I my schedule in Montréal. If I write directly, I might only interfere with arrangements made. Would you clarify that my lectures are offered to the Monastery of the Reparation by the Institut Scientifique Franco-Canadien? It would be wise I think to speak to M. Gardner too. I will give five lectures for the Institut, not just three, unless some change has perchance been made in our usual arrangements. (EG to Mme Thibaudeau, 35.11.24; tr.)

Mme Thibaudeau diplomatically solved the problem before anyone realized there was one. Gilson gave the five lectures.

It was a tired Gilson who sailed from New York late in December for Paris. Even as he boarded the ship he received the last of three letters from Professor Albert Balz, pressing him to revisit the Corcoran School of Philosophy in the University of Virginia. Balz had invited Gilson to give the fourth Richards Lectures at Virginia in 1936; Gilson had accepted the invitation, but for 1937.

Balz closed this last of his three letters with a humourous reference to his own cartesianism:

> I am venturing to enclose a document that may interest you. It will at least furnish an amusing story for you to tell in France, how an American student of philosophy (who is more thoroughly cartesian than any Frenchman – the French government should put me in a museum as the one genuine cartesian left alive) talked cartesian doctrine as the foundation of jeffersonian democracy before the officials of the Department of Agriculture in the USA. (Balz to EG, 35.12.23.)

9 HARVARD TERCENTENARY, 1936

Gilson's transfer in 1929 from Harvard to Toronto had by no means severed his Harvard connections, and he returned to Harvard on several occasions during the early 1930s. On 21 November 1933 he delivered a lecture on "The Social Function of Theology" at Harvard in the afternoon and at Wellesley in the evening. The following day he also participated in a Heidegger evening at Harvard.

Gilson had heard Heidegger lecture in Paris and had met him several times in Germany. Heidegger never failed to arouse in him stirring emotions: he had been embarrassed more than once by the tears Heidegger's words inevitably sent rolling down his cheeks. Gilson seems to have regarded Heidegger as a kind of *Thomas manqué*, who recognized the primacy of the act-of-existing over that which exists yet failed to recognize that his idea had historical precedents. His surviving notes on Heidegger include the following snatches:

It is ... quite natural that philosophers who discover their own notions analogous to those at the base of thomism should feel they are on to something new. Heidegger indeed pursues paths very different from those of St Thomas, but several of his affirmations, surprisingly enough, give one the impression of a curious misunderstanding on his part of his own intellectual antecedents.

Levinas asks in what the essential category of heideggerian existentialism consists. Does it consist in something which "projects its own particular beam of light on all those notions by which existentialists describe man and transform those old notions into a new philosophy"? The reply, "Certainly! I think that the new philosophical 'shiver' brought to bear by the philosophy of Heidegger consists in the distinguishing between *être* and *étant*." (Gilson Archives: re Heidegger.)

Ralph Barton Perry used this 1933 Heidegger evening to extract from Gilson a tentative commitment to take part in Harvard's 1936 tercentenary celebrations. It was some time before Gilson received a firm invitation from the Tercentenary Committee. He informed Phelan of his acceptance in April 1935, by which time he had also been invited to give the William James Lectures at Harvard:

Another question. You know Harvard wants me to go back there. You know, and they know, that I will not do it. At the same time I feel rather sorry to have nothing else to answer every year but "No." Moreover, they crowned this year their kind attentions with an invitation to attend the Harvard tercentenary celebration to be held in August to September 1936, and to receive on that occasion an honorary degree. Of course there was no question as to whether or not I should accept, and I did. Then came a few days later another invitation to stay there from October to December 1936 and to give the William James Lectures. I must confess that I have been wondering ever since if I should not accept it too. ... I would like to give them some sort of satisfaction by saying "Yes" at least once. (35.4.2.)

Phelan agreed that Gilson should go to Harvard for the fall of 1936. The Institute had hoped that Maritain could replace him at Toronto, but this proved impossible; Maritain's mother was ill that fall and he dared not leave Paris.

From April to August, Gilson's life was largely given over to preparing and revising his lectures for Harvard. His letters during this period deal constantly with tercentenary commitments. He looked forward to the lectures with some trepidation, and in July wrote Phelan that "I am finishing up the last of my Harvard lectures, and don't much like what I have done" (36.7.1).

Gilson left France on 19 August aboard the French liner *Lafayette*, sailing early to be in good time for the celebrations. His ship docked in Boston on 29 August and he moved into Harvard's Henry Adams House (E 21) to remain there until December. Between mid-August and mid-September various scholarly symposia, conferences and individual talks were to take place. These scholarly events would precede an elaborate programme of concerts, a service of thanksgiving, and a special convocation with the conferring of honorary degrees, all to take place from 16 to 18 September.

Gilson's lecture, on "Medieval Universalism and Its Present Value," was scheduled for 2 September. He was worried about this paper, as he well might have been. His new attitude toward idealist philosophy was not one that would be shared by most of his informed auditors. Moreover his paper was to be in English and would be broadcast on radio at the prime evening hour of nine o'clock. Gilson described his emotions during this lecture in a letter to Mme Thibaudeau:

> I finally delivered my paper last evening. I was trembling all over, before and during it, with the constant impression that I had lost the game and that the farther on I got, the worse things were going. I think St Thomas, to whom I said a prayer before commencing, took charge of the affair, because the results were of a kind to surprise me. I truly had no part in it because even now I can't so much as think of this lecture without experiencing that frightening terror which never left me for a moment while I was speaking. So it was until ten minutes before the end, when I completely forgot that I was giving a lecture. Well, ouf! It's over now. (36.9.4; tr.)

It was not over yet, however. The press gave the lecture extensive coverage, and Dorothy Thompson featured it in the *New York Herald Tribune*.

"Medieval Universalism and Its Present Value" (Cambridge, 1937; McG 342) analyzed the four foundations of medieval universalism – rationalism, realism, personalism, and the philosophical search for "truth universal in its own right." According to Gilson, medieval man possessed a strong feeling for the universal character of truths, including truths of faith. Medieval man probed truth with the aid of a reason that conformed to reality rather than struggling to determine reality through the laws of the mind. Modern man has only to gain, Gilson argued, by emulating this approach, and by comprehending truths through a knowledge that is intellectual, personal, universal: "What is rationally true is universally true, because the only thing that lies behind truth is reality itself, which is the same for all." This bare thesis was adorned with informed references to medieval texts, medieval history and modern circumstance in an attempt to move the contemporary audience, most of whom were unwilling to accept his position. The lecture revealed the essential Gilson of the late 1930s: the defender of Christian philosophy, the foe of idealisms, and the new disciple of the spirituality of St Bernard.

Shortly after giving his lecture, Gilson wrote of its success to Father McCorkell at the Toronto Institute:

> As you know by Dr Phelan and Father Muckle [who had attended the lecture], it went much better than I could feel while I was delivering it. So much so that, yielding as I believe to the suggestions of Dorothy Thompson in the *Herald Tribune* of New York, President Butler of Columbia has decided to get it printed and circulated by the Carnegie Endowment for International Peace. (36.9.12.)

Two weeks later, Gilson had to modify this report:

> Butler and his group were rather puzzled when they read the whole paper which they wanted to print. You know the newspaper had cut off a good deal of the religious part, and when [Butler et al.] saw what it looked like, they were a bit frightened. I offered to take it back and to relieve them from their engagement; they jumped at the proposal. (EG to McCorkell, 36.9.26.)

On the morning of 18 September, Gilson received his honorary degree from Harvard. He much appreciated the honour and carefully preserved both the diploma and E. K. Rand's impressive Latin *salutatio*. Gilson's most vivid recollection of the convocation was the deluge of rain that accompanied it: "I have never been so drenched in my life as for this doctorate" (EG to Mme Thibaudeau, 36.9.18; tr.). While Gilson was in Cambridge he visited several of his old friends including the Perrys, the Whiteheads, the Greenes, the Merciers, the Pickmans and the Rands. He also attended house dinners at Lowell and Adams and took automobile trips to Concord, Gloucester, Revere Beach, Lynn and Swampscott. He stayed busy socially right up until his first William James Lecture on 2 October. Later in the fall he had further dinners with most of the above, as well as the Fords, Wolfson and Mme Thibaudeau, who came to Cambridge to attend his last two lectures.

Gilson delivered his twelve William James Lectures in English to large university and public audiences. They were subsequently published as *The Unity of Philosophical Experience* (New York, 1937; McG 168). As an historian's statement of a philosophical position, *The Unity* is altogether unique. Its structure seems to reflect a technique Gilson had learned in a 1905 course by Bergson. Just as Bergson philosophized on the individual efforts of a sequence of philosophers, so Gilson examines a sequence of philosophical experiments or experiences: the logicism of Abélard's attempts to solve the nature of generalities; the theologism of Al Ashuri as set down by Maimonides, and of Bonaventure for whom no epistemology existed outside theology; the psychologism of William Ockham; the mathematicism of Descartes; and the physicism of Immanuel Kant. In the final chapter on the "Nature and Unity of Philosophical Experience," Gilson probes the full range of these diverse approaches as an historian and as a metaphysician.

In the final chapter of *The Unity* two major theses emerge. The first argues that the history of philosophy adds new dimensions to the accumulating statements of philosophers. The history of philosophy involves more than the biographies of philosophers or accounts of their philosophies. It also traces the development of philosophy itself. It notes recurrences and reveals the "abstract philosophical necessity," the "impersonal metaphysical determinism," that proceeds from the first principles of all authentic philosophies. It notes too the dissolution of most philosophies into scepticism, and the rise of new philosophies to replace them.

Gilson's second thesis maintains that a metaphysical quality lies behind all those philosophical approaches that agree on the need to find "the first cause of all that is." In other words, man is by his nature a metaphysical animal whose reason is empowered to overstep all sensible experience. Even when philosophers reject metaphysics as delusory, metaphysics remains the basis of the unity of their philosophical experiences. And philosophers have particularly depended upon metaphysics in their drive to find first causes: in Democritus' search for Matter; in Plato's for the Good; in Aristotle's for the Self-thinking Thought; in Plotinus' quest for the One; in the Christian philosophers' search for Being; in Kant's for Moral Law; in Schopenhauer's for Will; Hegel's for the Absolute Idea; Bergson's for the Creative Duration; and so on. In each of these cases a metaphysician has looked "behind and beyond experience for an ultimate ground of all real and possible experience."

The Unity of Philosophical Experience was the first of Gilson's major works to be published first in English. Even though his text was read and corrected by Perry, Phelan and a Toronto student, Daniel Walsh, it was a remarkable achievement. A fine feeling for the English language is revealed in apothegms like the following

> There is more than one excuse for being a Descartes, but there is no excuse for being a cartesian (p. 7).
>
> In theology, as in any other science, the main question is not to be pious, but to be right. For there is nothing pious in being wrong about God. (p. 52.)
>
> Philosophy always buries its undertakers (p. 306).
>
> Psychology is a science, psychologism is a sophism: it substitutes the definition for the defined, the description for the described, the map for the country (p. 90).

Although *The Unity of Philosophical Experience* was received warmly as a series of lectures and as a book, its reception as philosophical doctrine was somewhat mixed. Gilson was both elated and disturbed. In January 1938 he wrote to his friend Mortimer J. Adler of the University of Chicago Law School and asked him to outline the serious objections to *The Unity*'s positions on doctrine. Adler replied:

> Throughout the book and especially in the last and summary chapter you *seem* to identify philosophy with metaphysics, you *seem* to ignore the philosophy of nature as a quite separate division of philosophical knowledge. ... In short, the error with which you might be charged is metaphysicism, that is, reducing the whole field of philosophical knowledge to one of its parts, namely, metaphysics; and this I am sure you would say is just as bad an error as any of the others. (38.7.8.)

Adler's criticism probably made a strong impression on Gilson. At any rate he never again attempted to deal with modern philosophies in broad rhetorical settings.

During the fall of 1936 Gilson commuted three times to Toronto from Harvard. He lectured at the Institute and met with students on 10 to 14 October, 7 to 11 November and 6 to 9 December. During the second of these visits, on 11 November, the real inaugural of the Institute was quietly held with the chancellor, Archbishop James Charles McGuigan, presiding. On that day the Institute began to function under the provisionary statutes awaiting Rome's approval.

Gilson spent his last evening in Cambridge, 18 December, with the Perrys. He took the midnight train to New York where he had luncheon with his American publishers, Scribner's Sons. In the evening he dined at the Commodore with his oldest American friend, Richard McKeon, and on Sunday he sailed for France aboard the *Hansa*.

10 COURSES IN PARIS AND TORONTO, 1937-1939

Between 1937 and 1939 Gilson's courses in both Paris and Toronto were immensely successful. The first of these was given in the Collège de France on the love story of Héloïse and Abélard. Gilson drew his material from the letters supposedly exchanged by the lovers and from Abélard's *Historia calamitatum*. He presented it within the context of early medieval humanism, and with an animation stirred by the fascination of romance.

Gilson lectured on Héloïse and Abélard to a large Parisian audience that included Maman, Thérèse, the Georges Vaniers (then at Maison Canadienne), students from the University of Paris, and a large contingent from around the world. Indeed, the course was a kind of Petrarchan triumph, restoring to the Collège de France something of the aura of the Bergson years. Gilson presented the famous love story from two romantic perspectives: that of Abélard, the scholar, the teacher, the theologian who gave his heart to his young pupil and secretly married her; and that of Héloïse, an intelligent, well-read woman willing to sacrifice her reputation by concealing the fact of the marriage, and putting Abélard's career before moral and selfish considerations. In Gilson's complex psychological analysis, he weighted the balance in Abélard's favour. He did not question the authenticity of the letters, arguing that the story was too beautiful not to be authentic.

When Gilson's lectures were published as *Héloïse et Abélard* (Paris, 1938; McG 58), they were widely acclaimed and translated into many languages. Gilson had done much for the story. He had related it to twelfth-century legal, social and ecclesiastical settings, and he had submitted it to a plausible analysis which had removed many misunderstandings. Understandably however he was criticized on two grounds: he had been very hard on earlier critics, especially Mlle Charrier, and he had also failed to probe in depth the authenticity of the letters. However, if Gilson was hard on some who treated the story before him, he was more gentle with his successors. He later wrote to John F. Benton of the California Institute of Technology, who had raised a number of queries:

> The Abélard and Héloïse story is fascinating but I doubt a universal agreement on its meaning will ever be reached. Personal psychology is one of the limits of history. I don't know if there is one of my conclusions I would maintain *mordicus* and I do not feel able validly to oppose your own. (73.4.15)

Maman attended the first part of Gilson's course on Héloïse and Abélard at the beginning of 1937. In February she became ill and was confined to her room, and in March she died. At one of Gilson's last visits to her side, she told him with regret, and perhaps with humour, that now she would never know how that Héloïse-Abélard affair had turned out.

In Gilson's aide-mémoire for 1937 is this brief entry for Wednesday 24 March: "Mort de Maman à midi, dans sa 86e année." An undated fragment of a letter, probably to Father McCorkell, reveals some of Gilson's pain at the loss of his mother:

My old mother died on the 24 March in her armchair. She had been ill for about a month and she knew perfectly well that she was dying; but she suffered very little; and she was so well prepared, after such a splendid long life of eighty-six years, that God could not have dealt more sweetly nor more mercifully with her than he did. For all of us, and quite especially for me, her death is a terrible stroke. I thank God with all my heart for having kept me my mother until past my fiftieth year. For years and years I have done my best to get ready for that awful day of her death. I even imagined that I was ready, but I have now to realize that I had not the slightest idea what it would be like. It is hard to work and to think, life has lost so much of its taste; nothing can really help but prayer.

During this same prewar period, Gilson also conducted research courses with his Toronto students which broke new ground. Most notable were his "Intellect in the Work of Albert the Great" in 1937 and "Plotinus and Saint Augustine" in 1938. Gilson was always determined to involve his students in original work on primary texts, as his letters to Phelan show:

In order not to waste any time, I enclose a list of the subjects for the seminar. The texts which are indicated are mere suggestions, each student being invited to scout for other texts in other works of Albertus Magnus. There will be eleven meetings of the seminar: at each meeting, a lecture of forty-five minutes will be given by a student; I shall take care of the second part of the meeting. (37.7.1.)

Gilson's legend among his students largely derived from the "second part" of just such meetings. He could be very hard on his students, and not always justly so. He constantly looked to them for new insights into the texts they were analyzing, and he had little sympathy for the *déjà vu*. Indeed, the course on Plotinus and Augustine grew out of a desire to avoid any reliance on secondary materials:

The more I think of it, the less pleased I am with my seminar for next fall. I don't think the results could be good, because it covers much too wide a field. I am afraid the students will have to resort to second-hand information rather than to the texts if we keep that topic on the programme. Unless you have some definite objection to it, I would favour the following subject: "Plotinus and Saint Augustine." (EG to Phelan, 38.5.15.)

Gilson seems to have warmed to his students in the Plotinus-Augustine seminar. He no sooner returned to Paris after giving it than he sent back suggestions for two of them:

Mr O'Neil, Charles J., will find interesting suggestions as to the social character of the Greek notion of virtue in M. D. Chenu: "Les philosophes dans la philosophie chrétienne médiévale," in *Revue des sciences philosophiques et théologiques*, 36 (1937), esp. pp. 32-33. ... And it might interest Mr W. H. Walton to know that his subject happens to form the very centre of a contemporary controversy.

After passing on a reference to Walton and referring him with a caution to the work of Père Descoqs, Gilson turned his attention to a less fortunate student. He had just read David Host's paper in Paris and returned it. Yet even this harsh criticism was tempered by a helpful postscript:

> I feel sorry to say that his paper does not appear to me satisfactory. It is the very type of thing a student should not do after attending a seminar on Plotinus and St Augustine. ... I would not advise Mr D. Host to select the problem of "the opinion according to St Thomas." This, of course, is exactly what Father Régis is after. His book on *L'opinion selon Aristote* is but the first half of his work. (39.3.14.)

Gilson's students were never treated as cyphers: they walked with the great and were expected to aspire to greatness.

Professor Balz had for some time been after Gilson to give the Richards Lectures at the University of Virginia: these had been established to bring international scholars to Charlottesville to speak on a subject "within the range of Christianity." Gilson was fond of Balz and was grateful to him for having originally prompted his first trip to America.

For the Richards Lectures, Balz suggested three papers on "Scripture as Authority in Medieval Thought," but Gilson decided instead on "Reason and Revelation in the Middle Ages." This subject allowed Gilson to return to the challenging theme of double truth associated with the much-maligned Siger of Brabant. He had dealt with the theme once before* and was anxious to try again in the light of his own *The Unity of Philosophical Experience* and especially of Maritain's *Distinguer pour unir*, which had made a strong attempt to bring faith and knowledge into organic unity. Gilson became the fourth Richards lecturer, following his Harvard colleague Professor Hocking. The series was published as *Reason and Revelation in the Middle Ages* (New York, 1938; McG 136).

Back in France in 1938 Gilson bought a car and learned to drive. He took his training rather seriously and – for thirteen days between 11 and 27 May – entered carefully in his aide-mémoire the exact times he went out driving: "Wednesday 11 May, 5:15 AM, auto; Thursday 12 May, 11:05, auto," and so on. He suffered no delusions about his skill, and wrote Phelan:

> I hope I won't have killed myself before September, for I am now attempting to drive a car and I am very much afraid of that rearing monster. The thing makes a terrific noise, especially when I try to get it started, and it has its own way of jumping four or five times before taking its normal course, which attracts suspicious looks from the cops when I make Parisian exhibitions.

In the same letter he described a trip from Paris to Vermenton. After seeing four cars in the ditch along "la route meurtrière Nationale 6," he had started to pray:

> The inspiration I got as a reward was to keep to the middle of the road; but a fierce female driver called my attention to the fact that "snails" should keep to the right side of the road. Of course the family were delighted to see and hear the boss insulted. The poor things finally arrived at Vermenton all safe and sound, without realizing that they had courted disaster for two hundred kilometres. Blessed ignorance! Enjoy youself and pray for a belated disciple of St Christopher. (38.6.9.)

---

* See Gilson's early paper "La doctrine de la double vérité," *Etudes de philosophie médiévale* (Strasbourg, 1931); McG 467.

At the end of the 1930s two more deaths and a serious illness disturbed Gilson deeply. In 1939 he wrote Phelan:

> I am having an awful time, so I hope you will kindly excuse me for being a little too matter-of-fact in my way of stating things. ... I lost my friend Charles Blondel, the psychologist, two weeks ago. ... My old master, Lévy-Bruhl, died two days ago. ... And my wife has undergone a very dangerous surgical operation. (39.3.14.)

Blondel had been Gilson's dear friend from student days, and had shared with him a broad humanism and a rigid concern for detail. The two men had also shared a deep love of Bergson, and Blondel's widow now presented Gilson with her husband's notes on a series of Bergson lectures that Gilson had missed in 1911. In Blondel's death, Gilson lost much of himself.

The same was true of the death of Lucien Lévy-Bruhl. Gilson wrote immediately for his old *maître* a fine memoir acknowledging his debt to the man who had taught him how to become an historian of philosophy. Although Lévy-Bruhl had taught him nothing of metaphysics or theology, he had instilled in his student two crucial lessons. He had taught Gilson how to distinguish good sociology from bad: "When the extravagant systematizations of Durkheim have become part of the archeology of sociology, the acute penetrating analyses of Lévy-Bruhl will remain for investigators a never-failing source of information and reflection." Lévy-Bruhl had also taught his student how to appreciate the contributions to learning of scholars with whom he almost totally disagreed. And of Lévy-Bruhl the historian, Gilson wrote: "In a country where many have done well, none has done better." (*Les nouvelles littéraires*, 39.3.18; tr.)

Thérèse's illness had been of grave concern to Gilson for some time. She had always had poor health, but in 1937 an operation became almost certain; this was also the time of Maman's death and Gilson's own depression. Gilson decided to buy, with 14,200 francs saved from the Gifford and William James Lectures, a lovely house in Vermenton:

> I am in the country, in a house with a garden which ends with two rows of lime trees. My wife and the children arrive tomorrow evening, and we shall have the joy of several days together among trees and flowers. We have been afraid my wife will have to have a heavy operation. She is trying treatment first which we have been told is unlikely to be successful but right now seems to be helpful. I think I shall have to go to Lourdes before going to Toronto. If all goes well my wife will make both trips. (EG to Phelan, 37.5.12.)

Gilson travelled to Lourdes at the suggestion of his brother Maurice, now a radiologist; Maurice had a strong enthusiasm for Lourdes and had arranged for them to join a pilgrimage in August. Thérèse did not join them: "My wife was too well to come as a patient and not well enough to come as a member of the diocesan pilgrimage. ... She is still very weak and ... is living on her nerves." (EG to Phelan, 37.8.28.)

In the fall of 1937 Thérèse and the nine-year-old Bernard accompanied Gilson to Toronto. Thérèse enjoyed a splendid autumn and her health for the next year was relatively good. In Paris in March 1939, however, she had to have her operation; although she rallied after it, she never really recovered.

11 ON THE VERGE OF WORLD WAR TWO

Of several articles written by Gilson during 1939, one, published shortly before the outbreak of the war, is particularly remarkable. "Erasme: citoyen du monde" (*Les nouvelles littéraires*, 39.5.6; McG 648) was a profoundly personal statement and an attempt to assess, in the face of war, the moral factors attaching to world humanism. Although Gilson wrote other articles in defence of the war against Hitler, these were largely political statements in the service of the Third Republic.

Gilson's Erasmus was neither a theologian nor an exegete but, when he touched on exegesis, he was willing to accept what he could not reform. For Erasmus as for Gilson, theology and philosophy were *ancillae*. According to Gilson, Erasmus had much to tell us about our own times. He spurned "modernism" in religion as a failure to acknowledge the ills endemic to the church in all its periods. He shunned certitudes and jargon, and appreciated the indestructibility of the church, in spite of its shifty formulations. And most important, he brought a humanist perspective to bear on war:

> Erasmus hated war. He called it antichristian, inhumane, base, stupid. And he only knew the war of the good old days when, though it had its horrors to be sure, it was rather local. It was even then a resort for fools and brutes, and for mercenaries greedy for gain. As for booty, said Erasmus, speaking of the mercenaries, these fellows bring nothing home to their wives but disease and "a soul about as pure as a sewer on rue Maubert in Paris or a public latrine." However, war then was more a soldier's affair; now it extends to the unarmed civilian. Now whole nations suffer from war: humanists and everyone else carry haversacks. Protest as they may, none now escapes. (tr.)

This is a different and more despairing Gilson than the man who in 1924 at Naples read a paper on the humanism of Thomas. In that paper he had praised the Christian scholar as fulfilling man's highest potential, his intelligence, as he unlocked for himself and for humanity the highest and noblest truths, including those of the *revelabile*. Even in the early 1930s, when Gilson was specifying humanism as social and moral in *Les idées et les lettres* and in *Pour un ordre Catholique*, he had still held great hopes for mankind. By 1939, however, Gilson had come to identify himself with Erasmus, an *homme du monde* and one of the few surviving humanists; as he argued passionately for the defence of European culture, he saw himself as perhaps one of the last who would do so.

In the spring of 1939 Gilson and his colleagues in the Collège and the Institute struggled to carry on as usual. From France, Gilson announced a course on "The Classical Tradition" and sent Böhner to Toronto to edit a text. He also wrote the preface for Bernard Müller-Thym's *The Establishment of the University of Being in the Doctrine of Meister Eckhart of Hochheim* (New York and London, 1939; McG 522). Muckle went blithely off to Germany to photograph more manuscripts;

Phelan planned to spend the summer in Paris. Looking back, the period possessed an aura of unreality.

At least on the matter of Phelan's vacation, Gilson issued a firm warning:

> Nobody knows what is going to happen here. In fact the decision rests with two men, Hitler and Mussolini, and they are free. Humanly speaking, the probabilities now are: war ninety-five percent, no war five percent. Consequently, my advice is: stay at home! Besides, unless one is an interested observer of international crises, life is not very pleasant in Europe. We are rapidly moving toward a climax, and I see no point in your exchanging a restful vacation, which you certainly need very badly, for a visit to a lunatic asylum. (EG to Phelan, 39.4.15.)

In the same letter he told Phelan that, unless there were a change for the worse, he would sail from Europe on the *Montrose* on September 20.

According to his aide-mémoire, Gilson entered a Paris clinic for some minor surgery in mid-June and retreated to Vermenton for the summer. He was still there on 1 September when Germany invaded Poland, on 2 September when general mobilization was ordered, and on 3 September when France and Great Britain declared war. As an officer retired to the reserve, Gilson's services now became the property of La République.

12

World War Two, 1939-1944 (Incipit Senectus)

1 *LA DRÔLE DE GUERRE*, 1939-1940

Like most of his countrymen, Gilson was stunned by the declaration of war. Once again he was separated from his family:

> I left Thérèse at Vermenton on 12 September 1939 telling her I would return from Paris that evening. Instead of returning to Vermenton, I had to go directly to London and Liverpool to look for a boat. I have had no news since, but all was well with my family when I left them. (EG to Mme Thibaudeau, 39.10.5; tr.)

On 12 September Gilson probably visited one or more of the French ministries; he was likely advised to leave for London at once and to arrange passage to Canada on the next boat. No doubt he was told to give his regular courses in Toronto, to create as much sympathy as possible in North America for France and her allies, and to be available for such missions as the French government might arrange for him.

After Gilson crossed to London, he stayed for three nights in the Grosvenor, seeing friends and visiting the French embassy; he also arranged a first-class passage to Québec on the CPR liner *Duchess of York*. On the morning of 15 September, he took the boat-train from Euston station to Liverpool. And in the afternoon, as his ship set sail, he watched the children play on the docks while cruisers and submarines filled the harbour.

Gilson disembarked in Québec City on the afternoon of 22 September. Because he had only a few specific appointments, he found himself with time on his hands. During the next six days he visited several friends and officials, including Mgr Roy, Jean Bruchési (deputy minister in the Secrétariat de Québec) and Onésime Gagnon (Minister of Fisheries). He toured Lac Saint-Jean and Ile d'Orléans, and also visited Eva Bouchard, the model for Louis Hémon's *Maria Chapdelaine*; he asked her to send a postcard to Thérèse which survives in the family papers.

On 27 September Gilson met in Montréal with Mgr Maurault and Professor Montpetit to set December dates for his regular conferences at the universities, Le Cercle and the Institut Scientifique Franco-Canadien. On 29 September he called on the consul, Diné Broullette, at 3954, parc Lafontaine. He suddenly cancelled his other appointments for a quick trip to Ottawa; the next day he called on the Comte de Dampière and took an afternoon train to Toronto.

Although Gilson expected to be in Toronto only until mid-December as usual, he received word during the fall that, as courses in the Collège de France were suspended, he should prolong his stay. Accordingly he remained in North America from September 1939 until April 1940, roughly the period of the "phony war," the interim period between the declaration of war and the opening of hostilities in the West. Judging from his itinerary over these seven months, the subjects of his non-academic addresses, and the pace of his cultural pursuits, he took his war-related duties seriously. The staccato notes in his aide-mémoire are dizzying in the number and variety of activities they list.

Gilson was back in Montréal at the end of October "pour assister déjeuner Bruneau, parc Lafontaine 3954," and returned there again on 19 November to repeat a special lecture on "Société universelle" that he had prepared for St Michael's College, Vermont. In December his regular address to the Institut Scientifique Franco-Canadien was on "L'Europe et la paix" (*Revue trimestrielle canadienne*, 26 [March 1940]: 27-43; McG 657). In no autumn did Gilson appear so often in Montréal. He returned there after Christmas as well, from 23 to 25 January; this was followed by a trip to Ottawa for talks to the largely French-Canadian classical college, Saint-Alexandre d'Ironsides, and to the Ottawa Alliance Française.

Despite his war-propaganda efforts, Gilson's main motive during this period was to drive home to his Institute students his belief that in humanism lay the best antidote to the venom of war. For Gilson medieval universalism, or "true humanism" as Maritain called it, held the key to ultimate health in the human condition. Although he conceded that Christian humanism should first be analyzed philosophically, he also thought it imperative to present it in the context of the men who lived by it. During the fall of 1939 he therefore offered a public course of twelve lectures on "Roman Classical Culture from Cicero to Erasmus." This course followed in a direct line from his William James lectures of 1936, his lectures in the Collège de France on Héloïse and Abélard, and his recently completed monograph *Dante et la philosophie* (Paris, 1939; McG 12).

Gilson's lectures on humanism opened with a presentation of two Roman ideals: Cicero's *doctus orator* ("the man of learning and eloquence") and Quintillian's *vir bonus dicendi peritus* ("the good man who speaks from practical knowledge"). Gilson traced these ideals from the beginning of Christianity to the sixteenth century as they rose, fell, rose again, and were transformed. He led his students through the *translatio studii* ("the transmission of learning") into Northumbria, into the Palatine court of Charlemagne, into the monastery and cathedral schools, and into the universities of the thirteenth century. He dealt with individuals, with Aldhelm, Bede, Boniface, Alcuin, Abélard, John of Salisbury, Roger Bacon, Petrarch, Coluccio Salutati and Erasmus. And he dealt with cultural movements, with the renaissances of the ninth, twelfth and fifteenth centuries, each a corollary of expanding culture. In these lectures Gilson never mentioned the war, though he wondered aloud whether Roman culture had not already arrived at Armageddon.

During this fall of 1939 Gilson finally received good news from Rome. Ildebrando Antoniutti, the apostolic delegate to Canada, informed the chancellor that a Vatican decree of 18 October, the feast of St Luke, had granted the Institute its pontifical charter. Gilson was away lecturing at Burlington, Vermont, and at Montréal on the day the chancellor, Archbishop McGuigan, shared the news with the faculty. He returned however on 20 November to pass the good news on to the students and the public. In his speech he warmly welcomed the charter as a manifestation of the beneficence of divine Providence.

Gilson travelled tirelessly this fall. On 11 November he attended the opening of the Catholic University of America's fiftieth anniversary celebrations. On 14 November he visited the home of his old Cambridge friends, the Greenes of 10 Longfellow Park, the following evening he lectured on "Racine, tragédien de la fatalité," a lecture he repeated in Montréal.

Gilson's domestic concerns were quiet during this period. He wrote Thérèse some twenty-one letters in the fall; all were numbered, and their mailing dates recorded. By March he had sent her thirty letters in all, though neither these nor Thérèse's replies seem to have survived. Thérèse referred to these letters in a note to Mme Thibaudeau: "In my quasi-solitude, I find much comfort in the letters from my husband which have been arriving thus far with perfect regularity, while those I write him are much delayed" (39.12.18; tr.). The same letter also recorded the family's domestic arrangements during Gilson's absence: Thérèse was in Vermenton; Bernard, now eleven years old, attended school in the Benedictine monastery of La Pierre Qui Vire; Jacqueline, twenty-seven, was busy with her paintings in Paris; and Cécile, twenty-six, studied and taught at nearby Joigny while waiting to return to courses at the Sorbonne. Thérèse had seen the children only once: she had visited Jacqueline in Paris, stopping at La Pierre Qui Vire and at Joigny on her return to Vermenton. In her note, Thérèse also described two elderly relatives who were visiting her from Melun: "The ladies are infinitely sad, and I am doing what I can to distract them and bring them out of themselves, which is not always easy." All in all, domestic matters were fairly tranquil.

Rarely for him, Gilson fell ill in late January 1940, and spent a week in bed. He got up to prepare an unscheduled Toronto series of theologically-oriented lectures which he gave in late February; these were titled "God and Greek Philosophy"; "God and Christian Philosophy"; "God and Modern Philosophy"; and "God and Contemporary Philosophy." This series was really a preview of the Powell Lectures he was to deliver at the University of Indiana, March 2 to 8.

Gilson must have made at least part of the trip to Indiana with Jacques and Raïssa Maritain. On 19 March he wrote to Phelan from Harvard as follows:

> My trip to Bloomington was an uneventful one, save only for the tragicomedy of the Maritain family at Fort Erie. Raïssa was in a dark fury and I had a hard time

preventing the fierce offensive she obviously was meditating against that stupid immigration officer.

In the same letter, Gilson wrote enthusiastically of his reception by the university:

> The university had done things according to the highest standards of American hospitality. Their masterpiece was to invite Mgr Ritter, bishop of Indianapolis. He was actually in the university for a luncheon organized in honour of the Catholic Church on the very day of the second lecture, "God and Christian Philosophy." Mgr Ritter came and stayed for the lecture, accompanied by many priests and monks from the area, from St Meinrad's, Notre Dame, etc. (40.03.19.)

Besides Ritter, Gilson also met Father Kilfoil the university chaplain, Professor Gellema, Father Leo Ward, Yves Simon, Waldimar Gurian, J. B. Müller-Thym and Clare Riedl. This gala visit fittingly capped Gilson's long series of regular North American visits.

The Powell Lectures were published as *God and Philosophy* (McG 54) by Yale University Press in 1941. They initiated a new approach for Gilson to the history of philosophy and dealt directly with general themes rather than with individual texts and persons. In these lectures Gilson also attempted to develop the implications of Thomas' ontology for the entire problem of the existence of God.

From Bloomington Gilson went directly to Cambridge where he stayed in Winthrop House. His first activities there were of a diplomatic nature. As a result of meetings with the French Legation in Boston, he delivered several talks on "La France et la guerre" to Franco-Americans at New Bedford, Worcester, Woonsocket and Manchester.

At Harvard itself, on 11, 15, 22 and 28 March, Gilson repeated his lectures on "God and Philosophy" in Emerson Hall to audiences of about five hundred. In his relating of thomist ontology to the question of God's existence, Gilson was not yet fully aware that he was dealing with but one of a burgeoning array of existential philosophies. At Harvard, Professor Hocking forced him to realize that the time had come for making sensitive distinctions among these:

> In the spring of 1940, when I had just delivered the last of a series of four public lectures, Professor Ernest Hocking came to me, and shaking my hand said simply: "Very good! And what about Gabriel Marcel?" ... Ernest Hocking was right. Between the thomist ontology whose initial theses I had just been recalling, and that of Gabriel Marcel, there is a good deal more in common than the word "existence." ("Le thomisme et les philosophies existentielles," *La vie intellectuelle*, 13 [1945]: 144-155; McG 478.)

Hocking's brief remark anticipated Gilson's later probing of a number of forms of existentialism. He found that he and Marcel shared a good deal. Like Gilson, Marcel objected to the "progressive blindness to existence" of idealists and to idealism's neglect of "the rights of the object." He was also sympathetic to Marcel's insistence on the need to restore the proper "ontological weight" to human experience and to restore at the same time "the weight of human experience" to classical ontology. These statements may be wanting in thomist flavour, but they bear the earmarks of authentic ontology.

On 24 March Gilson left Cambridge for Montréal where he gave a six-lecture French version of his fourteen-lecture Toronto course on the humanist tradition: "L'idéal du *De oratore*," 26 March; "La culture patristique latine," 27 March; "La culture patristique au moyen âge, IX-XI," 28 March; "La bataille des Sept Arts, XII-XIII," 29 March; "Le conflit de l'éloquence et de la scolastique," 1 April; and "Culture patristique et origine de la renaissance (Erasme)," 2 April. On Saturday 30 March, he also delivered a radio address over CKAC on "Le français et la philosophie" (McG 670).

On 3 April Gilson went to New York, where he stayed for three days at the Commodore. At noon on 6 April he embarked aboard the Italian liner *Vulcania*. On 11 April the ship called at the Azores (Ponta Delgrada), and at six-thirty in the morning, 13 April, it arrived at Lisbon. At noon Gilson left Lisbon by train and on Monday 15 April at eleven-fifty-eight in the evening he arrived at the Gare d'Austerlitz. Gilson was now home for the war's duration, assured in conscience that he had performed at his best for country and for scholarship during the early months of conflict.

2 THE OCCUPATION OF PARIS

When Gilson reached Paris, he found his family reasonably calm, their situation unchanged. Cécile was back at the Sorbonne working on her *agrégation*, Bernard was still at school at La Pierre Qui Vire and Jacqueline continued to paint. Thérèse's health had somewhat improved, and she was "if not in brilliant condition, at least in an almost normal one."

At first Gilson was fairly optimistic about his chances for returning to North America the next fall:

> My present plans are to leave Paris next week and to spend four months in Vermenton preparing my next American campaign. I will have to be in Philadelphia on September 16 [for an honorary degree] and you will see me again at St Michael's around October as usual; that is, God and Hitler permitting. Please tell Father McCorkell, Father Muckle and all our friends that I am safe in France and that everything looks rather promising on this side of the water. Vrin will send Father Bondy's books as soon as possible, probably next week. (EG to Phelan, 40.4.20.)

Bondy's books – purchases for the French department – were not to be sent for another five years. The Nazi blitz through the Netherlands, Belgium and the French lines near Sedan began 10 May. On 10 June Reynaud's government moved to Tours and declared Paris an open city. Before the end of June Reynaud was out and Pétain (and Laval) in; in London Charles de Gaulle made his radio appeal on 18 June. An armistice was signed which split France into occupied and non-occupied zones and saddled the Vichy government with occupation costs.

The Vichy government quickly lost the confidence of its more thoughtful citizens, including Gilson who was "fundamentally against Vichy and Pétain from the first day of the disaster, that is, from the armistice. ... and I never looked for anything from that quarter." (EG to Mme Thibaudeau, 44.11.6; tr.) Twice the Germans approached Gilson to take part in their programmes, and twice he refused. "I must say," he also wrote, "that in spite of their complete failure, they never afterward molested me."

Except for two months in Angoulême between June and August 1940, Gilson spent most of the period of occupation with Cécile in Paris. Thérèse meanwhile passed most of it with Jacqueline in Vermenton. Both houses were also occupied by a succession of billets, as Thérèse recalled shortly after the liberation:

> After the war came, I lived almost continually at Vermenton, often alone, protecting the house from the invaders. At the moment of the exodus in June 1940, both our Paris apartment and our house in Vermenton were occupied. When we returned from Angoulême where we took refuge for two months, we found Vermenton fully occupied, turned inside out by seventeen ss personnel. We had to await their departure in a little house we had nearby [Cravant]. We could not go into our own house even to get clothes or other necessities. Several ss men kept strict surveillance over it. After they left, we had to share the house with a succession of non-commissioned officers, one officer, and even one ordinary soldier. In both our places we naturally suffered material losses. Had I left Vermenton it would have been completely ruined – the fate of all empty, uninhabited houses. (Thérèse to Mme Thibaudeau, 44.11.12; tr.)

Whether the billets in Vermenton and Paris were lodgers or spies, Gilson was never quite sure. He was sometimes inclined to be more sorry for the billet than for himself. One personable officer who was billeted with him in Paris never ceased to be embarrassed by his position. One day he walked in on Gilson seated at his radio listening to an English broadcast. Gilson hastily shut off the programme and awaited a reprimand. It never came, and the officer switched the radio back on. "I too," he said, "am interested in English broadcasts."

Cécile was less well-disposed toward the Germans than her father. She was often driven to near desperation, and one day destroyed all her diaries, including her full account of her wonderful autumn with her father in Cambridge in 1928. Cécile went out of her way to be unpleasant to the German billets. Once when one of them told her that the Germans were about to enter England, she snapped back that the English would make fish-food of them. On another occasion, he asked her to play ping-pong with him and she replied that there was no ball. When he handed her one from his pocket, she crushed it in her hand and coldly replied, "There is still no ball." His daughter's action made Gilson uncomfortable, but he said nothing.

Gilson was also worried about his son. Not only had Bernard's emotional health become somewhat precarious, but he had begun to become politically involved. Although Bernard loved the monks of La Pierre Qui Vire, he was openly critical of their collaborationist tendencies. Moreover at Vermenton, when he was home from school, he sometimes carried messages for the underground. Again Gilson said nothing and simply hoped that if the young boy were caught, he would merely be scolded and sent home.

Once the occupation was consolidated, Gilson found his intellectual situation quite tolerable. His enforced leisure allowed him to tackle some of those scholarly problems he had "set aside for a rainy day." Moreover the libraries were open, the presses functioning, and his colleagues more accessible than ever.

The major project Gilson took on during this period was the revision of his important books, some of which very much needed it. He turned his attention first to *Le thomisme*. Through its three previous editions the work had already become for Gilson a kind of intellectual autobiography. He now introduced into it his philosophical discoveries of the 1930s and in 1942 published a revised and greatly enlarged fourth edition (Paris, McG 160). No sooner was it off the press than he went back to it again; this time he paid even closer attention to his technical terminology and explored his deepening notion of *esse* as an act-of-existing distinct from essence.

During 1943 Gilson put out a second edition of his *Introduction à l'étude de saint Augustin* (Paris, McG 74). The new edition took into consideration the criticisms of Fernand Van Steenberghen and others, and sharpened Gilson's own statements of position. Although it also reflected his wider reading on Augustine, Gilson still thought of his book as only an introduction; he was still far from prepared to carry his study of Augustine into the related areas needed to provide the sort of thorough treatment that Augustine has since received from a succession of fine patristic scholars. For Gilson Augustine was a great Christian who philosophized; if he did not capture Augustine, at least he succeeded in tagging him.

In 1943 Gilson also published his second edition of *La philosophie de saint Bonaventure* (Paris; McG 122), a clarification and a confirmation of the positions which his friend Père Mandonnet had found so objectionable. Finally, he also reworked his *La philosophie du moyen âge des origines patristiques à la fin du XIVᵉ siècle* (Paris; McG 114) to incorporate his more recent philosophical thinking and his more mature sensitivities as an historian. When this new edition was published in 1944 it enjoyed an immediate vogue and it had to be reprinted in 1945, 1947 and 1948. Even when critics rejected Gilson's thomism as partisan, theological or unduly circumscribed by the bare text of Thomas, they recognized the work's timely scholarship, its vision, its common sense, its fine control and its value as a work of history.

Gilson also continued to deliver academic lectures during the occupation. Courses in the Collège de France had at first been suspended but were revived in 1941 so that life in Paris would remain as normal as possible. Gilson's extant papers contain two handwritten sets of notes for seminars at the Collège: "*Quaestiones disputatae* sur saint Thomas d'Aquin" (1941 to 1942); and "Albert le Grand" (1942 to 1943). There also survives a *leçon de clôture du cours* given 16 March 1943 on "Le christianisme et la tradition philosophique"; this lecture concluded a course in the Collège on "Les sources latines du platonisme médiéval."

The *"Quaestiones disputatae"* was a sequence of dense metaphysical analyses of questions raised in thomist metaphysics by Père Pedro Descoqs. These questions had been nagging at Gilson since the late 1920s, and concerned the object of metaphysics, existence, God and existence, the *esse* of substance, and being as being; indeed, the positions Gilson adopted to deal with these questions would dominate his philosophical writing into the 1960s. The course on Albert the Great reworked courses already given in Paris and Toronto, but also utilized a number of new texts. Some of these had been called to his attention by a critical edition of an Isaac Israeli text by J. T. Muckle in *Archives*; others had been submitted by Robert Miller* as a classroom exercise in Toronto as a result of Phelan's invitation to students "to scout for other texts in other works of Albertus Magnus" (EG to Phelan, 37.7.1).

Gilson published his *leçon de clôture* on "Christianity and the Philosophical Tradition" in both *Revue des Sciences Philosophiques et Théologiques* (30 [1941]: 249-266; McG 226) and in *Cherchez Dieu* ([Paris, 1943], pp. 61-81). This choice of two Catholic publications served notice that Gilson's perspective was shifting from philosophy toward religion. Touchstone sampling – the lecture is too vital for quick summary – demonstrates this shift: the neoplatonist is "less concerned to expound a science than to tell a story"; a Boethius moves "into high gear by questioning *philosophia* on the meaning of her own story"; certain aristotelians, or Christians "resigned to speak the language of Aristotle," fashion a *sacra docrina* or "abstract science of objective knowledge on the conditions of man's salvation." The article recounts how and why good, intelligent medieval Christians focused first on neoplatonic and then on aristotelian thought. These ways of philosophizing were pursued for other than "philosophical" reasons, and were important because their own internal integrity overlapped with and shed light on divine revelation.

Gilson's heightened interest in religion and spirituality had actually begun well before 1943. It may have started during the spring of 1940 when Gilson, just returned from his long visit to North America, began to pay frequent visits to Bernard's teachers, the monks of La Pierre Qui Vire. Gilson came to know the monks well and began to give them talks of an historico-spiritual flavour. There is no firm list of the dates on which he delivered them or any clue as to their frequency, but he was still giving them in 1949.**

---

* In 1938, when Miller had entered the novitiate of the Basilian Fathers, Gilson had written Phelan: "Thank you for the good news of the boys. Of course, the girls are crying, shaving their heads and lacerating their faces over the loss of Bob Miller. They say that all the best-looking ones become priests." (38.8.5.)

** The present writer well remembers how, at Gilson's request, he attended that year the *fêtes* held at Cluny to celebrate the anniversaries of Saints Odo and Odilon as well as the opening of a restored transept of the famous medieval abbey. He remembers especially how, after the papers by Cluny-lovers like Joan Evans, Kenneth Conant and Gilson himself, after Gustave Cohen directed from his

This new spiritual facet of Gilson's life is not at all unrelated to Thomas Merton's devoting several pages of his *Seven Storey Mountain* to Gilson (below, p. 309); it also had considerable bearing on the decision of Gilson's former and favourite student Dan Walsh, while still a layman, to give conferences to the monks of Gethsemani. Although his preoccupation with the spiritual life caused Gilson many new concerns, including impatience with the Holy See and the French hierarchy, it also brought him consciously closer to God.

In 1941 Gilson also encountered a very different kind of spirituality through renewed contact with Maurice Pradines (1874 to 1958). Pradines had been a colleague of Gilson's at Strasbourg, a professor of general philosophy with special interest in psychology; his important work along these lines was his *Philosophie de la sensation* published in the 1930s. He had been appointed to the Sorbonne in 1938, and his interest had shifted to the psychology of magic and religion.* In 1941 he published his *Esprit de la religion*, which attempted to specify religion as a mysticism, though with some minute and almost imperceptible source in nature, in man's emotions and nervous system. No doubt Pradines thought this would please Gilson, as it indicated some relaxation of his Protestant position that fallen nature was evil and played no role in salvation. Gilson however was not impressed by a psychological argument that threw together magic and religion.

Pradines seems to have written Gilson in early 1941 asking for favours. Would Gilson advise him how to conduct his candidature for the Collège de France? Would he look over and criticize his *exposé de titres*? And would he comment on his forthcoming *Esprit de la religion*? When Pradines wrote in February, he revealed the extent to which Gilson had influenced his work:

> I thank you very kindly for your letter, so cordial, so sincere. Let me say that I knew in advance that you would gladly comment on my work; and because I already know your views (I reread recently your *Christianisme et philosophie*), I am hardly surprised at your reactions to my thesis. As I wrote my book, you were often my implicit interlocutor, and I would have cited you oftener if I had not been avoiding throughout the appearance of engaging Catholic authors in heretical theories. ... This Catholic road, as you pursue it to the stars with such authority, seems to lead straight from philosophy to religion, and when I think of how forceful this notion can be, it is always some text you have used that comes to mind. (41.2.19; tr.)

Gilson did not agree that philosophy could lead to religion, and Pradines' comment may well have prompted him to write his "Sagesse et société" (*Témoignages*, 1 [1942]: 39-54; McG 792). This social essay dwelt on the true

---

wheelchair *Jeu d'Adam*, after the *vins d'honneur* in the châteaux of Burgundy and the visits to Paray-le-Monial and other places of special interest, Gilson unceremoniously whisked him off along with Armand Maurer, a Toronto colleague, and drove furiously to Vermenton by way of La Pierre Qui Vire. Gilson had promised to repeat his Cluny performance for the monks, and nothing, not even the *fêtes* of Cluny, were going to interfere; he left his guests to walk the monastery gounds while he went inside alone to give his talk in privacy.

   * While at the Sorbonne Pradines had been lavishly praised by one of his former students, André Grappe, in *La pensée de Maurice Pradines dans ses rapports avec celle de Paul Valéry* (Paris, 1938).

source of Christianity, the reason above all reason that guides all reason, the wisdom that is a gift of the Holy Ghost: "una sola sapientia perfecta, ab uno Deo data uni generi humano propter unum finem" ("one perfect wisdom, given by the one God to the one human race for one end"; p. 47, citing Roger Bacon). Gilson later returned to the issue in the introduction to *Le philosophe et la théologie* (Paris, 1960; McG 104): "You don't find the sources of religion at the end of a philosophy. If you want to talk about the sources of religion, you have to start from religion which, indeed, has no source but is itself the source. There is no other way of coming to it." (p. xxi.)

His contact with Pradines seems to have made Gilson aware of the need for research into the history of mysticism beyond what he had done for *La théologie mystique de saint Bernard* (1934). Even his recent harshness toward Abbé André Combes – who had abandoned him for the Little Flower – relented. On 15 November 1943 Gilson gave the inaugural for the establishing of a chair in the history of mysticism in the Institut Catholique de Paris: Abbé Combes was the first incumbent.*

Pradines never did become a professor of the Collège de France. Although Gilson somewhat reluctantly supported Pradines' candidature, Professor Lavelle, also of Strasbourg, eventually won the chair.

3 Père Chenu

In February 1942 Gilson received a number of disturbing letters from his Dominican friend, Père Marie-Dominique Chenu. After the prewar dispersion of the scholars and books of the Saulchoir, Chenu had gone to Etiolles. There he had learned that his brochure on Saulchoir methods of study had been placed on the Roman Index. Distressed, he wrote immediately to Gilson:**

> I don't want you to learn from someone else about my heavy sorrow. You may remember how, four years ago, I wrote a small thin booklet on the Saulchoir and its work, which drew bitter remarks from some Roman theologians. Although this

---

* The Combes-Gilson story is complex. Gilson had hoped that the gifted Abbé André Combes would one day join the teaching staff of the Toronto Institute. To that end Gilson obtained for Combes a government bursary so that he could work at the Centre des Recherches, Paris, on Jean de Ripa's *Commentary on the Sentences of Peter Lombard*. Much to Gilson's disappointment, Combes' interest shifted to the spirituality of Ste Thérèse de Lisieux, the Little Flower of Jesus. Combes complained that Gilson was hostile to the Little Flower. Gilson insisted rather that the accepting of a government bursary entailed the obligation of working on the subject specified. At a later stage, in 1945, Combes almost returned to medieval studies and even agreed to go to the Institute in Toronto. Gilson was elated. After reflection however, Combes said he would act in Toronto as "Theresian ambassador to Canada" (Combes to EG, 45.9.10). Combes even invited Gilson to give the closing address of a projected Canadian Theresian Congress on "Ste Thérèse et la philosophie." Gilson gave up and Combes never went to Toronto.

** Chenu's letters are available, Gilson's replies as yet are not; they are in boxes atop the bookshelves in Chenu's office on rue de la Glacière. "They are up there," says Père Chenu, "with thousands of others, and will become available when my things are sorted out after my death."

booklet has never been on the market, it has been dug up by someone and has just been placed on the Index. The blow reaches not only the booklet but the house as well, and will certainly remove me from teaching. ... You know enough about history not to be surprised by such tornadoes. You and I understand these things: deep down we are not scandalized. May your friendly confidence soften my sorrow and keep me from bitterness. May it give assurance to my spiritual freedom. (42.2.21; tr.)

Chenu and Gilson were not the only ones taken by surprise. In March Chenu wrote again:

Your two letters give me true strength in these difficult days. ... I hear it said here that the action has not been well received in high places. The cardinal of Paris refuses to let it be talked about during La Semaine Religieuse for this reason. And Mgr Beaussart (the auxiliary bishop) is furious. Your diagnosis as to what is happening is mine too: we have not yet liquidated the crisis of 1500 and are caught up in anti-Protestant reflexes. (42.3.7; tr.)

Gilson was never able to put Chenu's case out of his mind and he became sensitive to any displays of religious authority. He much disliked the tendency of his old friend Charles Boyer to set forth the right and the wrong about papal documents almost as though he had written them himself. Only the pope, Gilson said, has the right to interpret himself. And when on occasion at thomist congresses Boyer would presume to interpret papal documents to philosophers, Gilson would become furious.

On one occasion, Gilson told Mgr Montini (later Pope Paul vi) that he had found only three doctrinal issues in Chenu's brochure. Enumerating the doctrines he asked: "Which one of these, Monsignor, is out of line with Catholic doctrine?" Montini replied: "Le propre de l'autorité, c'est de ne pas se justifier." "His French," reported Gilson later, "was impeccable. That's the kind of man who is now pope."

Chenu's troubles no doubt contributed to Gilson's hard attitude toward those French Catholics including members of the hierarchy, who sympathized with Vichy and with collaboration and who were hostile to the Résistance. His language was sometimes strong enough to draw a cautionary letter from Henri Gouhier, his closest friend:

Are you not very hard on present-day Catholicism ? I have the impression that Rome still represents the only really spiritual power. ... As for the French episcopate, it has been able to maintain certain positions: its *non possumus* to the "jeunesse unique," its formula on "la jeunesse unie et non unifiée" have perhaps saved us from strong action out of line with our tradition and our convictions. Then there is a German episcopate which has not, I believe, ceased to remain "faithful." ... I am more optimistic for Catholicism than for France. More than ever, I believe their destinies are separate. We will do well not to make "the elder daughter" intervene too frequently in our discussion. Rather let us make Frenchmen understand that it is France that needs Catholicism, not Catholicism that needs France. (42.6.16; tr.)

A point of criticism in the charge against Chenu was that he had "discredited St Thomas." When Chenu completed his *Introduction à l'étude de saint Thomas d'Aquin* in 1950, he sent the first copy to Gilson. The two men remained close throughout Gilson's life. In 1959 Chenu succeeded Théry as codirector of the *Archives*, a position he continued to hold at Gilson's death in 1978.

4 CONTACTS WITH NORTH AMERICA

Several North American attempts were made to establish contact with Gilson during the occupation. The most concerted of these were Harvard's efforts during March and April 1941 to get Gilson a visa. Harvard wanted him to return immediately to Cambridge to give once more the William James Lectures. They also considered asking him once more to join the philosophy faculty permanently.

On 14 March 1941 Henry Copley Greene wrote to the registrar of St Michael's College:

> I am told that you have heard from our friend Professor Etienne Gilson. On July 10 he wrote me that he was with his family [Dr Henry Gilson] at Angoulême. Since then a rumour has reached me that he is in a concentration camp. Will you very kindly let me know whether you have heard from him, and when, and to what effect? (41.3.14.)

When Greene wrote this letter to Toronto, Gilson had already been reached in Paris by someone in the American consulate. Gilson had been summoned to the consulate for a visit and had then been requested by the vice-consul to return. Enclosed with the vice-consul's note was a letter written by someone in the American State Department to the Paris consulate. The top and bottom of Gilson's copy had been carefully removed by the censors before he received it:

> My dear friend: Could you get a message to Etienne Gilson, professor (of philosophy?) at the Sorbonne and the Collège de France. No address for him in ZNO [*zone non-occupée*]. In ZO: Paris, 2 avenue Emile-Accolas; Angoulême (Charente), 9 rue Waldeck-Rousseau; Vermenton (Yonne).
>
> Harvard University is offering him (it is trying to be helpful) a series of lectures in the spring. (It is really a question of a permanent chair: it is felt that the series of lectures will make getting an entry-visa easier).
>
> But no letters, no cables, to the above addresses appear to have reached him, and the State Department, it says, cannot pass the message along through the officers of the Paris embassy. Gilson should communicate with Jerome Greene, secretary of Harvard University (Cambridge, Mass.) and provide an address in ZNO where it will be possible to get in touch with him more easily. Everything that needs to be done will be to assure his getting an entry-visa into the United States through the Vichy Embassy without difficulty or delay. Tell him too that his friend and mine Henry Copley Greene of Boston will gladly guarantee the cost of his passage and that of any of the family he wishes and is able to bring with him. This formality, which Harvard does not assume, is indispensable for obtaining an American visa.
>
> For his part, Gilson will have to see to his own crossing into the ZNO and to his exit-visa from France. Perhaps my next letter may have a word in it for him. *Bien amicalement*. (nd)

On 9 April Ernest Hocking, Harvard's chairman of philosophy, wrote to Gilson via Clipper Air Mail. The letter got through, apparently directly:

> I am not sure that my previous letters have reached you but this pesent letter is to say that we have received authorization to invite you to give once more the William James Lectures next fall, that is, the first half of the academic year, 1941 to 1942 (41.4.4).

Gilson appears to have made some attempt to get a passport for his regular North American visit. When this failed, he seems to have reconciled himself to sharing the lot of his fellow Parisians. Eventually Phelan received the following note from Doris Anson, Jacques Maritain's secretary in New York:

> Professor Maritain, who is at present out of town, has asked me to write you and send you the following quotation which Dr Alvin Johnson received from the American Red Cross: "Professor Etienne Gilson and his family are very well. He is working at Vermenton and Paris. Was touched that you should make enquiries concerning him. He regrets he is unable to get his passport to enable him to go to the USA. Sends his kind regards."

At the end of 1943 Phelan received a more cheerful note through Madeleine Thibaudeau and the Canadian Red Cross:

> Tous parfaite santé. Jacqueline décore chapelle. Cécile assistante sociale. Bernard bachelier rhétorique, prépare philosophie. Espérons revoir bientôt cousins Phelan et McCorkell. Fidèle affection. Etienne. (43.12.5.)

5 Renewed Communications

In late August 1944, Paris was liberated, and in November Gilson broke four years of isolation with letters to Gerald Phelan, Edmund McCorkell and Mlle Madeleine Thibaudeau. His letter to Phelan was vibrant with joy at the war's conclusion:

> What a joy to write to you again! I can hardly believe it is true. And yet I have just been greeted by my wife with this joyful question: "Now guess what is waiting for you on your desk!" I tentatively made three guesses, one of which was the right one. Yes, we are all alive and in good health. There has been no tragedy in the family, which is more than many French families can say. Our material losses are small, and even insignificant.
>
> Soon after our national disaster, I received a German visit – an official one – and was asked to be a *kollaborate*. I answered that I had always collaborated as a Catholic and as a scholar, but that, as a Frenchman, I could collaborate only with those who were hoping for the liberation of my own country. That was all. I must add that, nevertheless, I have never been personally molested. Let God be thanked for it! I will not begin to tell you how we have lived during those dreadful years. Besides, we have forgotten it. THEY ARE GONE! We cannot think of anything else.
>
> My wife has been wonderful: she is well, although both of us are ten years older than we were four years ago. My daughters are very much as they were. Jacqueline

still painting (she has decorated the chapel of the hospital of Brevannes, near Paris),
Cécile getting ready for her diploma of *assistante sociale*. As for your friend
Bernard, who has never ceased to speak of you, of Father Muckle, of Father Bondy,
he is now sixteen (he will be seventeen next March) and, having successfully passed
his two baccalaureats, he is just beginning to prepare simultaneously two *licences*,
one in history and one in law. He is also very fond of modern languages; his
English has considerably helped him in the examinations (eighteen or twenty!) and
he is dabbling in Russian, Spanish (!!) and Italian. But he hates German, which is, as
I think, a huge mistake.

As for myself, I have been teaching, writing and praying, without ever forgetting
to pray for you, for the Institute and for all our friends. Toronto was in my memory
as an earthly paradise, full of good friends, and of good things. How many times
have we not evoked the memory of your own room at the Institute where there
always was a cup of coffee or tea for visitors! By the way, we have not yet tasted a
drop of either one since the end of 1940! It looks queer, does it not, even if it is a
fact. Now at least we can hope to see these things come back sooner or later, and it
makes quite a difference.

It was very kind of you to tell me that you hope to see me again in Toronto just as
soon as I can come. I cannot say that I am deeply surprised, but I am glad to *know* it.
On my own side there is nothing but desire to go back to the Institute. My Harvard
friends have tried and are still trying to get me back with them; I might perhaps give
them a second series of William James Lectures which I have been kindly invited to
do, but since you still wish to have me, I will stay with you so long as God keeps me
strong enough to do honest work. When will it be possible for a civilian to cross the
Atlantic by boat or plane? I don't know. I fancy that September 1945 will be the
earliest possible date. Just now everything here is exclusively for the army. I might
possibly get a "mission" but I know nobody in the new government (though I have
always openly been for de Gaulle and against the shameful armistice and the no-
less-shameful Pétain). Everything is starting again from the zero point, and it will
take some time before the Foreign Office gets interested in problems of intellectual
relations with foreign countries. So, I suppose that I must wait, without much hope
of getting suddenly "parachuted" onto some Toronto airfield. The first hot-dog and
the first Turret are not yet in sight. (44.11.3.)

The rest of the letter, a long postscript, arranges to revive his account at Eaton's
new store, asks that coffee and cigarettes be sent to him and speculates on the size
of the Royal Bank account in which his 1939 salary cheque has remained
untouched.

Gilson's letter took seven weeks to reach Phelan. He followed it with a *carte
postale* which revealed his rising spirits:

I have not yet received your letter nor any other from America since liberation day.
But I am just now smoking a Dunhill, two packages of which came recently to me
through the courtesy of Bill O'Meara, whom I proclaim to be a great boy. Unfortunately, Bernard is also puffing at them. *O tempora, O mores!* (what times, what
morals! – for the censor.) ... I am now trying to get all the French books published
during the pleasant prewar years and related to the Middle Ages, bought and given
to the Institute by our Foreign Office. I may succeed; if not they will remain at your

disposal until you can buy them. They are safe at Vrin's, together with Father Bondy's books. But I must not forget what was the purpose of my card ... to wish you and all ... a holy and happy New Year. (44.12.31.)

Phelan's reply to Gilson's letter was written the day he received it, and was full of the news Gilson most wanted to hear. It traced the story of the Institute since the spring of 1940:

Our student-body is now almost exclusively made up of priests. All able-bodied laymen have been taken into the armed services. The majority of our graduates who were teaching in the USA have likewise been drafted. Nevertheless the number ... has increased. ... Our staff has changed only slightly: Ignatius Eschmann OP and Dr [Anton] Pegis are now on the list of professors; Father Dwyer is no longer a member of the staff; Father Kennedy is superior of the [new] Institute House of the Basilian Fathers. ... Father George Flahiff has become secretary. ... Father Denomy has taken on the work of publishing *Mediaeval Studies* with the title of managing editor. ... The library has suffered from the impossibility of getting European books. ... Dr Ladner is in the Army Intelligence at Ottawa, on leave of absence from the Institute. The Canadian ambassador at Paris has received a message from the secretary of state for External Affairs conveying an official invitation to you to come as soon as possible. ... Marjorie Nazier and Lady Windle ask me so often for news of you; and Gordon Taylor is thrilled to know you are all well. (45.1.21.)

To his joy Gilson was still very much a part of Canadian academic life. Moreover the new Canadian ambassador to Paris was none other than his friend of many years, Georges Vanier.

13

Missions at War's End, 1945-1946

1 CUARF

Personally, Gilson wanted nothing more than to return to his teaching at the end of the war. Before this became possible however, he first had to overcome a series of hurdles thrown in his way by various national and international agencies. His first postwar mission was the chairmanship of one of the committees set up to administer monies collected by Canadian United Allied Relief Funds (CUARF). Gilson's committee surpervised relief to professors and students in some sixteen French universities. Mme Thibaudeau apparently suggested Gilson's name to Senator Vien, the head of CUARF, and the appointment was made by another friend, Georges Vanier. The committee members were all from the Collège de France and included, besides Gilson, Louis Justin-Besançon of the Faculté de Médecine (vice-chairman), Jules Marouzeau of the Faculté des Lettres, Gabriel Le Bras of the Faculté de Droit, Augustin Damiens of the Faculté de Pharmacie, Charles Maugetin of the Faculté des Sciences, as well as one student.

Although the work of this committee seems to have been supervisory and not especially demanding, the appointment started a trend which would soon snowball. There was, however, one important benefit for Gilson. In one of his letters, Justin-Besançon, who was also president of the Croix-Rouge, took time from committee business to discuss Gilson's suitability for the Académie Française:

> No, it is impossible you don't dream about the Académie [que vous ne songiez pas à la Coupole]. For you not to do so would be a betrayal not of yourself but of your friends. Will you allow me to speak about it to Pasteur Vallery-Radot when he returns? Unfortunately he was in Cuba yesterday and is in Caracas today. I am expecting him home by the end of May. (45.3.22; tr.)

When Justin-Besançon intervened with Pasteur Vallery-Radot, the first step was taken toward the most prestigious appointment of Gilson's life.

2 THE SAN FRANCISCO CONFERENCE, 1945

At the beginning of 1945 President Roosevelt, looking ahead to victory, told congress that this year would see the organization of a world at peace. Gilson was moved by this statement: an erasmian humanist at heart, he wanted to end all wars and to liberate men to work out their own salvation in the context of personal freedom. He believed that this could be achieved through the kind of education that fostered the acquisition of the moral virtues through the writings of Cicero and Seneca, and through the teachings of Christ. Now was the moment to work toward the realization of that *ordre catholique* he had advocated in the 1930s (above pp. 218-219). German hitlerism, Russian communism, Italian and Spanish fascism and American deweyism had stood in the way then; each of them had focussed on the production of their own brand of citizen, and none of them had seen a pressing need for the teaching of the moral and intellectual virtues. Now, at the moment of impending victory, real changes were finally possible.

Gilson first addressed some of these changes in an article entitled "Instruire ou éduquer?" (*Le monde*, 45.1.9; McG 686). The old French Ministry of Public Education was becoming the new Ministry of National Education. Did this change of name mean greater concern for students as individuals? Or would students still be prospective adherents to some political cause? Would they be "attached" beings, or would they once more be familiarized from infancy with moral imperatives like honour, duty, justice, love of God – the moral virtues of the individual?

The article in *Le monde* was followed quickly by several others for Stanislas Fumet's more religious *Hebdomadaire du temps présent*. This weekly had been started in 1937 to resist a tendency in the 1930s to speak of the spirit of France as one of anarchic liberty; according to Fumet, France's spirit was actually that of liberty moderated and tempered by reason. The day of liberation gave renewed vigour to *Temps présent*, and Fumet began a crusade, *ni politique ni confession- nelle*, to refashion French youth in the light of classical and thomist *amicitia*.

Gilson was actively interested in Fumet's campaign. He wanted to focus the attention of educators upon the virtues of persons rather than on power movements, and wanted France to learn from its own and from Hitler's mistakes in education. He also wanted France to become intellectually, morally and politically strong, to reject Vichy and Pétain and to fall behind Général de Gaulle. Between January and March of 1945, Gilson placed four articles in Fumet's *Temps présent*: "Hitler fera-t-il notre révolution?" (45.1.12; McG 679); "La circulaire 45 ou: comment l'on se propose de pervertir la vérité" (45.3.2; McG 588); "La révolution par l'amitié redressera la Cité" (45.3.9; McG 787); and "Le schisme national" (45.3.30; McG 798). The keynote theme appeared in the first of these, which declared "that the first step of any totalitarian regime is to seize the schools so as to have exclusive monopoly over the shaping of tomorrow's citizens" (tr.).

Gilson was inclined to look to Great Britain for a model of an educational programme that protected personal freedom. Among his papers is a copy of *La croix* (45.3.30) which contains an unsigned article entitled "La liberté de l'enseignement en Angleterre." This articles points out that Britain has both conformist (Anglican in England, Presbyterian in Scotland) and nonconformist (Catholic, Baptist, Wesleyan and so on) schools. Gilson admired this open kind of educational policy which contrasted sharply with the closed character of state-controlled education in France.

In the articles for *Temps présent*, Gilson formulated and articulated a position to which he gave classical expression a month later in his "Pour une éducation nationale" (*La vie intellectuelle*, April 1945; McG 404). In this article he argues that education, to be free, must not exclude religion.* The editor of *La vie intellectuelle*, according to Gilson's notation at the top of his corrected manuscript, "sent the text of this article before its printing to Général de Gaulle who read it in February 1945."

The series of articles in *Temps présent* was making a wide impression and Gilson found himself in close contact with post-liberation France, both friendly and unfriendly. He corresponded with Stanislas Fumet, Albert Camus, Emmanuel Mounier, Maurice Schumann and others, and on 15 March 1945 he addressed a large meeting of La Jeunesse Intellectuelle in the Grande Salle de la Mutualité. Increasingly Gilson was coming to be seen as a spokesman for a knowledgeable constituency of committed Frenchmen. Not surprisingly then, at the end of March, the Ministry of Foreign Affairs appointed him to the French delegation for the conference about to begin in San Francisco to plan a charter for the United Nations. A new phase of Gilson's career began, one which would keep him in the public eye and away from his Toronto teaching throughout 1945.

The delegation travelled from Paris to San Francisco by a curious route. First it went to Newhaven, Britain, on 3 April, then to Glasgow. On 6 April it boarded the *Neo-Hellas* and sailed from the Clyde Ports for Halifax, where it arrived on 17 April. In the midst of the crossing, on Sunday 15 April, memorial services, Protestant and Catholic, were held at ten in the morning for Franklin Delano Roosevelt.

Somehthing of the suddenness of Gilson's appointment, and of his role in the delegation, is evident in his first letter to Phelan from San Francisco:

> I will tell you some day by what chain of unexpected circumstances, after completing all my arrangements for a trip to Canada around 15 April, I was sent to San Francisco, and yet landed at Halifax. On 19 April the train of the French delegation stopped at Toronto for about twenty minutes. I could not really believe I was there and it seemed to me most unnatural to be in the Toronto depot without getting off the train and calling for a taxicab. The time was 11:15 PM. I rushed to the lower concourse, ran to a phone box, and dialled RA 3367. I even tried twice, but

---

* In this article Gilson drew on Augustine's *City of God*, Henri Marrou's "Protoschéma d'un plan de réforme universitaire" (*Esprit* [December 1944]), and Paul Seippel's *Les deux Frances et leurs origines historiques* (Paris, 1905). He also cited, for purpose of contrast, the monstruous *Catéchisme républicain romain de Poitevin* with its incredible questions and answers: "What is baptism? It is that regeneration of the French people begun 14 July 1789. What is communion? It is that association proposed for all reasonable people by the French Republic." And so on.

there was no answer. You were probably off philosophizing somewhere. At least I cannot imagine you already in bed at such an early time of the day.

Anyway, I am here, where I am supposed to act in the capacity of a technical adviser on all problems related to intellectual co-operation. There will be some problems, and we are already confronted with the curious reluctance of a great Eurasian state, a well-known champion of democracy in the world, to accept the principle of unrestricted freedom of information. Strange, is it not? But more about this later. (45.4.30.)

When Gilson called, Phelan had actually been in Halifax; Gilson later claimed to have had a "kind of queer feeling" about Phelan on landing in Halifax.

In San Francisco Gilson seems to have played a reasonably significant part in the important story of the founding of the United Nations; unfortunately however very little specific detail is available. For one thing, Gilson was one of the very few non-Russian delegates who knew Russian, and this made him useful in relieving the uncertainty and mistrust of some of his colleagues. For another, as his English had become positively literary, he was constantly being consulted on matters of exact wording.

Because the original drafts of the United Nations Charter were being prepared in English, Gilson also found himself a member of the committee formed to prepare the French version. He wrote Phelan in June:

> I am now sitting on a committee of six (including Canada, Belgium and Haiti) for the drafting of the French text of the charter. As they never cease to alter the English (or American) text, it is a heartbreaking job. And to respect the intentional vagueness of the English formulas is also very distressing, both literarily and morally. (45.6.11.)

Later, when Gilson was received into the Académie Française, he reminisced for the benefit of his colleagues:

> Future commentators, pouring over this curious document, which the French text of the United Nations Charter certainly is, will experience many a surprise, but too late for an explanation since its editors won't be around to explain. Reading there, for example, that the United Nations will "encourage respect for human rights and for fundamental freedoms for all without distinction as to race, sex, language or religion," any Frenchman will quickly grab his pencil and adjust the indispensible logical order to "without distinction of sex, race, language or religion." How is it that our delegates did not correct this awkward arrangement? They did correct it, I tell you, three times in a row, and nobody took issue with their point that the distinction between the sexes is more general than that among races, and should logically come first. But when the same English phrase came back to our committee for the third time, a glimmer of light got through the French brains. There was but one possible explanation, and appropriate prudence convinced everyone that it was a good one. If race continued to get into first place, it was in order to conceal something that could be heard but not seen. In this unequal battle between logic and modesty, who can blame logic for giving in? Of all the sacrifices France has made for peace in the world, none has cost less nor taught more. (*Discours de réception d'Etienne Gilson à l'Académie Française* [Paris, 1948], pp. 19-20; McG 19.)

Even the name "United Nations" was for many delegates difficult to accept: "Many Frenchmen present at San Francisco recoiled from this neologism. First we had to grow accustomed to it; eventually, it became as familiar as the name United States, from which indeed it derived." (Le monde, 45.10.28-29; tr.)

Gilson's official assignment from the French government as "adviser for all problems related to intellectual co-operation" brought him close to the core of the purpose for founding the United Nations. International intellectual co-operation was not a new idea; an Institut de Coopération Intellectuelle had been founded in 1926 to be a permanent organ of the old League of Nations. Now however the concept was no longer treated as an adjunct to world peace but, in theory at least, as one of its underlying principles.

The San Francisco Conference hoped eventually to initiate many cultural and artistic activities on an international scale. One of the regular conference events seems to have been the showing each evening of some first-run, unedited film. Hollywood, in Gilson's opinion, came out badly:

> From some fifty films I remember that, exclusive of the incomparable document-aries, two Russian films and one Mexican stood out in the mediocrity of the rest. There was one magnificent American film "San Francisco," but it was a rerun and a cruel testament to what Hollywood had once done and could do no more. (Le monde, 45.11.7; tr.)

Gilson's criticism however did nothing to abate the increasing influx of American films into France that began with the end of the war.

Gilson was also involved in the conference's French-language coverage. Shortly before he left San Francisco, the Office of War Information wrote to thank him for his co-operation throughout the conference, and particularly for his United Nations Day address, delivered 13 June.

In San Francisco the American delegation asked Gilson if he would act as an intermediary between the University of California and the small rural Académie de St-Hilaire de Harcourt in France. The university hoped to participate in the revival of France by sponsoring agriculture and archeology in this small French academy. On behalf of the conference, Gilson telegraphed the rector of St Hilaire to explain the offer. The rector had perforce to refer the proposal to the ministry in charge of agriculture, which told Gilson that it was already in the process of restoring agriculture in Normandy and that it regarded Harcourt as too remote for a school of agriculture. "I wonder," the minister wrote Gilson, "it if would not be better to switch the University of California project to the École Nationale d'Agriculture de Rennes" (45.10.15; tr.). Gilson checked with California, but the university was quite clear as to the specific school it wished to help. The minister relented a little, but asked that an École d'Industrie Laitière be considered rather than a full-fledged school of agriculture. Ultimately the University of California withdrew its offer. It had hoped to deal directly with St Hilaire's rector and had instead found itself faced with a government official. Gilson did not forget this experience when he later became a *conseiller*. In contemporary France, academies and universities had become the playthings of government; for education this spelled disaster. (*Le monde*, 47.7.20-21; tr.)

The United Nations Charter was signed on 26 June and the conference came to a close. On 28 June Gilson sent Phelan a telegram from Ogden, Utah, and on the morning of 30 June, he arrived in Toronto. With no lectures or courses to be given, this summer visit was largely a series of happy reunions with old friends. Among those he visited with at length were Alex Sampson and Gordon Taylor, who now lived side by side at Oak Ridges. He also visited Lady Windle, Marjorie Nazier and others.

Alex Sampson was an Acadian businessman, one of Ontario's first producers of native wine. Naturally Gilson teased him about his product: what Burgundian could credit an Ontario wine? Sampson, however, gave as good as he got. At one point he filled a French bottle with his own Château Gai, recorked it, and had it opened at table. Gilson tasted it and beamed: "Sampson," he said, that's what I call real wine!" Afterward he refused to believe that the wine wasn't French, even though Gordon Taylor had witnessed the substitution and vouched for it. Another time Sampson claimed that not only had Château Gai won an award in Paris but it was available in shops there. Gilson checked this out, and to his amazement found the wine in a Parisian shop to which Sampson had directed him. He never knew for certain however whether Sampson had planted the bottles there.

Gordon Taylor, a Toronto stockbroker and a convert to Catholicism, had been introduced to Gilson by Henry Carr, Taylor's mentor. Gilson and Taylor were as unlike in training and interests as an historian of medieval philosophy and a stockbroker could be, but they became fast friends. When Gordon lost his first wife during the 1930s, Gilson was deeply sorry for him. Sometime later, in France, Gordon met the woman he wanted to make his second wife, but could get nowhere with her. Then his stockbroker's intuition, which suspected that something of the broker exists in every man, led him to ask Gilson to intervene. Indeed Gilson proved a successful go-between, and Gordon won his bride.

Gilson's visit to Toronto was not entirely social; he also found time for sessions with Phelan and the priests of St Michael's about the Institute. The most pressing issue was how to further strengthen the staff at the Institute. Gilson also had to collect his salary for 1939, which he had not yet received; some administrative confusion attended this, but it was soon straightened out.

Both Gilson and Phelan felt that the permanent staff of the Institute required another strong international scholar. When Gilson told Phelan about Père Chenu's difficulties with Rome, Phelan thought he had found the solution. Jacques Maritain had returned from New York to Paris and had been appointed French ambassador to the Holy See.* Phelan thought that Maritain, in his new

---

* This appointment had pleased Gilson and had inspired him to place a strong article, "Jacques Maritain au Vatican," in the March issue of *La vie intellectuelle* ([1945], pp. 36-38; McG 325). Maritain deeply appreciated the article, and wrote Gilson that his "friendship had brought a ray of light" to him (45.11.15; tr.).

position, might be willing to intervene with the Holy See to ask that Chenu be permitted to teach in Toronto; after all, both Jacques Maritain and Mgr Ernesto Ruffini, secretary of the Sacred Congregation of Seminaries and Universities, were good friends of the Institute and might well engineer such a move. Gilson, who planned to go to Ottawa before returning to France, said he would speak to Père Regis, the Canadian Dominican closest to the Institute, and to M. Haute-cloque, the French ambassador.

On Sunday Gilson wrote from Ottawa that the French ambassador would "write to Maritain and ask him to negotiate that business with Mgr Ruffini" (45.7.8). From Ottawa Gilson travelled to Montréal, and a week later wrote from the Thibaudeaus' at La Pointe:

> I have seen Père Regis, who is quite pleased with your idea of bringing Père Chenu to Toronto. I am not sure that we will succeed, but if we fail ... no ecclesiastical problem will have been officially raised, and no harm done to Père Chenu. (45.7.14.)

Maritain's approach to Rome ultimately proved unsuccessful. When Gilson returned to Paris, he heard from Maritain directly:

> I received from the French ambassador to Canada your letter concerning our friend Père Chenu. My efforts, alas, have not been successful. I think I have carried out all the requests I possibly could, selecting the means offering the best chances and the least danger to him. (It seemed best not to speak to Mgr Ruffini who is leaving the Congregation of Studies for the See of Palermo, nor to Cardinal Pizzardo.) I would have preferred not to consult the responsible congregation, but could not get around it. The reply was: "Everyone has the greatest esteem and affection for Père Chenu, but because of this very affection and in his own interest, it is best he not go yet to teach in Canada." The worst, I dare say, is that there is no reason to doubt this esteem and affection, but they are penetrated with a kind of fear and trembling which gives "prudential" consideration an edge on all others. I can assert that Mgr Montini is personally well disposed toward Père Chenu, but even he can do nothing. No one can do anything. (45.11.15; tr.)

Gilson waited in Montréal until the freighter, *Ville de Strasbourg*, was ready to return to Marseilles. Reporters hounded him right up to the hour of departure on 26 July 1945, when his four months as a national delegate to San Francisco came officially to an end. At this point Gilson still thought of the mission as an interlude in his teaching and writing. He fully expected to return to Toronto in the fall to teach his course on "Being and Essence" in medieval philosophy.

3 THE LONDON CONFERENCE, 1945

On 14 September 1945, his plans for teaching in Toronto already completed, Gilson was informed by the Minister of Foreign Affairs that he had been named to yet another French delegation. This time he was to attend a London conference at the end of October. Having been involved from the beginning in the development of international intellectual co-operation, Gilson could hardly decline. He wrote Phelan the next day to postpone his autumn courses until next spring, after his lecture courses in the Collège de France. Although he suggested that Phelan invite Abbé André Combes in his place, Phelan and his colleagues were inconsolable; in the past they had been attacked for cancelling courses by Maritain at the last minute, and now risked criticism again for Gilson.

One of the decisions made at San Francisco, 25 May 1945, had been to implement the principle that "wars begin in the minds of men, and it is in the minds of men that the defences of peace must be constructed." The strategy for this implementation was, however, left unresolved. The London conference was originally to be a meeting of ministers of education from allied countries. It quickly became a preparatory conference to establish an international strategy to implement the United Nations principle. At first there was some doubt as to whether the London conference was an authentic act of the United Nations: Russia, for example, did not think so and did not attend. But whatever the initial technical irregularities, once convened in London the conference took on the character of a United Nations activity. Its specific aim was to draw up the constitution of what became thereafter the United Nations Educational, Scientific, and Cultural Organization, or UNESCO.

The London conference assembled the last day of October 1945, and remained in session for three weeks until 24 November. Gilson's role was a prominent one. He was the most multilingual delegate present, and one of the liveliest. On the request of Archibald MacLeish, who headed the American delegation, Gilson was placed on the committee to draft UNESCO's constitution. Gilson's special charge was again to work on the preamble to the constitution; this called for skills in both language and philosophy.

While at London Gilson wrote five articles on the conference for *Le monde*. Others appeared sporadically over the next four years in connection with various involvements in current affairs. In these articles Gilson was clearly less than satisfied with the conference. He considered the participants overly provincial and he was disappointed by the character of the UNESCO that was created. Even UNESCO's name was disappointing: while San Francisco had directed attention to "intellectual co-operation," London had translated this into "education, science and culture." American educators had pushed for "education" in the title to maintain the interest of their politicians in the issue, and British delegates had wanted science specified to appease their scientists. This meant that culture had to be specified for letters and the arts, even though, ironically, the word carried associations with German *Kultur*. In Gilson's view, such specifications arbitrarily restricted the much more liberal and universal expression, "intellectual co-operation."

Gilson also considered the delegates much too generous with the world's politicians:

> In brief, as between the organization of intellectual co-operation by government and its organization by governments and intellectuals, a majority of thirty nations against seven opted for the former. The representatives of Einstein, de Broglie,

Joliot will have, thanks to the insistence of France, some kind of chair between the benches of the public and the armchairs of the members. They can be consulted if governments consider such action necessary. ("L'UNESCO et ses membres," *Le monde*, 45.12.5; McG 815.)

In the light of such subsequent confrontations as those involving Israel, Ireland and Iran, Gilson's warning was prophetic: "There exist philosophical and religious explosives quite as powerful as those of nuclear physics: not all bombs are produced in laboratories."

Gilson's letters to Thérèse from London largely describe the things she wanted to hear about: the flight over the channel, the mix-up over his lodgings, the overcrowded conditions that made San Francisco's arrangements seem luxurious in contrast. He told Thérèse about the French ambassador's dinner and a conversation afterward with the wife of the *ministre plénipotentiaire*, Mme Paros, née Reine Claudel, daughter of the poet-ambassador. He also told her about the people he was working with at the conference: Ellen Wilkinson the chairman, Léon Blum the leader of the French delegation, the delegates from Colombia, Mexico, Holland, Poland and so on. Gilson reserved most of his warmth for his descriptions of the birds and cats he met:

Most days I pass through St James's Park where I stop before the ducks. There is even a cormorant there. This morning I walked to the conference by way of Piccadily. Who do you think I met there, perched in a Picadilly window? A magnificent black and white *mitonne* who was dying with desire to talk to someone. Unashamed, I entered into a long conversation under the noses of the passersby. The worst they can have thought is that I was not in a hurry.

Sometimes, not often, Gilson wrote Thérèse about conference business:

Yesterday, Saturday, meetings from 10:00 to 12:30, then with the French delegation from 3:00 to 7:00. The same old comedy: the three or four who had prepared the French project without consulting those who were going to have to support it, that is, me, must have recognized that several of its essential parts were insupportable, and that I would have publicly to disavow a good part of a project that should have been distributed beforehand.

And sometimes business and social events overlapped, as when he served as Léon Blum's interpreter at a grand reception in the Savoy – "Léon Blum who said he absolutely had to talk to me about St Thomas!":

Blum noticed my glancing around and asked: "Are you looking for someone?" I replied quietly: "Yes, for the Catholic archbishop of Westminster." Surprised, Blum asked: "Whatever for?" "Because," I said, "he will certainly want the centre for intellectual co-operation to be located in Paris rather than London. We have to see him." "How right you are!" replied Blum. "I would never have thought of that!"

Although the archbishop was not at the reception, Paris did indeed become the home of UNESCO.

At Claridge's one day with Miss Bosanquet, an English delegate, Gilson met Archibald MacLeish, who was chairing the Editing Committee. After MacLeish offered him a whisky and soda and some cigarettes, he showed Gilson an American draft of the UNESCO constitution and asked him, *tout cuit*, what he thought of it. Taken aback, Gilson asked for time to think about it; he had first to put it into French and show it to the French delegation. MacLeish was a little let down but took the delay with good grace.

Gilson and MacLeish appear to have been amiable co-workers. In 1966 F. R. Cowell was preparing material for UNESCO on the London conference. He wrote to both MacLeish and Gilson for permission to use this anecdote:

> The writer recalls ... a cold November morning in a small unheated room where a committee was drafting the final version of the constitution and endeavouring to ensure equivalent French and English texts. The energetic charmainship of Mr Archibald MacLeish, leader of the United States delegation, the deeply thoughtful contributions of M. Torres Bodet, leader of the Mexican delegation, and the fecund inspiration of M. Etienne Gilson from France, aroused an admiration which the passage of twenty-one years has not dimmed. It was then that M. Gilson minted the happy phrase, *the fruitful diversity of cultures*, and, on a more pedestrian level, the writer persuaded the committee to include *the promotion of the rule of law* among the primary purposes of the organization.
>
> The text of Article I had been agreed, everyone was cold and already late for lunch, but Mr MacLeish, who had never flagged in his enthusiastic pursuit of a form of language adequate to the high purposes of the proposed new organization, said that he thought that real progress had been made that morning. Turning to M. Gilson, who had never had any illusions about the strenuous difficulty of the committee's task, he added: "Well, M. Gilson, I think you will agree that it is better now ?" "No," replied Gilson amid general laughter, "it is no better but I am getting used to it." (66.7.7.)

4 UNESCO

The first general conference of UNESCO met late in 1946 in the *grande salle* of the Paris' Hotel Majestic with Gilson in attendance. If he had been disappointed in London by the limited role of intellectuals in UNESCO's structure, he was positively discouraged by the way the intellectuals themselves behaved in Paris. Sarvepalli Radhakrishnan, prime minister of India, who had at the opening of the conference called the delegates the "pionniers intellectuels du monde," was more than a little dismayed when one of the conference committees classified philosophy among the social sciences. Radhakrishnan promptly asked that it be reclassified with the humanities, and if necessary be dealt with administratively under the general rubric of culture. Julian Huxley, president of the conference, was unwilling to place philosophy among the humanities but consented to its administration as culture. One of the delegates quipped that so far as he was concerned philosophy could be classified with football; Gilson drily suggested that although his friend Alfred North Whitehead had been a football player in his youth, he thought it unlikely that Whitehead would consider the grouping appropriate (*Le monde*, 46.12.4).

Immediately after this first UNESCO conference, Gilson took part, along with Richard McKeon, J. B. Priestly and George Stoddard, in a broadcast discussion of the question "Can UNESCO Educate for World Understanding?"* Although Gilson took only a small part in the dialogue, his comments suggest that he considered the world far from ready for global understanding. He argued that it would only be possible to educate for peace when university education became more international than it was. He was also critical of nationalized universities, and commented on the unfavourable contrast between the University of Paris in the thirteenth century and present-day French institutions. Finally he made a plea, on the ground of practicability, for the establishing of international institutes in all important universities rather than the founding of brand new international universities.

5 TEACHING AND WRITING, 1945-1946

In 1945, the year of the San Francisco and London conferences, Gilson's teaching and publishing suffered from reduced priority. Even in this busy year, however, he managed to publish three brief put important papers clarifying his understanding of the relation between Thomas and twentieth-century existentialism. These were entitled: "Limites existentielles de la philosophie" (in *L'existence* [Paris]; McG 332); "Pierre Lombard et les théologies de l'essence" (*Revue du moyen âge latin*, 1 [1945]: 61-64; McG 396) and "Le thomisme et les philosophies existentielles" (*La vie intellectuelle*, 13 [June 1945]: 144-155; McG 478).

"Le thomisme et les philosophies existentielles" explains why Gilson's next courses for the Institute and the Collège de France took for their topic being and existence. The article explores three challenging contemporary questions. Can thomism be presented as an existential philosophy? What of Thomas is to be found in Kierkegaard, Heidegger, Jaspers, Scheler, Marcel, Sartre? And has the authentic thomism of Thomas anything to say to modern existentialists? Although Gilson indicates the directions in which answers may lie, he is careful to qualify his findings. For Gilson, the various philosophers are too different to permit a composite portrait; moreover, any thomist who pretends to be capable of solving problems for these philosophers is unacceptably apologetic.

In the opening paragraphs of the article, Gilson reviews his presentation of Thomas' ontology in the fourth and fifth editions of *Le thomisme*. First, existence is situated in the heart of the real; second, each thing has a being by virtue of its act of existing; third, each thing has its own proper act of existing; and fourth, the first act by which a being is placed as existing, or as an *existant*, is the source and cause of its unfolding operations, whether these are immanent or transient. Each statement is accompanied by appropriate texts from St Thomas. Clearly, the

---

* This was broadcast by NBC and published as No. 454 of the University of Chicago's *Round Table* (46.12.1).

answer to Gilson's first question is yes; the philosophy of Thomas is authentically existential.

Gilson then turns to Gabriel Marcel, whom he considers "perhaps the most authentic philosopher of these times: whatever he says comes from his very depths" (*Les nouvelles littéraires*, 46.12.26). Gilson had become increasingly interested in Marcel ever since a discussion with Ernest Hocking (above, pp. 241-242). Marcel shared enough thomisms to set him apart from other modern existentialists and, more than most, he kept a low profile as an existentialist. Gilson argues that although Marcel is at his worst when he falls back on an idealist critique of realism, he is somewhat redeemed by his ontology which speaks of the subject grasping the object in an unuttered "Je suis"; Marcel's "I" is the object's "seat" rather than its subject and is in a manner "passive." Marcel also, for Gilson, makes a constructive advance over Bergson when he finds hidden at the base of the real not an on-going *durée* but a stable act of existing by which every subject is placed within the very being of its object. Marcel's, says Gilson, is a "creative fidelity" rather than a "creative evolution." However, although Marcel concurs with much that is Thomas, he also professes much that is not Thomas: Marcel's *ce qui est* and *ce qui se profère* emphasize the *ce qui* and shove the act of being into the background. All in all, St Thomas' contribution to Marcel's existentialism is slight.

The case is different with Kierkegaard and similar existentialists. Kierkegaard's speculation grows out of a religious struggle against those who would make Christianity a knowing. No, Kierkegaard argues, Christianity is a life, it is founded on religious experience and cannot be thought. So, to *think* existence would be to conceive it *sub specie aeterni*, to make an abstraction of it and destroy it. In this, says Gilson, Kierkegaard is absolutely right. But he also lacks something, an ontology with which to carry on. Existentialists like Kierkegaard and thomists of Gilson's stripe face the same problem: they have somehow to avoid treating existence as a thing, a subject apprehended as object. Although existentialists have their psychology and their morality, they also need a metaphysics, a study of being, especially in terms of becoming. Can a phenomenology expand into an ontology for the existentialists? Thomism, argues Gilson, might help it to do so; in thomism existence is at the root of being and there are no pure objects, only subject-objects. Perhaps thomism, then, does offer a means of progress and development for some existentialist philosophies. Moreover, if an existentialist seeks anguish, he will find new sources of it as he crosses the threshold into metaphysics. He will find what Pascal called "the eternal silence of these infinite spaces" or will be led to ask with Leibniz: "Why is there something, rather than nothing?"

Gilson's three articles on thomism and existentialism led straight into the postwar courses he planned for the academic year 1945-1946. In the articles he pointed out that "the admirable conquests of existentialist phenomenology" were based on a "dialectic of the interior life" and "pushed the exploration of the *je* to bedrock depths perhaps never reached since the *Confessions* of St Augustine" ("Le thomisme et les philosophies existentielles," p. 145). In December 1945, as he opened his course on "La dialectique de l'être et de l'existence chez S. Augustin" in the Collège de France, he began: "We will read St Augustine simply to grasp his thought on the subject: and we shall choose his inexhaustible work, the *Confessions*" (lecture notes, 1945-1946). And in the spring of 1946 in Toronto Gilson called his lecture course "Being and Essence" and his seminar, "Texts Relating to the Distinction of Being and Existence in Medieval Philosophy." In both of them he dwelt heavily on Augustine and contemporary existentialism.

14

The Fulfilment of Being, 1946-1949

1 THE 1946 VISIT TO CANADA

Gilson had been forced to postpone his 1945 Toronto courses to accommodate the London conference. Now, pressed by Phelan, he asked the ministry for permission to leave for Toronto during February 1946, before his Paris course was quite over. In December 1945 he wrote Phelan that "I have just received my *ordre de mission*. I am therefore authorized to interrupt my teaching at the Collège de France and sail by the first available boat in February." This willingness to shift his priorities from France to Canada would later be criticized during *l'affaire Gilson*.

In late February 1946 Gilson travelled to Toronto alone, on a liberty ship via New York. It was over five years since he had last lectured at the Institute, and he had literally to be introduced to the students he found there; they knew about him, however, as many of them had studied introductory medieval philosophy under Gilson-trained men. Professor Desmond FitzGerald of the University of San Francisco later recalled the eagerness with which members of the Thomist Society, undergraduate and graduate students from all over the University of Toronto, waited to hear Gilson speak:

> I was chairman that Sunday afternoon as Brennan Hall filled with expectant students and faculty. Phelan was there to introduce Gilson, which he did with his usual grace and charm. The topic was "The Revival of Thomism in France in the Twentieth Century," the topic Gilson had proposed when we asked for a popular, non-technical talk. The substance of the talk was a history of the life and work of Jacques Maritain in which Gilson spoke of how Maritain had made thomism acceptable in the milieu of artists, poets, dramatists, etc., as well as Maritain's work in social and political thought. It was a remarkable tribute. Phelan in thanking Gilson prompted the audience to look forward to the day in which Maritain would return and speak of the life and work of Gilson. (FitzGerald to Shook, 78.4.28.)

The Institute was delighted to have Gilson back, and did not mind that his courses would last only two months, from early March until early May. Gilson's prolonged absence had made the Institute less dependent upon him, an independence that Gilson had desired from the beginning.

Around this time Gilson confided to close friends that his election into the Académie Française was a distinct possibility. François Mauriac, for example, had written him on the subject: "You belong in the Académie." Although Bergson's chair was certain to go to Edouard le Roy, "there are lots of other chairs. ... You belong among us." (45.3.16; tr.) The possibility of an Académie chair leant a new mystique to Gilson, especially in Montréal where Mme Thibaudeau had spread the news.

In Montréal in May Gilson became involved in a debate on Québecois literature. The debate had really begun back in Paris in January. George Duhamel of the Académie had toured French Canada and spoken on Québec's achievements. Back in Paris he had published a newspaper article on Québec letters, "L'arbre et la branche" (Le Figaro, 46.1.4). Gilson took exception to this metaphor and countered first with an article in Le monde entitled "L'arbre canadien" (46.1.6-7; McG 550); he followed this in Canada with a radio address (La 852e émission de la Société du Bon Parler) which was published in La patrie (46.5.12) as "L'arbre canadien: le canadien, notre égal." In these pieces Gilson argued that Québec could not be seen as a branch of the French tree. Canadian literature in French belongs to its own tradition, not France's. Certainly, like modern French literature, it owes much to France's past, but it owes nothing to present-day France. The arts in Québec belong no more to France than they do to England. The poetry of Saint-Denys Garneau, the painting of Alfred Pellan, are Canadian not French.*

Gilson's argument was taken up and published by Robert Charbonneau, editor of Montréal's La nouvelle relève. It was subsequently challenged in Paris by André Billy:

> If M. Gilson has expressed an opinion of this kind, he is wrong. ... It is always in France, it is always in Paris, that first matters of the intelligence appear. Our shortage of coal, of oil, of wheat, above all our shortage of dollars, should not let anyone be misled by articles by men who ought to get their information straight before they write. (La littéraire, 47.3.15; tr.)

2 THE ACADÉMIE FRANÇAISE

When Gilson returned to Paris in May, he was laden with purchases, and with gifts from the Thibaudeaus. Thérèse and the girls were delighted, and Thérèse wrote to Madeleine that she found her husband particularly well and cheerful after his visit. As for herself, she confessed to "a rather serious lassitude which takes the form of bouts of rheumatism and lumbago which I can't shake." She was obviously unwell and asked Madeleine to say nothing about it.

In June Gilson informed Phelan with some embarrassment that he would not go to Toronto the coming fall. He was tired, and his family needed him; his possible election to the Académie, he protested, had nothing to do with it. Gilson also wanted to avoid an upcoming election at the Institute. Phelan's second six-year term as president was now over, and council members disagreed on whether

---

* See also "Naissance du Canadien," Le monde, 46.5.15; McG 715.

he was eligible for a third under the statutes; there were also those who wondered whether he was the best candidate for the job. In the end the council voted in favour of Anton C. Pegis and Gilson, though he loved Phelan, agreed. Phelan was immeasurably disappointed and, rather than step down, decided to continue his work elsewhere. Although Gilson could not understand Phelan's preference for administration over research, he willingly wrote on Phelan's behalf to Father Moore, head of philosophy at Notre Dame.

Gilson's decision to remain in France meant that he was in Paris on 24 October 1946 when eighteen of twenty-four members of the Académie elected him into their midst. Two men were elected at the same meeting, Gilson to the chair last held by Abel Hermant, who had been expelled, and Maurice Genevoix to the chair held by Joseph de Pesquidoux, who had died. The two members-elect, like bishops, assumed their rank from the moment of their election. When Gilson's next article for *Le monde* appeared, "Les pionniers intellectuels" (46.12.4; McG 741), it was signed "Etienne Gilson de l'Académie Française." And when Paul Guth interviewed him for an article in his series "Les maîtres du Collège de France devant les problèmes d'aujourd'hui" (*Les nouvelles littéraires*, 46.12.28; McG 1127), he called Gilson "un grand personnage qui porte bicorne sous la coupole," one now entitled to wear the insignia of an *académicien*.

Gilson's election into the Académie was in recognition of a wide array of achievements: his role in the development of thomism; his grasp of languages and of language itself; his books and other writings; his manifest intelligence; his record in two wars, and especially his adamant refusal to collaborate with invaders; his missions to North America; and his unique strategies of education. Gilson explained to Guth that he considered his thomism of all these accomplishments to be the most significant:

> University, idealist philosophy, represented by Brunschvicg and Alain is dead. It speculated on a purely intellectual plane upon discarnate truth. For it, concrete realities did not exist, evil was a scandal. Today's philosophies, existentialism and marxism, are philosophies of the concrete and of evil. Thomism in the Middle Ages was also like this. It was a complete philosophy of the destiny of man: it was a philosophy of man endowed with reason and whose law is to seek fulfilment in human and divine society.

Guth then asked Gilson if thomism possessed the vigour, the muscular presence, to fill and toughen minds:

> Thomism is bursting with life. It is the philosophy of the future. Besides, it is absurd to talk about thomism: Saint Thomas but took up again Plato and Aristotle. For simplicity's sake, let us call thomism that new philosophy which, in no way eclectic, synthesizes philosophical capital and engages in a dialogue with existentialism and marxism.

Can there be and is there such a dialogue?

> There can be because these three philosophies take themselves seriously. If someone tries to tell me Sartre is all pornography, my reply is, "No! Sartre is looking honest-

ly for solutions, so let's pay attention." I also recognize as serious, marxism's attempt to create a better society.

What are thomism's solutions?

> Thomism (which, by the way, is an existentialism: I have myself rediscovered the importance of existence in St Thomas) starts from the notion of the human person. It shows that man, an individual engaged in a group, is also a person endowed with intelligence, and therefore engaged outside and beyond that group. One can indeed subordinate the individual to material interests, but one has also to respect the autonomy which is his through intelligence and soul.
>
> Aristotle said: "One able to avoid society is either a beast or a god." Man is neither but participates in both. Christian thomism considers him as an animal within society and as a reasonable being transcending it, a son of God.

And if thomism were to organize society?

> It would try at the same time to integrate what is still outside the social order into the social framework and to leave at liberty all the great activities of the mind – science, art, religion. It would establish the only collective happiness possible, that is, whatever satisfies the double nature of man. (tr.)

Felicitations on Gilson's election came to him from France and around the world, including some 275 letters. But however many he received, none could have pleased him more than his letter from France's ambassador to the Holy See, Jacques Maritain:

> Dr Phelan was with me in New York when we read the news of your election into the Académie in the *New York Times*. I hope you received our telegram. I don't know whether the Académie Française deserves the honour of having you among its members; however, in electing you it is returning to all that is noble and great in its traditions. For once a puff of pure air, of justice and loyalty, has passed over this aged body. I am filled with deep joy, as much for you, my dear friend, as for the dignity of our letters and the reputation of France. (46.11.14; tr.)

By Christmas 1946 Gilson was perfectly at home with his membership in the Académie and had begun to prepare for his formal reception. He wrote Mme Thibaudeau:

> I am preparing my *discours de réception*. I am to be received by Pasteur Vallery-Radot [professor of medicine, researcher in disease, grandson of Louis Pasteur]. The costume costs 100,000 francs, the cape 35,000, a sword 70,000, all of which is absurd; but when the wine is poured out, it should be drunk. Besides, it's all we have to drink: there is no milk to console us for its absence. We are aiming impatiently at the end of February – the month of the great cold. (46.12.25; tr.)

Gilson went on to say that he met Mme Thibaudeau's friend, Mme Archer, "chez vos délicieux Ambassadeur et Ambassadrice," the Vaniers. He had also just turned down a request to serve as a *conseiller de la République*:

> Last minute bulletin! I have been designated by the MRP for a seat in the Conseil de la République. I have not accepted. I do not know yet (and probably never will)

whether I am right or wrong not to. I believe I have acted rightly. In any case, that's what I have done. (tr.)

To mark Gilson's entry into the Académie, his friends formally presented him with his ceremonial sword. Vrin, his old friend and publisher, raised funds to pay for the sword, and Jacqueline designed engraved figures on the hilt and pommel to portray her father's wisdom flowing from his faith and intelligence. The creation filled Gilson with great joy. He allowed both sides of the sword to be reproduced on the title page and the jacket of a subsequent English work, *Elements of Christian Philosophy* (1960).

The presentation of the sword took place during May 1947 in the salons of Madame Demoge, rue de Presbourg. Gilson's family was there, as were professors from all faculties of the University of Paris and from the Catholic Institute. The Vaniers were there, and so was Jacques Maritain, in whom the occasion provoked uncommonly high spirits. Because travel was not yet easy and funds were severely restricted, overseas friends and colleagues were unable to attend. However several North American friends attended who were already in France, including Gilson's friend from University College and the Alliance Française in Toronto, Professor Andison. There was also a cheering group of Canadian students then in Paris, including Vianney Decarie, later professor of philosophy in the University of Montréal, and Pierre Trudeau, later prime minister of Canada.

The Académie's own formal reception was tendered "sous la coupole" during the afternoon of 29 May 1947. Gilson's *Discours de réception* (Paris, 1948; McG 19) was a masterpiece of style and diplomacy. Although new academicians customarily paid tribute to the predecessor in their chair, Gilson's predecessor had been expelled and was still living. Gilson instead paid tribute to all those scholars to whom he felt especially indebted for this honour. First he cited Lucien Lévy-Bruhl, who had first sent him to the Middle Ages to find the sources of Descartes' ideas. Then he turned to Henri Bergson, who had demonstrated for him that even after the critiques of Kant and the positivism of Comte, metaphysical knowledge remained possible: "How we loved him, that prophet pouring out the word of a God whose very name his noblest scruples long prevented him from so much as pronouncing." Gilson also acknowledged his debt to Joseph Bédier, who in 1919 in the *aula magna* of the University of Strasbourg had so impressed him with his paeon on the twelfth century, his descriptions of its first *chanson de geste*, its first *fabliau*, its first romance, its first pointed arch, its first *commune*; in his turn, Gilson had been inspired to look at the first grammar, the first logic, the first theology and the earliest mysticism. Only the other day said Gilson, Bédier had

> pointed at a book of mine which he loved, and joked that there was no reason why St Bonaventure too should not be entering the Académie! He is entering it today, Messieurs, and you have Joseph Bédier's word for it! Were you to permit me to step back and allow that humble Friar Minor to pass in ahead of me, be assured that I would gladly walk behind him. (tr.)

Gilson went on to recount what France owed to the Middle Ages, especially its logic through Abélard, its grammar, and yes, even the discovery of its wine. Was it not Salimbene who first recorded the news brought back by Gabriel of Cremona that he had seen in the tiny *finage* of the See of Auxerre "more vines and more wine than in the three countries of Cremona, Parma and Modena combined. ... And what wine! Golden and delicately scented, comforting; as rich in body as in bouquet, and so vigorous withal that even the very jugs it is kept in shed tears." (tr.)

Gilson managed also to pay a passing compliment to his unfortunate predecessor. After speaking about grammar and logic from Abélard to the present and remarking on the importance of both in French tradition, Gilson referred to a French grammarian Lancelot, whose *Grammaire générale* was so logical in character that its chapter on the verb became chapter 13 of the seventeenth-century *Logique de Port-Royal*. The academicians present could only detect here an oblique reference to Abel Hermant who, though not the grammarian of Port-Royal, was, as a *membre de l'Académie*, ipso facto a kind of grammarian; Hermant had long written regularly for *Temps* of Paris under the pseudonym *Lancelot*.

At least twice in his letters to Mme Thibaudeau, Gilson had promised to mention her beloved La Pointe at Beauharnois in his address. He was as good as his word, and included it in a recitation of French Canada's beautiful place-names: "Châteauguay, Beauharnois, Montmorency, Sainte-Anne de Beaupré, et tant d'autres." He well knew that Canada had played a role in his candidature and that he was much in debt to his Canadian friends.* He also praised the integrity of their speech in a statement that was picked up by the Montréal press a few days later: "Permit me to say here in your name: the Canadian people deserve well of the French language."

The *Réponse* (McG 1074) to this address was delivered by Doctor Louis Pasteur Vallery-Radot, Gilson's nominator. Vallery-Radot called attention to the wide range of Gilson's interests and competencies, and described him both as "one of the most perfect examples of the Frenchman," and as "a citizen of the world." He spoke of Gilson's liberality of thought and expression, citing Gilson's own words: "A good philosophical disagreement is better than a false agreement which ends in confusion." He then praised Gilson's "clarity and steadfastness" which, in the words of General de Gaulle, "are always the supreme skills."

Vallery-Radot also spoke of Gilson's uncompromising attitude during the occupation: "During sombre years, you never ceased, in private or public conversation, even in your courses, to express your faith in victory, refusing any compromise with the enemy." Gilson's resistance to collaboration during and after the war had loomed very large in Vallery-Radot's support of the nomination; he had himself been *rallié à la France libre* and had served as

---

* He had written to this effect to Jules Masse, president of Québec's Société du Bon Parler Français (*Le devoir*, 47.1.3).

secretary-general of Public Health in Algiers. In his *Réponse* he returned frequently to Gilson's role as a French citizen. Perhaps this twofold emphasis – on *France libre et Gilson français* – contained the seed of Vallery-Radot's later *volte-face* during *l'affaire Gilson*.

3 CONSEILLER DE LA RÉPUBLIQUE

Throughout the fall of 1946 Gilson was constantly fighting pressures to become politically involved with the Mouvement Républicaine Populaire (MRP). He mentioned this in his letters to Mme Thibaudeau, to Phelan and to the Institute's new president, Pegis, and insisted each time that his two absolute priorities at the moment were the Collège de France and the Toronto Institute. Although he acknowledged responsibility to the Republic, he was not sure that politics fell within his competence. Nevertheless the MRP's popular republicanism and its anticommunist position greatly attracted him, and he felt the lure of the public arena. In September 1946 he wrote Pegis:

> The minister of state, Francisque Gay, president of the MRP, is coming next Saturday to hold a council-of-war in my country house [Vermenton]. I have converted my curé [Abbé Breuil] to the MRP in spite of the decided opposition of my archbishop. Yet I have not accepted to run for deputy! (46.9.25.)

And in October:

> Intense political activity too. I think we should vote "yes" for the constitution, against de Gaulle's advice, and I have organized meetings in the country in favour of the MRP. Fighting with communists is really [fun]. (EG to Pegis, 46.10.9.)

In November, after Gilson flatly refused to run as an MRP candidate for a senatorial seat, he began to have second thoughts: "I am not sure I did my duty though, for indeed, *just now*, it might be the right thing." In January 1947 he gave a qualified "yes," but stipulated that he must be able to continue in the Collège de France and the Institute. He allowed his name to stand for nomination and was relieved when not nominated. However, the MRP also had, over and above its elective seats, a small number of appointive ones. On 28 March 1947 he was offered and accepted a two-year appointive seat on the Conseil de la République. Again he qualified his acceptance:

> I have accepted this new responsibility under two conditions: (1) that I keep my position at the Collège de France (which means two jobs for one salary); (2) that I be allowed to go to Canada next fall in my capacity of president of the Institut Scientifique Franco-Canadien, which is maintained by the French Foreign Office. (EG to Pegis, 47.4.1.)

In appealing to his Québec post rather than his work at the Institute, Gilson probably wanted to forestall objections to his trips to Canada.

More or less drafted, Gilson became, as he told Phelan, "senateur malgré lui." But he liked the idea too, particularly as it placed him in a position of influence at a time when reform of the national education system seemed likely to arise. If the future of Catholic schools was at issue, Gilson would even, he warned Pegis, miss a fall in Toronto: "If there is to be a fight, I should be among the fighters" (47.5.11).

Gilson remained a *conseiller* for two years, until early 1949. But from the beginning he found the venture disappointing and frustrating:

> Last Friday [47.3.28] a telephone call from the Assemblée Nationale informed me that ten minutes ago I had been elected a member of the Conseil de la République. The following day, or rather night, by 2 AM, I had already voted seven laws which I had not even read, including a particularly tricky one protecting democratic farmers (who are just now piling up huge stacks of money) against capitalist landlords who are getting practically nothing out of their farms. (EG to Pegis, 47.4.1.)

By June Gilson's public duties had escalated alarmingly: "Life is growing more and more absurd every day. I am beginning to wonder if I am not president of everything, except the French Republic. I am desperately fighting to keep in touch with philosophy." (47.6.21.) During Gilson's two years as a senator he had to limit his autumn visits to North America to two-month terms. He felt sometimes as though he had, as the peter principle later put it, been promoted to the level of his incompetence.

Gilson became deeply involved in two assembly bills pertaining to his own *métiers*. The first of these (law 482, 47.7.30) concerned schools. The Conseil asked the government to allow the collieries of central and southern France to lease out to the families of students the school buildings that had once been owned by the mines. This bill did not ask for subventions, merely that buildings now public be leased out for schools and that no competing state-supported schools be erected beside them. The bill was bitterly fought by the left, and defeated. As a result Gilson realized that the anticlericalism which some claimed had ended with the Résistance was as healthy as ever. The whole question of "free" schools would have to be fought at a higher and more abstract level than legal justice; it would have to be shown that religious freedom in the area of education was essential to the very survival of intellectual freedom. Gilson loaned his name as a patron to a newly-founded Secretariat of Studies, and spoke to its members on 10 May 1948 at the Cité-Club in Paris.* There he argued that the debate should be de-confessionalized and broadened to address the issue of worldwide educational freedom and liberty of teaching; the Gilson who had contributed to *Sept* in the 1930s had come to speak the language of the United Nations Charter.

The second bill (law 221, 1948) introduced a levy of taxes on books in the public domain after heirs could no longer benefit. Proceeds from this six-percent tax were to go to the Société des Gens de Lettres, and then be divided between the *société* and the government's own Caisse des Lettres. The *société* was a large writers' club, many of whose members practised another profession as well;

---

* See *Documentation catholique*, 45 (48.9.12): 1163-1169, for notes on the address.

among the writers who had not chosen to enrol were Gide, Malraux, Camus, Sartre and du Gard. The *société* would use its share of the tax to assist the families of destitute writers. The *caisse*, on the other hand, was a special treasury fund established in 1946 for paying the cost of gathering and preserving works of art.

Gilson's basic objection to the bill – known as *le domaine payant* – was that it permitted the government to turn over some of its own social responsibility to a private society. When the assembly eventually passed it, Gilson took issue with it in the *conseil*. He also placed an article, "Le domaine public," in *Le monde* (48.2.26; McG 620). This opened with a scathing attack on the bill:

> On 13 February 1948, within ten minutes and without debate, the National Assembly deprived the sovereign people of its rights over literary property held for all those works which have lapsed into the public domain. Moreover, it will make them pay tomorrow for things they owned yesterday, and pay out for the benefit of a corporation which, though itself a public utility, is not entirely dissociated from private interests. (tr.)

Gilson followed this a week later with a *reductio ad absurdum* entitled "Les héritiers du roi Salomon" (*Le monde*, 48.3.4; McG 676). Literary heirs, wrote Gilson, are no more identifiable than were the children of Solomon through his many wives, to say nothing of his concubines. Literary works can have temporary heirs, but ultimately such works must, when the heirs become too numerous, fall into the public domain. Taking as his authority the jurist Planiol, Gilson urged the government to restore such literary works to the rightful possession of the public.

Gilson was never really comfortable in the field of law. On 3 March *Le monde* published a public letter to him from Gérard Bauër, president of La Société des Gens de Lettres. Bauër gently reminded him that, although the law had been passed in one morning and without debate, it was nonetheless, like the well-known painting by Whistler, the result of thirty years of experience. The law was not, Bauër said, very different from other copyright laws governing drama and music, and in many ways did serve the interests of writers. Gilson also heard privately from J. P. New, civil administrator to the Ministry of Economic Affairs and author of a doctoral thesis on "Le domaine public moral," and also from Paul Olagnier of the Court of Appeals; both concurred that public domain must include works of the mind in order to justify the existence of obligatory depositories like the Bibliothèque Nationale, to justify government grants to theatres and so on. Other letters were less cautious in their support for Gilson's position, and agreed with him entirely. The question itself, however, fell into stalemate as a series of crises struck parliament and governments rapidly began to fall.

Between 31 August and 18 September 1948, just before going to Canada for two months, Gilson submitted five politically-based articles to *Le monde*, all of them suggesting his discouragement with politics. Upon his return to Paris in December, Gilson's two-year stint in the senate came officially to its close. At this time new laws stated that everyone had to be elected to the Conseil. Gilson did not wish to run for office, and quit. In the postscript of a letter to Phelan at Notre Dame, he wrote with relief: "I am using old envelopes, but I am no longer an MP [Member of Parliament]. Blessed be God!" (49.1.5.)

Looking back on his political career from his retirement retreat in Cravant, Gilson mused:

> What I realized most is that there is no difference at all between being a senator and being nothing. In a few cases I risked giving advice to some minister, but I was not listened to. I said this to a minister – Bizot, I think – and was told that it is the same with ministers. ... I feel I got nothing at all out of my experience as a senator. It might have been better had I been able to do something ... but I felt no satisfaction. For the most part, in France, deputies and senators don't count for much. (interview, 1974.)

4 COPING FROM PARIS, 1946-1947

Because Gilson was not in Toronto during the fall of 1946, he had to cope by mail with President Pegis' administrative problems. Substitute courses were needed to replace Gilson's, and unfinished theses had been left behind by Phelan when he moved to Notre Dame. Father O'Donnell was the *deus ex machina* in finding Gilson's replacement: he simply told Père Regis of Montréal that he would have to come to Toronto and Regis acquiesced. Gilson was relieved:

> Thank you for the good news, and while Regis is there don't fail to ask him to let you know when Father Thomas Philippe OP is in Montréal. According to His Excellency, the French ambassador to the Holy See (secret!) you should invite Philippe for a lecture – in French. Doing so would only be a pretext for him to discuss with you the possibility of Father Chenu's coming to the Institute. (46.10.9.)

As for the unfinished theses, Gilson himself stepped in to solve some of the problems of the abandoned students. He provided Pegis with firm information on the whereabouts of manuscripts of Henry of Ghent, Richard Holkot and Marius Victorinus.

Gilson also corresponded with Pegis in connection with his own recent work on being and existence. Gilson looked to Pegis for help in clarifying a number of details as he completed his two very important studies: his *L'être et l'essence: problèmes et controverses* and his *Being and Some Philosophers*. These works were to present Gilson's mature positions on the philosophy of being. They would not simply be French and English versions of the same text, but would be adapted to the intellectual climate of their readers in each language. The French work would be published by Vrin in 1948, and the English by the Toronto Institute in 1949.

By staying in Paris this fall of 1946, Gilson could give important public lectures to audiences he had been neglecting. He travelled to England and on 20 November delivered the Philip Maurice Deneke Lecture at Lady Margaret Hall, Oxford: this was entitled "Pétrarque et sa muse" (London and New York, 1946; McG 103). On 21 and 22 November he gave two lectures for the Faculty of

Divinity, University of London, on "The Judgment of Existence in Its Relation to the Problem of God." He was also invited at this time to give the Clark Lectures at Cambridge, but later had to cancel when he took his seat on the senate.

Most of Gilson's activities during the first eight months of 1947 were divided among the Collège de France, the Conseil de la République, and the Académie Française, though he did manage to accept some independent invitations. In January 1947 he went to London briefly where, at the suggestion of Robert Speaight (another friend of Georges Vanier), the BBC had asked Gilson to give a radio lecture on 26 January. Speaight wrote Gilson afterward to thank him warmly for accepting:

> I heard splendid reports from all sides of your visit. People were excited about it. I am sorry I was not at the dinner where you became acquainted with many of my friends. Right now I am preparing a revival of *Murder in the Cathedral* to follow the Saroyan about the end of February. When I return to Paris this summer, I very much hope to see you again – perhaps in your wonderful corner of Burgundy which I keep close to my heart. (47.1.27; tr.)

In March Gilson gave talks in Liège and in Brussels. While in Liège he interviewed Dom Henri Pouillon OSB of Mont-César Abbey, Louvain, for the Institute. With Combes and Chenu both unavailable, Pegis had independently approached Pouillon about an appointment as visiting professor for the term beginning January 1948. After the interview Gilson wrote to Pegis that he thought Pouillon would work out well. As for Chenu:

> The situation of Père Chenu is still deteriorating, nobody knows why, except that three French-Canadian bishops have raised objections to his teaching in Montréal or, *a fortiori*, Québec. ... It is a great pity and my heart is bleeding for my friend. ... He is just in the situation where Maritain and I would be, were we priests. God seems to be saving a few laymen to very definite purposes. Let this be off the record. (47.4.1.)

In April Gilson attended meetings in Rome of the Pontifical Academy of St Thomas Aquinas. He also took part there in an international gathering to set up Pax Romana as an international movement, engaging intellectuals in the service of God. According to Maritain, Gilson's presence in Rome at this time was essential:

> Your visit to Rome will be very important ... and I will make a point of receiving you in the salons of this ancient Palais Taverne, an incomparable old barracks in the hands of the most avaricious of proprietors. (Let's hope there won't be a storm that night. Last night rain came through the roofs and ceilings, and every room was flooded.) (46.11.14; tr.)

Gilson and Thérèse planned to leave for Rome on Easter Sunday evening, 6 April, and would not arrive until Tuesday; as he wrote Mme Thibaudeau, "you can't imagine what travelling is like in Europe since the war."

Once in Rome Gilson quickly became involved in the two congresses, which took place between 8 and 14 April. His theme for the Academy of St Thomas expanded upon his latest interest, "The Knowledge of Being." For Pax Romana he spoke in the Palazzetto Venezia, 12 April, on "Les intellectuels dans la chrétienté" (*Travaux et documents* [May, June 1947], pp. 3-15; McG 312). He pleaded with intellectuals to keep the church in the world where, according to Dante, it was as much at home as fish in the sea. At present the secular rather than Christian world was struggling hardest to promote Christian ideals. UNESCO, for example, was a noble secular effort to establish the same intellectual co-operation that the Middle Ages had found through the church but which rampant nationalism had since all but destroyed.

While in Rome, Gilson and Thérèse had an audience with Pope Pius XII. Upon his return to Paris, Gilson wrote Pegis:

> I am just back from Rome, where I have been received by the Holy Father. ... Twenty-four hours after my visit, the Holy Father promised me to send to the Institute a word of approval and encouragement. ... My wife was with me, and I could not well tell you everything that happened during those unforgettable minutes. Had I found my own father alive, I don't believe he could have shown me more fatherly love. I was more deeply moved than I can say, and I truly believe that the Holy Father was as deeply moved as I was. (47.4.25.)

A "Letter of Praise" from Pius XII arrived in Toronto a few months later, toward the end of Pegis' first year of presidency. This letter praised the work of the Institute throughout the difficult years of the war.

This same spring Gilson also wrote Pegis that a Premonstratensian canon, Astrik Gabriel, had approached him about conducting some personal research at the Institute in Toronto. Canon Gabriel and Gilson were old friends, and had met in the 1930s when Gabriel had followed Gilson's lectures in the Collège de France; Gabriel had then been director of the French lycée in Budapest. Gilson responded warmly to the request:

> I have just had the visit of a certain Father A. Gabriel, coming from Hungary to see me with a very definite object in mind. He is a Hungarian, and I cannot make a long story shorter than by telling you, rather reminding you, that Hungary is occupied by the Russians. Father Gabriel simply wants a scholarship to spend three months at the Institute of Mediaeval Studies. ... Father Gabriel is now working on a catalogue of all the medieval manuscripts to be found in Hungary. ... He has already published five or six books – in French – on the medieval history of Hungary and intellectual relations between Budapest and Paris during the Middle Ages. I have one of them on my desk: *Les rapports dynastiques franco-hongrois au moyen âge* (University of Budapest Press, 1944). ... It is beautiful (plates of mss, monuments, illuminations, etc.) and it really looks good. I think the proposal ... very much in the line of the Institute as a "catholic" institution. ... I would be grateful to you for ... a not too long delayed decision." (EG to Pegis, 47.4.28.)

Canon Gabriel reached Toronto in the late summer of 1947 and quickly became a lively and respected member of its teaching staff. Like other staff members he went occasionally to Notre Dame to lecture for Phelan, who appreciated his talents. When Gabriel decided in 1948 to go permanently to Notre Dame, Gilson assured him he could return to the Toronto Institute at any time.

In 1946 and 1947 Gilson refined for himself the difference between being an historian of philosophy and being a philosopher. He put the distinction succinctly, thinking primarily of his own case: "The only task of history is to understand and to make understood, whereas philosophy must choose" (*Being and Some Philosophers* [Toronto, 1949], p. x; McG 3). Although Gilson continued to argue often that he was "only an historian," he realized that with *Being and Some Philosophers* he was writing as a philosopher and putting forward his own kind of existentialism.

5 THE MCMASTER CONFERENCE, 1947

When Gilson visited Toronto in 1947, he was not only an academic but also a foreign statesman of senatorial rank. Paul Martin, Minister of Health and Welfare in Mackenzie King's Liberal government, invited him to come early to address a Young Liberals' Conference, 1 to 5 September at McMaster University in Hamilton, Ontario. Martin had attended Gilson's lectures at St Michael's in 1927 and 1928, had met him again at Cambridge University, and had run into him recently a number of times at the Canadian embassy in Paris. Martin had already acquired C. D. Howe and Louis St Laurent for the conference, and asked Gilson to prepare an address on the subject of democracy. Gilson accepted; apparently, a remark of Martin's had first prompted him to enter the senate.

Before Martin's invitation Thérèse had already decided not to come to Toronto this year; no boat was available around 15 September and she did not want to fly. Bernard, however, now nineteen, was anxious to go to the conference and offered to act as his father's secretary. Thérèse consented, on the condition that Gilson write often with full accounts of her son's activities.[*]

Father and son left Paris for London on 26 August, and flew from Prestwick for Gander and Montréal two days later. During the trip Gilson wrote much of his address. As a senator, and the guest of a cabinet minister, he was treated with more than usual ceremony. When the plane landed in Montréal, father and son were whisked off the plane and through immigration and customs. The airport's public address system announced that the "Messieurs Gilson" were welcome to Canada, and would they move directly to the Ottawa plane which had been delayed for their convenience. In Ottawa they were met by the French ambassador's cadillac, and taken to dine and lodge at the embassy. The next day they moved on to Toronto more humbly by train, and were met by a committee of two: the Institute's diminutive President Pegis had found it advisable to bring along Father George Flahiff, who was tall enough to do the spotting. A day later

---

[*] This explains why Gilson's letters to her during this fall are carefully numbered one to fifteen. Until Bernard's return to France they were almost completely given over to his son's affairs.

the two Gilsons arrived in Hamilton, where both were invited to participate fully in the sessions.

Gilson's address drew a tremendous response from his audience. He reported to Thérèse that "never have I received such an ovation" (47.9.2). Wilfrid Egglestone wrote in *Saturday Night* that the impact of the lecture had been profound: "Young Liberals at Hamilton greeted the eminent French philosopher's remarks with loud and prolonged enthusiasm and more than one of them said afterward that his speech had led them to decide to dedicate themselves to a life of public service" (47.9.13).

"The Philosophy of Liberalism" was later published as "The Task of the Democratic State" (in *Canada Looks Ahead* [Ottawa, 1948], pp. 78-91; McG 810); the talk was repeated in the fall to the Political Science Club of the University of Toronto. It was basically a philosophical analysis of marxism, contrasting it with that healthy state intervention that protects the personal liberty of its citizens. Gilson called on the young audience to keep their principles straight: they should not condemn marxism's correct attempt to expand politics into economic and social spheres, but should condemn it when it allowed the state to oppress the individual. According to Gilson the most pressing problem of the day was to invent some means by which to grant personal freedom to everyone:

> Is it too ambitious to will a society where man will remain the master of the machines he makes instead of becoming their slave? Where the right to private property would mean the right of *all* men to private property? Where the state would take a hand in everyone's business, not to dominate him but to help him? When the authority would seek no other justification than to facilitate and guarantee the flowering of all personal liberties? (author's draft, p. 49.)

Political liberty must now be expanded to encompass economic and social liberties; only then might economic and social justice be offered to all. This address reinforced the moderate social policies becoming popular among many Canadian Liberals.

Gilson's political and social acumen was well respected by political leaders in France and Canada. When Maurice Schumann visited North America in 1948 he asked Gilson to join him in Ottawa and accompany him to Toronto (48.9.1); in mid-September Gilson brought the French premier to a civic reception in Toronto, and to a private luncheon at St Michael's College. Similarly, when Louis St Laurent became prime minister of Canada in 1949, he wrote a warm letter to Gilson urging him to call on him personally in Ottawa (49.6.30).

On 2 September, the day of his father's address, Bernard made the noon radio broadcast in Hamilton. Some underlying tension between father and son emerges in Gilson's account:

> I am beginning to understand why Bernard is enjoying himself here. I have just heard – not from Bernard himself – that during a committee meeting yesterday, he answered questions for twenty minutes on the political situation in France. It appears that he was excellent and he made the noon programme today on the

Hamilton radio. It all took place in English, naturally. Bernard has not said a word to me about it. He has spent the afternoon sleeping, resting on his laurels, as it were. He is entirely on his own, which I like. I can now miss some meetings, being represented by him. ... Unfortunately, it is now 11 PM and the rascal seems to have gone off somewhere in a car with his Canadian friends [the Comery boys]. Just let's see what time he comes in. I have left a piece of cake for him on the table. There were no sandwiches left in the snackbar. [Next day] Where do you think Bernard and his friends with the big Buick went? To Toronto, to the Canadian National Exhibition. (EG to Thérèse, 47.9.2; tr.)

6 IN SEARCH OF JEAN DUNS SCOT

After the McMaster conference Gilson returned to Toronto to devote three full weeks to preparing the courses he was to begin there around St Michael's Day. These courses had originally been announced as "Early Anglo-Saxon Humanism" and "Seminar on the Formation of the Augustinian Notion of God." He had originally intended to revise his lectures on Anglo-Saxon humanism for the Clark Lectures at Cambridge, which he had called off when he joined the senate. Rather than prepare the lectures for Toronto alone, he decided to substitute a more philosophical seminar on the prologue to the *Opus Oxoniense* of Duns Scotus. "I have got," he wrote Pegis, "sixteen pages of the new Quaracchi text (but don't say a word about it!) and may get more during the coming months" (47.4.25).

The decision to turn his attention to Duns Scotus had significance for Gilson's philosophical career at this time. He was already very familiar with the philosopher's work and had presented it in various histories of medieval philosophy. In 1932 he had devoted a whole course in the École Pratique des Hautes Études to Scotus' *Natural Theology*, and through Philotheus Böhner he had dipped widely into Scotus' metaphysics and theology.* In 1938 Gilson had also demonstrated, to his own satisfaction if not to Ephrem Longpré's, the authenticity of the first sixteen theoremata (above, p. 226). Scholars working on Franciscan philosophy had long wanted Gilson to produce a work on Duns Scotus similar to those he had done on Bonaventure and Augustine.

The new Quaracchi text of the *Opus Oxoniense* spurred Gilson's return to Duns Scotus. The Franciscan Doctor was to be the subject not only of the 1947 seminar, but of both Gilson's course and seminar in 1948: "The Infinite Being According to Duns Scotus" and "Texts Relating to the Notion of Infinite Being." Once into the subject, Gilson could not put it from him. In 1949, although he returned to St Thomas in his lecture course for the Institute, his seminar was on Scotus' *Quaestio quodlibetalis VII*. Even though Gilson's courses this year were cut short by Thérèse's illness, Gilson buried his sorrow as he prepared a major text on the philosopher:

---

* These inquiries however were neither as deep nor of quite the same nature as those Böhner had indicated in his translations of Gilson or in his "Metaphysik und Theologie nach Duns Scotus" (above, p. 212).

I am muddling through Duns Scotus' angelology. It is full of texts on everything, including intuitive knowledge. How can a Franciscan be both an occamist and a scotist? The *de potentia absoluta* has nothing to do with it. The *visio intuitiva rei non existentis* is to Duns Scotus a contradiction in terms! (EG to Pegis, 49.11.26.)

In January 1950 Gilson grew excited by new insights that had come from Matthew of Aquasparta, and he was wading through everything he found even remotely helpful:

I still have three chapters of my "Duns Scotus" to write. The title, I believe, will be "Duns Scot et la philosophie," though in fact it should be "Duns Scot et les philosophes." I think it will take a few years for its conclusions to sink into Franciscan minds. Scotism is indeed very different from Scotus. (50.1.8.)

This year Gilson's Toronto courses again focused on Scotus: "Lectures: The Human Soul in Duns Scotus (Intellect and Will)," and "Seminar: Thirteenth-Century Answers to the Problem of the Divine Illumination from Thomas Aquinas to Duns Scotus."

By this time the book was completed:

The Duns Scotus is done, a slow meandering book, the least constructed and conducted of all those I have ever written. I think, however, that it expresses a most sincere effort to understand him as he was. What the result is worth I don't know. At any rate it has helped me through the worst months (at least, I hope so) of my life. (EG to Pegis, 50.2.25.)

The book finally appeared in 1952 as *Jean Duns Scot; introduction à ses positions fondamentales* (Paris; McG 81). It was a good book but not everything Gilson had hoped it would be. He told Father Maurer, for example, that he regretted not having paid more attention throughout to the influence of Henry of Ghent; he only recognized this flaw when the critical edition of Scotus, published just as he finished his own work, revealed a surprising frequency of references throughout to Henry. However, despite its flaws, *Jean Duns Scot* stands as an important milestone in Gilson's mature years.

7 DOMESTIC LIFE, AUTUMN 1947

Following the McMaster conference Gilson attempted to provide a profitable six-week vacation for Bernard without sacrificing his own need for study and quiet. First he sent the boy to the Thibaudeaus at La Pointe for ten days, a visit from which Bernard returned tanned and full of enthusiasm. Then Gilson arranged for Alex Sampson to take Bernard along on a business trip across Canada to the Pacific coast. Sampson was an excellent travelling companion for Bernard, and an ingenious instructor. He made a point of introducing everyone he knew well to the son of his friend Etienne Gilson, distinguished philosopher, celebrated wine connoisseur and resident of Burgundy – all this helped to promote Sampson's own Canadian Château Gai wines. Bernard was noticed everywhere he went, shook hands with Canada's clergy, mayors and business-men in all the major cities, and spoke over Western Canada's French-language station in St Boniface.

Bernard returned to Toronto regenerated and refreshed. On 19 October he departed for New York to embark on the *De Grasse* for France in time for school. Gilson hated to see Bernard go, and wrote sadly to Thérèse that "the bird has flown for good and the cage is empty. I was desolate when he left but knew he had to go home." (47.10.20; tr.) Back in Paris Bernard launched into the best academic year of his life, crowned with a brilliantly won *licence de philosophie*. Gilson was so pleased that he recompensed his son with two summer months in Oxford and London.

At around the time of Bernard's departure, perhaps because of Thérèse's deteriorating health, Gilson developed an acute sense of his entire family's vulnerability. The Cold War was underway, and he was worried that Europe might become the theatre of yet another world war, this time between the United States and Russia. He wondered whether he should not keep Bernard with him in Toronto, even have him finish his education there, but Thérèse would have none of this. Gilson also worried for Jacqueline's safety in Spain and sent her the addresses of friends in Montréal with whom she could seek refuge if life in Madrid became too dangerous. Already his attitudes were beginning to reflect that politic of aggressive neutralism that would eventually cut him off from many Frenchmen.

Something of that neutralism can also be seen in Gilson's opinion at this time of the Académie:

> Curiously, I have no sense of being part of [the Académie]. I hardly ever think of it, and when I do it is to recall being elected and afterward received. I seem some-how to have been taken into it as a kind of supplement rather than as a true Academician. I am under no illusion about the Académie: the name surpasses the reality. I am not sure that most members, apart from four or five like Claudel and Mauriac, are Academicians at all. No doubt I shall accommodate myself to it all, and ultimately accept the Académie for what it in reality is. (EG to Thérèse, 47.10.20; tr.)

If Gilson felt the Académie failed to exert a profound influence on French thought, he did respect its work on language. His own explorations in this area had begun in his youth under Abbé Thorelle and would continue throughout his life. For Gilson the Académie was the inventor and preserver of good French, and its work on vocabulary, syntax and usage caught his interest. He wrote to Mme Thibaudeau on the issue of rendering neologisms into French:

> The Académie Française is authorized to sanction good usage, not to create words. Why create words for things which are English? Why and how? A "grill" is quite simply *un gril*. This is an easy one. A "snack" is *un casse-croûte*; and so is a "snack-bar." Yet no one would think of saying "*Je m'arrêtai à un casse-croûte*," which is, however, quite good. Proposing words which will not be accepted is, in my opinion, a waste of time. (50.1.5; tr.)

Gilson sometimes got tripped up in this area of usage, however. Once when a Montréal taxi-driver spoke of *un building*, Gilson countered with *un bâtiment*. "But the Académie Française approves of *un building*," said the driver, and Gilson shut up. Back in France he checked the word, and found that the taxi-driver had indeed been right.

The autumn of 1947 was a busy one in Toronto, with two new courses on Duns Scotus and several outside lectures. Gilson lectured in October at Regis College where he had many Jesuit friends and to the Alliance Française in Toronto, which he never turned down. The next month was filled with more distant commitments. From 12 to 14 November he was in Montréal, where the university was inaugurating a new annual lecture in medieval thought, to be known as the Albert the Great Lecture; Gilson delivered the first in this series, choosing as his topic "Philosophie et incarnation selon saint Augustin" (Paris, 1947; McG 124). On 19 November he lectured in Windsor. From 20 to 22 November he was at Notre Dame in South Bend, where he gave three lectures on "Being and Existence" and an informal talk on "Philosophy in France." On 23 November he gave the Aquinas Lecture for Father Smith at Marquette on "The History of Philosophy and Philosophical Education." On 30 November he was back lecturing in Montréal and on 1 December at Laval in Québec City. He would have accepted even more invitations if he could have, for with the fall of the franc he needed the money; Thérèse had just written him that one "pot-au-feu, légumes compris" had cost her a disastrous 930 francs, and this, as he wrote Mme Thibaudeau, "did not include the eggs" (47.11.17; tr.). Besides, Gilson enjoyed the work and infinitely preferred it to "les paperasses du conseil." "I have become a philosopher again," he told Pegis, "and hope to be able to remain so."

The return trip to Paris this year was fraught with anticlimax. As Gilson waited at the Thibaudeaus' to leave for the airport, Jacques came in to tell him that his plane would not leave until the next day, 3 December, at three PM. The next afternoon the three Thibaudeaus drove him to Dorval and saw him off. Four hours later his plane was grounded at Gander for "mechanical adjustments" to an engine. On 4 December the plane took off again at nine forty-five AM:

After an hour's flying over the Atlantic, it turned about and landed at Dorval at 4:00 PM. A bus took us to dinner at Pointe Claire on Lac Saint-Louis, I think. From there I sent you a card [47.11.4]. Our trip thus far, not counting meals, has set TCA back over $100. At 6:45 we boarded a new plane, but one of its motors was not working. Later we climbed aboard again. The motor had been fixed (!) and we took off at 8:00 arriving in Gander at midnight. We left Gander at 1:15 – it was now Friday the 5th – and arrived at Shannon at 10:00 AM. We were supposed to take off again at 11:00 but the same motor stalled. We got off once more, the motor was fixed again (!). We left at noon and reached London at 1:30 PM – really now 6:30 PM. There was no plane to take us to Paris, so we spent the night in a hotel. On Saturday 6 December we left London at 8:30 AM with a full plane, arrived Paris at 9:45. I was home at 10:00 AM. (EG to Mme Thibaudeau, 47.12.7; tr.)

Further tragicomedy awaited him at home:

> The nylons were a great success. But what drama! I had found only one white
> blouse (plain-white) tailored by Tooke, size thirty-four. Now both Thérèse and
> Cécile wanted it. Thérèse, you might know, gave in. Do you think this injustice can
> be remedied? If Madeleine could send Thérèse a blouse, size thirty-four, plain
> white, but *tailored by Tooke* (this is essential), Thérèse would be enraptured. If you
> find two of them, send two, preferably by air, after taking them out of the cartons,
> to be sure. Put it on my bill. (ibid.; tr.)

Gilson carried two accounts, one with Mme Thibaudeau, one with Tony Pegis.
Both had been sending food parcels to the Gilsons since the end of the war.

8 THE ROLE OF THE INTELLECTUAL, 1948-1949

As a *conseiller* in 1948, Gilson was interested in all political and diplomatic
issues. Very early in the year his friend Jacques Maritain told him he was about to
leave the diplomatic service and return to teaching. Gilson regretted this move
and felt that, as French ambassador to the Holy See, Maritain had been valuable
to the church and to France; just this past year Maritain had headed the French
delegation and delivered the *discours d'ouverture* at the Second International
Conference of UNESCO in Mexico City.

Gilson would have liked such a strong intellectual, if he had to leave diplomatic
circles, to enter the French educational system. He offered to support Maritain's
candidature for the Collège de France but was turned down. Princeton had
already made an offer and Maritain, who had consistently steered clear of the
French educational network, found this privately-supported chair more attractive.
Gilson wrote cryptically to Pegis that "Maritain is not going to the Collège de
France but to Princeton. Wild ducks don't make such mistakes." (48.3.26.) He did
however see a useful side to Maritain's error: "J. Maritain will certainly come to
Toronto, that is, given the proper incentive [a decent honorarium], and barring all
opposition on the Princeton side" (48.6.25).

While Maritain the intellectual moved away from the detail of ecclesiastical
business, Gilson moved toward it. The director of the Secretariat of the French
Episcopacy, Mgr Henri Chappoulie, issued an appeal for help from the laity in
handling church problems. Gilson's response was a letter to Cardinals Suhard and
Liénart expressing his filial attachment to the church and offering to share with
them whatever intellectual experience and competence he had. This letter was
read to the Assembly of the Cardinals and Archbishops of France. Gilson received
a formal reply from Chappoulie, which both cardinals signed, informing him
that the episcopate's present problem was the recruiting of diocesan clergy;
Chappoulie asked that Catholic intellectuals generally promote a positive image of
the priesthood. A few days later, Emmanuel Cardinal Suhard replied personally,
and more to the point:

> I am particularly interested in the judgment you bring to bear by the very reason of your indisputable competence in the domain of Catholic thought, and on thought *tout court* (47.3.30).

Suhard went on to suggest that, in their various fields of knowledge, Catholic intellectuals could be of considerable value to the Catholic hierarchy.

The next year accordingly found Gilson giving one of the major talks at the renewed series of Semaines des Intellectuels Catholiques. Paul Claudel presided over the opening session on Sunday April 11, Cardinal Suhard over the closing one on April 18. Each night had its own theme; on the first night this was "Les intellectuels devant la charité du Christ" and on the last "Les intellectuels et la paix." * This final night had an international flavour. Robert Speaight (represented by Jacques Herissay) spoke first and Romano Guardini, the first German to speak publicly in Paris since the war, spoke second. Gilson spoke third and last.

Gilson's address on the topic "Intellectuals and Peace" examined peace in terms of the Nietzschian atheism that permeates the thought of Jean-Paul Sartre; for Sartre existentialism was the will to extract the necessary consequences from a coherent atheism. Gilson used his own historical method to draw a comparison between the outlook of men of 948 who were expecting the Antichrist and of men in 1948 who have been told there is no God. If there is no God, as Dostoevski had Karamazov say, then everything is permitted. The terrors of the year 2000 would become a dominant theme for Gilson over the next few years.**

In the following year Gilson remained enthusiastic about this kind of collaboration with the episcopate. He took two of his young Toronto colleagues, Maurer and Shook, who were on sabbatical, to sessions of the Semaine. This time Gilson spoke only from the floor, although he talked and felt like a cofounder of the Semaines, he did not play an important part in them every year.

In the 1949 Semaine, Gilson presided over the meeting of Monday 9 May addressed by Etienne Borne, Henri Gouhier and Aimé Forest on the "Situation des philosophies actuelles devant la foi." In his summation he commented on the extraordinary changes that had taken place in Christian philosophy since St Augustine, and on the corresponding constancy of that philosophy's dedication to the wisdom of Christ even in the revolutionary renewal of Thomas Aquinas: "It is still ours to create, certainly, and to invent, but we must conserve too."

During the first half of 1948 Gilson also became involved in more secular intellectual activities. He attended the meeting of the Congress of Europe, 7 to 10 May in the Riddezaal square of The Hague. The objective of the congress was to plan for a united Europe, an idea which went back to Alexis de Toqueville and was gaining new urgency for Europe in the Cold War; the European Union of

---

* For the text of all addresses see Pierre Horay, ed., *Semaine des intellectuels catholiques* (Paris, 1948).

** See *The Terrors of the Year Two Thousand* (Toronto, 1949; McG 148) and "Les terreurs de l'an deux mille," in *La revue* (2 [1949]: 193-206; McG 149) and in *Revue de l'Université d'Ottawa* (19 [1949]: 67-81).

Federalists, headed by H. Brugmans, had taken up the idea and a loose type of congress had been called to look into the matter. Various European nations were represented by informal groups without firm delegation from their respective governments.

Some thousand persons gathered at The Hague, about a hundred of them from France; these hundred Frenchmen, of whom Gilson was one, never actually met together before, during or after the congress. Among those assembled were men of considerable political, economic and intellectual stature, and in the foreground with Brugmans were Winston Churchill, Henri Spaak and Henri Ramadier. Gilson described the meeting in an article for the Paris paper *"Une semaine dans le monde"* (48.5.15) and in a typescript to be found in his files, "Existe-t-il une culture européenne," written during 1950.

Gilson's description of the congress in The Hague begins with his departure from Paris on 6 May and his trip north across Belgium into Holland. Since the group had no diplomatic status, its members had to pass through the regular customs and immigration bureaus, spending longer in the stations of Esschen and Rosendael than in travelling from Paris to the Belgian border. This *colossale brimade* reminded the *congressists* of the absurdity of European travelling conditions and fueled their desire for a united Europe.

The congress worked in three large committees, economic, political and cultural. Members attended the committee of their choice, and the big names attended the political one. Gilson joined the smallest of the three, the cultural committee, with such *seigneurs de moindre importance* as Salvador de Madariaga, Denis de Rougemont and Charles Morgan. They called their committe *Cendrillon*, the Cinderella section, with its writers and professors "who could have nothing of practical importance to say."

Of the three committees, the one on economics proved the most boisterous as liberals, socialists and trade unionists squared off on such intricate questions as tariff reduction and the relative importance of monetary and industrial unification. The political committee was best attended while it tried to determine whether members of the European federation would have to give up any of their powers and whether there should be a common parliament. One particularly thorny issue was whether deputies to the federation's parliament should be appointed by the various governments or elected directly by the people. Paul Reynaud moved in favour of direct election and Gilson agreed: his experience in the Canadian federation had shown him that people often elected one party to govern their province and another for the country at large, a dualism he found salutary. Nonetheless, British opposition to direct election prevailed and the Congress of The Hague recommended that deputies be named by national parliaments. For Gilson, this "was the only mistake made by the congress, but it was a serious one."

Gilson's position on the cultural committee was a careful one that shied away from simplification. He had always been impressed by the importance of European culture, and the same concern that had produced his early articles for

L'européen still continued in articles for *Le monde.* * Gilson was reluctant, however, to draw a line around European culture. For him culture in Europe had several sources, many of them Eastern. It had also been continued in countless ways in other parts of the world, such as America and Russia, and it belonged wherever it manifested itself. In his typescript essay he wrote:

> The notion of "culture européenne" is a false window. A Europe politically and economically united could become a reality as distinct as the USA. Everything in it would be European, except its culture. ... Europe's sole task in this domain is to work from its side to keep the intellectual culture of the world alive. (p. 7.)

Gilson reiterated this position in June 1948 at the time of the *Congrès mondial des intellectuels pour la paix* held in Wrocław (formerly Breslau), Poland, in an article called "Un lever de rideau" (*Le monde*, 48.6.10; McG 699); and again, when a similar assembly was held in Lausanne. He referred to his position once more in 1949 when the First International Congress of the European Movement was called to the Brussels Palais des Académies in February; this article was entitled "Cendrillon" (*Le monde*, 49.2.20-21; McG 580).

Whatever his reservations culturally, Gilson stood firmly in favour of European federation and was distressed by apparent indifference on the part of France. He insisted that federation was less a choice than a necessity, and urged his readers to realize that the idea had originally been a French one: "As the Belgian member, M. Bohy, so generously pointed out, the project of a European federation is a French idea. Will we, who conceived it first, be the last to turn it into a reality?" (*Une semaine*, 48.5.15, p. 2; tr.)

9 L'ÊTRE ET L'ESSENCE

Gilson's activities as an intellectual also had their less public aspect during the late 1940s. In 1948 he completed *L'être et l'essence* (Paris, 1948; McG 42) which remains one of his best historical and philosophical studies. Its ten chapters trace the rise and decline of metaphysics and conclude with a plea for its resurrection. Gilson had devoted a good deal of his time during the later war years preparing this book. His shorter articles during this time had largely been attempts to clarify his own mind on points of metaphysics.

The epigraph chosen by Gilson for *L'être et l'essence* announces the book's theme with devastating concision: "Reason has only one way of explaining what does not come from itself: it is to reduce it to nothingness." **

In his introduction, "Le vocabulaire de l'être," Gilson then points out the main problems currently besetting metaphysics. First, its function as the science of primary reality has often been usurped by other less general and less basic sciences. Second, the object of metaphysics, the study of being as being, cannot

---

* See for example "Pour la culture européenne," *Le monde*, 48.4.1; McG 756.
** This was taken from E. Meyerson, *La déduction relativiste* [Paris, 1925], p. 258; tr.

be conceptualized, and few modern philosophies can operate without concepts. And finally, metaphysics requires a more rigid semantic control than modern languages seem able to provide. Gilson notes that he would have liked to call his work on metaphysics "L'être et l'existence," a title that had been pre-empted by Kirkegaard and others. He has settled on his present title because it is the French form of the title of an important little work by St Thomas, *De ente et essentia*. Gilson cautions his readers that the *être* of his title is sometimes a noun, sometimes a verb, depending on the context. The *essence* is also used in a specialized sense to mean "essence as concretely actualized by *esse*." Gilson's *essence* is always either *un être* ou *l'acte d'être*, a being or the act of being.

In the book's first chapter, "L'être et l'un," Gilson examines three Greek philosophers, Parmenides, Plato and Plotinus. Parmenides was the first to reduce the world, not to one of the elements, but to being. Plato refined the use of *being* to mean "reality in itself" and first included ideas among the real. Plato's ontology was not limited to beings in Parmenides' sense, but extended beyond the real to essences in general, including artistic creations; as Gilson points out, even Mrs Gamp and Tartuffe exist as types. Plotinus' world, like Plato's was a world of knowledge. Thinking engenders an object, and an object is thinkable. This sequence, from Parmenides to Plato to Plotinus, offers an idealism – all is within the life of the mind.

Gilson's second chapter "L'être et la substance," is given over to Aristotle, Averroës, Avicenna and Siger of Brabant. Their view rejects ideas in the platonic sense and designates as substances only things that actually exist. It groups the things that are, and studies them as sciences. These thinkers developed the science of ontology as handed on to the late Middle Ages; theirs was a substantialist ontology.

The key chapter of *L'être et l'essence* is the third, "L'être et l'existence." It is devoted mainly to the differences between the science of ontology as defined by Aristotle and that developed by Thomas. Because this science of ontology deals mainly with first causes, it was sometimes called *prima philosophia*, first philosophy. It was also called "metaphysics" because investigators, in their search for the causes of effects, were forced to search beyond the physical and sensible. This chapter is rich in texts from Thomas and Aristotle, and its unravelling of their meanings is beyond summary.

Throughout the remaining chapters of the book, Gilson provides a dictionary of the problems that have beset metaphysics from the thirteenth to the twentieth centuries. The work was well received, and Gilson later considered it his finest. In 1949 his English version of *L'être et l'essence* was published as *Being and Some Philosophers* (Toronto, 1949; McG 3); this was not a translation but it presented much of the same material.

In the fall of 1948 Gilson also published what would become the first chapter of his book on Duns Scotus as "L'objet de la métaphysique selon Duns Scot" (*Mediaeval Studies*, 10 [1948]: 21-92; McG 371); this committed him irrevocably to completing the project. In the spring of 1949 he made a short trip from Paris to

Toronto for a meeting of the Mediaeval Academy. This was the first annual meeting the academy had ever planned outside of Massachusetts, and Pegis had insisted that Gilson read a paper. Although Gilson had demurred at first, he delivered a paper on Saturday morning, 9 April, entitled "Doctrinal History and Its Interpretation," (*Speculum*, 24 [1949]: 483-492; McG 256).

Meanwhile Thérèse was both sad and failing:

> Thérèse speaks to me more about others than herself. I know she is sad to have two daughters, neither married, and that she is in love with Bernard. I share her chagrin [as to their daughters] and am not jealous of Bernard, who will be the great consolation of her old age. She is now dividing her time between Paris and Vermenton, which the car makes easy; but I think she will soon be closing Vermenton for the winter and returning the Parisian piano. (EG to Mme Thibaudeau, 48.11.6; tr.)

Gilson hoped Thérèse would accompany him to Toronto in 1949. He suspected, however, that her insistence upon the difficulties of travel arrangements was an attempt to conceal her deep-seated illness.

When Gilson arrived in Toronto in September 1949, he was alone. He had lined up several outside talks but gave only one of them, which had been promised St Thomas More College of Saskatoon a full year before. He went to Saskatoon earlier than proposed so that he could make the trip west with the superior of St Michael's, who was attending the installation of a new president at the University of Saskatchewan. This meant that Gilson would be speaking in Saskatoon on the day of the installation, and some – including Dean Francis Leddy and Father Paul Mallon – thought the conflict inappropriate. Gilson agreed to lecture in the morning and to attend the installation in the afternoon as a delegate of the University of Paris and of the Académie. In the end he gave two talks: one on Friday night in the Catholic College on "Thomas More and the Law;" and the second on Saturday morning in the university on "Politics and Philosophy."

The address on "Politics and Philosophy" takes as its topic the freedom of the intellectual to speak his own mind. Gilson questions whether we actually possess such freedom. Currently, scepticism in philosophy is thought to be the only position consonant with liberalism and democracy in politics. Gilson argues however that "there is no necessary connection between philosophical dogmatism and political tyranny, any more than between philosophical scepticism and political liberty." Indeed, only those who hold something as true are in a position to be tolerant; sceptics cannot be tolerant, only permissive. Moreover, "tolerance is a moral virtue, not an intellectual one; it is founded on what Aristotle called the two moral virtues of political life – justice and friendship." Our only duty toward ideas is to seek truth for its own sake; tolerance and intolerance simply do not apply to the order of ideas, but to the order of politics. Thus, concludes Gilson, if we want to keep our countries safe for democracy, we don't need less philosophical dogmatism but more.

When Gilson returned to Toronto immediately after the lecture, he left behind him a campus controversy. Some students objected to linking tolerance with dogma, intolerance with scepticism. One of them, H. F. Jones, later leader of the Conservative party in Saskatchewan, dismissed Gilson's lecture as "philosophical fun" and argued that political dogmatism had led to Spanish inquisitions and St Bartholomew's Day massacres. He was answered editorially by Blair Neatby and James McConica, who pointed out that Gilson was speaking as a philosopher. Philosophical dogmatism simply held for the basic truth of things, and was an intellectual virtue in the Aristotelian sense producing clear and hardheaded thinking. Justice and friendship were another issue entirely. (See *The Sheaf*, University of Saskatchewan, 49.10.10-14.) Gilson later repeated his lecture in a somewhat more polished form at Rutgers University and elsewhere, and published it under the title *Dogmatism and Tolerance* (New Brunswick, N.J., 1952; McG 22).

10 THE DEATH OF THÉRÈSE, 1949

Over the years Thérèse had become accustomed to Gilson's absences in North America and elsewhere. She saw them as annoyances to be endured for the sake of her husband's career, respites from the tensions which were the product of his genius, and occasions when she could completely own herself and her family. It is not always easy to be the wife of a philosopher: he is too often aware of Francis Bacon's adage that "he who hath a wife and children hath already given hostages to fortune." Some of Gilson's close friends still remember him standing on the porch of his house on Elmsley Place in Toronto with a taxi waiting while Thérèse bundled up Bernard inside; he envied aloud the carefree lives of his priest-friends and muttered to all and sundry that "Cicero was right – a philosopher should never marry." Thérèse was no doubt used to such tantrums and quite up to handling them – if anything she was more French than he was, as she had no Viking blood in her veins.

Thérèse could never be at home in a foreign country. Like her daughter Jacqueline, she refused to become a linguist, and compensated with a beautiful patient French articulation which any foreigner could understand. She liked little trips to almost anywhere, provided they were only vacations, but she could never accept Canada as another home. She went there for vacations a few times before the war, never after it; when perfect accommodations by ship were unavailable in 1947 and 1948, she remained behind.

If in her later years Thérèse sometimes gave the impression of hypochondria, it was because she was in fact unwell. In those years, each time her husband left home she was afraid she would not be alive to receive him back. Gilson had some sense of her suffering. When during the fall of 1948 Mme Thibaudeau wrote of her lumbago, he replied that he too suffered from the disease. But "when it afflicts me, I think of Thérèse who suffers almost continual rheumatic pains – hers is a true martyrdom (48.11.6). Gilson knew that Thérèse's real illness was leukemia, and that he was going to lose her; hence his desire to take her with him to Toronto in 1947 and 1948, and his reluctance to attend the meeting of the Mediaeval Academy in 1949.

Gilson and Thérèse did manage to take three leisurely trips together in the spring and summer of 1949. Between 10 May and 17 June they spent over a month in Spain visiting Jacqueline, who was again in Madrid on an extended bursary. Gilson had received a government-approved invitation to lecture in philosophy; he reported drily to Pegis that "Catholicism has now replaced racism as the official language in the Spanish state. You can guess the rest." (49.6.25.) In July Gilson took Thérèse with him to the fêtes at Cluny held to celebrate the anniversaries of Saints Odo and Odilon (see above, p. 245 n.). And in August Gilson received a surprise invitation to serve as a judge in the Cannes Film Festival, 2 to 17 September, just before leaving for Toronto:

> What could I do? My wife is quite in favour of those two weeks at the Carlton, the more so as she will not have to see the [sixty] films. I suspect she does not trust me completely, in spite of my old age, in a city where my vote can mean so much to stars or starlets of all creeds and nations. (EG to Pegis, 49.8.24.)

The trip to Cannes was enjoyable, but the hectic pace took its toll: "We passed fifteen very agreeable days in Cannes, but in a distracting social excitement which was not very good for Thérèse, nor for me either, for that matter" (49.8.24). Of the winning films that year at Cannes, only Carol Reed's *The Third Man* endures in its appeal.

In the fall of 1949 Gilson left France for Toronto once more alone. He left Thérèse in bad health and wrote to Madame Thibaudeau:

> I give you her exact words: "I no longer have any desire to go to America, save for one thing, to see the Thibaudeau women again and to spend some days with them." But her entire system is truly impaired, and I think her condition serious. My only reason for doubting this is that her doctors seem to think it is not serious right now. I would be reassured if only people who live together in intimacy didn't sometimes know such things better than the doctors do. (49.8.24.)

Despite this strain Gilson carried on in his usual manner. He gave two courses, one on the "Applications of *Esse* in St Thomas," the other on "The Seventh *Quodlibetal* Question of Duns Scotus." He also prepared his lectures for Montréal, Notre Dame and, this year, for St Thomas More College in Saskatchewan (above, pp. 289-290). Because he went there early, this last was the only commitment he had time to keep. Shortly after returning from Saskatoon to Toronto, he received bad news from Paris and wrote Phelan immediately to cancel his lectures at Notre Dame:

> I have just received a cable from Paris, signed by my children, and telling me that my wife is dangerously ill. Their exact expression is "maladie aiguë." They add that the doctor advises me to come back "très rapidement." I will therefore leave Toronto tomorrow and fly back to Paris via New York. (49.10.20.)

Thérèse was still alive when Gilson reached Paris. There was even an outside hope that her life could be saved, if thrombocytes could be obtained. He wrote Pegis an urgent letter on 4 November:

> What we cannot get is the drug I have asked for and which I have even been asked to bring back from Canada, namely *an American* (i.e., made in the USA) *injectable extract of blood platelets*, alias *thrombocytes*. Nobody here can give us the brands of this drug. Our doctor knows that it exists in America, but does not know the American name. I imagine that Lederle makes it, but I don't know. Yesterday I mailed two requests, one to Dan Walsh the other to John Nef. If I fail with them I will write to my friend the wife of the Canadian consul in Boston, Mrs. P. Beaulieu. Just now we need this very badly and no substitute. *Only blood platelets* could help in stopping this dreadful bleeding. We have a blood transfusion every other day. (49.11.4.)

At five-thirty on the morning of 12 November, surrounded by her family, Thérèse died. She had received Holy Communion the same day. "All that could be done," Gilson wrote Phelan, "has been done. Jacqueline and Cécile have been admirable and Bernard is very courageous. But I am a wreck. This is an innermost devastation. I accept everything, but there is much to be accepted. Thérèse had a great affection for you. I know she will have your prayers." (49.11.12.)

Thérèse had been everything to Gilson – his dear companion, his eager student, his *chouchette*, his *femette*, the mother of his children, the manager of his household. They had loved one another deeply and irrevocably. Two weeks after her death Gilson wrote Pegis:

> I am writing to you from the new desert and wasteland wherein I now have to live, but don't imagine that such affection as yours brings me no comfort. With prayer, *amicitia* is the only consolation. ... Common tragedy *is* tragedy. And now, the best I can do is to say nothing more about it. Deep sorrow is a slow discovery and one feels ashamed to discover it at sixty-six, while it is as commonplace, but as important, as the sun and the moon or day and night. (49.11.26.)

15

A Year of Depression, 1950-1951

1 CONTINUING POLITICS

After the death of Thérèse, Gilson entered a deep depression. He found the prospect of a lonely future unbearably bleak. To make matters worse, he was becoming increasingly estranged from Bernard. Since childhood, Bernard had been troubled by occasional bouts of emotional instability; these had served to aggravate the tensions that normally underlie relationships between fathers and sons. Gilson blamed himself for Bernard's illness, and regretted his long absences from home when Bernard was a child. Gilson also blamed his own shortcomings as a father for the fact that his daughters, now nearing forty, were not married – as a Frenchman, he considered unmarried daughters to represent a parental failure.

During this time Gilson did manage to find some distraction in work. The book on Duns Scotus was nearing completion and, because he had left Toronto early to be with Thérèse, he was able to teach at the Collège de France as soon as it opened in December. Early in January 1950 he attended a philosophical conference in Lausanne, then rushed back to Paris to address a regional rally in the fifteenth *arrondissment* for the MRP.

This address, which survives unpublished, was on the assigned topic of "Political Liberty and the Parties." Some political parties in France, and especially the communist party, expected blind loyalty from all their deputies.* Parties often forced the resignation of a difficult member, assigning his seat to the next person on the priority list. Gilson considered this kind of action an infringement both on the rights of the deputies and those of the electorate. He applauded the MRP's respect for the liberty of its deputies, even at the risk of seeming over-idealistic.

According to Gilson, the programme of the *Mouvement Républicain Populaire*, a movement rather than a party, would regard the family, and never the political party, as the true core of any social organization in France. The MRP would only nationalize industry where normal production and distribution called for it, never on principle. It would only support unions whose objectives were authentically

---

* Deputies are those representatives in the French Assembly elected by proportion rather than *nominatim*.

revolutionary, rather than anarchical or marxist. And it would treat every French citizen as a moral individual with intellect, will and power of choice, not merely a registered number. Under such a programme there would be no state religion, no official philosophy or science, and no discrimination in the realm of teaching.

Questions came from the floor: What is a deputy's course where political action is contrary to the moral law? Are there not too many elected representatives of the people? Why did M. Gilson call monarchists "historical paleontologists" and Charles Maurras [of Action Française] a "traitor"? Why did he accuse Maurras of advising collaboration? M. Calzan, a disciple of Maurras, came armed with the previous day's *Le monde* in which an article had appeared by Gilson on "1940 to 1950" (50.1.14; McG 717). Calzan had been enraged by the piece. We monarchists, he cried, are not fossils, we are very much alive! And Maurras never advised collaboration! How can Gilson call the MRP the defender of the *école libre* when the *école libre* is being allowed to collapse? And why did Gilson criticize the Marshall plan?

In reply to the charge that he had maligned Maurras, Gilson rose rhetorically to his own defence:

> [Gilson:] You complain that I call Maurras a collaborator. When I use such an expression, I am sure to have the text before me – an old habit whether I happen to be talking about the twentieth or the thirteenth century. What I said came from *La France seule*, written by Charles Maurras and published in 1941 by Librairie Ardenché, Lyon. I was using the sixty-fourth edition.
>
> [Calzan:] May I tell you, Monsieur, with the same praiseworthy care for exactitude as you manifest, that this book is called *La seule France*, not *La France seule*.
>
> [Gilson:] I hope then you will be able to rearrange my quotation from the text which you are about to hear, because I don't flatter myself that I can recite it exactly from memory. It was not part of my preparation for this lecture. What Charles Maurras said (and he was perfectly within his rights, the question being simply to know whether he said it or not) was, according to Montoire: "The Marshall [Pétain] decided he had to collaborate with Germany. Do we refuse him? No. Do we acquiesce? No. Do we accept? No. We do it *without discussion*."
>
> [Calzan:] We follow the Marshall *without discussion*, and you write in *Le Monde* – I have it with me, because I too keep my texts in front of me – that we have advised collaboration. Nothing could be more false.
>
> [Gilson:] You haven't advised collaboration, you have simply advised following the Marshall without discussion in his decision to collaborate.
>
> [Calzan:] In all his decisions.
>
> [Gilson:] Including this one. The case is historical. It's simply a matter here of knowing whether I invented it. No, I did not invent it.

Clearly, Gilson's politics had forced him to stand well outside the ivory tower of learning.

As Calzan's anger made clear, Gilson's political articles in *Le monde* were making their point. In them he regularly challenged statements by the American secretary of state, by government ministers and by leading senators, and he operated like the better American columnists, James Reston, Walter Lippman, and his old friend and admirer of the 1930s, Dorothy Thompson. Gilson was read for his clarity, precision and innuendo, and held a strong influence over those who took their politics from *Le monde*. Brisson and the staff of *Le Figaro* disagreed with him, and Maurras and the monarchists detested him.

Gilson's articles reflected his personal conviction that a high level of self-interest governed American foreign policies, and that the same self-interest dominated Europeans who reached out to America for credit and pacts. Alignment, he thought, with either Russia or America must lead directly to war; France would be invaded and subdued in a week and her people crushed as never before. Gilson feared for France, and feared for his family. Indeed fear was the thrust of his every statement until he began to see some hope in a politic of neutralism.

Gilson's first articles in defence of neutralism pointed out the weakness of those moral arguments that viewed neutralism as a shameful form of cowardice, a defeatism; he also argued against those who believed neutralism wouldn't work because Russia wouldn't respect it. Gilson maintained that neutralism was no more cowardly than the braggadocio of Cyrano de Bergerac's "I fight, I fight, I fight" was brave; nor was neutralism shameful because *neutre* happened to rhyme with *peutre*. Countries like Switzerland and Sweden did not consider neutrality the least bit unrespectable. Moreover neutrality demands neither disarmament nor defeatism, and involves no rejection of national responsibility. Victors in war never win anyway: as Frank Monaghan points out in his history of the Second World War, "For each dollar of reparation paid by Germany to France and England, Germany received two dollars from the USA." It is all very well for the British to say "Give us the arms and we will finish the job," but in sober afterviews "les morts sont morts; les survivants doivent payer les armes." The moral victor in a war emerges at best as a gallant cripple. (*Le monde*, 50.4.28). And, as to whether Russia would violate France's neutrality, she did not violate the neutrality of Japan in 1941; indeed, Russia's will to complete the Soviet revolution might well rule out aggression from her.

Gilson's positions in April 1950 were not very far from those of Erasmus. They were shared by many of Gilson's fellow veterans who had experienced both war and prison, and they reflected also the *cui bono* mood of a man who had lately lost his wife. Politics like philosophy may try to appeal to reason alone, but perspectives spring from the whole being.

Several objections were raised to Gilson's arguments when they appeared. The secretary-general of the French Ministry of Foreign Affairs wrote to him the day after one of his articles was printed, pointing out the weakness of his statements: Russia was too busy elsewhere in 1941 to take action against Japan, and Russia's policy could hardly be presented as in any sense *pacifique* because she had in a single given circumstance not gone to war (50.4.28). Also on 5 May, an apologetic editorial in *Le monde* cautiously dissociated the politics of the paper from that of its contributors. But many other readers agreed with Gilson. Walter Gyssling, for example, sent him a copy of his own "Atlantische Union oder Neutralität" from the *Tages-Anzeiger* of Zurich, which took a position like Gilson's: "You are," Gyssling wrote in an accompanying letter, "a thousand times right!" Gilson also received a thoughtful response from his old Harvard friend, Ralph Barton Perry, who was feeling the weight of American McCarthyism:

> It has been a long time ... since I have heard from you or written you. The recent extracts published in the *New York Times* ... furnish me an incentive! If the ... articles had been unsigned I would have guessed that they were by you, remembering the last conversation we had in 1938 or 1939. My only improvement on your proposals would be to have *all* countries become neutral. We have suffered serious physical damage from war. But wars, and the last continuing war, have greatly injured our political, social and cultural life. We are living in a kind of reign of terror imposed by anticommunism which is almost as terrifying and repressive as communism. (50.5.4.)

Meanwhile the Atlantic Pact was ratified. Although to Gilson's dismay, America offered no assurances that it would prevent another invasion of France, the pact together with the American army of occupation in Germany was thought to offer assurance enough. The Russians would not now attack and, in the stalemate that followed, Gilson found himself strategically and uncomfortably aligned with French communism and its leader, M. Thorez. As Gilson wrote Pegis, "I am not very popular with your [American] administration. I have written three papers on the possibility of a European neutrality in case of war. So I have become (1) a crypto-communist, and (2) anti-American. Yes sir. Me. In person! Wonders will never cease!" (50.6.1; letter 1). These three papers belonged to a series entitled "En marge des négociations atlantiques" and appeared in *Le monde*, 28 to 30 April 1950, under the headings "Défaitisme et neutralité" (McG 636), "La neutralité vers l'est" (McG 637), and "La neutralité vers l'ouest" (McG 638).

2 Preparation for the September Congresses

All spring and summer of 1950 Gilson had on his mind two important congresses – the *Congressus scholasticus internationalis* and the *Congressus thomisticus internationalis* – to be held in Rome in September. The congress on modern scholasticism had been conceived by the eminent Francisan scholar, Père Carlo Balić, *rector magnificus* of the Collegio Antoniano and world authority on Duns Scotus. Balić was a good friend of Gilson's and had made many attempts to turn him into a scotist against his will; Gilson considered Balić "straight, perfectly honest, sincerely friendly, and a great scholar" (EG to Pegis, 50.8.22). The thomist congress was the third in a recurring series held under the auspices of the Pontifical Academy of St Thomas Aquinas. This year it would take place under the presidency of Charles Boyer SJ who, along with Père Garrigou-Lagrange, formed the backbone of the Holy Office; though Boyer was feared and generally unloved, he was a bulwark of the Holy See.

In his present depression Gilson dreaded attending these congresses. At one stage in January he decided not to go, though he insisted that Pegis be there as president of the Toronto Institute. By March Gilson had become reconciled to attending as well, and both men began to prepare their papers. By June they had settled on their subjects. At the scholastic conference Gilson would speak twice, and once privately to Franciscan professors. His papers would be: "Duns Scotus in the Light of Critical History," "Critical-Historical Research and the Future of Scholasticism," and "The Prologues of the *Opus Oxoniense*." At the thomist congress he would speak once on "La preuve du *De ente et essentia*." Pegis would speak on "Matthew of Aquasparta and the Cognition of Non-being" for Balić, and would explore intellectual nature and final causality for Boyer.

The spring of 1950 was otherwise unencumbered. At sixty-six and alone in Paris, Gilson began to long for his retirement. He wrote Pegis that he might discontinue his courses at the Collège de France in early 1951, which he was now entitled to do: "I don't know but I am thinking about it. Paris is now meaningless to me. I am craving for peace. But is not the very idea of peace a laughable one for any man now to entertain." (50.2.24.) He also found himself resisting pressure from Balić to get involved in the movement to have Duns Scotus canonized:

> I am now reading the consultation of the Roman congregation on the possible canonization of Duns Scotus. It is a theological libel, just garbage. Personally I wholly disagree with Duns Scotus. His is a climate of thought in which I cannot live. But I cannot understand what there is against him from the point of view of faith. Not even of ethics. The trouble is that scotists are, in their controversies, no more honest than the thomists. (EG to Pegis, 50.2.25.)

In the spring of 1950 Gilson's old adversary, Fernand Van Steenberghen, paid him a visit at Vermenton. (See above, pp. 190-191.) Van Steenberghen was setting out on an extensive tour of North America which was to include both Toronto and Notre Dame. He was worried – as Gilson himself had been years ago – about his spoken English. Gilson wrote Pegis and Phelan encouraging them to be helpful and receptive to the distinguished professor from Louvain who had done so much for philosophy. To Phelan he wrote:

> Van Steenberghen is a saintly priest, a hard worker and a very great scholar. He has a literal mind ... out for scientific demonstrations and clarification in a field where they don't work. The main trouble is that the Lovanienses have turned the formal distinction between philosophy (*in divinis*) and theology into a practical separation. (50.5.22.)

And later to Pegis:

> I am glad to know that Father Van Steenberghen's visit turned out to be a good thing. As for his own philosophical ideas, they are indeed fantastic. Tony, let me tell you something: the *only* chance for a Catholic to be a great philosopher is to be, above all, a theologian. This is what I am going to tell them in Rome; and very few will like it. (50.6.1; letter 1.)

Gilson's course in the Collège de France continued into March, and was followed by a trip to Sweden from 12 March to 2 April to deliver a series of eight lectures on St Augustine. He then withdrew to Vermenton to rest and recover from his depression. His daughters, who had preceded him to the country house, were also in need of a rest, especially Cécile who had borne the strenuous burden of nursing Thérèse through her final illness. Gilson was beginning to worry about financing his two residences, as death duties had cut deeply into his capital. Eventually he was to sell his large home on Émile Accolas and take a smaller one with Jacqueline on rue St Romain; he would also exchange his place in Vermenton for the little cottage his mother had left him in Cravant.

During this year's rather longer stay in Vermenton, Gilson limited himself to preparing his papers for Rome and giving thought to his duties as director of studies in Toronto. Things were going well at the Institute; as Pegis grew into his role of president, the faculty and student populations continued to flourish. A young Basilian, Ambrose Raftis, had just completed his doctorate in economics at Laval and had been approached to join the Institute as a professor of medieval economics after working for a time in the field under M. M. Postan at Cambridge University. Gilson was pleased and wrote Pegis enthusiastically: "As to your young man, the history of medieval economics would be a wonderful and promising field. They do it well in England, better I think than in France. This would be very good for the future of the Institute." (50.6.1.)

By August, as the congresses grew near, Gilson's depression had lifted somewhat and his high humour had begun to return. He decided to take Bernard with him to Rome, where the three of them would stay with the Franciscans at Cara Pax. His advice to Tony Pegis was affectionately mocking; Pegis revelled in raising questions beforehand, and was travelling to Rome for the first time:

> 1 (a) Don't bring any chocolate for us in Rome. ... The heat is that of New York in August. (b) Custom duties we ... pay, first in Rome, second in Paris.
> 2 A taxicab from Rome airport will be throatcutting. ... Use the airport bus – if there is one. Stick your money as deep inside as you possibly can, short of eating it. ... All you can pay for ahead in time, ... tickets, bus fares from and back to the terminal, ... will be a positive gain.
> 3 I am trying to get you a room.
> 4 As a gift to Father Balić, I would not risk Teacher's Highland Cream. I don't know that he likes it ... or would be allowed to drink it. ... Custom duties [are] likely to double the price of the bottle. ... I would suggest one or two volumes of the Institute's publications.
> 5 As to seeing the Holy Father, I suppose the letter from the cardinal will have some weight, but you had better phone at once to Alec Sampson, who knows the ropes. He will get ... *the* right letter.

3 THE SEPTEMBER CONGRESSES, 1950

Gilson went to Rome intent on making two points. He intended to show that scholastic philosophies had grown out of medieval theologies. He would also argue that Thomas' perceptive philosophizing *in divinis* had created a unique metaphysics, well worth mastering if scholasticism were to go on developing in an authentic, healthy tradition.

"Les recherches historico-critiques et l'avenir de la scholastique" was first published in *Acta Congressus Scholastici Internationalis Romae Anno Sancto MCML Celebrati* ([Rome, 1951], pp. 131-142; McG 419); it also appeared in Gilson's own adapted English version as "Historical Research and the Future of Scholasticism" in *The Modern Schoolman* (29 [1951]: 1-10; McG 420). Gilson argues that true scholastic philosophy must always be, as it was in the Middle Ages, an attempt to integrate acquisitions made by science and philosophy in order to correct and purify them. Scholasticism must not claim to be what *de facto* it is not, a philosophy in its own right functioning apart from theology: "scholastic philosophy must return to theology."

To defend his position, Gilson uses dogmatic as well as historical arguments. Theology "corrected Aristotle" so effectively during the Middle Ages that it generated a new metaphysics of being, one not only different from Aristotle's but also more philosophically tenable. Theology achieved this by turning the light of revelation on the "first philosophy" of the ancients. Gilson concludes that the ongoing role of theology must be to continue turning the light of revelation on the transitory achievements of science, whether science in its constantly changing modern senses, or science as metaphysics.

Gilson's analysis was offensive to many scholastic philosophers because it argued that they must be theologically inspired in order to be valid. Gilson knew that his paper would be devastating; and even before delivering it he had described it as "an H-bomb, but it came to me" (EG to Pegis, 50.6.1; letter 1). Gilson's own thomism would henceforth be dominated by this view of the role of scholastic philosophy as a "handmaid" to theology.

When Phelan read Gilson's argument, he was also annoyed, particularly by the implication that philosophy could not be learned from a theologian:

> I do not like what you have written in *The Modern Schoolman*. This is the first time in my life that I have not been able to say to my students: "Read what Gilson has written in his most recent article!" ... I ask you: How is a philosopher to be a good philosopher if he does not learn philosophy through history? Can he not learn philosophy from theologians? Theologians have learned theology from the Fathers who were not "theologians" but commentators on Holy Scripture. (51.11.2.)

The second of the September congresses, the Congressus Thomisticus, lay largely in the hands of two powerful members of the Holy Office, Père Garrigou-Lagrange OP and Père Charles Boyer SJ. These men were generally thought to have authored the encyclical *Humani generis* which Pope Pius XII had released only a few days before the congresses. Although by no means a *Syllabus of Errors*, the recent encyclical had mentioned certain theological "aberrations." Scholars present for the congresses suspected that the Congressus Thomisticus might be used to promulgate the encyclical, perhaps at the expense of their liberty of discussion.

According to Fernand Van Steenberghen, the first of two tense episodes took place after the closing session of the scholastic congress. A number of participants – Van Steenberghen himself, Gilson, De Raeymaeker, and others – were standing and talking when Garrigou-Lagrange approached them and hailed Gilson:

> Ah, my dear Gilson! I am going to attack you on Monday morning when the thomistic congress opens. You have spoken in your recent book, *L'être et l'essence*, about the metamorphosis of metaphysics. It is very dangerous to talk about the metamorphosis of metaphysics. It is as if metaphysics is not always the same, as if the eternal truths themselves change.

Gilson, no doubt thinking back to Chenu, was not amused and replied sharply: "Mon père, if you do that, I will leave the congress and return to Paris the same day." Garrigou was startled and thought, as did Van Steenberghen, that Gilson was speaking out of fear that his book would be placed on the Index. In reality Gilson wanted to avoid embarrassment for the church in front of his colleagues in the Académie Française. He was also disgusted that the Holy Office, in a learned congress, would even consider more or less official objections to the kind of ratiocination proper to living scholarship.

When the second congress opened, Gilson was not challenged by Garrigou-Lagrange. However both Van Steenberghen and De Raeymaeker were confronted with censorial remarks by Boyer. Van Steenberghen gave the first paper and Boyer chaired the meeting. Pegis later recollected the session:

> After Van Steenberghen's paper, Boyer made some critical remarks about orthodoxy and talked as though Van Steenberghen should be censured. I was on the point of getting up and asking Boyer his authority for insulting Van Steenberghen, when that magnificent man, Canon De Raeymaeker, intervened and brought Boyer to a test. He marched onto the platform in his splendid robes and asked by what authority Boyer was acting as censor. And challenged, Boyer retreated. He did more than retreat, he said that he had not meant to censure anyone. (Pegis to Shook, 75.6.24.)

Van Steenberghen recalled approximately the same story. Exceptions were taken to his paper on the *quinque viae* of Thomas Aquinas, and Boyer spoke briefly in Latin against some points made in the paper: "Ergo: objectiones clarissimi domini professoris nil valent." As chairman, Boyer then called immediately for the next paper, as there were still three to be heard. Van Steenberghen added to Pegis' account of De Raeymaeker's subsequent actions, and recalled something of what De Raeymaeker had said: that university professors in a learned congress ought not to be treated like children in a catechism class, and that if such treatment continued the professors of Louvain would have no choice but to go home. After Boyer's assurance that he was only trying to get on with a crowded agenda, Gilson was heard to blurt out that Boyer had "accepté de remords."

A deeper issue lay behind all this tension. Following *Humani generis* the Holy Office, spurred on by Boyer, was considering placing Père de Lubac's recent book, *Surnaturel* (1946), on the Index. Pegis recalled:

My relations with Father Boyer remained rather impersonal throughout the congress. In his office he showed me a copy of the *Osservatore Romano*, turned to the text of *Humani generis*, pointed to a paragraph in the text and asked me whether I knew against whom that paragraph was written. I said I did not, whereupon I was told that it was directed against Father de Lubac. I regret now that I refrained from asking how Father Boyer knew this. I was not entirely unprepared when the same evening Gilson told me at dinner that, according to reliable sources, people like Boyer were trying to drum up a condemnation of Father de Lubac's *Surnaturel*. (Pegis to Shook, 75.6.24.)

In an attempt to put Boyer's hostile actions into a larger context, Gilson wrote de Lubac some years later:

I think this kind of thing is an after effect or a man:festation, of the philosophism endemic in the church from its earliest days and which gripped scholasticism in the thirteenth century. While St Thomas and some others soar above it, hundreds of low-flying rationalizers falter along beneath. ... How frightening it is to find orthodoxy placed in the hands of its own destroyers. Modernism's tragic scenario implies that theology was corrupted by adversaries largely responsible for their own errors. Not so! Repression was the work of men who were simply wrong: their pseudo-theology rendered a modernist reaction inevitable. (65.6.21; tr.)

In 1956, six years after the September conferences, Boyer again asked Gilson for a paper, this time for a volume of *Doctor Communis* to be dedicated to Pius XII (below, p. 330). In his letter of acceptance Gilson complained to Boyer that his paper for the thomist congress had never been published. Boyer replied:

If you are asking about your communication on the *De ente et essentia*, it is printed in the *Acta, Doctor Communis*, 1950, fasc. 2 to 3, pages 257-260 [McG 406] and the discussion ... pages 281-282. I can send you this volume if you don't have it. Just ask me, and I will sent it to Vermenton. (56.8.26.)

Much later Gilson scribbled a note on Boyer's letter: "I never received the volume, neither before this letter nor after" (tr.). Boyer was perfectly right however: the published article was there in the *Acta*.

4 *L'affaire Gilson*

After the September 1950 congresses, Gilson went as usual to Toronto where he planned to deliver courses on "Intellect and Will" and "Illumination in Duns Scotus." The disturbances in Rome behind him, Gilson found relative peace in Toronto, and reached a decision to retire from the Collège de France. In his remaining years he planned to pursue at a less hectic pace his private studies and to oversee the welfare of the Institute. He would be happy to escape the melee of international politics, where so many of his own friends disagreed with him.

During the fall of 1950 Gilson as usual took on a few outside commitments. As a friendly gesture to Fathers Carr and Muckle he agreed to give a few lectures at the University of British Columbia. He also consented to requests from Phelan of Notre Dame in South Bend and from Father Gerard Smith of Marquette in Milwaukee.

The University of British Columbia had always been a nonsectarian university. Archbishop Mark Duke of Vancouver planned to establish in it a Catholic college which the Basilian fathers would administer. Gilson went to Vancouver in mid-November 1950 and gave a total of four lectures. The most significant of these dealt with "The Place of Medieval Studies in the History of Western Civilization,' and was given 16 November at noon when students from all faculties could attend. After the lecture Gilson took part in student discussions throughout the afternoon and evening dealing with whether academic liberty was really assured by non-sectarianism. The visit modified the climate of opinion within the university and was an important step toward the incorporation and affiliation of St Mark's Theological College in 1956.

Some ten days after his visit to Vancouver, Gilson went to Notre Dame. In 1949 he had cancelled his visit there because of Thérèse's illness. This year his visit was more urgent than ever; Phelan's institute was short-handed while Astrik Gabriel took leave for private research at the Princeton Institute for Advanced Study. Gilson's four public lectures were actually incorporated into the year's programme, and were subsidized by the new Michael P. Grace II Trust; he received a handsome honorarium of nearly six hundred dollars.

The four lectures for Notre Dame were given over three days, November 30 to December 2. They were basically the lectures given for Balić in Rome in September. Three were entitled "The Fundamental Positions of Duns Scotus in the Light of Historical Research" and were held in a classroom of the Law Building. The fourth was an evening lecture, given on Thursday 30 November in the Law Auditorium, entitled "Historical Research and the Future of Scholasticism."

Phelan went out of his way to make this visit a memorable one. He surrounded the lectures with a dizzying sequence of social events. Selected groups of professors and students took part in luncheons in the university dining halls on Thursday, Friday and Saturday. On Thursday a small dinner meeting in the Blue Room of the Oliver Hotel preceded Gilson's evening lecture. President Cavanaugh of Notre Dame gave a dinner party on Friday evening in the Trustees' Room, and on Saturday afternoon a tea was held for some Chicago students brought in by Yves Simon. Finally, on Saturday evening, Jim and Suzanne Corbett gave a small dinner party attended by Professor and Mrs Simon, and one or two others; as he often did, Gilson became highly impassioned during the after-dinner conversation and spoke of the dangers that an unarmed, partisan France faced from Russia. Phelan himself was at all these functions.

On Sunday morning after mass, Fathers Phelan and Peter O'Reilly drove Gilson to Milwaukee. On Sunday night at Marquette University Gilson repeated the public lecture of Thursday night at Notre Dame. Tired and numb from academic and social exposure, he returned to Toronto on Monday 4 December, the same day that Jacques Maritain arrived to pass "une dizaine de jours à Toronto" (EG to Mme Thibaudeau, 50.11.25).*

On 12 December Gilson wrote the French Ministry of Public Instruction that he would like to retire from his professorship in the Collège de France as of 1 January 1951. In applying for retirement Gilson was thoroughly within his rights. A professor in the French university system was entitled to retire after thirty years of service and fifty-five years of age. Gilson was now sixty-six. If he reckoned his service from his first post in Bourg-en-Bresse in 1907, he had now put in forty-four years; if from his first university post at Lille, he had put in thirty-eight years. Moreover, as Gilson later argued, a professor's reasons for retirement are his personal concern. He need not plan to do anything again; he could plant cabbages, go fishing, or even accept, with a government stipend, a cultural mission abroad:

> I chose another way: consecrating the two or three years of teaching still left to me to serving that same Toronto Institute which I saw born, watched grow, and to which, as any observant person could see, I had become in the course of more than twenty years work there strongly attached (EG to Albert Béguin, *Esprit*, Jan.-April, 1951, p. 594; tr.)

Despite Gilson's objections, however, there were valid grounds for some criticism concerning the manner of his retirement. His decision was rather sudden, and he seems not to have talked it over with his friends in the Collège.

On 15 December *The Commonweal* published as a major article an open letter from Waldemar Gurian to Gilson on "Europe and the United States" (McG 1124). Gurian was a Russian who had fled the revolution to Germany, then the Nazi Reich to America. At the time of his open letter he was professor of political philosophy at Notre Dame, head of the Committee on International Relations in that university, and editor of the *Review of Politics*.

Gurian accused Gilson of using Notre Dame to spread that political doctrine of neutralism which he had aired in his *Le monde* articles the previous spring. He reproached Gilson for "spreading the sad gospel of defeatism," for accusing a respected French publicist of being "a paid American agent," and for predicting that, in the event of war, "France will be occupied by the Red Army without much resistance and that the United States will not do much about it." According to Gurian Gilson had already "told us" that he planned "not to return to France": although Gurian could understand Gilson's preferring "the haven of the New World to threatened Europe," he could only condemn Gilson for trying to speak out on an international issue as though he were a statesman. Should war come there could be no neutrals: by undermining "the will to resist" Gilson was helping the cause of world communism. In his conclusion Gurian hoped fervently that Gilson would abandon his "campaign of despair and incrimination."

---

* These "dizaine de jours" included a particularly delightful private dinner when Gilson and Maritain sat down together at Norah Michener's table in Rosedale.

Gurian's letter contained a complex mixture of truth and error. Certainly Gilson's Atlantic-Pact politic, like that of *Le monde* and many in France, was neutralist. He believed that if America wanted to use France as a bulwark against Soviet imperialism, she would first have to arm her: if France remained unarmed, as she currently was, she would surely fall before the Red Army. Gilson felt Gurian had wronged him, especially in the accusation that Gilson had claimed he would never return to France. Gilson's friends knew he was discontinuing his courses at the Collège the France, but they also knew he intended to divide his time almost equally between France and North America. Although he probably did not want to be caught in France during a Russian occupation, he seems never to have said, even in his angriest moments, that he would never return there. Perhaps his excited remarks three weeks earlier at the Corbetts' in South Bend had been misunderstood; nonetheless Gilson considered impassioned dinner conversation the personal privilege of any man among friends and believed it should be kept strictly off the record.

When Gilson read the open letter in *The Commonweal*, he wrote immediately to Phelan:

> This is just to ask you if I had any conversation with Monsieur W. Gurian, or in his presence, while I was at Notre Dame? I cannot remember having seen him once during these three days, but I would be glad to know that I am not mistaken in this belief, for it would explain to me how our colleague may have ascribed to me such incredible and, indeed, dishonourable opinions. If he was present at any of my conversations, or if I spoke to him without recognizing him, there is very little I can do to repair the damage which will be done by his calumnies. This, at least, will teach me to stay in Toronto. (50.12.17.)

Phelan told Gilson over the telephone that he had held no conversations either with Gurian or in his presence while at Notre Dame (memo to President Cavanaugh, 51.1.8). Clearly then the basis of the attack must have been hearsay, and Gurian's letter constituted an infringement on Gilson's personal privacy.

For the first two weeks of January 1951 Gilson tried in relative calm to get some kind of retraction from the editor of *The Commonweal*. He refused to make any public statements himself: to Phelan he wrote, "You are naturally free to tell everybody that I dissuaded you from intervening in the Gurian incident" (51.2.16); and to Father Moore of Notre Dame, "As you have perhaps noticed, I have answered nothing. This is what I will continue to do" (51.1.28). As events unfolded, however, it became imperative to answer Gurian's charges.

On 27 January Gurian's open letter reappeared in French in *Figaro littéraire* and Pierre Bernus produced a summary of its charges in the *Journal de Genève*. Thereafter, the presses of Paris buzzed with "l'affaire Gilson." Especially virulent were attacks by disciples of Charles Maurras (Action Française) in *Aspects de la France* (51.2.9) and by Gaullists in *Carrefour* (51.2.13). Works like *traître, déserteur* and *fuyard* cropped up again and again. Gilson, one article suggested, had to be a villain. Had he not years ago spoken disrespectfully of de Gaulle? Particularly painful to Gilson was a personal rejection by Pasteur Vallery-Radot, who had sponsored him into the Académie; Vallery-Radot now said Gilson was no longer a Frenchman and should be excluded from the national community.

Shortly after this virulent anti-Gilson offensive had reached its peak in the press, the Collège de France met in its general assembly of 11 February and took up the matter of their colleague's retirement. The ministry had already processed Gilson's notice of retirement, and had officially announced it in its journal of 11 January. For some reason in February the Collège did not follow its usual assembly procedure for a retirement. It deferred such technical matters as the title of Gilson's now-vacant chair and the identity of his possible successor to the general assembly of March, and turned immediately to the matter of their colleague's honorariat. After a discussion of the *qualité* expected of an honorary professor, the Collège decided, in a surprise vote, not to solicit this honour for Gilson. Sixteen members voted in favour of the honorariat, nine against, and seven abstained: a positive recommendation required seventeen votes in favour. "The rumour then spread that the honorariat had been refused 'for moral reasons'. Only *Le monde*, 51.2.24, re-established the facts." (EG to Béguin, *Esprit*, Jan.-April, 1951, p. 591; tr.)

There was a world of pathos, confusion and frustration in Gilson's two letters to Phelan upon receiving this incredible news in Toronto:

> I have just received communication of an article published in *Figaro* 16 February. It informs its readers that I have been refused the honorariat by my former colleagues at the Collège de France. The vote was: for eight, against six, abstentions sixteen [*sic*]. The professors, the article says, arrived at the assembly "avec un journal dans leur serviette." The journal, of course, was the article of Professor Gurian as published in the *Figaro littéraire*. I only want you to know that I have invented nothing when I hold him responsible for this new development. There are more to come. And all this for three lectures on Duns Scotus! (51.2.20.)

And the next day:

> The last development is that in *Carrefour* Pasteur Vallery-Radot suggests my exclusion from the Académie Française. If things are allowed to go any farther, I don't know what may happen. The editor of *Commonweal* sticks to his point: that I did say what Gurian makes me say. ... I really believe that I should not have prevented you from publicly re-establishing the truth, but I was afraid for yourself more than for me. ... You may consider yourself as free to publish the letter which you had prepared for *Commonweal*. (51.2.23.)

Phelan did prepare such a letter (51.2.26), sending it to Skillin and, in a shorter French form, to Mauriac. Phelan pointed out that Gilson had made no political remarks in any of his public sessions, and that Gurian had not been present at any of the private sessions. As a consequence Gurian could only be relaying on hearsay; certainly his specific charges – that Gilson had accused a French journalist of being a paid agent and (notably) that Gilson had said he would never return to France – were untrue. This letter seems never to have been published either in North America or France, though it was sent to both New York and Paris.

Gilson also wrote two explanatory letters to the editors of the two leading Paris newspapers: Pierre Brisson of *Figaro littéraire* and Hubert Beuve-Méry of *Le monde*. Brisson published Gilson's letter on 17 February under the headline: "M. Etienne Gilson rompt le silence" (McG 703). He introduced it with a resounding welcome, as though wondering where Gilson had been since 17 January when *Figaro littéraire* had done him the favour of publishing Gurian's open letter in French: what did Gilson mean by keeping everyone waiting so long for a reply?

Gilson had expected to be mocked in this way, and used as his opening gambit a curt objection to the open letter's subtitle "champion du neutralisme." He denied having campaigned politically in the United States and having ever oriented his words politically. And why was Brisson ignorant of the dates of the controversial articles on neutralism, assigning them to the late fall of 1950 rather than to the preceding April? They were old stuff indeed when Gurian falsely picked them up as though they had been freshly uttered at Notre Dame. No doubt Brisson was stung: bright journalists don't like to be out-done by academics. He sharply replied that dates were insignifiant and mattered far less than context. His attack became more personal as he called Gilson a loser whose political influence would always add up to zero: he said he was sorry he had called Gilson a "champion," for the word was too grandiose by far. In all, Gilson did not feel that he had achieved much with his letter to *Figaro littéraire*.

The *Le monde* letter, published a few days later on 22 February, fared rather better, possibly because Beuve-Méry was a friend and had a real interest in the issue. In this letter Gilson took a more intellectual, if still somewhat bitter, approach. He claimed to be intrigued that his most prominent attackers in North America and France were always Catholics who had embarked upon what they obviously saw as a holy war: the particularly virulent form of political fanaticism they displayed clearly arose out of misplaced religious feeling. In their insistence that the real enemy was communism, they alienated those who knew better. The real enemy was Moscow imperialism, and Catholics played straight into Moscow's hand when they equated all communists with Moscow imperialists. This inability to distinguish the two was driving into the Moscow camp millions of people who were only in search of religious, intellectual, civic and national liberty.

Gilson's position infuriated a good many Catholic editors who liked to pretend there was almost no sectarianism in their stances. *The Commonweal* in particular took issue with Gilson's attack upon Gurian's open letter as "part of a campaign undertaken by a group in the United States ... to defame any fairly well-known Catholic who does not hold that war against Russia is a sacred duty, in the strict religious sense of the word" (tr.). Clearly the letter in *Le monde* had stung Skillin; the editorial took some pains to cite texts from Gurian's earlier articles that "give the lie to M. Gilson's unfounded charge" (51.3.9). The editor of *The Tablet* of London seems also to have been stung – Gilson's letter provoked one of the most carelessly inaccurate responses in the long history of that excellent Catholic journal:

M. Étienne Gilson, until about the middle of last year one of the leading exponents in *Le monde* of the untimely and fallacious neutralism with which that newspaper has come to be associated, and who is now in Canada at University College, Kingston, Ontario, has recently said in an interview appearing in the *Journal de Genève* that he "will never set foot in France again ...." His apologia in *Le monde* was a sorry document, leading M. Mauriac in *Le figaro* to regret that a man accustomed to handling historical texts should have been inveigled into political journalism so late in life. (51.3.3.)

Gilson had never given an interview to the *Journal de Genève*. And he had certainly never been on the staff at Queen's University, Kingston. It was this kind of confused and entangled inaccuracy from which Gilson began to try extricating himself in March.

When *l'affaire Gilson* cooled a little in mid-March, Brisson at *Figaro littéraire* tried to revive it. He prepared a short diversified article, "Où en est l'affaire Gilson?" (51.3.17; McG 1143). In it he quoted from a letter in which Gurian admitted that he had not personally been present at the conversations reported. Gurian insisted that the important point was not whether he was present, but whether the conversations had taken place and whether they had injured France's reputation in America; he also promised shortly to name names. A week later an article by Gurian entitled "Des précisions de W. Gurian sur l'affaire Gilson" appeared in *Figaro littéraire* (51.3.24). Here Gurian cited his source for the conversations as Professor James Corbett of the Notre Dame Institute, *diplomé* of the École des Chartes. As proof of the disastrous effect of the conversations throughout the United States, he also cited a young French student at Notre Dame, a M. Labbence (Labbens); however, although Corbett's would have been strong evidence, the opinion of a boy away at college was hardly significant.

On finding himself named, Corbett denounced Gurian in a letter to Brisson. He also sent copies of his denunciation to *Le monde* and to Phelan. In a covering letter he told Phelan that he and his wife were trying "to forget the whole business which has made us both sick" (51.9.2). His letter to Brisson at *Figaro* was a sharp one:

In reply to the letter of M. Gurian published in the *Figaro littéraire* of 24 March 1951, I have this to say:

1. I formally protest the accusation of having, in M. Gurian's words, "spread" the conversation attributed by him to Gilson. It is M. Gurian's own responsibility.

2. I confirm that the conversations on which M. Gurian based the letter printed in *The Commonweal* were strictly private and took place before a small group of M. Gilson's friends. If M. Gurian were an honourable man he would not have made use of these conversations without the permission of M. Gilson and without having asked M. Gilson to verify that the account of them he had written was exact. M. Gilson's public replies clearly show he did neither.

3. If there was an "effect désastreux sur le prestige de la France en Amérique" – greatly exaggerated in that the major American press did not even feature the incident – M. Gurian alone is responsible for it. In this affair M. Gurian has

only sought publicity. Honest people find such a procedure revolting, and it is fortunate that the French and foreign press have given such importance to a letter inspired by such particular motives.

4. In these conditions, I categorically refuse to act as a witness for M. Gurian. Having only scorn for his methods of getting publicity, I forbid him to introduce my name into his bare polemic. Moreover, M. Gilson needs no help to make his mind known to the public.

My numerous French friends are pained and surprised at the very thought of the role M. Gurian is assigning me: accordingly, I will be most grateful if you will publish this letter in the usual way in its entirety as you have the letters of M. Gurian, Veuillez, etc. (51.4.1; tr.)

The content of this letter became common knowledge, but never appeared in *Figaro littéraire*. The explanation currently held by many is a surprising one. After some time, when the letter had not yet appeared, word was sent to Father Reginald O'Donnell, then at Oxford, to call at the *Figaro* office and enquire why not. He called and was passed about from one official to another until the obvious runaround was complete. He intended to try again, but received a cable from Father Kennedy in Toronto to forget it. Apparently Gilson had told his sad story to his longtime stockbroker friend, Gordon Taylor. According to report, Taylor was outraged and exclaimed, "Is *Figaro* doing this to you? It's got to stop." Gilson smiled at the little man who did not, he thought, really understand the seriousness of the situation. But if anything, Taylor understood too well. As one of *Figaro*'s largest shareholders, he sent off a brief cable: "Gilson articles must stop or heads will roll." With Taylor's cable *l'affaire Gilson*, which had been declared closed in *Le monde* on 10 March, was also dropped by *Figaro littéraire*. Ironically, however, Corbett's disclaimer was never published.

The best single summary and analysis of the Gilson affair appeared in April in *Esprit*, Emmanuel Mounier's leftwing Catholic journal. *Esprit* had published an article entitled "La neutralité française: utopie ou solution?" which had concluded that a plausible case could be made for French neutrality toward Russia and the United States. As early as 17 February 1952 Albert Béguin, director of *Esprit*, had written to Gilson in Toronto expressing his sorrow about "the hurtful campaign waged against you by la presse d'A.F. [Action Française]." Béguin advised Gilson to set the matter straight:

I cannot believe that you have said the things people are saying you said. It is very necessary that you straighten things out, giving the true reasons for your departure and being precise about the meaning of the conversations in which people are making points against you. I will publish whatever you say on this subject in *Esprit*. The affair is a grave one, even beyond your own person, because the meaning people are giving to it ... is causing trouble in many minds. (51.2.17; tr.)

Béguin was as good as, even better than, his word. When he received Gilson's long and beautiful *apologia pro vita sua* in March, he published it in its entirety in the April issue along with his own summary and analysis, "L'affaire Gilson"

(*Esprit*, 19 [1951]; pp. 590-596; McG 695, 1093). In this apologia Gilson explained his attachment to North America, telling why he had "fled" there twenty-two times since 1926 and why he had chosen to retire from the Collège de France before retiring from the Toronto Institute. He explained that the medieval programme of the Institute was his personal interpretation of how to proceed with a discipline created within his own lifetime. The Institute allowed him to transport to Canada that part of France that he carried within him always. (See especially pp. 595-596.)

Ultimately the tumultous events of 1950 and 1951 caused Gilson to become a more spiritual man. He had lost his wife, watched his son become ill and turn from him, and seen his beloved Paris grow cold toward him. He had only one place to turn and that was to God within him. He remembered what St Bernard had meant to him in the 1930s, and his visits to La Pierre Qui Vire during the occupation of the 1940s. He recalled his friendship with his student Dan Walsh and his associations with Father Thomas Merton of Gethsemani. He tried the catharsis that came immediately to mind, and wrote Father Merton to pour out his soul. Father Merton's reply was a document of salvation:

> Deeply moved by your beautiful letter I want at last to do what I should have done long ago – write you a line to assure you of my recognition of a spiritual debt to you which I too sketchily indicated in the pages of the *Seven Storey Mountain*, and in a rather badly constructed section of the book at that. To you and to Jacques Maritain, among others, I owe the Catholic faith. That is to say I owe my life. This is no small debt. Can you feel as abandoned as you do when you are handing out to other people as great a gift as is the Kingdom of Heaven? But indeed, it is the privilege of those who bear such spiritual fruit to feel abandoned and miserable and alone, for poverty of spirit is the patrimony of the children of God in this world, and their pledge of glory in the world to come: "for theirs is the Kingdom of Heaven." Please do not fail to come and see us if you are ever around Chicago or any of the middle-western cities which are "near" Gethsemani. ... Meanwhile we will meet before the holy altar of God, and I promise to remember you. (51.11.12.)

Subsequent to this letter, Merton dedicated to Gilson a book dealing with St Bernard and the recent encyclical: "I can think of no one," he wrote, "to whom I owe this dedication more fittingly than to you who first introduced me, by your own writings, to St Bernard of Clairvaux" (54.6.2).

It was while in this ferment that God's hand seemed providentially to touch Gilson's life. On 2 October 1951 he received a welcome letter from Waldemar Gurian offering an authentic apology: "At odds with you on certain primordial questions of international politics, I ought to have cited in a public discussion only your public expressions of your views. In citing from private conversations I was at fault and beg your pardon." (51.9.29.) By return mail Gilson wrote from St Michael's: "I thank you for your letter of 29 September which has just arrived. It was not necessary, but I appreciate it all the more sincerely for the very noble feelings which inspired it." (51.11.2.) Both letters, each in character, were long ones and went into circumstantial details. Gilson urged Gurian to forget the affair – "what's done is done; all that remains is for you to forget about it as completely as I have now forgotten." When Gilson said "forgotten," he no doubt meant "forgiven"; the masses he later had offered for Gurian, including those after Gurian's death, signalled his forgiveness but also his remembrance.

The reconciliation with the Collège de France came more slowly. An old axiom says that it is harder to forgive someone you have hurt than someone who has hurt you: the Collège had wronged Gilson and certainly found it hard to forgive him. The Collège also found it difficult to endure the shame occasioned by its treatment of Gilson. Later, when Eugène Vinaver was in Toronto, he claimed that this action of the Collège de France had made him for the only time in his life ashamed to be a Frenchman.

Technically the Collège's only sin was to have taken up the matter of Gilson's honorariat too soon. De facto this could be easily remedied. Pressed especially by its younger and newer members, the Collège opened the matter again at its assembly of December 1956. The assembly recommended that Gilson be given his honorariat, and Le monde published the recommendation on 26 December 1956 (below, p. 332). By this time, Gilson was already receiving the state pension which, although delayed, had never been refused. And though he had been returning to France each year, he had for some years been spending most of his time in Toronto.

16

Retirement to Work, 1951-1957

1 REDISCOVERING ACADEME: L'ÉCOLE DES MUSES

During the early part of 1951, while *l'affaire Gilson* was alive in Paris, Gilson lived with Jacqueline, Cécile and Thérèse's two cats at Elmsley Place on the campus of St Michael's College in Toronto. In the old Victorian house put at their disposal by Father Louis Bondy, the family lived a quiet life. Gilson gave his lectures and seminar, took part in the activities of the Institute and the university's graduate school, and wrote continuously. Jacqueline painted and Cécile found professional employment as a social worker. Bernard, meanwhile, was with the army in Fès, Morocco.

During this period Gilson was externally calm, internally tense; he was embarrassed not to feel that he had Paris behind him. His aide-mémoire recorded few commitments this spring: a meeting with the French consul at the King Edward Hotel, another with Father Parsons, SJ of Georgetown University, and one more with an Ottawa friend and counselor, John J. Connolly. Gilson accepted at this time only one outside lecture invitation: on 22 April he delivered a centennial lecture at St Francis Xavier University in Antigonish to fulfil a promise to a friend, probably Alex Sampson. Three weeks later he sailed with his daughters from Québec City on the *Scythia*, and arrived in Le Havre and Paris on 24 May.

This was Gilson's first return to France since the previous September, and he immediately sought out the company of friends he knew to be sympathetic. Richard McKeon and Henri Gouhier were both able to brief him on events in Paris and at Notre Dame in Illinois. He attended a lecture by McKeon on 28 May, lunched with him on 6 June, and dined with him on 13 June, Gilson's sixty-seventh birthday; he dined with Gouhier on 29 May. Gilson also saw Vrin about his *Duns Scot*, and Vrin and Thérèse d'Alverny about the *Archives*; Mlle d'Alverny, in charge of manuscripts at the Bibliothèque Nationale, was becoming increasingly involved in running the journal. At Vrin's Gilson met another good friend, Henri Marrou, authority on patristic education and another frequent visitor to Canada. He also saw his younger brothers, Doctor Maurice and Abbé André: Maurice was still taking his annual pilgrimage to Lourdes, and André had just had his first heart attack. Most of these appointments were entered in Gilson's aide-mémoire, some he passed on viva voce; they are listed here to combat the stubborn notion that Gilson was entirely absent from France for several years after the Gurian affair.

Gilson was also in Europe at this time to receive an honorary doctorate at the grand convocation to mark the five hundredth anniversary of the founding of the University of Glasgow. This visit to Glasgow combined with the solicitude of his Paris friends to brighten Gilson's spirits. On 20 June, the day of this important convocation, the chancellor at Glasgow conferred twelve honorary doctorates in divinity, fifty-six in the laws. Over half of those honoured were personally known to Gilson, including Maurice Goguel of the Protestant Faculty of Theology in Paris, Alfred Ernout also of Paris, Paul Tillich of New York and Ernst Curtius of Bonn. Several Canadian acquaintances were also honoured or present as delegates, including Maurice Lamontagne of Laval, Harold Innis of Toronto, and Norman McKenzie, Gilson's recent host in Vancouver. Besides attending the academic ceremony in St Andrew's Hall, Gilson went with delight to every one of the luncheons, dinners and receptions held in Bute Hall, Trades Hall, University Union and the Grosvenor Restaurant. He took part in a long intellectual discussion with J. S. Dawson, a professor of moral theology soon to be teaching philosophy at Memorial University, Newfoundland. In short, Gilson rediscovered his own world.

On 26 July, after a relatively short stay in Europe, Gilson returned to North America with his daughters again aboard the *Scythia*. Back in Toronto the fall of 1951 was relatively peaceful. Gilson delivered a lecture course in the "History of Medieval Philosophy" and a seminar on the "*Confessions* of St Augustine"; both were spread, as they had been last year, over the better part of two semesters. During this fall Gilson made his peace with Gurian and began to pick up his outside lectures again, travelling in December to Rutgers.

Although 1951 was an emotionally trying year for Gilson, it did produce a number of books. One of these had been largely written in France since the war's end, and was a blend of literary criticism, psychological analysis, classical Greek thought, and art theory. *L'école des muses* (Paris, 1951; McG 24) included three items previously published, yet remained largely a new work. It was quickly and well translated into English by Maisie Ward as *Choir of Muses* (New York, 1953; McG 25). With this work Gilson turned to a consideration of the functions of the muse in artistic creation.

Choir of Muses is not, like *Les idées et les lettres* (1932; McG 70), a simple collection of earlier pieces nor, like *Dante* (1939; McG 12), an analysis of the art and thought of a single genius. Rather it is a thoughtful, philosophical and psychological study of great art in its relation to erotic love on the one hand and religious reflection on the other. For the Greeks, the poet's muse was the source of his inspiration; muses were divinities invented to account "for that ordered design which confers upon certain of the ideas and works of men a superhuman loveliness" (p. 11). De-divinized, the poet's muse became either his inspiration in general, or the particular character of his poetic genius. Later on, poets began to speak of certain women as their muses, finding in their love a source for inspiration. It is these women who form the subject matter of *Choir of Muses*, as Gilson attempts to discover whether they actually contributed to the art of their lovers. Gilson's analysis is historical and pragmatic in its method and is not, for the most part, ontologically based.

Six of the nine chapters of *Choir des Muses* deal with specific muses well known in history: Petrarch's Laura; Baudelaire's unidentified Marie and Mme Sabatier; Wagner's Mathilde; Comte's Clotilde de Vaux; Maeterlinck's Georgette Leblanc; Goethe's Lili Schöneman and Ulfrike von Levetzay; and Robert Browning's Elizabeth Barrett, a special case in that she was married to Browning and a poet herself. In these chapters Gilson raises several questions: Is a muse, as Petrarch claimed, more a dream figure than a reality, a false image of a promise that cannot be kept? Is the real bond between an artist and his muse mere lust, as Baudelaire's seemed to be, or at best lust that only becomes love when the muse refuses to comply? Does separation from the muse produce the poet's greatest art, as when Wagner created *Tristan* and *Parsifal* after Mathilde rejected him? Does a poet owe anything of his art to his muse? Can a muse also be an artist's wife in a happy marriage?

Gilson's answers to most of these questions are ambivalent, but on one he is firm. The muse is not the source of the poet's art, and does not enter into the essential nature of her lover's achievement. Gilson concedes that the muse may help an artist to keep alive his desire to achieve – as Petrarch said of Laura: "I shall ever see you shining with the same brightness" (p. 61). But the achievement must be his own or it is no longer art. Gilson even hazards an ontological guess: "To create life, a man needs a woman. To create the perfection of beauty, it may be that the man must also *be* the woman" (p. 81).

Although Gilson's explanations of this subject are not entirely satisfying, they do in part demonstrate his own definition of art. Art, in Gilson's view, is an aesthetic and a creative activity falling, in the artist's awareness, somewhere between erotic love and religion. Art's beauty is linked at one end with the fecundity of nature which the artist struggles to discover in Eros, and at the other with religion, where the artist probes the meaning of language and the word. The last chapter of the *Choir*, "The Artist and the Saint," contains some of Gilson's finest writing. He examines the artist's fascination with the divine and grieves with Franz Liszt, the spoiled priest, in exclaiming: "Poetry, music and a touch of rebelliousness in my nature have ruled me too long. *Miserere mei Domine.*" (p. 118.) Gilson marvels that even the irreverent C. F. Ramuz can describe himself as a man with "a vocation" who is "obedient to grace"; according to Ramuz, "what is called poetry is the sense of the *sacred*, and the need, once the sacred is seen, of helping others to share it. ... All poetry is religious, all poetry is a kind of religion." (p. 188.)

Gilson's reflections on the writings of artists on the process of their creation were of considerable interest to practising novelists and literary critics. Charles Morgan, whom Gilson had first met during the London conference in 1946, wrote Gilson an interesting letter acknowledging several references in *Choir* to his own book:

I am grateful. ... No one has understood as well as you what *Portrait in a Mirror* was really about. I remember that George Moore, when he read it, or dipped into it, came away with the impression that my young man, Nigel Frew, had been physically unsuccessful when at last he found himself in bed with the girl he loved. But that of course was precisely the kind of impression that poor George Moore would invent for himself." (53.9.29.)

And Lionel Trilling of Columbia University grew excited when Mel Evans of Doubleday informed him of Gilson's interest in his literary criticism. Trilling wrote Evans:

Gilson has long been my idea of the great – the real – scholar, the man who always knows what he's talking about. ... For him to take a book of mine into account and actually like it is a little like getting the Order of the Garter would be like to the kind of person who gets the Order of the Garter. (54.3.29.)

The following year Gilson apparently told Trilling that his criticism was creative rather than literary. Trilling responded: "Your letter touched and gratified me more than I can say. There isn't, I think, any comment on my work as a literary critic that I would rather have, than the one you make, that I am not a literary critic." (53.3.18.)

2 Practical Humanism, 1952

By 1952 Gilson had, on the surface at least, recovered from his depression. He began to accept invitations with abandon. On Candlemas Day he gave his celebrated lecture for St Michael's Adult Education Programme on *The Breakdown of Morals and Christian Education* (Toronto, 1952; McG 6); this was repeated at St John Fisher College, Rochester, and other places, and was twice published. On 22 February he gave the first of several talks this year to the Alliance Française of Toronto, renewing his dedication to his lifelong French cultural mission. On 5 March, his Toronto courses finished for the year, he began an American tour which took him to Chicago, River Forest, St Louis, New Orleans and Houston. From 27 to 31 March he delivered his regular lectures in Montréal, three for the university and one for the Institut Franco-Canadien. On 15 April he attended the twenty-sixth annual meeting of the American Catholic Philosophical Association in Cleveland where he was awarded the Cardinal Spellman Aquinas medal and tendered a warm citation by Anton C. Pegis, president of the Toronto Institute. Gilson read a paper on "Science, Philosophy and Religious Wisdom" (*Proceedings*, 26 [1952]: 5-13; McG 443); he also delivered a version of this paper, "Religious Wisdom and Scientific Knowledge" over CBC Radio (in *Christianity in an Age of Science* [Montréal, 1952], pp. 15-22; McG 786). On 23 April he flew to Belgium to inaugurate the Cardinal Mercier Chair at Louvain; he delivered a course of ten lectures there between 29 April and 19 May.

Most of Gilson's lectures during these months focused on one of three themes: morality and education; philosophy and contemporary science; and christendom as the city of God. The moral issues in contemporary education was not really a new lecture-subject, but was marked by a new apocalyptic tone. In reading Nietzche in the context of popular figures like Sartre and Potin, Gilson had become increasingly concerned at the impact of the new non-morality on modern youth. Existential atheism had dispensed with God and eternal life and had invited man to make his own distinctions between right and wrong. Considering the plight of modern education, Gilson lamented: "The real trouble of our times is not the multiplication of sinners, it is the disappearance of sin" (*The Breakdown*, p. 4).

Gilson had been struggling with the second theme, philosophy and contemporary science, since the early years when he had prepared his thesis on Descartes. Why had it been, and why was it still, so difficult for a philosopher to cope with science and vice versa? Gilson concluded that the problem lay in the increasing rapidity of scientific development, which even scientists found it impossible to keep up with. In Newton's world, science had accepted a high degree of "previsibility": there was complete determination among physical phenomena, and scientists believed themselves capable of arriving at and defining truth. Since 1905 however two non-newtonian models of the world had emerged: Einstein's of relativity, and Bohr, Heisenberg's and Louis de Broglie's of undulatory mechanics. Are physical phenomena determinable in these worlds? Or do phenomena escape the determinism of time and space?

Around the beginning of 1952 Gilson wrote to de Broglie asking him whether there was still room for determinism in quantum physics. De Broglie replied in a long detailed letter (52.3.9) which inspired Gilson's papers for the American Catholic Philosophical Association and the CBC. De Broglie not only recognized the validity of a philosophical inquiry and the need for a philosophical answer, but also agreed with Gilson that the answer must come from things, from nature itself, rather than from reason or from critiques. For Gilson, Kant was dead, and science was alive.*

The third theme of Gilson's papers this year was the role of christendom in the universal community of men. This theme was particularly evident in the ten lectures given at Louvain to inaugurate the new Cardinal Mercier Chair. Gilson was especially pleased to be invited to Louvain in view of his years of philosophical disagreement with many members of the Louvain community.

At Louvain Gilson elected to deal with the changing notions of the city of God to be found in seven historical periods. The first of these, antiquity, Gilson presented through the vision of Fustel de Coulanges as a gradual process of spiritualization. During the second period, the late Roman empire, the city of God became universalized through grace as envisioned in Augustine. In the Middle Ages the trend toward universalism continued, as in Roger Bacon's presentation of the city of God as a Christian republic, the *res publica fidelium* founded on wisdom. During the Imperial Monarchy the city of God fell within the terms of

---

* See "Le jubilé de Louis de Broglie: en marge d'un texte," *Le monde*, 53.1.8; McG 689.

autonomous reason, as seen in Dante's *humana civitas* or *civitas humani generis*. In the fifteenth century, the city of God was seen as the peace of faith, which Nicholas of Cusa would snatch from the Wars of Religion or Campanella would extract from a platonic city of the sun. Eventually a more modern, philanthropic concept of the city of God emerged in the notion of a united Europe as spelled out by Abbé de Saint-Pierre and developed by Jean Jacques Rousseau and the Congress of The Hague. And finally the city of God came to be viewed as the philosopher's city of Leibniz, home of the science-oriented Auguste Comte.

Gilson's lectures at Louvain were warmly praised by scholars there, especially by Fernand Van Steenberghen and Gérard Verbeke (interviews, 1975). For ten days the large university lecture hall was filled to capacity. The lectures were published as *Les métamorphoses de la cité de Dieu* (Louvain, 1952; McG 91). This book was undeservedly disregarded, perhaps because of *l'affaire Gilson*, perhaps because it rarely mentioned either scholasticism or St Thomas.

After the Louvain series Gilson went to Paris, where he arrived 24 May. During the last week of August he returned to Toronto with his two daughters. He had with him drafts of two papers: a short one for Université Laval, and a longer for St Michael's College.

The first of these papers was for Laval's centenary and was on behalf of the Académie Française; it was given in Palais Montcalm, Québec City, 22 September 1952. Gilson was present by personal invitation of the rector, Mgr. Vandry, and as president of a large French mission to the convocation – he was also among those to receive honorary doctorates. His address, which was limited to fifteen minutes, concerned the first French book ever published in Canada: *Catéchisme du diocèse de Sens*, by Mgr. Jean-Joseph Lenguet, printed in Québec by Brown and Gilmore ("noms bien français") in 1765. Gilson explained that he had been reading this catechism in Vermenton during the past summer, knowing nothing at all about its author, Mgr. Lenguet. When he had investigated he had found to his surprise that Lenguet had actually been a member of the Académie Française, "an immortal like me," the sixth incumbent of the first chair "flanked in time, if not in glory, between Boileau his predecessor and Buffon his successor." Alas "Lenquet l'oublié" had been in most respects far from immortal, "sauf pour son catéchisme," and "sauf pour Québec" where "in the classical prose of an immortal, generations of young Canadiens had learned their *grand catéchisme*, the elements of their religion." With these words Gilson introduced his warm greetings from the Académie Française to Laval. ("Hommage à l'Université Laval," *La revue des deux mondes*, 52.11.1; McG 681; tr.). In an article for *Le monde* a few weeks later, Gilson criticized the lack of government representatives in France's official delegation to the centenary; Robert Schuman, who was to have come, had received his honorary degree *in absentia* to prolonged applause ("À propos de l'Université de Laval: le sens d'un centenaire," *Le monde*, 52.11.14; McG 534).

On 6 October Gilson gave the inaugural address for the centennial of St Michael's College. The lecture was delivered before two thousand people in

Convocation Hall, University of Toronto, and was entitled "Education and Higher Learning" (*The Norton Reader* [New York, 1969], pp. 317-328; McG 628). In this paper Gilson objected to the modern tendency of democratic governments to present education as though it were simply another commodity.

In the fall of 1952 Jacques Maritain visited the Institute, one of the relatively few occasions when he and Gilson were on the Toronto campus at the same time. Norah Michener always took advantage of these occasions to invite Gilson and Maritain to her home, and these dinner parties were invariably memorable affairs. Norah Michener was highly thought of by both men. She was one of their continuing students, was philosophically knowledgeable, and had already, with her husband, Roland Michener, served Canada well;* she had also been especially kind to Gilson and his daughters at the time of Thérèse's death.

Norah would invariably place Gilson on her left, Maritain on her right – she had written her doctoral thesis on Maritain. She would then raise some controversial issue, which this fall was Jean-Paul Sartre. Maritain asked Gilson if he had attended Sartre's Toronto lecture. Indeed Gilson had. And did Sartre take notice of his presence? "No, he did not," answered Gilson, "but he mentioned a greater than I." Another time Gilson arrived for dinner with two bottles of wine, one rather better than the other. "Be sure," he said loudly as he came in, indicating the better wine, "that this bottle is poured on my side of the table."

Gilson and Norah could always be completely open with each other. During the summer of 1954 Norah wrote a plaintive letter to Gilson at Poitiers. She was unwell, spiritually disturbed and her thoughts had turned, as those of high Anglicans sometimes do, nostalgically to Rome. She consoled herself by plunging into work on her lovely Rosedale garden. Gilson replied:

> I don't know why, but it seems to me the time is near when you may and can follow ... your own heart. ... You need only consult yourself and God. ... The fence around the garden seems to me to betray the spirit of the New World. It's so very European. The main thing is that it please you. ... Why are you not now in Poitiers writing a cookbook here? The Poitiers table is unbelievably abundant and refined. (54.8.14.)

Whether the desire to write a cookbook was inspired by Gilson or had already been expressed by Norah, she actually did publish a gourmet cookbook two years later under a pseudonym. *Janet Peter's Personal Cookbook* (Toronto, 1956) includes among its desserts recipes for both a *gateau maritain* and a *gateau gilson*.

Another episode reveals both Norah's generosity and Gilson's frank and rather scornful impatience. She had just sent him a note enclosing tickets for *Die Fledermaus*. He replied immediately:

> If you do not mind it too much, just forget about ... *Fledermaus*. Music has always been for me something very important, quasi-religious, and I know enough of

---

* Roland Michener, aided by his wife, would go on to occupy the high commissioner's office in India and to become governor-general of Canada.

Fledermaus [to consider it] the kind of third-rate music that makes me feel too miserable for words. I simply cannot stand it. Incidentally, this is part of the Toronto tragedy in the field of intellectual culture: everywhere to substitute some dummy for reality. Your conservatory of music has no money to bind its scores, nor even shelves to store them. Yet Toronto is going to offer itself a performance of *Fledermaus* because opera is a social function. I am afraid I shall not even succeed in making myself understood, but you will forgive me, won't you? (55.2.1.)

3 Pegis and Doubleday's Catholic Textbooks

In March 1953 Gilson paid his first visit to Princeton. He had been invited by the university chaplain, the Dominican Father Halton, to lecture for the Aquinas Foundation on 5 March, the day prior to the opening of the foundation's week-long Princeton Conference. Gilson chose as his subject "Thomas Aquinas and Our Colleagues" (McG 154). It was a good lecture and was twice published: first as an Aquinas Foundation Lecture (Princeton, 1953) and later by Pegis in *A Gilson Reader* (New York, 1956).*

Gilson was pleased to go to Princeton because he wanted to see how Maritain was getting along there. The two spent an evening together on Thursday 12 March, and Gilson later reported to Pegis:

> [Maritain] thinks Princeton is a small provincial place. Like the bees, the Princetonians have no conversation. He does not believe in John of St Thomas any longer but does not want the rumour to spread. He vaguely suspects that Cajetan is no better. He is planning to contact Bañez. (55.12.16.)

Actually, neither Maritain nor Gilson saw much need for these commentators except to confirm their own judgements on St Thomas.

During the spring of 1953, one year into his second term as president of the Institute, Pegis became deeply interested in an offer from Doubleday and Company of New York to help them establish a Catholic Textbook Division (CTD) of their publishing business; with some qualms, he went to New York. Curiously enough, Gilson who had been an enemy of the textbook approach to either theology or philosophy, encouraged Pegis and even volunteered to act as a consultant. Perhaps he had somehow become convinced that bad textbooks, not good ones, were the real enemies of education. Also Doubleday was using the term "textbook" widely to cover the placing of all kinds of good books with pertinent prefaces in the hands of Catholic students.

---

* When Pegis was preparing his *Reader* he discovered that Father Halton had copyrighted the paper. Gilson was surprised because he had, on learning of the chaplaincy's precarious financial condition, refused Halton's promised $500 fee; he was "as surprised ... as Romain Rolland when after giving his *Jean-Christoff* to Péguy, he noticed that Péguy had reserved to himself all rights of reproduction: *si licet parva componere magis*" (EG to Pegis, 57.3.6). Gilson wrote Halton, whom he considered "a nice man," and was quickly granted "unreserved rights" for what Halton described as "a gift of your own giving" (57.4.7).

Pegis wrote Gilson enthusiastically from New York:

> The CTD is growing. One manuscript is now ready for the printer, and we have a second one in hand. The third will be in during October. All three are science manuscripts. We shall also have an American-history manuscript in January or February. (53.7.7.)

These works were far removed from medieval studies and, indeed, functioned as modern apologetics.

In 1953 Gilson was fairly indifferent to the project. By the following year he was better disposed toward it, and even agreed to do two prefaces: one for a collection of social encyclicals by "my very dear friend Pope Leo XIII," published as *The Church Speaks to the Modern World* (New York, 1954; McG 507); the other for a textbook edition of J. H. Newman's *Grammar of Assent* (New York, 1955; McG 524). However, much as Gilson liked Leo XIII, Cardinal Newman, and Pegis, he found his first foray into the CTD tedious and frustrating. He wrote to Pegis about the first preface:

> You were not pleased with what I wrote first, so I changed it. ... Here, at any rate, is the abortive fruit of my Saturday vigil, the revised preface. It is yours for whatever you may wish to do with it: rewrite, correct, shorten, lengthen etc. ... I was tempted to become personal, toward the middle of the paper. I would have liked to quote the words of Van Dusen to Julian Huxley at the Arden House Conference on the Unity of Knowledge: "You are the most arrogant dogmatist I have ever heard." But I don't think such barbed shafts ever do any good. Besides, in the matter of arrogance, we Catholics don't always do badly. (54.2.21.)

The summer of 1953 was spent in France and was doubly exhausting. Gilson's daughter Jacqueline had to have a major operation which, though successful, made an invalid of her for much of the summer. Gilson was not well either. He had a number of dizzy spells which his brother, the radiologist Maurice, assured him resulted from his obesity; Gilson's girth had reached an uncomfortable extreme. Maurice urged his brother to diet strenuously.

During this summer, the Eleventh International Congress of Philosophy was held in Brussels from 20 to 26 August. Gilson did not feel like attending but, on pressure from Louvain, consented to give a paper on the last day of the congress; this was entitled "Remarques sur l'expérience en métaphysique" (*Actes du XIᵉ congrès international de philosophie* [Amsterdam and Louvain, 1953]; McG 429). At the congress Gilson became even more acutely aware of the urgency of his weight problem. On the day the speakers were to meet the king of Belgium, Gilson literally got stuck in his bathtub and had to ring for emergency assistance. He almost missed, he said afterward, shaking hands with the Belgian king. The situation was also complicated by an attack of sciatica, though Gilson never mentioned this when he told the story. (EG to Pegis, 53.9.2.)

4 NORTH AMERICAN DEMANDS, 1954

During the winter-spring term of 1954 in Toronto, Gilson was preoccupied with his work for the CTD and with the preparation of his six Mellon lectures for the National Gallery in Washington the next year. The CTD work was both a burden and a worry; he disliked the project, yet was consulted on every move Pegis took. Gilson judged manuscripts, prepared long lists of items suitable for textbook publication or as Image Books, and made quick trips to New York for consultations. He also planned books of his own for the textbook series, books that did ultimately appear (*Elements of Christian Philosophy, A History of Philosophy*), though in a different and more suitable context.

Although the preparation of the Mellon Lectures was equally trying, it was considerably more satisfying. Gilson had long wanted to undertake a major work on the relation between philosophy and art. In 1953 he was highly pleased when invited to give the fourth series of Mellon Lectures at the National Gallery in Washington during 1955; his lectures would follow series by Jacques Maritain, Kenneth Clark and Herbert Read. The lectures were highly paid but had to meet rigid conditions: Gilson had to prepare a detailed plan of the lectures well in advance, deliver a sample lecture, and then produce a publishable text worthy of an expensive Bollingen format.

In January 1954, over a year before the lectures were to be given, Gilson lunched with the Bollingen editor, Huntingdon Cairns, in the Cosmos Club of Washington to go over in detail the plan of his talks. The following day, Sunday 17 January, he and Cairns lunched with David E. Finlay, director of the National Gallery, in Finlay's Georgetown home. Later in the afternoon, Gilson delivered a sample lecture before an audience at the gallery on "The Aesthetic Doctrines of Maurice Denis." Denis was a friend of Gilson's: he was also Jacqueline's painting master and a disciple of Delacroix, some of whose philosophical notions Gilson planned on using in his other lectures. No one was leaving the success of the series to chance, and Gilson had a heavy year of preparations ahead of him.

Not surprisingly then, during the winter and spring of 1954, philosophy and art began to fill Gilson's private reflections; they also inspired many informal talks, such as the one he gave at a Jesuit seminary on 24 February. This seminary, on Wellington Street in downtown Toronto, was the residence of such fine advanced graduate students as Linus Thro, Robert Henle and Leo Sweeney. This year Gilson also attended all the sessions of the Mediaeval Academy of America, which again had chosen to meet in Toronto. Although he did not himself give a paper, he was particularly drawn to the session of Saturday morning, 10 April, in which Nevill Coghill addressed the academy on "Medieval Literature and the BBC." Gilson was intrigued by the title, which promised the kind of ingenious medieval-modern interplay he liked to engage in himself. He was also drawn to Nevill Coghill. Gilson had met Coghill's distinguished relative, the paleontologist Sir Bertram Allan Coghill Windle, in Toronto in 1927, and was still a good friend of Windle's widow.

At the end of April Gilson visited the Thibaudeaus in Montréal. He went on to Halifax to lecture at Mount St Vincent College on 29 April, and returned to Paris on 30 May. Just as the previous year, he was in France from late May until late September. The summer was marred by uncertain health and a number of commitments which, to his frustration, competed for his attention and interfered with his work on the Mellon lectures.

The first of these distractions concerned the new Centre d'Études Supérieures de Civilisation Médiévale at Poitiers. A. Loyon, rector of the Académie de Poitiers, had in January asked Gilson to serve on the new centre's council (54.1.15). Gilson had consented and had also agreed to provide six lectures during the centre's first session between 19 July and 22 August. Even as he prepared these lectures, however, Pegis begged him to take on more work for CTD; Pegis wanted Gilson to accept an invitation from Mgr Elwell, schools superintendent in Cleveland, to speak to his teachers on the nature of high-school education:

> There are many people in American Catholic Education who think that education consists in what they call adjustment, or life-adjustment, social adjustment, etc. They do not like to think that education in the school consists in instruction, that is, has intellectual purposes and objectives, and that it should respect the need of the child to undergo the discipline of learning. Right now it is important to say something on the nature of teaching and learning, especially at the high-school level where a curriculum is in the process of being built. (54.6.28.)

Gilson's first answer was a refusal, his second a compromise. He eventually lectured for Elwell in October 1955, a year later than the invitation specified.

There were other distractions for Gilson this summer as he struggled to return to work on the Mellon lectures. The most obtrusive was an invitation to join the Third Annual Congress for Peace and Christian Culture in Florence, 20 to 26 June:

> So far I have spent a week reading manuscripts for my friend Vrin. Then I came here [Vermenton] to join Jacqueline. We shall go back to Paris on Wednesday and fly to Milan next Friday. A train is supposed to take us to Florence the same day. Besides toning down my Florence lecture, I have done very little since coming to Vermenton. Yesterday and today I have played a little with my painters. Problem: Is a hierarchy of the genres of painting a justifiable notion? Oh! My head! (EG to Pegis, 54.6.14.)

At the congress Gilson delivered a paper on "L'universalisme et la paix" which was given over to the themes of revelation and unity. Other lecturers at the congress included Mme B. R. Sen, Indian ambassador to Italy, Père Jean Daniélou of Paris, Allen Tate of the United States and Father Martin Darcy of England; the Holy See was represented by Monsignor Castelli. After this congress, Gilson and Jacqueline went on to Venice for eight days where Jacqueline could explore Venetian art. Indeed Gilson devoted almost a month largely to his daughter's interest in art; as the Mellon lectures were to focus on painting, Jacqueline's career was useful to him.

Gilson also took Jacqueline along on his cartrip to give his six lectures in Poitiers between 2 and 13 August. As at most summer programmes, any slack in lecture hours was taken up by local tours and social functions, most of which Gilson and Jacqueline attended. At a *déjeuner* with the Dominicans, Gilson met the authority on the *Sentences*, Father Moos, who directed him to two important articles that he didn't know existed.* Gilson's aide-mémoire listed other entries too: "Cabaude-de Templiers" [Hotel]; "diner R. Crozet, thé Jollivet"; "soirée Cité-Universitaire."

From 17 August to 8 September Gilson and Jacqueline stayed in Vichy where both of them took the waters. His comment, in a letter to Pegis from Villa des Lotus, Vichy-Allier, is typical: "It is raining cats and dogs practically every day. Vichy water is a sad drink. Besides, there are too many different wells, all of them specialized in the healing of different ailments, except (alas) mental sterility." (54.8.20.) This "mental sterility" reflected Gilson's frustration concerning his lack of work for either the CTD or the Mellon lectures.

Pegis had become so involved with Doubleday that he had been forced to resign his presidency of the Institute so he could go to New York for a few years to work on his new mission. He resigned in the spring of 1954 and was replaced in the fall, after Gilson's return from France. The new president was Father E. J. McCorkell, who had been a professor of English, a college head, a founder of the Institute and, until recently, superior-general of the Basilian Fathers. Joseph Owens, a young Redemptorist father, was hired to replace Pegis in the teaching work of the Institute; Gilson was the prime mover in the acquisition of Owens from the Redemptorist Seminary in Woodstock, Ontario.

The election of Father McCorkell was generally approved, though some objected that he was not a medievalist. However, the Institute was in serious financial straits and many rightly considered McCorkell able to solve its problems; though Gilson liked Pegis he was not sorry to see him resign. For Gilson the issue of the presidency was largely a matter of dollars and cents:

> We spent the traditional [Christmas] afternoon at our friend Sampson's. After dinner, when he was well in his cups – after all they were his – he expressed his disgust at what the poor Institute was doing and not doing. He was for a layman as president, not a damned Basilian. I asked [Sampson] how many dollars he had contributed to the success of this cause. Then he got foxy. I dared him to sign over to me a cheque for $20,000, which, of course, he didn't do. Thus I could conclude: "If the Basilians are paying for it, let them do what they please. If you want your say, sit down at your desk and make out your cheque. You will have the right to talk up to the amount of your gift." He was so frightened he ran out of the room. So, we got peace on earth to the extent it can be got. (54.12.26.)

---

* These were both by Ramirez: "De propria indole philosophiae S. Thomae Aquinatis" in *Xenia Thomistica*, Rome, 1923; and "De ipsa philosophia in universum ..." in *Ciencia Tomista*, July 1922-Jan. 1924. Gilson was excited about these articles which renewed his interest in Bañez, the Spanish commentator on St Thomas who had been so useful to him on the meaning of *esse* when preparing the fifth edition of *Le thomisme*. (EG to Pegis, 54.8.15.)

Three days later Sampson gave a small dinner to mark Father Phelan's fortieth anniversary. The next morning Father McCorkell called at Gilson's office to report that he had just been given two thousand dollars for two Institute scholarships. Gilson was delighted: "That's what I call fast work. The rebuking of Alex Sampson was not entirely in vain." (EG to Pegis, 54.12.30.) Sampson, incidentally, was always a generous and loyal supporter of the Institute project. Throughout the fall of 1954 Gilson worked at top speed on the Mellon lectures. They moved well but, as late as December, he did not know toward what conclusion:

> The Mellon lectures are going at a good pace. While in the middle of what is now chapter 8, I suddenly jumped to the conclusion, that is, to chapter 10, but I am afraid that fifteen pages in two days is not a normal philosophical rate. True enough, I have been thinking about the problem for two solid years, unless it is forty. I also know I have not yet written the end of the conclusion, and that when I do the whole book will have to be rewritten in the light of the last chapter. (54.12.30.)

This fall Columbia University invited Gilson to take part in celebrating the bicentenary of its founding. A Conference on the Unity of Knowledge was held at Arden House in Harriman, New York from 27 to 30 October 1954. This was to be followed by a charterday dinner in the Walfdorf-Astoria with Queen Mother Mary of England and many of the world's leading statesmen and educators in attendance; there would also be a bicentennial convocation in the Cathedral of St John the Divine. Gilson was invited to speak at the conference and would also receive an honorary degree, as would the Queen Mother, Julian Huxley, Archibald MacLeish, Paul-Henri Spaak, Konrad Adenauer and Dag Hammarskjöld.

On the morning of 28 October, Gilson, Niels Bohr and John Herman Randall spoke at Arden House on the subtheme, "The World for Knowledge." Gilson's paper was one of the most important of his career. Although it was not heard or read by very many, it offered a digest of his views on theology in the 1950s. What was writ large in *The History of Christian Philosophy in the Middle Ages* was writ small in this paper, published under the title, "Theology and the Unity of Knowledge" (in *The Unity of Knowledge* [New York, 1955], pp. 35-46; McG 477).

In his paper Gilson approaches the unity of knowledge from the point of view of medieval theology rather than of science or philosophy. The medieval theologian was not a Greek philosopher in that his God was unknown, nameless and a creator. Medieval theologies debated, for example, whether the infinity attributed to God was negative or positive, an imperfection or a perfection. Some, such as Henry of Ghent and Duns Scotus, suspected that infinity was a positive perfection; nonetheless, neither of them concluded either that God or the world He freely created could be totally known. Later, however, Descartes and others who thought like Greeks used the idea that infinity was a perfection to speak of knowledge of the world in terms of a totality.

According to Gilson, medieval theology – or any theology for that matter – makes no attempt to tell us whether the world is a chaos, a cosmos or something between the two. It tells us simply that we cannot know God, and that "a unified world of knowledge escapes cognoscibility." As Gilson explained to the Arden Conference, unity of knowledge for a medieval theologian is simply not an issue:

> Assuredly we still believe that there is order in reality and that, without order, no world of knowledge is in any sense possible, but we have ceased to think that the relation of countable parts to a whole is the highest type of intelligible order. We have even ceased to imagine that what is deepest and best in any finite part can be expressed in terms of quiddities and exhaustively expressed by means of abstract definitions. The world in which Christians have learned to live is no less perfect than the Greek cosmos ever was in the minds of the Greeks, but its perfection comes to it from the infinity of its cause which, being beyond all, perfects all. No conceivable image could picture to us such a world, yet we do need images and, since our preferred image of the world is a perfect sphere, let us also remember that it is a sphere whose centre is in infinity. (p. 46.)

5 ART TO THEOLOGY, 1955-1957

Early in 1955 Gilson wrote to Mme Thibaudeau that he was overwhelmed by "a horrible dread that never leaves me." Thérèse was gone, his daughters, now well into their forties, were still unmarried, and Bernard was unwell. Gilson buried himself in his projects for CTD in New York, and in his preparations for the Mellon lectures. Only work, he lamented, "lets me drift a little closer to equilibrium" (55.2.1; tr.). Gilson was also feeling the beginning of the prostate trouble which would soon require surgery; he was continually reminded of death as a series of heart attacks forced his younger brother André into a convalescent home for priests near Paris.

Besides these woes, there still nagged the injury done him by *The Commonweal*. Although the *Commonweal* staff tried in small ways to repair the damage, Gilson did not consider this enough:

> The only thing they have never done is to say that Waldemar Gurian had neither seen me nor heard me during the four days I spent at Notre Dame. That was the only thing I wanted them to acknowledge because it was the bare truth. I still do not believe their honesty and I do not think their disgraceful behaviour should be encouraged in any way. I feel a victim to moral or character assassination. I still am dishonoured in my own country, I am still refused honorable discharge from the Collège de France. ... For them this is a thing of the past, for me it remains present in its consequences. (EG to Pegis: 55.2.1.)

There were also financial concerns this year. Gilson sent Jacqueline to Paris to sell the properties on rue Émile Acollas and in Melun that had belonged to her, Cécile and Bernard since Thérèse's death. Selling the houses turned out to be a characteristic financial mistake; Gilson greatly missed Thérèse's shrewd business judgment.

In January Gilson published his *History of Christian Philosophy in the Middle Ages* (New York, 1955; McG 65). The *History* was very different from Gilson's previous books on medieval thought. It had been "entirely taught and written at the Pontifical Institute of Mediaeval Studies" and took the form of a kind of textbook. Gilson charged his notes and bibliographies with fascinating profiles similar to the thumbnail sketches of thirty years earlier in his edition of Descartes' *Discours de la méthode*. A typical example is the book's lively and personal treatment of Alcuin. Enthusiastic historians had long conferred upon Alcuin all kinds of skills he never actually possessed, presenting him as an impossible paragon in politics, diplomacy, paleography, liturgy and so on. Gilson modified this view to present Alcuin as the essential teacher, an intermediate humanist, a lover of learning, and the principal agent in an eighth-century *translatio studii* from York to Aachen and from Aachen to Tours.

Gilson submitted his lecture notes to Random House for publication without taking the precaution of showing them to some of his colleagues. He did not like what he found in the galley sheets and set about making extensive revisions. Saxe Commins, his editor, was not as tolerant as Vrin usually was, and objected strenuously to the book being rewritten in galleys. Commins complained bitterly to Pegis, who passed the complaint on to Gilson in an ameliorated form:

> I had lunch with Saxe Commins yesterday noon. He told me about the very friendly feud you two have been carrying on by correspondence. ... I can add that Saxe is very anxious to have the *History* out this fall. (54.3.24.)

Gilson replied later the same month:

> I have received and corrected the first hundred pages or so. Father Maurer is reading the galleys after me. ... If they push the work ... I shall have corrected all the galleys of the text and part of the notes before flying to Europe. (54.3.24.)

The book was ready in the fall and released in January 1955. The high costs billed to Gilson for author's alterations were nearly met by the royalties from the first printing of 6,500 copies.

When the book was finally published, Random House made certain Gilson got some personal publicity. Both *Time* and *Newsweek* sent reporters to interview him on current topics. What, the *Time* reporter asked, did Gilson think of the results of the recent Gallup Poll on the extent and nature of belief in God in the United States. Though Gilson recognized the poll for what it was, a survey of off-the-cuff opinions solicited with journalistic thoughtlessness, he agreeably tried to locate them in the history of thought. He claimed that he saw much sense in the public's replies, most of which were derived through the "proof from order." St Paul himself had recommended this proof in Romans 1:20 when he spoke of the "invisible things" of God being "clearly seen" from "the things that are made." However, Gilson thought that most people were too neglectful of St Augustine's argument for God as derived from moral conscience, "which leads men to God through consideration of the presence of truth in the mind." (*Time*, 55.1.10.)

The *History of Christian Philosophy* was reviewed by prestigious critics, including Walter Lippman and Reinhold Niebuhr. After Lippman published his review he sent Gilson a copy of his own *The Public Philosophy*; Gilson found this work excellent, though it showed "how far modern states are from being directed by philosophers." As for Niebuhr's review:

> I thanked him, and assured him that if he considered my position as that of the "thomists" he still has some illusions to lose. His paper was really very good. He was caught between two duties: either as a Protestant to tear the book apart, or else to follow ... his heart so as not to look like a Protestant. ... He acquitted himself remarkably well. (EG to Pegis, 55.1.28.)

The second significant event of Gilson's career in 1955 was the delivery of his six Mellon Lectures in March and April at the National Gallery in Washington. Essentially his lecture format followed the philosophical catechism he had acquired from his Sorbonne masters forty-five years earlier: he asked himself pertinent questions, then proceeded to answer them from his own ontological positions. Does a painting exist? Does it exist in the same mode as things exist in nature? Does it exist in the realm of knowing or of being? Can its mode of existence be specified, for example, by origin? What have painters said about the origin of their paintings?

For answers to his questions Gilson first turned to particular paintings themselves, just as he had done on his walk-day outings to the Louvre as a Champist some fifty years earlier. He then turned for answers to the writings, journals and jottings of painters. Finally he consulted his own experience, not as a painter himself but as the loving father of a painter whose work he had often followed from earliest sketch to finished canvas. In each case the answers were the same. A painting does exist, and its mode of existence and the origin of its existence are different from those of the realities of nature; the specifying factors are the origin of each painting's active existence and the uniqueness of that act of being. Moreover, it had suddenly struck Gilson that these answers came more clearly from non-representational paintings which did not confuse the issue by appearing to imitate something else.

Gilson was in no sense the first art critic either to begin his analysis with paintings themselves or to move from these into deeper philosophical questions. He was, however, the first to move from paintings into the context of their *être et essence*. Moreover he was able to point out that many painters – Gaugin, Delacroix, Secusier, Denis – had reflected deeply on their own paintings with not dissimilar results; the opinions expressed by these artists provided much of the "stuff" of the Mellon lectures.

Gilson does not propose any thomist philosophy of painting, and does not believe any existed in St Thomas. He sees no point in torturing an art criticism out of Thomas as James Joyce does in chapter 5 of *Portrait of the Artist as a Young*

Man or Jacques Maritain in *Art and Scholasticism*, or Eric Gill in *Beauty Looks After Herself*. Far better, decides Gilson, to admit that Thomas knew very little, possibly nothing, about fine art and, a fortiori, about painting.

According to Gilson those who have previously attempted a philosophical definition of art, most notably Jacques Maritain, have never succeeded in taking art outside the philosophy of knowing. Painting, according to Gilson's personal synthesis, is not a knowledge but what Aristotle called a *habitus operativus*, an operation of the entire man, not just a perception. Gilson does not agree with either John of St Thomas or Maritain that a formula like *recta ratio factibilium* could ever define art or take it beyond knowledge into reality.

Gilson also points out the limitations of phenomenology and cites Leibniz' remark that "systems are true in what they affirm and false in what they deny":

> Phenomenology is a very important discovery and is here to stay. Even if its arrival should not prevent the survival of ontology, the fecund investigation of the manifold modes of phenomenological existence deserves to be carried on, as it has been ever since the time of Hegel, with increased care, but the aesthetic implications of this new philosophical attitude are not so simple as they seem to be in the eyes of some contemporary aestheticians. (pp. 13-14.)

In other words, beauty is not only in the eye of the beholder, but also in the mode of existence of the painting. This mode emerges from the creative work of the artist, and is unique to the existence of each painting.

Throughout *Painting and Reality* Gilson attempts to bring sound ontology to bear on art criticism without ever claiming that he has reached definitions or solved problems. He also provides a forthright defence of the journey of art away from the representational toward the abstract, that is, away from natural toward man-made realities. As a philosopher Gilson fully approves of the ascetic effort of contemporary artists to strip art of the allurements on which it has traditionally relied for the favour of the public. He believes that as art moves toward more abstract forms it also moves away from the order of language toward the order of being: "It is more important to create a being whose justification is in itself than to turn out clever images of such beings." And again: "Images add nothing to existing reality; artistic creations do increase the sum total of the objects whose reality is as certain as their intelligibility." And still again: "Being comes before knowledge. Because painting is art, painting stands on the side of being." (pp. 282-284.)

Painting and Reality (New York, 1957; McG 99) was published in English in the Bollingen Series with many colour plates. The book remained true to the oral and visual presentation of the lectures themselves. The French version, *Peinture et réalité: problèmes et controverses* (Paris, 1958; McG 102) was better organized and used further scholarly material, notably *The Transformation of Nature in Art* by Ananda K. Coomaraswamy; however, the French version lacked the fine indexing and the panoply of visual materials that the Bollingen edition supplied. *Painting and Reality* was one of Gilson's more original achievements. Its spirit soon flowed over into other important, though lesser, books, into *Introduction aux arts du beau* (Paris, 1963; McG 79) and *Matières et formes* (Paris, 1964; McG 88). It also influenced many an address, notably Gilson's memorable 'L'énigme de la peinture" for the Alliance Française de Montréal, 2 February 1957 (see *La presse*, Montréal, 57.2.9).

Six weeks in Washington with only one lecture a week left Gilson with time on his hands. Monsignor Hart, whom Gilson had met at meetings of the American Catholic Philosophical Association, invited him to speak to the students of his regular philosophy seminar at Catholic University. Gilson was delighted. He knew he was persona non grata at Catholic University, at least with the administration, just as he was at Louvain and Laval; because he had been Sorbonne-trained and committed from youth to the French university system he was still viewed with suspicion in some narrowly Catholic circles. Hart knew that the dean of philosophy, Father Ignatius Smith, was not disposed to be friendly to Gilson; in fact, he doubted that Smith would even authorize Gilson's honorarium. Hart counted on Gilson's far-ranging reputation and prudently moved the lecture to McMahon Auditorium which could seat 450 students; also prudently, he asked Smith to deliver the introduction. On the afternoon of the lecture 750 persons packed the auditorium, its doorways and beyond. Smith introduced Gilson, carefully pointing out that he personally held no brief for Christian philosophy and citing texts from Thomas in his own support. There was tension in the audience, and some considered the introduction insulting to Gilson. As for Gilson himself, Smith's remarks provided precisely the stimulus he needed to produce one of the major classroom performances of his life. His lecture was followed by long rousing cheers, then by a lively question period. The event capped his Washington sojourn, but left some bad feelings in its wake (below, pp. 386-387).

Gilson spent the summer of 1955 quietly and relatively happily in Vermenton. All four Gilsons were there together in July, and went as a group to Lourdes. Gilson worked hard all summer, mostly on chores for Pegis at CTD: he prepared the Cleveland lecture for Monsignor Elwell that Pegis had asked him for; drew up a plan for a Catholic Nurses' Library as a CTD project; prepared an introduction for a CTD edition of St Augustine's *Confessions*; and played with an invitation to do a "Maritain Reader," a companion volume to Pegis' *A Gilson Reader*. He also tried to get Maritain to do a major CTD volume, and spoke to Maritain about it personally when the two were together in Toronto the next winter:

> Jacques Maritain has just left for Union Station. I snatched about thirty minutes of free conversation with him. Naturally I approached him on the matter of the book. One point is clear; he likes the idea of four thousand dollars, but he wonders about the meaning of the formula – a book of about three hundred pages on a subject of general interest. He asked me if a book on "the sin of angels" would be considered a topic of general interest. I replied by asking if this would introduce the notion of sin in man. His answer was, "No! It is sin in *angels* ...." The book (I said) would have a tremendous sales appeal for citizens of the Empyrean ... but not in this sublunary world. And that was that. But he sure wants the dollars, and there is nothing quite like them to fecundate a man's intellectual imagination. (55.12.16.)

Gilson was not exactly disinterested in dollars himself, like Maritain, he was far from wealthy. He had begun to act as a consultant for Pegis' Image Books, a reprint series run jointly with CTD. However, when he came to make out his income tax returns for Canada, France and the United States, he found that his consultant's fees were entirely wiped out. He dramatically resigned from his consultantship, which he considered at any rate an unwelcome intrusion on his life as a scholar. He did agree to keep his commitments to Pegis, which he was not to escape until 1961.

In 1956 Gilson embarked upon a new adventure when he was invited to lecture in Bogota, Colombia. At first he refused:

> They asked me for a certificate of good conduct, to be obtained from the police, and of good health from my doctor. My health is so good I have no doctor. I don't want to ask for a certificate from the police: what if they refused it? So politely I wrote that I am a very busy man. (EG to Pegis, 56.3.14.)

He soon relented and arranged a flight to Bogota via New York, where he was to hand over to his Bollingen publisher the second half of his manuscript for *Painting and Reality* on April 12. No sooner were these plans finalized than a letter arrived from his brother Maurice in France. Maurice and his second wife, Bernadette, were arriving in Montréal on 27 March to begin a long tour of American hospitals. Undaunted, Gilson changed nothing. Already scheduled to be in Montréal that day for a radio broadcast, he simply went the night before to meet his brother's early-morning plane. He gave his radio talk for CKAC, took his brother and sister-in-law on a tour of Montréal's two largest hospitals, introduced them to doctor-friends and arranged dinner for them at the Thibaudeaus'. He then took Maurice and Bernadette to Québec City for a two-day trip and returned them to Montréal to continue their tour. He flew home to Toronto at once and worked furiously on the Bollingen manuscript. On 12 April he left as scheduled, with the manuscript under his arm and a suitcase in his hand, for two days in New York and two months in South America.

In New York Gilson went directly to his publishers, unburdening himself of his manuscript. Then, to unwind, he visited Radio City Music Hall – an old love – to hear Mario Lanza whom he found "stupide." He also went to the Roxy to hear – or rather watch – *une chanteuse française* named Vicky Aubier: "Ballet les filles de Paris sont les girls qui patinent sur la glace et montrent leurs tutus rouges." His last evening in New York was spent gossiping with Pegis over dinner at Chez Cézanne.

Gilson flew out of New York at ten o'clock the next morning, 14 April, and reached Bogota the same evening. After mass the following day, he entrusted himself to the embassy man, J. M. Chavez, who was to accompany him around Colombia. In Bogota Gilson was to deliver twenty-one lectures in twelve days, and in São Paulo Brazil, he was to give six lectures in nine days. These talks would largely be on "Being According to St Thomas Aquinas" with now and then a Mellon variation – "tableaux et existence" "The Labyrinth of Painting."

Gilson's tour through Bogota's nine universities was a kind of triumphal march. "My lectures," he wrote Pegis, "caught like a prairie fire" with few rooms large enough for the crowds; his audience "seemed to understand something for the first time" (56.7.23). Brazil wanted his lectures published as a book, and asked him to have his text translated into Portuguese; although this didn't happen, the text appeared in Spanish as *La existencia en Santo Tomas de Aquino: conferencias pronunciadas en Bogota durante los dias 16 a 20 de abril de 1956* (tr. by Fernando Rivas Sacconi [Bogota, 1956]; McG 48). Pegis also wanted a book of the lectures in English, but had to make do with the special paper Gilson had already written for *The Gilson Reader*.

On 11 June Gilson left São Paulo for France and arrived, via Africa, at Orly for his seventy-second birthday. The next day, Thursday 14 June, he attended the regular weekly meeting of the Académie Française. He had rushed back to Europe because he had an appointment in Bonn, Germany on 18 June to receive "Der Orden *Pour le Mérite* für Wissenschaften und Kunste." This was a gratifying award, and reminded him of a lifetime of German experiences:

> In Bonn I saw Werner Jaeger. A better example of the helpless German scholar cannot be found. And was he wonderfully happy! Harvard could easily lose him in the future. I too was wonderfully happy, because on Sunday night, June 17, I heard *Fidelio* in Beethoven's own city at the Stadtheater. Those Germans are musicians indeed. We just play around music. (aide-mémoire, 56.6.17.)

That summer Gilson again shared Vermenton with Jacqueline and Bernard. All three drove together to Poitiers where Gilson gave a summer course of six lectures. At Poitiers he met a young Benedictine, Callistus Edie, from Collegeville, Minnesota, who was writing a doctoral dissertation at Louvain on Gilson's thought. Gilson was amazed at the thoroughness of Edie's bibliography and promised to help make it complete. Through 1956 and 1957 he corresponded at length with Edie, whose bibliography later became the lead-off item in the *Mélanges ... Gilson* (Toronto, 1959; McG 945).

Following the Poitiers sojourn, Bernard had a serious nervous breakdown. He was driven to leave his home and his broken-hearted father behind him. "De profundis ... fiat voluntas Sua," wrote Gilson in his aide-mémoire (56.8.25), "du côté de l'homme, il ne reste que désespoir." Further jottings record some of his son's words.

During this summer of 1956 Gilson was invited by Charles Boyer to prepare a paper for the Roman Academy of St Thomas Aquinas; the paper would be published in a future number of *Doctor Communis* dedicated to Pius XII. Boyer suggested some nineteen possible themes. Gilson, who had not been much impressed by Pius XII's philosophical statements, was annoyed to find Boyer's *temi* distributed in Italian and to find them rather contradictory. He threw letter and list into the wastebasket, but sensibly rescued them after further reflection – he had always found popes irresistible.

Gilson prepared a paper for Boyer covering two of the contradictory themes: "raccomandazioni della dottrina di S. Tommaso" and "la filosofia fondamentale a tutti necessaria." He suggested that accommodation was possible only if one took "filosofia fondamentale a tutti necessaria" to refer to any naturally knowable truth which also happened to be revealed by God. Gilson implied that this accommodation was at best facile, and was surprised when Boyer missed the irony and accepted the article. He wrote to Pegis:

> This very morning I received my answer: "Your article deals with a real problem, and I don't think it can be better handled than you do it. The expression 'filosofia fondamentale a tutti necessaria' is probably too abrupt. As applied to *Humani generis* it ought to be reduced to something like this: there is a base in traditional philosophy which no Christian can reject. See my 'Lectures on *Humani generis*' in *Gregorianum*, 31 (1950): 535. What you are saying is correct and rightly said. Once more my thanks." (EG to Pegis, 56.8.29.)

Gilson was uneasy about Boyer's letter and worried that he had somehow left the impression that he had accommodated his real position to the wording of Boyer's theses (below, pp. 354-355). The paper was published as "Sur deux thèmes de réflexion" (*Doctor Communis*, 10 [1957]: 155-164; McG 458).

On 12 September 1956 Gilson went to Spain to participate in a three-day Pax Christi congress held in Valladolid. Speaking at the congress besides Gilson were President Pella of Spain, Professor Milat of Bonn, and others. The congress' theme was the religious aspect of patriotism and good citizenship at national and international levels; this explored some of the issues faced at The Hague and at subsequent European congresses at Geneva. Gilson spoke last, in an address entitled "Cité des hommes et cité de dieu" (*Documentation catholique*, 53 (1956): 1437-1447; McG 589). In this paper he returned to themes that had run through his successful Louvain lectures and that he had met again in his recent paper for Boyer. He pointed out that philosophy in the strict sense was "of this world" while the peace of Christ was a grace; in appealing to God's promise of peace Gilson maintained he was strengthening rather than weakening his reason. Important for this practical exercise in Christian philosophy was Gilson's first footnote, which dealt with the *Aeterni patris* of Leo XIII:

> Those who link their philosophical endeavours with Christian faith philosophize best: "qui philosophiae studium cum obsequio fidei christianae conjungunt, ii optime philosophantur." The same pontiff sometimes called this "Christian philosophy," by which he meant the proper way for Christians to philosophize. (p. 1438, n. 1.)

At the end of September, Gilson returned as usual to Toronto where he again offered his popular course on "Christian Humanism" (above, p. 239); this time he placed more than usual emphasis on Anglo-Saxon England, though he continued the theme, as previously, through to Petrarch. Gilson's heavy work this term was reading proofs for *Painting and Reality* which was soon to appear. He wanted particularly to avoid the lawsuits that might result from his lectures' descriptions of the Hahn *Belle ferronière* as a fake, and of the Louvre *Belle ferronière* as "attributed to Leonardo da Vinci." His editor William McGuire was also worried:

> Concerning the Hahn painting, the point of view at the gallery was that labelling
> your plate specifically a fake would entail risk of a lawsuit ... while labelling it
> specifically genuine, as its owners would wish, would be repugnant both to the
> gallery and yourself. A court would, I think, consider you to be speaking as an
> expert (and paid). (56.12.11.)

Germain Bazin of the Palais du Louvre advised that their painting be labelled
simply "Leonardo da Vinci"; Bazin regarded the Louvre painting as genuine and
thought it was labelled as such. Gilson was sure it had been labelled "attr. à
Leonardo" and asked Mlle d'Alverny to check for him. She wrote:

> I went to the Louvre this morning with three of my nephews. ... They allowed me
> five minutes in the Grand Gallery to interrogate *La belle ferronière*. This painting
> bears a label; it is not a recent one, and reads "attr. à Leonardo da Vinci." You don't
> have to alter your proofs. (56.12.30; tr.)

Not for nothing had Gilson been visiting the Louvre since his schooldays as
a boy in Paris. Three weeks later a second letter came from Bazin, agreeing that
the label read "attr. à," but reiterating that the painting was almost certainly
Leonardo's. Bazin complained that the public always took "attr. à" to certify that a
painting was not the master's when in fact it usually meant the opposite.
(57.1.17.)

In December 1956, the assembly of the Collège de France at last recommended
that Gilson be given his honorariat. On 26 December, the day of the announcement, Francisque Gay, ambassodor of France, who had first brought
Gilson into political office, wrote him an exultant letter. Clearly Gilson had
withdrawn almost completely from public life during the intervening years: "I
have scrupulously respected over these last few years your desire to be left in
silence. I cannot tell you how much I have sometimes wanted to break in upon it.
I am sure that you will allow me to express all the joy I felt on opening *Le
monde*." (Gay to EG, 56.12.26; tr.)

Gay gave Gilson a quick rundown of political activities during the chaotic
postwar years in France: François Mauriac continued to practise his extraordinary talent for polemic, for pulverizing adversaries, for closing his eyes to
nothing; Étienne Borne and Bidault were still releasing incredible articles to their
respective journals, *Forces nouvelles* and *Carrefour*; the socialists, in an uncomfortable parliamentary position, managed to join easily with the opposition
they had just finished condemning; the right, divided and obtuse, still tolerated
any stupidity and any shoddy deal; General de Gaulle and his block of faithful still
struggled to explain the kind of regime they would like to substitute for "le
système." As for the MRP, an apparent conformity could not conceal deep
divergencies. Although Pierre Emmanuel and others sometimes wrote brilliantly
in *Témoignage chrétien*, *Esprit*, *Exprès*, *La vie intellectuelle*, *Le monde* and so on,
a few burdened, isolated voices could not offset all the rubbish in these same
papers: "I thought I had myself a certain gift for reacting strongly to events: but
unfortunately I have not the talent needed to express – to have heard and

understood – the judgments and feelings shared by so many" (56.12.26). Gay's commentary was not likely to lure Gilson back into French politics.

Between the announcement of the decision of the Collège de France and its finalization by the ministry, Gilson received a letter from his friend André Rousseaux. Rousseaux had visited Gilson the previous year in Toronto, and had recently been discussing him with Father Bondy in Paris:

> Since then [last August] your name keeps turning up in Paris. Some speak of your eventual return. Some say the students want you back and are complaining that France, which possesses the world's greatest *philosophe-médiéviste*, allows him to remain buried under snow in Toronto. And this reintegration of your honorariat is provoking! Could anyone have wanted this? Is the bulletin a mistake? Only for *Figaro* is the hunting down of neutralism not yet closed. (57.1.3.)

Some four weeks later, 5 February 1957, the Collège's action was finalized by the ministry. Gilson was at last *professeur honoraire*. The administrator of the Collège, M. Bataillon, wrote him shortly thereafter:

> My personal feeling on this matter has never been in doubt where you are concerned. But when an institution, exposed from all sides, commits a grave and scandalous error, it is hard for it to make amends without reviving the old scandal. We have not escaped. *Le monde* characteristically continues to dog us, and *Combat* too with all the stupidity of its managing editor. (57.2.11.)

Such, for Gilson, was the conclusion to a long and sad affair.

6 RETURN TO PARIS

In 1957 Gilson began to turn down almost all invitations to give outside lectures: the only exception was for two unpaid lectures for the Alliance Française de Montréal in February 1957. He turned down prestigious and well-paid offers from Whitney Oakes at Princeton, and from the Pax Monastère de Tioumlelino in Morrocco as well as from colleges in St Paul, Kansas, and Rochester, New York. He even turned down men he knew well, like Sidney Hook of New York and Malcolm Ross of Kingston. The same steady line of refusals continued in the spring of 1957, when he turned down Gaines Post of Wisconsin and others.

Gilson's refusals stemmed partly from his preoccupation with his publishing activities and partly from his dissatisfaction with the tax laws of Canada, the United States and France; these rendered outside lectures financially unprofitable. He was also beginning to suffer a deterioration in his health; for the first time he knew he was aging, and he wrote to André, his priest-brother:

> Each week I refuse invitations to travel to American universities to give lectures. The old rule persists: you have to be old to be known; you get invited when you no longer have the strength to accept and when you hate to waste your strength where you won't produce results. I hate sometimes to refuse because I still have some taste for adventure, but I am satisfied to accept only a few during the summer when it is a kind of holiday and doesn't hurt me. It doesn't do much good either. (57.11.21.)

Gilson did accept two invitations of a different nature in 1957. The first was from Kirtley Mather, president of the then 177-year-old American Academy of Arts and Sciences. The Academy had recently launched a new quarterly, *Daedalus*, and was now trying to consolidate a policy to promote some unity among the scattered intellectual communities inside and outside academe. Gilson agreed to let his name stand on the proposed board of twelve scholars; his entire life had been testimony to such an ideal. The second invitation was an especially gratifying one:

> I have received an invitation to attend the fiftieth anniversary of the University of Freiburg-im-Breisgau. The invitation came from the Faculty of Theology and they offer me an honorary doctorate – in theology! Tony! I shall feel very proud of this one. (EG to Pegis, 57.4.10.)

Gilson regarded this honorary degree as the most significant in his life because it was in theology. His only fear – and a passing one – was that the idea of honouring him in this way had come from Rome, particularly from Boyer:

> I have learned from an extremely reliable and well-informed source that the doctorate in theology conferred by the Catholic University of Lille upon Frank Sheed was a purely Roman initiative. I don't know whether I should hope or fear that the same is the case at Freiburg. ... Lille just got an order and complied with it. *Le propre de l'autorité* ... etc. (EG to Pegis, 57.5.27.)

The Freiburg convocation had to be moved from the auditorium of the Albert-Ludwidgs-Universität to the University Church. There were two other honorary graduands: Abbot Anselm Maria Albareda, prefect of the Vatican Library; and Dr Simon Hirt, apostolic protonotary and chancellor of Freiburg. Each candidate was permitted to address the convocation for fifteen minutes or less from either the ambo or the lectern as he preferred; "And if the speakers are not applauded, don't be surprised!" said the faculty dean as he opened convocation. "The undemonstrative Germans rarely render this kind of approval in church."

The convocation was only one of many anniversary events held in Freiburg at this time. Of special interest to Gilson was an address delivered by Martin Heidegger in the Stadthalle, 27 June at ten-fifteen, entitled "Der Satz der Indentität"; Gilson held reserved seat 469. He always knew he was listening to a great philosopher when tears of emotion ran down his cheeks – he had cried before at Heidegger (above, p. 227) and at Bergson. Some seven months later, when this address was printed along with Heidegger's "Die Onto-theo-logische Verfassung der Metaphysik," Gilson wrote to Pegis:

> The first pages, dealing with Plato and Parmenides would catch your attention at once: "Plato says not only *ekaston auto tauton – jedes selber dasselbe* [each thing itself is the same] – but more especially *ekaston eautò tauton – jedes selber ihm selbst dasselbe* [each thing itself is the same as itself]." Tony, we may not agree with all the answers given by all the great philosophers, but a real philosopher rarely fails to ask the right question. The problem of intellectual communication becomes acute in this wonderful lecture. We ought not to dismiss Heidegger by saying he doesn't

realize what he is saying. He also knows full well what he is largely failing to say. He is taking us to the only real metaphysical problems. I believe he could, with more mental leisure and ability, help us not only to deeper insights into his own thought, but even into that of your own dear Thomas Aquinas. His thought is different, less rooted in negative metaphysics. But it is where it is [and it's] good exercise for the mind to be taken there by his new and unfamiliar way. (58.1.26.)

Gilson also commented on this same Heidegger lecture to Maurer. After speaking of its technical perfection, he added:

I do not think it fair to judge his words from any other perspective than the German language. In French [what he is saying] is unthinkable. But what a problem this raises about relations between language and metaphysics! (57.7.21.)

In 1957 Gilson also attended, with Jacqueline, the twelfth Rencontre Internationale de Genève, from 4 to 14 September. These now regular *rencontres* had grown out of the UNESCO and Hague conferences at which Gilson had been a French delegate. This year the meetings fell at a good time for him and he was eager to speak. The theme was "L'Europe et la liberation de l'art," a theme so in keeping with Gilson's recent Mellon lectures that he may actually have suggested it. In 1957 Europe's international role was in decline, and it had ceased to be the force that held the world together. Gilson argued that its leadership in art may have become "the last hope for a United Europe." Other speakers were André Philip, Max Borne, Paul Henri Spaak and Berredo Carneiro. All spoke on unity, and Philip joined Gilson in emphasizing unity through the creativity of art.

Gilson wrote three other significant pieces at this time, all of considerable beauty. "What is Christian Philosophy?" was originally intended as a preface for the second edition of Aimé Forest's *La structure métaphysique du concret de Saint Thomas*. "Le centenaire d'Auguste Comte" was written for *Le monde* (57.9.4; McG 581) to mark the hundredth anniversary of Comte's death. And "Amicus amicis" was Gilson's warm address to his students as they prepared their *Étienne Gilson Tribute* (Milwaukee, 1959; McG 198) for his seventy-fifth birthday in 1959.

On 15 November 1957, back again in Toronto, Gilson wrote starkly to Pegis: "My friend Joseph Vrin died last Sunday and was buried yesterday. No comment! I am taking it very hard. Once more, I shall get used to it." (57.11.15.) Gilson was deeply upset. Vrin had been his close friend, adviser and publisher. Their careers had risen together and their affection for one another had withstood the trials of forty years. If there was any third party to their friendship, it was Père Chenu, who wrote a consoling letter to Gilson following the funeral in Rouen of their *commun ami* (57.11.14.) Medievalists everywhere were saddened. Stegmüller wrote Gilson from Freiburg that "Vrin's sudden death was hardly shattering, but it touched medievalists deeply" (57.12.10).

Vrin's death was the first of a number of events that by the end of 1957 led Gilson to curtail his teaching in Toronto. Since retiring from the Collège de France in 1951, Gilson had scrupulously spent seven months each year at the Pontifical

Institute and five in France. Now he found himself confronted with heavy complications funnelling upon him from Pegis' publishing ventures in New York. Financially he was caught in a crisis arising from Canadian income-tax policies. He was also becoming increasingly lonely in Toronto and more keenly aware of his old age.

In April 1957 Gilson had been named general editor of a four-volume Catholic textbook to be entitled *History of Philosophy*. A search had been undertaken to find authors to produce volumes on ancient, medieval, early modern, and recent philosophy: suggestions had included Anton Pegis, Armand Maurer, Charles O'Neil, Vernon Bourke, Elizabeth Salmon, A. De Waelhens, Thomas Langan and others. On 15 April Gilson had issued for prospective authors his "Notes on the CTD *History of Philosophy*":

> Let your philosophers speak for themselves as often as can be done. ... Each philosopher will have to be met on his own terms. ... Do not substitute philosophical continuity for historical continuity. ... Historical continuity admits of a fair proportion of discontinuity. ...
>
> Three historical conditions are important: (1) the philosophical situation ... e.g. Socrates was a determining factor in shaping the doctrine of Plato. ... (2) the cultural situation: the conditions of religion and science at the time the philosopher lived. ... (3) the personal situation ... although this often disappears behind the philosophy. These three historical situations are important but not all-important. ...
>
> The substance of the book should consist of a continuing exposition of doctrinal history, simply presented. The best sources for a history of philosophy are the writings of philosophers themselves. ... Never write anything about a philosopher without having one of his books in front of you.

From the beginning of the project Anton Pegis undertook to write the volume on ancient Greek philosophy and Armand Maurer that on medieval philosophy; Gilson himself would not write anything. By December it was apparent however that authors for the third and fourth volumes were not going to be easy to find: acceptable people did not want the job, and those who did want it were unacceptable. Gilson saw the handwriting on the wall, and realized that as general editor he was going to have to rescue the project and fill in as contributing editor as well.* In many ways the fault was his own. His stipulations had been forbidding, and his comments on proferred work had been harsh, offering such judgments as "philosophically weak," "less clear than the original," "still unregenerated," and "in need of preambulatory metanoia," to mention but a few.

In December Gilson also realized, as he assessed his income-tax returns, that his seven months each year in Canada were simply not financially feasible. Because he was in residence for over half the year, he had to pay taxes in Canada

---

* Ultimately it was the first volume, the Pegis volume, that never came out: Pegis was overworked while with CTD, was deeply troubled after his resignation from Doubleday, suffered nagging ill-health and eventually died prematurely. Gilson was extremely disappointed by the volume's absence, particularly when the other three volumes, published in 1962, 1963, 1966, were so successful.

on his entire income – Canadian, American, French – which was nearly $19,000. In 1956 he had paid the Canadian government alone over $5,000, all of which he had paid out of his Canadian income. So he grumbled:

> Unless I am mistaken, $3,860 is what I am actually being paid for seven months work in Canada. Raising my salary here would not help. It would just put me in a higher bracket, which I do not want because here no earning of a writer or teacher is reckoned as costing him anything. Nothing is deductible: attending the meetings of the Academy, going to a foreign university to be honoured, attending international meetings, spending two or three months in countries where the intellectual atmosphere has higher density, nothing of all this is deductible even by token. I have been told the law, and choose not to discuss it. Socrates was right, and his respect for the law cost him more than money. My only conclusion is that I have put myself in the wrong place. ... It is essential for my work here that I be considered a messenger of European culture to Canada, for this is what I am. (EG to Pegis, 57.12.22.)

If he stayed in Canada only three months a year, as he once had done, he could claim most of his professional deductions in France.

During this period loneliness also became increasingly worrisome for Gilson. He was not as close to his Canadian colleagues now as he had been in his early years in Canada. At the Institute he was growing more dependent, while his colleagues grew more independent; this proved that his mission had been successful, but was nonetheless difficult to accept. In the same letter to Pegis Gilson wrote:

> There was a time when I could enjoy intellectual communication with Father Phelan; now we do not communicate any longer. Our mental worlds have been drifting apart. Then there was you. Now there is nobody.

Phelan had retired to Toronto from Notre Dame and, though it was not quite true that he and Gilson did not communicate at all, their mode of communication had become argumentative. Phelan felt that Gilson had always taken Maritain's philosophy of art too lightly. After one of their debates Gilson sat down and wrote a letter to Phelan – who was living in the same college – to try to state more clearly his quarrel with Maritain. First, he points out in the letter, the subject matter of their respective books differs: Maritain's books deal with poetry – *poiesis* – while his own deals with painting as a plastic art. Second, Maritain's use of the expression "creative intuition" is in error; an intuition cannot be creative in the order of material things because it has no hands. Third, Maritain extends the teaching of St Thomas to cases where it does not work and where St Thomas himself never took it.

Maritain, writes Gilson, follows John of St Thomas and applies the notion of *recta ratio factibilium* (reasoning correctly about things that are or can be made) to works of art as though it is a *definition* of art, which it is not. St Thomas' only definition of art, which follows Aristotle exactly, is that art is a *habitus operativus cum recta ratione* (an operative habit rightly understood). On those occasions where St Thomas uses *recta ratio factibilium* he is not defining art, he is simply distinguishing practical arts from morals; John of St Thomas mistakes this for a definition, and so does Maritain. In fact St Thomas knew nothing about painting, and never thought about that art. Had he done so, Gilson argues, he would have connected art to being, to the entire man, and not to some form of knowledge – to take art to knowledge is to indulge in the sophism of misplaced intellectualism. Cognition stands on the side of the intellect but, if art is operative, *habitus operativus*, it does not stand entirely on the side of the intellect; knowledge alone neither makes nor operates. Maritain then is sometimes a neothomist, in that he regards the *neoterici* – "modern" writers like Cajetan and John of St Thomas – as speaking for the master himself. At the three orders of human operations – knowing, doing, making – none can be completely reduced to any of the others. Their unity is to be found in their common root, the act of being.

Much of Gilson's loneliness lay in his having come to his unique perception of Thomas' philosophy as a philosophy of being. He realized he was almost alone in understanding this, and closed his sad letter to Phelan:

> Jacques has been looking at art. I have been looking at art. Why should anybody be looking at us instead of at art itself? Simply because philosophy is about reality, and philosophical lectures are about philosophy. The utter sterility of neoscholastic philosophy during the last fifty years (at least) has no other source. (57.11.16.)

Another long letter written in December reveals Gilson's intellectual ferment as he entered his mid-seventies. He was again at work on the *quinque viae*:

> I know something very good remains to be said. ... Trying to rid myself of all sorts of historical and philosophical prejudices leaves me with insufficient light to catch the blinding evidence I feel all around me. We are too far now from Thomas to make people accept him as he was.

He then went on, with a good deal of irony, to discuss Father André Hayen's *La communication de l'être après saint Thomas d'Aquin* (1957), which had just appeared:

> He is splashing about in our pool. ... He finally understands the true meaning of causality in St Thomas. You know where he has learned it! Only he does not think I realize the bond between ... efficient cause and creation! I don't dare tell him this is an old story. ... In contending there is only one metaphysical truth ... he is not thinking of Duns Scotus and Thomas ... but of *Thomas et Blondel*!

Finally he turned to yet another source of intellectual irritation:

> I just bought a copy of the newly published treatise of Coluccio Salutati, *De seculo et religione*. ... How eager I was to see what the Florentine humanist had to say in praise of man and the world! Are you ready? Listen then to Salutati: "This world is a dirty sewer of turpitudes: deceptive birdlime, sorry pleasure of false joys, foolish exultation, bed of tribulations, lake of miseries, shipwreck of virtues, kindling-wood of evil, inciter of crime, road of darkness, rugged bypath, mountain ambush, horrid prison" etc.; there are nine more lines of such abuse against the world ... thirty-six

insults, thirty-six chapters. As the editor of the treatise rightly says: "In this treatise, Coluccio seems to be a medieval rather than what I call a modern man." You bet! But what is he doing in a collection of *testi umanistici*? This problem, Tony, should keep you busy during your empty hours. (57.12.15.)

Burdened with a *History of Philosophy* for CTD, beset by tax-collectors and weary of intellectual isolation, Gilson suddenly decided to retire from his retirement. Once again he would spend only three months a year in Canada, and would pass the rest in France. As soon as Gilson revealed his decision, Pegis wired him from New York: "Hold everything. If possible try not to cross any Rubicon before I come to Toronto January 11. Letter follows." (57.12.19.) But Gilson had already crossed his Rubicon and, Pegis notwithstanding, his new retirement pattern became effective immediately.

17

Sexta Aetas: Senium, 1958-1962

1 THE ONSET OF ILLNESS, 1958

Early in January 1958 Gilson had Pegis reserve two one-way first-class plane tickets to Paris for Jacqueline and himself. They would fly from New York on 30 April to be back in Paris for the regular Thursday meeting of the Académie Française, 1 May. Gilson was growing eager to work once more in the "French style," paying tributes to contemporaries and marking the anniversaries of giants of the past. He was also looking forward to resuming his former yearly-pattern – three months in Canada and nine in France. He expected to be in New York for a few days in late April for a last-minute meeting over CTD business, especially to discuss details of the projected four-volume *History of Philosophy*. He also hoped to deliver a promised lecture on some aspect of medieval philosophy for New York's Fordham University; he wanted to encourage Professor Elizabeth Salmon – or "Queen Bess" as he called her – who was Fordham's leading thomist and a possible contributor to the *History*.

As the winter progressed Gilson's resolve to re-establish himself in France grew stronger, and his desire to visit New York waned. Eventually he cancelled his Fordham appearance, called off his end-of-the-year CTD meeting, and rebooked his flight to Paris from Toronto through Montréal; he intended not to return to Toronto until January 1959. One of the sources of Gilson's restlessness was his increasing distance from the objectives of the CTD. This came sharply home to him when he was asked to prepare some digests of classic Christian texts:

> The director of Image Books [John Delaney] sent me a new crop and I thanked him for the gift. At the same time I thought it charitable to tell him how I felt about his digest of the *City of God*. On the other side, in connection with *Superstition Corner*, I called his attention to the usefulness of a proofreader acquainted with Latin grammar. One must not print *Introibo ad altare Deo*, nor *De profundus clamavi ... exaudi vocem meum*. Finally, Christianity cannot be learned from textbooks only, or else we shall never have more than a textbook Christianity. (EG to Pegis, 58.1.26.)

Despite his disenchantment, Gilson still planned this year to prepare with Pegis an original text, *Elements of Christian Philosophy*. He also continued to believe that CTD's intention to counterbalance the influence of Dewey in schools and teachers' colleges was a valid one.

Gilson's nine months in Paris were almost happy ones this year. On 5 May he was pleased to be named a Membre de l'Académie Royale de Belgique, Section des Sciences Morales et Politiques. In June, when Gabriel Marcel was awarded Le Prix National, Gilson provided, as he often had for others in the past, the leading article on the event. In "Un philosophe singulier" (Les nouvelles littéraires, 58.6.19; McG 738), Gilson attributed to Marcel's work all the best qualities of his own: he wrote that Marcel's thought does not take philosophy for its object or even bear on philosophy, but is philosophy, and that Marcel cannot be "systemized," "summarized" or "answered" because he refuses "to falsify the real in order to create a system." Marcel mailed Gilson a letter the same day thanking him for his "magnifique et pour moi émouvant article."

By the summer Gilson was happy and relaxed, almost his old self again. He was taking renewed interest in French politics despite his intentions to the contrary; he had a growing admiration for Charles de Gaulle, though he often made fun of the general. During May he completed a long article that he called "Autour du thomisme." Although he did not intend to publish it, he sent it to Pegis as requested. Pegis urged Gilson to publish it, for he knew its historical approach to thomism would provoke controversy among thomists: "It is a lesson for the future of Christian philosophy" (Pegis to EG, 58.7.31). The substance of the article was later powerfully expressed in a recorded lecture for the Institute entitled "The Future of Christian Philosophy" (60.3.29; McG 1201).

June and July were spent in furious work on the manuscripts for *Elements of Christian Philosophy*, which Gilson had promised to CTD. In this book Gilson was bringing philosophy back within the boundaries of theology where, under whatever title, it had flourished in Thomas' day:

> The book's place is in a series on religious knowledge. The popes say: "Ite ad Thomam." We do. The old boys object: "This is not philosophy." We say: "All right, then, let it be religion." There should be in the curriculum of a Catholic school one place where it is possible to comply with the formal position of the popes and the decrees of canon law. (EG to Pegis, 58.7.14.)

Gilson was tempted to drop from this book any treatment of the five ways, the five proofs or demonstrations of the existence of God. They didn't seem to belong in a metaphysics of being that only began after God had been accepted by faith; the question of the existence of God is a philosophical one. Nonetheless he retained the section, as its omission would have provoked sinister interpretations. Gilson's concise summary of the text to Pegis is informative:

> *Object of the book*: to convey to minds the meaning of the notion of *esse*. *Method of the book*: to show the notion at work in the thomistic treatment of being, of the transcendentals, of causality, of man, of intellection, of love and of social life (i.e., the *being* of society). ... At the centre, the omnipresent notion that only one single object fully answers the notion of being, namely God. (58.7.14.)

During this summer at Vermenton Gilson's son returned to him after an absence of two years. The entry in Gilson's aide-mémoire is terse and emotional:

"Hier, vendredi, 20 juin, arrivée de B. après deux ans de séparation. Bonheur. Laudetur J-C." (58.6.21.) Another worry was also ended for Gilson this summer. Thomas Langan of the University of Indiana visited him on 20 July and 6 August and agreed to become involved in the third and fourth volumes of the *History of Philosophy* for CTD: "He will do it well. ... He is clever. ... His wife, who is French, has led him to believe that she is deeply interested in philosophy. So she too is clever." (EG to Pegis, 58.8.3.)

Late in the summer Gilson attended two congresses and a symposium. Because the three took place almost continuously, he made them the occasion of a motor trip to northern Italy with Jacqueline and Cécile. The first was the Congress on European Culture at Bolzano from 31 August to 9 September. This was the fifth meeting for a united Europe, and had as its theme "European Unification: The Reality and the Problems." On 12 September the three Gilsons drove from Bolzano to Venice for the week-long International Congress of Philosophy. Gilson complained to Pegis about the size of this event, which featured some thirteen hundred delegates and three hundred and fifty papers; in the session he chaired alone, there were four main speeches and fourteen speakers from the floor. The congress also had some good features: for variety, members were free to go to Rome to hear Pius XII; and the locale was moved to Padua for the closing. Gilson did not go to Rome, though he was sorry afterward; he was running out of traveller's cheques, and tired. The day after the congress, 18 September, Gilson read a paper at the Symposium d'Esthétiques in Venice on "L'œuvre d'art et le jugement critique" (*Lettere Italiana*, 10 [1958]: 405-416; McG 372).

At Rome Pius XII had read a communication to philosophers from the Venice congress and had spoken to them in tone and substance along lines taken by Leo XIII in *Aeterni patris*. He had urged philosophers to end the separation between philosophy and theology. Gilson read an abstract of the talk, and found the pope's remarks "a source of consolation and inspiration. We are not alone feeling that the separation of philosophy and theology has been for philosophy a downright evil."

In October, when Gilson was quietly working in Vermenton, word arrived that Pius XII had died. Gilson was saddened, and wrote Pegis that he found himself

> missing Pius XII much more deeply than I imagined I would. I am haunted by the memory of our audience (my wife's and mine) when he received us both. I wrote an expression of my regret to Archbishop Montini, choosing to write him because he had arranged our visit to Pope Pius XII. The archbishop answered by a nicely-worded telegram. I expected nothing of the sort. Was anyone placed to know Pius XII better than Monsignor Montini, as we used to call him? (58.10.17.)

In the late fall, at about the same time as Jacqueline took a house of her own in Paris, Gilson became quite ill with prostatitis. He cancelled the courses scheduled for Toronto in January, and on 4 and 10 December visited a Dr Westphal. He also began to keep a detailed log of his symptoms and treatments: on 4 December for example he noted "tension 23, mictasol, prostatidousse." On 19 December he was given *un examen radioscopique* by his brother Maurice, and on 23 December he visited a surgeon, Dr Michon.

On 9 January 1959, Gilson underwent surgery in the Clinique des Frères de Saint-Jean-de-Dieu, 19, rue Ondinot. Although he had noted his symptons in detail for several days before the operation, he recorded only the briefest comments after it. On 9 January his entry was simply "les heures dolentes," and for several succeeding days this was abbreviated to "id." On 15 January he noted "bien," but then "mauvaise nuit." By Monday 19 January he was more himself, and wrote laconically: "Vie principalement urinaire et sans aucun plaisir." It was late in January before his violent skin eruptions subsided and his sedative could be cut. All in all, he had a very rough time.

Throughout Gilson's ordeal, Jacqueline was, he said, his *providence*. Cécile, who was also with him, was his English amanuensis. To Gilson's letter to Pegis on the day of his operation, she appended the first official bulletin: "Operation successfully complete. Patient full of Rabelaisian spirit!" (59.1.8.)

2 Convalescence

When Gilson left hospital at the end of January he moved into Jacqueline's home at 9, rue Saint-Romain and advised his correspondents to write him there. Although the apartment was sparsely furnished, in his condition it was a godsend. It placed him in the heart of Paris where he could regale his spirits with interests that Vermenton couldn't provide. It also placed him near the Académie and close to medical help should he need it.

February was spent in bed and in a chair: "I am not out of the woods yet. ... I am being drugged with antihistaminic products. These leave me four or five hours of lucidity each day." (EG to Pegis, 59.2.20.) On his sickbed he was haunted by a number of spectres. He had a foreboding that Pegis, *per impossibile*, might not take a hard enough line with CTD personnel. He was also worried that Institute professors might forget that their scope was the whole of Christian culture in the Middle Ages. With some vexation he recalled being misunderstood in the past, and by one of the Institute's most valued professors: "Two years before Father Denomy's death, he asked me with plaintive misgivings if it was true that I intended to turn the Institute into a school of philosophy" (EG to Pegis, 59.3.6).

Father McCorkell acted quickly to anticipate and swathe Gilson's anxieties. McCorkell was a supreme consoler; although not a medievalist, he knew men, whether intellectuals, simple souls, saints or *minus habentes*. He invited Pegis to come to Toronto to offer a course during Gilson's absence. Pegis immediately agreed to change his plans, and prepared a course of ten lectures on Gilson's positions in his *Elements*. Gilson was delighted, as he had wanted his Institute students to know his latest positions before they became public property.

McCorkell also soothed Gilson's financial worries by putting him on a pension of $5,000 a year; this could be changed back, next year or whenever, to the usual $4,000 plus expenses for three months teaching (McCorkell to EG, 59.1.22). Pegis began to send Gilson his CTD consultation fees on a monthly basis so that he could meet emergencies as they arose; this charity was known to Doubleday, but was not general knowledge. As Pegis' son Richard put it, Pegis was "a very private person" but also a thoughtful one. He even asked Gilson if he could send him advance royalties on *The Elements*; Gilson refused, insisting that with French pensions and his Toronto and New York supplements he was holding his own.

From rue Saint-Romain, Gilson found it easy to get to the Académie, and some Thursdays the de Paulhacs, Vrin's daughter and son-in-law, picked him up and drove him there. Gilson's attendance record at meetings reached a new high this year, and between March and December he was designated, by internal appointment, to fulfil the functions of chancellor of the Académie.

As early as April Gilson was a walking convalescent. Jacqueline felt free to leave him and go to Toronto to fetch her paintings and other possessions for permanent return to Paris. She was away all April and her absence was good therapy for her father. He began to do his own shopping again and to walk more; on 18 April his aide-mémoire noted: "walked to visit André, and walked home again." Gilson's attention now began to focus increasingly on André's needs rather than his own; he regularly shuffled over to the nursing home with little presents for his brother.

As Gilson recovered, people began to call on him more frequently. He took many of them across the street for *déjeuner au* Petit Lutetia, a delightful restaurant which served good meals. Solicitous waiters and interested patrons enjoyed overhearing, indeed participating in, Gilson's conversations with his guests. During April and May alone he took Father Flahiff* there twice and Father Vincent Kennedy once, his son Bernard several times, Maurice and his second wife, Bernadette Clouet, and several others. This semi-salon pattern soon became a distinguishing mark of Gilson's declining years. Music came back into his life, too. On Saturday 2 May he attended – "fifth tier boxes with no view" – the opera *Tannhäuser*, which he thought "excellent but for the horrible choruses." Horrible or not, he returned to hear them again on Monday, two days later: "same seats; a marvel; enthusiasm and deep emotion; the third act has tonic beauty, but the added opening ballet is still grotesque; does no one dare suppress it?"

By May Gilson was deep into metaphysics again. Les Sociétés de Philosophie de Langue Française had decided to mark the centenary of Bergson's birth with a Bergson Congress, to be held 17 to 20 May at the Sorbonne.** Gilson declined an invitation to read a paper, but attended the sessions and spoke from the floor on two occasions. On Monday morning, in the Amphithéâtre Turgot, Mme Rose-Marie Mossé read a paper on "Sources et histoire du Bergsonisme." The paper

---

* Gilson had directed the studies of Flahiff and Kennedy back in the 1930s. Flahiff was now superior-general of the Basilians and would eventually become the archbishop of Winnipeg and a cardinal.

** See *Congrès des Sociétés de Philosophie de Langue Française* (Paris, 1960).

was analyzed by Marc-André Bloch, then discussed by the panel while Gilson repeatedly waved his hand from the audience. At last, at noon, the chairmen threw open the discussion and called first on the still-signalling Gilson. For Gilson, the so-called historical method had definite limitations:

> To speak of Bergson's sources is legitimate, but one must always be dealing with Bergson's own thought. Thus where there is some resemblance between him and platonism, it is still Bergson one is dealing with. In such a case Bergson is the source of Plotinus, not Plotinus of Bergson. Anyone can read Plotinus. But this is not the way to find out what Bergson read in Plotinus.

This observation was much appreciated, and Jean Guitton wrote Gilson a few days later thanking him for a beautiful intervention: "You saw how it was received" (59.6.19; tr.). Gilson intervened a second time in the afternoon session of the same day in Amphithéâtre Richelieu. He explained how Bergson had actually dealt with metaphysics:

> You had to observe his intonation in order to be sure just when he was having some fun, as on the day when he said that for Plotinus "l'action est un accès de faiblesse de la contemplation – [action is a weakened form of contemplation] – ἀσθένεια θεωριας." He was enjoying himself as he spoke these words. Why? Because this was exactly the contrary of what he had been teaching us all along.

3 Books, 1959-1960

This year of sickness, surgery, and convalescence proved ultimately to be anything but idle. After this Bergson Congress Gilson began to write *Le philosophe et la théologie* (Paris, 1960; McG 104), which helps to explain why Bergson is so prominent in this book. Gilson undertook *Le philosophe* at the request of the Académie Française:

> The forty fellows of the Académie Française ... are all invited (in turn!) to contribute one volume to the series [*Les quarante*]. They like memoirs, which I feel unable to write. So I answered in the negative, saying that a life spent in rediscovering the true meaning of the word "theology" was not a fit subject for such a collection. But Daniel-Rops (de l'Académie Française) replied: "Oh, but yes! You sit down and write a book entitled *Le philosophe et la théologie*. Do it without opening a single book." (59.7.22.)

Gilson finished the first 145-page draft of *Le philosophe* in only twenty-three days. August to December were largely spent on revision. He expanded three short sections into full chapters: *Universitas magistrorum* became "The World of Secular Learning"; *Le désordre* became "Confusion in the City"; and *Le cas Bergson* became "The Bergson Affair." Most of his time was spent pulling out little passages, then putting them back in again.

In August, near the beginning of this revision, André passed away. Gilson was glad he had been able to spend time with his brother in the last years of his life. He wrote Pegis:

My brother André, the priest, died on 25 August. His great fear was that he would become completely paralyzed and unable to read and listen to music. God has mercifully spared him this twofold calamity. We had to go to Paris and spend four days there for the funeral. (59.8.31.)

This year Gilson was also saddened by the death of Gabriel Théry; he wrote a warm "In Memoriam" for Théry that appeared in the *Archives* (26 [1959]: 7; McG 306; see above, pp. 137-139). Gilson insisted that Père Chenu* succeed Théry at the *Archives*, and passed on the invitation by way of de Paulac, who had succeeded Vrin as editor. Chenu at first objected that the job required a younger man, but was finally happy to accept. He and Thérèse d'Alverny were still codirectors of the *Archives* when Gilson died in 1978.

In his intellectual autobiography, Gilson did not know how to treat Jacques Maritain; though Maritain was his very good friend, the two sharply disagreed on a number of essentials. Eventually Maritain was generously dealt with in the second-last chapter, "L'art d'être thomiste," which offered an objective treatment of thomism. Gilson did not want to create a controversy between himself and his friend, nor did he want to pretend to endorse concepts that were anathema to him. He wrote Pegis:

> *Re* Jacques Maritain, the truth is that what he has written has played no part at all in my intellectual history. Were I to get started on him, for whom I have a brotherly affection, I would have to raise problems better left untouched. I thought the few things I said about him in [the chapter on] "L'art d'être thomiste" would suffice to make it impossible to ascribe to me any unfriendly feelings about him. Still, there is one thing that cannot be done: to condone his book on Bergson. ... There would be no problem if Maritain didn't wield thomism like a bludgeon. ... I have never had to take Maritain's positions into account until recently in *Painting and Reality*. The result is that I have been expelled from earthly paradise by an angel of wrath who is especially charged to protect by flame and sword the truth about poetry. (59.12.7.)

The angel of wrath was Raïssa who, Gilson felt, had been responsible for most of what Maritain had written about poetry – a good poet and a mystic, she had turned her husband toward an aesthetic that bore little relation to Thomas. In a second letter, written the following day, Gilson continued:

> *Art and Scholasticism* has been the breeding soil of a number of notions proper to Maritain, very original, ... foreign to my mind, ... profitable to meditate upon. I profit from Maritain, as I profit from Bergson, and as I am sure I would profit from Heidegger, if I understood him better. To what extent [Maritain] agrees with St Thomas does not enter into my preoccupations. Only, when I see him falling upon Bergson in the name of Thomas Aquinas, and perhaps misunderstanding Thomas himself on the very points under discussion, I cannot refrain from saying it. And since I don't want to say it, I shut up. (59.12.8.)

---

* Père Chenu was no longer, in 1959, in trouble with the Holy Office.

When *Le philosophe et la théologie* appeared early in 1960 it was not received well by the new pre-conciliar theologians. During the 1940s Gilson himself had explained to Maurice Pradines that philosophy properly learned did not lead a man to faith and theology (above, pp. 246-247); now his very title suggested that philosophy had brought him, the philosopher, to theology. The title had been urged by Daniel-Rops and accepted against Gilson's better judgment (EG to Pegis, 59.12.8); given the mood of theologians at the time, it was a mistake. Even Henri de Lubac, still grateful for Gilson's defence of his *Le surnaturel* in *La croix* (above, pp. 300-301), thought *Le philosophe* an "unfortunte book." Gilson's writing it so quickly as a convalescent reminded de Lubac of Doctor Johnson's rejoinder when Boswell called a woman's preaching remarkable: "It is remarkable, as is a dog's walking on two legs, not in that it is well done but that it is done at all." (interview, 1974.)

If *Le philosophe* was too hastily written to be great Gilson, another book, written at about the same time, came much closer. Gilson had been working on the *Elements of Christian Philosophy* (New York, 1960; McG 27) since Pegis had asked him for a Catholic textbook in 1958. The *Elements* had been well thought out and carefully submitted chapter by chapter for criticism; there was nothing hasty about it.

4 Late 1959

It was becoming usual in these years for Gilson to make some gathering of scholars the occasion of a motor trip from Vermenton with his daughters. This year he interrupted his revisions of *Le philosophe* to drive with Jacqueline to Cologne for two congresses at the Thomas-Institut: a symposium on the "History of Moslem Philosophy" from 6 to 9 September; and a meeting of the International Society for the Study of Medieval Philosophy from 10 to 12 September. Gilson spoke enthusiastically about the former:

> The first, on Moslem and medieval philosophies, was extraordinarily good: an example of perfect intellectual co-operation between Moslems and Catholics. Two or three Egyptian scholars [probably Anawati and Ibraham Madkour, possibly also Vajda] put all the rest of us to shame by their intellectual culture. I cannot find the slightest difference between a Moslem philosopher and the kind of Christian philosopher we wish to be. The point where we part company is quite clear, but we can go a long way together, in fact we have in common the whole of *De Deo uno*. (EG to Pegis, 59.9.15.)

Gilson had little to say about the International Congress of Medieval Philosophy, except that he was disappointed that Doctor Joseph Koch was not there and pleased that Canon Astrik Gabriel was. What he remembered best was good wine, lively conversations and much gossip: the intellectual fare was ordinary in contrast with that furnished by the Moslem and Egyptian scholars.

In November, Gilson went to Brussels to give two public lectures at the Faculté Universitaire Saint-Louis. As his announced titles he used two subheadings discarded from chapter 3 of the first draft of *Le philosophe*: "Un théologien devant les philosophes: St Thomas d'Aquin" and "Un philosophe devant les théologiens: Henri Bergson."

During this visit to Brussels Gilson was also inducted into the Royal Academy of Belgium and delivered his maiden communication, "Philosophie du Plagiat" (*Bulletin de l'Académie Royale de Belgique*, 49 [1959]: 556-572; McG 386). He held the academy spellbound by philosophizing for an hour in the Bergson manner on the meaning of plagiarism. When Nathaniel Hawthorne repeated ten lines from Edgar Allen Poe almost word for word, yet without saying the same thing at all, was he guilty of plagiarism? And if Albert Kann and Paul Arbelet actually anticipated ideas held afterward by Bergson and Stendhal respectively, had they not long since placed them in the public domain? Indeed, is plagiarism possible? In citing these celebrated cases Gilson also shared with other scholars personal reflections on two incidents in his own life, the socalled plagiarisms of Louis Rougier in 1925 and, currently, of Risieri Frondisi.

The case of Louis Rougier had proved oddly persistent. When Rougier had asked Gilson to help him become his successor in Strasbourg in 1921, Gilson had not done so (above p. 101). Then in 1925 Rougier published *Le scolastique et le thomisme* (Paris), a book in which he borrowed so lavishly from Gilson's writings that Père Théry publicly scolded him in *M. Rougier et la critique historique* (Paris, 1925). Rougier apparently still wanted Gilson's place in the world of scholarship and next attempted to discredit Gilson's historical approach as overly sympathetic to the scholars it dealt with.* Rougier was a strange character, a sensationalist. Some years later, in 1940, he appeared on the international scene by claiming to have negotiated a secret "gentlemen's agreement" early in World War II among Pétain, Weygand, Churchill and Lord Halifax.** Rougier briefly entered Gilson's life once more at the time of the San Francisco Conference in 1945. When Gilson visited the Université de Montréal at this time and learned that a certain Louis Rougier had been invited to lecture in international politics, he quickly and unceremoniously quashed the invitation.

Rougier's 1925 work had been studded with unacknowledged phrases and passages from Gilson. Was this plagiarism, as Théry had claimed? If Gilson had ever thought so, he did not think so now. By 1959 the memory of Rougier's antics had lost its sting. Even Gilson, who in the 1920s had been so frustrated and disturbed by them, now considered them simply amusing anecdotes for mention in passing before the Belgian Academy.

Gilson's other experience with plagiarism was still in progress at the time of the Belgian address. As an innocent third party he was not in the least disturbed. In Buenos Aires a political power struggle was taking place in university circles between "progressives" and "humanists." The "humanists" in the Argentinian

---

* See Rougier's "Le thomisme et la critique sympathique de M. Gilson," *Mercurie de France*, 31.10.15, pp. 340-378; McG 1057.
** See William L. Langer, *Our Vichy Gamble* (New York, 1947).

government wanted to oust the university rector, Risieri Frondisi, and had accused him of plagiarizing Gilson's 1930 edition of Descartes' *Discours de la méthode*. Both sides approached Gilson – Jose Marcia Sciurano of the Humanist League as well as the badgered Frondisi – and presented him with pages of words, phrases and sentences alleged to have been plagiarized from his work. Sciurano urged him to take the case to court, and told him that "it would not be considered an attack on the present Argentinian government" (59.2.29). This government happened to be presided over by Rector Frondisi's own unfriendly brother, and the rector wrote: "The idea is to discredit me intellectually. ... I want to put in your hands all the materials. ... You may write to (among others) Professor Paul Weiss at Yale." (59.4.26.) Gilson decided not to act, though he was happy to use the incident as material for his Bergsonian philosophizing before the Belgian Academy.

Gilson's last Paris function this year was to chair on 21 November the meeting of La Semaine des Intellectuels Catholiques. Père Chenu discussed *mystère et raison* with M. Jean Lacroix; again Gilson could well have been responsible for the topic. Before the papers were heard, he speculated:

> I imagine that the first speaker [Lacroix] will examine the problem starting from reason and moving toward the mystery, and that Père Chenu will begin with the mystery of faith in the word of God, and will come back from this summit toward reason. (tr.)

At the end he saw the two men in agreement on the "essential conclusion," namely the "absolute transcendence of religious mystery over faith." But for Gilson, Chenu's progress from mystery to reason was the true one. In his summary Gilson argued that Christian mystery "does not follow reason, it precedes it, accompanies it as it moves along; it wraps it round and eventually shows it salutary perspectives which reason left to itself would never suspect possible. Theology transcends philosophy because it is founded on faith." In this summation Gilson presented his last, refined judgment on theology in relation to the thought of man. He came very near to saying that, for the believer, philosophy in the generally accepted sense of the word is an impossibility. He also offered one of his best explanations of why he now insisted so adamantly that Thomas had been a theologian who had used philosophy as a theologian:

> While Père Chenu was speaking I remembered a passage in St Thomas which he was no doubt thinking about too. The passage is in Thomas' *Commentary on the De Trinitate of Boethius*. St Thomas was (even then) being accused of pouring the water of philosophy into the wine of Holy Scripture. He replied simply that theology was not a mixture in which a constituent kept its own nature. A theologian doesn't mix water with wine, he changes water into wine. We ought not be disturbed by this manifest allusion to the miracle at Cana. St Thomas is here speaking for all theologians conscious of the supernatural function they are performing. A discipline founded on faith in God's word must share in the privileges of divinity. It would be surprising if its operation had nothing of the miraculous about it. (*Semaine des Intellectuels Catholiques*, Paris, 1959.)

Gilson, then, had come to see theology as the meeting place of reason and the Christian mystery seeking understanding of itself: "haec credendo, incipe, procurre, persiste ... intellige incomprehensibilia esse" (Thomas Aquinas, quoting St Hilary, *Summa contra gentiles*, 1.9.2). Gilson, grown in his faith and its mysteries, hoped that he had become, like Thomas, a theologian. Had he dared he would have called *Le philosophe* "Le théologien et la philosophie."

Following this encounder with *mystère*, Gilson met with Father Carlo Balić from Rome. Balić was working on the beatification of Duns Scotus and arrived in Paris on 27 November to enlist Gilson's support in this Franciscan cause. The two men met for *déjeuner* at La Closerie des Lilas where Balić passed on to Gilson the latest Roman gossip. Balić reported to Gilson that "the dominant wind in the Roman Curia is blowing against our friends the Jesuits, so we have to stand by them if occasion arises," and that "*Esprit*, founded by the late Emmanuel Mounier and by noncommunist leftist Catholics, is likely to be stricken first." Balić went on, extravagantly:

> Jacques Maritain is considered a heretic. He would already have been condemned – on the twofold ground of *progressismus* and *laicismus* – were it not that he has been French ambassador to the Holy See. ... He will not be condemned ... never! Still progressism and laicism are heretical. *Integral Humanism* is a dangerous book.

In his letter to Pegis, Gilson added:

> Father Balić ... is all taken up with the cause of the beatification of John Duns Scotus and he wanted to enlist my good will. Personally, I am in favour. I do like Scotus very much; I hope the new attempt will prove successful, I shall do my utmost to help the Franciscans, but they are so clumsy that I doubt they will succeed. ... In my mind, the *only* problem is: Does the holy servant of God, John Duns Scotus, deserve to be beatified? And my answer is: Yes. Will they succeed? They will to the extent they approach the problem with a pure heart, that is, without trying ... to get the doctrine canonized along with the man. ... Besides, I like him, and have been praying to him myself for many years. (59.12.1.)

This year Gilson experienced considerable satisfaction when he received from his students and friends three rewarding *festschrifts* to mark his seventy-fifth birthday. One of these was the 1959 volume of *Mediaeval Studies* dedicated to him and contributed entirely by his Toronto colleagues. The second was the large *Mélanges offerts à Étienne Gilson* consisting of thirty-four papers, all but one by his European friends; it was edited by Alex Denomy and published simultaneously by Vrin and the Pontifical Institute. The third was a volume of papers written by Gilson's North American students, *An Étienne Gilson Tribute*. The *Tribute* was edited by a committee of five former students in North America: Charles J. O'Neil and Gerard Smith, SJ of Marquette; Linus Thro, SJ of St Louis; Armand Maurer, CSB of Toronto; and William O'Meara of the University of Chicago. Gilson himself contributed to the *Tribute* a beautiful paper on wisdom for which Anton Pegis supplied the title, "Amicus amicis." In all, the three volumes totalled some

1500 pages comprising sixty-seven papers, tangible evidence that Gilson's scholarly influence had been wide, deep and lovingly recognized.

5 THE SPIRIT OF THOMISM, 1960

From the end of 1959 until the fall of 1962, Gilson lived a year at a time. His surgery had made him realize how precarious his health had become, and he made a sustained effort to complete his commitments and to tie together the loose ends in his intellectual positions. His first objective was to get his CTD commitments under control. He had promised an English translation of *Le philosophe* to Pegis at Doubleday, and as general editor of the four-volume *History of Philosophy* textbook, he still had many problems to resolve.

When Gilson arrived with Cécile in Toronto on Christmas Day 1959, his first move was to set his daughter to work translating *Le philosophe*. While she translated aloud from his French manuscript, he typed out the English "as it came into existence" and modified the original sense as the spirit moved him. By 24 February they had together Englished a French manuscript of 232 pages:

> Cécile finished her task yesterday night. We celebrated with a glass of [Ontario] Liquor Commission port wine. Awfully jolly it was! as Monsignor Ronald Knox would say. She would now like to tackle the *Metamorphoses de la cité de Dieu*. (60.2.25.)

For several reasons *The Philosopher and Theology* was not to appear for another two years. Pegis thought a translation should render the original French text, and not be a relatively independent book. Moreover Pegis was shortly to leave the CTD and Doubleday. At Gilson's insistence, Pegis controlled the copyright for this book personally; as a result *The Philosopher* became one of the pawns in the disputes surrounding Pegis' departure.

Around this time Gilson also wanted to settle once and for all who the four authors of the *History* were to be and how they were to divide the work; things were so unresolved that he could not even sit down and write his general preface to the series. Only Maurer's volume – volume 2 – was on schedule. Charles O'Neil had taken over the first volume from the overworked Pegis, but ill-health was preventing him from meeting deadlines. Elizabeth Salmon was producing for the third volume, but not meeting Gilson's stipulations, particularly his requirement that she write exclusively from the perspective of specific philosophical texts. Volume 4 meanwhile was completely up in the air, as author after author considered the proposition and withdrew: they found the prospect of producing a contemporary volume in a series controlled by medievalists, and especially by Gilson and Pegis, unattractive. Thomas Langan had begun to enter the picture, but largely in a revising capacity.

To arrive at some resolution, a meeting of all parties concerned was planned for early April in New York. From the beginning Gilson was apprehensive about this meeting, and thought it would only delay things further; even when he arranged for his visa, he expected no co-operation and was amazed to be granted entry for four years; "it may still be valid in the other world!" (EG to Pegis, 60.3.14.) Present in New York were Gilson and Pegis, other personnel from Doubleday, Elizabeth Salmon from Fordham, Maurer from Toronto, and Thomas Langan from Indiana. Nothing at all was resolved. For Gilson the main saving feature of the trip was that it allowed him to slip up to Hartford on Thursday 7 April to deliver a McAuley Lecture for Father Lescoe at St Joseph College. He also managed to get a good seat for *Parsifal* at the Metropolitan Opera House on Saturday 9 April.

The Hartford lecture provided Gilson with an opportunity to examine closely one of those loose-ended intellectual positions that he wanted to tighten. Sure as he was that Thomas was primarily a theologian, he still wanted to look hard at the "five ways." Did they belong in the *Summa theologiae*? He had nearly dropped them from his *Elements of Christian Philosophy*, reconsidering only at the last minute. Now he thought the problem through once more for "Can the existence of God still be demonstrated?" (*St Thomas and Philosophy* [Hartford, 1961]; McG 222). This lecture was a superb meditation on *Summa theologiae*, I.2.2. The validity of the five ways had actually been the problem of Pope Leo XIII and had only become one for Gilson when he committed himself to Christian philosophy; it had never been a problem for St Thomas, who had neither raised nor answered it. Gilson later returned to the five ways in "Trois leçons sur le problème de l'existence de Dieu" (*Divinitas* 5 [1961]: 23-87; McG 485) and in "La possibilité de l'athéisme" (*Il problema dell'ateismo* [Brescia, 1962], pp. 39-42; McG 402). He also returned to West Hartford a number of times.

Gilson left New York for a command performance in Toronto. General de Gaulle was to visit the city on 21 April and had asked that Gilson be there. He was indeed: at noon Gilson attended a civic ceremony at the Toronto City Hall, and at five-thirty he appeared at the reception given by John Keillor MacKay, the lieutenant-governor of Ontario, in his suite on Queen's Park. Gilson also took part in a state dinner that evening in the Crystal Ballroom of the King Edward Hotel.

When Gilson returned to France on 23 April, he turned at once, in solitude, to the problems facing the *History*. Convinced that Elizabeth Salmon had no intention of conforming to his prescriptions, he started writing a few isolated chapters for volume 3. Langan suddenly presented a solution when he wrote in August to say that he would accept the co-editorship of volume 3 if it were offered to him. Langan had cancelled the summer course he was to give in St Louis and was spending the summer in Yorktown Heights, New York, experimenting on his own with chapters and meeting Gilson's requirements:

> My labours have brought forth the following chapters: Montaigne (20 pages), Bacon (30 pages), Hobbes (25 pages), Descartes (5 pages) etc. ... for a total of approximately 255 pages. ... I would be happy to contribute any or all of the completed chapters. (60.8.3.)

Gilson was delighted and relieved. He wrote Langan that he would turn over to him "control of the language; I like your English. I don't even have one of my own to dislike." (60.8.6.) As was expected Elizabeth Salmon resigned from the project.

Shortly afterward Charles O'Neil, still unwell, also resigned, and volume 1 once more lacked an author. Then Pegis wrote, and re-offered his services:

> What about Greek philosophy? Being weak, and no doubt profiting by your example [writing experimental chapters] I would like to think about doing the volume myself. Doubleday is serious about giving me time to work. I would still like to consider this if you, being more realistic than I am, do not veto the idea. (60.8.23.)

The *History* still had four authors – Pegis, Maurer, Langan and Gilson. The three latter now shared responsibility for volumes 3 and 4.

For the rest of 1960, and for the next three years, Gilson spent a considerable portion of his time writing chapters for volumes 3 and 4. He wrote in furious bursts at his large desk in Vermenton, and each Thursday, when he went to Paris for meetings of the Académie, he slipped over to do research at the library of the Institut de France, the country's best philosophical library. As he completed sections, he forwarded them through Mary Baldwin, Pegis' secretary. Gilson even came to enjoy salvaging volume 3, and wrote to Mary Baldwin: "I am ashamed to say, I am getting interested in the work. It would take too long to tell you why. My next instalment will probably consist of a footnote on Voltaire." By reading Thomas Reid, Cardinal Gerdil and Wolff, especially in their relation to Malebranche, he was discovering significant links among French, Italian and other European philosophers. The *History* was beginning to assume "philosophical sense" of its own.

Gilson and his two daughters drove together to Venice a number of times these years, travelling from Vermenton via the Simplon Pass through Lugano, Bergamo, and Padua. All three were inordinately fond of Venice; Gilson once called the city "my only mistress" (EG to Pegis, 65.3.25). For Gilson Venice was a dream-city, not so much for its ideas or its books, but for such associations as its nearness to Mantova, the birthplace of Virgil: "Tale tuum carmen nobis, divine poeta / Quale sopor fessis in gramine" (EG to Pegis, 60.9.8).

This year Gilson travelled to Venice in September to consult several books there. He spent four full mornings in the Marciana with the early editions of the works of Pompanazzi. Renaissance scholars had been critical of remarks he had made about Pompanazzi on the immortality of the soul; for example, Gilson had claimed that positions like those of Pompanazzi and Spina had been derived from Cajetan and not from Thomas. Gilson had spoken on this matter the previous year during the Congress of Venice in a lecture to the Fondazione Cini.* His lecture had gone unchallenged and Bruno Nardi, his chief critic, had not been present. Now, at work on his *History*, Gilson continued to be uncomfortable about his treatment of Pompanazzi:

---

* See "L'affaire de l'immortalité de l'âge à Venise au début du xvi⁰ siècle" in *Umanesimo europeo e umanesimo veneziano* (Florence, 1964), pp. 31-61; McG 194.

> I think I have done all I can for Pompanazzi-Cajetan-Spina. It is far from satis-
> factory. Others will have the pleasure of improving upon it. ... I wish I were ten
> years younger. ... I am digging into Gerdil, a key man. Do you know the number of
> volumes in his complete works? Twenty! Gosh! as Macaulay would exclaim. (EG to
> Pegis, 60.10.10.)

Venice was not entirely given over to work, however. At one dinner Gilson
met Clare Booth Luce, who owned the English publishing house, Sheed and
Ward. Gilson had quarrelled with these publishers, complaining about their slow
schedules and accusing them of underpayment:

> Lots of good concerts and a few social functions. At the table of Count Cini, it was
> my privilege to sit near Mrs Clare Luce. She was good enough to declare to me that
> *she* was Sheed and Ward Inc. With my usual tactfulness, I thanked her for warning
> me. I might otherwise (I said) be volunteering information about the curious
> relations obtaining between her firm and its authors. She was interested but made
> no comment. (EG to Pegis, 60.9.19.)

In early November Raïssa Maritain died, and Gilson attended the funeral. As
he and Jean Marx talked together, each realized that with Raïssa had passed a
"large slice" of his own life. Gilson experienced a certain remorse, as he had never
much liked her.

From 9 November through 15 December Gilson was caught up in UNESCO
business almost daily. Between 7 and 11 December he interrupted his work to
give three lectures at the Lateran University, Rome. This visit was a short but
stirring one. On Friday 9 December, following the second of Gilson's talks, he and
Jacqueline had a private audience with Pope John XXIII:

> The present pope (the third I have met) is unlike either of the others. For thirty-five
> minutes he talked away almost as though giving reasons for what he was doing.
> One thing, he cannot account for his decision to call a council. ... He had asked
> himself: "Why not call a council? It would be a good thing to do. ... Still, for the life
> of me, I don't understand how the idea came to me." "Perhaps," I suggested, " it
> was what the catechisms would call a case of special assistance of the Holy Ghost to
> the pope." Indulgently, he agreed that the explanation was possible. He went on to
> say that his deepest suffering, as pope, was not being able to relieve so many poor
> priests from the "martyrdom" of celibacy. Nothing, he said, forbade his doing so,
> neither in scripture nor dogma, only the thought of the heroic effort of the church
> to become *sancta, casta*. He did not feel he had the right to undo what the church of
> her own free will had done at the cost of so much suffering. All this he said
> voluntarily. It followed from no previous words. It was just something he wanted
> me to know: that it was his most acute pain as pope. (EG to Pegis, 60.12.12.)

In December the articles that Gilson had written for Charles Boyer's *Omaggio*
to Pius XII appeared in print (above, p. 330). Boyer published "Sur deux thèmes de
réflexion" (*Documentation catholique*, 10 [1957]: 155-164; McG 458) just as
Gilson had written it, but indicated in his preface that he, Gilson, and Leo XIII's
Humani generis were united in the opinion that there was a fundamental

philosophy which a Christian required for salvation. Gilson had neither spoken of nor intended to convey such an opinion.

Before he even received his copy of *Omaggio*, Gilson received a letter from Gerald Van Ackeren, editor of *Theology Digest*, asking for permission to publish an English translation of the article. Van Ackeren also asked for a reference to the specific passage in *Humani generis* in which Gilson had based his statement on the need for a fundamental philosophy to achieve salvation. Gilson was furious. His first fear was that Boyer had made a change in the text of his article, which was not the case. Nonetheless, he asked Van Ackeren not to publish the article. If he was already committed to do so, then he was to append a note:

> Professor Gilson says he does not know of a passage in *Humani generis* containing the sentence in question. He does not even remember writing that "the encyclical *Humani generis* asserts that a fundamental philosophy is necessary for men if they are to achieve salvation." How that sentence got in his manuscript he professes not to know. (60.12.1.)

Although the translation was already in typeset, it did not appear in *Theology Digest*.

When Pegis heard about the controversy, he was prompted to write Van Ackeren himself:

> Your summary, as I read it in the galleys, [imputed] to Gilson a view he ... dislikes; you were [misled] by Father Boyer's note on the first page of the article. Father Boyer created an impossible problem when he (and not *Humani generis*) talked about a fundamental philosophy that was necessary for salvation. ... Father Boyer does not know that the philosophy that is part of theology is theology. (60.12.29.)

By the end of 1960 Gilson was back in Toronto, bracing himself for his winter lectures in the Institute. He was resolved to make no outside commitments other than one lecture, out of gratitude to Father Ackeren, at Rockhurst College, Kansas City, on "Paths to Peace." This lecture and an English version of "Sur deux thèmes de réflexion" were published as the concluding and opening chapters respectively of *The Spirit of Thomism* (New York, 1964; McG 147). The intervening chapters were the four lectures on "The Spirit of Thomism" later delivered at Georgetown University on the occasion of its 175th anniversary in March 1964 (below, p. 366).

6 Turbatio, 1961-1962

The years 1961 and 1962 brought some discord into Gilson's publishing life. By early 1961 Pegis had clearly fallen out with Doubleday over internal policies. Early in February he wrote Gilson that he was about to resign his post as director of CTD, effective 1 March. He planned to return to teaching in Toronto the next year:

> I do regret leaving – I should not say abandoning – CTD, but it would be a little inhuman to feel otherwise after nine years. It would be particularly inhuman in

view of that generous help that you have given me since the day I first came to
discuss with you Bennett Cerf's "crazy idea." (Pegis to EG, 61.2.8.)

Gilson was angry with Doubleday even though he was pleased that Pegis was
leaving the company. He told his friend staunchly that he "had been pushed into
rectitude" and that "the Institute would not be the loser" (61.2.23). Arrangements
were made to transfer Pegis' interests to Random House, including Cécile's
translation of *Le philosophe et la théologie*, her unfinished *Les métamorphoses de
la cité de Dieu*, and the four unfinished volumes of the *History of Philosophy*.

A number of issues arose at this stage between Pegis and Gilson. Pegis still
thought Cécile's translations were so free as to constitute new books, substantially
different from the original French texts; although this had been Gilson's doing,
the translations were Cécile's and she took some umbrage. Pegis also had to pass
on to Gilson a reminder from Doubleday that he had not turned over to Langan
his share of a typing bill for the *History*, which presumably had been sent to
Gilson as general editor; with age Gilson had become increasingly intolerant of
such trifles, and he huffily wondered why anyone should pay someone else
through him. Two months later Gilson had entirely forgotten both issues, and he
blithely continued to send translation items to Pegis, presuming they would be
looked after. But once bitten, twice shy: Pegis was taking no more chances. The
very whereabouts of the translated manuscript of *Les métamorphoses* was
forgotten for a time, and Gilson's changes in that manuscript were lost.

In late summer a new source of contention arose. The scheme for volume 4 of
the *History* had called for a section on French Catholic traditionalists such as
Bonald, Maistre and Lamennais, as well as another on the neoscholastics. Gilson
emphatically disliked this part of the plan, and wrote Pegis a sharp letter saying
that volume 4 was getting too Catholic in content. If this material might be
acceptable in a specifically Catholic textbook, it was utterly useless in one
intended also for state universities. "So," he said,

> I have simply removed all sections concerned with Christian philosophy:
> traditionalism, neoscholasticism etc. ... I removed 248 pages of text and notes from
> my volume 4 and sent my manuscript off to Random House. It still weighed 2 kilos
> 330 grams. (61.6.29.)

Pegis was furious, and suspected that Langan was behind the deletions. Pegis also
knew that Random House intended the *History* for the Catholic college market:

> It was part of the significance of the *History* you undertook to edit that it should be a
> monument of Catholic scholarship – honest, free, balanced, unprejudiced – and
> was to exercise these virtues toward all thinkers, including Catholic thinkers. ... If
> these were not the reasons for the *History* ... I don't know what we were doing.
> Having spent a life-time fighting rationalism in France, are you now going to yield
> to it for the sake of appeasing American state universities? (61.10.3.)

Gilson replied in four crammed pages to what he called Pegis' "nuclear letter."
He explained his changes, arguing that the deleted Catholic philosophies were
inferior to Thomas as well as to the secular philosophies of their own day. He

compromised a little by telling Pegis that the deleted sections still existed. Random House was always welcome to use them but if they did, they would have a volume of over 2,000 pages. He concluded with a low dig: "*Quod scripsi scripsi and stet*, and all that. God bless you dear Tony, and think of volume 1." (61.10.7.) Nearly two years later, Gilson was still adamant on the issue. He wrote Maurer:

> Two weeks ago I panicked, thinking I had omitted from volume 4 the Swiss Protestant philosopher Secretan. So I collected four volumes of his work to do some rewriting. Now, however, I realize that I discarded them along with the Catholic *philosophantes* of the nineteenth century. In fact, his mediocrity equals theirs, so no harm was done. (63.7.9.)

Although Pegis and Gilson continued their bickering through most of 1961, the two by no means became enemies; indeed, in some ways they were never closer friends. Gilson realized that Pegis' split from Doubleday had been an ordeal, and Pegis recognized that Gilson was suffering from the unreasonable irritability of his years.

In spite of charged emotions, the year's events passed almost normally. As usual in Toronto Gilson gave a public course and a seminar during the winter. He lectured for Father Ackeren at Rockhurst College, Kansas on 7 March, and he paid his usual visit to Montréal. Finally he returned to Paris in early April for the Académie elections.

As in the last two years, Gilson was most attentive to Académie affairs. In May he acted as Académie delegate to the Prix de la Vigne et du Vin at Mâcon. This was a gala affair: he spent the morning of 29 May on the jury of wine tasters, walked in the parade, attended the fair and gave out the prizes during the grand banquet. He received, for all these services, a huge decorated diploma, bestowed amid much laughter, which he kept among his honorary degrees and his Académie-membership documents.

In May Gilson proposed Maritain's name for the Grand Prix de l'Académie, its highest award. In spite of competition he succeeded in getting it through. Maritain received the award on 22 June, and wrote Gilson the following day:

> Before checking out of the hotel, I am hurriedly sending you these few lines to offer you my warmest thanks. I was very surprised to receive this Grand Prix de l'Académie, and I know through Jean Marx that it was all due to your initiative and insistence. I suppose that in the mind of most of your Académie colleagues the prize is mostly for longevity. What counts most with me, however, is your part in it, the token of esteem and intellectual fraternity of which it is the sign. What else matters for me in this world except a little tenderness? This witness of friendship from you and those who joined you has given me joy, and is precious to my old heart. I am truly grateful: believe me. (61.6.23; tr.)

Maritain received another distinguished award through the Académie in 1963, the Grand Prix in Belles Lettres from La République. Gilson was not on the awards committee on this occasion. (EG to Shook, 63.11.25.)

In the summer of 1963, when Maritain was passing briefly through Paris, the two men met unexpectedly. Gilson was entertaining friends at the Hotel Lutetia:

Yesterday night, July 3, I had the pleasure of entertaining Miss Pauline Bondy and a friend of hers at the Hotel Lutetia. We had reached the middle of the meal when I realized that an oldish man, sitting alone in his overcoat and having dinner, was no other than Jacques Maritain. He was busy working on a *plateau de fromages*, making a judicious selection. The cheese was followed by a plateful of strawberries, well-sugared judging from the white spots on the fruit. He was drinking no wine, just mineral water, always a bad sign in France. When he was leaving, I stopped him. He was surprised but seemed pleased. He was charming but downhearted. ... I found him aged, with an unhealthy pallor, a slightly puffed face like a person whose heart was not as it should be. In fact he complained about the old ticker from his first words, and also of other troubles he had had this year, all with that expression of a hurt child he often has. I was a little sad to see him down, yet glad to have seen him. Maritain is above the common measure. His biographers – and there will be more than one – will find him a fascinating personage and, if I am not mistaken, a man of action in the order of the intellectual life. (EG to Pegis, 62.7.4.)

Gilson himself had just represented the Institut de France at the reception held in Paris for Konrad Adenauer:

I never could have believed, back during the German occupation, when I was being walked around the Champs de Mars at the tail of a Feldwebel's horse, that I would see this day! Only a de Gaulle could lose Algeria, achieve a kind of reconciliation between France and Germany, and get away with it. (EG to Pegis, 62.7.4.)

The summers of 1961 and 1962 were spent at Vermenton. In 1961 the family took its annual trip to Italy so that Gilson could give a twenty-minute address at Bolzano. Later, in the fall, he attended a congress in Cologne, visiting for a second time the Royal Belgian Academy in Brussels where he intended "to sing the glory of old man Parmenides. Now, there *was* a philosopher!" (EG to Pegis, 61.11.3.)

In 1962 Gilson's lecture course in Toronto was a departure from his usual medieval topics. In "From Traditionalism to Thomism" he presented the work of De Bonald, Joseph de Maistre, Gerdil, Rosmini, Giobert, Lamennais, Bautain and *Aeterni patris*, much of the Catholic material he had recently excluded from the *History* over Pegis' objections. Whether he was trying to prove a point is not clear; he claimed he was simply trying to introduce philosophy students to the *Annales de philosophie chrétienne* where they could find "theses galore for dissertation topics." At any rate, by consensus, the result was the dullest and poorest-attended course Gilson ever offered in Toronto.

Gilson met far more success with his seminar on books 11 and 12 of the *Confessions* of St Augustine; he also gave brilliant lectures for the Paulists in Boston, for St Mark's College in Vancouver and for the University of California at Berkeley. During this term Gilson's publishing projects also began to bear fruit with the appearance of *The Philosopher and Theology* (New York, 1961; McG 105) and of volume 2 (the first to be published) of *The History of Philosophy* (New York, 1962; McG 186). Volumes 3 and 4 of the *History* were now advancing rapidly as Maurer, Langan and Gilson stepped into all troublesome breaches.

Gilson returned to Paris in April, and in May had more good news about his publishing projects:

I handed over to Pierre de Paulhac yesterday the final text of "Art et métaphysique." The book is very abstract. So much so that I decided in favour of a short appendix, a *secteur philistin*. The book will never go over with Dale Carnegie. (EG to Pegis, 62.5.26.)

"Art et métaphysique" appeared under the modest title of *Introduction aux arts du beau* (Paris, 1963; McG 79). Gilson issued it with some trepidation but with considerable emotion. It was his first book to look at all the fine arts through the ontological prism employed in *Peinture et réalité*; the second would be *Matières et formes* (Paris, 1964; McG 88; below, pp. 362-363). Gilson was still longing to achieve what Thomas had never even considered, a presentation of the work of artists from the perspective of art itself. "I find myself," he wrote, "in deep agreement with Henri Focillon, author of *The Life of Forms*, who rightly said that, in the case of the plastic art, *the hand thinks in the mind*" (EG to Shook, 62.5.25). *Introduction aux arts du beau* was dedicated to Focillon, "who knew the art of translating into the language of knowledge the forward thrusts of creation."

In May Gilson received a welcome invitation to give a course during the fall in the Harvard Divinity School. "I will enjoy speaking of a theologian," he wrote Maurer, "without having to conceal the fact that he is a theologian" (62.5.25). He accepted with relish, and promised Harvard Divinity to include "a lecture in the master's theology," modestly entitled "An Introduction to the Theology of St Thomas Aquinas" (62.5.25). He even offered to include a seminar on the *Contra gentiles*, book 3, "for students with reading knowledge of Latin" (EG to Pegis, 62.6.1).

By the summer of 1962 both Gilson and Pegis were returning to themselves as they realized they would soon be working together again in the Institute. The substance of their letters took on a new tone and depth, far removed from the mundane concerns of publishing. In May Pegis was in Toronto for the holiday, and wrote to Gilson in Paris:

> For St Thomas *ens inquantum ens* has two transcendental communities in it: likeness (analogy) and causality, and the latter contains in a special way a pull toward the cause whose effect it is. I ask naïvely: "Is Heidegger's problem [his urge to transcend metaphysics] the fact that being is *over*-shadowed by God and therefore that its upward openness cannot be reduced to its downward inclusiveness as the object of metaphysics? *Mutatis mutandis* (which is saying a lot), is not this true of Old Thomas himself?
>
> Would you look again at *De Trinitate*, 5.4 (especially Decker, pp. 193-194)? Maybe Heidegger is forcing us to re-emphasize that transcendence within being that leads to the negative theology. (62.5.23.)

This was the sort of question Gilson loved to receive, and he soon replied in kind:

> Your questions, Man! If I could answer them, I would be a philosopher indeed! Why don't you write to Heidegger directly? I think he would answer. Personally, I often contemplated the move [of writing Heidegger]. I never made it because,

honestly, *my* first question to him would have to be: "When you first wrote that the object of metaphysics was being *qua* being, were you aware of the authentic position of Thomas Aquinas, or did you intentionally neglect it?" I don't dare ask him that question because it is too personal. (62.6.26.)

His discussion with Pegis was only one of several serious intellectual exchanges that Gilson took part in during this period. Others were with Paul Weiss, whose book, *Why People Want to Know the Past*, was coming out in October, and with André Metz, who was writing an article on "Causalité scientifique et cause première"; a few months later, Gilson also helped Metz to publish *Science et réalité* (Metz to EG, 63.3.19). Gilson and de Lubac were also in correspondence around this time (above, p. 301) – Gilson always loved to be consulted by theologians.

Gilson stayed on in Paris until 6 July to attend the closing session of the Académie. He had a word to say about the second-last meeting, which must have seemed anticlimactic after the intellectual communications of the previous two months:

> The Dictionary of the Académie Française is in the middle of the letter *C*. To our great dismay, last Thursday we had to find a definition of the verb *chier*. The definition is followed by this simple comment: *Il est bas. Il* means the verb. (EG to Pegis, 62.2.26.)

As events turned out Gilson did not go to Harvard for the fall of 1962. During the summer at Vermenton, he had a relapse of his earlier prostate trouble; in September he again underwent surgery. Cécile wrote Pegis:

> My father's operation was performed yesterday, and everything went well. Knowing how strongly he reacts to medicine, they did not give him any. Therefore his temperature is running high today. ... When we visit him he carries on a conversation as if nothing has happened. He quotes Molière a good deal – his witticisms on the medical profession. (62.9.4.)

Gilson made a good recovery and could say in November that his life was normal again – certainly it was normal in the order of his wit and ability to take things as they were. In early November he was asked to contribute a paper for a 1965 congress in Florence to celebrate the seventh centenary of the birth of Dante. "I hastened to write it without waiting any longer than was necessary. So they will have the paper even if I am not there to read it." (EG to Pegis, 62.11.5.) Gilson would be there. Though he was already seventy-eight, he had many productive years ahead of him yet.

18

Senium Post Quod Est Mors, 1963-1978

Twice in his letters after 1962 Gilson referred to himself as having entered the last of the ages of man, *senium post quod est mors*, the extreme old age after which comes death. Still, though his powers were in decline, these were relatively good years for him. Mostly they followed a consistent pattern; ten months in Paris and Vermenton writing furiously, and two months each winter in Toronto, sharing his reflections and providing a brief series of talks. At six or fewer lectures, these courses were too short to be counted for credit, but they recorded Gilson's considered final positions, and drew crowds of undergraduates who had been told by their professors that they would never see the like of them again.

In 1961 and 1962 the last of Gilson's strictly philosophical works had appeared: "De la connaissance du principe" (*Revue de métaphysique et de morale*, 66 [1961]: 373-397; McG 242); "L'être et Dieu" (*Revue thomiste*, 62 [1962]: 181-202, 398-416; McG 276); a few articles in *Mediaeval Studies*; and some incidental congress papers. He had also produced one major revision, the second edition of his *L'être et l'essence* (Paris, 1962; McG 45), originally published in 1948; over the years Gilson had come to consider this his best philosophical work. Now, in Vermenton and Paris, Gilson began to shift his attention to new themes, and in 1963 his Vermenton books began to appear. All six Vermenton books were consciously philosophical studies in disciplines other than strict metaphysics. In Gilson's view these disciplines were essential complements to a philosophical life.

In *Introduction aux arts du beau* (Paris, 1963; McG 79) Gilson brings to bear on the other fine arts the ontological analysis he had developed for painting in *Peinture et réalité* eight years earlier. He begins by quoting Lucien Febvre from the *Encyclopédie française* that "art is a kind of knowledge," and goes on to argue that it is nothing of the kind. Rather, art is that fashioning virtue or power by which an artist makes a thing of beauty. Although the perception of this beauty by a beholder is knowledge, art itself is a *making* – this is the doctrine of Thomas on art and also of Aristotle. Gilson goes on to explore the poietic or making arts and the poietic being, functioning throughout as an historian. He examines the positions of Locke and Kant and finds both inclined to fear beauty, preferring to focus on art's usefulness and morality through truth. He also looks at the words of such thoughtful artists as Paul Valéry and Edgar Allen Poe, trying to make philosophical sense of the things they say about their work.

*The Arts of the Beautiful** is an abstract and difficult book, and its substantial contribution to the study of poietics has yet to be recognized. It did receive some notice, largely from people close to Gilson. Pasteur Vallery-Radot, Gilson's nominator into the Academy and hostile critic during *l'affaire Gilson*, wrote a warm letter in praise of these new pages, "each one of which was a subject for meditation":

> Don't you think your book should have still another fine chapter called "Joy Comes to Man Only in Creation." I think the principal reason for the present social malaise is that workmen no longer create. They fashion links in a chain, they never complete a work they can take pride in. (63.4.28.)

Another friend, Colonel Champeaux of Versailles, begged Gilson to turn again to the social themes of *Pour un ordre catholique*; "You are one of France's two most important catholics – the other is Péguy – and you owe us *une explication de notre temps*" (63.7.3). And Henri Gouhier, not unexpectedly, thought *Les arts du beau* "must rid us of so many confusions" (63.7.3).

Matières et formes (Paris, 1964; McG 88) completed the trilogy on fine arts that Gilson had begun with *Peinture et réalité*, and was published quietly in 1964. In his introduction to *Matières*, Gilson tests the abstract conclusions of his *Introduction aux arts du beau*, and illustrates why he called that book "introductory." In the first chapter he reviews Kant's method for distinguishing the fine arts through their respective relations either to space or time as perceived by a knower. Gilson disagrees with this categorization because all the fine arts have, without exception, relations to *both* space *and* time. He argues that the arts are distinguished by their "matter" and by the natural forms which their various artists impose upon them; as a thomist he takes his artifacts not to a mode of knowing but to a mode of being – to matter and form. Gilson proceeds to distinguish *les arts du beau* by his own criteria, and then to examine the full range of arts, including sculpture, architecture, painting, music, dance, poetry and theatre; his original observations are of the sort only a man who has spent nearly eighty years close to the arts could have written.

Matières et formes has gone largely unread by critics, despite its original and controversial positions. Gilson, for example, ridicules Croce's *Aesthetica in nuce* (aesthetics in a nutshell) as a sort of handbook on art for grown-up children (p. 15). He even criticizes Bergson's (or perhaps Felix Ravaisson-Mollien's) somewhat Delphic formula that "it is the same intuition, diversely utilized, which makes both the profound philosopher and the great artist" (p. 16); Gilson complains that this tells us nothing and gets us nowhere, and is, besides, too flattering to the philosopher.

---

* At an earlier stage Gilson had wanted to call the book "Art et métaphysique" (above, p. 359) and at a later stage "The Making of Beauty."

In a letter to Pegis, Gilson adopted an almost apologetic tone in describing his work on the book:

> I spent a pleasant summer in Vermenton ... overhauling my French book *Matières et formes* which will be printed this winter. With it I shall have said all I wanted to say about the fine arts. It is (I suppose) triumphant hylomorphism all along the line. (63.9.12.)

In another letter Gilson told Pegis that he expected the book to meet with considerable critical controversy:

> I am reading the proofs of *Matières et formes: poietiques particulières des arts majeurs*. It does not seem stupid, but will create a hue and cry among critics, professors and other *loquentes*. I will be hurting poor Jacques again, by saying that I don't think Thomas much liked the fine arts. (63.12.18.)

Instead of inspiring criticism, however, *Matières et formes* was largely neglected. It did receive praise in some unexpected places. Eugène Vinaver, for example, an international authority on late medieval romances, found it the most useful treatise on the principles and practice behind medieval art yet to appear.*

With *La société de masse et sa culture* (Paris, 1967; McG 146), Gilson transferred his attention from *homo artifex* to *homo faber*, and dealt with the more practical and technical arts of man. *La société de masse* took more than two entire Vermenton seasons, and also involved the preparation of a paper for a conference in Florence. Gilson wrote the book from a sense of social obligation, having been urged by friends "to do something more for this world too" (Champeaux to EG, 63.4.15).

Gilson wrote three more Vermenton books in these final years of his career. *Les tribulations de sophie* (Paris, 1967; McG 167) was really a byproduct of his private life as a Catholic during these post-conciliar years and can be seen as Gilson's version of Maritain's reflective *Paysan de la Garonne* (1966). Pegis even dubbed Gilson the "fisherman of the Seine." *Les tribulations*, and with it *Linguistique et philosophie* (1962) and *D'Aristote à Darwin et retour* (1971), will be dealt with later in the context of the years in which they were written (below, pp. 376-378; 383-384).

2 LECTURES AND CHRONICLE, 1963-1964

The Vermenton books were a remarkable feat for a man in his eighties, but by no means represented Gilson's only activities during the period. Having delivered a dull course in the winter of 1962, he seemed to have resolved never to be dull again. He told Father Shook, the new president of the Institute, that after 1961 he would keep coming to Toronto for as long as he could and was wanted;

---

* Professeur Vinaver was visiting professor in medieval literature at the Centre for Mediaeval Studies, University of Toronto, during 1972.

thereafter, as he and French sailors put it, "A Dieu vat!" By December 1962 in Paris, in spite of a bout of influenza, he was quite himself again. He was even walking doggedly if unsteadily twice a day from rue Saint Romain to UNESCO headquarters, a "two-hour walk in all" (EG to Shook, 62.12.1).

Gilson arrived in Toronto for his 1963 lectures at the end of January and stayed until early May. During these months he delivered only six public lectures, no more than one in any given week, most of them extracted from his Vermenton book, *The Arts of the Beautiful*. He found this programme easy, and took on two other chores for the Institute. On 3 March, for the approaching feast of Thomas, he held a seminar called "Prolegomena to the 'Prima Via'." * Now that he was formally dealing with Thomas as a theologian, he felt able to play down the philosophical significance of the five ways, much to the annoyance of some of his more philosophically-oriented colleagues.

On 9 May, just before returning to Paris, Gilson spoke at an Institute convocation on the pertinent topic, "Research Schools in the Context of St Thomas on Education." He first recalled how Aristotle, in chapter 4 of the *Nichomachean Ethics*, had cited with approval Hesiod's view that the very best students are "those who understand by themselves." Then he cited Thomas' "optimus ... scilicet potest per ipsum intelligere" ("the best, to be sure, can understand on his own"). Such research students, continued Gilson, are really colleagues; with them a master can raise questions to which he doesn't know the answer, and feel confident that some of them either do know it or will. The authentic pattern of instructional research, said Gilson, is what Albert North Whitehead rightly called an "intellectual adventure." When Gilson gave this talk he was aware that the Institute fellows, senior and junior, were immersed in a statutory review of the Institute's programme. He had been following their considerations closely from France *nihil dicens* by design; he was gratified that the Institute no longer depended on its director for its decisions.

Gilson believed that the Institute had come structurally of age this year with the conferral of the licence in medieval studies on Stanley Cunningham, Stuart Martin, Astrid Salveson and Albert Wingell, all laics, and with the conferral of its first doctorate in theology on Walter H. Principe. At the end of the convocation Chancellor Pocock confided that, although he perforce spoke in these circles as a plagiarist, he now for the first time grasped the profound significance of research students for the Institute.

Gilson visited few other places in North America this year. Later in May he was back in France moving between Paris and Vermenton, and preparing both *Matières et formes* and *The Spirit of Thomism*. He was also finishing at least his part of volume 4 of the *History*, highly pleased that Langan and Maurer were proceeding equally well.

Both these younger colleagues were providing Gilson with the most rewarding collaboration of his life. Langan was on the continent this year, consulting with

* Cf. "Prolégomènes à la 'Prima Via'," *Archives*, 30 [1963]: 53-70; McG 411.

thomists in Poland and phenomenologists in Freiburg-im-Breisgau, and visiting Sicily with his wife Janine and their two children. He was in particularly good form, and lifted Gilson out of his doldrums with warm, brash letters like the following, written just after seeing proofs for volume 3 of the *History*:

> Cher Monsieur le Professeur: Don't fear that I am lavishing my time and *Anstrengungen* to render the Random House bazaar prosperous! Rather, Ya know! As this project has proceeded, I have come to appreciate its possibilities more and more. There is a real philosophical service – not merely didactic – to be rendered by telling the story of what has happened these last 150 years – in fact, what better way to gain a glimpse of the soundest way of bringing its discoveries into line with the perennial truths. (63.8.9.)

Maurer, with less *éclat*, also delighted Gilson this year. Not only did he take over the American and English sections of the *History* – "now that's what I mean by a medievalist!" – but he completed his assignment in the right number of pages, and ahead of schedule.

During these months of 1963 Gilson was again scrupulously attentive to events at the Académie. He attended all the meetings, even when he had to commute to Paris from Vermenton:

> I attend the weekly meetings of the Académie, whose fellows are no chickens. Our conversation largely consists of an exchange of news about health. We also watch one another and say: "Poor so-and-so does not look well ... etc." This week – next Thursday – I shall be acting-chancellor at the reception of Henry de Montherland, a well-known novelist and playwright. He suffers a perpetual breakdown, which, so he says, makes it impossible to read his speech publicly. Yet he can talk on the radio! So we have organized a private reception. ... This has not happened since Richelieu's time, 1634, I think. (EG to Maurer, 63.6.1.)

A further reminder of Gilson advancing years was the death of the third pope he had known personally:

> The death of *le bon pape* Jean XXIII occupies the minds and hearts of everyone. Nothing like him has happened to the church before. (EG to Shook, 63.7.9.)

Gilson also personally knew his successor, Paul VI, as Cardinal Montini:

> *Habemus papam!* I know him and like him. Since they could not elect Cardinal Bea, they made what is probably the best choice. I cannot help smiling when I hear him praised as a liberal, whatever that means. Applied to him it must somehow be compatible with that memorable statement he once made to me: *le propre de l'autorité est de ne pas se justifier* (EG to Maurer, 63.7.9; see above p. 248.)

This fall Gilson spent three days, 11 to 13 November 1963, teaching the monks of Fleury. Abbot Grégoire had invited him to live in and give six conferences, two each day, in Abbaye Saint Benoit de Fleury at Saint-Benoit-sur-Loire, on the mutual importance of theology and philosophy. Gilson must have been reminded of the tenth-century Abbo, who had taught the monks of Fleury the importance of the sciences for theology; this was long before the philosophy of the schools came to be known as theology's handmaid. Gilson, who loved the medieval masters, must haved dreamed about the Fleury of books and scribes in which Abbo had walked.

A few weeks later, on 13 December, Gilson was invited to participate in the public homage to Père Sertillanges at the Institut Catholique. Gilson was one of five speakers; the others were Père Chenu; Bishop M. Blanchet, the rector; Robert Garrie from Cité Universitaire; and Père Lelong op, the radio priest of Paris. Sertillanges had been important to Maman, and to Gilson too as a boy. In "Souvenir du Père Sertillanges" he claimed that, even in 1963, he still considered Sertillanges the most authentic thomist of the preceding generation (Gilson Archives, Toronto).

During this year Burt Franklin in New York announced an unauthorized reprint of Gilson's 1913 complementary dissertation, *Index scolastico-cartesien* (above, p. 54). Gilson was deeply upset. Under American law he was powerless to block the reprint because the copyright had run out. He by no means considered the *Index* a complete work of scholarship, and had refused two hundred dollars for the rights when it had been offered to him:

> It is the public that is victimized in a deal like this. I am opposed and refuse to be responsible. I am not through with the work until I am dead. While I am alive I owe it to the public not to allow to appear under my name something I am not teaching my students. Intellectual honesty requires no less. If I live, I will surely do this book over again. (EG to Morot-Sir, cultural attaché, French embassy, NY, 64.1.14.; tr.)

Gilson's visit to Toronto from late February to April 1964 was, like his visits of old, full of varied activity. He left France on 12 February, went to Québec City via Montréal for a conference, and returned to Montréal for several days. On 22 February he reached Toronto in good time to keep a dinner invitation from Archbishop Philip Pocock, chancellor of the Institute; as president of the Institute, Father Shook was also in attendance. During dinner the chancellor reiterated his deep interest in research; Vatican II had impressed on him the futility of attempting anything serious without it. Toward the end of the dinner, the chancellor turned and asked Gilson to receive for the Institute his gift of a hundred thousand dollars for financing research scholarships in the Institute. After all, he said, the secret of effective research is to be able to attract top scholars. So far the Institute had focused its attention on its book collection and on the training and hiring of competent instructors. The chancellor now provided a substantial financial base on which to establish a Mediaeval Studies Foundation to deal with its research needs. For the first time Gilson began to be confident that his work in Toronto would continue after his death.

Between 28 February and 20 March Gilson gave four lectures on "The Spirit of Thomism" at the Institute. These were the trial run for the lectures he was to give at the 175th anniversary of Georgetown University in April. The Georgetown lectures formed the core of Gilson's *The Spirit of Thomism* (New York, 1964; McG 147), a book which presented the thomism of the later Gilson.

Shortly before leaving for Georgetown University, Gilson gave another memorable lecture to the University College Literary and Athletic Society which was sponsoring lectures on present-day morality: Paul Tillich was the other invited speaker, though not on the same day. Gilson worried a good deal over this lecture – the topic, "On Moral Progress," was unusual for him. In the lecture he located morality within its aristotelian and thomistic frameworks, and presented it in the disparate contexts of Lévy-Bruhl's sociology, of slavery and brutality, and of the moralities of UNESCO and of Simone de Beauvoir. Gilson charted man's moral progress through historical times as a sequence of five discoveries: man's discovery that he has a history; his discovery of himself as good; his discovery of himself as a social animal; his discovery of law; and lastly his discovery, in the Judeo-Christian tradition, of interiorized love – man's love for man as one with his love for God and of God's love for him. Gilson repeated this lecture later in the year at Temple University (Philadelphia), at St John Fisher College (Rochester), and elsewhere. However, although he thought it good when he first delivered it, he made light of it some years later.

Gilson returned to Paris 4 May 1964, leaving behind his own English version of *Les arts du beau* to be polished by Institute colleagues and the editors of Scribner's Sons. In Paris and then Vermenton, Gilson carried on with volume 4 of the *History*, with his Venice lectures for September, and with the preparation of his Dante lectures for the next year. In June he quietly marked his eightieth birthday.

For some time Gilson had been worried that the Vatican II Council was downplaying Thomas Aquinas. In late May he read that Père Congar at the Saulchoir had talked about "the church of the future" and had suggested that modern Christians show some sympathy for Teilhard de Chardin on the grounds that de Chardin "at least succeeded in catching the attention of the contemporary world." Gilson was furious: "Had I been there," he wrote Pegis, "I would have observed that Luther too had caught the attention of his contemporaries. What a criterion!" (64.5.30.) At eighty Gilson was no longer the tactful and generous critic whom Louis Rougier had once dubbed the proponent of "La philosophie sympathique" (above, p. 348). Now he simply lost his temper at Congar, though he also resolved to give four lectures on Luther the next year in Toronto. These along with all his other commitments made the rest of 1964 impossibly busy.

In August Gilson's family joined him in Vermenton, and in early September he, Jacqueline, Cécile, and Thérèse d'Alverny motored together to Venice. On 5, 7 and 8 September, for the Fondazzio Georgio Cini, he delivered three lectures on the plastic arts, writing and music under the general title "Industrialization of the Arts" (*Arte e cultura nella civilta contemporanea* [Florence, 1966]; McG 308). These lectures were not an extension of the Vermenton trilogy on the fine arts, but a new analysis of the effects of technology upon them.* On 9 September,

---

* This theme wold have come in part from Marshall McLuhan. The two had held conversations in the Institute office and in McLuhan's Communications Centre in the University of Toronto, where a

following the lectures in Venice, he took part in another seminar on the industrialization of the arts.

This was a particularly happy visit to Venice for Gilson. Both daughters were with him, as was Mlle d'Alverny, who was busy with a multiplicity of projects that took her back and forth between Fondazzio and St Mark's Library. Armand Maurer also arrived in Venice on his return from the Settimana Nella Internazionale di Studi, which he had attended with Nikolaus Häring. Amid all these goings and comings, Gilson even made a discovery of sorts. He found that Sigismund Gerdil – now readmitted to volume 3 of the *History* – was part of a "philosophie savoyarde," the existence of which explained the history of ontologism from Malebranche to Rosmini:

> Remarkably, I found in Venice that Professor Di Noce had reached the very same conclusions: there is a "filosofia de Savoia" with Turino at its centre and extending to Milano, an Italo-French line of Christian philosophers spawned in the wake of Malebranche. (EG to Maurer, 64.9.21.)

Gilson returned to Canada in November, one of the few times he visited Toronto twice in one year; possibly he was inspired by the optimism he felt as a result of the chancellor's gift. He paused in Montréal to read in preview his newest paper, "Saint Thomas et nous," written for non-Dante invitations during the coming Dante year.

Gilson's Toronto lectures this fall took place in late November and early December in the theatre of the Royal Ontario Museum; the lectures of the preceding winter had drawn more people than Carr Hall could hold. The subject of the lectures was "The Birth of the Lutheran Reformation." Of all the Protestant reformers, Luther had taken the most intransigent attitude toward speculative theology; witness his early "Disputation Against Scholastic Theology" in which he had urged that no man could become a theologian unless he did so without Aristotle.* Gilson could understand Luther's sweeping dismissal of all medieval theology, but considered the recent softening of the Council Fathers toward Luther to be weak and wrong-headed. Gilson's lectures were entitled: "Luther's Starting Point"; "Personal Experiences and Theology"; "The Freedom of a Christian"; and, with an eye on Erasmus, "The Fly and the Elephant." In them he dealt sympathetically with Luther's personal psychology, but sternly with the anti-intellectual theology attaching to it.

Gilson was considerably upset that the French bishops were, in a sense, following Luther's lead by allowing free entry to new confusions without compensating with doctrinal directives:

> Luther damned himself in vain. Last week I attended at Saint-Sulpice an entirely new, two-hour-long liturgy invented by the director of a Catholic school. It was a

---

McLuhan-Gilson interview was taped. They had subsequently exchanged letters on technology, though no "meeting of minds" can be said to have taken place.

* See *Luther: Early Theological Works*, ed. James Atkinson, Philadelphia [c. 1962], 19: 266-272, especially theses 43 and 44.

> Solemn Profession of Faith intended to replace the now defunct First Communion: Bible readings, songs and exhortations and, in the middle, a (frankly) improved mass. Those priests are saints. (EG to Pegis, 64.6.7.)

In other words the new reforms created much hard work over nonessentials, and offered little for the mind.

This was the beginning of the painful reaction to the winds of "renewal" which were to prove so upsetting to himself and Maritain over the next few years. Too many old mistakes were being made again:

> Maritain says that even in the days of Aristotle philosophy had already gone full cycle. I think he is right. The only difference between men and dogs is that while both like to chase their own tails, dogs never forget they have one. ... The important point to be remembered – one not found in books – is that man, in a sense, is not made up of soul and body; he *is* an animated body, a body animated by an intellect. Now we *say* this, but don't believe it. We acknowledge the unity of man without being convinced of it. (EG to Pegis, 64.6.26.)

The lectures on Luther came to grips at one extreme with the inhuman emptiness of philosophies that have no metaphysics. Gilson knew however that, when he got through with the Dante activities of 1965, he would return in his formal lectures to the thought of Thomas.

3 THOMAS AND DANTE, 1965-1966

From early January until the end of October, Gilson spent the year 1965 in Europe. He had two dominating interests: to resist the assaults on Thomas and thomism that were becoming common, and to promote the appreciation of Dante during this seven hundredth anniversary of the poet's death.

Gilson was aware that his own handling of Thomas' teachings had changed much over the years, and that he had often been critical of thomists. This struck him full force in early 1965, as he made revisions for the sixth and last edition of *Le thomisme* (Paris, 1965; McG 165). He began to have some doubts about his work. Had he been right in trying to package Thomas in successive editions of this book? Thomas had never tried to organize his own teachings, probably realizing that it couldn't be done. Thus some of the few changes Gilson introduced into his sixth edition of *Le thomisme*, such as his way of handling the *quinque viae* disturbed him. He wrote Maurer:

> I hope Father Owens is not too concerned about what I have said about the proofs of the existence of God. ... He should not hesitate to tear my book to pieces if he thinks I am harming the truth of the doctrine. St Thomas first! Besides, I feel pretty sure that certain very important aspects of his admirable doctrine still escape me. (65.5.1; see further, Gilson's "Prolégomènes à la 'Prima Via'," *Archives*, 30 [1963]; McG 411.)

This scruple also affected Gilson's important "St Thomas et nous" lecture which he gave several times this year; he changed the lecture almost as often as he gave it. When he delivered the paper in Rome on 13 April, he was so sensitive that he abused Boyer unnecessarily at a reception afterward at the French embassy. Boyer had congratulated Gilson on his lecture and had gone on to say he simply must read a paper at the Sixth International Thomistic Congress in Rome in September. Gilson did not want to get further embroiled in thomist bickering over theology and philosophy, and the pent-up emotions that had simmered since his 1956 embarrassment over "les deux thèmes" suddenly exploded. "In an embassy," he wrote Maurer, "I should have been more diplomatic" (65.5.1). Nonetheless, Boyer had the last word. Nearly two months later he issued Gilson a second invitation, explaining that the Holy Father had expressed displeasure with Gilson's refusal and had asked that he reconsider. "What else could I do?" wrote Gilson. "I complied." (EG to Shook, 65.6.18.)

At the September congress Gilson read an excellent paper, "De la notion d'être divin dans la philosophie de saint Thomas d'Aquin" (*Doctor Communis*, 18 [1965]: 113-129; McG 243). Gilson's was the only paper given at the Solemn Inauguration of the congress on the evening of Monday 6 September; Cardinal Pizzardo presided and Boyer introduced both theme and speaker. Gilson had to confess that, at this second meeting of 1965, Father Boyer was charming. He had gone out of his way to please Gilson by placing de Lubac on the programme; Gilson had once staunchly defended de Lubac's *Surnaturel* when Rome had questioned it. Ironically, however, de Lubac spoke on Teilhard de Chardin. "Ah!" Gilson wrote, "that I could cure our friend Father de Lubac of his acute 'Teilhard-de-Chardinism.' Teilhard is a gnostic." (EG to Pegis, 65.7.20.)

For Gilson, the pièce-de-résistance of this September congress was the reception of the members by Paul VI at Castel Gandolfo:

> The pope spoke in French. He was obviously laying down the law for the council [about to begin its final session]. ... Thomas is, was, and always will be the Doctor Communis ... the master of all and for all. Then [the pope] said what I have always been waiting for: that by making him the Common Doctor, the church did not intend to exclude other doctors whose teachings are theologically sound. ... Milk and honey to Father Balić: he was beaming. ... I was living through a historical moment in the development of thomism. At that moment the devil got so angry he unleashed one more diabolical storm; a soaked congress returned to its buses. (EG to Pegis, 65.9.17.)

Gilson would refer frequently to this allocution in the remaining lectures of his life. He considered it a new papal position that broadened the church's outlook on the various theologies. One day, he said, it would be acclaimed as the best thing ever to have happened to thomism.

During this year Gilson continued to react strongly against theologians and liturgists who were attempting to reduce the instructional role of thomism in the life of the church. On 2 July 1965 he released his "Suis-je schismatique?" (McG 805) in *La France catholique*. Three days earlier he had written:

> I am going to create a scandal with a paper to be published by *La France catholique* under the title "Suis-je schismatique?" And why should I be such a monster?

Because I refuse to say that in the new French version of the mass the Son "est de même nature que le Père." I am creating a new schism, that of the Nicaean paleocatholics who believe that the Son is of the same "substance" as the Father, and that both are of the same nature only because they are "consubstantial." In short, I am asking our liturgical authorities to re-establish in the Creed the old *consubstantialem patri*. Everybody tells me that there will be an outcry; the notion of substance is rejected by the modern mind. (EG to Shook, 65.6.29.)

An outcry indeed there was from supporters, opponents and the indifferent; French liturgists, including the bishops of France, were caught completely offguard. A fortnight later Gilson was backing down, protesting that his "interrogation about the schism was a purely rhetorical question" and that he "was surprised at the number of persons who took it literally" (EG to Shook, 65.7.11). Some correspondents, such as Jean Godest, berated Gilson for not supporting the French-speaking hierarchies around the world, and for bringing his objections into the public forum. Nonetheless, many significant French Catholics wrote Gilson to express their agreement. Yves Congar wrote that he had himself supported a similar protest, sent to the Centre de Liturgie, taking exception to the Arianism of this phrase and others in the new French translation of the mass. The reply from the Centre had maintained that Arianism was no longer a problem. This could be so, wrote Congar to Gilson, but as you say, "it is also necessary to express faith correctly" (65.7.6).

Another "thomist" issue to occupy Gilson during 1965 was a challenge to a dialogue issued by the marxist Roger Garaudy on the flyleaf of a complimentary copy of his *De l'anathème au dialogue: un marxiste s'addresse au concile* (Paris, 1965). Gilson started to write something but put it aside, declining the invitation as too difficult – marxists, he said, don't really dialogue, they preach. However, as he prepared a three-part article for *Seminarium*, "Trois leçons sur le thomisme et sa situation présente" (17 [1965]: 682-737; McG 486), Gilson introduced a brief oblique reply to Garaudy.* He wrote as follows to Pegis:

> In the latter part of my reply, I had to revive the Teilhard de Chardin problem since Garaudy quotes him at great length to make clear that dialogue is possible between communists and Catholics. He means, of course, "intelligent" Catholics like Teilhard. I don't count myself one of them. I am now considered retrograde because "nature" is leftist whereas "substance" is rightist, ... a fascinating way of putting it because it makes a terrifying kind of sense. I just heard the French version of the Preface for Trinity and Sundays. It uses "nature" everywhere and I cannot stand it. I have no choice, however. These [modern liturgists] are so naïve that they find "nature" easier to understand than "substance." By Jove, if they ever succeed in making the dogma of the Trinity even slightly intelligible, they will have done a remarkable thing. (66.7.17.)

---

* This piece in *Seminarium* was preliminary to Gilson's larger "un dialogue difficile" to appear the next year in *Les tribulations de Sophie* (Paris, 1967; McG 167). See below, pp. 376-378.

During 1965 Gilson had delivered several lectures on Dante to mark the seventh centenary of the great poet's death. He had begun to plan these lectures the previous year when early, urgent invitations arrived from Florence and Cornell. He had prepared three original papers – "Dante's 'Mirabile Visione'," "What is a Shade?" and "Poetry and Theology in *The Divine Comedy*"; these were published as "Trois études dantesques" (*Archives*, 32 [1965]: 71-126; McG 484). He also prepared an article, "À la recherche de l'Empyrée" for the *Revue des études italiennes* (11 [1965]: 147-161; McG 189). Gilson delivered one or more of these papers in many places: Florence (21 April), Montréal (29 October), Cornell (1, 2 November), Toronto (5, 12, 19 November), Berkeley, Augsburg, and elsewhere. Where he gave only one lecture, it was usually "Dante's 'Mirabile Visione'," his own favourite, which had created some sensation in Italy:

> This lecture had already, in Italy, been excerpted from my English manuscript and widely quoted as a kind of revolutionary interpretation of the *Vita nuove*, which in a way it is. I hold in it the bold view that things happened to Dante exactly as he says they did. What real scholar could ever believe this? (EG to Maurer, 65.9.24.)

As the year went on Gilson widened his list of topics. The next year he was still involved with Dante:

> I shall go to Venice, Padua and Verona for the last leg of the Dante centennial pilgrimage. Deserted by my drivers, I shall go by train, alone save for the company of the romantic shades that still haunt the countryside. (EG to Pegis, 66.3.4.)

Gilson gave lectures in 1965 on other topics as well. In September he lectured for Count Cini in Milano on "L'industrialization des belles-lettres." He gave his "Saint Thomas et nous" in Turin, Rome, Naples and, with variations, at Soisy-sous-Étioles, where he pointed out "how the naughty Dominicans are misbehaving" by abandoning St Thomas (EG to Shook, 65.2.24).

In 1966 Gilson's months in France were busy ones. At least twice he wrote up his fall lectures for Toronto in an effort to render them more metaphysical. He was also, as he put it, "wasting my precious remnant of life playing around with a treatise on the 'Platonic Essence of Photography.' It's silly, I know, but I can't stop." * In Paris, the student-worker riots were underway: "The whole country is going on strike; from railroads to electricity to university professors and, of course, students. The philosophers have quit thinking and nobody notices the difference." (EG to Pegis, 66.3.25.)

Gilson was invited this year by Balić to attend a scotist congress. He decided not to go and pleaded family difficulties. By this he meant he wanted to join a parish pilgrimage to Lourdes; although the two events did not quite overlap, they were close enough to make conflicting demands on a man of eighty-two. His real reason for refusing, however, was that antiscotism was no longer serious enough

---

* This is a reference to "Photographie et beauté" published in the UNESCO journal, *Diogène* (55 [1966]: 34-53; McG 394).

to require his attention. He had no intention of allowing himself to be drawn intellectually into the scotist camp:

> I have done all the fighting I can for Scotus. Now that suffering scotism has been succeeded by triumphing scotism, I have no more interest. I want scotists to be free within the church; I have been disgusted by the calumnies against them and him. Now all this is in the past. Scotism now is simply a doctrinal position in opposition to the true metaphysics of being of St Thomas. Since I have to choose between *ens* without *esse* and *ens habens esse*, I choose the latter. I now foresee a Scotus era that is philosophically and theologically anti-Thomas, so I prefer to abstain. This will be taken as just another instance of "late Gilsonism." ... Freedom for me is not the freedom of indifference: I am against the metaphysics of universal being. (EG to Maurer, 66.10.3.)

Far from being difficult, Gilson's family situation was good this year. On 27 August he went with the Vermenton parish on its pilgrimage to Lourdes:

> I have to thank Our Lady for a great grace and to ask for another one. The pilgrimage will be back on 4 September. Cécile just announced her coming for 9 September. She will stay with us till 9 October. Bernard is now at Geneva, working for the UNO as a translator of English, German, and occasionally Russian. He will join the New York staff next August. He likes the work but finds it very heavy. Anyway, this is my reason for going to Lourdes next month in the spirit of thanksgiving. The other grace I shall beg for is spiritual. (EG to Pegis, 66.7.17.)

Cécile had now taken up residence in Toronto and was working for the Children's Aid Society there.

Before going to Toronto in October for his 1966 lectures, Gilson decided to sell his large house at Vermenton, and to dispose of the library he had gathered there:

> I have no space for books in Paris. None of my children will be able to keep the Vermenton house; I shall not even leave them enough money to pay the death duties. So I am preparing the small house at Cravant (five kilometers from Vermenton) for a shelter during my last years – or months. It has a nice garden, but no place for books – except my Marietti editions of St Thomas. (EG to Maurer, 66.10.3.)

Gilson did not tell his children of this decision beforehand, and they were taken aback when faced with the *fait accompli*. Cécile thought the family might well have pooled their resources to finance the Vermenton house as "a more suitable retirement home for papa."

Gilson planned to sell his books to the Institute in Toronto or to de Paulhac, who had taken over from Vrin. Some years ago he had already sold his superb, strictly philosophical library to the Institute, claiming that he could use it there just as effectively as in France. The remaining books – some four thousand in number – were not, for the most part, philosophical:

> There is a fair collection of modern Italian philosophies, good books on and by Dante, modern French literature and criticism, books on aesthetics, the Descartes Adam-Tannery, all the editions (deluxe and otherwise) of the French Bible de

> Jerusalem,* etc. etc. I shall keep practically nothing. You can't take those things
> with you. But matter has *partes extra partes*: so there are good Claudels, Valérys
> and such delightful French literature! Bernard has picked up my Schopenhauer and
> selected writings of Auguste Comte! I watched them go *siccis oculis*. I think I have
> written as much as I want to. I can live with one Bible, an *Imitation of Christ*, and
> enough pent-up malice to fill thirty volumes. What I want is peace! (EG to Maurer,
> 66.9.3.)

Eventually the Institute bought his books for $10,000 plus packing and shipping
costs. In April 1967 the Institute librarian, Father Harold Gardner, and Pierre de
Paulhac met with Gilson in Vermenton to evaluate, pack and ship the entire
collection to Toronto. Not strictly a medieval collection, the books represented
Gilson's wide range of interests during the Vermenton years. (See Gardner to
Shook, 67.4.24.)

Just before leaving for Toronto in late October, Gilson presented a paper *sous la
coupôle* to all five Académies de l'Institut de France on *Les arts ou les lettres*
(Paris, 1966; McG 1). He arrived in Toronto with a wretchedly typed dossier of
seven papers. Six of these were on the "Renewal of Metaphysics" and would be
delivered as one, two or three lectures to the Pontifical Institute, to St Joseph's in
West Hartford, to Assumption in Windsor and to other centres. There was also a
lone historical paper entitled "The Cultural Revolution of the Thirteenth Century"
(*Distinguished Lectures Series* [Durham, 1968], pp. 124-142; McG 239); this was
to be given at the University of New Hampshire in Durham, 5 January 1967.

The thrust of the papers on metaphysics was set forth in Gilson's introduction
to the three – two on "Metaphysical Knowledge," one on "The Will to Meta-
physicize" – given in Toronto:

> First, that there is such a thing as metaphysical knowledge; secondly that there is a
> valid metaphysical knowledge; thirdly, that no genuine philosophical knowledge is
> possible without a minimum of metaphysical speculation. ... There is a meta-
> physical knowledge whose truth is as unchangeable as the structure of the human
> mind. ... The contrary view is the popular one: it is now considered evident – which
> to Plato would have been a scandal – that Becoming, not Being, is the core of
> reality. ("On the Renewal of Christian Philosophy," Gilson Archives, additional
> page 23.)

The word "renewal" in the title of these papers clearly refers to the Vatican
Council that had just finished in Rome. The council's influence can be detected
throughout the lectures, particularly where Gilson speaks of Heidegger, Maurice
Blondel, Maritain and others. In these papers Gilson articulated the respective
roles of philosophy and theology as he would have liked the council fathers to
have done.

---

* As a member ot the advisory board, Gilson received fascicules as they appeared.

4 CANADIAN CENTENNIAL CONGRESSES, 1967

During 1967 Gilson delivered no lecture series in Toronto, and limited his Canadian appearances to two important congresses. In Toronto he attended, from 2 to 25 August, the International Congress on the Theology of the Renewal of the Church sponsored by the bishops of Canada as their participation in Canada's centennial celebrations. And in Montréal he attended the Fourth International Congress of Medieval Philosophy from 27 August to 2 September. Gilson's featured role in these two centennial congresses was in recognition of his intellectual contributions to Canada since 1926. Under his patronage two institutes of medieval studies had flowered in Toronto and in Ottawa and Montréal. In the eyes of Canadian medievalists Gilson was – to adapt Pliny – "although over eighty years of age, a truer, more authentic and a better scholar than the world had thus far known."

Gilson travelled to Canada this year with Jacqueline, Pierre de Paulhac and Anne-Marie de Paulhac, Vrin's granddaughter. Anne-Marie had just completed her master's degree in philosophy at the Sorbonne. Gilson, who had got his equivalent degree from the Sorbonne in 1907, made a predictable comment: "What they are being taught there now is beyond imagination!" (EG to Maurer, 67.4.23.)

Gilson found the Toronto congress gratifying on several scores, not least that it was hosted by his own Institute. He took pleasure in reading a paper at a theological congress – though it didn't make him into a theologian, at least it made him feel like one. He also enjoyed a moment of gratifying irony when he was asked to read the paper of Yves Congar, who had fallen ill in South America. Congar had been one of Gilson's students in the 1930s, and had become a notable Dominican theologian and a leading force during Vatican II; as a council figure, Congar was more liberal than Gilson could wish for, as seen by his defence of Teilhard de Chardin (above pp. 212, 367). At the Institute's congress, Gilson stepped easily into the breach created by Congar's absence and read Congar's paper with such vigour, clarity and aplomb that Convocation Hall vibrated with the applause.

Gilson's own paper was entitled "On Behalf of the Handmaid" (*Theology of Renewal*, ed. L. K. Shook [New York and Montréal, 1968], 1: 236-249; McG 373). Essentially it applied the central point of his 1966 Toronto lectures to theology. Gilson argued that when theology uses philosophy, philosophy is placed in a subordinate position because natural reason is subordinate to faith. This process does not permit a proper definition of philosophy, which has its own nature, methods and ends, all of which theology must respect when it uses philosophy. Theology should not demand more of philosophy than philosophy can give. Nonetheless, theology can make strong demands: it can ask, for example, that philosophy return to metaphysics and to the natural notion of finality, the natural notion of God.

The Fourth International Congress of Medieval Philosophy took place in Montréal immediately after the Toronto congress, and took for its theme "The

Liberal Arts and Philosophy in the Middle Ages." Gilson presided over the congress as a whole, and over an afternoon session devoted to "The Liberal Arts and Humanism Today." In his opening remarks for this session, Gilson returned to his Toronto theme, this time on behalf of the liberal arts. Again, Gilson insisted that there must be a return to metaphysics:

> Now we might say that the arts and encyclopedic sciences are, in fact, subordinated to a higher speculative end, to a wisdom; not however to a practical wisdom like Seneca's but to a speculative wisdom. The spirit and content of this speculative wisdom are those of philosophy properly so called. This speculative wisdom is distinct from the liberal arts. This wisdom uses the liberal arts for its own purposes, that is, it considers their ends. The ancients called this wisdom "first philosophy." We call it "metaphysics." (*Arts libéraux et philosophie au moyen âge* [Paris, 1969], p. 271; McG 387.)

Both before and after his brief Canadian tour this year, Gilson's activities in Europe were limited. He flew to Bologna in February to receive an honorary degree, and in April superintended the packing and shipping of his Vermenton library. On 11 May he spoke in the Panthéon where a tablet to Henri Bergson was unveiled, and on 29 May he flew to Berlin for a week for the annual chapter of the Orden Pour le Mérite. On 6 November he went to Liège to receive his second honorary degree of that year: "I have too many ex-pupils at Liège not to accept their invitation." And on 15 November he took part in a radio tribute to Jacques Maritain: "le vieux Jacques" thanked him for his participation, happy that a broadcast could provide "such splendid public statements on faith and reason and the intuition of being!" (Maritain to EG, 67.11.15; tr.)

If Gilson's physical activities were relatively light in 1967, not so his intellectual efforts. In the series "Essais d'art et de philosophie," he published two short Vermenton books: *La société de masse et sa culture* (Paris, 1967; McG 146) and *Les tribulations de Sophie* (Paris, 1967; McG 167). *La société* offered a final extension of Gilson's ontologies into the production-line world of the practical and technical arts. *Les tribulations* presented the personal and cathartic causerie of a practising thomist during the maelstrom that had risen in the wake of the Vatican Council.

The title of *Les tribulations de Sophie* had a history:

> To give credit where it is due, Mme la Comtesse de Segur, née Rostopschine, published *Les malheurs de Sophie* back in 1864. So my title is incontestably from hers. Her Sophie was a little girl, presumably real, whose misfortunes were not entirely undeserved. Paul Claudel dramatized her into the symbolic and scriptural incarnation of the formidable Judith, the moving Esther, and other persons in sacred history who, according to Saint Hilary, in some way prefigure Christ. My Sophie – la nouvelle Sophie – is not a little girl or an allegory, but that wisdom which is, according to St Thomas, supreme among the human wisdoms ... *sapientia ... simpliciter*. (Pp. 11-12.)

Les tribulations picks up the theme of "Trois leçons sur le thomisme et sa situation présente" (*Seminarium*, 17 [1965]: 682-737; McG 486) in which Gilson dealt with metaphysics and touched in passing upon the work of Teilhard de Chardin; Dino Staffa, editor of *Seminarium* had told Gilson he should write more of the same. The book also draws upon Gilson's "Saint Thomas et nous" lectures in all their variations. The first part of *Les tribulations* substantially repeats the three chapters of "Trois leçons" adding a fourth on Teilhard. Gilson then casts away caution and offers two supplements. The first of these, subtitled "Le dialogue difficile," is really addressed to the marxist, Garaudy. The second supplement, "Divagations parmi les ruines," consists of some rambling, angry postconciliary reflections.

"Le dialogue difficile" was a response to a challenge to a dialogue issued by the marxist Roger Garaudy (above p. 371). Gilson at first declined this challenge, but decided to accept after reading in an article by David Rousset (*Le Figaro*, 66.6.18) that Garaudy's book, *De l'anathème*, was only part of a more comprehensive survey of marxist thought. Gilson selected for debate four of Garaudy's arguments: that marxism is a humanism which puts man before and against God; that marxism's task is to cure the thousand ills caused by religion; that dialectical materialism is a philosophy; and that marxism offers a scientific position. In his answers Gilson argues that he prefers Maritain's integral humanism to Garaudy's in that it gives man the greater honour.* He finds Garaudy's "thousand ills," where plausible, irremediable, and finds Garaudy's philosophy of "matter as being" even more untenable than Descartes' and quite as antiquated. Gilson considers scientific evolution, or passive creation, philosophically insipid beside the *Dei cooperatores* of Thomas. He also professes surprise that Garaudy could speak highly of Teilhard de Chardin's science, which had always struck him as a sequence of "massive undemonstrated and undemonstrable affirmations": Teilhard's "tout ce qui monte converge," for example, Gilson had seen verified by "no jet of water and few trees" (p. 129).

In the second supplement, "Divagations parmi les ruines," Gilson offers a selection of the unpleasant ramifications of the postconciliary church; these concern celebrations, vernacular masses and defections by priests over celibacy. The supplement was seen by some of Gilson's friends as a lapse of taste, sensitivity and the power to discriminate. Maritain replied first:

> I think too much of you, regard you too highly, and love you too much, not to caution you. You seem to be putting absolutely essential questions, those touching on your truth, faith, theology, philosophy, "in the same bag" with lesser matters like the celibacy of priests. (I am as attached to this as you, but my goodness! there are married priests in the Greek rite and in the Russian Orthodox Church whose wives are no more indiscreet than are the maidservants of the curés.) Then there is the matter of that wretched "*messe farfelue*" where you showed yourself not very community-minded; and that abominable mingling of consecrated and nonconsecrated hosts by some priests; and there are those masses in the vernacular where a foreign visitor follows nothing. (But this was also the case of the unlettered attending a Latin mass!) Am I unnecessarily "liberal" in pointing this out – I who

---

* Garaudy apparently had been replying to an address by Maritain to UNESCO in Mexico City.

am also pained by the French translation of the canon? No! I only point out that
there is a certain hierarchy in these problems. (67.11.15; tr.)

Congar also cautioned Gilson:

> Your *Tribulations* poses problems which again have a sting in them for me too.
> First, there is the place of St Thomas. Our own young Dominicans are not
> neglecting Thomas, but they think the most real problems are to be met in other
> philosophers ... especially in the anthropologists – and cannot be conceptualized in
> the philosophy of St Thomas. ... Secondly, there is the post-conciliary church. I
> don't deny the excesses you deplore. But I wish you and M. Maritain would take the
> positive role of the postconciliary church into consideration. What you are saying
> about the liturgical reform loses much of its weight because you don't balance it
> against the many very beautiful celebrations where the priestly people really do
> participate. (67.10.24; tr.)

If Gilson was negative in matters concerning the day-to-day life of the postconciliary church, he could be positive enough when it came to metaphysics as a
sine qua non of properly functioning theology. He and Maritain suffered
personally when Père Poupard wrote *Les vieillards de l'après-concile* and left his
order, and also when Père Geffré, op, regent of studies, announced that he had left
Thomas and would not return. Gilson's and Maritain's sense of abandonment
was real, and they could not help fighting back against what they saw as changes
for the worse.

5 THE CASE FOR METAPHYSICS, 1968-1969

For his Toronto lectures of early 1968, Gilson took his theme from "Le
dialogue difficile." He was determined to deal with what he saw as a gaping hole,
not only in marxist thought but in all matter-oriented sciences. If the existence of
God left the Christian with problems, the non-existence of God left him with
other even more difficult problems. In Carr Hall between 23 February and 16
March Gilson presented four lectures on "The Problem of the Non-Existence of
God": "The Difficulties of Atheism," "Is God Dead?" "The True Problem" and "Is
the Non-Existence of God Even Thinkable?" These drew heavily on Gilson's
detailed knowledge of French philosophy since Descartes, and referred
extensively to Kant, Hegel and Nietzsche. At this time Gilson planned to produce
a large study on atheism and the idea of God. He drew up a list of its chapters and
prepared a good deal of material, but seems not to have completed it. After his
death parts of this book, which he had meant to call *Constantes philosophiques de
l'être*, were made available by his good friend Henri Gouhier as *L'athéisme
difficile* (Paris, 1979; McG 2). Gilson did not allow himself to get caught up again
in any wretched "divagations parmi les ruines."

At the end of March 1968 Gilson returned to France and began to work on still
another metaphysical front, language in relation to philosophy. He had certain
equipment for the task: his metaphysics, his knowledge of living languages, and
his lexicographical experience from the Académie Française. But, although Gilson

knew what earlier philosophers had said about language, he was seriously handicapped by his unfamiliarity with contemporary linguistic science.

Gilson's linguistic interest first manifested itself early in the year when he took another look at Siger of Brabant. At St Michael's College, Armand Maurer – to whom Gilson had drawn very close – was collaborating with Professor William Dunphy on the editing of new Siger manuscripts they had located. As both men had been Gilson's students, he followed their project closely, even passionately. He wrote Maurer from Vermenton:

> Is the deep point of differences between Siger and Thomas really over the nature of *sacra doctrina*, about which Thomas said: "Non ergo est scientia practica, sed magis speculativa" (ST, I.1.4, *Sed contra*)? What does this mean? Is this *magis* a kind of English "but rather," or does it mean, as I have always thought, that theology is "more" speculative than practical? (68.1.21.)

At eighty-four, Gilson had found a new approach to texts through the asking of linguistic and semantic questions. He had paid little attention to Siger since his two papers on averroism and thomism some thirty years earlier for *Dante et la philosophie* (Paris, 1939; McG 12). Now he was finding a not-uncommon little word like *magis* raising questions about the nature of the opposition between thomism and averroism.

When Maurer went to England to transcribe the Peterhouse manuscript he was editing, he found occasion to visit Gilson at Vermenton. There the two talked a good deal about the "philosophical constants" of language. Gilson was already working on a book on the subject and was worried about it. Before returning to Toronto, Maurer urged caution and advised Gilson at least to read Noam Chomsky on the subject. Gilson promised to be careful, and also said he would give his next Toronto lectures on language.

When Maurer returned to Toronto, he met Dorothea Sharp, who was lecturing at the Institute on Marsilio of Padua. He wrote Gilson that Professor Sharp recalled his coming to Oxford for her thesis defence. Gilson also remembered the occasion clearly: "That was the day when I had to rush hurriedly out of an Oxford college to buy myself a white necktie. Otherwise the doctoral examination would not have been valid." He also recalled drily that "she had converted to scotism at the same time as to Catholicism, only to discover that, according to some eminent thomists, she could not possibly be both a scotist and a Catholic. Today it would be the other way round!" Gilson closed this letter on a more serious note: "Next Sunday, I shall represent the Académie Française at the Solemn Mass at Notre Dame for all the dead of two world wars. I could myself have been one of them." (68.11.1.)

A year or two earlier Gilson had agreed to go to Berkeley, California, for two or three months at the invitation of Professor Charles Witke of the Classics Department. During 1968, when campus feeling was running high at Berkeley and elsewhere, Gilson decided to keep his promise. He wrote Madeleine Thibaudeau that he would be in Berkeley for two and a half months from early

January to mid-March "with a three-day detour, San Francisco to Toronto, sometime during February" (68.6.17); this allowed him to keep two commitments at the same time, though the sojourn in Toronto was sharply curtailed.

On 3 January Gilson flew from Paris to Berkeley and took rooms in the Faculty Club. He offered two courses on Thomas to Californian students. His public lecture course on the authentic thomism of Thomas based on the *Summa theologiae* twice required moves to larger classrooms to accommodate the students; meanwhile, a seminar on texts of Avicenna and Thomas had an official registration of six. The public course required little new preparation beyond the normal updating of earlier lectures. For the specialized seminar, Gilson had Maurer xerox for his students the appropriate texts from Vandenkiste's "Avicenna citaten bij S. Thomas" (*Tijdschrift voor Philosophie*, 15 [1953]: 437-507). Beyond these small preparations he had only to sit down at his desk,* introduce his topic, then reveal his matchless involvment in the writings of medieval thinkers to win total rapport with his students for the duration of each lecture or seminar.

Gilson enjoyed Berkeley. In his first short letter to Maurer he wrote: "This country is what little was left of earthly paradise, except that Yahweh has permitted the sinners to re-enter it" (69.1.4). In the next he added that "babies and dogs can attend lectures so long as they behave, which in fact they do. There is a great deal of actual confusion beneath a thick coating of technical organization." (69.1.12.) Gilson had friendly former students in the area, such as Vincent Moran and Desmond FitzGerald, and he made new friends each day. In some ways the novelty of the experience took him back to 1926 when he first arrived, like a pioneer, at Virginia and then Harvard. Once again he became involved in the details of daily life, coping with Sunday meals, getting to Sunday mass, opening a bank account:

> Thanks for the Bonaventurian [royalty] cheque. I will take it to Wells Fargo, the nearest bank, and proudly open an account in the amount of the cheque. That will help until my first salary instalment. I have enough money, thank you! I hear mass at the Newman Club. Apart from guitars – now liturgical instruments – the only innovation I remark is an intermission at the Moment of the Offertory, in fact for the collection. The priest invited us to avail ourselves of the opportunity to become acquainted with our neighbours. Everybody else engaged in a lively conversation, but I was as shy as the young girls between whom I was sitting. We sat it out. In fact *we did not want to talk*. ... The weather here? It's raining cats and dogs. ... The Faculty Club is a kind of funeral parlor, especially on Sundays, when they serve absolutely no meals. But I have fat to spare. (EG to Maurer, 69.1.12.)

Gilson included with his letter a typed copy of a poem left by a student in his office and signed: "Lindee Reese, AXOLOTL, Merritt College, 1968, p. 31." The poem was called "Flying Fish" and contained the lines:

---

* Gilson had begun lecturing from a chair in 1968.

> To be the flying fish who bursts his head
> Above the confines of his world
> and knowing there is something more to know.

"I would add," wrote Gilson, a subtitle: 'or, The Metaphysician." I made copies of it for you and Father Shook because I liked it."

At Berkeley Gilson developed an amusing if stubborn objection to the expression "people of God," which since Vatican II had been used to refer to the church congregation:

> While at Berkeley I had a discussion, at a meeting of Catholic professors, with a rather talkative woman who set my nerves on edge with her constantly repeating "the people of God, the people of God." I finally told her that in the good old times, the people of God were called the church. Suddenly, I found myself confronted with [a reference to] *populus Dei* in *Contra gentiles*, IV, ch. 76! I felt much ashamed! By way of penance I forced myself to consult the text. Well, *populus Dei* is not there. How do you like that? The Jews were a people, the Jewish people, and in virtue of their election by God (sorry! by YHW) they truly were the people of God. But since the time of Paul – my parish priest now calls him Paul – the Christians are not one people. Well *you* know that. (EG to Maurer, 69.12.2.)

The phrase continued to bother him for some time, particularly when Congar's name came up. Eventually he forgot it.

Gilson flew to Toronto as planned and gave three lectures on language and metaphysics: "Language is Metaphysical," "Words and Meanings," and "Poetry and Metaphysics." He omitted a fourth, "What is a Word?" as he thought it his poorest and was pressed for time. Gilson strongly suspected he was too old to have undertaken this series on language. When he sent the four lectures to Maurer in November, he wrote:

> I am worried about my projected small book on "Les constantes philosophiques du langage" (the book is an extended version of the Toronto lectures you now have in hand). I am afraid of becoming ridiculous by making the mistake of treating, be it philosophically, technical questions with which I am not familiar. In such cases one always gets caught and harms the philosophical truth he is trying to establish. (68.11.1.)

Later he seems only to have considered his typing unacceptable; he had taught himself to type in middle life, and his style was speedy and erratic:

> The typescript I sent you was abominable, and I am ashamed of it. When I mailed it, I was overwhelmed by all sorts of other obligations. I regret the time you spent on the footnotes. I have no intention of publishing the lectures. The longer book in French will be enough to relieve me of my linguistic fit. (EG to Maurer, 69.1.12.)

Gilson's lectures on language were not devoid of sense. Like Aristotle, he started from the meaningful word as the basis of language, and saw no need to reduce the word to its sounds as, for example, the phonemicists did. Gilson took the position that language is tied to thought and meaning and must therefore be metaphysical. Because he did not tie language to sound, or matter, he largely left linguistic science alone, except on small points where it seemed to argue in his favour. To defend this position he referred to Edward Sapir's observation that man has no specific organ of speech, and he cited Noam Chomsky's opinion that structural linguists and psycholinguists were on the wrong track through overconfidence. The two best aspects of Gilson's lectures were his running commentary on selected texts from Aristotle, St Albert, Descartes and Condillac, and his astute use of such lexicography as he had picked up in Académie debates on French usage.

Gilson had promised to take part in a symposium on "Oriental and Occidental Medieval Philosophy and Science" to be held at the Accademia dei Lincei of Rome, 9 to 15 April 1969. He prepared a paper entitled "Avicenne en occident au moyen âge" (*Archives*, 44 [1969]: 82-121; McG 209), but decided ultimately not to attend. Thérèse d'Alverny read a compendium of the lecture and published it in the *Archives* with an added section on "Y a-t-il eu un avicennisme latin?" The paper was complementary to Gilson's important earlier essay on "Les sources gréco-arabes de l'augustinisme avicennisant" (*Archives*, 4 [1929]: 5-149; McG 451). It represents Gilson at his best in coping with Arabic thought, probably thanks to the watchful scrutiny of Thérèse d'Alverny, whose grasp of Arabic was superior to his. By 1969 much of the responsibility for *Archives* had devolved upon Mlle d'Alverny. Although Gilson and Chenu continued their supervision and maintained a lively if intermittent concern, such tasks as handling correspondence, examining manuscripts and preparing them for the publisher had become mainly hers.

In July 1969, in the lovely church at Vermenton, Gilson delivered the homilies at high mass on two successive Sundays. According to Gilson the curé had wanted to "submit to a period of *recyclage*"; he had engaged a Dutch priest for the Sunday masses and had asked Gilson to preach:

> I did it last Sunday. It was not too hard. It was the feast of Saints Peter and Paul. With a Pope named Paul in the chair of Peter, I had something to go on. Next Sunday, however, I will have to give a homily on the miracle of the multiplication of the loaves and fishes. I shall explain the difference between a wonder (which only happens in a world in which there is no nature) and a miracle, involving walking, hearing, seeing, living, eating; that is, a supernatural restoration of nature in its integrity. I imagine that the five thousand men (fifteen thousand according to Michel Menot who includes also the women and children at a ratio of three to one) did not even realize that a miracle was taking place. A layman *cannot* preach! He can only give a short lecture, which is something different. (EG to Maurer, 69.7.3.)

In his homily the following Sunday Gilson added a reflection of his own, suggesting that in multiplying the loaves Christ recreated for a short time the natural conditions of earthly paradise, where man had not to work in order to eat: "I am not quite sure of my exegesis, but if laymen start preaching anything can happen" (EG to Maurer, 69.7.7). A postscript to Gilson's brief preaching career arose a few weeks later in conversation with the curé of Vermenton:

It was then I learned that the archbishop of Sens had not been consulted in the matter of a layman preaching homilies in one of his churches. I demurely expressed disapproval of the procedure. I am for bishops, against priests when conflicts arise, and for the pope, against bishops who oppose him. So I asked: "Did you at least keep the archbishop informed of what you had done?" "Yes!" "What did he say?" "Nothing." "Well, if I had been the archbishop I would have said something." I have to suppress frequent tempations to meddle with "the present state of the church." But I think it is none of my business, and I go back to my usual work. (EG to Maurer, 69.8.5.)

The summer of 1969 had other pleasure for Gilson. In the week between his two homilies, Jacqueline drove him to Chablis:

I visited the cellars of J. Moreau, a local wine merchant. I asked him for six bottles of Vaillons. ... He asked me where I had become acquainted with his wine. I answered: in Rochester, New York, USA, which was true. I had been intending to renew my acquaintance with that good wine ever since first making it at St John Fisher College. It is still a good wine, and costs one dollar fifty a bottle. But the bottles (*bourguignonnes*) are regrettably small. (EG to Maurer, 69.7.7.)

And later in the summer, *Linguistique et philosophie: essai sur les constantes philosophiques du langage* (Paris, 1969; McG 84) appeared, though Gilson was far from happy with it:

I stumbled on eighteen misprints. I had read and reread the proofs so many times that I must have become unable to focus my attention. Worse, two of those misprints were faults of style! Those two sentences don't stand on their feet: they have no feet to stand on. That I did not notice ... is an indication that the time has come to lay down my pen. That is what I did many years ago when I took away my own driver's licence: I found myself driving on the left side of the road, without knowing how I got there. (EG to Maurer, 69.8.5.)

6 THE SCIENTIFIC TRILOGY, 1970-1972

Gilson devoted his last three series of Toronto lectures to a sharpening of his presentation of the role of metaphysics as complementary to the sciences of nature. The first of these series, "Finalism Revisited," comprised four lectures: "The Case for Final Causality," "The Case for the Mechanical Cause," "Finalism and Physical Probability," and "Evolution: Teleology and Theology." They were delivered on 6, 15, 22 and 29 January 1970, respectively.

"Finalism Revisited" presented selective but representative aspects of the history of finalism since Aristotle, and covered material later published in *D'Aristote à Darwin et retour* (Paris, 1971; McG 15). These were strong lectures, and harked back to Gilson's earlier years; they sustained and implemented such earlier positions as those found in *Études sur le rôle de la pensée médiévale dans la formation du système cartésien* (Paris, 1930; McG 47), and in volume 3 of *History of Philosophy* (New York, 1963; McG 186). The dominant theme of the lectures was "the pull of creation toward the causes whose effect it is," the *ens in quantum ens* and its two communities, analogy and causality (Pegis to EG, 62.5.23). Gilson's classroom technique was typical of him. He began with Aristotle's *History of Animals* and moved through Thomas's *Quaestiones disputatae de veritate*, 1.1, to Francis Bacon's *Advancement of Learning* and Newton's *Optics*; he then moved into nineteenth-century research by Claude Bernard and recent work by Walter M. Elsasser on the biological sciences. Detailed, humorous, profound, skilfully argued, and utterly beyond summary, the series worked inexorably to its conclusion that the finalism of nature is a defensible constant in the philosophy of living rational beings.

Throughout 1969 and 1970 Gilson had been pursued by Otto Bird, Eyvind Ronquist, and the Hutchins-Adler Great Books team of Chicago.* In 1970 Gilson allowed himself, at the age of eighty-six, to be drafted into a vast Great Books project to create on microfiche a *Library of Mediaeval Civilization*. Others involved in the project were Giles Constable, Astrik Gabriel, C. H. Taylor, and Armand Maurer, who worked with Gilson. The estimated number of volumes to be put on fiches was first said to be forty-five hundred. By August this estimate had risen to nearly eight thousand, and the editors were contemplating expanding the original plan from an undergraduate to a full research library.

Gilson became impatient as the project expanded, particularly in June when he found himself overwhelmed with requests. He was writing up a short address for the tercentenary of the Académie de Savoie, and another, "Propos sur le bonheur," for the December meeting of the Académie Française. There was also a twelve-page paper for a Great Books project on world society for which he was trying to grasp the use of "common good" in *Pacem in terris*:

> What is the common good of Jews, Arabs and Christians in Palestine where the Jews are trying to steal from the Arabs the very territory they had once stolen from them when Yahweh Sabaoth delivered them into Israel's hands? I am fascinated by present events. Unless I am mistaken, Palestine is the land of the Philistines and everything is beginning all over again. (EG to Maurer, 70.6.13.)

As Gilson wrote this paper for Great Books with one hand, he was trying to do their bibliography with his other. One day he received from Bird 1,001 blank cards on which he was asked to fill in, correctly and fully, the nominations he had already forwarded as brief titles. This was not easily done in Vermenton, and no clerical help was provided. Gilson wrote Maurer angrily:

> Since you will undoubtedly have to pay for what our friend calls "clerical help," I expect to be in for at least fifty percent of the operation. Is not this what the Americans call "a dirty trick?" Are you sure that our combined fees [$6,000] will be enough for filling out a thousand fiches? Yes, I suppose it will. It comes out to six

---

* Gilson's position on metaphysics had much in common with that defended by Mortimer J. Adler in *The Difference of Man and the Difference It Makes* (1967). Gilson had spoken favourably of Adler's "long first step toward the proper assessment of an immaterial element in material reality" (EG to John N. Deely, 68.9.18; see Gilson-Deely correspondence, 1968-1974 *passim*; see also above, p. 231).

> dollars apiece. In good old antiquity an educated slave would have done this for his grub. (EG to Maurer, 70.6.13.)

A few weeks later, he was still fuming:

> Only bad historians like this kind of bibliography. It is pretense. When I sent [to Bird *et al*] my article on the "Difficulties of Atheism," they added an absurd bibliography. I doubt they had read their additions. I had read practically none of them. The whole thing is fake. (EG to Maurer, 70.7.6.)

In September Gilson still felt himself hopelessly overworked and regretted ever getting into the mess. Not surprisingly then, in November he turned down an invitation from René Habachi and Mme Herzog to collaborate on their UNESCO project, "Culture et science." Quite apart from his lack of time, Gilson felt that to include philosophy among the human sciences, as UNESCO was doing, was to turn it into a kind of "displaced person" (EG to Habachi, 70.11.24).

In 1971 Gilson's lecture series for Toronto was "In Quest of Evolution": the three component lectures were "Darwin without Evolution," "Evolution without Darwin," and "From Malthus to the Twilight of Evolution." The general topic had clearly grown out of last year's series on finalism. Gilson now wanted to show how antifinalism had actually produced nineteenth-century evolutionism; in his third lecture he provided a summary of the steps for such a demonstration. According to Gilson, Darwin's theory, at least in its beginnings, was not intended as a philosophical theory but as a scientific theory to explain the origin of species by natural selection; Darwin had originally been inspired by his reading of Malthus on the principle of population. The first philosophical theory of evolution was presented not by Darwin, but by Herbert Spencer. The general public, however, confused the two theories, and began to misread Darwin's scientific demonstration of the origin of species as a demonstration of the origin of being; Darwin himself was too good a scientist to ever mistake his scientific theory for a philosophical one. Nonetheless, once the transference was made, the enemies of the revealed notion of creation quickly accepted the origin of species as demonstrating the origin of being, and Darwin never contradicted them. For Gilson theories of evolution had never proven themselves scientifically tenable, and had raised many questions that science could not answer. Leibniz, said Gilson, once asked how it is that there is something rather than nothing – surely it is easier to understand nothing than something. Here, argued Gilson, lies the philosophical problem with evolution.

The conclusion of "From Malthus to the Twilight of Evolution" extends Gilson's argument into current debates in physics:

> Beginning February 4, the Canadian Broadcasting Corporation network will broadcast a programme under the general title "The Violent Universe." On 23 February the final broadcast of the series will look at what they call the two major theories of the universe: the "Big Bang" (evolutionary universe) and the "Steady State" (continuous creation) theories. Since I don't look to Genesis for scientific information, I don't ask scripture which theory we should prefer. At first blush, the

universe of Genesis looks like a violent universe: "Let there be light. And light was made" – a very big bang! Other things are ambiguous: when water "produces" fishes, and when the earth "brings forth the living creature in its kind" (Genesis 1.24), these may or may not be sudden and unexpected. All this, of course, is not scientific. But if God had said, "Let a hydrogen cloud be made!" would that be more scientific? If we are content to say that in the beginning, there was a big bang, the next question will be: A big bang of what? Then, how did all that explosive stuff happen to be there? Science cannot give answers to nonscientific questions. Scientific or not, the questions have always been there, and always will be. Scripture soars high above science and philosophy. With a bang, or with a whimper, heaven and earth will pass away, but the words of the Lord will not pass away. (pp. 12-13.)

Later in 1971, after Gilson returned to Vermenton, the School of Philosophy of Washington's Catholic University of America unanimously submitted Gilson's name for an honorary degree. The nomination was quietly dropped at the committee stage and did not reach the academic senate for consideration. In a strong intervention from the floor of the senate, Dean Jude Dougherty of the School of Philosophy expressed surprise that the unanimous nomination of a man of Gilson's stature and service in the Catholic community had been dropped. The senate listened and in a secret ballot gave Gilson the highest number of votes of all candidates proposed that year.

In due course Gilson was invited by President Clarence C. Walton to receive an honorary degree in humane letters from Catholic University. Gilson was pleased but had to confess the bitter truth that he could not afford the transatlantic fare. Dougherty again expressed surprise that no compensation had been offered, an oversight President Walton quickly put right. Dougherty then urged the president to invite Gilson to give the convocation address, but this was turned down – Gilson was, after all, eighty-seven years old. Undaunted, Dougherty wrote Gilson, still in France and unaware of all this byplay, inviting him to deliver a "post-commencement" address for the School of Philosophy on the afternoon of Saturday 15 May in Keane Auditorium. Gilson accepted and brought from France an address on the theme closest to him this year, "Evolution: From Aristotle to Darwin and Back." Dougherty sent out invitations to the faculty and students of Catholic University and of the other universities and colleges in the Washington area. As he expected, even though it was the day after convocation and a Saturday afternoon, a wide spectrum of listeners came from all corners of Washington and remained with rapt attention right through to the end of the question period.

That evening a small dinner was held in the Montpellier Room of the Madison Hotel for Gilson and a number of longtime, close friends including Paul Weiss, who had first heard Gilson lecture at Harvard, and his fiancée Marcia Gultentag; Leo Sweeney, sj; Kenneth Schmitz, who had studied under Gilson in Toronto; Cécile Gilson; Antonio and Mrs Cua; and Allan B. Wolter. For four short hours the room radiated with warm humour and affection. Each person present, in response to the chairman's invitation, rose and spoke. Ten times Gilson briefly replied telling them how much each had meant to him and expressing pleasure at his new title, Doctor of Humane Letters of the Catholic University of America.

In January 1972 Gilson gave his last series of lectures in Toronto. "In Quest of Species" probed philosophy for some means of reconciling Darwin's findings on the origin of species; the three lectures in the series were called "Species for Experience," "Species for Science," and "Species for Philosophy."

Gilson very nearly didn't finish these lectures. He had planned on devoting all of 1971 to preparing them, but the year was busier than projected. His move from Vermenton to Cravant was an ordeal, and the small cottage, though comfortable, did not lend itself as easily to his writing. Moreover his subject – species – turned out to be particularly intractable. Nothing he wrote satisfied him:

> I now shall type up a third redaction. I am afraid it too will be boring by contrast with last year's. That was *un sujet en or*. What I now want to say is that *species* is not a scientific notion either. Hence the endless perplexities of naturalists about it. ... I have touched upon the point in my book. ... I would like to clear it up. I have suffered "aches and pains" reading and rereading Adler and Deely on the subject. ... What they say is irrelevant to the authentic thought of St Thomas. ... Little children can tell cats from dogs unerringly. We don't know any more about the notion than they. Adler, however, saw and pointed out the mistake of those scholastics who confuse logical with biological species. (EG to Maurer, 71.8.20.)

In preparation for this third version of the lectures Gilson reread Dickens' *Pickwick Papers* for its English style. He also reread Ockham, who of all medieval thinkers had immersed himself most thoroughly in the problem of universals. Gilson found this a heavy chore: "I cannot use Ockham without first assimilating his conception of substantial form. I have not enough life left for such a task. I'll ask him when I meet him." (EG to Maurer, 71.9.5.) Ultimately, it was to Aristotle that Gilson turned for inspiration: "[Aristotle] merely says: 'No part of an animal is purely material or purely immaterial.' Drop the immaterial and the notion of species makes no sense; it is not a scientific notion but a philosophical one." Gilson's "In Quest of Species" led to this same conclusion:

> True species can be found in zoos. There are no others. Darwin despaired of trying to differentiate species from varieties. Adler is driven to affirm that there are *three* species: plant, brute, man. The only explanation I can see for the very possibility of species is the notion of substantial form. (EG to Maurer, 71.10.4.)

Gilson opened the first lecture of the series with a strong assertion. At eighty-six he was still, as he had been throughout his life, profoundly convinced of the specificity of the philosophical order: "I call specifically philosophical," he said, "those problems that arise *in* science from science, but have no scientific conclusion"; such problems, he argued, can only be specified in philosophy, and only in a philosophy which accepts metaphysics. Gilson was addressing those scientists who needed to be convinced that anything could remain for human consideration after they had pushed their science to its *ultima thule*; he had earlier

reminded philosophers of their responsibilities to truth in a similar context.*
Though time and strength were not on his side, Gilson hoped next year to open
one last subject with scientists – the philosophical nature of the matter with
which they worked.

Gilson's lectures on species were the last he was to deliver in North America.
After they were finished he made his final journey across the Atlantic, arriving in
Paris at the beginning of February 1972. He immediately turned his attention to a
naïve question put to him by the president of his Institute, who was preparing a
report on research for the Canada Council. Where would one find St Thomas
discussing what is today called research? Gilson's reply was concerned primarily
with ends:

> I think one can properly distinguish research from education, even from teaching.
> The English universities are distrustful of researchers as teachers. The end in view
> of the researcher is the success of his research, of the teacher the good of his pupil.
> The Institute of Mediaeval Studies has for its proper end the training of researchers
> by researchers. The end of college teaching is the formation of minds equipped with
> the general culture befitting what Montaigne called "une tête bien faite." Education
> goes further still because it includes the formation of the whole man, including
> character and will, in view of his highest end both natural and supernatural. I don't
> think the distinction between teaching and research was part of Thomas'
> problematic. (EG to Shook, 72.2.20.)

On 7 March 1972 Gilson received in Paris the Gulbenkian prize for philosophy
(in cruzeiros) from the Brazilian Academy of the Latin World in recognition of the
honour in which he was still held in Brazil. He was pleased and amused by the
award – he had won his last prize in philosophy in 1903 as a boy in Lycée Henri
IV. Gilson used the occasion to speak briefly about Professor Dereux who had
introduced him, as well as Jacques Maritain, to philosophy (above, pp. 10-11).

In Cravant, on 30 July 1972, Gilson finished his preparation of his next three
lectures for Toronto, "In Quest of Matter." The papers surveyed three ways of
examining matter: the Greek method, the Christian philosophers' method, and the
scientific method followed since Descartes.

For the Greek approach to matter, Gilson looked at Aristotle's *Metaphysics*. He
called the Greek approach "matter for sense experience," and argued that the
Greeks were not interested in submitting a thing to calculation and measurement
for possible practical uses. They wanted to understand it as it struck them, and
then, if possible, to define it. Matter to the Greeks was the obscurity out of which
a thing was produced by a form. Matter was a mode of being; it was not nothing
but was an incomplete, a potential being.

The Christian philosophers presented matter through a variety of depictions.
Augustine called it, beautifully if inadequately, the mutability of mutable things.

---

* See "De la connaissance du principe," *Revue de métaphysique et de morale*, 66 (1961): 373-397;
McG 242.

Albert the Great called it an "order toward a form," a kind of halfway post between nonbeing and being. Thomas called it "being *in potentia*," a could-be-but-not-yet being. Some scholastics, for example Scotus, saw matter as a *res*; they located this *res* in nature however, where it could be made the object of a science.

Although Descartes and his scientific successors have presented many varying opinions on matter, most have thought of matter as a thing discoverable in its properties and uses, and as useful and profitable to science. For them matter is no longer an obscurity, a mutability, or a potency; rather, matter is an extension, a quantity, a figure or situation, a movement. For the sciences the distinguishing mark of matter is its usefulness. The ancients and the medievals asked themselves the philosophical question, "What *is* matter?" The moderns merely pry into its properties:

> The result of Descartes' victory is that modern scientism leaves us without any metaphysical notion of matter .... Science has discovered an unbelievable quantity of truth concerning the structure of material bodies; it has pushed beyond the notion of atom and discovered in elemental molecules an infinitely small universe of unbelievable complexity. ... Because [scientists] are busy investigating the nature of matter, they believe they are examining the question of what it is.

In Gilson's view, despite all such progress, "the nature of reality is other than our knowledge of it." To illustrate he repeats Einstein's reply to the wife of physicist Max Born, who asked him if he believed that absolutely everything could be expressed scientifically. "Yes," he replied, "it would be possible, but it would make no sense. It would be description without meaning – as if you described a Beethoven symphony as a variation of wave pressure." * The philosophy of Aristotle and the scholastics was always concerned with reality as perceived by the senses and translated into such terms of conceptual knowledge as being, cause, becoming, quantity, quality, relation and so on. The peculiar satisfaction the mind derives from matter arises from reality as given to the senses, and is as obscure as reality itself. As presented by the philosopher, matter is only one of all those philosophical translations of sensory experience that science spurns as incapable of quantification within clear and distinct categories. Philosophy prefers to keep reality as it truly is – to suppress reality's obscurity is to remove one of its essential parts.

As Gilson sent these three lectures to the Institute, he felt his teaching had reached some point of completion:

> I probably would have modified them if I had felt able to deliver them but the substance would have remained the same. Anyway, these were the last lectures I intended to give. They deal with the last of the metaphysical concepts I had wanted to clarify in my own mind. In a sense, the thought satisfies me. To realize that the moment has come when I no longer have anything personal to say leads me to hope that there was something in these lectures. I felt an urge to deliver them before the end.

* See R. W. Clark, *Einstein: The Life and Times* (New York, 1971), p. 192.

Gilson had just returned alone – Jacqueline was ill – from a difficult trip to Venice for the xiv Corso Internazionale d'Alta Cultura. He had been made helplessly aware of his failing strength:

> I managed to give them two days and two lectures. The Corso had then to continue without me. I say "managed" but not without the help of friends, colleagues, and even fellow travellers who had only to look at me to see I was in trouble. The experience convinced me that I should not attempt another trip to Toronto.

Even regular attendance at the Académie was no longer within his powers:

> Yesterday, coming back from Paris to Cravant after the weekly meeting of the Académie, I failed to climb aboard the railway carriage. I was helpless to get either up or down. A good Samaritain helped me up and pushed me inside the car, rather unceremoniously but most effectively .... I visibly stand in need of help. This began about six months ago. My conclusion now is that I must stay home. (EG to Shook, 72.9.30.)

7 Cravant: Last Years

In 1971 Gilson had moved his country home from Vermenton to "the cottage of my grandparents" at Cravant. At first his life there remained much the same as in recent years. He spent each winter in Paris, and the rest of the year in the country, travelling each week to the city for Académie meetings and for research in the Institut de France and the Bibliothèque National. Gradually however he became more dependent on his daughter, who was herself approaching sixty: "Jacqueline takes care of me, and I more and more need such care. Or, perhaps, I take more pleasure in being pampered." Each year Cécile came from Toronto to spend a month's vacation with them, and Bernard came too from time to time.

As Gilson's sight failed and he more easily became drowsy, he had to spend less time reading and more listening to music; he found himself limited to "dwindling hours of lucidity" while "sleeping the rest away by narcolepsy" (EG to Shook, 72.6.5). The little reading he could manage tended to be lighter than in the past: "I am in a period when I like to read Plato: delightful reading, to be sure, although it doesn't take you anywhere." He read Plato in Jowett's English translation because he found himself forgetting his English:

> I was delighted to find one of the most admirable English sentences I have ever met: "*Callicles*: Why not give the name yourself, Socrates? *Socrates*: Well, if you had better that I should, I will." Commentaries by a scientific linguist are welcome! (EG to Maurer, 71.11.9.)

Gilson's demobilization was not complete however. For some years after moving to Cravant he could still undertake a certain amount of writing, and he could go on short trips if driven. In early 1972 he wrote a short and rather frustrated paper to answer a query that Marshall McLuhan had sent him through Father Shook. Was there anything in Christianity, McLuhan had asked, that committed it to Western thought and culture? Was not the electronic revolution in effect terminating the church's marriage with the West? Gilson's thinking had little in common with McLuhan's but he tried to answer. For Gilson Christianity had arisen from the East, and its basic theology was Eastern; the present threat was coming from the West which was submerging both Christianity and the East. He did not think of the church as married to either the East or the West – was it not catholic? – Nor did he really know what the effect of the electronic revolution was likely to be. This was in early 1972.

Early in 1973 Jacques Maritain died. Gilson had loved his friend, and he experienced deep sorrow at his passing:

> As is the case with the angels of Thomas Aquinas, he was a species all his own. There will never be another thomist quite like him. I don't think we need pray for him. We can pray with him and to him. ... We can thank God for keeping his intelligence intact to the end. (EG to John Deely, 73.5.4.)

The death of Maritain, some two years his senior, must have reminded Gilson of the approach of his own. His letter to Edward Synan, the Institute's new president, held a note of grim humour:

> I am reading the last [posthumous] book of Jacques Maritain, *Approches sans entraves*. ... I am afraid he was wrong here, unless of course I am. In both our cases the situation is discouraging. ... I shall be turning ninety on 13 June, which is no joke, or if it is, it is a bad one. (73.12.13.)

In 1973 Gilson took on a small number of projects. In February he wrote a four-page introduction to the Book of Wisdom for a third edition of Canon Osty's translation: "They wanted it to be short, unscientific and by a layman." Gilson had been on the advisory commission for the Jerusalem Bible, and had made a significant contribution, not as an exegete or scripture scholar, but as a master of French prose and a member of the Académie. A brief introduction to the Book of Wisdom presented little problem, and he gladly wrote it. Soon after, in April 1973, Gilson agreed to represent the Académie in Rochefort where the *maison de Loti* was declared a public monument; the event carried him back to his second year of teaching in the lycées and to his lectures on Loti in Tours and Lille.

In 1 June 1973 Gilson received a letter from John Hellman, historian at McGill University. Hellman was preparing his *Emmanuel Mounier and the New Catholic Left: 1930 to 1950* (Toronto, 1981), and wanted to know about Gilson's own involvement in the activities of Catholic intellectuals in the 1930s. Hellman already knew and admired Gilson, and had named his son "Etienne" after him. At the age of eighty-nine, Gilson had still not softened his opinion of the left:

> Unfortunately I am not able to tell you anything likely to be helpful. I have never been interested in Catholics of the extreme left, the more so in that the question strikes me as vitiated by a fundamental confusion between communism and marxism. ... I have no religious objection to a given priest, ... even a bishop, looking kindly on communism. I have, however, economic and political objections to their doing so, because I once visited communist Russia and know that widespread impoverishment follows the introduction of the system. ... Marxism is an atheistic

communism and its atheism is an essential component. ... It has always seemed to me that Catholics who collaborate with marxists are guilty not only of political miscalculation but utter absurdity. I have never been able to share their interest.

These sharp judgments were followed by more poignant reflections on the present:

I have now for some time been in my *senium*, which St Thomas puts after *senectus*. To be quite frank, *senium* spells decrepitude, and it is painful enough. Even thinking is no longer possible. Jacques Maritain found the best solution, but for me to do the same would be a pretence. Luckier than he, I will, thanks to you, leave behind me still another Etienne with a long life ahead of him. People used to think that the blessing of an old man had some efficacy. At least I pray that he will learn and never forget his catechism, the most useful of all books after the gospels. (73.6.1.)

In September Thérèse d'Alverny and Pierre de Paulhac approached Gilson with a plan to collect some of his Dante papers not well known in France. At first Gilson was not enthusiastic, but when he discovered that the volume would have a theme of its own, Dante and Béatrice, he became quite eager. The result was the highly presentable *Dante et Béatrice: études dantesques* (Paris, 1974; McG 11).

On 11 November 1973 Gilson spoke over French radio for the Les Anciens Combattants; he taped the address in Jacqueline's apartment in Paris and placed its text carefully among his papers. This was a moving, patriotic talk, an emotional address on *la patrie*, and drew strongly on Gilson's war experiences and his profound attachment to the soil of Burgundy. The talk revealed, once again, Gilson's remarkable feeling for the meaning of words: *la patrie* evoked for him, through phrases like *le sol de la patrie* and *la mère patrie*, the warmth attaching to *le pays*. A great nation, said Gilson, is an assembly of its many *pays*, and in moving to Cravant, he had returned to his own:

The happy vacationland of my childhood, ... the home of my mother's parents, ... is a beautiful *pays*. Its capital is Auxerre. My home now is in one of its tiniest villages, Cravant. But *mon pays* has large towns too: Avallon, Vézelay, Joigny, Chablis, Saint-Florentin, Tonnerre. People there speak only French – the French of Buffon, of Rétif de la Bretonne, of Colette, and of Marie Noël. I find it quite natural that nearby Toucy should have given Pierre Larousse to France. Ask him for the meaning of any word in our language and he will give it to you. A *pays* with a long memory it is too, and of ancient rancours: I still hear an angry young mother calling her child *un marmot d'Armagnà*. There, between Auxerre and Avallon, I learned what a meadow is, a field, that quasi-sacred thing a vineyard, but also that place of mystery a forest, hills crowned with their *meurgers*, ancient witnesses of the great pain of men. I have also loved and passionately explored those back roads running from village to village, all different, each with its own church quite unlike any other. ("L'émission des Anciens Combattants," Gilson Archives; tr.)

Not surprisingly, Radiodiffusion-Télévision Française invited Gilson to set up another programme, "une conversation dialoguée" (André Chanu to EG, 73.1.22). There is no record that he accepted.

Near the end of 1973 a certain Grisette arrived to assume control of the Cravant household. Gilson welcomed the takeover:

> A kitten jumped over the wall into our Cravant garden. She at once performed the surrendering rite. Naturally that meant she was taking possession of the garden including the house, Jacqueline, and everything else in it. A month later she presented us with four splendid kittens. We had to get her sterilized, which is a crime, but we had no other choice. She is at the moment in Paris, letting us share her modest suite of three rooms plus bath and kitchen. We call her Grisette. She provides me with my constant and inexhaustible motive for wonder, in addition, that is, to Thomas and *esse*. What is it for a nonspeaking animal to think, to know, and to give all appearance of reasoning? Chains of images without concepts may be an answer, but I don't know. Even the *aestimativa*, which so closely resembles the *cogitativa*, are to me just two symbols for unknown quantities. I never tire of watching the simili-mind of that cat at work. (EG to Maurer, 73.11.26.)

Gilson's visitors at Cravant were many, and included Thérèse d'Alverny, Henri Gouhier, Pierre and Gerard de Paulhac, Astrik Gabriel, Fathers Maurer and Morro, Father Shook and his Nassau cousin Mary Diane, and others. Each in turn suffered at some time Grisette's close inspection as she turned her "simili-mind" to determining her approval.

In 1974 Gilson was particularly pleased when two commemorative volumes were published by the Toronto Institute to mark the seven hundredth anniversary of St Thomas' death. Gilson had first moved that the project be undertaken at a council meeting in May 1972. He had wanted the anniversary to be marked on time, by 7 March 1974, and had also wanted all submissions to focus primarily and authentically on Thomas himself. From the Institute's outset Gilson had demanded that it encourage and pursue all medieval studies in as much depth as possible. Now, as an editor of the anniversary volumes, he had insisted, over some opposition, that the project honour St Thomas directly and not become a mere miscellany. He called his own article, prepared at Cravent, "Quasi definitio substantiae" (*St Thomas Aquinas, 1274-1974, Commemorative Studies* [Toronto, 1974], 1: 111-129; McG 413). When the volumes appeared early in March 1974, just before the feast of St Thomas, Gilson was very pleased:

> The two volumes commemorating the seventh centenary of the death of St Thomas more than fill my ambitions and hopes. They are exceptionally good and contain nothing that was not worth the trouble of writing and printing. Such works easily contain too many pages written by people with nothing worthwhile to say. ... I reread my own article with satisfaction. I do not think it will change the established habit of defining the substance as an *ens per se*, but Frater Thomas must be pleased that two or three people will at least have paid attention to his own language on that point. It gives me great satisfaction in that this one detail so marvellously illustrates the meaning of his notion of *esse*. (EG to Maurer, 74.3.6.)

Over the years life for Gilson became gradually more restricted and lonely, though he never admitted any unhappiness beyond the wistful impatience of old age. In 1975 he and Jacqueline began staying in Cravant year-round; he was no longer able to stand the exertion of travelling to and from Paris, even with assistance. But despite the isolation of Cravant, he maintained contact with many friends during his declining years. On one occasion, when Jacqueline had to be absent in Paris, Henri Gouhier paid him a particularly unusual visit:

> I am to confer on him this afternoon the insignia of the Ordre pour le Mérite. I have not received this myself, but it appears that any Commandeur de la Légion d'Honneur can confer the grade of Commandeur de l'Ordre pour le Mérite. There will be three of us on hand for the ceremony: Henri, my cat Grisette, and myself. Neither fanfare nor ringing of bells is anticipated. (EG to d'Alverny, 74.3.11; tr.)

On 20 February 1975 Gilson was driven by car to the Académie in Paris to receive the gold medal conferred on members during their ninetieth year. At this time Jacqueline wrote to Madeleine Thibaudeau that her father could "no longer read or write – or very little." (75.2.25). Madeleine wrote familiarly to Gilson this year, sending "the greeting of my angel to yours." Gilson had sometimes chided her about her excessive familiarity with her angel and Jacqueline replied for him: "The greeting from your angel to his makes good fun. You seem to handle your angel with authority." (75.7.1; tr.)

This same year, 1975, Gilson's younger brother Maurice, the doctor, died. Gilson became relatively inactive thereafter, going out only by car for Sunday mass, otherwise spending a good deal of time with his head close to the television or drowsing. He never became comatose, however, and was invariably intellectually alert when friends or acquaintances called.

In September 1978, in his ninety-fifth year, Gilson had to be moved from Cravant to the Centre Hospitalier in nearby Auxerre. Even during the five days he spent there before his death, he frequently became sharp and talkative, especially with the hospital chaplain. Gilson had always known how to be at home with priests, no doubt because his memory was a storehouse of the truths and records of their sacerdotal nobility throughout history. In the hospital the chaplain, Abbé Bernard Gallet, asked Gilson if he might call him "maître." Gilson answered immediately, and in Latin, "unus est enim Magister vester" from Matthew 23.8. Then, reflecting on what Christ had meant by these words, he said he would be happy to be called "maître."

Gilson died on Tuesday morning, 19 September 1978. He was buried the next Friday with mass from, appropriately, La Cathédrale de Saint-Etienne in Auxerre. He was laid in the north cemetery of Melun, beside Thérèse.

Appendix

The four seminars that Gilson offered in the École des Hautes Études during his first two years of teaching at the University of Paris were critical in establishing patterns of thought that would persist throughout his long career. (See above, p. 106.) Gilson's own anticipatory summaries of these seminars are presented here in translation. Two of the seminars were to deal with St Augustine (1921 and 1922) and one with Descartes (1922):

1. *A study of the texts of Augustine on divine illumination*

The examination of these texts in their chronological order shows that the problem of knowledge in Augustine is inseparable from his moral and religious development. The reform of morals and manners made possible by the act of faith is now the very condition of every correct solution of the philosophical problem which he proposes. As to this problem itself, it is resolved by a method of interiority, observation making clear that all knowledge comes from within. This assertion is verified in his notion of teaching: in reality we never learn anything from outside (*de magistro*); also in his notion of sensation: sensible images are formed by the soul from its own substance when it reads material impressions made by the body. This presents a double problem: if all knowledge comes from within, are we its sufficient reason? If nothing passes from one created spirit to another, not even from an angel to a man, how can harmony be established among spiritual beings? This is the point at which it becomes possible to understand the theory of illumination. God's wisdom passes over things as a two-pronged ray. First, as an intelligible ray, in that the absolute Likeness (the Word) of God introduces into things likeness at the level of species (making individuals resemble one another); unity at the level of the individual (making one part of an individual resemble another); and number at the level of matter – the last and least of wisdom's participations. Second, as an intelligent ray, in that the Word presides immediately over our thoughts, enabling us to judge things by eternal reasons. Thus knowledge is presented as God's quickening of the meaning of our thought. It is the immediate and purely interior experience of this quickening that constitutes the proof par excellence of the existence of God and which explains our knowledge of things, the possibility of sensation, and even the possibility of that harmony which we establish among spiritual beings.

2. *The influence of the Franciscan spirit on medieval theology*

A close examination of all the texts of St Francis, of all the witnesses of the early historians of St Francis, and of the documents bearing on the development of the order from its beginning, show that Felder's thesis is untenable and that the founder of the order did not want studies. It does not follow that his thought did not exert a profound influence on the development of medieval philosophy and theology. St Bonaventure is penetrated by a Franciscan spirit: his *Legenda S. Francisci* and the opening of the *Itinerarium* show how he was preserving the Franciscan spirituality by upholding (1) the universality of the mystical vocation; (2) that the active life is a preparation for the contemplative; (3) that love goes farther than knowledge; (4) that the universe is one vast system of symbols in which the face of God appears. From these flow immediately the essential theses of his theology and his philosophy – insofar as it is a legitimate philosophy – a *via* toward a higher state, a doctrine of universal analogy, a theory of knowledge, a notion of the role of grace and the importance of the gifts of the Holy Ghost. Moreover, the study of the texts of St Bonaventure relating to the Franciscan rule show him preoccupied above all in deriving from it a conception of the Franciscan spirit (imitation of Christ, taste for contemplation, the winning of soul) which will allow him to retain its ideal while sacrificing its letter and also enable him to justify the extraordinary development of theological studies which took place within the Franciscan order.

3. *St Thomas' critique of St Augustine*

The guiding hypothesis of the research presented in these lectures is that the development of a Christian philosophy inspired by Aristotle in the thirteenth century is not adequately explained by the intrinsic superiority of aristotelianism. To interpret the birth of thomism as due to the superiority of aristotelianism is in line with the well-known thesis that thomism's rise was a partial defeat of the Christian spirit and a victory of Hellenism over the tradition which St Augustine represented. It may well be asked, however, whether this kind of reformation would have been possible if Christian thought had found no Christian interest to bring it about. To know whether there was such a Christian interest, one should interrogate the very authors of the reformation asking them what they found unsatisfactory in augustinian philosophy. The task is a delicate one because St Thomas is particularly careful to retain augustinian terminology while giving it a new meaning. This fact has fostered the delusion that the two doctrines are in agreement with each other, an agreement which I have not been able to substantiate.

The method I followed in my research was to gather as a base the fundamental texts of the *Quaestiones disputatae de veritate*, x-xi, and to group around them all analogous texts from the time of the *Commentary on the Sentences* right up to the *Summa theologiae*. I have examined these texts chronologically and can now affirm that the idea circulated in recent years that there was an evolution in St Thomas from a survival of augustinianism in the *De veritate* to the aristotelianism of the *Summa* cannot be verified on any point I have examined. St Thomas' aristotelianism was fully formed from the beginning.

I first established Thomas' teaching on each point; next I set Thomas' quotations from Augustine against Augustine's own text; and then I compared with this text the interpretation Thomas gave it. From my many detailed analyses and comparisons, I was able to conclude that on the central problems about truth, about the relation between the essence of the soul and its faculties, about the role of sense knowledge in the forming of general ideas, about the soul's way of knowing itself, about the acquisition of first principles and about divine illumination, St Thomas was profoundly transforming the meaning of Augustine's statements while retaining his words.

I then sought to find out how this transformation was made and concluded that it always depended upon a new concept of the relations between the first cause and second created causes. In St Thomas, man receives from God everything he receives from Him in St Augustine, but not in the same way. In St Augustine God delegates his gifts in such a way that the very insufficiency of nature constrains it to return toward him; in St Thomas God delegates His gifts through the mediacy of a stable nature which contains in itself – divine subsistence being taken for granted – the sufficient reason of all its operations. Accordingly, it is the introducing into each philosophical problem of a *nature* endowed with sufficiency and efficacy that separates thomism from augustinism. This teaching troubled augustinians because it seemed to confer on creatures a dangerous sufficiency. It enabled one to define with rigorous precision the respective domains of the natural and supernatural, indeed of philosophy and theology. Both of these had something to gain from such a delimitation, or at least such can be affirmed from a summary examination from the delimitation introduced into the traditional teaching about seminal reasons, divine subsistence and original sin.

4. *Descartes and the religious thought of his time*

Here the practicalities of mathematical physics inclined Descartes to suppress forms; his metaphysical reflections in 1629 led him to distinguish between soul and body; and the systematic application of this distinction to the explanation of natural phenomena in the *Monde* (1629-1632) confirmed his metaphysical conclusions, which had surprised him. At the same time as this *Monde* (founded by metaphysics) confirmed metaphysics, it took on for him apologetic significance of the highest importance because, as the history of his thought on this point shows, he had been of the opinion that physics gave the only rational interpretation conceivable for the biblical account in Genesis.

[During the first semester, M. Henri Gouhier collected, classified, and interpreted texts from Descartes on the subject of faith and reason. These texts were discussed. Gouhier then established a sort of intellectual biography of Descartes in terms of his metaphysical, scientific and apologetical preoccupations. These three preoccupations, in Descartes, seemed to interact: in responding to one, he responded to all three.

During the second semester, Gilson discussed the actual proofs which Descartes had worked out for his blend of metaphysics, science and apologetic, and looked closely at Descartes' critique of the substantial forms of the scholastics. It appeared that Descartes did not proceed by three parallel currents of thought; rather he pursued now one, now another through the same intellectual activity, thus imparting unity and organic accord to the whole.]

Index

Published during the
Sesquicentennial of the
City of Toronto (1834-1984)